For Reference

Not to be taken from this room

NOVELS
for Students

Advisors

Erik France: Adjunct Instructor of English, Macomb Community College, Warren, Michigan. B.A. and M.S.L.S. from University of North Carolina, Chapel Hill; Ph.D. from Temple University.

Kate Hamill: Grade 12 English Teacher, Catonsville High School, Catonsville, Maryland.

Joseph McGeary: English Teacher, Germantown Friends School, Philadelphia, Pennsylvania. Ph.D. in English from Duke University.

Timothy Showalter: English Department Chair, Franklin High School, Reisterstown, Maryland. Certified teacher by the Maryland State Department of Education. Member of the National Council of Teachers of English.

Amy Spade Silverman: English Department Chair, Kehillah Jewish High School, Palo Alto, California. Member of National Council of Teachers of English (NCTE), Teachers and Writers, and NCTE Opinion Panel. Exam Reader, Advanced Placement Literature and Composition. Poet, published in *North American Review, Nimrod,* and *Michigan Quarterly Review,* among other publications.

Jody Stefansson: Director of Boswell Library and Study Center and Upper School Learning Specialist, Polytechnic School, Pasadena, California. Board member, Children's Literature Council of Southern California. Member of American Library Association, Association of Independent School Librarians, and Association of Educational Therapists.

Laura Jean Waters: Certified School Library Media Specialist, Wilton High School, Wilton, Connecticut. B.A. from Fordham University; M.A. from Fairfield University.

NOVELS
for Students

Presenting Analysis, Context, and Criticism on Commonly Studied Novels

VOLUME 31

Sara Constantakis, Project Editor

Foreword by Anne Devereaux Jordan

GALE
CENGAGE Learning™

Detroit • New York • San Francisco • New Haven, Conn • Waterville, Maine • London

Novels for Students, Volume 31

Project Editor: Sara Constantakis

Rights Acquisition and Management: Jennifer Altschul, Margaret Chamberlain-Gaston, Leitha Etheridge-Sims, Kelly Quin

Composition: Evi Abou-El-Seoud

Manufacturing: Drew Kalasky

Imaging: John Watkins

Product Design: Pamela A. E. Galbreath, Jennifer Wahi

Content Conversion: Katrina Coach

Product Manager: Meggin Condino

For product information and technology assistance, contact us at
Gale Customer Support, 1-800-877-4253.
For permission to use material from this text or product, submit all requests online at **www.cengage.com/permissions**.
Further permissions questions can be emailed to
permissionrequest@cengage.com

While every effort has been made to ensure the reliability of the information presented in this publication, Gale, a part of Cengage Learning, does not guarantee the accuracy of the data contained herein. Gale accepts no payment for listing; and inclusion in the publication of any organization, agency, institution, publication, service, or individual does not imply endorsement of the editors or publisher. Errors brought to the attention of the publisher and verified to the satisfaction of the publisher will be corrected in future editions.

Gale
27500 Drake Rd.
Farmington Hills, MI, 48331-3535

ISBN-13: 978-1-4144-4169-6
ISBN-10: 1-4144-4169-X

ISSN 1094-3552

This title is also available as an e-book.
ISBN-13: 978-1-4144-4947-0
ISBN-10: 1-4144-4947-X
Contact your Gale, a part of Cengage Learning sales representative for ordering information.

Printed in the United States of America
1 2 3 4 5 6 7 14 13 12 11 10

Table of Contents

The Informed Dialogue: Interacting with Literature

When we pick up a book, we usually do so with the anticipation of pleasure. We hope that by entering the time and place of the novel and sharing the thoughts and actions of the characters, we will find enjoyment. Unfortunately, this is often not the case; we are disappointed. But we should ask, has the author failed us, or have we failed the author?

We establish a dialogue with the author, the book, and with ourselves when we read. Consciously and unconsciously, we ask questions: "Why did the author write this book?" "Why did the author choose that time, place, or character?" "How did the author achieve that effect?" "Why did the character act that way?" "Would I act in the same way?" The answers we receive depend upon how much information about literature in general and about that book specifically we ourselves bring to our reading.

Young children have limited life and literary experiences. Being young, children frequently do not know how to go about exploring a book, nor sometimes, even know the questions to ask of a book. The books they read help them answer questions, the author often coming right out and *telling* young readers the things they are learning or are expected to learn. The perennial classic, *The Little Engine That Could, tells* its readers that, among other things, it is good to help others and brings happiness:

"Hurray, hurray," cried the funny little clown and all the dolls and toys. "The good little boys and girls in the city will be happy because you helped us, kind, Little Blue Engine."

In picture books, messages are often blatant and simple, the dialogue between the author and reader one-sided. Young children are concerned with the end result of a book—the enjoyment gained, the lesson learned—rather than with how that result was obtained. As we grow older and read further, however, we question more. We come to expect that the world within the book will closely mirror the concerns of our world, and that the author will *show* these through the events, descriptions, and conversations within the story, rather than *telling* of them. We are now expected to do the interpreting, carry on our share of the dialogue with the book and author, and glean not only the author's message, but comprehend how that message and the overall affect of the book were achieved. Sometimes, however, we need help to do these things. *Novels for Students* provides that help.

A novel is made up of many parts interacting to create a coherent whole. In reading a novel, the more obvious features can be easily spotted—theme, characters, plot—but we may overlook the more subtle elements that greatly influence how the novel is perceived by the reader: viewpoint, mood and tone, symbolism, or the use of humor. By focusing on both the obvious and more subtle literary elements within a novel,

Novels for Students aids readers in both analyzing for message and in determining how and why that message is communicated. In the discussion on Harper Lee's *To Kill a Mockingbird* (Vol. 2), for example, the mockingbird as a symbol of innocence is dealt with, among other things, as is the importance of Lee's use of humor which "enlivens a serious plot, adds depth to the characterization, and creates a sense of familiarity and universality." The reader comes to understand the internal elements of each novel discussed—as well as the external influences that help shape it.

"The desire to write greatly," Harold Bloom of Yale University says, "is the desire to be elsewhere, in a time and place of one's own, in an originality that must compound with inheritance, with an anxiety of influence." A writer seeks to create a unique world within a story, but although it is unique, it is not disconnected from our own world. It speaks to us *because* of what the writer brings to the writing from our world: how he or she was raised and educated; his or her likes and dislikes; the events occurring in the real world at the time of the writing, and while the author was growing up. When we know what an author has brought to his or her work, we gain a greater insight into both the "originality" (the world of the book), and the things that "compound" it. This insight enables us to question that created world and find answers more readily. By informing ourselves, we are able to establish a more effective dialogue with both book and author.

Novels for Students, in addition to providing a plot summary and descriptive list of characters—to remind readers of what they have read—also explores the external influences that shaped each book. Each entry includes a discussion of the author's background, and the historical context in which the novel was written. It is vital to know, for instance, that when Ray Bradbury was writing *Fahrenheit 451* (Vol. 1), the threat of Nazi domination had recently ended in Europe, and the McCarthy hearings were taking place in Washington, D.C. This information goes far in answering the question, "Why did he write a story of oppressive government control and book burning?" Similarly, it is important to know that Harper Lee, author of *To Kill a Mockingbird,*was born and raised in

Monroeville, Alabama, and that her father was a lawyer. Readers can now see why she chose the south as a setting for her novel—it is the place with which she was most familiar—and start to comprehend her characters and their actions.

Novels for Students helps readers find the answers they seek when they establish a dialogue with a particular novel. It also aids in the posing of questions by providing the opinions and interpretations of various critics and reviewers, broadening that dialogue. Some reviewers of *To Kill A Mockingbird,* for example, "faulted the novel's climax as melodramatic." This statement leads readers to ask, "Is it, indeed, melodramatic?" "If not, why did some reviewers see it as such?" "If it is, why did Lee choose to make it melodramatic?" "Is melodrama ever justified?" By being spurred to ask these questions, readers not only learn more about the book and its writer, but about the nature of writing itself.

The literature included for discussion in *Novels for Students* has been chosen because it has something vital to say to us. *Of Mice and Men, Catch-22, The Joy Luck Club, My Antonia, A Separate Peace* and the other novels here speak of life and modern sensibility. In addition to their individual, specific messages of prejudice, power, love or hate, living and dying, however, they and all great literature also share a common intent. They force us to *think*—about life, literature, and about others, not just about ourselves. They pry us from the narrow confines of our minds and thrust us outward to confront the world of books and the larger, real world we all share. *Novels for Students* helps us in this confrontation by providing the means of enriching our conversation with literature and the world, by creating an *informed* dialogue, one that brings true pleasure to the personal act of reading.

Sources

Harold Bloom, *The Western Canon, The Books and School of the Ages*, Riverhead Books, 1994.

Watty Piper, *The Little Engine That Could*, Platt & Munk, 1930.

Anne Devereaux Jordan
Senior Editor, TALL (Teaching and Learning Literature)

Introduction

Purpose of the Book

The purpose of *Novels for Students* (*NfS*) is to provide readers with a guide to understanding, enjoying, and studying novels by giving them easy access to information about the work. Part of Gale's "For Students" Literature line, *NfS* is specifically designed to meet the curricular needs of high school and undergraduate college students and their teachers, as well as the interests of general readers and researchers considering specific novels. While each volume contains entries on "classic" novels frequently studied in classrooms, there are also entries containing hard-to-find information on contemporary novels, including works by multicultural, international, and women novelists.

The information covered in each entry includes an introduction to the novel and the novel's author; a plot summary, to help readers unravel and understand the events in a novel; descriptions of important characters, including explanation of a given character's role in the novel as well as discussion about that character's relationship to other characters in the novel; analysis of important themes in the novel; and an explanation of important literary techniques and movements as they are demonstrated in the novel.

In addition to this material, which helps the readers analyze the novel itself, students are also provided with important information on the lit-erary and historical background informing each work. This includes a historical context essay, a box comparing the time or place the novel was written to modern Western culture, a critical essay, and excerpts from critical essays on the novel. A unique feature of *NfS* is a specially commissioned critical essay on each novel, targeted toward the student reader.

To further help today's student in studying and enjoying each novel, information on media adaptations is provided (if available), as well as reading suggestions for works of fiction and nonfiction on similar themes and topics. Classroom aids include ideas for research papers and lists of critical and reference sources that provide additional material on the novel.

Selection Criteria

The titles for each volume of *NfS* are selected by surveying numerous sources on notable literary works and analyzing course curricula for various schools, school districts, and states. Some of the sources surveyed include: high school and undergraduate literature anthologies and textbooks; lists of award-winners, and recommended titles, including the Young Adult Library Services Association (YALSA) list of best books for young adults.

Input solicited from our expert advisory board—consisting of educators and librarians—guides us to maintain a mix of "classic" and contemporary literary works, a mix of challenging and engaging works (including genre titles that are commonly studied) appropriate for different age levels, and a mix of international, multicultural and women authors. These advisors also consult on each volume's entry list, advising on which titles are most studied, most appropriate, and meet the broadest interests across secondary (grades 7–12) curricula and undergraduate literature studies.

How Each Entry Is Organized

Each entry, or chapter, in *NfS* focuses on one novel. Each entry heading lists the full name of the novel, the author's name, and the date of the novel's publication. The following elements are contained in each entry:

Introduction: a brief overview of the novel which provides information about its first appearance, its literary standing, any controversies surrounding the work, and major conflicts or themes within the work.

Author Biography: this section includes basic facts about the author's life, and focuses on events and times in the author's life that inspired the novel in question.

Plot Summary: a factual description of the major events in the novel. Lengthy summaries are broken down with subheads.

Characters: an alphabetical listing of major characters in the novel. Each character name is followed by a brief to an extensive description of the character's role in the novel, as well as discussion of the character's actions, relationships, and possible motivation.

Characters are listed alphabetically by last name. If a character is unnamed—for instance, the narrator in *Invisible Man*—the character is listed as "The Narrator" and alphabetized as "Narrator." If a character's first name is the only one given, the name will appear alphabetically by that name.

Variant names are also included for each character. Thus, the full name "Jean Louise Finch" would head the listing for the narrator of *To Kill a Mockingbird*, but listed in a separate cross-reference would be the nickname "Scout Finch."

Themes: a thorough overview of how the major topics, themes, and issues are addressed within the novel. Each theme discussed appears in a separate subhead and is easily accessed through the boldface entries in the Subject/Theme Index.

Style: this section addresses important style elements of the novel, such as setting, point of view, and narration; important literary devices used, such as imagery, foreshadowing, symbolism; and, if applicable, genres to which the work might have belonged, such as Gothicism or Romanticism. Literary terms are explained within the entry but can also be found in the Glossary.

Historical Context: this section outlines the social, political, and cultural climate *in which the author lived and the novel was created*. This section may include descriptions of related historical events, pertinent aspects of daily life in the culture, and the artistic and literary sensibilities of the time in which the work was written. If the novel is a historical work, information regarding the time in which the novel is set is also included. Each section is broken down with helpful subheads.

Critical Overview: this section provides background on the critical reputation of the novel, including bannings or any other public controversies surrounding the work. For older works, this section includes a history of how the novel was first received and how perceptions of it may have changed over the years; for more recent novels, direct quotes from early reviews may also be included.

Criticism: an essay commissioned by *NfS* which specifically deals with the novel and is written specifically for the student audience, as well as excerpts from previously published criticism on the work (if available).

Sources: an alphabetical list of critical material used in compiling the entry, with full bibliographical information.

Further Reading: an alphabetical list of other critical sources which may prove useful for the student. It includes full bibliographical information and a brief annotation.

In addition, each entry contains the following highlighted sections, set apart from the main text as sidebars:

Media Adaptations: if available, a list of audiobooks and important film and television adaptations of the novel, including source information. The list also includes stage adaptations, musical adaptations, etc.

Topics for Further Study: a list of potential study questions or research topics dealing with the novel. This section includes questions related to other disciplines the student may be studying, such as American history, world history, science, math, government, business, geography, economics, psychology, etc.

Compare and Contrast: an "at-a-glance" comparison of the cultural and historical differences between the author's time and culture and late twentieth century or early twenty-first century Western culture. This box includes pertinent parallels between the major scientific, political, and cultural movements of the time or place the novel was written, the time or place the novel was set (if a historical work), and modern Western culture. Works written after the mid-1970s may not have this box.

What Do I Read Next?: a list of works that might give a reader points of entry into a classic work (e.g., YA or multicultural titles) and/or complement the featured novel or serve as a contrast to it. This includes works by the same author and others, works from various genres, YA works, and works from various cultures and eras.

Other Features

NfS includes "The Informed Dialogue: Interacting with Literature," a foreword by Anne Devereaux Jordan, Senior Editor for *Teaching and Learning Literature* (*TALL*), and a founder of the Children's Literature Association. This essay provides an enlightening look at how readers interact with literature and how *Novels for Students* can help teachers show students how to enrich their own reading experiences.

A Cumulative Author/Title Index lists the authors and titles covered in each volume of the *NfS* series.

A Cumulative Nationality/Ethnicity Index breaks down the authors and titles covered in each volume of the *NfS* series by nationality and ethnicity.

A Subject/Theme Index, specific to each volume, provides easy reference for users who may be studying a particular subject or theme rather than a single work. Significant subjects, from events to broad themes, are included.

Each entry may include illustrations, including photo of the author, stills from film adaptations, maps, and/or photos of key historical events, if available.

Citing Novels for Students

When writing papers, students who quote directly from any volume of *Novels for Students* may use

the following general forms. These examples are based on MLA style; teachers may request that students adhere to a different style, so the following examples may be adapted as needed.

When citing text from *NfS* that is not attributed to a particular author (i.e., the Themes, Style, Historical Context sections, etc.), the following format should be used in the bibliography section:

"*Night*." *Novels for Students*. Ed. Marie Rose Napierkowski. Vol. 4. Detroit: Gale, 1998. 234–35.

When quoting the specially commissioned essay from *NfS* (usually the first piece under the "Criticism" subhead), the following format should be used:

Miller, Tyrus. Critical Essay on "*Winesburg, Ohio*." *Novels for Students*. Ed. Marie Rose Napierkowski. Vol. 4. Detroit: Gale, 1998. 335–39.

When quoting a journal or newspaper essay that is reprinted in a volume of *NfS*, the following form may be used:

Malak, Amin. "Margaret Atwood's *The Handmaid's Tale* and the Dystopian Tradition." *Canadian Literature* 112 (Spring 1987): 9–16. Excerpted and reprinted in *Novels for Students*. Vol. 4. Ed. Marie Rose Napierkowski. Detroit: Gale, 1998. 133–36.

When quoting material reprinted from a book that appears in a volume of *NfS*, the following form may be used:

Adams, Timothy Dow. "Richard Wright: 'Wearing the Mask.'" In *Telling Lies in Modern American Autobiography*. University of North Carolina Press, 1990. 69–83. Excerpted and reprinted in *Novels for Students*. Vol. 1. Ed. Diane Telgen. Detroit: Gale, 1997. 59–61.

We Welcome Your Suggestions

The editorial staff of *Novels for Students* welcomes your comments and ideas. Readers who wish to suggest novels to appear in future volumes, or who have other suggestions, are cordially invited to contact the editor. You may contact the editor via e-mail at: **ForStudentsEditors@cengage.com.** Or write to the editor at:

Editor, *Novels for Students*
Gale
27500 Drake Road
Farmington Hills, MI 48331-3535

Literary Chronology

1771: Sir Walter Scott is born on August 15 in Edinburgh, Scotland.

1819: Sir Walter Scott's *Ivanhoe* is published.

1835: Mark Twain is born Samuel Langhorne Clemens on November 30 in Florida, Missouri.

1865: Emmuska Orczy is born Emma Magdalena Rosalia Maria Josefa Barbara Orczy on September 23 in Tarna-Örs, Hungary.

1881: Mark Twain's *The Prince and the Pauper* is published.

1896: Betty Smith is born Elizabeth Lillian Wehner on December 15 in Brooklyn, New York.

1904: Graham Greene is born on October 2 in Berkhamsted, Hertfordshire, England.

1905: Emmuska Orczy's *The Scarlet Pimpernel* is published.

1910: Mark Twain dies of a heart attack on April 21 in Redding, Connecticut.

1920: Frank Herbert is born on October 8 in Tacoma, Washington.

1924: Olive Ann Burns is born on July 27 in Banks County, Georgia.

1928: Robert Pirsig is born on September 6 in Minneapolis, Minnesota.

1931: William Goldman is born on August 12 in Chicago, Illinois.

1932: Sir Walter Scott dies of the lingering effects of a stroke on September 21 at Abbotsford, his home near Melrose, Scotland.

1937: Bessie Head is born on July 6 in Pietermaritzburg, Natal, South Africa.

1940: Graham Greene's *The Power and the Glory* is published in the United Kingdom and under the title *The Labyrinthine Ways* in the United States.

1943: Betty Smith's *A Tree Grows in Brooklyn* is published.

1947: Emmuska Orczy dies on November 12 in London, England.

1952: Amy Tan is born on February 19 in Oakland, California.

1961: Laurie Halse Anderson is born on October 23 in Potsdam, New York.

1965: Frank Herbert's novel *Dune* is published after being serialized in the science fiction magazine *Analog* between 1963 and 1965.

1966: Sherman Alexie is born on October 7 in Wellpinit, Washington.

1967: Jhumpa Lahiri is born Nilanjana Sudeshna Lahiri on July 11 in London, England.

1969: Bessie Head's *When Rain Clouds Gather* is published.

1972: Betty Smith dies on January 17 of pneumonia at a nursing home in Shelton, Connecticut.

1973: William Goldman's *The Princess Bride* is published.

1974: Robert Pirsig's *Zen and the Art of Motorcycle Maintenance: An Inquiry into Values* is published.

1984: Olive Ann Burns's *Cold Sassy Tree* is published.

1986: Bessie Head dies of alcohol-induced hepatitis on April 17 in Serowe, Botswana.

1986: Frank Herbert dies while recovering from pancreatic cancer surgery in a hospital on February 11 in Madison, Wisconsin.

1990: Olive Ann Burns dies of congestive heart failure on July 4 in Atlanta, Georgia.

1991: Graham Greene dies of heart failure on April 3 in Vevey, Switzerland.

1995: Sherman Alexie's *Reservation Blues* is published.

1999: Laurie Halse Anderson's *Speak* is published.

2000: Jhumpa Lahiri is awarded the Pulitzer Prize for Fiction for *Interpreter of Maladies*.

2001: Amy Tan's *The Bonesetter's Daughter* is published.

2003: Jhumpa Lahiri's *The Namesake* is published.

Acknowledgments

The editors wish to thank the copyright holders of the excerpted criticism included in this volume and the permissions managers of many book and magazine publishing companies for assisting us in securing reproduction rights. We are also grateful to the staffs of the Detroit Public Library, the Library of Congress, the University of Detroit Mercy Library, Wayne State University Purdy/Kresge Library Complex, and the University of Michigan Libraries for making their resources available to us. Following is a list of the copyright holders who have granted us permission to reproduce material in this volume of *NfS*. Every effort has been made to trace copyright, but if omissions have been made, please let us know.

COPYRIGHTED EXCERPTS IN *NfS*, VOLUME 31, WERE REPRODUCED FROM THE FOLLOWING PERIODICALS:

ANQ, v. 19, winter, 2006. Copyright © 2006 by Helen Dwight Reid Educational Foundation. Reproduced with permission of the Helen Dwight Reid Educational Foundation, published by Heldref Publications, 1319 18th Street, NW, Washington, DC 20036-1802.—*The Bloomsbury Review*, v. 15, July-August, 1995 for "'Reservation Blues' by Sherman Alexie," by Abigail Davis. Reproduced by permission of the author.—*CRITIQUE: Studies in Contemporary Fiction*, v. 50, fall, 2008. Copyright © 2008 by Helen Dwight Reid Educational Foundation. Reproduced with permission of the Helen Dwight Reid Educational Foundation, published by Heldref Publications, 1319 18th Street, NW, Washington, DC 20036-1802.—*ETC: A Review of General Semantics*, v. 55, fall, 1998. Copyright © 1998 by the International Society for General Semantics. Reproduced by permission.—*Extrapolation*, v. 26, spring, 1985. Copyright © 1985 by The Kent State University Press. Reproduced by permission.—*Journal of Adolescent & Adult Literacy*, v. 43, March, 2000; v. 52, September, 2008; v. 47, October, 2003. Copyright © 2000 International Reading Association. All reproduced by permission of the International Reading Association.—*Journal of Modern Literature*, v. 26, winter, 2003. Copyright © 2003 Indiana University Press. Reproduced by permission.—*The Lion and the Unicorn*, v. 2, 1978. Copyright © 1978 The Johns Hopkins University Press. Reproduced by permission.—*MELUS*, v. 31, summer, 2006. Copyright *MELUS: The Society for the Study of Multi-Ethnic Literature of the United States*, 2006. Reproduced by permission.—*The Nation*, v. 260, June 12, 1995. Copyright © 1995 by *The Nation* Magazine/The Nation Company, Inc. Reproduced by permission.—*National Review*, v. 37, April 5, 1985. Copyright © 1985 by National Review, Inc., 215 Lexington Avenue, New York, NY 10016. Reproduced by permission.—*The New Criterion*, v. 8, October, 1989 for "Graham Greene: The Catholic Novels," by Bruce Bawer. Reproduced by permission of the author.—*The*

Contributors

Bryan Aubrey: Aubrey holds a Ph.D. in English. Entry on *The Power and the Glory*. Original essay on *The Power and the Glory*.

Catherine Dominic: Dominic is a novelist and a freelance writer and editor. Entries on *Zen and the Art of Motorcycle Maintenance: An Inquiry into Values* and *The Prince and the Pauper*. Original essays on *Zen and the Art of Motorcycle Maintenance: An Inquiry into Values* and *The Prince and the Pauper*.

Joyce Hart: Hart is a published author and creative writing teacher. Entries on *Speak* and *When Rain Clouds Gather*. Original essays on *Speak* and *When Rain Clouds Gather*.

Michael Allen Holmes: Holmes is a writer and editor. Entries on *Reservation Blues* and *The Scarlet Pimpernel*. Original essays on *Reservation Blues* and *The Scarlet Pimpernel*.

Sheri Metzger Karmiol: Karmiol holds a Ph.D. in English Renaissance literature. She teaches literature and drama at the University of New Mexico, where she is a lecturer in the University Honors Program. She is also a professional writer and the author of several reference texts on poetry and drama. Entry on *A Tree Grows in Brooklyn*. Original essay on *A Tree Grows in Brooklyn*.

David Kelly: Kelly is a writer and an instructor of creative writing and literature. Entry on *The Princess Bride*. Original essay on *The Princess Bride*.

Michael J. O'Neal: O'Neal holds a Ph.D. in English literature. Entries on *Cold Sassy Tree* and *Ivanhoe*. Original essays on *Cold Sassy Tree* and *Ivanhoe*.

Bradley A. Skeen: Skeen is a classics professor. Entry on *Dune*. Original essay on *Dune*.

Leah Tieger: Tieger is a freelance writer and editor. Entry on *The Namesake*. Original essay on *The Namesake*.

Carol Ullmann: Ullmann is a freelance writer and editor. Entry on *The Bonesetter's Daughter*. Original essay on *The Bonesetter's Daughter*.

The Bonesetter's Daughter

The Bonesetter's Daughter, published in 2001 by Putnam, is Amy Tan's fourth novel. It spans two continents and more than one hundred years of history. Like Tan's other novels, *The Bonesetter's Daughter* is about family—specifically the relationship between mothers and daughters—and cultural identity. It tells the tale of three generations of women: how they loved, how they suffered, and how they survived. Precious Auntie was raised in privilege and love but lived out her life in grief and obscurity, and died trying to save her daughter LuLing from an abusive man. LuLing bridged the transition from a traditional Chinese rural life to a modern American life full of conflicting messages but she is distanced from her daughter Ruth by their different upbringings. Ruth, disconnected from her past and upset at her superstitious mother, wants to understand and reconcile her roots with who she is as a Chinese American woman.

Although it is not Tan's most famous novel, *The Bonesetter's Daughter* has received accolades. It was named a Notable Book by the *New York Times* and nominated for the prestigious Orange Prize and the IMPAC Dublin Award. Framed by war, self-discovery, and superstition, *The Bonesetter's Daughter* ultimately delivers truth and peace from the ashes of history.

AMY TAN

2001

Amy Tan (© Christopher Felver / Corbis)

AUTHOR BIOGRAPHY

Amy Tan was born on February 19, 1952, in Oakland, California, to John and Daisy Tan. Her parents had left China only a few years before, fleeing the new Communist government. After settling safely in the United States, John changed careers from electrical engineer to Baptist minister. Daisy worked as a vocational nurse. Tan, the middle child, had two brothers. Her parents had high expectations of her, deciding by the time she was six years old that she would be a medical doctor and play piano. She showed interest in language and writing early on but was discouraged from pursuing English as a course of study.

When Tan was fifteen, she lost both her father and older brother to brain cancer within six months of each other. Superstitious that their home in California may have contributed to their deaths, Daisy moved the family to Switzerland for a year where Tan finished high school. In college she began as a premed student but threw off her parents wishes, earning a bachelor of arts degree in English in 1973 and a master of arts degree in linguistics in 1974, both

from San Jose State University. Also in 1974, Tan married her college sweetheart, Louis DeMattei.

Tan had several jobs dealing with language and writing before she settled into a successful career as a freelance technical writer. When she began to suffer exhaustion from working eighty to ninety hours each week, Tan took up jazz piano and fiction writing to balance her life. Her first short story, "Endgame," was published in the prestigious *FM* literary magazine in the mid-1980s and, with her second story, was impressive enough to get Tan the attention of a literary agent.

Tan's first book, *The Joy Luck Club*, often called a novel but considered by Tan to be a collection of connected short stories, was published in 1989 to great critical acclaim. It was named a Notable Book by the American Library Association (ALA). Tan's other books, including *The Kitchen God's Wife* (1991), *The Hundred Secret Senses* (1995), *The Bonesetter's Daughter* (2001), *Saving Fish from Drowning* (2005), her two children's books *The Moon Lady* (1992) and *Sagwa: The Chinese Siamese Cat* (1994), and her memoir *The Opposite of Fate* (2003) have garnered her many award nominations. Her books have often been recognized as Notable Books by the *New York Times* and as Editors' Choice by *Booklist*. Her signature combination of history, family saga, and multicultural struggle have made Tan's books popular with teachers, who find that these novels are accessible to students.

Tan is an outspoken advocate for people suffering from Lyme Disease, which she contracted in 1999. She lives in San Francisco, California, and New York, New York, with her husband.

PLOT SUMMARY

Truth (Prologue)

The Bonesetter's Daughter begins with LuLing's childhood memory of waking with her nursemaid, Precious Auntie, when she is six years old. Precious Auntie helps LuLing bathe and dress, like they do every morning, then they go to the ancestral hall to pray before breakfast. Precious Auntie, who is mute, uses her hands to tell LuLing that her family name, the name of the bonesetters, is written on a paper and she shows it to LuLing, asking her to remember, before leaving the paper on the altar. LuLing cannot remember Precious Auntie's family name and begs her forgiveness, calling her mother.

MEDIA ADAPTATIONS

- *The Bonesetter's Daughter* was made into an unabridged audio book in 2006, read by Tan and Joan Chen and published by Phoenix Audio. It is available on eleven compact discs.
- *The Bonesetter's Daughter* was made into an opera. The libretto was written by Tan and the music was composed by Stewart Wallace. It premiered at the War Memorial Opera House in San Francisco on September 13, 2008, directed by Chen Shi-Zheng, conducted by Steven Sloane, and performed by the San Francisco Opera company.

Part One

ONE

Every year for the past nine years, Ruth loses her voice for a week. She embraces this event as a kind of vacation from her life. As the novel begins, Ruth is emerging from her week without a voice. She and her boyfriend Art are in a rut, his teenage daughters are rude and distant, and her mother LuLing is forgetful and difficult. In Ruth's desk, amongst her pile of things to do, is a memoir written by her mother, LuLing, of which Ruth resolves to translate a small amount each day.

TWO

After taking Art's daughters to the skating rink, buying groceries, working, and getting Art's water heater fixed, Ruth goes to LuLing's house to pick her up for a doctor appointment. Ruth has noticed that her mother has been behaving strangely. Although elderly, she is physically healthy, but she has become forgetful and that compounds the confusion in her life because LuLing does not speak English well.

THREE

Ruth takes LuLing to see Dr. Huey for her checkup. He pronounces LuLing strong and healthy but after asking her some questions, he tells Ruth her mother may have dementia. Ruth

does not want to hear this and tells her boyfriend it might be depression.

Ruth remembers a time from her childhood when she defied her mother and performed a playground stunt that resulted in a broken arm. During her convalescence, Ruth refuses to talk and instead uses a sand table to communicate. One night, her mother becomes convinced that Ruth is channeling the spirit of Precious Auntie. LuLing feels terrible guilt about Precious Auntie's death and young Ruth, posing as Precious Auntie, reassures LuLing that she is not cursed.

FOUR

Ruth has organized her family's annual reunion, which is held at a Chinese restaurant during the Full Moon Festival. In addition to her family, Ruth has also invited her closest friends. At Art's insistence, she has invited his ex-wife Miriam and her husband and children. Ruth is angry about their inclusion, feeling that Art continues to misunderstand what is important to her. At the end of dinner, Ruth gives out gifts. To the adults in her family, she gives framed enlargements of an old photo of her mother and her aunt, standing with their mother. LuLing insists that the woman is not her mother and that GaoLing is her sister-in-law and not her sister. Ruth takes this as further sign of her mother's confusion.

FIVE

Following more tests, the doctor confirms that LuLing has Alzheimer's disease, a type of dementia. Ruth tries to tell her mother about the diagnosis but LuLing insists her memory is fine. Her mother now joins Ruth, Art, and Art's teenage daughters for dinner every night and Ruth tries to maintain her current busy lifestyle by hiring a housekeeper for LuLing. LuLing's abrasive personality chases all caretakers away and Ruth has no choice but to send Art alone on their romantic vacation to Hawaii while she stays in San Francisco to take care of her mother. Ruth feels the distance between herself and Art growing. After a bad episode where LuLing wanders away from her house, Ruth sends her mother to stay with GaoLing so that she can work.

SIX

Ruth remembers back to a time when she and her mother lived in a rented bungalow and Ruth had a crush on their landlord Lance. He and his wife Dottie invite Ruth to come over and watch *The Wizard of Oz* on their new color TV.

Ruth uses their bathroom after Lance and accidentally sits in urine that he has left on the toilet seat. A few days later she becomes convinced that Lance has impregnated her through his urine. Her friend Wendy tells Dottie that Ruth is pregnant and Lance and Dottie separate before they figure out Ruth's misunderstanding. Lance now frightens Ruth. Her mother knows nothing of what's going on and Ruth, pretending to channel the spirit of Precious Auntie, convinces LuLing to move to another part of town.

SEVEN

Ruth cleans her mother's house while LuLing is staying with GaoLing. After she makes a dent in the clutter, Ruth begins exploring her mother's old hiding places, where LuLing has stashed valuable jewelry, cash, and sentimental items in case of emergency. She also unearths her own teenage diary, remembering the events surrounding the last few entries. Teenaged Ruth, tired of her mother secretly reading her diary, dares LuLing to commit suicide instead of just talking about it all the time. After school the next day, GaoLing rushes Ruth to the hospital to see her mother, who has fallen from a second story window and hit cement. Ruth is devastated and devotedly takes care of LuLing while she heals. For Ruth's birthday, LuLing gives her daughter an heirloom gold and jade ring that Ruth covets, a Chinese bible, and a photo of LuLing's mother as a young woman. LuLing immediately takes the gifts back to hold on to until Ruth is older and this makes Ruth angry. At the time she was only concerned with the beautiful ring. Now she realizes the photo of LuLing's mother is the same picture of Precious Auntie that LuLing was showing at the family reunion, insisting that this woman, her childhood nursemaid, was her mother. With these items, Ruth also finds another copy of her mother's memoir, although this one is different. Ruth resolves to take care of her mother and make the translation of her story a top priority.

Part Two

HEART

The point of view is now LuLing's, as told in her memoir. She grew up in Immortal Heart village with the Liu clan. When she was a girl, the mountain village of Immortal Heart had already ceased to be a lucky place, but the Liu clan made ink sticks of famous quality and were comfortable in their profession. LuLing also recalls her mother's story. Precious Auntie is the only daughter of a famous bonesetter from the nearby village of Mouth on the Mountain. She falls in love with Baby Uncle, the youngest son of the Liu clan, but is also sought after by Chang, the coffin maker, an abusive, greedy man. Her indulgent father turns down Chang and arranges for her marriage to Baby Uncle. On her wedding day, Precious Auntie's caravan to Immortal Heart is robbed by Chang in disguise and her father and bridegroom are killed as a result. Having no other family, she continues on to Immortal Heart and the Liu clan takes her in as charity. In her grief, Precious Auntie swallows hot resin, scarring her beautiful face and making herself mute. When it becomes clear she is pregnant with Baby Uncle's child, Great-Granny devises a story by which Precious Auntie and her child can stay with them without causing scandal. Precious Auntie becomes her daughter's nursemaid and at Great-Granny's insistence, Mother reluctantly claims LuLing as her eldest daughter.

CHANGE

In 1929, Mouth of the Mountain is the site of the famous archaeological discovery of Peking Man. The archaeologists seek more old bones to complete their skeleton and pay people to give up their artifacts. Precious Auntie, through her father, knows of a place where old bones can be found but will not sell them for fear of being haunted by the ancestor they belonged to. Chang the coffin maker rises in importance by selling the bones he stole from Precious Auntie. Following Great-Granny's death, LuLing is sent to Peking to be matched with a husband, who turns out to be Chang's son Fu Nan. Chang is hoping to get more bones through LuLing. LuLing and Precious Auntie have a fight when Precious Auntie learns who LuLing is betrothed to.

GHOST

Precious Auntie writes down the story of her life while the rest of the clan is busy with LuLing's wedding preparations. LuLing glances at the first few pages but refuses to read anything bad about her intended husband. Unable to stop LuLing's marriage to Chang Fu Nan any other way, Precious Auntie kills herself, sending a note to the Changs, threatening to haunt them if the marriage happens. LuLing finally reads the rest of Precious Auntie's story and learns that she was her real mother. Grieving anew, LuLing goes into the wild lands known as the End of the World behind her clan's compound, looking for Precious Auntie's body. Her only friend is GaoLing, who still treats her as a sister while GaoLing's mother, angry at Precious Auntie, gives up all pretense. Not long thereafter, the clan's shop in Peking burns down and the family fears ruin from damages owed to the adjacent shopkeepers. A man claiming to be a ghost catcher comes to their compound and secures Precious Auntie's ghost in a jar and immediately the family's luck turns around. Mother sends LuLing to an orphanage as an extra measure of security against Precious Auntie's ghost returning.

DESTINY

LuLing arrives at the orphanage on Dragon Bone Hill, which is hosted at an abandoned monastery and run by American missionaries. The orphanage shares its space with scientists working at the nearby quarry where Peking Man was found. LuLing, who can read and write thanks to Precious Auntie, is both student and tutor at the orphanage school. Time passes and LuLing gets a letter from GaoLing. GaoLing married Chang Fu Nan instead and is very unhappy because she spends all her time finding money for her husband to buy opium. More years pass and LuLing and Kai Jing, a geologist and son of one of the teachers, fall in love.

EFFORTLESS

LuLing and Kai Jing talk of marriage as the Japanese attack Peking. The morning following the first conflict, GaoLing appears at the orphanage and chooses to stay rather than return to her husband. Months later, a wedding is held for LuLing and Kai Jing but their happiness is fleeting; later that winter Kai Jing and his fellow scientists are conscripted into the Communist army to fight the Japanese. Two months later, they return, on the run from opposing forces. Kai Jing has a few tender hours with LuLing before Japanese soldiers find him. He refuses to tell them where the Communist army has gone and is executed along with thirty other recalcitrant villagers.

CHARACTER

LuLing only survives her husband's death because other people at the orphanage need her. When the United States joins the war against the Japanese, the orphanage is no longer safe and the girls escape in small groups, making the dangerous journey to Peking, where they find sanctuary with former students from the orphanage. LuLing, GaoLing, Teacher Pan, and Sister Yu live in the quarters at the ink shop. Together the four make the ink shop more successful. The war ends in 1945 and Chang Fu Nan returns home. Miss Grutoff, one of the Americans who ran the orphanage school, is released from a Japanese war camp and is very ill. GaoLing is chosen to accompany her back to the United States, for which LuLing is intensely jealous.

FRAGRANCE

LuLing moves to Hong Kong to wait to hear from GaoLing. GaoLing writes to tell her that Miss Grutoff died soon after arriving in the United States. She is finding life in the United States to be difficult and expensive but she is trying to find a way to sponsor LuLing to join her. LuLing wants to return to Peking, far away in the north, but the train ticket is too expensive. She eventually takes a job working as a maid for an elderly Englishwoman and her daughter. GaoLing writes to tell her that she has met a pair of brothers, one of whom she would like to marry so she can be an American citizen. LuLing runs into Fu Nan who thereafter regularly pesters her for GaoLing's address. When GaoLing tells LuLing she can be sponsored as a visiting artist, LuLing sells her mother's oracle bone to afford her boat passage.

Part Three

ONE

The point of view returns to Ruth, who is now living with her mother. Art has finally realized that his relationship with Ruth needs attention. Over the next few months, Art and his teenaged daughters come to miss and appreciate Ruth more now that she is not in their daily lives. The translator of her mother's memoir, Mr. Tang, is infatuated with LuLing after reading her story. Ruth invites him over for dinner so that he can meet LuLing. They chat as if they are old friends reunited. Ruth is finally able to read the story of her mother's life and learns more than she realized she did not know. She shares the memoir with Art as they draw close to each other again. Art suggests an assisted living home for LuLing but they have to trick her into going there because she would not go along with it if she knew what it really was and how much it costs.

TWO

The family gathers at GaoLing's house for her birthday. Ruth finds a private moment with her aunt to reveal to her that she now knows Precious Auntie is her grandmother and understands their whole history in China before emigrating to the United States. GaoLing is relieved that it is no longer a secret and tells Ruth what became of the different people they left in China. She also reveals to Ruth that LuLing used to successfully trade on the stock market and now has a large amount of money tucked away in an investment account. They are interrupted when LuLing falls into the pool after seeing a vision of her mother, Precious Auntie; Art rescues her. The following evening, Ruth and Art celebrate ten years together over dinner at a restaurant. Their relationship is on the mend.

THREE

Ruth, Art, LuLing, and Mr. Tang visit the Asian Art Museum for an exhibit on Chinese archaeology. Ruth and Art delight in watching the affection between LuLing and Mr. Tang. They come upon an oracle bone and talk about LuLing's grandfather, the famous bone doctor. She suddenly remembers her mother was called Liu Xing, "shooting star," and her grandfather's family name was Gu or "bone." Ruth is not impressed—these names are descriptive rather than actual. Later that day, Art casually suggests they marry and Ruth agrees.

GaoLing contacts relatives back in China and learns of Precious Auntie's family name. Like LuLing said, it is Gu but GaoLing explains to Ruth that in Chinese this spelling of gu means "gorge" and not "bone." Precious Auntie's personal name was Liu Xin, which means "remain true." She was called Liu Xing by some people because comets, which look like shooting stars, indicate bad luck. Ruth's grandmother's name was Gu Liu Xin.

EPILOGUE

The events of the novel take place over the course of a year. It is August again, but Ruth does not lose her voice for the first time in many years. She feels free, finally, of the superstition her mother brought her up with. LuLing seems to grow happier as she forgets all the bad things that happened to her. Ruth is happy for her mother and feels connected to her past. Although she has not lost her voice, she still takes this time for

herself to write a story for herself, her mother, and her grandmother.

CHARACTERS

Auntie Gal
See GaoLing Liu Young

Baby Uncle
Baby Uncle, whose real name is Liu Hu Sen, is the youngest son of Great-Granny. He is thin and good-looking. He falls in love with Precious Auntie and a marriage is arranged between them but Baby Uncle dies on their wedding day when a horse kicks him in the head. He is the father of LuLing.

Catcher of Ghosts
The Catcher of Ghosts is a con artist who pretends he is a Taoist priest. He performs a ritual in which he claims to catch Precious Auntie's ghost in a vinegar jar and cure the Liu clan of her haunting. He is later arrested and proved to be a charlatan but the family still believes they have been cured.

Chang
Chang is a local coffin maker. He is an abusive man who repeatedly brings evil into the lives of the Liu clan, beginning with his involvement in the death of Baby Uncle. His first wife falls from a roof and dies, which is probably a lie to cover up her death by his hands. He is publically executed in 1950 after being found guilty of various crimes including fraud and drug trade.

Chang Fu Nan
Chang Fu Nan is the fourth and youngest son of Chang the coffin maker. LuLing is briefly betrothed to him when she is fourteen years old; he later marries GaoLing. He is apprenticed in his father's trade but, as GaoLing learns when she lives with him, he is addicted to opium and spends all his money buying more.

Doggie
See LuLing Liu Young

Father
Liu Jen Sen is known as Father. He is married to Mother and is the son of Great-Granny. He has three brothers, Big Uncle, Little Uncle, and Baby

Uncle, but as the eldest son he is the leader of the Liu clan. He is largely absent from LuLing's life because he lives and works at the family's ink shop in Peking. He helps to arrange LuLing's betrothal to Chang Fu Nan when she visits Peking. During a terrifying nighttime vision of the ghost of Precious Auntie, he knocks over a lamp and burns down the ink shop.

Great-Granny

Great-Granny is the mother of Father, Big Uncle, Little Uncle, and Baby Uncle and is the matriarch of the Liu clan. LuLing remembers Great-Granny had a clever tongue but as Great-Granny ages, her memory deteriorates. She wanders the clan compound, looking for her youngest son, Baby Uncle, who is dead. Precious Auntie describes her condition as Confusion Itch and LuLing, more than sixty years later, wonders if she has the same disease. Great-Granny dies after a fall.

Ruth Grutoff

Ruth Grutoff is an American Christian missionary who is nurse and headmistress at an orphanage school housed in an abandoned monastery on Dragon Bone Hill. Miss Grutoff has curly hair and is in her early thirties when she and LuLing first meet around 1929. She is resourceful and keeps the orphanage running during the early years of the war with Japan. She bravely goes with the Japanese soldiers as a prisoner when the United States declares war on Japan. LuLing and GaoLing remain close friends with Miss Grutoff until her death in the late 1940s. LuLing's daughter Ruth is named after Miss Grutoff.

Art Kamen

Art Kamen is Ruth's boyfriend; they've been together for ten years. They met in a yoga class, where she mistook him for a gay man. He has a Ph.D. in linguistics and works as an American Sign Language specialist. He is amicably divorced with two teenaged daughters, Fia and Dory. Ruth lives with him and his daughters in his Edwardian townhouse. Art has become careless about letting Ruth take care of everything, leaving her feeling tired and unappreciated. When Ruth leaves to stay with her mother, Art realizes how much he misses Ruth and works with her to convince— even trick—LuLing into moving into an assisted living home. Near the end of the novel, he calmly asks Ruth to marry him and she agrees.

Dory Kamen

Dory is the daughter of Art Kamen and his ex-wife Miriam. She is thirteen years old and in the sixth grade. She is a little heavy with chestnut-colored hair and has been diagnosed with Attention Deficit Disorder.

Fia Kamen

Sofia, known throughout the novel as Fia, is the daughter of Art Kamen and his ex-wife Miriam. She is fifteen years old and has chestnut-colored hair.

Old Widow Lau

Old Widow Lau, a distant cousin to Mother, is a matchmaker who is paid to pair LuLing with Chang Fu Nan. She takes fourteen-year-old LuLing to Peking for an arranged "chance" meeting with Mrs. Chang in the family's ink shop.

Liu Hu Sen

See Baby Uncle

Mother

Mother is married to Father and is head woman of the Liu clan. She is GaoLing's mother, and LuLing's aunt, although for the first fourteen years of LuLing's life she poses as her mother also. She hates Precious Auntie for bringing bad luck into their household and sends LuLing away to an orphanage as soon as she believes Precious Auntie's ghost to have been captured. She dies after 1972 when the remainder of the Liu clan house is swallowed by a sink hole.

Pan Kai Jing

Pan Kai Jing is a geologist working at the Peking Man archaeological site and living with other scientists at the same monastery where the orphanage is housed. His father is Teacher Pan, an educator at the orphanage. He is attractive but suffers from a limp from a childhood bout with polio. Kai Jing and LuLing fall in love and marry but their happiness is short-lived. Kai Jing is conscripted into the Chinese Communist army, then later captured and executed by the Japanese when he will not reveal army secrets to them.

Teacher Pan

Teacher Pan teaches the older girls at the orphanage school. His son is geologist Pan Kai Jing, of whom he is very proud. He becomes LuLing's father-in-law when she marries Kai Jing and they have a very happy small family. His skill with calligraphy and scholarship helps the Liu family ink shop succeed following the end of the war. After the ink shop is sold, Teacher Pan remarries and lives out the rest of his life in China.

Precious Auntie

Precious Auntie, one of the main characters of this novel, is the daughter of a famous bonesetter but her real name is one of the mysteries of this novel. She is LuLing's mother and Ruth's grandmother. She is a passionate, clever woman who has deep reverence for traditional Chinese beliefs. After her father's ghost visits her in a dream, Precious Auntie is convinced that her family is cursed for disturbing the bones of her ancestors. At the same time that scientists are gathering ancient bones to put together Peking Man, Precious Auntie is trying to find all the bones left by her father to return them to her family's secret cave, called Monkey's Jaw. Overcome with grief at the loss of her father and bridegroom, Precious Auntie swallows hot resin, scarring her beautiful face and making herself mute. She should have died from these wounds but Great-Granny nurses her back to health, directed to do so by the ghost of Baby Uncle. Her life thereafter is a shadow of her former status and happiness. She acts as a nursemaid to her own daughter to avoid scandal and provide for LuLing. Fifteen years later, Precious Auntie commits suicide to prevent her daughter from marrying Chang's son. Over the years, LuLing has forgotten Precious Auntie's real name and this distresses her. Ruth, in coming to terms with her background, seeks out her grandmother's name, with GaoLing's help: Gu Liu Xin.

Dottie Rogers

Dottie Rogers is Ruth and LuLing's landlady when Ruth is eleven years old. She and her husband Lance rent them a barely legal bungalow on their property. Ruth doesn't like Dottie because she is loud and bossy. Dottie leaves Lance when she thinks he has molested Ruth.

Lance Rogers

Lance Rogers is married to Dottie and is Ruth and LuLing's landlord when Ruth is only eleven. She has a crush on him and mistakenly believes that he has impregnated her, which breaks up his marriage to Dottie. Later, he does start to touch her inappropriately and this drives Ruth to manipulate her mother into moving to a new house.

Mr. Tang

Mr. Tang is the linguist who translates LuLing's memoir from Chinese into English for Ruth. Over the course of this work, he comes to admire LuLing for her strength of character. He meets LuLing in person and they behave as if they are old friends with great affection between them. Mr. Tang takes LuLing out several times each week and has great patience with her lapses in memory.

Miss Towler

Miss Towler is the director of the orphanage school on Dragon Bone Hill. She is sixty-four years old when she meets LuLing around 1929. She is Miss Grutoff's best friend, plays piano for the students to sing along with, and leads Sunday service. Miss Towler dies in her sleep in the early 1940s, not long before the United States declares war on Japan.

Wendy

Wendy has been Ruth's best friend since childhood. She is with Ruth throughout the pregnancy fiasco with Lance Rogers when they are eleven. Over twenty years later, they take yoga together and this is where Ruth meets Art. Wendy is a colorful personality and expresses her emotions without reservation, acting as something of a foil to Ruth's reserve.

GaoLing Liu Young

GaoLing—known as Liu GaoLing while she lives in China and often called Auntie Gal by Ruth—was born in 1916, five months after LuLing but her birth date is recorded for nine months later, in 1917. She and LuLing grow up as sisters although they are actually cousins. GaoLing marries Chang Fu Nan and lives for several miserable years as his wife, supporting his addiction to opium. The war with Japan gives her an opportunity to disappear. Fu Nan finds her after the war but GaoLing is able to escape with Miss Grutoff to the United States, where she reinvents her life, marrying and starting a family with Edmund Young, the younger of two brothers and a dental student. Her children are Billy and Sally.

GaoLing has always taken care of LuLing, from when Precious Auntie died and no one wanted anything to do with her, up to the present time of the novel when LuLing's dementia makes it increasingly difficult for her to live alone. GaoLing is relieved that LuLing has told the truth of their life in China to Ruth; she has more readily adopted a Western lifestyle than LuLing has and wishes to let the past go.

LuLing Liu Young

LuLing was born in 1916, the daughter of Precious Auntie and Baby Uncle. Throughout her childhood, she thought she was the daughter of Mother of the Liu clan and does not learn the truth of her parentage until after Precious Auntie's death. LuLing's life as a young woman in China is difficult, full of great happiness as well as sadness, but the strength she learned from Precious Auntie and the support of the people she loves, like Pan Kai Jing, GaoLing, and Miss Grutoff, help guide her and keep her going. She marries Pan Kai Jing for love but he dies during the war with the Japanese. She travels to the United States as a Famous Visiting Artist and marries Edwin Young, the elder of two brothers and a medical student. Ruth is their daughter but Edwin is tragically killed in a hit-and-run accident when Ruth is two years old. LuLing's relationship with Ruth is both dependent and combative as LuLing holds her traditional beliefs and Ruth grows up as an American teen in the 1960s.

As she enters her eighties, LuLing is diagnosed with Alzheimer's disease, a type of dementia. Ruth is floored that her strong, if difficult, mother is unable to care for herself on a daily basis any longer. But LuLing seems happier as she forgets more, letting go of all the bad things that happened in her life while retaining the good.

Ruth Luyi Young

Ruth is the daughter of LuLing and the granddaughter of Precious Auntie. She is named after Miss Grutoff and Sister Yu. When the novel opens, her life is sliding out of balance as she loses touch with her boyfriend Art and her mother LuLing, and works too much. Her mother's Alzheimer's diagnosis forces Ruth to face the issues she has with her mother and her childhood. In the process, she finally learns the entirety of her mother's history before LuLing emigrated to the United States and this brings them closer together. On her mother's behalf, as well as for herself, Ruth investigates and learns the real name of her grandmother. This gives her a sense of closure and enables Ruth to move forward with her life. She and Art decide to marry after ten years together; her mother is happy for the first time in sixty years; and Ruth is finally giving voice to her own creativity.

Sister Yu Luyi

Sister Yu works at the orphanage school in China and is in charge of Cleanliness, Neatness, and Proper Behavior. LuLing finds her bossiness tiresome during the start of her life at the orphanage but soon learns to appreciate Sister Yu's cleverness, determination, and wit. She is especially close with GaoLing. After the war, Sister Yu lives and works in the ink shop with LuLing, GaoLing, and Teacher Pan until Chang Fu Nan kicks her out, disturbed by the sight of her hunched back. Sister Yu goes on to have a successful career in the Communist party of China. Ruth is, in part, named after Sister Yu.

THEMES

Family Relationships

The Bonesetter's Daughter tells the story of three generations of women, mother to daughter to granddaughter. Tan does not hesitate to reveal the pain and conflict in these relationships that cause the women to struggle with each other, as well as the love and loyalty that keeps them together. Throughout the novel, family relationships are defined with some fluidity, starting with LuLing being adopted by Mother to cover up the scandal of her birth outside wedlock. Many years later, after LuLing and her cousin GaoLing have settled in the United States and are married to a pair of brothers, the stigma of being born outside wedlock is much less significant and yet the lie is maintained so as not to disturb their new husbands. In the contemporary setting of the novel, Ruth's unmarried relationship to Art and his daughters is not typical but it is very stable and her fluid sense of family is represented by the variety of friends included in Ruth's family reunion.

LuLing and GaoLing grow up as sisters although they are technically cousins. When LuLing is cast off by the Liu family and sent to an orphanage, the two girls swear to stand by each other as sisters and indeed do so for the rest of their lives. Like all sisters, there is an element of competition but they never hesitate to help each other. In her novel, Tan represents healthy family relationships as important to a happy life. Ruth and LuLing struggle with this as their different values—American and Chinese—drive them apart. As a child, LuLing is very close to her mother, Precious Auntie, just as Precious

TOPICS FOR FURTHER STUDY

- Tan's novels focus on family relationships, especially those between mothers and daughters. Watch the 1993 movie adaptation of *The Joy Luck Club*. Which themes and symbols are similar to those in *The Bonesetter's Daughter*? Write your own short story or teleplay centered around family relationships, drawing upon inspiration from Tan's characters, setting, or organization.

- Read Sandra Cisnero's young-adult novel *The House on Mango Street* (1984). What parts of Esperanza Cordero's life are reminiscent of LuLing's childhood or even Ruth's? Write an essay that compares and contrasts Cisnero's coming-of-age novel with *The Bonesetter's Daughter*.

- Peking Man was an important archaeological discovery that was unfortunately lost during the war with the Japanese. The region where these bones were found, Zhoudoukian, China, has been the site of many other important finds. What other archaeological evidence has been uncovered in this region? What do these items signify? Write a short paper about the scientific significance of this locality.

- Superstition was an important part of the daily lives of people living in China during the early twentieth century. Research the psychology of superstition. What purpose do superstitions serve for people who believe them? What superstitions are common in North American society? What superstitions do you or your family members hold and why? Share the results of your research in a PowerPoint presentation.

- Cuisine is an important part of Chinese ethnic identity and varies widely from region to region in this vast nation. Tan describes different traditional Chinese foods throughout her novel, such as spicy turnips and jellyfish. Research the cuisine of the mountain region near Peking (also known as Beijing), where Ruth's family is from. Which dishes are familiar and which are unusual? Which ingredients are unknown to you? Create a recipe book.

Auntie was close with her father following the untimely deaths of her mother and brothers. Through these strings of relationships, a heritage is built. When Ruth finally learns the truths of her past, she is buoyed up and this strength is reflected in her relationship with Art, her business life, and her creativity.

Superstition

Traditional Chinese culture is rich with superstitions that guide people in the choices they make in their everyday lives. One type of superstitious activity in the early twentieth century in China was fortune telling. The fortunes told could be good or bad but were often so vague that they could be interpreted in multiple ways. For example, Baby Uncle has a fortune-teller read the omens for his marriage to Precious Auntie. The fortune-teller sees nothing but calamity; nonetheless, Baby Uncle is so smitten with Precious Auntie that he pays the old woman to reinterpret the omens so that they can be married.

Ghosts are also prevalent in traditional Chinese culture and often bring bad luck. Many behaviors are used to prevent or drive away ghosts, such as proper burial and respectful treatment of their wishes. In *The Bonesetter's Daughter*, ghosts are more real in China than in the United States, visiting people in their dreams or in the latrine. Baby Uncle threatens to haunt his mother unless she saves Precious Auntie's life. Precious Auntie's vengeful ghost frightens Father, causing him to knock over a lamp and burn down the family's ink shop. These superstitions have less hold when LuLing and Gao-Ling move to the United States. GaoLing readily embraces Western life, leaving behind the old ways, whereas LuLing, sure that her family has been cursed, clings to traditional beliefs. Chinese superstitions often revolve around bad luck and its avoidance. Ghosts are feared largely because they bring bad luck; ghosts do not stay behind to haunt mortals if they are happy and peaceful.

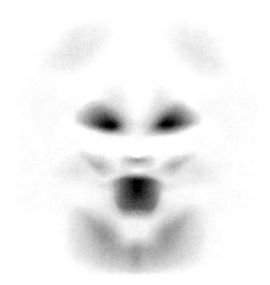

Ghost *(Image copyright Dic Liew, 2009. Used under license from Shutterstock.com)*

STYLE

Foreshadowing

Foreshadowing is a literary device used by writers to present hints about events yet to happen. Foreshadowing creates dramatic tension as the reader anticipates what is to come without always knowing exactly how it will come to pass or even if it will happen for sure. In *The Bonesetter's Daughter*, for example, Baby Uncle receives bad omens for this marriage to Precious Auntie and later dies on his wedding day, leaving Precious Auntie to live out a difficult and unhappy life, and Ruth's first worry about her mother's health is dementia but she immediately disregards this and is taken by surprise when the doctor gives a diagnosis of Alzheimer's (a type of dementia).

Setting

Setting is a literary term encompassing the location, the time period, and the cultural milieu that provides not just a backdrop for the story but also a context. For example, *The Bonesetter's Daughter* has two main settings, which correspond to its two major characters, pre-war rural China and early twenty-first century San Francisco. The setting in China starts off gentle and sleepy and probably foreign to most Western readers but builds in danger and consequence as Peking Man is discovered and the war with Japan breaks out. In parallel to these events, LuLing grows from childhood to adulthood. The setting in San Francisco is probably familiar to Western readers, even if they have not been to the city, making Ruth the character readers will more readily identify with. Her struggles, although not life-threatening as LuLing's sometimes were, are the kinds of things people deal with in contemporary Western society: difficulty balancing work and personal life, multicultural families, stepchildren, and elderly parents who need assisted living. In this way, setting enhances the story being told.

HISTORICAL CONTEXT

Peking Man

Peking Man is an assemblage of Homo erectus fossilized bones found on Dragon Bone Hill, amidst the Zhoudoukian cave systems, thirty miles (fifty kilometers) southwest of Peking, China, from 1921 to 1936. Dragon Bone Hill was called such because local people knew it as a place to find the fossils they called dragon bones—an important ingredient in traditional Chinese medicine. Excavation by Swedish geologist Johan Andersson and American paleontologist Walter Granger began in 1921 after the pair was directed to Dragon Bone Hill by local men as a place where old bones could be found. Two molars were the first human fossils discovered. As more scientists became involved, more fossils were uncovered, including a jaw and skull fragments. Excavation temporarily ceased after 1936 when hostilities between China and Japan made work dangerous. In 1941, the bones were packed up and sent away for safekeeping until China's war with Japan was over, but they mysteriously disappeared before they left China. Despite ongoing attempts to find them, the original Peking Man bones have not been recovered. Luckily, paleontologist Franz Weidenreich made casts of the original bones and paleontologist Jia Lanpo copied the site drawings, preserving important evidence that would otherwise be entirely lost.

Dragon Bone Hill is a very important archaeological and geological site because it has very deep stratigraphy, or layers, which help scientists to accurately date their finds. The site is particularly

Statue of Liberty in New York City *(Image copyright Vhrinchenko, 2009. Used under license from Shutterstock.com)*

significant for the Paleolithic, or Stone, Age. The fossils of Peking Man come from more than forty different people, most of them women and children, and are believed to be 750,000 years old, making these remains part of the Lower Paleolithic, or Old Stone, Age. Scientists theorize that Homo erectus is the direct ancestor of modern humans, although how Homo erectus transitioned to Homo sapiens is hotly debated, with Peking Man being of central importance to those theories because of its distance from Africa, where hominids originated.

The Bonesetter's Daughter takes place, in part, during these years of discovery and war southwest of Peking. Precious Auntie, daughter of a bonesetter, knows of a secret place containing human and "dragon" bones but she will not tell the scientists because she believes her ancestors reside there and it would bring restless ghosts and bad luck if they were disturbed. LuLing lives in an orphanage on Dragon Bone Hill and marries a Chinese geologist who works there. Periodic

excavations resumed in 1949, after the war. Additional pieces of Peking Man have been recovered, as well as 17,000 stone artifacts, which include stone tools and tool-making debris. The United Nations Educational, Scientific, and Cultural Organization (UNESCO) declared this archaeological site a World Heritage Site in 1987, confirming its importance to humanity.

CRITICAL OVERVIEW

Tan catapulted into the literary world in 1989 with the publication of her first book, *The Joy Luck Club*, which was lauded by critics and, in 1994, made into an equally well-received film of the same title. *The Bonesetter's Daughter* is her fourth novel, published in 2001. Donna Seaman, in her review for *Booklist*, describes the book as "polished and provocative" and "compulsively readable." A reviewer for the *Economist* gives both praise and criticism: "Ms. Tan is a powerful and sensitive writer, but if she has a fault it lies in her tendency to weigh down every element of her story with meaning." Troy Patterson, reviewing for *Entertainment Weekly*, finds fault with *The Bonesetter's Daughter* as compared to Tan's other works. "The rich sources of vivid detail that Tan has evoked so successfully in previous novels are undermined here by hackneyed images and feeble descriptions," he writes. Patterson's scathing opinion is uncommon. Poet Nancy Willard, in a review for the *New York Times*, praises Tan's "marvelous characters" and "superb storytelling."

Altogether, Tan has published five novels, two children's books, a memoir, and a libretto. Critics have generally praised her work and her books are popular with readers. Tan remains a dominant figure in the genre of multicultural literature.

CRITICISM

Carol Ullmann

Ullmann is a freelance writer and editor. In the following essay, she examines the significance of ghosts in Amy Tan's The Bonesetter's Daughter.

Ghosts are an important motif in Amy Tan's *The Bonesetter's Daughter*. A motif is a recurring object, idea, or other element that the writer uses to reinforce the theme of the work. This novel has two distinct settings, contemporary San Francisco and early twentieth-century China. In China, as represented in the novel, ghosts have a very real, often threatening, presence, whereas most of the characters in San Francisco are unaffected by ghosts.

The most important ghost of the novel is that of Precious Auntie. She commits suicide when LuLing is fourteen years old to frighten the Chang family into calling off LuLing's marriage to Fu Nan. LuLing does not learn that Precious Auntie is her mother until after Precious Auntie is dead and spends the rest of her life trying to contact her, a sort of haunting in reverse. First, LuLing searches for her mother's body; later in life LuLing comes to believe that her daughter Ruth can communicate with the spirit of Precious Auntie. Ruth does not know that Precious Auntie is her grandmother and is annoyed and embarrassed by her mother's desire to talk to ghosts through her. Ruths feels that her mother's superstitious beliefs are antiquated

and backwards. For Ruth, LuLing's superstitions have no power.

The only true hauntings that reportedly happen occur in China; for example, Baby Uncle's ghost threatens to haunt his family if they do not care for Precious Auntie in her grief; the ghost of the bonesetter visits his daughter and warns her to return the bones of their ancestors to the family's secret cave; Great-Granny's ghost haunts the latrine, making Mother maintain the household (including Precious Auntie and LuLing) as she did before her death; Precious Auntie's ghost visits Father in the middle of the night in Peking, causing him to knock over a lamp and burn down the family's shop. LuLing also believes that Precious Auntie communicates with her through a fortune-teller shortly before she goes to live in the orphanage. In China, ghosts have a terrible power. Restless spirits are considered bad luck and must be appeased. Overwhelmed by misfortune, the Liu family tries another approach: they hire a priest who calls himself the Catcher of Ghosts to trap Precious Auntie's ghost in a jar of vinegar so that she cannot bring them bad luck any longer. Young LuLing is convinced that her part in the ritual is a betrayal of Precious Auntie and she never fully recovers from that guilt. The Catcher of Ghosts later turns out to be a charlatan but regardless, the Liu clan believes her ghost is gone.

In San Francisco, LuLing is the only character who really believes in ghosts. When Ruth is a young girl, she becomes convinced that Ruth is able to channel the spirit of Precious Auntie and write for her on a sand table. This brings great solace to LuLing, who feels guilty about Precious Auntie's death and misses her. Ruth, who is pretending to speak for a ghost, finds the sand table sessions both liberating (because she can say things she normally is not allowed to voice) and imprisoning (because she can never refuse to use the sand table and is forced into these fake conversations, increasing her feelings of guilt). Ruth privately calls Precious Auntie "the crazy ghost," knowing only her own personal torment.

In *The Bonesetter's Daughter*, several characters make appearances as ghosts. Precious Auntie's father, the bonesetter, and her bridegroom, Baby Uncle, are the only two male ghosts to make an appearance. They deliver warnings meant to guide their families to better care for their ancestors or each other. The other men who die in this novel, LuLing's two husbands, Kai Jing and

WHAT DO I READ NEXT?

- *The Joy Luck Club* (1989) is Tan's acclaimed first novel about four Chinese women who flee to the United States during World War II and remain close friends in an effort to preserve their heritage. The novel also tells the stories of their four daughters, who struggle with their identities as first-generation Chinese Americans.

- Maxine Hong Kingston's *The Woman Warrior: Memoirs of a Girlhood Among Ghosts* was published in 1976 and is a unique blend of autobiography, fiction, myth, and history. It tells the tale of a Chinese American girl (Kingston) growing up in San Francisco during the mid-twentieth century.

- Li-Young Lee is an American poet who was born in Indonesia to Chinese parents. *Rose* (1986), his first book of poetry, draws inspiration from his family and his Chinese background.

- *American Born Chinese* (2006) by Gene Luen Yang and Lark Pien is a graphic novel about a teenage boy, Jin, who suddenly finds himself to be a minority when his family moves to a different part of town and he must deal with racism and self-hate before coming to terms with his distinct heritage.

- *China A-to-Z: Everything You Need to Know to Understand Chinese Customs and Culture* (2007) by May-lee Chai and Winberg Chai covers crucial cultural information for a Western audience in brief chapters, making this complex culture with a deep history more accessible.

- *The Moon Lady* (1992) by Amy Tan and illustrated by Gretchen Shields is a picture book about a young girl's adventures on the night of the Full Moon Festival, after she is separated from her family.

- *The House of the Spirits* (1985) by Isabelle Allende is a novel about four generations of women surviving political upheaval in South America. It is one of Allende's most famous works as well as her first novel.

- Ella Leffland's *Breath and Shadows*, published in 1999, is a mystery about three generations of a Scandinavian family. The youngest generation is trying to understand their ancestry and identity as they search for the name of their father. Leffland's novel was a *Booklist* Editors' Choice for 1999.

Edwin Young, never reappear as ghosts. Kai Jing, in fact, implores LuLing to give up her superstitions when he is alive. "[A] superstition is a needless fear," he tells her after they are married. As a scientist, he only believes in what he can observe. These Western, scientific sensibilities are slowly supplanting traditional beliefs during LuLing's childhood. The archaeologists assembling Peking Man ask people to give them their own bones and, lured by fame and money like Chang, they do. Although all are proud to claim ancestry from someone so ancient, none seem worried that disturbance of these ancient bones will anger the ancestors. Precious Auntie's fear of the curse of her ancestors is far greater than any

earthly desires. As the ghost of her father warns her, "There is nothing worse than having your own relative out for revenge."

The women ghosts in this novel are Great-Granny and Precious Auntie. Great-Granny's ghost is more of a residual haunting, "making sure everyone still followed her rules." In this way, Precious Auntie's position in the household is maintained. Precious Auntie's haunting is vengeful. She appears thirty miles away from where she died, in Peking, to tell Father, "Did you value camphor wood more than my life? Then let the wood burn as I do now." Ghosts not only function as a fear incentive to keep people behaving within acceptable boundaries, but are also a vehicle, literally or figuratively depending on one's beliefs, by which individuals can do things in death that they could not do in life because of station, gender, or other social restriction. Traditional Chinese culture is carefully structured; ghosts are feared because they are not bound by the same rules as the living. They bring bad luck, which is another way of saying confusion, disharmony, or destruction.

Ruth's career as a ghost writer introduces an American concept of ghosts. In the United States, ghosts are sometimes malevolent, but are more often weak residuals with limited power to affect the living: ghosts can sometimes speak, move through rooms, or, in rare instances, move physical objects. Therefore, as a ghostwriter, Ruth's creative life is only half alive and weak. Art delivers an interesting twist when he reinterprets her work and calls her a "book doctor," which is reminiscent of her great-grandfather, who was a famous doctor in China—a bonesetter. LuLing never really loses the sense that Ruth can communicate with the dead because of Ruth's work as a ghostwriter. "Her mother thought it meant that she could actually write to ghosts."

Ruth's annual muteness is an echo of her grandmother's disfiguration. Tan emphasizes this connection by having the week of speechlessness coincide with the Pleiades meteor shower, a group of shooting stars, or "melting ghost bodies," as described by LuLing. Mid-August is also approximately the time when the Chinese Ghost Festival occurs each year. The Ghost Festival is a holiday during which people venerate their ancestors by putting out special foods and burning paper objects. If one fails to pay attention to their ancestors then they will become angry, hungry, and restless and cause trouble for the living. Ruth's week of muteness is the only time she ever gives to herself until the conclusion of the novel. It is a way, unconsciously, of honoring her ancestors, especially Precious Auntie. The discovery of her heritage through LuLing's memoir spurs Ruth to take hold of what she wants in life. Inspired by her grandmother and mother, she finally begins to write creatively for herself. She is no longer a ghost writer for other people's ghosts. The lesson of *The Bonesetter's Daughter* is to come to terms with and cherish your family members while they are alive because when these loved ones become ghosts, it is too late to say what was left unsaid.

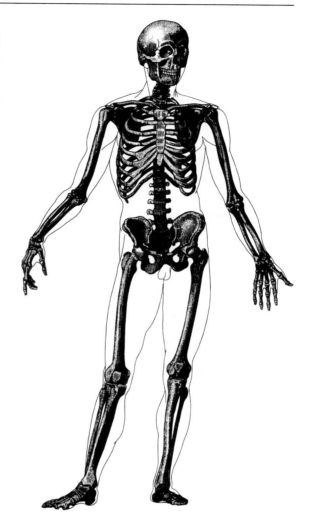

Human skeleton (*Image copyright Betacam-SP, 2009. Used under license from Shutterstock.com*)

Source: Carol Ullmann, Critical Essay on *The Bonesetter's Daughter*, in *Novels for Students*, Gale, Cengage Learning, 2010.

Lisa M. S. Dunick

In the following essay, Dunick examines the relationship between writing and cultural identity in The Bonesetter's Daughter.

In the past twenty years, novels such as Maxine Hong Kingston's *Woman Warrior*, Leslie Marmon Silko's *Ceremony*, and works by an array of African American women writers have become relatively common occurrences on university syllabi. The inclusion of these female authored texts is often a function of their difference from the grand narratives of "traditional" American literature.

IN *THE BONESETTER'S DAUGHTER*, TAN CREATES THE POSSIBILITY FOR THE RECEPTION OF CULTURAL AND PERSONAL MEMORY IN THE AMERICAN DAUGHTER BECAUSE THE DAUGHTER, IN EFFECT, BECOMES THE READER OF HER MOTHER'S TEXT."

University instructors and literary critics alike have tended to highlight traditionally oral forms of narration, especially women's oral story-telling, found in many of these ethnic women's texts as equal to the traditional grand narratives of Western literature. While the attention given to these authors has broadened our definitions and understanding of what we consider literary, it has at the same time highlighted these authors' difference to such an extent that they remain always in some respect outside of or in opposition to a traditional conception of the canon. In some cases, the effect of this limitation has been to valorize texts that fit into the neat models of what writing by ethnic American authors should do and has relegated writers who do not fit into these models to the outskirts of our critical interest. Thus, certain writers become naturalized as intrinsically important, while others are relegated to the realm of the popular.

In the realm of Asian American women's literature, we can see this exclusionary effect in discussions about Amy Tan's works. The criticism about Tan's works centers on the way that the dialogic nature of talk-story functions either to create or to bridge gaps between bi-cultural, bilingual immigrant mothers and their Americanized second-generation daughters. In particular, since Maxine Hong Kingston's *Woman Warrior* underscored the Chinese tradition of "talk-story" as a major trope in Chinese American women's narratives, focus on this specific oral tradition has become the center of much of the critical work being done about Chinese American women writers. However, in the case of Tan's texts, this critical focus on the importance of talk-story serves to limit the interpretive work to be done on these texts. Studies of Amy Tan's first three novels,

The Joy Luck Club (1989), *The Kitchen God's Wife* (1991), and *The Hundred Secret Senses* (1995), have correctly identified patterns of tension in her texts that result from the conflict between the oral storytelling of Chinese mothers (what has been identified as talk-story) and their American daughters' initial resistance to and eventual acceptance of that mode of narration. Critical work on Tan's texts has largely ignored aspects of that corpus which separates it from the work of writers like Kingston—the importance of written texts and the literacy of Chinese mothers. Consequently, by failing to recognize that Tan highlights the crafting of written texts as important, critics also have failed to appreciate fully Tan's representation of her Chinese mothers and the work that these texts do within a broader context of literature.

This critical shortcoming may be recognized and perhaps rectified with a reassessment of her work through the lens of *The Bonesetter's Daughter* (2001). This novel's intense focus on the literary quality of women's writing may allow us to recognize that literacy in the form of writing and written texts represents an important and often more effective means of transmitting cultural memories and cultural identity across generational lines than talk-story. Furthermore, *The Bonesetter's Daughter* is not a completely new development in or deviation from Tan's previous themes, but represents a more fully developed reworking of issues about identity and language than we can find in many of her works. Through an analysis of the importance of written texts, this study will demonstrate the ways that Tan's works present literacy and writing in order to reveal the critical problems with identifying non-Western narratives only through an understanding of oral traditions. The misreading of authorship in *The Bonesetter's Daughter* mirrors the mechanisms of inclusion and exclusion necessary in both forming and reacting to the literary canon and the silencing function that imposes limits on the possibilities of recognizing literary value.

Throughout Tan's novels, talk-story promotes multiple levels of misunderstanding between both Chinese-speaking mothers and English-speaking daughters and between persons who speak different Chinese dialects. As a linguistic strategy, talk-story in Tan's novels often fails to convey clearly the speaker's message to her audience. Some critics have attempted to complicate the use of talk-story in their analysis of Tan's work, but they never see literacy and written narrative as an alternative. Judith Caesar indicates that while Tan's use of a multi-voiced talk-story narrative is noteworthy, even more significant is who speaks in the texts. Following the usual line of argument that privileges orality, Caesar specifically argues that by privileging the accented and fragmented speech of Chinese immigrants, Tan gives their voices validity in the same way that African American writers have validated the vernacular speech of black communities. Caesar's arguments demonstrate the way that literary critics have found value in Tan's work through an interpretation of Chinese speech as a rhetorical device. Chandra Tyler Mountain recognizes that the memory fueling these stories "becomes the agent involved in redeeming cultures; it becomes a political struggle against the negation of cultures." Consequently, many critics have recognized talk-story as a source of agency for Asian American women writers because it allows them a mode of discourse not constricted to the confines of traditional Western narratives.

In her article "The Semiotics of China Narratives in the Con/Texts of Kingston and Tan," Yuan comes closest to recognizing the limits of talk-story in Tan's novels by arguing that they embody a distinct aspect of loss. Throughout her novels, Tan's characters emphasize that their immigration to the United States after World War II caused an erosion or loss of their cultural memories. Throughout her texts, Chinese-born mothers attempt to perpetuate these cultural memories in the stories told to their American-born daughters, but often with mixed results. For the daughters, these talk-stories do not represent a stable text but depend solely on the mothers' memories. Thus, the mothers' continual revision of their stories often signals an erasure or loss of China as referent for the American-born listeners. As Yuan argues, "In short, China lies at an absolute distance from the present remembrance, irretrievably lost beyond recall, made present only through a narrative that invites forgetting instead of remembering" (293). Using China as the missing "prior text," Yuan calls attention to the inability of oral talk-story in Tan's novels to establish and maintain an intergenerational cultural memory of China as a cultural homeland, but she does not attempt to find alternative contexts within Tan's work.

The problems caused by talk-story, or oral communication in general, occupy a major place in Tan's first novel, *The Joy Luck Club*, when Jing-Mei describes not understanding her mother's story about the time her mother spent in Kweilin during World War II. Jing-Mei states that she never saw the story as anything more than a "Chinese fairy tale" because "the endings always changed." Her mother's constant revision of the story's ending did not provide a narrative that Jing-Mei was able to recognize and claim as her own. Jing-Mei understands what her mother was attempting to tell her only after Suyuan finishes the story for the last time. Gasping with the stunned realization that the story had always been true, Jing-Mei asks her mother what happened to the babies in the story. Suyuan "didn't even pause to think. She simply said in a way that made it clear there was no more to the story: 'Your father is not my first husband. You are not those babies.'" Jing-Mei can only begin to understand the story's significance when her mother gives it a recognizable ending and imposes on it a narrative structure that Jing-Mei recognizes.

The misinterpretations and misunderstandings of Suyuan's story are representative of those throughout the body of Tan's work. In part, these miscommunications are a result of faulty translation. Translation, as Ken-fan Lee points out, "suggests not only literal transformation but also cultural and psychological interaction." A successful translation entails more than a desire to understand; a successful translation also entails ability and cultural knowledge. Throughout Tan's novels, these failed attempts at communication are in part produced by a tension between persons who have different understandings of how stories, culture, and language are supposed to work.

Far from being complete failures, the tensions produced by competing forms of narration are somewhat alleviated through Tan's portrayal of the didactic nature of the mothers' voices. Winnie Louie's narrative, which comprises the bulk of Tan's second novel, *The Kitchen God's Wife*, provides a specific example of a mother who must teach her daughter how to listen and understand her stories as she speaks. In this text, Winnie narrates secret pasts and truths "too complicated" to tell to her American daughter, but can only speak in the English she has not wholly mastered. Winnie says that she will tell her daughter "not what happened, but why it happened, how it could not be any other way." In the narrative that follows, Winnie uses talk-story to narrate her own history, but as she talks she must help her daughter understand both her broken English and what remains untranslatable. While the story chronicles the life of a young Winnie from orphan to abused wife, the narration consciously draws attention to the language that it uses.

Though Winnie speaks to her daughter in English, she must attempt to teach her the Chinese words that when spoken have no translation. When Winnie is in urgent need of money from her dowry account, she sends a telegram to her cousin Peanut that reads "Hurry, we are soon taonan." She continues with her explanation of the necessity for funds, but is cut off with a question about what the word means from her listening daughter. Winnie tries to answer her daughter by explaining the significance of the word since she cannot translate its literal meaning. She says,

> This word, taonan? Oh, there is no American word I can think of that means the same thing. But in China, we have lots of different words to describe all kinds of troubles. No, 'refugee' is not the meaning, not exactly. Refugee is what you are after you have been taonan and are still alive. And if you are alive, you would never want to talk about what made you taonan.

This passage demonstrates the voice that Tan develops for her Chinese mothers by balancing the simplicity of diction with vivid imagery to illustrate the narrative. It also demonstrates the confusion and misunderstanding common in exchanges between Tan's mothers and daughters. However, once she has explained and developed the idea of taonan, she can use the word throughout the rest of her narrative in place of a less specific English translation. Later, when she tells her daughter how fear can change a person, she says "you don't know such a person exists inside of you until you become taonan." While the true significance of the word is always missing from the narrative, her daughter can begin to understand the importance of the word through her mother's instruction. Therefore, talk-story cannot be read as a complete failure, nor should it be ignored in Tan's texts. However, talk-story cannot function properly for these Chinese mothers and American daughters without a source of mediation.

In Tan's novels, often the source of that mediation comes through the vehicle of the written text. For instance, in *The Joy Luck Club* the differences between Chinese dialects become evident when Lindo Jong cannot communicate with her future husband, Tin, because of his Cantonese dialect. Although they are both in a class to learn English, even that mode of communication is not wholly available because they can only speak the "teacher's English," which consists of simple declarative sentences about cats and rats. During English class, the two must use written Chinese characters to communicate with each other. Lindo sees those written notes as an important conduit for their relationship. She tells the reader, "at least we had that, a piece of paper to hold us together." Though Lindo and Tin cannot understand the Chinese dialects that each one speaks they can understand Chinese characters written on paper. While the two may be unable to speak to one another, the universality of a written Chinese character allows them to communicate clearly across the boundaries of speech.

This use of written texts reoccurs in the relationship between Lindo and Tin as they use written texts to facilitate their courtship. An-mei tells Lindo that in the movies, people use notes passed in class to "fall into trouble," so they devise a plan to "pass a note" to Tin. Because they work in a fortune cookie factory and can control the fortunes, the women decide to arrange a marriage proposal by putting the message in a cookie. Earlier, these fortunes were seen as both powerful and foolish by Lindo and An-mei, but appropriated for their own use, the fortunes become a valuable form of written communication. Sorting through the many Americanized fortunes, they settle on "A house is not a home when a spouse is not at home" to cross the boundaries of both translation and propriety. Because it breaks with Chinese custom for a woman to initiate a marriage proposal, Lindo uses the fortune cookie to "ask" Tin to marry her in a language and a custom that is not her own. The English writing must be translated (because Tin does not know the meaning of "spouse"), but the physicality of the text allows Tin to take the message and translate its meaning outside of the immediacy of speech. The use of a text, in this case an English text, allows Lindo to determine her future using the silence of the writing at a point when the vehicle of talk-story could not work, even with another Chinese-speaking person.

Lindo's use of the fortune cookie is an example of how we can find small, but important places where the tensions and misunderstandings between speakers must be alleviated through writing or written texts. Like Lindo Jong, Winnie

Louie in *The Kitchen God's Wife* is highly aware of the importance of writing and authorship. Winnie demonstrates her ability to create meaning through writing the banners that she designs for her floral business. As Pearl tells the reader, the red banners she includes with each floral arrangement did not contain typical congratulatory sayings. Instead, "all the sayings, written in gold Chinese Characters, are of her own inspiration, her thoughts about life and death, luck and hope." These inspirational banners with their creative sayings like "Money Smells Good in Your New Restaurant Business" and "First-Class Life for your First Baby" represent more than a creative outlet. For Winnie Louie, their authorship is the very reason for her business's success and an expression of her identity.

Winnie continually stresses the importance of her literacy and that of her mother. As a child on a trip to the market with her mother, Winnie tells the reader that she could not read and therefore could not tell what the paper her mother purchased was. Unable to read, she misses vital information about events that will eventually change her life. However, by the end of her narrative, her ability to write letters to her future husband enables her to escape from China before the Communists take power. In a society where the "traditional way" deems that "the girl's eyes should never be used for reading, only for sewing," the fact that Winnie's mother was both highly educated and bilingual represents an important difference. Winnie's ability to write in both Chinese and English indicates that her use of oral narrative was a conscious choice rather than the result of some limitation. That Winnie can choose between the two languages and modes of expression demonstrates that talk-story works only in selective situations and that it is not the only choice Chinese women have for authentic self expression. Instead, literacy—the ability to both read and write—marks Tan's mother figures as powerful forces in her texts.

Though Tan asserts the voice of Chinese immigrant women through her own writing, the written texts that appear throughout her works endow Chinese and Chinese-immigrant women the agency to write themselves, an agency that critics have not yet recognized in the over-emphasis on talk-story. Tan has intentionally fashioned a complexity of voice for her Chinese mother figures. In her essay, "Mother Tongue," Tan emphasizes her conscious desire to give validity to the voice of those who speak "broken" or non-standardized Englishes in her novels. She tells her reader that she writes her stories with all of the Englishes she has used throughout her life. Most importantly, she says that she "wanted to capture what language ability tests can never reveal: her [mother's] intent, her passion, her imagery, the rhythms of her speech and the nature of her thoughts." Tan attempts to capture what no language ability test would reveal: the fundamental literacy of her Chinese mothers. In addition, she also captures their literary ability. Tan's emphasis on the aesthetic power of nonnative speakers emphasizes the art inherent in their narrative. Instead of representing the reclamation of voice, as some studies have suggested, Tan's portrayal of Chinese women's use of written texts demonstrates a less marginalized presentation of Chinese mothers than the critical focus on talk-story would indicate.

In *The Bonesetter's Daughter* Tan focuses her attention even more closely on the possibilities for communication in written texts. In his article on *The Joy Luck Club*, Stephen Souris argues that the Chinese mothers in that text speak into a void and that "no actual communication between mothers and daughters occurs." He goes on to suggest that it becomes the reader who establishes the connections between the dialogic voices of the text and in whom the prospect for reception of the stories resides. In *The Bonesetter's Daughter*, Tan creates the possibility for the reception of cultural and personal memory in the American daughter because the daughter, in effect, becomes the reader of her mother's text.

The Bonesetter's Daughter focuses intently on the permanence of written texts and writing's most basic materiality through the recognition of ink's physicality. The connections between the physical nature of ink, the process of writing, and the lasting nature of text resonate throughout the narrative. Pan, LuLing's teacher and father figure, recognizes that writing preserves the moment in a way that cannot easily be retracted or erased and through this recognition stresses the effect of permanence in written texts. He believes that written texts become artifacts, and so he emphasizes the importance of writing one's "true purpose" when he reminds LuLing that "once you put the ink to paper, it becomes unforgiving."

Precious Auntie also specifically connects the act of writing with the quality of the text produced. She teaches her daughter, LuLing, that when you use the modern bottled ink,

> You simply write what is swimming on the top of your brain. And the top is nothing but pond scum, dead leaves, and mosquito spawn. But when you push an inkstick along an inkstone, you take the first step to cleansing your mind and your heart. You push and you ask yourself, What are my intentions? What is in my heart that matches my mind?

Precious Auntie thus stresses the physical process of writing by drawing attention to the amount of work entailed in preparing an inkstone for writing. She believes that the use of an inkstone, a more physical process of writing, forces the writer to be conscious of her true purpose, rather than the immediate feeling of the moment. Through repetition of this idea, the novel emphasizes the importance of intent in writing and indicates that the type of writing important to the characters in the novel is not the unthinking act of recording immediate thoughts but the conscious and deliberate act of preserving and communicating specifically selected messages.

Consequently, the writing and texts in *The Bonesetter's Daughter* are represented as having power and importance because they are conscious and deliberate rather than haphazard. Precious Auntie teaches LuLing that when writing "a person must think about her intentions," and LuLing recognized that when Precious Auntie wrote, "her ch'i flowed from her body into her arm, through the brush, and into the stroke." Each stroke, then, becomes representative of the energy and character of the writer, and the words on the page can signify more than the ideas that the shapes represent; they come to signify the intent and character of the author. The marks on the paper do more than represent words because they also somehow embody the life and person of the writer. The autobiography that LuLing writes so precisely does more than tell her life story; the perfection of the vertical rows and complete absence of mistakes alerts Ruth to the clearly evident care taken with its creation and the text's consequent importance. Although Ruth cannot understand the meaning of the manuscript's Chinese characters, she can understand that they are important through their presentation.

Ruth could only understand this deeper significance because she had developed a respect for writing's importance as a child through her sand writing and her diary. The young Ruth recognized that she "had never experienced such power with words," as she wrote "messages" from Precious Auntie to give her mother instructions. As a child Ruth used words to gain power over her mother by pretending to write the words she said Precious Auntie's ghost told her. Her "ghost writing" had the power to move her family and upset her mother's daily life, even though the words were only her own. A similar power was also available to Ruth when she wrote out the hate she felt for her mother in her diary because she knew that her mother would read the diary and she knew that the words would affect her mother in a specific way. As she wrote the words in her diary, she was conscious of her intent and recognized that

> what she was writing was risky. It felt like pure evil. And the descending mantle of guilt made her toss it off with even more bravado. What she wrote next was even worse, such terrible words, which later—too late—she had crossed out. [. . .] 'You talk about killing yourself, so why don't you ever do it? I wish you would. Just do it, do it, do it!'

When Ruth discovers the next day that her mother has fallen out of a window, her worst fears about the power of her writing make her believe that she has killed her mother. She comes to believe that words and writing have importance because of their potential power, a belief that will affect her throughout her life.

As an adult, Ruth states that her childhood guilt and fear has prevailed over her desire to write her own words. She knows that by writing a novel in the high style of writers like Jane Austen, she could "revise her life and become someone else. She could be somewhere else." But the possibility of erasing those parts of her life she does not like through revision frightens her, and her fear of imagining her life differently through the vehicle of a novel stops her from writing her own texts and restricts her to writing texts for others as a ghostwriter. Even as an adult, she believes that "writing what you wished was the most dangerous form of wishful thinking." The fear that revising her mother out of her fictional life may erase her from reality hinders Ruth from claiming any sense of agency she might find through original authorship. Ruth's career as a ghost writer allows her to mold the words of others without the possibility of affecting her own life. Her fear also emphasizes other characters' perception of writing's power in this text. She has no personal investment when writing the words of others; they remain "safe" for Ruth.

Ruth eventually comes to recognize the importance of original authorship through the discovery of her mother's autobiography. Just as Precious Auntie saved LuLing through writing her autobiography, LuLing's writing replicates that rescue through her autobiography's effect on Ruth. By the end of the text, Ruth will continue the tradition started by Precious Auntie and begin to write her own stories. These Chinese women use written autobiographies to reveal and establish lasting conceptions of their individual identities. The text reveals Precious Auntie's identity to the reader through the autobiography that LuLing writes for Ruth, even though LuLing never actually reveals this secret to her daughter. Thus, Tan's palimpsest-like layering of written autobiographies in *The Bonesetter's Daughter* highlights the specific connection between authorship and the articulation of self and the importance of written text over oral narrative.

The written nature of these autobiographies illuminates each woman's sense of identity, while it also emphasizes the stability and power of written narratives over the oral. For LuLing, writing has a cultural and an ancestral importance. By replicating her own mother's autobiographical writing, she displays reverence for the importance and power of literacy. However, writing also has a practical importance for LuLing because she understands that her memory—and thus her ability to orally narrate those memories—is failing. She begins her narrative with the statement "These are the things I must not forget." This opening line of her autobiography indicates that through her writing she will be able to preserve the past beyond her own memory of it. LuLing's narrative achieves a physical permanence like that of an artifact that the constant revisions and indeterminacies of talk-story lack. Although her speech (like that of Tan's other mothers) often results in misunderstandings and an estranged relationship with her daughter, her written narrative allows Ruth finally to understand her story.

Unlike the oral narratives told by the Joy Luck mothers, Winnie Louie, and Kwan Li in Tan's first three novels, LuLing's written narrative allows Ruth to be prepared to consciously understand and internalize the cultural importance of the story. Because LuLing's stories are written, they retain a possibility for translation beyond the immediacy of a mother-daughter exchange; the text's materiality allows LuLing's

memory to be uncovered and read at a point when her dementia prohibits her from orally passing on her story and memories to her daughter. The written text also differs from oral narratives in that it allows for later translation and mediation—the only way that Ruth is able to understand the text—while an oral narrative's immediacy creates a transitory moment in which the story must be understood. Ruth's inability to read Chinese highlights a specific form of illiteracy and makes tangible the necessity for the specific knowledge necessary to translate meaning between mothers and daughters, a need that parallels that of other daughter figures in Tan's work. The written text's permanence and physicality allow Ruth to give the manuscript to someone who has access to both English and Chinese for translation.

This translation comes through Mr. Tang, who is only able to recreate LuLing's voice in her text because he understands both the Chinese and English language systems. Using a photograph of LuLing when she was younger, Mr. Tang uses all of his senses to interpret LuLing's manuscript. He tells Ruth that "seeing her would help [him] say her words in English the way she has expressed them in Chinese." Telling Ruth that he will need two months to translate the narrative completely, Mr. Tang declares, "I don't like to just transliterate word for word. I want to phrase it more naturally, yet insure these are your mother's words, a record for you and your children for generations to come. They must be just right." His declaration that he does not only "transliterate" LuLing's writing signifies a move beyond a strict interlingual translation to an incorporation of textual mediation. It also should remind of us both of Precious Auntie's earlier statements about writing and of Tan's own position as a writer who translates Chinese and Chinese American culture for a larger audience. Mr. Tang recognizes the importance of giving Ruth access to her mother's words through the embedded signals inscribed in the process of writing. Mr. Tang's desire to capture LuLing's "essence" in the text is a recognition of writing's ability to preserve a moment, an intent, and the character of both. Mr. Tan recognizes that LuLing's text is more than a simple historical account, but can contain evidence of LuLing's entire self. This recognition leads him to emphasize the preservation of both the meaning of the text and of LuLing's aesthetic voice in the process of translation.

Tan clearly succeeds at giving a legitimate voice to the Chinese immigrant mothers in her texts through the representation of their storytelling, both oral and written. Her articulation of women's authorship and the emphasis on the power and importance of written words throughout her novels should signal that Tan works from an aesthetic tradition broader than that of talk-story or even of oral narrative; she works also from a literary tradition. In the conclusion of *The Bonesetter's Daughter*, the image of Ruth using her recognition of Chinese identity by actively engaging in the act of writing emphasizes the importance of the literary tradition in Tan's own work. "Ruth remembers this [her mother's story] as she writes a story. It is for her grandmother, for herself, for the little girl who became her mother." The production of an ecriture feminine—of women writing women and of woman writing herself—becomes repeated and amplified through the written autobiographies of Precious Auntie, LuLing, and eventually Ruth by means of the writings of another American daughter, Tan herself.

As I have already argued, *The Bonesetter's Daughter* does not represent a divergence from an earlier pattern, but the amplification of an often ignored pattern in Tan's work. The misunderstanding of these patterns may have oversimplified analyses of Tan's works. For instance, if we recognize LuLing's narrative as a written text because it lacks the verbal markers of other narratives, perhaps the reading of *The Joy Luck Club* as an experiment in talk-story and the voices as actual oral voices does not take fully into account the possibility that each voice has in effect authored its own written text. In the mothers' sections of *The Joy Luck Club*, we do not see the same stylized representation of speech that we find in Tan's texts when someone hears a Chinese immigrant speak. The mothers' voices do not seem to speak directly to their American daughters, as Winnie Louie's or Kwan Li's voices do, but instead seem to create texts that their daughters do not read. In certain sections of those texts, the voice of each mother becomes the narrative voice, and each woman effectively authors her own autobiography. Although it is Tan who actually writes these autobiographies, the narrative voices are highly literate and highly literary in their use of highly stylized and manipulated language. The importance of inscribing one's self on paper resonates most powerfully in *The Bonesetter's Daughter*, but it is speech's failure and the appearance of texts throughout Tan's other novels that should serve to suggest new ways to interpret written representations of Chinese immigrant women.

Tan's Chinese mothers not only verbally convey their stories, but also use writing to assert their identity. Their understanding of literacy, the power facilitated by the permanency of writing, and their active engagement with and use of written texts demonstrate that Tan's mothers do more than talk-story. Scholarship about Chinese American literature became more recognized and integrated into the university curriculum after the highly successful *Woman Warrior* by Maxine Hong Kingston, but imposing the same critical paradigms on the works of Amy Tan (and perhaps other Chinese American women writers) has confined and distorted the discussion of Tan's texts. The lack of critical recognition of Tan's Chinese mothers' literacy has produced studies and analyses that depended on an assumption of marginalization or silence. Many critics have assumed that the mothers' fragmented English represents their only means to impart a specifically Chinese cultural memory and identity to their American daughters. These studies have been important in opening the discussion of Tan's work, but they have missed the complexity of the representations of Chinese American immigrant women available in Tan's work. Amy Tan's novels do not demonstrate the inability of Chinese mothers to communicate with their American daughters but the artistic complexity of these interactions. Tan has created a literary tradition apart from Kingston. Not dependent on speech alone, Tan's mothers are able to move between speech and writing, voice and silence, through their literacy rather than their limitations.

More importantly perhaps, the misreading of authorship within these texts serves as a potent metaphor for the misreading of Tan's own authorship. In fact, the relative lack of favorable critical attention that Tan's work has received as compared to Maxine Hong Kingston's displays the effects of canon formation and canon critique. In his chapter "Material Choices," Robert Dale Parker argues that arguments critiquing the canon often rest on a notion of representation, and it is because of this reliance on the idea of representation that they ultimately fail. The idea of representation assumes that "there is a stable and coherent entity to be represented" and that "there can be an equation or one-to-one relation between signifier and signified, and that the signified (e.g., identity) somehow rests independently of and underneath the process (e.g., a novel) of signifying it" (171). Thus, the critical inclination to recognize oral narratives, like talk-story, assumes a certain identity politics—by representing one voice in the canon, we represent a constitutive identity (a good and noble endeavor, certainly). But if the canon is expanded or obliterated to make room for, based on some notion of difference from a master narrative (i.e., representative of a majority identity), then there exists the risk of limiting based on the very exoticism of that difference. The terms of the discussion have not changed to be more inclusive, but instead use difference as a new policing mechanism.

Twenty-five years after Lyotard introduced a critique of grand narratives in *The Postmodern Condition*, the syllabi of university courses have expanded to include women's writing and the writing of women of color, but as this analysis of Tan's work demonstrates, this inclusion often comes at the cost of silencing the multiplicity of voices that challenge notions of identity representation on which critiques of the canon have been based. The focus on and near-fetishization of oral narratives, or other "non-traditional" narrative strategies, can produce the same limiting effect that those attempting to expand or abandon the canon critique. The failure to recognize what should be considered a major theme running throughout Tan's work and the pervasive focus on oral narrative demonstrate the way that critical practice informs reception and eventual recognition of texts. If, as John Guillory argues, the canon—composed of those works that appear on syllabi—serves as an ideological tool to teach the masses, we must also understand that this tool, which so many have used to represent the minority or ethnic voice, at the same time keeps it safely contained.

Source: Lisa M.S. Dunick, "The Silencing Effect of Canonicity: Authorship and the Written Word in Amy Tan's Novels," in *MELUS*, Vol. 31, No. 2, Summer 2006, p. 3.

Akasha Hull

In the following review, Hull discusses the roles of writing and gender in The Bonesetter's Daughter *and considers the novel in the wider context of Tan's literary oeuvre.*

> THE MOTHERS AND MOTHER-FIGURES HAVE ALWAYS BEEN THE MAGIC OF AMY TAN'S FICTION. AT THIS POINT IN HER LIFE AND CAREER, PERHAPS SHE WILL BEGIN TO GIVE US THAT SAME GREATNESS AND GRACE IN THE DAUGHTERS."

Two writers fill the pages of Amy Tan's latest novel, *The Bonesetter's Daughter*. The first and most talented is LuLing, an 82-year-old Chinese woman who, in a tragically beautiful narrative, tells the story of her life before she emigrated to the United States following World War Two. At the heart of her story is Precious Auntie, the ill-fated mother she grew up calling her nursemaid, who was scarred and mute from a suicide attempt and who finally succeeded in killing herself after LuLing's blind rejection of her. LuLing is writing because Alzheimer's disease is robbing her of memory and she wants to set down before it is too late the things that must not be forgotten. The second writer is LuLing's daughter, Ruth, a 46-year-old professional "book doctor" who earns a living ghostwriting New Age self-help texts. As a writer, she originates nothing, only uses her talent to make the egotistical and commercial ideas of her clients successful.

The writer who stands behind both of these two is the author, Amy Tan. When she writes for LuLing, she is inspired and superb. When she writes for Ruth, she is, like Ruth, competent and clever, but the result lacks comparable mystery and verve. In what she herself has called the most intensely personal" of her four novels, Tan stands at a crossroads. Her next level of growth, it seems to me, is to do for the daughters what she has so eloquently done for their mothers: make them heroic and sympathetic women with fiery stories of their own that they themselves passionately tell.

A fine and highly readable novel, *The Bonesetter Daughter* is essentially about writing and the act of writing, what fuels it and how it is created. More specifically still, it is about how we, as women, creatively express our selves via language.

When the story begins, Ruth has lost her voice, an annual occurrence that initially happened when she moved in with Art, her boyfriend, and accepted the work-laden role of caring for him and his two teenaged daughters. Ruth does not effectively speak up for herself, allowing herself to be manipulated into compliance and servitude by Art as well as her clients. When she writes, she squeezes herself into a cubbyhole of a pantry with her notes and her laptop computer.

Ruth's aphasia was presaged when she broke her arm in a playground accident at six. Suddenly silent, she received her first positive attention as others tried to guess what she wanted and waited on her. It was then that she became a kind of writer—first scratching with a chopstick on a tray of sand to communicate her wishes, and then using that same means to convey messages from her dead grandmother, messages that her mother, LuLing, compelled her to receive (or devise). Ruth was always a facilitator, translating her mother's Chinese to American teachers, grocers, the official world—and vice versa. As a grownup, she has a troubled history of silence, frozen emotions, submerged anger, guilt—and of hiding herself even as she craftily uses words.

When she belatedly recognizes LuLing's dementia, she decides that it is time to listen to her mother and try to understand who she is, a resolve which leads her to the pages that LuLing has written about her life. These pages constitute Part Two of the novel, its brilliant center. Whereas Part One is written in objectifying and analytical third person, this second part is an immediate and vibrant first-person voice.

Writing and reading in many forms play a major role in the narrative. LuLing's family, the Lius, earn their livelihood by selling fine quality ink made by the women of the clan. LuLing acts as translator for the mute Precious Auntie, who devised extravagantly creative ways to communicate with her:

> She had no voice, just gasps and wheezes, the snorts of a ragged wind. She told me things with grimaces and groans, dancing eyebrows and darting eyes. She wrote about the world on my carry-around chalkboard. She also made pictures with her blackened hands. Hand-talk, face-talk, and chalk-talk were the languages I grew up with, soundless and strong.

LuLing's story of Precious Auntie's early life comes from a sheaf of pages that Precious Auntie herself has written. Unlike other women of her time, Precious Auntie is literate and can even execute flawless calligraphy because her widowed father, the famous bonesetter of the Mouth of the Mountain, had "spoiled her," letting her grow up as a free-spirited girl. These pages reveal the secret of LuLing's birth—that she is, in fact, the bastard daughter of Precious Auntie and the youngest son of the Liu family Though Precious Auntie thrusts these pages upon her, LuLing does not read them. She only pretends to, wanting to distance herself from the crazy, disfigured woman she thinks she has now outgrown. When Precious Auntie tries to get LuLing to acknowledge her as her mother, LuLing can only give a cruel and uninformed answer; Precious Auntie returns to the room where she had years earlier swallowed flaming pitch, this time to slit her own throat.

The orphaned LuLing survives both marriage and widowhood. In tandem with her Liu clan "sister," GaoLing, she eventually comes to the United States, where she repeats elements of her mother's story and enacts an equally painful and troubled relationship with her own daughter, Ruth.

The shorter third section of *The Bonesetter's Daughter* returns to third-person narrative and to Ruth. It is a somewhat huddled ending in which Art is transformed from a cad to a generous and loving man, LuLing finds happiness with the old Chinese scholar who translated her text, and Ruth and LuLing make peace with one another. In the epilogue, we find Ruth sitting in her San Francisco cubby with a picture of Precious Auntie in front of her. Though it is the time of year when she usually loses her voice, she can still speak, and she is writing—only now, it is an original story. With her grandmother guiding her to "Think about your intentions," "what is in your heart, what you want to put in others," Ruth and Precious Auntie write of what has been and what could be, making the choice not to hide the past but to "take what's broken, to feel the pain and know that it will heal."

In the early March "Good Morning, America" interview in which she called *The Bonesetter's Daughter* "the most personal novel" she had ever written, Amy Tan talked to host Charles Gibson about the role her mother played in this work. Like LuLing, Tan's mother was stricken with the memory loss and delusions of Alzheimer's disease. Like all the mothers in Tan's books, she had a traumatic life and passed on that trauma to her daughter "like a legacy"—from Tan's grandmother, who had killed herself, and perhaps even further back. Before she died in 1999, Tan's mother, also like LuLing, apologized to her daughter for the terrible things she thought she had done to her but could now no longer remember, and encouraged her to write honestly about their relationship. Tan had struggled with *The Bonesetter Daughter* for four and a half years; she was so transformed by the redemptive quality of her mother's death that she, in turn, had to transform her book, with "help from a new ghostwriter."

The mothers and mother-figures have always been the magic of Amy Tan's fiction. At this point in her life and career, perhaps she will begin to give us that same greatness and grace in the daughters. Writing in the first person, using her own strong "I," what will Ruth tell us about her thoughts and feelings, what inspirational story will she offer the world? I and many others of Tan's devoted following are eagerly waiting to read that book.

Source: Akasha Hull, "Uncommon Language," in *Women's Review of Books*, Vol. 18, No. 9, June 2001, p. 13.

SOURCES

Boaz, Noel T., and Russell L. Ciochon, "The Scavenging of 'Peking Man,'" in *Natural History*, Vol. 110, No. 2, March 2001, p. 46.

Bower, Bruce, "Peking Man Ups His Age," in *Science News*, Vol. 175, No. 8, April 11, 2009, p. 14.

Huntley, E. D., *Amy Tan: A Critical Companion*, Greenwood Press, 1998, pp. 1–11.

Kosman, Joshua, "Opera Review: *Bonesetter's Daughter*," in the *San Francisco Chronicle*, September 15, 2008, p. E1.

Kramer, Barbara, *Amy Tan: Author of the Joy Luck Club*, Enslow Publishers, 1996, pp. 10–34.

Melvin, Sheila, "Archaeology: Peking Man, Still Missing and Missed," in the *New York Times*, October 11, 2005.

Patterson, Troy, "The New Age Club: Amy Tan Mines the Spirit World in Her Latest Novel, But Readers May Find the Journey All Too Familiar," in *Entertainment Weekly*, Vol. 583/584, February 23, 2001, p. 154.

"Oh, Mama: Chinese American Fiction," in the *Economist*, Vol. 359, April 28, 2001, p. 5.

Rincon, Paul, "'Peking Man' Older than Thought," in *BBC News*, March 11, 2009, http://news.bbc.co.uk/2/hi/science/nature/7937351.stm (accessed May 1, 2009).

Seaman, Donna, Review of *The Bonesetter's Daughter*, in *Booklist*, December 1, 2000, p. 676.

Tan, Amy, *The Bonesetter's Daughter*, Ballantine Books, 2001.

Willard, Nancy, "Talking to Ghosts," in the *New York Times*, February 18, 2001, sec. 7, p. 9.

FURTHER READING

Birch, Cyril, *Tales from China*, Oxford Myths and Legends series, Oxford University Press, 2001.

   In this English translation of traditional stories, Birch presents more than a dozen familiar Chinese myths that describe the creation of the world, and the characters—often magical—who then inhabit it.

Tan, Amy, *The Opposite of Fate: A Book of Musings*, Putnam, 2003.

   Tan's memoir is a loose narrative touching on the various areas of her life, including her mother, her family, her heritage, and her experiences as a writer. She provides insight into biographical elements of her fiction and her motivation for crafting fiction.

van Oosterzee, Penny, *The Story of Peking Man*, Allen & Unwin, 2001.

   Science writer van Oosterzee retells the discovery of the Peking Man fossils during the early twentieth century, including the controversies that arose among anthropologists and the mysterious disappearance of the fossils during World War II.

Williams, Tom, *The Complete Illustrated Guide to Chinese Medicine*, Thorsons, 2003.

   Williams's book is an accessible source for information about herbs, acupuncture, acupressure, massage, meditation, and other forms of alternative health therapy. This authoritative volume is a classic introductory text into Chinese medicine.

Cold Sassy Tree

OLIVE ANN BURNS

1984

Olive Ann Burns's *Cold Sassy Tree*, published in 1984, is a poignant and comic coming-of-age novel set in Cold Sassy, Georgia, in the years 1906 and 1907. It is told in the first person from the point of view of Will Tweedy, who is fourteen years old when the novel's action begins, although he is narrating the story from a more adult perspective in 1914. The novel centers on the scandal caused when Will's grandfather and mentor, Rucker Blakeslee, suddenly marries a much younger woman, Miss Love Simpson, just weeks after the death of his first wife. Will observes the community's reaction to the marriage, the deaths of his grandmother and ultimately his grandfather, and changes in the town brought by modern conveniences and new attitudes. He examines the nature and source of prejudice, ponders the role of God in the lives of individuals, and develops a more mature, adult perspective on life.

AUTHOR BIOGRAPHY

Olive Ann Burns was born on a farm in Banks County, Georgia, on July 27, 1924, the youngest of four children. Because of hardship caused by the Great Depression, her father had to sell the farm, which had been in the family for generations, and move to the small town of Commerce, Georgia, which became the model for the town

Richard Widmark as Enid and Neil Patrick Harris as Will in the 1989 made-for-television film version of the novel (*The Kobal Collection. Reproduced by permission*)

of Cold Sassy. She attended school in Commerce and later went to high school in Macon, Georgia. She enrolled at Mercer University in Macon, which she attended for two years. She then transferred to the University of North Carolina in Chapel Hill, graduating with a journalism degree.

Burns was originally a journalist. After completing college in 1946, she took a job as a staff writer for the *Atlanta Journal and Constitution* magazine, which later became the *Atlanta Journal* magazine. She held this job for ten years until she married in 1956 and gave birth to two children. She continued, though, to work as a freelance journalist, and until 1967 she wrote an advice column under the name Amy Larkin for the *Atlanta Journal Magazine* and the *Atlanta Constitution* newspaper.

The genesis of *Cold Sassy Tree* came in 1971, when Burns's mother was diagnosed with cancer. Burns decided to begin accumulating materials for a family history and relied on her mother for stories about the family's past. After her mother died in 1972, Burns turned to

her father for his recollections of life in Commerce. She discovered that her grandfather had remarried just three weeks after the death of his first wife. A fictionalized version of this story became the premise of *Cold Sassy Tree*, which Burns began writing in 1975 after she herself was diagnosed with cancer. She worked on the novel until it was published in 1984. The book was an immediate success, and in 1985 the American Library Association named it a best book for younger readers.

During the final years of her life, Burns worked on a sequel to *Cold Sassy Tree*. In 1987, however, she was again diagnosed with cancer. The effects of chemotherapy consigned her largely to her bed for the last three years of her life. During those years she dictated *Leaving Cold Sassy* to a neighbor. The novel remained unfinished, but the thirteen chapters Burns completed were published in 1992, two years after her death on July 4, 1990.

PLOT SUMMARY

Chapters 1–4

In 1914, the novel's narrator, Will Tweedy, recalls events in Cold Sassy, Georgia, that took place primarily in the summer of 1906, when he was fourteen years old. On the night of July 5 that year, Will's grandfather, Rucker Blakeslee, arrives at Will's home to have a drink of corn whiskey; Rucker's wife, Mattie Lou, had never allowed him to keep whiskey in the house. But Mattie Lou has been dead for three weeks. Rucker asks Will to gather his mother, Mary Willis, and his aunt, Loma Williams. When the women arrive, Rucker makes a startling announcement: he is going to marry Miss Love Simpson, a hat maker who works at the general store he owns and who is young enough to be his daughter. Loma reminds Rucker of Mattie Lou's recent death, but Rucker's only reply is, "Well, good gosh a'mighty! She's dead as she'll ever be, ain't she? Well, ain't she?" After Rucker leaves, the two women express their outrage. Miss Love is a Yankee (a northerner), and the marriage will disgrace the family in the eyes of the town.

Will reflects on what has just happened. He recalls that Rucker lost a hand in a sawmill accident and that he needs someone to look after him. He thinks about mourning and reflects that there is a difference between being "in mourning" and actually mourning the loss of a loved one. He worries that his mourning clothes will prevent him from going fishing and taking part in other boyish activities. His reflections are interrupted when his father, Hoyt Tweedy, arrives to announce that Rucker and Miss Love have gone off to get married. Will then thinks about his grandfather, a quick-tempered, domineering old Confederate. He also thinks about Miss Love, whom he has always liked. Miss Love is unlike most of the women in Cold Sassy. She is pretty, wears colorful clothing, and designs fashionable hats. She advocates the right of women to vote. Will believes that Aunt Loma does not like Miss Love because she is jealous of Miss Love's good looks. Finally, he reflects that he does not like his aunt Loma, who married Campbell "Camp" Williams to spite Rucker, her father, after he refused to allow her to pursue an acting career.

Chapters 5–10

This group of chapters looks back at events surrounding Mattie Lou's death. Will thinks about his grandmother and her passion for gardening.

MEDIA ADAPTATIONS

- A 1989 film version of *Cold Sassy Tree*, starring Faye Dunaway, Richard Widmark, Frances Fisher, and Neil Patrick Harris (as Will Tweedy) and directed by Joan Tewkesbury, was released by Turner Home Entertainment in 1990 and rereleased in 1998. Running time is 97 minutes.

- A comic opera version of the novel was written by Carlisle Floyd and produced by the Houston Grand Opera Orchestra and Chorus. It was released as an audio CD by Albany Records in 2005.

- An audiobook version of *Cold Sassy Tree*, read by Tom Harper, was released by Audiofy/Blackstone in 1993 and rereleased by Playaway in 2008. The reading runs thirteen hours.

He remembers that her final illness began with a stroke. During her illness, Rucker took good care of her, but the only family member he allowed to visit her was Will. One day, Will stole into the room but backed out because his grandfather was crying. Later, Rucker appeared in the room with one of Mattie Lou's roses as a reminder of their courtship. He asked Will to pray with him. In his prayer, Rucker asked God to forgive his sins against Mattie Lou.

Mattie Lou's condition seemed to improve, but a week later it worsened, and she had hallucinations as Will sat by her bed. That night, she died, and Rucker seemed heartbroken. Mattie Lou had treated Miss Love with kindness when the younger woman was ill with the flu, so Miss Love wanted to return the kindness and cleaned the house for Rucker. On the morning of the funeral, Rucker asked Will to help him gather all of Mattie Lou's roses. The two then took the roses to Mattie Lou's grave, which they lined with a bed of roses. The day after the funeral, Rucker returned to work at his store, but he treated everyone coldly. Will's recollection of past events concludes with the town's Fourth of July parade. No U.S. flags were in evidence; all of the flags were Confederate Civil War flags. Participants in the parade included Civil War veterans, who normally would have been led by Rucker. However, Rucker declined to take part because of Mattie Lou's death.

Chapters 11–16

This group of chapters details Will's near-death experience on the town's railroad tracks. He decides that because Rucker has gotten married, the mourning period must be over, so he decides to go fishing. He takes along with him his dog, T.R., named after President Teddy Roosevelt. To get to the fishing creek, he has to pass through Mill Town, the area of Cold Sassy where poor laborers at the cotton mill live. Although the mill is a major contributor to the town's economy, people look down on Mill Town residents, calling them "lintheads." Will has feelings for one of Mill Town's residents, Lightfoot McClendon, a girl in his class at school. Will hopes that he does not run into Hosie Roach, a much older boy from school who fights Will.

On impulse, Will decides to cross the train trestle over the creek. When he is halfway across, though, a train comes. As Will is about to dash to safety, his fishing pole becomes entangled. He lies down on the railroad bed between the tracks, and the train passes over him. Lightfoot appears to help him off the tracks. The train stops, and Will boards it to ride back to town. Back home, everyone is elated by Will's escape. A crowd gathers at his home to talk about the incident, recall past train wrecks, and gossip about the marriage of Rucker and Miss Love. Rucker appears, and in the kitchen, Will tells Rucker about the train incident. The two then have a discussion about God's will and the power of prayer. Rucker asks the family and guests to join him in prayer, astonishing them by asking God to help Miss Love realize that any good in him was because of Mattie Lou. Everyone hugs Miss Love except Loma, who leaves in a jealous huff.

Chapters 17–20

These chapters include hints of Will's adolescent development and his growing relationship with Miss Love. Will has a dream in which Lightfoot takes off her clothes just before being hit by a train. In the same dream, he sees himself running from the train, but his path is blocked by Aunt Loma. After Will awakens, he remembers why he hates Aunt Loma. His aunt is only six years older than he is, and when they were children they played together. But on Loma's twelfth birthday, she broke all of his lead soldiers. He thinks of other people he hates, including his Grandfather Tweedy, a lazy farmer who does little more than spout religion from his porch.

Will goes to Rucker's house to help Miss Love clean and go through Mattie Lou's things. Before he announces his arrival, he watches Miss Love playing the piano and is aroused by the sight of her figure. He discovers that Miss Love has her own bedroom, so he concludes that her marriage with Rucker is a marriage of convenience. Rucker arrives and allows Miss Love to give him a haircut and shave off his beard. Will is then struck by how alike he and Rucker look. Later, Will asks Miss Love why she married his grandfather. He thinks that Miss Love will be offended by the question, but she is not. She replies that she married Rucker to keep house for him. In exchange, Rucker has promised to leave her the house and some money. The two also discuss Miss Love's former boyfriend, Son Black. Will asks why she did not marry him; she replies that she has decided not to marry because of something bad that had happened to her in Texas, though she does not say what. Cold Sassy's town gossips believe that she rejected Black because he had gotten Miss Love's best friend pregnant.

Chapters 21–27

A cowboy appears, who turns out to be Clayton McAllister, another of Miss Love's old boyfriends. A neighborhood gossip, Miss Effie Belle Tate, sees McAllister kissing Miss Love passionately. Rucker arrives, and surprisingly, the two men get along. Rucker invites McAllister to spend the night, but McAllister declines. He leaves behind a saddle as a present for Miss Love. Rucker tells her that if she wants to marry McAllister, he would be willing to annul their own marriage. He asks her whether she would like to have a horse, and when she brightens at the prospect, Rucker sends Will to fetch a horse from a cousin in the country. Will decides to combine the errand with a camping trip. He visits his Grandpa Tweedy to borrow a wagon to use on the trip, which turns out to be a disaster. On the way back home, he makes up stories about his aunt Loma. After the stories are spread around town, Rucker scolds Will. Meanwhile, Miss Love has been removed from her position as piano player in the church because of her presumed improper behavior.

Chapters 28–31

Everyone in town knows about the nature of Rucker and Miss Love's marriage. Mary Willis tells Will that while Will was camping, Miss Love herself announced in the store where she works that she and Rucker were sleeping separately. This revelation is further evidence to the town that Miss Love married Rucker for his money. Loma's resentment of Miss Love grows after Loma and her husband, Camp, visit Rucker's house to lay claim to Mattie Lou's piano and other items. Miss Love refuses to relinquish them. Will concludes that Miss Love has declared war on the family.

Will's friendship with Miss Love continues to grow as he goes to Rucker's house to help her train her horse. In their conversation about Queenie, the Tweedys' black cook, Will learns that some of his assumptions about Queenie's position may be untrue and naive and that she is the victim of racism. Will goes to Loma's house to apologize for the stories that he told about her. There he is dismayed by how poorly she treats her husband. He is astonished to discover that she found the stories funny, and the two of them actually get along during the afternoon. Loma gives Will a journal and urges him to write, but Will is resolved to become a farmer.

Chapters 32–35

Rucker has offered Hoyt and Mary Willis tickets for a trip to New York. Mary Willis is reluctant to go, still mourning the death of Mattie Lou. Just as she changes her mind, though, Rucker announces that he and Miss Love are going to use the tickets to go to New York to buy stock for the store. Rucker invites the entire town to a church service at his house. He invites Loomis, Queenie's husband and an employee at the store, to preach at the service. Hoyt declines to attend the regular Sunday service at the Presbyterian church, which mystifies everyone until he appears on Sunday morning with a new Cadillac, the first automobile in Cold Sassy. After practicing driving for a week, Hoyt and Will offer rides to the townspeople, but Hoyt pointedly refuses to offer Miss Love a ride.

Miss Love begins to win friends in Cold Sassy. From New York, she sends postcards, telling the women of the dresses she has picked out for them. Will takes Lightfoot for a drive in the car. They park at a cemetery and talk. Lightfoot cries because of the death of her father. She cannot afford a grave marker for him, and her aunt has taken her out of school. Will kisses her passionately, imitating the kiss he saw Clayton McAllister give Miss Love. A nosy townswoman sees them kissing, forces Lightfoot to leave, and lectures Will.

Chapters 36–41

Hoyt learns that Will and Lightfoot have been kissing and punishes Will by whipping him. After Rucker and Miss Love return from New York, Mary Willis invites them for dinner. At dinner, Rucker talks about the New York trip, particularly his newfound interest in automobiles. It also becomes clear that Rucker and Miss Love have become closer during the trip and that their marriage of convenience is evolving into a true marriage. Rucker and Miss Love tell Will that they have bought a car and that they intend to sell cars in Cold Sassy. Miss Love begins to put together a plan for selling the cars. Will is saddened that Lightfoot no longer attends school, but he is surprised that Hosie Roach, his former enemy, has become friendly with him.

Will begins to notice that Rucker and Miss Love are treating each other with a great deal of affection. As the three drive to the county fair, Will feels that he is intruding on them. After an accident that damages the car, the three spend the night at the home of a local family. Will and Rucker share a room, but during the night Will hears Rucker going into Miss Love's room and overhears their conversation. Miss Love rejects Rucker's romantic overtures, saying that she has a secret that would make her repellent to any man. She confesses that when she was twelve, her mother was dying. Her father was a drunk and accused her mother of having an affair. He claimed that Miss Love was not his daughter, and to prove it, he raped her.

Chapters 42–46

Rucker wins a drawing that allows him to rename the town's hotel. The name he chooses is the Rucker Blakeslee Hotel. Rucker spends more time at home with Miss Love; although he says that he is ill, and indeed has a cough, his appetite is unaffected. He and Miss Love go on buggy rides together and seem to become much closer. Aunt Loma directs the school's Christmas play, but Will plays a practical joke by releasing rats in the school auditorium. He later apologizes to Loma, and he is gratified that his relationship with Loma is back on its old footing of hatred.

Camp sends Loma away on a trip to Athens, Georgia, claiming that he wants to use her absence as an opportunity to fix the plumbing. He asks Hoyt to help him. When Hoyt and Will arrive at Camp's home, they hear a gun blast and discover that Camp, who always felt like a failure, has committed suicide. Some townspeople believe that Camp does not deserve a funeral because he committed suicide, but Rucker arranges a funeral and insists that Camp be buried at Mattie Lou's feet in the family plot. Loma, with her baby, Campbell Junior, moves into Will's home, where she gets help with the baby and uses her time to write plays and poetry. Miss Love's birthday is on Valentine's Day, and to celebrate her birthday, she resolves to get indoor plumbing. Rucker agrees, and in addition he buys her a record player. Rucker hires Hosie Roach to replace Camp at the store and allows Loma to work at the store as a milliner (hat maker). On his fifteenth birthday, Will shaves for the first time. He runs into Lightfoot, who tells him that she is going to marry Hosie.

Chapters 47–50

During a robbery at his store, Rucker is shot. As he is convalescing, Will overhears him conversing with Miss Love about Jesus and whether God answers prayers. He says to Miss Love, "They ain't no gar'ntee thet we ain't go'n have no troubles and ain't go'n die. But a God'll forgive us if'n we ast Him to." They also discuss changing the name of the town to something more up-to-date. Will sees Rucker and Miss Love kissing and concludes that their union is a real marriage. Rucker's condition takes a turn for the worse when he catches pneumonia and begins to hallucinate. Miss Love reveals that she is pregnant with Rucker's child. Later that day, Rucker dies. He has ordered that his funeral be a simple one. He has left his house and some money to Miss Love, and he has divided his other money and property between Mary Willis and Loma, who, Will reflects, are likely to be upset that some of the money will go to Miss Love's child. Rucker has appointed Hoyt manager of the store and left Will money for college that he can collect if he works at the store for ten years.

Miss Love decides to remain in Cold Sassy so that her child can grow up around family. She tells Will that she hopes he can be a father to the child. A month later, the town changes its name to Progressive City. To make room for improvements in the town, the Cold Sassy tree, a sassafras tree, is cut down. People, including Will, take chunks of the tree's roots to make tea. Years later, Will notes that he still has his piece of the tree, along with the newspaper story of the incident on the train trestle; a photo of Rucker, Miss Love, and himself; and a buckeye that Lightfoot gave him as a memento to remember her by.

CHARACTERS

Mattie Lou Blakeslee
Mattie Lou is Will Tweedy's grandmother and the wife of Rucker Blakeslee. She dies before the novel's action begins and does not appear directly in the story. She was a good wife to Rucker and earned the respect of the town for her kindness. She was an avid gardener and loved her rosebushes.

Rucker Blakeslee
Rucker is a veteran of the Civil War, the patriarch of his family, and the owner of the town's general store, which becomes the hub of gossip. He has a commanding physical presence, and he enjoys shaking up Cold Sassy by violating its norms and defying its conventions, particularly by marrying a much younger woman, Miss Love, just weeks after his first wife's death. He likes to puncture the pretensions and hypocrisies of the townspeople. He is depicted as stubborn, cantankerous, and brash. At the same time, he is more open-minded than most of the people in Cold Sassy, including his own daughters. He is a man of great integrity, and as such he has a profound effect on his grandson, Will Tweedy. He is an intensely religious man, but his religion, unlike that of many of the townspeople, is not just for outward show. Rather, he thinks deeply about spiritual questions. After his beard is shaved off, it is discovered that he and Will bear a marked physical resemblance to each other. The two characters are in a sense mirror images. Will grows and develops by becoming a bit more like his grandfather; Rucker grows and develops by becoming a little more like Will. He becomes more easygoing and less stingy as his marriage to Miss Love grows into one of genuine affection.

Aunt Carrie

Although Will Tweedy refers to this woman as "Aunt" Carrie, she is not his aunt but simply a close family friend. She is regarded as a bit of an oddball, and other than Miss Love, she is the only woman in Cold Sassy who advocates women's suffrage.

Loomis

Loomis, an African American, works at Rucker Blakeslee's general store and is the husband of the Tweedys' cook, Queenie. He is a kind man and is regarded as a good preacher.

Clayton McAllister

Clayton is a rancher from Texas. He is charming, but he treats Miss Love badly; his past treatment of her caused her to resist love and marriage.

Lightfoot McLendon

Lightfoot is a studious girl in Will Tweedy's class at school. She and Will have feelings for each other, but later, after her father dies, she announces to Will that she is marrying Hosie Roach.

Queenie

Queenie, an African American, works as a cook for the Tweedy family and is the wife of Loomis. She feels the effects of racial prejudice in Cold Sassy.

Hosie Roach

Hosie is a much older boy who still attends Will Tweedy's school. The two boys are enemies, though the townspeople generally think highly of Hosie. Eventually, Lightfoot McClendon agrees to marry him after he takes a job at Rucker's general store.

Miss Love Simpson

Miss Love works as a hat maker in Rucker's general store, and she marries Rucker three weeks after his first wife, Mattie Lou, dies. She is depicted as kind, openhearted, exuberant, spirited, and a breath of fresh air in Cold Sassy. Like Rucker, she defies the town's conventions. Questions arise as to the nature of the marriage. Many of the townspeople believe that she marries Rucker for his money. Will suspects that Rucker simply needs someone to take care of him. Questions also arise about whether Rucker and Miss Love were having an affair before Mattie Lou died. As the novel approaches its climax, though, it becomes apparent that their marriage has developed and deepened. Miss Love's initial resistance to entering into a real marriage is the result of a childhood incident: When she was twelve, she was raped by her drunken father. Her relationship with Will Tweedy, the novel's narrator, is important in depicting the growth of Will's character. He has always liked Miss Love. As the two get to know one another, Will comes to understand her more. His support of Miss Love and the marriage is key to his ability to outgrow the moral and social constraints of Cold Sassy.

Effie Belle Tate

Miss Tate is Rucker Blakeslee's next-door neighbor. She is representative of the nosiness and narrow-mindedness of the Cold Sassy community.

Hoyt Tweedy

Hoyt is Will Tweedy's father and Mary Willis's wife. As Rucker's son-in-law, he works at Rucker's general store. He is depicted as a religious man who treats Will with sternness. He is interested in modern technology and buys the first automobile in Cold Sassy.

Mary Joy Tweedy

Mary Joy is Will Tweedy's younger sister.

Mary Willis Tweedy

Mary Willis is Rucker Blakeslee's elder daughter, Will Tweedy's mother, and Loma Williams's sister. She is depicted as a nervous woman who is deeply affected by the death of her mother. She leads a very conventional life and shares many of the prejudices of the town.

Will Tweedy

Will is the novel's narrator and protagonist. He narrates the events of the novel from the perspective of 1914, though the events take place primarily in 1906 and 1907, when he is fourteen years old (he turns fifteen near the novel's end). The novel focuses on Will's growth and development as he passes from childhood to early manhood, marked symbolically by the first time he shaves. The point of view of the novel is complex because Will is telling the story when he is twenty-two years old, but he tells it from the perspective of his adolescent self. Thus he can show and understand his maturation as he deals with a wide range of complex issues: love, death, sexual awakening, prejudice, narrow-mindedness, social constraints, modernization, and the ways of the South in the decades after the Civil War. His physical resemblance to his grandfather, Rucker, helps suggest that the two characters are mirror images whose lives move in opposite directions. Will becomes more like his grandfather by growing braver and more direct; Rucker becomes more like Will by becoming more youthful and exuberant.

Campbell "Camp" Williams

Camp is Loma's husband. He works at Rucker Blakeslee's general store. He is depicted as generally incompetent and the object of Rucker and Loma's scorn. He is eventually driven to despair and commits suicide by shooting himself.

Loma Williams

Loma is married to Campbell Williams. She is Rucker Blakeslee's younger daughter and thus Will Tweedy's aunt. Just twenty years old, she earlier wanted to pursue a career as an actress. She treats Camp poorly, and Will has long hated her. She is bossy, irritable, and given to fits of jealousy, though she encourages Will to become a writer.

THEMES

Death

Death plays a prominent role in *Cold Sassy Tree*. Before the action of the novel begins, Rucker and Will are faced with the death of Mattie Lou, Rucker's wife. Will himself has a near-death experience when he is caught on a train trestle and the train passes over him as he lies between the tracks. Later in the novel, Lightfoot's father dies; Will's uncle, Campbell Williams, commits suicide; and Rucker is shot during a robbery at the general store and later dies.

These events force Will to contemplate the meaning of death. After his grandmother dies, he reflects on the difference between being "in mourning" for someone's death and actually mourning that person's death. His thoughts that his mourning clothes will prevent him from fishing and other activities reflect an early immaturity, but the deaths of Camp and his grandfather lead to deeper and more dignified reflections on death. It is through Rucker that Will comes to examine death from a religious perspective. Rucker frequently ponders the issue of God's involvement in human affairs and serves as a mentor to Will on such issues. Rucker has concluded that God does

not involve himself directly in human matters and that no amount of prayer can persuade God to change his mind about anything, including death. Rather, humans can pray to God for strength to deal with life's hardships. His lessons even rub off on Miss Love. In Chapter 48, for example, Miss Love says to Rucker,

> Tell Will that sometimes God has to say no for our own good, or to teach us something, or show His power. Sometimes it's just not His will to give us a certain thing. Or He wants to test our faith and see if we trust Him no matter what.

While death is depicted as a sad event, it also opens the possibility of renewal and new life. Rucker is able to find happiness with Miss Love, Loma is released from a marriage she hates and is able to write poetry and plays, and Miss Love will give birth to a new baby after Rucker's death. In this sense, death gives rise to new possibilities, just as Cold Sassy "dies" and is "reborn" as Progressive City.

Modern Life and Technology

Cold Sassy Tree shows the introduction of more modern ways to the town. Hoyt Tweedy brings to the town its first automobile, a shiny new Cadillac. The car attracts a great deal of interest among the townspeople, most of whom have never even seen a car. Rucker operates an old-fashioned general store, but after his trip to New York, he and Miss Love decide to become auto dealers, and Miss Love's business acumen is seen as more modern. The cars stand in contrast to the railroad, the older form of transportation that almost kills Will. Many people in Cold Sassy do not have telephones, but many do, and telephone service is spreading. Miss Love decides that for her birthday she wants indoor plumbing in Rucker's house; Rucker agrees, and additionally he buys her a record player—again, something that most people in the town likely have never seen.

These items, though, are only the outward signs of modernity. More important are more modern attitudes. One clear example is the issue of women's suffrage. Miss Love and Aunt Carrie are the only two women in town who support the right of women to vote. In this way they challenge the town's old-fashioned prejudices. Another is the issue of racial prejudice. Will naively assumes that Queenie, the family's African American cook, accepts her position in life, but Miss Love, who comes from outside Cold Sassy, convinces him that his views might be wrong and that Queenie

TOPICS FOR FURTHER STUDY

- Conduct an interview with someone who has encountered a situation similar to that depicted in *Cold Sassy Tree*. The interview can be held with a relative, a neighbor, a family friend, or anyone else who has encountered prejudice or social taboos in a community, questioned those taboos, and grown as a result. An example might be a grandparent who grew up in a small town or an immigrant who questioned traditional ways in his or her culture. Transcribe your interview and share it with classmates.

- Conduct Internet research on new technology in the United States in the early years of the twentieth century. In particular, search for images of the cars that were being introduced, such as Hoyt Tweedy's new Cadillac, or the telephones that were spreading through the country. Share the results of your search in a PowerPoint presentation that uses as many visuals as possible.

- During the early twentieth century, Jim Crow laws kept African Americans in an inferior position by segregating them and denying them civil rights. Trace the history of Jim Crow laws and write an essay on precisely how African Americans might

have been treated in some small southern American towns in the first decade of the twentieth century.

- Miss Love Simpson was a "suffragette," that is, a woman who advocated the right of women to vote. (Today, the term "suffragist" is preferred.) Conduct research into the history of the women's rights movement in the early twentieth century. Who were some of the most prominent suffragists? What actions did they take to change thinking about voting rights? Prepare a time line of key events in the suffrage movement during these years.

- Perhaps the most famous American novel about race relations, small-town prejudice in the American South, and the observations of young people on the issues of social class, gender roles, and similar matters is Harper Lee's *To Kill a Mockingbird*. Read Lee's novel or watch the widely available movie version and report on its similarities to and differences from *Cold Sassy Tree*, focusing on a single aspect of the two stories. Possibilities include the use of humor, the point of view, or the depiction of community attitudes.

---

suffers from discrimination. More generally, the relationship between Rucker and Miss Love challenges the old-fashioned attitudes of the townspeople—attitudes that Will Tweedy in part learns to question and outgrow. Will also acquires a deeper religious faith, one based not on rituals and outward show, as represented by his grandfather Tweedy, but on contemplation, God and the relationship between God and humanity.

At bottom, the entire novel depicts a society and culture on the cusp of new ways of thinking brought about by the advent of modern life—by the still new twentieth century. The old Cold Sassy is symbolized by the Fourth of July

parade, with its Civil War–era Confederate flags. Cold Sassy still adheres to the traditions and values of the Old South at the time of the Civil War, but those traditions and values are challenged by Miss Love, a northerner. The old Cold Sassy is also symbolized by the sassafras tree; this old town is replaced by a new Cold Sassy, where the tree is cut down to make room for modern improvements and the town's name is changed to Progressive City. However, the old Cold Sassy is not forgotten; Will still has his piece of the tree in 1914, when he tells the story of Cold Sassy and when the world changed forever with the start of World War I.

A family gathered on steps, early 1900s (© *Augusta National | Masters Historic Imagery | Getty Images*)

Social Constraints

Closely related to the theme of modernity is that of social constraints. Cold Sassy is depicted as a closed-minded community where everyone pays attention to everyone else's business and where people have strong feelings about social matters based on prejudice and tradition. When Rucker announces to his daughters that he is going to marry Miss Love, he knows that he is violating these social conventions and does not care. He is going to remarry when he wants to, not when "society" tells him it is acceptable. A counterpoint to Rucker is his daughters Mary Willis and Loma. They object to the marriage not because they believe that Miss Love is wrong for their father but because they believe that the marriage will make the family an object of ridicule in the town. They also worry that the townspeople will think that Miss Love is marrying Rucker for his money. Other characters, such as Effie Belle Tate, are representative of the social constraints of Cold Sassy. She is depicted as nosy, and when she catches Will kissing Lightfoot in the car at the cemetery, she feels compelled to drive Lightfoot away, scold Will, and tell his father what she witnessed. The townspeople believe that it is not proper to have a funeral service for Camp Williams because he committed suicide.

Will, as a young boy, does not understand these social proprieties. He does not understand, for example, why his grandfather cannot marry Miss Love when he wants to—and indeed he cannot understand why it would not have been possible for Rucker to love Mattie Lou and Miss Love at the same time. Will represents the overturning of social constraints: he accepts the marriage of Rucker and Miss Love. Rucker is a product of the past; he is a Civil War veteran. Miss Love is a product of a more modern world. Their marriage and the birth of their baby suggest that old and new can blend, that social constraints can be overcome, and that people such as Will can grow and change to overcome their prejudices. In time, Miss Love becomes more accepted by the townspeople, and her use of the southern dialect "y'all" ("you all") near the end of the novel, unusual for her because she speaks "properly," suggests that she is becoming part of the fabric of the town.

STYLE

Point of View

Point of view refers both to the narrator of a work of fiction and to the perspective from which the novel is being narrated. The narrator is Will Tweedy, who narrates the novel from a first-person point of view, that is, from his own perspective using the pronoun "I." The perspective, though, is more complex. At the time of the novel's events, Will is just fourteen years old, though he turns fifteen near the end. As an adolescent, he is not always able to comprehend the implications of the events that he narrates. Thus, rather than having him tell the story from the fourteen-year-old's perspective, Burns makes her narrator older. Thus, Will tells the story in 1914, by which time he would be twenty-two years old. This technique gives Will more of an adult perspective on events. He is still young enough to capture the innocence and incomprehension of the teenager but old enough to understand the meaning of what has occurred and communicate that meaning to the reader. Thus, the novel blends the two perspectives. Some events would have little meaning if they were narrated by the fourteen-year-old, but if the novel had been narrated entirely from the twenty-two-year-old's perspective, it would have lost much of its poignancy, its ability to capture the perceptions of a character who stands at its center and who has to outgrow his more childish perceptions on his road to adulthood.

Symbolism

Symbolism, a device in which something concrete represents something abstract, can be used in fiction in at least two different ways. Sometimes symbolism occurs in the form of symbolic objects. The symbolism of these objects can be universal, but often it is contextual, meaning that the symbolism derives from how the object is framed in the story. Two prominent symbolic objects in *Cold Sassy Tree* are the Cold Sassy tree itself and the automobiles that Hoyt and Rucker acquire. The Cold Sassy tree is the last remaining tree of a grove of sassafras trees. The town's settlers cut down the grove to make room for the town, but one tree remains. The tree then is symbolic of the town itself and its link with the past. However, as the town moves into the more modern age, the tree has to be cut down to make room for improvements. Thus, the town's link

with its past, including its traditions and prejudices, is severed. It is not severed entirely, though. Townspeople, including Will, take pieces of the tree, and Will still has his eight years later at the time he tells the story of Cold Sassy.

In the context of *Cold Sassy Tree*, cars become symbolic objects. Until 1906, the town relied entirely on horses and horse-drawn carts and wagons for transportation. The railroad went through town, but even that is beginning to seem old-fashioned, the product of the previous century. Cars, though, are a symbol of modern progress. They point not only to technological change but to changes in attitude as Cold Sassy moves into a modern age with more modern ways of thinking.

Actions, like objects, can have symbolic overtones. Early in the novel, Will is on the railroad trestle that crosses over the creek where he is fishing. A train approaches, and Will is caught on the trestle with no means of escape. He lies down between the tracks so that the train passes over him. Although he emerges unharmed, the experience is frightening and could have led to his death. In the context of *Cold Sassy Tree*, this scene could be regarded as symbolic. Just as Will is caught on the trestle, so too he is caught between two ways of life in Cold Sassy. Will himself becomes a kind of bridge (like the train trestle), connecting these two ways of life. In the process of surviving his passage over the bridge, he becomes a bit of a hero in the town, just as readers may regard him as heroic for safely negotiating his passage into adulthood. This passage is suggested by another symbolic act: Will's shaving for the first time.

Dialect

Burns uses a great deal of southern dialect, a distinct form of language and grammar particular to a region or community, in *Cold Sassy Tree*. Thus, for example, late in the novel, Rucker says to Miss Love, "They ain't no gar'ntee thet we ain't go'n have no troubles and ain't go'n die. But . . . God'll forgive us if'n we ast Him to." Translated into standard English, this passage would read, "There isn't any guarantee that we aren't going to have any troubles and aren't going to die. But God will forgive us if we ask Him to." Will even gives the reader a bit of a lesson in Cold Sassy dialect in Chapter 17: "You need to understand that in Cold Sassy when the word 'aunt' is followed by a name, it's pronounced aint, as in Aint Loma or Aint Carrie." Will goes on to provide further examples. The chief purpose of this use of dialect pronunciation and grammar is to add color to the novel. The reader is invited into the Cold Sassy community and can "hear" the characters speaking in their characteristic ways. Cold Sassy thus becomes more real. In contrast, Miss Love, a northerner, speaks more properly, using standard English grammar and pronunciation. Near the end of the novel, though, she uses the phrase "y'all," dialect for "you all" or simply the plural "you." This hint of dialect suggests that she is becoming part of the Cold Sassy community.

HISTORICAL CONTEXT

Cold Sassy Tree is one of many works—novels, short stories, and plays—that examine small-town life in the American South, particularly during the early years of the twentieth century. Chief among American writers who chronicled small-town life was William Faulkner, who created a fictional county in Mississippi that he used in many of his novels and short stories. Other American writers who have taken up this theme include Eudora Welty, Flannery O'Connor, Thomas Wolfe, Tennessee Williams, Harper Lee, and many others. One of the most famous novels set in the rural South and written by a southern writer is *Gone With the Wind* by Margaret Mitchell, and certainly no survey of writing about the rural American South can ignore such novels as Mark Twain's *Adventures of Huckleberry Finn*.

Southern American literature is often considered a distinct genre in American letters. These works tend to be steeped in the past, in a former pastoral age that is imagined to have existed in the agricultural South before the Civil War. The American South was, and to some degree still is, regarded as unique because of its distinct history and culture. In writing *Cold Sassy Tree*, Olive Ann Burns drew on this tradition of southern writing, steeped in a sense of history and uniqueness. Her perspective is not that of 1984, the year of the novel's publication, although the themes of her novel are universal and are just as applicable in 1984 or any year as they would have been at the turn of the twentieth century. Rather, she draws on stories related to

her primarily by her parents to reconstruct a historical past. More to the point, in reconstructing this historical past, she illuminates the clash that takes place when that past is confronted with more modern realities.

The roots of this type of historical writing extend back into the nineteenth century. As tensions in America began to mount over the issue of slavery—tensions that culminated in the Civil War—American writers began to explore the unique characteristics of southern culture: its language, its social institutions, its economy, its religion, and others. Many of these works tried to recreate a pastoral idyll, a world where everyone knew his or her place in the social order and where home, family, and particularly the soil were paramount. Many other novels, including Harriet Beecher Stowe's *Uncle Tom's Cabin*, took the opposite tack, emphasizing the horrors of the South's rigid social structure. In the twentieth century, many writers, including Burns, took a comic view of the South. On the one hand, they examined the South with a great deal of affection, recognizing that they themselves were shaped by the cultural institutions of the region. On the other hand, they were well aware of the limitations and peculiarities of southern culture and revolted from it in what Lucinda MacKethan, in *Southern Space*, has called the "revolt from the village" school of writing. Accordingly, they were able to lampoon its rigid social structure, taboos, and traditions, often by creating grotesque characters and situations. Those tales that emphasize the grotesque are often regarded as belonging to a tradition called Southern Gothic. This tradition arose, many scholars argue, because traditional southern culture had allowed few outlets for reasoned protest and disagreement.

That Burns made use of these traditions of southern writing is immediately clear. She lovingly recreates the dialect and unique patterns of speech in her southern small town, whose citizens have a love of oral storytelling. Characters are given odd names, such as Rucker, Lightfoot McClendon, and Hosie Roach; there are no "John Smiths" in her novel. Many of these characters have features that border on the grotesque; Rucker, with his commanding physical presence, his penchant for fighting, and his general brashness, is the central example. Through her depiction of Mill Town and its poverty,

COMPARE
&
CONTRAST

- **1900s:** Racial prejudice is widespread throughout the nation but especially entrenched in the post–Civil War South. African Americans are segregated and routinely denied their civil rights.

  1980s: The condition of African Americans is greatly improved as a result of the civil rights movement and legislation enforcing civil rights.

  Today: Prejudice against African Americans continues among some people, but ongoing civil rights gains have led to greater acceptance and less discrimination. The United States elects its first African American president in 2008.

- **1900s:** The movement to grant voting rights to women is gathering steam through the work of such suffragists as Susan B. Anthony and Alice Paul.

  1980s: As a result of the Nineteenth Amendment, which was ratified in 1920, women have enjoyed the right to vote for six decades. In 1984, women cast 53 percent of the votes in the presidential election, and Geraldine Ferraro is the first woman ever to run on the ticket of a major political party in a presidential election.

Today: Women continue to make gains in employment, government, and such institutions as the military. In 2008, Hillary Rodham Clinton becomes the first woman candidate to have a legitimate chance to win the U.S. presidential election.

- **1900s:** The United States, particularly in the rural South, is just beginning to enjoy modern technology, including automobiles, indoor plumbing, electricity, and telephone service. Roughly 33,000 cars are produced in the United States in 1906, including 3,500 Cadillacs. Gasoline costs 6 cents a gallon.

  1980s: Modern plumbing, cars, and telephone and electrical service are commonplace in all but the poorest homes. U.S. auto production is about eight million cars in 1984. Gasoline costs about $1.20 a gallon.

  Today: A new technological revolution, marked by home computers, wireless Internet, cell phones, digital television, and many other innovations, is changing the way Americans live and work. The United States produces 8.7 million cars in 2008. Gasoline prices temporarily spike to over $4.00 a gallon in 2008.

Burns reminds readers that the Old South was built on cash crops such as cotton.

The community's rigid social structure—perhaps the most common theme in southern historical literature—is illustrated on virtually every page. Traditional religion is to some degree lampooned through such characters as Will's Grandfather Tweedy, though it must always be recognized that through Rucker and his relationship with Will, a nontraditional, more thoughtful religious outlook is emphasized. Although the Civil War has ended some four decades before, the war and its aftermath are still a felt reality in the community. The Fourth of July parade route is lined with people waving Confederate flags, not

U.S. flags. Miss Love is a threat to the community not just because she is an outsider but because she is from Baltimore, and therefore "practically" a Yankee. It is worth noting, too, that after Rucker and Miss Love travel to the big city—New York—thus leaving behind the small town, Rucker shows more affection to Miss Love and to some extent enters the modern world by deciding to become a car dealer, buying Miss Love a record player, and agreeing to the installation of indoor plumbing.

Many writers who follow the traditions of southern writing have taken an ultimately pessimistic view. They regard southern traditions and taboos as so entrenched that they cannot be resisted or overcome. They ultimately swallow the

Fishing trip (© *H. Armstrong Roberts | Retrofile | Getty Images*)

individual and determine the individual's fate. Others take a more optimistic view, emphasizing the epiphanies, or moments of revelation, when characters recognize the realities around them and are capable of change—and of changing others. *Cold Sassy Tree* clearly belongs to the latter camp. Through Will, Burns stresses that historical realities are not imprisoning. And in connection with the child that Miss Love will give birth to, Cold Sassy can become Progressive City.

CRITICAL OVERVIEW

Cold Sassy Tree continues to enjoy a wide and enthusiastic audience and has become part of the reading curriculum in some middle schools, high schools, and even colleges. Nevertheless, at the time of its publication and since then, critical reactions to it have been somewhat mixed.

Many critics admire the book. Writing in the *Christian Science Monitor*, for example, Ruth Doan MacDougall calls the novel "captivating" and "joyous." A *Publishers Weekly* reviewer cites the novel's "fine characterization and rich detail," concluding that "it hurts to turn that last page." In the *Washington Post*, Jeanne McManus praises the novel highly, calling Will Tweedy a "sophisticated and astute observer of adults" and describing the book as "rich with emotion, humor and tenderness."

Other critics, though, have been more restrained. Writing in the *New York Times Book Review*, Jason Berry calls some of the novel's black characters "preposterous" and faults the book as a "narrative riddled with clichés." Berry does, however, acknowledge that "the author effectively conveys the world view of an adolescent boy." Perhaps the most negative review of *Cold Sassy Tree* was written by Loxley F. Nichols for the *National Review*. Nichols places the novel in the tradition of other writing about the American South, with its mixture of "pride and . . . insecurity." He argues that "Miss Burns's love of local color, mixed with a certain defensiveness, and edge of uneasiness, leads her to excesses that the reader may find tiresome." As an example, he notes the novel's overemphasis on explanation, on "spelling out the obvious," and he regards Will Tweedy as an "officious commentator who, all too frequently, intrudes unnecessarily to interpret events . . . for the reader." He further argues that Burns "overwrites the regional idiom"—that is, relies too heavily on dialect—and that Rucker Blakeslee's homilies are "ponderous."

CRITICISM

Michael J. O'Neal

O'Neal holds a Ph.D. in English literature. In this essay on Cold Sassy Tree, *he examines the novel as part of the literary tradition of the* bildungsroman, *or novel of development.*

Within the broad category of novels, critics and literary historians identify numerous types, each with its own conventions and each arousing certain expectations in the reader. While readers are usually told that they cannot judge a book by its cover, the fact is that readers begin to make judgments about books on the basis of the book's type, which they typically know before reading it. Modern romance novels, for example, are defined by their adherence to certain conventions. So are westerns, science fiction novels, police procedural novels, and murder mysteries.

One important subgenre in the history of fiction is the *bildungsroman* (pronounced BILL-doongz-row-MAHN). This is a German word that is generally translated as something like "novel of development." The German word continues to be used among English speakers, though, because translations into English seem slightly inadequate. In breaking down the German word, *-roman* is easy: it means "novel." *Bildung*, though, is more complicated. It is etymologically related to the English word *building*, used not in the sense of an object but in the sense of a process of construction. It is variously translated as "development," "formation," "education," "apprenticeship," or "growth." Hundreds of years ago, the word's connotations included the notion of spiritual or religious development. In the twentieth century, the word came to include artistic development, that is, the development of a writer's or artist's artistic sensibilities. All of these meanings are folded into the word bildungsroman.

The bildungsroman originated in the late eighteenth century in, appropriately, Germany, and the word itself was used by early-nineteenth-century German critics. The first such novel is generally thought to be Johann Wolfgang von Goethe's *Wilhelm Meister's Apprenticeship* (1795–1796). In the years that followed, many German authors followed in Goethe's footsteps by writing similar novels. Inevitably, the tradition of the *bildungsroman* was transplanted to the English-speaking world. In England, Charlotte Brontë's *Jane Eyre* is regarded as an early English bildungsroman. Later, Charles Dickens adopted the tradition in *David Copperfield* and *Great Expectations*. In the United States, Mark Twain's *Adventures of Huckleberry Finn* makes use of many features of the bildungsroman. In the twentieth century, young-adult novels widely make use of the conventions of the bildungsroman. A common theme in young-adult fiction is the process of maturation as the child or adolescent takes tentative steps into adulthood.

While any literary genre or subgenre can be a broad tent that includes variations, scholars generally agree that the bildungsroman has four important characteristics. Each of these characteristics can be found in *Cold Sassy Tree*. The first, and most important, is that such a novel traces the moral and social development of a single individual who lives within a clearly delineated social order. Will Tweedy fits the bill. He narrates the novel, and his perceptions of life in Cold Sassy define the novel's emotional and physical space. He begins the novel as a fourteen-year-old who has unthinkingly absorbed the conventions and attitudes of his community, though there are hints that he is a sensitive boy who is predisposed to question those conventions and attitudes. The social order is defined by numerous characters: his mother, Mary Willis; his aunt, Loma Williams; and gossipy neighbors, such as Effie Belle Tate. His grandfather's general store is the hub of town gossip, where the community's moral and social codes are articulated and reinforced. Within this context, Will searches for meaningful spiritual and social truth.

WHAT DO I READ NEXT?

- After *Cold Sassy Tree* was published, the author received many requests for a sequel. Before her death she completed thirteen chapters of *Leaving Cold Sassy* (1992), which examines Will Tweedy's early adulthood and marriage to a schoolteacher. The book contains an extensive biography of Olive Ann Burns.

- *Green Days by the River* (2000) is a novel by Michael Anthony, an author from Trinidad. It tells the story of Shell, a fifteen-year-old boy who, like Will Tweedy, faces confusion as he grows into adulthood, has to make difficult choices, and learns about the people around him.

- Jerry Amernic's *Gift of the Bambino* (2004) is a coming-of-age tale about a boy and his special relationship with his grandfather.

- *America in the 1900s and 1910s* (2005), by Jim Callan, presents a nonfiction portrait of America—its politics, art, and culture—during the years in which *Cold Sassy Tree* is set. The book's audience is young-adult readers.

- "A Rose for Emily" is a short story by William Faulkner, first published in 1930. It is set in a small southern town, where the townspeople are bound by traditional ways and intrude into the business of others.

- Rudolpho Anaya's *Bless Me, Ultima* (1972) is a coming-of-age novel set in a small town in New Mexico during World War II. It tells the story of a young Hispanic boy who encounters death and confronts religious and moral issues. He is caught between his two families: his father's family, made up of untamed nonconformists, and his mother's family, farmers who are quieter and more religious.

- J. D. Salinger's 1951 novel *The Catcher in the Rye* is widely considered one of the best novels of the twentieth century. It is a coming-of-age novel about a disaffected teenage boy, Holden Caulfield. The character's name is widely known as representative of teenage rebellion, but his story is ultimately optimistic.

A second characteristic is that some event occurs that spurs the character into searching for truth. In this sense, the bildungsroman is related to the theme of the quest. *Cold Sassy Tree* begins with two such events that are crucial to Will's development. The first is the death of his grandmother, Mattie Lou. This death, along with the later deaths of Camp Williams by suicide and of his grandfather (and to a lesser extent of Lightfoot McLendon's father), launches Will into a quest to understand the meaning of death and, more importantly, the meaning and role of God in the individual's life. The second event is Rucker's hasty marriage to a much younger woman, Miss Love Simpson. The marriage violates every convention in the rural southern town of Cold Sassy and becomes the topic of endless gossip and speculation. Miss Love herself, a northerner

and advocate of women's suffrage, is a challenge to the social order. Part of Will's quest is to get to know Miss Love and to understand the motives behind her marriage to the much older Rucker.

A third characteristic of the bildungsroman is that the central character's quest for growth and self-development is long and arduous. It does not come easily. The character makes missteps and misjudgments. He encounters obstacles on his quest, and he has to find ways to overcome them. In *Cold Sassy Tree*, the obstacles are not earth shattering; they consist of the normal challenges that a boy in a small southern town, or any boy, might encounter. Examples include Will's near-death experience on the train trestle, his feelings for Lightfoot McLendon, the awakening of his sexual awareness through Miss Love, his disastrous camping

1906 Cadillac (*Image copyright Rob Wilson, 2009. Used under license from Shutterstock.com*)

trip and the false stories he tells about his aunt Loma on his return from the trip, the suicide of his uncle, and ultimately the death of his grandfather. Often, the quest comes to involve religious doubt, even spiritual despair, but Will arrives at a more profound relationship with God through the example of Rucker. All of these events conspire to bring Will to a more mature outlook on life.

The final characteristic of the bildungsroman has to do with the resolution of the central character's relationship with the social order. Here is where these types of novels tend to follow differing paths. In the older German tradition, the tendency was for the book to present the apprentice character as naive. In the end, after serving his "apprenticeship," he becomes part of the social order. In the English tradition, though, such novels tend to present the social order as limiting and ultimately destructive to the individual. The central character's ideals are often presented not as naive and childish but as liberating. The character does not accommodate himself or herself to the social order but rather finds a way to escape its limitations while leaving a personal stamp on it.

The resolution of *Cold Sassy Tree* is much more optimistic than that of other novels in the genre in which the character has to sever himself from the social order. In *Huckleberry Finn*, for example, Huck can only escape. The social order that surrounds him is incapable of change. Will, though, witnesses ways in which Rucker and Miss Love transform the culture of Cold Sassy, at least in part. Cold Sassy may be dragged kicking and screaming into the modern age, but it does change. Will can leave the community behind, knowing that its development has paralleled his own. And "Will," with his future-oriented name and its implications of resolution and determination, can keep with him his souvenir piece of the Cold Sassy tree as a reminder of his roots.

Source: Michael J. O'Neal, Critical Essay on *Cold Sassy Tree*, in *Novels for Students*, Gale, Cengage Learning, 2010.

Katrina Kenison

In the following essay, Kenison, Burns's editor, reflects on the author's life and death, the writing

> **SOON AFTER SHE EMBARKED ON A SEQUEL TO *COLD SASSY TREE*, HER CANCER RETURNED. ALTHOUGH SHE CONTINUED TO WRITE, AND LATER TO DICTATE, FROM HER BED, THE BOOK WAS UNFINISHED WHEN SHE DIED ON JULY 4, 1990."**

and publication of Cold Sassy Tree*, and the inspiration she found in a note written by Burns.*

We have become experts at documenting the lives of our children. From the instant my sons made their first appearances in the delivery room, they have been the stars of our home movies and our favorite photographic subjects. But the most precious moments of my family's life are not the ones illuminated by birthday candles, Christmas lights, or amusement park rides, and they cannot be captured on film or tape.

The moments I hold most dear are those that arise unbidden in the course of any day—small, evanescent, scarcely worth noticing except for the fact that I am being offered, just for a second, a glimpse into another's soul. If my experience as a mother has taught me anything, it is to be awake for such moments, to keep life simple enough to allow them to occur, and to appreciate their fleeting beauty: a lip-smacking good-night "guppy kiss"; a spoonful of maple syrup on snow, served to me in bed with great fanfare on a stormy winter morning; a conversation with a tiny speckled salamander discovered, blinking calmly, under a rock. . . . These are the moments that, woven together, constitute the unique fabric of our family life. Herein lies the deep color, the lights and shadows, of our days together.

I am fortunate to have had a mentor in the art of living in the moment. In fact, I received my most precious lesson from her after her death. My older son, Henry, was a year and a half old, and I had left him for the first time, to spend four days in Atlanta, going through the papers of my friend Olive Ann Burns. When Olive Ann and I had first met, eight years earlier, I was an ambitious twenty-five-year-old, eager to make my way in the world of New York publishing. She

was a sixty-year-old housewife about to publish her first novel after a ten-year battle with cancer. In retrospect, I suppose I was of some small help to Olive Ann, suggesting ways to cut pages from her enormous manuscript or sharpen a character, but I now know that she had much more to offer me, namely an unforgettable example of how life ought to be lived, even in the face of tremendous pain.

Cold Sassy Tree surprised everyone by becoming a best-seller, and Olive Ann Burns became a national celebrity. Having been confined to the house during all those years of illness, she thoroughly enjoyed her moment in the spotlight. But it was not to last. Soon after she embarked on a sequel to *Cold Sassy Tree*, her cancer returned. Although she continued to write, and later to dictate, from her bed, the book was unfinished when she died on July 4, 1990.

By the time of Olive Ann's death, I had left publishing to edit an annual short-story anthology from home. Much as I had loved my career, I knew that I could not sustain that kind of commitment to my work and to children, too. But my relationship with Olive Ann had long since transcended that between editor and writer. She was my friend and my teacher as well, for she embodied the kind of courage and spirit that I aspired to. On the other side, she had come to trust my editorial judgment, and she knew that I would be honest with her about the new book.

Olive Ann had completed twelve chapters when she died and had made notes for others. She had also left explicit wishes for the manuscript: She wanted it to be published somehow, so that the hundreds of people who had written her asking for a sequel would not feel let down. Olive Ann had told me this story many times; we had sat side by side on her couch as she showed me the family photo album, introducing me to the real-life characters who had inspired her work. So, with her family's encouragement, I agreed to supplement Olive Ann's chapters with a reminiscence of their author, telling how *Cold Sassy Tree* came to be written and fleshing out the story of the sequel. This was the task that brought me to Atlanta.

Every mother remembers the first night she spends away from her first child. Settling into the familiar little inn a few blocks from Olive Ann's house, where I had always stayed when visiting her, I felt that I had been yanked out of my current life, as a wife and mother, and hurled back into my former one. I was rereading *Cold Sassy Tree* as preparation for the work ahead, and—wonder of wonders—I was alone. For the first time since my son was born, I had time to reflect, to become reacquainted with myself, apart from my husband and my baby. I tried to appreciate the solitude, for I had always loved it, but now I felt unmoored, free-floating in a hotel room while my real life went on without me, someplace else. I realized how grateful I was for all the connections that usually held me in place, and I couldn't wait to get home.

It was in this mood that I sat down in the middle of a room filled with Olive Ann. There were all the drafts of *Cold Sassy Tree*, every typed page densely scribbled with her revisions; there were boxes of fan mail; manuscript pages of the new book, ideas she had jotted on the backs of envelopes and shopping lists, love letters from her late husband, and, perhaps most poignant of all, notes Olive Ann had written to herself to bolster her own courage during the hard times.

Late in the afternoon of my last day in Atlanta, I came across a sheet of yellow-lined paper on which Olive Ann had written these words:

> *I have learned to quit speeding through life, always trying to do too many things too quickly, without taking the time to enjoy each day's doings. I think I always thought of real living as being high. I don't mean on drugs—I mean real living was falling in love, or when I got my first job, or when I was able to help somebody, or watch my baby get born, or have a good morning of really good writing. In between the highs I was impatient—you know how it is—life seemed so Daily. Now I love the dailiness. I enjoy washing dishes. I enjoy cooking, I see my father's roses out the kitchen window, I like picking beans. I notice everything—birdsongs, the clouds, the sound of wind, the glory of sunshine after two weeks of rain. These things I took for granted before.*

It seemed that Olive Ann was speaking directly to me. I copied the lines down and then taped them above my desk when I got home, where they remain to this day. For many weeks I found myself blinking back tears every time I read them, for my own life with an infant was about nothing if not "dailiness," but mine was just beginning, while hers had ended. The fact that she was gone was a powerful reminder to me to pay attention while I had the chance, and to respect the fact that our time here is short.

In a way, those words launched me on the journey into what I have come to feel is my authentic adult life. The idea of living in the moment is not new, of course, but the piece of paper that I carried home from Atlanta and hung above my desk was the inspiration I needed to begin to turn an idea into a way of life. Those simple words seemed to hold out to me a practice, a way of being, that was worth striving for. I didn't want to learn this lesson as a result of ten years of cancer and a few brushes with mortality, as Olive Ann had done—I wanted to learn it now, to be aware of life's beauty even before fate threatened to take it away.

Ours is a society that places high value on achievement and acquisition. The subtle rewards of contemplation, quiet, and deep connection with another human being are held in low esteem, if they are recognized at all. As a result, mothers are constantly pulled in two directions: Can we negotiate the demands of our careers and the world at large, and meet our own emotional and physical needs—not to mention those of our children—at the same time? Can we keep our sights on what is important in any given moment? Do we know how to shut the door, stop the noise, and tune in to our own inner lives?

We all have fallen victim at one time or another to the relentless cycle of our children's playdates and after-school lessons, to the push for their academic and athletic accomplishments, and to their endless desires for the latest toy, video game, or designer sneakers. The adage of our age seems to be "Get more out of life!" And we do our best to obey. Grab a snack, round up the kids, and we're out the door—to do, or buy, or learn something more.

But in our efforts to make each moment "count," we seem to have lost the knack of appreciating the ordinary. We provide our children with so much that the extraordinary isn't special anymore, and the subtle rhythms of daily life elude us altogether. We do too much and savor too little. We mistake activity for happiness, and so we stuff our children's days with activities, and their heads with information, when we ought to be feeding their souls instead. I know a mother who came upon her two-year-old sitting alone, lost in a daydream, and worried that he was "wasting time."

Over the years, I *have* learned to quit speeding through life, but it is a lesson I must take up and learn again every day, for the world conspires to keep us all moving fast. I have found that it is much easier for me to stay busy than to make a commitment to empty time—not surprising, perhaps, in a culture that seems to equate being busy with being alive. Yet if we don't attend to life's small rituals, if we can't find time to savor "dailiness," then we really are impoverished. Our agendas starve our souls.

Like all mothers, I harbor dreams for my children, and sometimes I fall under the spell of my own aspirations for them. We want our children to do well! But when I stop and think about what I *truly* want for them, I know that it is not material wealth or academic brilliance or athletic prowess. My deeper hope is that each of my sons will be able to see the sacred in the ordinary; that they, too, will grow up knowing how to "love the dailiness." So, for their sakes as well as my own, I remind myself to slow down and enjoy the day's doings. The daily rhythms of life, the humble household rituals, the nourishment I provide—these are my offerings to my children, given with love and gratefully received.

> *When I stop speeding through life, I find the joy in*
> *each day's doings, in the life that cannot be bought, but*
> *only discovered, created, savored, and lived.*

Source: Katrina Kenison, "Dailiness," in *Mitten Strings for God: Reflections for Mothers in a Hurry,* Warner Books, 2002, pp. 7–14.

Loxley F. Nichols

In the following mixed review, Nichols argues that although Cold Sassy Tree *is "a genuine Southern novel in substance, form, and voice," the author "simply tries too hard."*

"You can't understand it. You would have to be born there." So says Quentin Compson in *Absalom, Absalom!,* dismissing Shreve McCannon's efforts to define the Southern identity. That the outsider—the "yankee"—cannot *know* the South is a belief deeply ingrained in the Southern consciousness. This assumption is both the consolation and the curse of the Lost Cause. What results is, as Henry James noted, "half a defiance and half a deprecation"; or, to put it another way, a pride and an insecurity—a pride felt partly in the distinction of being different, and an insecurity born largely of the isolation of being misunderstood.

In *Cold Sassy Tree* these dual strains of Southern consciousness are readily discernible, and they account for much of what is good and not so good in the novel. Olive Ann Burns cashes in quite profitably on the Southern oral tradition; tale-telling is the heart of her book. Stories are embedded in stories, and the raconteur seems to enjoy his recitation almost as much as the listener relishes the inventiveness of action and richness of detail. However, Miss Burns's love of local color, mixed with a certain defensiveness, an edge of uneasiness, leads her to excesses that the reader may find tiresome.

Olive Ann Burns seems to believe that kernels of truth are better explained than intuited. In a sense, this tendency reflects both her journalistic background and her lack of previous experience as a writer of fiction. But, on a deeper level, the author's commitment to explication—her insistence on spelling out the obvious—raises a barrier of condescension between writer and reader that bespeaks the characteristically Southern attitude toward the outsider. Will Tweedy is not just a narrator but a rather officious commentator who, all too frequently, intrudes unnecessarily to interpret events and details for the reader—the "damn-yankee"—who cannot assimilate the Southern milieu:

> You need to understand that in Cold Sassy when the word "aunt" is followed by a name, it's pronounced *aint,* as in Aint Loma or Aint Carrie. We also say *dubya* for the letter "w," *sump'm* for something, *idn'* for isn't, *dudn'* for doesn't', *raig'n* for reckon, *chim'ly* for chimney, *wrench* for rinse, *sut* for soot, as in train or chim'ly sut, and *like* for lack, as in "Do you like much of bein' th'ew?" Well, I know that how we speak is part of what we are. I sure don't want Cold Sassy folks to sound like a bunch of Yankees. But I don't want us to sound ignorant, either, and pronunciations like *sump'n* and *id'n* [sic] sound ignorant. So I'm trying to remember not to use such—except right now to tell how Loma became Aint Loma.

Excesses and insecurities inherent in the Southern ethos are inadvertently, yet overbearingly, displayed in the author's emphasis on dialect. A person, even a native Georgian, cannot help feeling that Miss Burns overwrites the regional idiom. The authenticity of the curious names of many of the characters and the curiosities of their speech are indisputable, but well-placed expressions that punctuate rather than dominate dialogue are generally all a reader needs to capture the flavor of the spoken word.

Olive Ann Burns would do well to follow the example of Flannery O'Connor in this regard.

Miss Burns is at her best when she lets her characters indulge in what they like best, namely gossip: an abundant natural resource for the Southern writer, as Eudora Welty has acknowledged in her memoir, *One Writer's Beginnings.* And religious reflections in this form are more effective than Grandpa Blakeslee's rather ponderous homilies. Thus, two Presbyterians muse about predestination as they pay their respects to the Tweedys after Will's train accident:

> "Dear boy, hit just wadn' his time to die," Miss Looly said softly.
>
> "S'pose it wadn' his time to die but it was that trestle's time to fall?" her sister breathed, touching my cheek. "Or what if it was that train engineer's time to die? What would of happened to Will?"
>
> "Shet up, Cretia," whispered Miss Looly. "Hit ain't for us to ast sech questions. Hit were the Lord's will for the boy to live. All we got to do is be thankful."

Compare the suggestiveness of this with Grandpa's "profound" analogy: "Livin' is like pourin' water out of a tumbler into a dang Coca-Cola bottle. If'n you skeered you cain't do it, you cain't. If'n you say to yoreself, 'By dang, I can do it,' then, by dang, you won't slosh a drop."

Cold Sassy Tree is amusing, but Miss Burns's treatment of the comic is exceedingly rich. She plays the joke for all it's worth, and in the process she sometimes plays out. We can hardly muster even a smile when we are forced to hear yet once again about Grandpa's turning over the privy with the Yankee railroad bigwig inside. And the repetition of detail with which characters are reintroduced detracts from the humor of the original description: "Aunt Carrie, remember, was the one who read poetry, studied Latin and Greek, talked cultured, believed in human excrement, and put mourning dye on Mary Toy's hair for Granny's funeral."

Cold Sassy Tree is a genuine Southern novel in substance, form, and voice. Set in an historically accurate background, it is a story about death—the death of an era, as well as the little deaths of individuals. It is also about religion, caste, and—of course—The War. Throughout her book, the author humorously harnesses the old-fashioned to the new-fangled, and in so doing creates a tension of forces that is similarly embodied in her 14-year-old narrator, who, on the brink of change himself, is torn between nostalgia and curiosity.

As a novelist, Olive Ann Burns will need to learn to put greater trust in her audience, as well as in herself. In her efforts to combat what she considers Northern provinciality and ignorance of the ways of the South, she simply *tries* too hard; and so, rather than drawing the reader into her confidence, she deepens the chasm with patronizing and apologetic explanations. We may, however, finally excuse her for her clannishness; for what true Southerner, writer or not, does not in his heart believe that only someone who was "born there" can truly know the South?

Source: Loxley F. Nichols, "Going to Excess," in *National Review*, Vol. 37, No. 6, April 5, 1985, pp. 54–55.

SOURCES

"1906," in *Antique Automobile Club of America*, http://local.aaca.org/bntc/mileposts/1906.htm (accessed May 27, 2009).

Berry, Jason, Review of *Cold Sassy Tree*, in *New York Times Book Review*, November 11, 1984, p. 32.

Burns, Olive Ann, *Cold Sassy Tree*, Ticknor & Fields, 1984.

"China Outperforms U.S. in 2008 Auto Production," in *EE Times Asia*, April 2, 2009, http://www.eetasia.com/ART_8800568569_499495_NT_0a8a4485.HTM (accessed May 27, 2009).

"How Groups Voted in 1984," in *Roper Center* Web site, http://www.ropercenter.uconn.edu/elections/how_groups_voted/voted_84.html (accessed May 27, 2009).

MacDougall, Ruth Doan, Review of *Cold Sassy Tree*, in *Christian Science Monitor*, December 7, 1984, p. B12.

MacKethan, Lucinda, "An Overview of Southern Literature by Genre: The South's Literatures of Resistance," in *Southern Spaces*, February 16, 2004, http://www.southernspaces.org/contents/2004/mackethan/5d.htm (accessed April 19, 2009).

McManus, Jeanne, "Southern Comfort," in *Washington Post*, November 25, 1984, pp. 3, 11.

Nichols, Loxley F., Review of *Cold Sassy Tree*, in *National Review*, April 5, 1985, http://findarticles.com/p/articles/mi_m1282/is_v37/ai_3719798/ (accessed April 21, 2009).

O'Dell, Jay, "Trucks, Six-cylinder Engines Gain Popularity in 1906-07," *Herald-Dispatch* (Huntington, WV), December 11, 2008, http://www.herald-dispatch.com/news/

x1133222293/Trucks-six-cylinder-engines-gain-populari ty-in-1906-07 (accessed May 27, 2009).

Purcell, Kim, "Olive Ann Burns (1924–1990)," in the *New Georgia Encyclopedia*, http://www.georgiaencyclopedia .org/nge/ArticlePrintable.jsp?id = h-1230 (accessed April 16, 2009).

Review of *Cold Sassy Tree*, in *Publishers Weekly*, September 21, 1984, p. 90.

Tilton, John, *World Metal Demand: Trends and Prospects*, Resources for the Future, 1990, p. 179.

FURTHER READING

Goldfield, David R., *Still Fighting the Civil War*, Louisiana State University Press, 2004.
> This volume surveys the impact that the Civil War had on "southern memory" and its influence on the South in the decades following the war.

Gray, Richard, and Owen Robinson, *A Companion to the Literature and Culture of the American South*, Wiley-Blackwell, 2004.
> This volume is a comprehensive survey of the literature and culture of the American South, with emphasis on literary works, music, art, politics, and social issues.

Loughery, John, ed., *Into the Widening World: International Coming of Age Stories*, Persea Books, 1994.
> This book is a collection of coming-of-age short stories from a wide variety of cultures around the world. The introduction provides insights into the nature and characteristics of coming-of-age fiction.

Millard, Kenneth, *Coming of Age in Contemporary American Fiction*, Edinburgh University Press, 2007.
> Millard's book focuses on recent coming-of-age fiction across a range of racial, class, and gender settings.

Otfinoski, Steven, *Coming of Age Fiction*, Chelsea House, 2009.
> The writer explores the issue of young-adult coming-of-age novels that have been challenged in schools and public libraries because of their frank portrayal of controversial issues such as drug use and sexuality.

Dune

FRANK HERBERT

1965

Dune, published in 1965, helped transform the genre of science fiction from one of adolescent adventure to one of exploration of ideas. It was an unprecedented success in mainstream culture, becoming the first piece of genre science fiction to appear on the *New York Times* best-seller list. The importance of *Dune* in Herbert's career was paramount, ensuring his financial success, but also dooming him (and his son Brian Herbert) to a lifetime of writing sequels, since no other project could match its popularity. *Dune* has become the source of many media projects, including comic books, a feature film, a television miniseries, and a proposed new film series. *Dune*'s influence has spread even further, becoming the inspiration for such media projects as *Star Wars*.

Created in the 1960s, *Dune* bears the marks of the counterculture of that time in its concern for ecology. It also reflects the counterculture's distrust of authority and power in its portrayal of corrupt and manipulative institutions such as the Bene Gesserit, the CHOAM corporation, and the Spacing Guild that rule its fictive world. It also shares the optimism of the 1960s that human powers of imagination and perception could transcend and displace materialistic culture. However, *Dune* is, above all, an exploration of the role of religion and quasi-religious forces in human culture in the wake of the fascist hero cults of the 1920s and 1930s.

Frank Herbert (AP Images)

AUTHOR BIOGRAPHY

Herbert was born on October 8, 1920, in Tacoma, Washington. After a brief service in the army during World War II, he attended the University of Washington, but he did not obtain a degree because he refused to take required courses that he considered personally uninteresting and unnecessary. This marked the independence of thought that dominated his adult life. He took highly original viewpoints to arrive at highly creative solutions in his writing, but at the same time he was prone to imagine that his expertise extended to many areas in which he had no formal training. This led him to accept many pseudoscientific ideas in his own thought as well as exploring them in his writing; for instance, he believed that human can be stored in genetic material. Unusually for a science fiction author, he rejected the scientific method in favor of more holistic approaches to knowledge, whose results are, to say the least, unverifiable.

Herbert worked as a journalist in the Pacific Northwest throughout the 1950s and 1960s, eventually becoming an editor at the *San Francisco Examiner*. At the same time, he occasionally published short stories in the science fiction pulp magazines, and in 1955 he published his first novel, known variously as *Under Pressure* or *The Dragon in the Sea*. This novel takes place during a future war between the United States and the Soviet Union and concerns a psychologist evaluating the effects of combat stress on the crew of an American nuclear submarine assigned to steal oil from the Soviet-occupied Persian Gulf. The theme of scientific psychological evaluation is typical of Herbert's work.

Herbert took six years to write his next novel, *Dune*, which grew out of his convergent interests in religion, the psychology of totalitarianism, and ecology. It was serialized in *Analog* magazine between 1963 and 1965 and published in book form in 1965. It immediately won the two most prestigious awards in science fiction, the Nebula, awarded by the Science Fiction Writers of America, and the Hugo, awarded by the attendees of the annual World Science Fiction Convention. It is generally considered to be, if not the greatest science fiction novel ever written, certainly the first to attain a new level of literary achievement within the genre. With brisk book sales and the sale of film rights to the book in 1971, Herbert retired from journalism to write and lecture full time. Though he produced many independent projects, his most successful literary work was a series of five sequels to *Dune*, completed before his death from pancreatic cancer in Madison, Wisconsin, on February 11, 1986. His son Brian Herbert has written a biography of his father and several more novels continuing and expanding the story related to *Dune* based on his father's notes.

PLOT SUMMARY

The text of *Dune* is divided into three books of unnumbered chapters. Each chapter is headed by an epigraph that is a quotation, not from an existing literary work but from a pseudoscholarly work attributed to Princess Irulan, whom the reader learns only at the very end of the novel becomes Paul's wife. The various works named are supposedly historical treatises concerning her husband's early career that she wrote some time after the conclusion of the novel. Read retrospectively, these pseudoquotations reveal important points of the story that occur either in the chapter they head or in a later chapter. This violates a basic principle of ordinary

MEDIA ADAPTATIONS

- The first film adaptation of *Dune* was made in 1984 and was directed by David Lynch.

- In 2001, *Dune* was adapted as a miniseries on the Science Fiction Channel of American cable television in three two-hour-long installments, directed by John Harrison. This version is sometimes known as *Frank Herbert's Dune*.

- In 2008, it was announced that Peter Berg would begin directing a new film adaptation of *Dune*; this version is scheduled for release in 2010.

- Several video games have been based on *Dune*: *Dune* (1992; based on graphics from the 1984 film), *Dune II* (1992), *Dune 2000* (1998), *Emperor: Battle for Dune* (2001), and *Frank Herbert's Dune* (2001; based on graphics from the 2001 miniseries).

storytelling: it gives away key elements of the plot. In a way, Irulan allows the reader to share in Paul's prophetic ability and see glimpses of what will happen later in the narrative.

Dune

The first several chapters are devoted as much to the exposition of the story's world as to traditional plot elements. The civilization of *Dune* spans the galaxy and is approximately ten thousand years old (how far in the future it might be from the present is never revealed). This Imperium took on its present form in response to the "Butlerian Jihad." This conflict is never clearly discussed, but it is hinted that it was a crisis in which intelligent computers attempted to exterminate or enslave the human race. Since that time, all computers have been forbidden. Perhaps as a result, there has been little technological advance since that time. Instead, various human potentials have been developed to ever greater heights of perfection. Several institutions based on human abilities rule the galaxy in concert with more traditional power structures. The central source

of political power is the Combine Honnete Ober Advancer Mercantiles (CHOAM), a joint-stock corporation whose stockholders are granted absolute rule over entire planets in proportion to their stock. The expression of this rule is feudal: the chairman calls himself emperor, the other stockholders dukes and barons. Each member maintains a large military establishment that is used for protection in feuds with other magnates (under the code of *kanly*, or vendetta) and protection from the power of the emperor. The Great Houses are organized into the *Landsraat*, or parliament. Together their military power is only about equal to the emperor's since he controls the Sardaukar, a large force of soldiers whose superhuman military skill make them nearly invincible. Each Great House also has a cache of nuclear weapons (the "family atomics") that may only be used if the legal functioning of the power structure is violated. Another vital component of civilization is the *mentats*, men whose minds are trained to function as computers. Without their aid, controlling civilization on a galactic scale would be impossible, although as a class they have no independent access to power apart from the nobles they serve.

The rule of the Great Houses, however, extends only across the surface of planets. The Spacing Guild has complete control of all spacecraft (even weather and communications satellites can be put into orbit only with their approval). Beyond this, they have a monopoly on travel between star systems (and their final authority is to withhold this service from a Great House that might pose a challenge to them). In the absence of computers, Guild ships are guided though hyperspace by navigators who can see into the future because they take massive doses of a drug known as spice. This spice (the source of wealth of the CHOAM) is a natural product of a single planet, Arrakis (Arabic for "the dancer"). It is generally referred to as the "geriatric spice," since it is taken in lower doses by all aristocrats who can afford it for the purpose of extending life. Another powerful group is the Bene Gesserit Sisterhood (Latin for "she will have performed well"). Just as mentats and navigators are only males, the Bene Gesserit is a purely female institution. Disciplined according to a system of physical and psychological training derived from the martial arts, Zen, and yoga, the Bene Gesserits use the water of life, a spice-poison that uses the biochemistry of their own bodies to metabolize into a drug that induces a higher state of consciousness. The Reverend Mothers who have performed this rite are able to perceive the world around them absolutely (for instance, they are called truthsayers, since they can detect from the smallest telltale sign whether someone is lying) and can also see into human consciousness as a whole. The role of the Bene Gesserit in society seems to be to provide wives and concubines to the Great Houses, and they often educate daughters of the nobility. In short, Herbert presents the human civilization of the future as a finely balanced system in a state of homeostasis (constantly staying the same). However, it is a frozen system, not a dynamic one in constantly rebalanced change, and therefore it will tend to break if pressure is applied.

Dune opens with a scene in which Paul Atreides, the son of Duke Leto and his Bene Gesserit concubine Jessica, is being tested by the Reverend Mother Gaius Helen Mohaim. The test consists of having a poison dart (the *gom jabar*) held to his throat with the threat that it will instantly kill him if he removes his hand from a box that seems to be destroying his appendage in an excruciatingly painful way. When he passes the test and realizes that the pain was an illusion, Paul is told that his experience reveals that he is a human being, able to govern his response to pain and fear with reason, rather than an animal. Over the course of the first book of *Dune*, Herbert reveals that in accordance with the Bene Gesserit breeding program, Paul was meant to have been a girl (Bene Gesserits can control the sex of their children), but out of love for the Duke, his mother Jessica bore a son in defiance of the orders of her superiors. Paul, in addition to being the heir of a duke, has been trained as a mentat by his father's mentat Thifur Hawat. He was also trained by his mother as a Bene Gesserit, although training a man in this fashion is forbidden. Paul has also been taught fencing by Gurney Halleck, the most loyal of his father's military retainers.

Paul's family is being led into a trap. Arrakis, the planet that is the sole source of geriatric spice, has been controlled for many decades by the Baron Harkonnen, an ancestral rival to the house of Atreides. Supposedly, the Emperor has removed him from control of this huge source of income on the grounds of mismanagement. The planet will instead be given to Duke Leto, who is universally admired by members of the Landsraat for his uprightness and honor. The duke is

well aware, however, that this is most likely a plot to destroy him. The second chapter reveals every detail of this scheme in a staff meeting between the Baron Harkonnen, his nephew and chosen heir Feyd-Rautha, and his sadistic mentat Piter de Vries. Once the duke is established in his new holding, the baron will invade the planet in a surprise attack. Although his forces could probably be defeated by the superior training and valor of the Atreides military, the Harkonnens will be supported by sixty thousand Sardaukar from the Emperor's guard, the greatest soldiers in the galaxy.

The plot is duly carried out within a few days of Duke Leto taking possession of Arrakis, and although the matter might seem quite straightforward given the element of surprise and the overwhelming military force used, the nearly two hundred pages of the first book are used to spin out the elaborately Byzantine plot of the Harkonnens. Ruses and deceptions are used at every turn to feed the suspicions of the leaders of the House Atreides about each other. The Harkonnen plot succeeds in effecting the military defeat of the Atreides forces (they are virtually annihilated) and in killing the Duke. Baron Harkonnen believes that he has also killed Paul, the heir, and his mother Jessica, by forcing them to fly an ornithopter into a sandstorm, but in fact they survive, aided by the Imperial planetologist Pardot Keynes, whose mother was a Fremen, a member of the mysterious native population of Arrakis. Kynes is secretly Liet, the leader of the Fremen. He guarantees that the Fremen will protect the fugitive nobles.

During their escape, Paul reveals to his mother a prophetic vision of the future that he has had. He authenticates this vision by telling her that she is pregnant with a daughter, Alia (which only she knew), and with the revelation that she is the Baron Harkonnen's daughter, a fact that she has denied as unthinkable but that she now must accept based on family resemblance. She suggests that he is the Kwisatz Haderach, the male Bene Gesserit bred from thousands of years of eugenics experiments by the sisterhood; if Jessica had obeyed her Bene Gesserit orders and borne a girl, that girl would later have been the Kwisatz Haderach's mother. However, Paul tells his mother, "Put that out of your mind. I'm something unexpected." Paul does not precisely have the power to see into the future but rather to see all of the possible futures and take actions that make certain possibilities more likely. He sees two main pathways to the future, one in which he enigmatically confronts Baron Harkonnen, and another in which he unleashes a jihad, a holy war, across the galaxy to serve the purpose of remixing isolated human gene pools, but at the cost of billions of deaths. He fears pursuing either possibility.

Muad'Dib

Liet-Kynes also escapes from the Harkonnen forces, but he dies in the open desert. During his death agony he has a vision in which he obliquely reviews the ecology of Arrakis with the ghost of his father. The elder Kynes gained control of the Fremen by promising to turn Arrakis into a fertile paradise. Alluding to information that is scattered throughout the novel, Kynes realized that there was no shortage of water on Arrakis. The whole planet was a desert because its water had been trapped by an alien life form that had long ago been introduced there. This is the sandworm, referred to as the Maker or Shai-hulud by the Fremen. It is an enormous creature hundreds of meters long that swims through sand. Kynes discovered that it has a complicated natural history. The first stage of its existence is as a "little maker," a microscopic creature with both plant-like and animal-like properties that lives in the sand and sequesters any available water in cysts. Because this life was alien, it had no natural predator and so ran wild, trapping nearly all the water on the planet. The spice is a by-product of its life cycle in the desert sands. The next stage is the larva or sand-trout, a small animal that lives in the sand, feeding on the microbial form. These eventually pupate into full sandworms. Kynes devised a plan to build up green areas in the desert with water taken from the atmosphere and protected from the little makers by plants that are poisonous to them. Of course, only selected areas could be reforested or else the spice-making ecology would die out. The Fremen have been secretly carrying out this plan for several decades.

Among the Fremen, Paul and Jessica are protected by their assimilation to roles in religious mythology that the Bene Gesserit sowed among the Fremen thousands of years before through the Missonaria Protectiva. Paul is recognized as Lisan al-Gaib, the promised messiah. He uses his authority over the Fremen to lead them in a guerilla war against the Harkonnen occupying forces. He utilizes the potential of what his father called "desert power." Not only are the Fremen

the greatest warriors in the galaxy thanks to the harshness of their living conditions and able to utilize the resources of the desert (such as the sandworms) for warfare, but their ultimate power is the control of the spice. Using the logical insight of his mentat training, Paul quickly deduces, "The Fremen [are] paying the Guild for privacy, paying in a coin that's freely available to anyone with desert power—spice." With their unlimited access to spice, the Fremen are able to bribe the Spacing Guild into ignoring their ecological work in the deep desert and also into denying intelligence to the Harkonnen military forces. The baron, however, cannot see the potential of the Fremen and discounts them as "rabble" He blinds himself to his greatest danger because of his arrogant, prejudiced assumptions. He pursues a course of harshly oppressing Arrakis using his nephew Glossu, so that he can later put his favored nephew Feyd-Rautha in power as a beloved savior. His ultimate aim is to position Feyd-Rautha as successor to the emperor. The baron attempts to build his nephew Feyd up to superhuman stature by making him a popular gladiator. The Bene Gesserit nevertheless do not wish to lose his lineage from their breeding program and so arrange for one of their agents, the Countess Fenring, to seduce Feyd-Rautha.

Paul and Jessica are taken in by Stilgar, the Fremen leader of Sietch Tabr. There Paul meets Chani, the daughter of Liet-Kynes and takes her as his concubine. During the fighting, Paul and the Fremen adopt many terrorist tactics, such as kamikaze attacks on troop transports that exchange the life of one pilot for the lives of hundreds of the enemy. His followers become known as Death Commandos. Jessica becomes the Reverend Mother (high priestess) of the Sietch in a ceremony in which she drinks a poison created by drowning a young sandworm. She is able to consciously control the biochemistry of her body to metabolize it into an intoxicant that is shared out among the community as a sacrament. This process calls her unborn daughter Alia to consciousness, with the result that she is able to think and speak in an adult fashion shortly after birth. Jessica also gains access to the memories of all the Fremen Reverend Mothers in the chain of succession before her.

The Prophet

Thifur Hawat has agreed to work for the Baron Harkonnen as his mentat chief of staff because he realizes that the Atreides's main enemy has been the emperor, and serving the Harkonnens puts him in the best position to directly attack the throne. Hawat reveals to the baron what the Atreides learned about the Fremen and convinces him that they should be cultivated as allies to produce a fighting force superior to the Sardaukar. He has also deduced that the reason the emperor destroyed Duke Leto was that the military proficiency of the Atreides armed forces was approaching that of the Sardaukar. The baron imagines that this new scheme of cultivating the Fremen can be effected by his original plan of replacing Glossu as governor of Arrakis, with Feyd-Rautha in the role of a liberating hero.

As commander of the Fremen resistance to Harkonnen occupation, Paul, despite his unparalleled military success, must prove himself by the conventional measures of Fremen manhood: for instance, by riding a sandworm. In the traditional Fremen order, Paul would have been forced to call out and kill Stilgar to succeed him as leader of Sietch Tabr, but he manages to convince his followers that such a waste is unnecessary since his claims to power as the duke extend over the whole planet, not a single community. Paul also tests himself by transforming the sacramental poison in the same manner as a Reverend Mother, something no male has ever done. During one of his military actions, Paul is reunited with Gureny Halleck, who has been living since the coup as a spice smuggler, plotting for the day he can assassinate Glossu Harkonnen.

Once it becomes clear that the Fremen are on the verge of winning their war against the Harkonnen, the Spacing Guild transports to Arrakis Emperor Shaddam IV, together with five legions of Sardaukar and military contingents from all the Great Houses of the galaxy. However, Paul has foreseen this day and developed a plan to overcome this vast military expedition and to secure his own position not only as duke but as emperor. Before his plan goes into action, however, the Sardaukar raid Sietch Tabr, kill Paul's son Leto, and take Alia captive. While Alia is being interviewed by the emperor, she kills Baron Harkonnen. Paul defeats the invading Sardaukar by using his arsenal of nuclear weapons to blow a hole in the shield wall, the mountains that surround the north pole of Arrakis. This allows a devastating desert storm to roll through the imperial encampment. This is followed by the Fremen army, riding sandworms

that make short work of the imperial spacecraft and the Sardaukar they shelter. Paul takes a group of nobles captive, including the emperor and representatives of the Spacing Guild. He explains to them that if the Guild does not disperse the main elements of the invasion fleet still in orbit, and if the emperor does not abdicate in his favor (giving Paul his daughter Irulan in an official marriage that would legalize the succession), he will destroy the spice, which can be easily done by interrupting the life cycle of the sandworms. Faced with this terrorist threat that would end interstellar travel in the Imperium, Paul's adversaries must accept his conditions. The climax of the novel comes in a duel fought between Paul and Feyd-Rautha in satisfaction of the vendetta between their families. Paul's virtue easily overcomes Harkonnen treachery. Although it does not begin within the scope of the novel, the Fremen jihad across the galaxy will shortly take place because it is an imperative of human evolution.

Appendices

Four appendices contain pseudodocuments supposedly produced within the Dune universe, similar to the chapter epigraphs. They explain in a more systematic fashion material already presented in the novel concerning the ecology of Arrakis, the Bene Gesserit, and the religious history of the Imperium, and they supply brief biographies of the main characters holding ranks of nobility.

CHARACTERS

Alia Atreides

Alia is the daughter of Leto and Jessica. She was conceived only a few days before her father's death. As a result of Jessica drinking the water of life, the sacramental poison of the Fremen, while pregnant with her, Alia becomes fully self-aware while still in the womb and has an adult consciousness. She becomes known as St. Alia of the Knife because she takes revenge for her father by assassinating her grandfather, Baron Harkonnen.

Duke Leto Atreides

Duke Leto is Paul's father. The family name derives from the family that led the Greek forces in the Trojan War (perhaps because of the fulfilled prophecy concerning Agamemnon's treacherous death). Leto is aware that a member of the nobility is supposed to act in the ideal—with honor, justice, and courage—and does so to the best of his ability. His genuine virtues make him popular among the other noble houses of the Landsraad. Even the emperor, ultimately his deadly enemy, secretly wishes that Leto were his son. However, the duke's very popularity creates jealously among other houses, such as the Harkonnens, and the emperor, whose lack of a male heir makes him nervous of any potential rival. Overwhelmed by the Byzantine plots in which he finds himself enmeshed on Arrakis and disgusted by what he views as his own hypocrisy in promoting his image through propaganda, the duke finally tells Paul, "I'm morally tired. The melancholy degeneration of the Great Houses has afflicted me at last, perhaps." After his assassination by the Harkonnens, he becomes a venerated martyr in the new political and religious order instituted by Paul.

Paul Atreides

Paul is the son of Duke Leto Atreides and his concubine Lady Jessica. His birth was part of the Bene Gesserit breeding program to produce the Kwisatz Haderach, a male Bene Gesserit. However, he was intended to be born a girl who would breed with Feyd-Rautha Harkonnen and complete the program. When Jessica used her prana-bindu training to produce a son to satisfy the desires of the Duke, the birth completely upset the Bene Gesserit plans and the static system of the Imperium. Trained as a Bene Gesserit and a mentat and a user of the prophecy-inducing spice, Paul combines in himself all of the mental disciplines developed to expand human potential in place of technology. In a development completely unforeseen by the Bene Gesserit, he discovers he has the ability not only to see into the future but to shape it, realizing that small decisions of his will produce disproportionate changes in events as they unfold. His abilities are not unlimited, but he eventually chooses a path that makes him emperor and allows the fulfillment of what Herbert considers to be the primary human instinct, to indiscriminately mix pools of genetic difference. The cost, however, is the unleashing of a galaxy-wide war that will cause billions of deaths.

At the beginning of the story, Paul is a fifteen-year-old boy who must rapidly face the death of his father, his exile into a community of the desert, and the realization of his unique powers and position. Becoming a guerilla leader fighting against the Harkonnen, he must come to terms with the necessities of killing, as well as with the new experience of love with his mistress Chani. Among the Fremen, he is given the personal name Usul (meaning "base of the pillar") and the public name Muad'Dib (after the constellation of the mouse). As the plot of the novel develops, the presentation of Paul's character becomes less distinct and immediate; many of the sayings attributed to him in the epigraphs by Irulan cannot easily be reconciled with his character as portrayed in the novel. Perhaps these developments are deliberate, emphasizing Paul's movement beyond the sphere of the comprehensibly human.

Chani

Chani is the daughter of Liet-Kynes. Once Paul takes up life among the Fremen, she becomes his concubine and the heir to his mother as Reverend Mother. She also bears his son Leto II, who is killed in a Sardaukar raid. Paul praises her for her wisdom.

Count Hasimir Fenring

"A dapper and ugly little man," Count Fenring had been the imperial agent on Arrakis before the transferal of the planet to the Atreides. The closest friend of Emperor Shaddam IV, he is a "Genetic-eunuch and one of the deadliest fighters in the Imperium." His sterility was a failure of Bene Gesserit breeding. He had been intended as a candidate to become the Kwisatz Haderach. In the climax of the novel, he saves his friend Shaddam's life by refusing to duel with Paul.

Countess Margot Fenring

Countess Fenring, a Bene Gesserit, is the wife of Count Fenring. As a fellow member of the sisterhood, she leaves in the ducal residence in Arrakeen a document warning Jessica of various traps and plots prepared on Arrakis by the Harkonnens. She is later assigned by the Bene Gesserit to become pregnant by Feyd-Rautha Harkonnen so as not to lose his genetic material for their breeding program.

Gurney Halleck

Halleck is a senior officer in Duke Leto's military; he serves as fencing master to Paul. His personality possesses curious, contrary features: "a head full of songs, quotations, and flowery phrases ... and the heart of an assassin when it [comes] to dealing with the Harkonnens." He survived the Harkonnen coup and led a small remnant of Atreides soldiers who worked as spice smugglers. He eventually rejoins Paul and his Death Commandos. After Paul becomes emperor, Gurney is made Earl of Caladan.

Feyd-Rautha Rabban Harkonnen

Feyd-Rautha is the younger nephew of Baron Harkonnen. Though he has been corrupted by his uncle's influence, his genetic material is vital to the Bene Gesserit, and when it proves impossible to breed him with a daughter of Duke Leto, his line is preserved by having Countess Fenring seduce him. He is chosen by the baron not only as his successor but as a potential heir to the imperial succession. His public persona is based on his prominence as a gladiator on the Harkonnen home world of Gedei Prime. Like the ancient Roman emperor Commodus, he has won more than a thousand matches, all of which were rigged in his favor. At the climax of the novel he is anxious to resolve the feud between the Houses of Harkonnen and Atreides in a duel with Paul (a scene based on the ending of Shakespeare's *Hamlet*, complete with poisoned swords), in part because he longs to test himself in a relatively fair fight. He proves no match for Paul, who is hardened by years of actual combat experience.

Count Glossu Rabban Harkonnen

Rabban is the older nephew of Baron Harkonnen. He was the ineffectual governor of Arrakis before the plot of the novel begins, becoming known as Beast Rabban because of his excessive cruelty. He was restored to that post after the baron regained control of the planet and given instructions to maximize revenue at all costs. This is part of the baron's plan to make his eventual replacement by his younger brother seem like a deliverance.

Baron Vladimir Harkonnen

Vladimir Harkonnen is the chief villain of *Dune*. While many names in the novel were chosen to evoke Arabic culture, the baron's is decidedly Russian, to evoke the Cold War hostility toward the Soviet Union prevalent in the early 1960s. In contrast to Duke Leto's asceticism, the baron devotes himself to every kind of depravity in pursuit of physical pleasure. One result of this is that he is immensely fat and has to support his weight with "suspensors." Also in contrast to Leto, the baron believes that people can be ruled only by manipulation and cruelty. He sets in motion the action of the novel by involving the emperor in a complicated

scheme of treachery and deception that he hopes will destroy his ancestral enemies, the Atredies, and eventually maneuver his nephew Feyd-Rautha into a position to succeed the emperor. His motivation is largely simple hatred of the Atreides, of whose more legitimate and popular position he is jealous, and because "an Atreides had a Harkonnen banished for cowardice after the battle of Corrin." His family is nevertheless of great interest to the Bene Gesserit eugenics program to breed the Kwisatz Haderach. Accordingly, the Bene Gesserit lured him into fathering a child who eventually became Lady Jessica. She was later ordered to produce a daughter with Duke Leto, whose offspring from Feyd-Rautha would hopefully become the male Bene Gesserit. This makes Baron Harkonnen not only Jessica's father but the grandfather of her children, Paul and Alia. His granddaughter Alia eventually assassinates him in revenge for her father's death.

Thufir Hawat

Hawat is Duke Leto's mentat, effectively his chief of staff. He is recognized as one of the greatest mentats in the galaxy and has served the Atreides family for generations. Once he is taken captive by the Baron Harkonnen, he begins to work for him as a mentat in exchange for the possibility of taking revenge against the emperor. Remaining loyal to Paul to the last, he reveals in the final meeting between Paul and the emperor that the latter has been foolish enough to order him to assassinate his rightful lord.

Duncan Idaho

A top official in Duke Leto's military, Duncan is made ambassador to the Fremen once Leto takes control of Arrakis. During Baron Harkonnen's coup, he dies fighting Sardaukar to buy time for Paul and Jessica's escape. He is later venerated as an important martyr of the Atreides regime.

Princess Irulan

Irulan is a Bene Gesserit and the daughter of the emperor. She plays a relatively minor role in the text of the novel. Paul must marry her to legitimize his succession as emperor. The marriage is entirely for form's sake, and she will live out her days in the fashion of a wife sent to a convent in the Middle Ages. However, she devotes the rest of her life to the production of scholarly works about Paul, and it is from these that the epigraphs at the head of each chapter are drawn.

Lady Jessica

Jessica is the concubine of Duke Leto Atreides and mother of his heir, Paul. A Bene Gesserit, she betrays her order's plan to breed the duke's daughter with Feyd-Rautha Harkonnen. Escaping to the desert Fremen with Paul, she becomes his closest adviser and mentor. She becomes a Reverend Mother through the biochemical transformation of poison, a Bene Gesserit practice that has been preserved among the Fremen. Jessica shapes Paul's life into the pattern of messianic expectation among the Fremen. This pattern of belief was in turn sown as myth among them thousands of years before by Bene Gesserit agents of the Missonaria Protectiva so that it could be exploited by any future Bene Gesserit marooned among the Fremen.

Muad'Dib

See Paul Atreides

Pardot Liet-Kynes

Pardot Liet-Kynes is the Imperial Planetologist on Arrakis. As an imperial official, he holds the position of Judge of the Change for the transition of power between the Harkonnens and Atreides. He inherited his position as planetologist from his father, also named Pardot. The elder planetologist had convinced the Fremen that by following his plan they could convert Arrakis into a paradise with open water and large tracts of vegetation. In deference to this plan, he became their de facto leader, using them as a work force to plant and protect plants in the southern hemisphere. He married a Fremen woman, and his son also has the Fremen name, Liet. During the coup, Liet-Kynes saves Paul and Jessica by sending them to the Fremen of the deep desert, but he dies while trying to escape the Sardaukar

Gaius Helen Mohaim

She is a Bene Gesserit Reverend Mother and the emperor's truthsayer. She has had the mind-expanding experience of consciously using her body's biochemistry to neutralize the water of life poison, the highest level of Bene Gesserit training. As a result, she has a heightened awareness of subtle cues in her perceptual field, and can easily tell whether someone speaking to her is lying or not. She makes a special trip to Caladan to test Paul with the gom jabr. Ordered to evaluate Paul to see whether he is the Kwisatz Haderach, she unconsciously blinds herself to the evidence. She is present in the final audience scene with Paul, principally as the representative of the Bene Gesserit order, so that Paul can gloat to her over his complete destruction of their breeding scheme.

Emperor Shadam IV

Shadam is the emperor of the galactic Imperium. He sets the plot of *Dune* in motion by conspiring with the Harkonnens to destroy the Atreides family, something he feels is a political necessity because they have trained their own military to a standard equivalent to his Sardaukar corps, upsetting the balance between emperor and nobles. Nevertheless, he idealizes Duke Leto more than anyone else, and his daughter Irulan perceives that her father wishes the duke were his son. When he is utterly defeated, Paul offers him the face-saving way out of accepting Paul as heir through marriage to Princess Irulan. Irulan prevents her father from rejecting Paul's mercy by using the Bene Gesserit trick of appealing to his deepest unconscious wishes at a moment of crisis, telling him of Paul, "But here's a man fit to be your son."

Stilgar

Stilgar is the leader of the Sietch Tabr. (This community is probably named after Mt. Tabor, the hill outside Jerusalem where tradition says the Transfiguration of Christ took place, and an important name in medieval messianic movements in Central Europe.) He originally led the Fremen embassy to Duke Leto and created a stir with the duke's bodyguard by spitting at his feet, but this was a sign of desert honor rather than a challenge. He becomes Paul's protector among the Fremen after the Harkonnen coup. Although Stilgar becomes Paul's chief lieutenant during the guerilla war against the Harkonnen and governor of Arakkis after Paul becomes emperor, Paul considers that he is inherently diminished to something less than human to the same degree Paul himself must play the role of the more than human: "Paul saw how Stilgar has been transformed from the Fremen nain to a *creature* of the Lisan al-Gaib, a receptacle for awe and obedience. It was a lessening of the man."

Usul

See Paul Atreides

Piter De Vries

De Vries is the sadistic mentat of the Baron Harkonnen. Before being killed in Duke Leto's final attempt to assassinate the baron, De Vries invents a poison that will remain in the body indefinitely with no effect so long as an antidote is regularly administered. This is later used by the baron to control Thufir Hawat.

Wellington Yueh

Yueh is the personal physician of Duke Leto. He was a Suk Doctor, meaning he has undergone psychological conditioning to make it impossible for him to betray his master, an important consideration among nobles who live in constant dread of assassination. His betrayal of the duke makes the swift advance of the baron's coup possible. The baron believes he has broken Yueh's conditioning by torturing his wife and securing his treachery in exchange for stopping the torture and the promise returning her to him. However, the actual factor involved was Yueh's hope for revenge against the baron, which he nearly achieves by implanting a false tooth filled with poison gas into Duke Leto's mouth, to kill the baron as he gloats over him in triumph. However, this plan does not ultimately work.

THEMES

Religion

The main theme of *Dune* is the disastrous effect that messianic religious belief can have on human society. Herbert's original inspiration was the messianic cult of personality that was attached to Adolf Hitler, who exploited the power it gave him to start World War II and the Holocaust. Herbert treats this through fiction in the messianic role Paul plays for the Fremen and the eugenics program of the Bene Gesserit, as well as in the anti-eugenic disaster unleashed across the galaxy by the Fremen.

Technology and Human Development

The fantastic advance of technology has always been a common theme of science fiction. There are certainly some instances of superscience in *Dune*, but Herbert's treatment of such marvels stands far apart from most science fiction. Many of the technological ideas used in *Dune* in 1965 have already been surpassed by modern science. For instance, the ornithopters used as aircraft on Arrakis underperform modern helicopters and

TOPICS FOR FURTHER STUDY

- Draw some sketches of your favorite characters from *Dune*. Then, compare them to the way the characters were drawn in the 1984 *Dune* comic book (*Marvel Super Special 36*) by Bill Sienkiewicz. Report to your class on the differing artistic approaches.

- George Lucas, the writer and director of the *Star Wars* movies, does not deny that much of the fictional world and plot of that series was derived from *Dune*. View one or more of Lucas's films and give a PowerPoint presentation explaining some items that are similar to material in *Dune*.

- Robert Heinlein's 1961 novel *Stranger in a Strange Land* arguably did as much to change the nature of the science fiction genre as *Dune*. The novels are very different in form, style, and language, but they treat many of the same themes. Write a review comparing and contrasting the two books.

- Religion plays an important, if unorthodox, role in *Dune*. Present an oral report to your class on some similarities between the religions presented in Dune and the real-world faiths of Christianity and Islam.

- Choose one of the short stories from *The Year's Best "Science Fiction" and Fantasy for Teens: First Annual Collection*, edited by Jane Yolen and Patrick Nielsen Hayden (2005). Look for comparisons to *Dune* in terms of theme and style. Write an essay that sums up your findings.

jets. In general, the level of technology in *Dune* is relatively primitive; the water reprocessing stillsuits used by the Fremen have a "green" rather than a high-tech feel. Even items such as the interstellar travel used by the Spacing Guild and the shields used as personal protection by soldiers function rather strangely in the book. They can hardly be said to be technological marvels since they have no conceivable basis in physics and so are more nearly devices of fantasy than of scientific extrapolation. In fact, Herbert uses the ships and navigators of the Spacing Guild to avoid having to deal realistically with the effect of space travel on society. The characters might as well be magically transported from Caladan to Arrakis so that they can get on with the action. The shields work similarly: they make firearms and energy weapons such as lasers practically useless, so soldiers have reverted to fighting with swords, whose relatively slow movements can penetrate the shields. Herbert purposefully ignores technological advancement to emphasize the development of purely human potential. The initial objection to the use of firearms in war at the end of the Middle Ages was that a knight who had trained at arms for ten years could be killed on the battlefield by a peasant with a musket who had trained for ten minutes. Herbert wanted to reverse that development and imagine to what heights and extremes the training of human abilities could reach. The exploration of technological advancement is rejected in favor of the exploration of human advancement. The abandonment of computers during the Butlerian Jihad "forced *human* minds to develop. Schools were started to train *human* talents." This is manifested in the prophetic abilities of the Spacing Guild navigators, in the seemingly magical powers of perception and self-control perfected by the Bene Gesserit, and in the computing ability of the mentats. All of these qualities are combined in Paul, who as the Kwisatz Haderach of the Bene Gesserit and the messiah of the Fremen represents a new level of human evolution and potential.

Eugenics

Inasmuch as the historical phenomena of the rapid rise to power and striking initial success of Adolph Hitler were among Herbert's inspirations, it is not surprising that eugenics is an important theme of *Dune*. Eugenics (literally "wellborn") is the effort to breed human beings like domestic animals to achieve some apparently desirable new trait or to shift the composition of a population. It involves controlling which human beings may breed with others or even the sterilization or culling (i.e., murder) of supposedly undesirable specimens. It is one of the most outrageous violations of human rights imaginable. There are nevertheless two important eugenics programs in the *Dune* universe.

The civilization depicted in *Dune* has endured for over ten thousand years; during that time, the imperial family has controlled Salusa Secundus, a planet whose environment is extremely hostile to human life. The planet was originally used as a prison, and the emperors relied on the environmental conditions there to select for "tough, strong, ferocious men" who were naturally suited for warfare. This eventually created the Sardaukar guard of the emperor, the greatest soldiers in the empire. Or rather, the second greatest, since the even more extreme conditions on Arrakis produced the Fremen, who were correspondingly better fighters, only in this case by an entirely natural evolution. "God created Arrakis to train the faithful" is a Fremen saying. The fact that human intentions to imitate or control nature are doomed to ultimate failure is an important point of the novel: artificial breeding cannot outdo evolution. Although Herbert intended the Sardaukar as a thought experiment to play out something like the Nazi eugenics program on a larger scale (it is clear that the Sardaukar are modeled after the Nazi SS), it is quite fantastic. In fact, the human cultures of the most extreme desert environments, the Bushmen of the Kalahari and the Australian Aborigines, depend for survival on cooperation and altruism, with the result that they are remarkably unwarlike.

The primary purpose of the Bene Gesserit Sisterhood was to breed a man who could look into some part of the human consciousness that they, as women, were blind to (the part that takes and is inherently male, as Paul later describes it). This was the Kwisatz Haderach (Shortening of the Way), whom they hoped could see where the Reverend Mothers could not. To this end, the Bene Gesserit established a social position for themselves wherein most young aristocratic women joined the Bene Gesserit, and the Bene Gesserit supplied wives and concubines to the aristocrats of the empire. By keeping track of the often secret paternity of children born to these unions and carefully interbreeding the various families, they control the genetic destiny of the whole imperial aristocracy and manipulate the nobility for the purposes of their covert eugenics program. Their final plan is to produce the Kwisatz Haderach by breeding the daughter of Duke Leto and Jessica (secretly the daughter of Baron Harkonnen) with the baron's nephew Feyd-Rautha. However, out of her love for Leto, Jessica instead bears a boy, Paul. He upsets all of the Bene Gesserit plans by becoming the Kwisatz Haderach (and much else besides) entirely outside of their control. Paul eventually realizes that his destiny, which the Bene Gesserit have been breeding for without

British musician Sting as Feyd Rautha and Kyle MacLachlan as Paul Atreides in the 1984 film version of the novel (AP Images)

realizing it, is to unleash a devastating war across the galaxy. This war, countering every effort at eugenics, will indiscriminately mix the genetic material of all human populations: "They were all caught up in the need for their race to renew its scattered inheritance, to cross and mingle and infuse their bloodlines in a great new pooling of genes." Herbert views eugenics as a system that is ultimately self-defeating, aside from its moral repugnance, because it is contrary to a nature that will not be denied. Herbert told his biographer Timothy O'Reilly, "I can state it for you very straightly: human beings are not through evolving. And if we are going to survive as a species, we're going to have to do things that allow us to keep on evolving."

Ecology

In the 1960s, it was becoming increasingly apparent that modern industrial society was transforming, even damaging, the natural world, as population increased dramatically and industrial processes were carried out on ever larger scales, using irreplaceable resources and generating increasing amounts of dangerous waste. *Dune* was of great interest to the nascent environmental movement because, in the Fremen's attempt to restore open water and green areas to Arrakis, it offered a model of ecological repair.

STYLE

Science Fiction

Science fiction and the closely allied genre of fantasy (*Dune* is often said to have elements of both) is difficult to define. A simple definition based on elements common in the genre, such as space travel, stories set in the future, and so on, or even a more sophisticated attempt at definition such as a 'literature of ideas,' is not sufficient, since many books contain those elements but are not science fiction. Works by authors such as Doris Lessing, Anthony Burgess, or Margaret Atwood meet those simple criteria and yet they have never been considered science fiction by critics, and the authors themselves more or less vociferously deny that their works are science fiction. A historical definition of the genre is more useful (leaving aside the works of authors such as H. G. Wells or Jules Verne, which are best seen as precursors of the purely genre development). Science fiction developed in the 1920s in the United States along with a series of pulp (mass-marketed) journals that capitalized on the increasing public perception of the transformation being effected in society by the hastening pace of technological change (such as radio and the dispersion of the automobile). The creator of the science fiction magazines was Hugo Gernsback, who had long published journals devoted to amateur radio enthusiasts. Gernsback began publishing *Amazing Stories* in 1926; this and similar magazines were called "pulps" after the cheap paper stock on which they were printed. The formula of the science fiction genre was established by John W. Campbell, who from 1938 to 1971 edited *Astounding Science Fiction*. The genre originally consisted of relatively simplistic stories whose interest was generated by fantastically advanced technology (indistinguishable from magic as Arthur C. Clarke said) such as robots with intelligence and feelings comparable to human beings or interstellar space flight. The primary audience for these magazines in the 1920s to the 1950s consisted of teenage boys, and many of science fiction's themes of adventure, warfare, and heroism—fantasies of power—catered to that audience. Most decisively, there was only a superficial contact between the language and style of science fiction and the wider world of literature as a whole. It was the isolation of a small, self-contained world of science fiction authors (such as E. E. Smith, Robert Heinlein, and Isaac Asimov) and readers (fans) that created science fiction as a genre, while at the same time other authors, such as Aldous Huxley, George Orwell, and William Golding, were treating very similar themes in writing intended for a more general audience. Herbert's work, before and after *Dune*, corresponds to the profile of genre science fiction, as noted by critic David Miller: "Most of Herbert's novels seem designed to be read once; hence story lines are clear, there is little parallel action, genre markers are unequivocal, and proleptic [anticipatory] clues are relatively obvious." *Dune*, however,

broke out of this generic mold in a way that had never been seen before in science fiction. While *Dune*'s characters remain for the most part stereotypes, Herbert was successful in making the plot and its meaning arise from the characters, and especially from the character of the narrative world he created, thus introducing new levels of literary sophistication while staying within the genre. This made it possible to do real literary work in the science fiction genre, and while science fiction still maintains its distance from other literature and still produces a great deal of material that follows the old pulp formulas, it was forever transformed by the presence of *Dune* within it.

Series Fiction

It is a peculiarity of science fiction publishing that a popular novel will often initiate a series of sequels (by the same author or others). The resulting series of books may not all contain the same characters or discuss the same themes, but they will take place in the same "universe." That is, the books will all share the same premise about the development of future history and technology, take place in the same alternative universe, or share other essential features of the original's setting. This trend exists largely because of the economic realities of publishing. It is easier to sell readers books that they already have some familiarity with, and writers frequently have extensive background notes compiled for the original novel that can be exploited in this way. Perhaps the prototype for this kind of publishing is L. Frank Baum's *The Wonderful Wizard of Oz*, to which Baum wrote thirteen sequels and, after his death, other writers an additional twenty-six. The sequels are aimed at a specific fan base who read the original book and not at new readers. The pattern has been repeated endlessly in science fiction publishing (and to a lesser degree in mystery novels and other genres). Fans pride themselves on their knowledge of the "canon" of particular series, and a technical literature of encyclopedias and dictionaries relating to a series is often produced as well (though usually not by the writer or writers of the series). Herbert resisted this trend in some respects in that he introduced radically new concepts in his sequels, ideas that often undercut or reinterpreted material in the original novel and that many of his readers found distressing, but that he had deemed integral to the overall story from the original inception of the project. In *Dune*, Herbert included several appendices of reference material and a glossary of terms used in the languages he

COMPARE
&
CONTRAST

- **1960s:** Computer technology is primitive and has little direct impact on people's lives; the absence of computers in *Dune* is not very noticeable.

  Today: A majority of people use a computer and the Internet every day for work and pleasure; the absence of computers in *Dune* is striking.

- **1960s:** The United States is committed to a rapidly escalating and ultimately unsuccessful guerilla war in the rain forests of Vietnam.

  Today: U.S. forces are fighting in Iraq and Afghanistan, areas where the climate and culture provide striking parallels to the guerilla war in *Dune* and its ideological and geographical setting.

- **1960s:** Although the space race is widely followed in popular media, it is something to be watched almost as a drama on television rather than a concrete reality in people's lives.

  Today: The use of space is widespread and completely integrated into mainstream culture through the use of weather prediction satellites, telecommunications, global positioning systems, and many other areas. These space-based technologies are ubiquitous and are sometimes taken for granted.

---

fabricated for *Dune*. He also encouraged his colleague Willis McNelly to create additional fabricated historical documents in *The Dune Encyclopedia*, although he eventually repudiated the new fictional material in this work as "noncanonical." However, Herbert finally became trapped in a situation in which he had to write more Dune sequels because sales and therefore publishers' advances were much larger for books in the Dune series than for anything else he could write. His son, Brian Herbert, has found himself in the same position; he has written eleven additional sequels and announced plans to produce about one novel a year indefinitely. Each sequel goes onto the *New York Times* best-seller list, while his original books enjoy lesser popularity.

HISTORICAL CONTEXT

General Semantics

In the 1930s, the Polish American engineer Alfred Korzybski developed the discipline of general semantics (not to be confused with ordinary semantics, the study of the meaning of words) and founded a school for instruction in his system. General semantics holds that language is a metaphorical abstraction that actually separates the human mind from objects of thought. He wished to use mathematics as a model for a new way of thinking that would suspend ordinary semantic categories (words) and allow the mind to deal directly with reality. For instance, a rose is not the word *rose*. Korzybski believed that a tremendous advance in understanding could be achieved through comprehending the thing itself rather than by using the symbolic value of its name as an intermediary. Herbert was deeply influenced by Korzybski's thought. In fact he ghostwrote a syndicated newspaper column on the subject for U.S. Senator S. I. Hayakawa. Herbert's biographer Timothy O'Reilly finds that "much of the Bene Gesserit technology of consciousness is based on the insights of general semantics." The same is true of mentat training. Whereas mentat identify themselves with the flow of the process of any phenomenon that comes under study, Bene Gesserit focus on controlling perception. They use conscious intent to control what is otherwise determined unconsciously, to truly perceive what is before them instead of filtering it through memory and other mental processes that normally suppress most possible perceptions (and of which language

Illustration of a desert planet (Image copyright Andrea Danti, 2009. Used under license from Shutterstock.com)

is only the most superficial, in Herbert's exaggeration of general semantics). By extending this practice they can control autonomic functions, such as heat rhythm and the ability to metabolize chemical substances in the body, and achieve a subtlety of perception that makes them human lie detectors (an idea that fascinated Herbert) through their perception of changes in expression and biological function of the speaker. One of the most interesting things for Herbert, though, is when a system fails to operate correctly. An example of this is Jessica not realizing that she and Paul are descended from Baron Harkonnen. Despite the telltale physical similarities, she never suspects her ancestry until Paul reveals it to her. It is not that she cannot see the resemblance—indeed, she obviously can—but she refuses to do so because it is contrary to her preconceived ideas.

Systematics

Systematics, or system thinking, is an approach to problem solving derived from mathematics and engineering. It treats any problem as part of a larger system and considers the possible effects throughout the system from changing one element of it, as well as the possibility of effecting system-wide change by making small changes in one or a few system components. In the course of his work as a journalist, Herbert became fascinated with an example of what he considered a systematic approach to problem solving, namely the stabilization of sand dunes that constantly threatened to engulf the town of Florence, Oregon. Rather than a massive public works project involving hauling away millions of tons of sand (which would not have solved the problem of the natural forces that formed the dunes to begin with), the dunes were stabilized by a very small-scale planting of specific plant species. This was one of the most important sources for his conception of *Dune*, which essentially scales the process up to transforming a whole planet, as Herbert explains in detail in the first appendix to the novel. Another influence of systematics in *Dune* is seen in the epigraphs from Irulan's scholarly works at the beginning of each chapter. By revealing the "future," that is, key points of the plot, they act like the connective arrows on a flow chart, showing how the various parts of the plot are to be connected. Understanding, rather than surprise, is Herbert's aim. The same applies to Paul's visions of the future. He does not see specific unalterable events that must come to pass. Rather, he sees "a spectrum of possibilities...from the most probable to the most improbable." That much is actually no different than anyone else trying to estimate probable outcomes, but there is more to Paul's vision: "*I have another kind of sight. I see another kind of terrain: the available paths.*" In other words, Paul sees the future as a system and can see the (possibly large) outcome of small changes that occur based on his decisions. In other words, he does not so much see the future as how to shape the future he wants through systems analysis.

The characters in Dune are for the most part clearly defined stereotypes. This is not a result of lack of skill on the author's part but rather of Herbert's interest in systematics. If the characters are in the familiar cookie-cutter shapes of the 'good nobleman,' the 'decadent monster,' the 'gruff but loveable loyal old soldier,' the 'peasant girl who becomes a princess,' and even the 'messiah,' then Herbert can build his story in the same fashion as assembling the pieces of a jigsaw into an organized pattern, all interconnected with each other like the boxes on a flow chart, rather than developing the chaotic plot that might arise from more fully developed characters.

CRITICAL OVERVIEW

Brian Aldiss's *Billion Year Spree* is the seminal work of genre science fiction criticism. Writing only six years after the publication of *Dune*, Aldiss already stresses that Herbert's novel breaks out of the science fiction mold perfected in the 1930s by author and editor John W. Campbell:

> Its readers can indulge in a fantasy life of power and savour a strange religion. But there is more than that to *Dune*.... Although Campbellian science fiction is still present, so, too, is an attention to sensuous detail which is the antithesis of Campbell.

Aldiss realizes the novel has depths that repay careful reading, but also judges its ecological themes to be trendy.

One of the earliest academic assessments of *Dune* came in David Miller's critical monograph on *Frank Herbert*. In Miller's view, the main theme of all of Herbert's work, especially of his greatest novel, is the necessity for balance:

> 1.) If man does not achieve a balance within himself and with his environment, existence is merely a version of chaos. 2.) If man freezes an achieved balance, decadence sets in and life yields to entropy. Thus the problems to be solved by Herbert's characters require that chaos be organized and stasis disturbed. The desideratum is dynamic homeostasis.

This nicely captures Herbert's interest in systematics. One of the most important sources of information about Herbert's own views of *Dune* and the process of its composition is Timothy O'Reilly's 1981 biography, *Frank Herbert*. O'Reilly's discussion is based on extensive interviews with Herbert. Peter Minowitz, writing in *Political Science Fiction*, compares the actual political deeds of the Atreides and Harkonnens and finds that they are not so different as the novel's appeal to a stark dichotomy of good and evil might suggest, but that rather both sides follow Machiavelli's statements regarding the use of power.

A theme of recent criticism has been to view *Dune* as, far from radical, old-fashioned. Michael R. Collings's contribution to *Aspects of Fantasy* speculates that while the poetic epic form died out in English after reaching its apex with John Milton, much of the essential content might survive in the modern form of the novel. Citing *The Lord of the Rings* as an obvious example and suggesting that *Dune* is another, he demonstrates that the surface narrative of Herbert's novel is composed of traditional epic themes of valor, camaraderie, hierarchy, and the drawing-out of strong emotion. Julia List, in her article "Call Me a Protestant," in the 2009 issue of *Science Fiction Studies*, points out that although Herbert rejects the radical messianism depicted in *Dune* as destructive, he embraces nevertheless the values of 1960s elite mainline American Protestantism without examination to "serve as a secular cultural code that unites the elite." Adam Charles Roberts, in his *Science Fiction*, views Herbert's presentation of a traditional male ideology of power through royal lineage, messianism, warfare, and aggression as an implicit criticism of such power structures.

CRITICISM

Bradley A. Skeen
Skeen is a classics professor. In this essay, he explores the importance of religion in Dune.

Despite its obvious theme of ecology, which has generated much of the book's popularity,

WHAT DO I READ NEXT?

- Much of the culture and religion of *Dune* is derived from Arab culture and Islam. An overview of this background for younger readers is provided by Mitchell Young's 2005 compilation *Religions and Religious Movements: Islam.*

- *The Saviour God: Comparative Studies in the Concept of Salvation Presented to Edwin Oliver Kames,* edited by S. G. F. Brandon and published in 1963, provides a cross-cultural survey of messianic figures, representing the state of scholarship on the question at the time Herbert wrote *Dune.*

- In 1969, Herbert published his first sequel to *Dune, Dune Messiah,* which had been planned as a continuation of the original novel.

- In 1976, Herbert completed the *Dune* trilogy with *Children of Dune.* Although this completed his original concept, the popularity of the series led him to write several more *Dune* novels.

- The official *Dune* Web site (http://www.dunenovels.com) hosts a Web log written by Brian Herbert and Kevin J. Anderson, the authors of the continuing "Dune" series, along with a discussion forum and a variety of *Dune* resource materials.

- *The Best of John W. Campbell,* published in 1976, collects the most important work by arguably the most important and influential writer in traditional science fiction in the era before Herbert's *Dune.*

and the ornate gothic surface that attracts so many of its readers, the main theme of *Dune* is religion, and especially the interaction of religion with human culture as a whole. The presentation of religion in the book is quite remarkable. Given the feudal character of the social structure of the novel, with its emperors, dukes, and barons, one might expect to see noble households with a chaplain and a church hierarchy that

> HERBERT USES HITLER AS AN EXAMPLE OF THE IDEA THAT SOMEONE COULD RISE TO POLITICAL POWER BECAUSE HE PLAYS THE PART OF A HERO, BECAUSE HIS LIFE AND CAREER SEEM TO PARALLEL NATIONAL OR ETHNIC MYTHS."

parallels the political hierarchy, but there is nothing of the kind. No noble character ever attends a religious service. The existence of a chapel or church building is never hinted at. The book's aristocratic characters seem for the most part to live in a secular world in which religion plays no role. The only exception to this pattern is the common use of a scripture, the Orange Catholic Bible. Gurney Halleck is thought eccentric because of the readiness with which he quotes from it, yet the book is considered an appropriate and meaningful gift from Doctor Yueh to Paul. Herbert supplies the history of this document in an appendix. The book was produced after the Butlerian Jihad with the goal of producing a synthesis of older sacred scripture, such as the Bible and the Koran, but also to combine this with elements of other religions, such as Obeah, Buddhism, and Hinduism.

In the same appendix, however, Herbert provides a resolution to this difficulty. The Orange Catholic Bible is seen as an important signifier of cultural tradition, but to indulge in it excessively is superstitious. Scripture may contain some vestige of truth and beauty, but only if it agrees with other philosophies. Religion has practically ceased to exist among the aristocrats of the galactic empire, "the agnostic ruling class . . . for whom religion was a kind of puppet show to amuse the populace and keep it docile, and who believed essentially that all phenomena—even religious phenomena—could be reduced to mechanical explanations." This attitude toward religion as a tool of social control used by the elite class to manipulate society was first put forward by the Greek philosopher Plato in *The Republic.* It was enthusiastically taken up during the Enlightenment and later, finding expression equally in the writings of Thomas Paine and Karl Marx, and it is manifestly Herbert's own attitude to religion. Herbert's original conception for *Dune* was to explore the effect of religion, viewed in this light, upon human civilization and especially how it can, or even must, lead to disaster.

Herbert told his biographer, Timothy O'Reilly, about the origin of *Dune*: "It began with a concept: to do a long novel about the messianic convulsions which periodically inflict themselves on human societies. I had this idea that superheroes were disastrous for humans." But this idea had a specific origin in Herbert's life also. One of Herbert's closest friends was the psychologist Irene Slattery. She was a German who had left her home to escape the Nazis but not before personally observing the rise of Hitler. According to Brian Herbert in *Dreamer of Dune*, his biography of his father, Slattery's reminiscences about Hitler made a profound impression on Herbert:

> Hitler terrified her from the moment she first gazed upon him. He was a skillful demagogue, she said, an expert at couching twisted angry thoughts in words that sounded convincing. He was a hero to the German people, and terribly dangerous in that position, she felt, because of the way his people followed him slavishly, without questioning him, without thinking for themselves.

These ideas were incorporated into the plot of *Dune* at several levels. Herbert uses Hitler as an example of the idea that someone could rise to political power because he plays the part of a hero, because his life and career seem to parallel national or ethnic myths. Another use of Hitler is in the idea of the Voice, the power of the Bene Gesserit to probe the psyche of any individual and find a way of speaking that is absolutely persuasive from rhetorical, intellectual, and physiological perspectives so that the listener cannot resist the persuasion of the speaker, even if ordered to do something contrary to his or her own will. This is based on the widely reported and apocryphal power of Hitler's rhetoric to hypnotize his listeners and control their wills. When Lady Jessica uses the Voice on the mentat Thifur Hawat, he reacts in much the same way Irene Slattery did to Hitler: "*Does every human have this blind spot? he wondered. Can any of us be ordered into action before we can resist?* The idea staggered him. *Who could stop a person with such power?*" Herbert put his general treatment of messianic political leaders quite plainly in *Dune* in the mouth of the elder Pardot Kynes: "No more terrible disaster could befall your people than for them to fall into the hands

of a Hero." Nevertheless, the Fremen accept Paul as their messiah, and Herbert explicitly says that in his political addresses to his followers Paul uses the Voice to control their reactions and decisions.

According to O'Reilly's biography of Herbert,

> For years he researched the origins and history of religions, trying to understand the psychology by which individuals submit themselves to the juggernaut of a messianic myth. He continued to study psychoanalysis and philosophy, and added history, linguistics, economics, and politics, trying to grasp the whole pattern.

In other words, he tried to understand all of human existence as a system prone to being upset by hero worship. The academic critic David Miller nicely summarizes Herbert's approach to politics and religion in *Dune*:

> Much of the complexity and depth of Herbert's ... *Dune* ... derives from an elaborate system of power structures; hence, a good question with which to begin is "Who's in charge?" Ultimately the answer is "No one," but several organizations think that they control both tactical and strategic flow. One may think of the power structures as a system of overlays, each level of which believes that it is using all the others.

Each faction believes that it is in control of the system because the balance benefits that faction, but in reality it is the balance itself that controls each element of the system. It is religion and especially, in Herbert's view, the rise of a messianic figure that can most easily upset the delicate balance of the system.

Unlike the elites of emperors and dukes, the Fremen, standing at the very bottom of the social hierarchy of the Imperium, very definitely have a religion and a religious worldview. They think of their religion as the native foundation of their own culture. It is a religion based on many elements of Islam and Christianity, yet it is also polytheist and embraces many deities other than the supreme god. Its strongest element is hope in the coming of a messianic figure, the Lisan al-Gaib, "The Voice from the Outer World," the Mahdi who will lead them to paradise. Herbert is very specific about the true origins of this religion, however. For the last ten thousand years, the Bene Gesserit Sisterhood has run an operation called the Missionaria Protectiva. In this program, a Bene Gesserit is sent to each of the thousands of different worlds of the Imperium to found an artificially created religion among the uneducated common masses, gaining converts through preaching (no doubt using the Voice) and performing what seem to be miracles utilizing her prana-bindu training, "seeding the known universe with a prophecy pattern for the protection of B.G. personnel." The organization has created a religious mythology that can be exploited by any Bene Gesserit who might find herself marooned among converted peoples at any time in the future. Jessica, well aware of the activities of her order, is able to exploit the Fremen's religious beliefs exactly as intended, and she quickly becomes a Reverend Mother among them, a position that not only gives her high status and a claim to protection, but gives her great sway and influence over the population of an entire planet, but especially in positioning Paul as their messiah.

The manipulative and secretive Bene Gesserit Sisterhood grew in Herbert's imagination from the anticlerical stereotypes of his youth. In his memoir of his father, *Dreamer of Dune*, Brian Herbert explains the origin of the Bene Gesserit.

> His Irish Catholic maternal aunts, who attempted to force religion on him, became the models for the Bene Gesserit Sisterhood of *Dune*. It is no accident that the pronunciation of "Gesserit" and "Jesuit" are similar, as he envisioned his maternal aunts and the Bene Gesserit of *Dune* as female Jesuits.

The Bene Gesserit become Herbert's archetype of the religious domination of society by elites.

For Herbert, the most important element of religion is messianism. Paul is immediately identified with the Fremen messianic figure of the Lisan al-Gaib because he is the son of a Bene Gesserit, a belief that becomes the source of his political control over the Fremen tribes. He can become a dictator over people who recognize him as the embodiment of their ideas about the epiphany of the divine in the world. He does not have to win the right to lead; he lets himself be identified as the leader they have been waiting for. This dictatorial level of control, based originally in Herbert's mind on the rise of Hitler, is nevertheless not a judgment on the leader, as he explains in "Dune Genesis": "People tend to give over every decision-making capacity to any leader who can wrap himself in the myth fabric of the society. Hitler did it." However, he considers the same to be true of John F. Kennedy. The problem, Herbert says, is with the nature of the social control that messianic figures wield,

whether for good or evil: "It's the systems themselves I see as dangerous." But this introduces a paradox. The religion of the Fremen is by definition false, the result of manipulation by the Bene Gesserit, yet Paul is a truly messianic figure. Ironically, he is unknowingly created by the Bene Gesserit with powers to shape the future to his will, moving far beyond anything the sisterhood intended. So how can a false religion give rise to a true messiah? The answer is directly related to the problem of the Bene Gesserit eugenics program, but not in an obvious way. Carefully created by selective breeding, Paul uses his powers to overturn all of the sisterhood's work and stir up an indiscriminate mixing of human genetic material. For Herbert, all of this has been arranged by a higher power, the human need to evolve: "The race knows its own mortality and fears stagnation of its heredity. It's in the bloodstream—the urge to mingle genetic strains without plan." But it is just here that Herbert falls into the trap of religious thought that he is so manifestly trying to avoid and analyze from outside. A mechanistic process such as evolution does not have an end goal; it does not seek any one particular end rather than another. Nature is incapable of caring whether isolated populations mix their genetic material or not. Isolation does not mean "stagnation," but rather the possibility of speciation; in any case, the genes do not care how they do or do not change. However, Herbert cannot escape the apocalyptic religious model by which any process, even a mechanistic one such as evolution, leads toward a fixed goal. The teleological thinking that Herbert ascribes to evolution in ultimately creating Paul and using him as its tool is entirely the product of human imagination—of Herbert's imagination—and its religious impulse. Paul's destiny is not understood through the scientific process of evolution but through a religious worldview. While Herbert tries to transcend religion, he cannot quite make a final separation from it, even at the deepest level of his fiction.

Source: Bradley Skeen, Critical Essay on *Dune*, in *Novels for Students*, Gale, Cengage Learning, 2010.

Ronny W. Parkerson

In the following essay, Parkerson argues that Herbert utilized general semantics—a doctrine that emphasizes the critical use of words and other symbols—to support a theme on power, a notion of consciousness, and a structure for human thought and behavior.

A man looking into space (© Panoramic Images / Getty Images)

Frank Herbert's *Dune*, a thematically rich and varied work of science fiction, is the first novel in a trilogy about the desert planet Arrakis, or Dune, and the rise to power of Paul Atreides, its messianic leader. Herbert initially conceived of writing one long novel about "the messianic convulsions that periodically overtake us. Demagogues, fanatics, con-game artists, the innocent and the not-so-innocent bystanders—all were to have a part" ("*Dune*Genesis" p.72). Ultimately, Herbert produced six novels about Dune comprising what has become known as *The Dune Chronicles*. The intricate ecology of the planet, encompassing the Fremen natives' desire to turn Dune into a "green and fertile world" and the need of the Empire for the indigenous spice melange to facilitate space travel, forms the backdrop for Paul's struggle to overcome his enemies, control the planet, and fulfill his personal destiny. Throughout the novel Paul must meet and overcome challenges that serve to confirm him in the minds of the Fremen as being their messiah. Paul does not seek this position but is instead caught up in the events that lead to his deposing of the Emperor and control of the throne.

Herbert's decision to examine the messianic superhero against a backdrop of ecological concerns was no accident. Drawing on his experience in journalism, he noted:

> I had already written several pieces about ecological matters, but my superhero concept filled me with a concern that ecology might be the next banner for demagogues and would-be heroes, for the power seekers and others ready to find an "adrenaline high" in the launching of

a new crusade. I could begin to see the shape of a global problem, no part of it separated from any other—social ecology, political ecology, economic ecology. I find fresh nuances in religions, psychoanalytic theories, linguistics, economics, philosophy, theories of history, geology, anthropology, plant research, soil chemistry, and the metalanguages of pheromones. A new field of study arises out of this like a spirit rising from a witch's caldron: the psychology of planetary societies. ("*Dune*Genesis" p.74)

It seems, therefore, evident that a central theme of the novel is not only ecology, but ecology examined in many different contexts. In addition to exploring environmental ecology, the study of the relationship and interaction between organisms and their environment, *Dune* explores social, political, economic, and language ecologies as well (Touponce pp.13–14). Herbert compared these variations on a central theme to a musical fugue:

> Sometimes there are free voices that do fanciful dances around the interplay. There can be secondary themes and contrasts in harmony, rhythm, and melody. From the moment when a single voice introduces the primary theme, however, the whole is woven into a single fabric.

> What were my instruments in this ecological fugue? Images, conflicts, things that turn upon themselves and become something quite different, myth figures and strange creatures from the depths of our common heritage. ("*Dune*Genesis" p.74)

These various ecologies evolve out of their respective relationships and interactions with the planetary environment of Arrakis. Specifically,

Herbert believed language mirrors the ecosystem from which life evolves: (Touponce p.2)

> ... we commonly believe meaning is found— in printed words (such as these), in the noises of a speaker, in the reader's or listener's awareness, or in some imaginary thought-land between these. We tend to forget that we human animals evolved in an ecosystem that has demanded constant improvisation from us. In a mirror sense, we reflect this history of mutual influences in all our systems and processes. ("Listening" pp. 98, 100)

Another major theme of the novel is that of power, and the nature of the superhero or leader who emerges to discover that he or she must wage war to gain and maintain that power. Herbert strongly believed war to be the logical consequence of any struggle to gain and maintain power whether political or economic. He also believed history supports the emergence of a superhero in such situations: "... people tend to give over every decision-making capacity to any leader who can wrap himself in the myth fabric of the society. Hitler did it. Churchill did it. Franklin Roosevelt did it. Stalin did it. Mussolini did it." ("*Dune* Genesis" p.72). Dune explores the wielding of political, economic, and military power, and, by incorporating aspects of general semantics, their common thread: the power of language.

During the period he was writing *Dune*, Herbert studied general semantics in San Francisco, and for a time worked as a ghost writer for the late S. I. Hayakawa, a renowned writer on language and major proponent of general semantics (O'Reilly pp.59–60). Mona Campbell has defined general semantics as "the scientific study of the use and abuse of language, the study of the effects of communication on behavior, and the application of the scientific method to problem solving" (Campbell p.45). Alfred Korzybski (1879–1950), who developed general semantics in the 1930s

(O'Reilly p.59), theorized, according to Campbell, "that language reflects only imperfectly and incompletely the actualities of the external world, that there is a wide gulf between the word and the thing it stands for, and that the word is intimately related to human behavior" (Campbell p.45).

Herbert's use of general semantics in *Dune* becomes doubly important for it "emphasize[s] the importance of language and other cultural givens in providing a fundamental, unconscious structure for human thought and behavior; and it insist[s] that it [is] possible to train human beings into new semantic habits and an orientation toward first-order experience" (O'Reilly p.60).

An excellent example of how Herbert brings the principles of general semantics to life in *Dune* is found in the Bene Gesserit, "an ancient school of physical and mental training for females" (Touponce p.18). For centuries, the Bene Gesserit have conducted a human breeding program with the objective of eventually producing a person with superior mental powers whom they refer to as the "Kwisatz Haderach" or "one who can be many places at once." All signs indicate that Paul Atreides might be that person. To create Bene Gesserit training Herbert combined principles of general semantics with yoga, Zen, biofeedback, and nonverbal communication to produce these powerful beings of superior intelligence and ability (O'Reilly p.60). Indeed, the whole of the Bene Gesserit technology of consciousness is based on general semantics, and Herbert illustrates this notion of consciousness along with the power of language and gesture very early in the novel when Jessica, Paul's Bene Gesserit mother, brings him to be tested by the Reverend Mother Gaius Helen Mohiam:

> Jessica stopped three paces from the chair, dropped a small curtsy, a gentle flick of left hand along the line of her skirt. Paul gave the short bow his dancing master had taught—the one used "when in doubt of another's station."
>
> The nuances of Paul's greeting were not lost on the Reverend Mother. She said: "He's a cautious one, Jessica."

Meaning in this passage stems almost exclusively from gesture and not from spoken language. Both Jessica and Paul show their respect for the Reverend Mother, but only minimally and without wasted effort. This economy of gesture and language provides for effective communication with a minimum of effort, and is the foundation of "ecological semantics." Paul's actions serve as proof for what the Reverend Mother already knows about Jessica's training of the boy.

While gestures effectively used are excellent communicative tools, language, both written and spoken, has greater power, as demonstrated by Paul's reaction to the way the Reverend Mother treats Jessica:

> Paul faced the old woman, holding anger in check. "Does one dismiss the Lady Jessica as though she were a serving wench?"
>
> A smile flicked the corners of the wrinkled old mouth. "The Lady Jessica was my serving wench, lad, for fourteen years at school." She nodded. "And a good one, too. Now, you come here!"
>
> The command whipped out at him. Paul found himself obeying before he could think about it. Using the Voice on me, he thought. He stopped at her gesture, standing beside her knees.

Paul is powerless and under the control of the Reverend Mother in this situation. She controls him with the "Voice" and, shortly thereafter, with the threat of the gom jabbar. Here, the capitalized term "Voice" refers to an aspect of Bene Gesserit training where, through shadings of tone in voice utterances, a user can control others.

Herbert also draws on general semantics to explain Paul's reaction to the combination of the Reverend Mother's words and the nerve induction pain caused by the gom jabbar, the poison tipped needle used by the Bene Gesserit to administer the "death-alternative test of human awareness":

> Paul looked down at the hand that had known pain, then up to the Reverend Mother. The sound of her voice had contained a difference then from any other voice in his experience. The words were outlined in brilliance. There was an edge to them. He felt that any question he might ask her would bring an answer that could lift him out of his flesh-world into something greater.

This passage reveals Paul's understanding of the power of language. Assigning physical qualities to the words personifies their power. The words are "outlined in brilliance," have "an edge," and are capable of lifting Paul "out of his flesh-world."

Even Herbert's emphasis on the power of language found in the ordinary spoken word, (i.e. lower case "voice") is evident throughout the novel. At times it is subtle; at others it is overtly stated. An examination of the episode in which Paul makes himself known to the Fremen reveals Herbert's emphasis on language in action. In the epigraph preceding the chapter, a quotation from the "Private Reflections on Muad'Dib," the Princess Irulan, chronicler of Paul's life and times, overtly acknowledges the power of language: "Does the prophet see the future or does he see a weakness, a fault or cleavage that he may shatter with words or decisions as a diamond-cutter shatters his gem with a blow of a knife?" The episode that follows represents a pivotal point in the novel for it vividly recounts the Fremens' capture of Jessica and Paul after their ordeal of escape into the desert. More importantly, however, this experience marks Paul's entry into the Fremen culture to whose leadership he eventually will ascend.

The entire episode is charged with tension. Night has fallen and Jessica and Paul are defenseless except for Jessica's superior sensory awareness and ability to analyze the danger by utilizing semantic judgments. A close reading reveals the word "voice" is used thirty-three times in the chapter. Most often it is used as a referent to or personification of the speaker. Rather than directly identifying the speaker by name or gender, this technique more effectively adds power and an air of mystery to the text, as the following excerpt from early in the episode shows:

> "It would be regrettable should we have to destroy you out of hand," the voice [emphasis mine] above them said.
>
> That's the one who spoke to us first, Jessica thought. There are at least two of them—one to our right and one on our left.

By using "the voice above them said" instead of "the man above them said," or some other similar wording, Herbert strengthens the impact of the scene. What unfolds from this technique is Jessica's urgent need to rely on her superior abilities to analyze the semantics of the situation and subdue their captors. The following passages illustrate the emphasis Herbert places on voice and semantics:

> "What have we here—jinn or human?" he asked.
>
> And Jessica heard the true-banter in his voice, [*sic*] she allowed herself a faint hope. This was the voice of command, the voice that had first shocked them with its intrusion from the night....
>
> "Do you also speak?" the man asked.
>
> Jessica put all the royal arrogance at her command into her manner and voice [emphasis mine]. Reply was urgent, but she had not

heard enough of this man to be certain she had a register on his culture and weaknesses. . . .

I have his voice and pattern registered now, Jessica thought. I could control him with a word, but he's a strong man worth much more to us unblunted and with full freedom of action. We shall see.

Jessica has heard enough from the speaker to know she "could control him with a word." She knows she has the upper hand in the confrontation, but her captors remain unaware of her power.

Using the powers of her Bene Gesserit training, Jessica subdues her captors by convincing their leader, Stilgar, to accept them rather than harm them. Herbert then, through Jessica, reveals the power found in individual words:

> Their destination was Sietch Tabr—Stilgar's sietch.

> She turned the word over in her mind: sietch. It was a Chakobsa word, unchanged from the old hunting language out of countless centuries. Sietch: a meeting place in time of danger. The profound implications of the word and the language were just beginning to register with her after the tension of their encounter.

Jessica's thoughts reveal the connotative power of words. Here within the context of the immediate situation the sound of the word interacts with Jessica's knowledge of its origin and history to reveal to her the essence of Fremen existence, an existence enveloped in danger and requiring vigilance and communal refuge.

From this pivotal point forward, Paul faces many challenges and tests over a period of time which serve to solidify his position as leader of the Fremen in their quest for control of Arrakis. Paul matures and develops into manhood. In the novel's climactic scene, Paul and the Fremen are victorious in their battle with the Emperor's forces and have come to the governor's mansion to depose the Emperor. Paul is now able to use his linguistic power to control even the Reverend Mother.

> "Silence!" Paul roared. The word seemed to take substance as it twisted through the air between them under Paul's control.

> The old woman reeled back into the arms of those behind her, face blank with shock at the power with which he had seized her psyche. "Jessica," she whispered. "Jessica."

> "I remember your gom jabbar," Paul said. "You remember mine. I can kill you with a word."

> The Fremen around the hall glanced knowingly at each other. Did the legend not say:

> "And his word shall carry death eternal to those who stand against righteousness."

Again, language receives its power through personification. The word "silence" took "substance," and "twisted through the air." The word takes the deadly qualities of an arrow unleashed at its victim. Linguistic power, then, has come full circle. Paul needs no needle tipped with poison to exercise control; he needs only a word.

Paul, however, cannot complete his rise to power without destroying the Harkkonens, if not absolutely, at least symbolically. In a final attempt to maintain control, Baron Vladimir Harkkonen's nephew and heir, Feyd-Rautha, calls Paul out in "kanly," or vendetta, to fight. The deadly consequences of language use and the power of silence are illustrated during the subsequent combat between Paul and Feyd-Rautha:

> They circled each other, bare feet grating on the floor, watching with eyes intent for the slightest opening.

> "How beautifully you dance," Feyd-Rautha said.

> He's a talker, Paul thought. There's another weakness. He grows uneasy in the face of silence.

> "Have you been shriven?" Feyd-Rautha said.

> Still, Paul circled in silence. . . .

> "Why don't you speak?" Feyd-Rautha demanded.

> Paul resumed his probing circle, allowing himself a cold smile at the tone of unease in Feyd-Rautha's voice, evidence that the pressure of silence was building.

These two passages reveal the ecological semantics of silence. Paul exercises control not by using language, but by avoiding it. Here Herbert shows that meaning is found not only in the use of language, but in its absence. The word is truly not the thing, and the map is not the territory.

Heretofore we have seen ample evidence in *Dune* of the power of language in action. *Dune* is also a novel of language in thought. It is a novel of dialogue, and the narrative voice supplements the internalized and externalized speech of the characters. Herbert weaves the narrative voice with externalized and internalized speech to effectively add a kind of linguistic mortar to the action of the characters. Hence, the metaphor of the musical fugue comes into full bloom. Ecological semantics involves the relationship and interaction of the users or communicators of language in context in a manner similar to how environmental ecology involves the relationship and interaction of organisms and their environment. The episode describing the death of the architect of the planet Arrakis' ecological transformation, Liet-Kynes, contains excellent examples of both narration and the use of internalized and externalized speech in a semantic fugue. Like small changes in the environment, the way in which language is used or not used can be beneficial or detrimental depending on the situation, and general semantics, as stated earlier, concerns itself with the uses and abuses of language. Although this scene appears at approximately the mid-point of the novel, it penetrates to the novel's thematic heart, and serves to foreshadow events to come. Liet-Kynes speaks and he hears the voice of his father. Appropriately the utterances of both voices appear in quotation marks. The following passages appear:

> "I am Liet-Kynes," he said, addressing himself to the empty horizon and his voice was a hoarse caricature of the strength it had known. "I am his Imperial Majesty's Planetologist," he whispered, "planetary ecologist for Arrakis. I am steward of this land." . . . .

> "To the working planetologist, his most important tool is human beings," his father said. "You must cultivate ecological literacy among the people. That's why I've created this entirely new form of ecological notation."

> He's repeating things he said to me when I was a child, Kynes thought.

> He began to feel cool, but that corner of logic in his mind told him: The sun is overhead. You have no stillsuit and you're hot; the sun is burning the moisture out of your body.

> His fingers clawed feebly at the sand.

> They couldn't even leave me a stillsuit!

> "The presence of moisture in the air helps prevent too-rapid evaporation from living bodies," his father said.

> Why does he keep repeating the obvious? Kynes wondered. . . .

> "No more terrible disaster could befall your people than for them to fall into the hands of a Hero," his father said.

> Reading my mind! Kynes thought. Well let him. . . .

> Then, as his planet killed him, it occurred to Kynes that his father and all the other scientists were wrong, that the most persistent principles of the universe were accident and error.

As Liet-Kynes dies listening to this polyphony of voices of which his own, externalized and internalized, is a part, he foresees the ecological disaster to come resulting from his and the Fremen dream of "greening" Arrakis. This passage sharply focuses Herbert's theme of ecological change falling prey to the desires of would-be-heroes and power seekers. Small changes, whether ecological or semantic, frequently produce unwanted results.

The power of choice, environmental or semantic, and the power of accident and error all affect the consequences of life. Herbert understood the value and power found in both environmental ecology and semantic ecology. He understood how language is used and abused. *Dune* serves to show the reader the effect language can have on a variety of situations. Life and death, *Dune* reveals, often hang precipitously on a word.

Source: Ronny W. Parkerson, "Semantics, General Semantics, and Ecology in Frank Herbert's *Dune*," in *ETC.: A Review of General Semantics*, Vol. 55, No. 3, Fall 1998, p. 317.

Jack Hand

In the following essay, Hand examines the male-dominated society presented in Dune, *outlining how the novel's female characters are limited to traditional roles.*

It is no surprise to anyone who has read *Dune* or its sequels that the universe Frank Herbert posits is male-dominated. A majority of science fiction writers seem to mine the human past in order to find patterns through which to express their hopes and fears for the human future. One may be condemned to repeat past mistakes through a lack of knowledge of history; but a knowledge of history may also force, or at least tempt, one into extrapolating backward as well as forward. In the single novel *Dune*, which is the cornerstone of that series, Herbert creates both an interplanetary empire and planetary societies which, no matter how bizarrely changed at times, derive from past or present cultures which we know in our own world. The breadth of Herbert's knowledge of both Western and non-Western societies enables him to combine them in his societies to create a freshness which fascinates the reader, like some dream in which our common world has undergone Prospero's sea changes.

It is the women of *Dune* who suffer most from this past-as-future effect, but not them alone. The Padishah Empire in *Dune* seems

> THEY EXPRESS THEMSELVES AS WIVES,
> MOTHERS, SISTERS, AND LITERARY WOMEN, BUT
> ALWAYS DEFINE THEMSELVES BY MALE STANDARDS."

almost medieval in its reliance on political intrigue, marriages of state, and *force majeur* as its instruments of power, although the existence of male-led Houses Major and Minor, and the rather ineffectual Landsraad, might be seen as the beginnings of a pre-Magna Carta parliament. The Sardaukar, or male soldier-fanatics of the emperor, have the flavor of samaurai or jannisaries. They show the kind of reflex loyalty drummed into Japanese school children before World War II, who, according to the Japanese novelist Keno Oé, when asked, "What would you do if the Emperor asked for your life?" were trained to respond, "I would rip open my belly and die."

The glue which holds the Padishah Empire together on an interplanetary level is the Space Guild, once again a male preserve, and one of the few forces which must be wooed rather than pressured into functioning for the whole. However, the guild's dependence on melange makes its members cooperative in matters concerning Arrakis or *Dune*. Melange is needed for guild navigators to "see" in an unspecified way, through time nexuses which enable faster-than-light flight, without which this human-settled galactic empire could not function or cohere. The spice-addicted navigators also gain a limited prescience through the melange.

One of the few provinces left in Herbert's world in which women can operate is religion. In the Western world, women have always exerted official or unofficial power in the area of religion. Women have been involved in the making or breaking of many male preachers; they have themselves become religious leaders gathering large followings, as in the case of Mother Ann Lee of the Shakers, Aimee Semple McPherson, or Madame Helena Petrovna Blavatsky; and in some cases they have wielded power more indirectly. (For example, the nun, Sister Pascalina, called "La Popessa," was a power behind Pope Pius XII.) Thus, in the light of Western history,

religion is the most natural and traditional method for women in a world like that of *Dune* to gain and wield power. Herbert's Bene Gesserit, without Blavatsky's "Ancient Masters of Tibet," developed the techniques of modern psychology into trance states which allow them limited future visions, command by voice control alone, and enough other arcane powers to have acquired the general title of witch, among even the agnostic ruling classes for whom religion is simply a means to pacify the peasantry. Herbert himself describes the Bene Gesserit as a group "who privately denied they were a religious order, but who operated behind an almost impenetrable screen of ritual mysticism, and whose training, whose symbolism, organization and internal teaching methods were almost wholly religious...." With this information from the author, one wonders how many of the women trained in this manner could any longer distinguish religion from political action and from their centuries-long plan of human eugenics.

An irony, although perhaps a necessary one, in the Bene Gesserit's secret breeding plan is that they are aiming at a male as the end product. This male, the Kwisatz Haderach, would have the potential of vision forward and backward in time, and a way of sensing crucial departure or splitting-off points in humanity's path, thus enabling him possibly to control the path of social and political evolution for the entire human race, not in the manner of, but with at least the effectiveness of, Asimov's psychohistorians in the *Foundation* series. This would be a prescience greater than that achieved by either Space Guild navigators or the Bene Gesserit themselves. The Bene Gesserit sisterhood seems confident that, through their unseen conditioning, they can control and direct such a seer. This hope, for a male with the powers they expect, seems, in fact, a rather foolishly optimistic wish and, in a way, an unconscious admission, especially considering Paul's career, that they have not really grasped what powers this male Bene Gesserit would have.

It is, in Herbert's male-dominated society, a condition of the Bene Gesserit's survival and acquisition of power that their order remain closed to the scrutiny of male authority and operate behind the scenes as advisors, information gatherers, and preparers of the way for Kwisatz Haderach. They are seen publicly only in their religious guise, as supporters of the male status quo who help to keep the masses more easily controllable. As with any powerful religious group, however, it is straining one's imagination to believe that the civil authorities do not continuously attempt to track the machinations of the order.

In line with their eugenics plan and the society in which they operate, the Bene Gesserit carefully condition young women, such as Lady Jessica, as vehicles in their secret breeding plan. These women are then sold as concubines, but only to those men or houses whose own bloodlines match the secret breeding plan. The women, always physically attractive, are sought after avidly, because they have been conditioned as perfect concubines and companions, seeming to bend to their lord's every wish, but conditioned secretly to obey the Bene Gesserit without question. Despite the larger plans of the order, this method of operation amounts to an acquiescence in the dominant male value system to the point of approving a kind of female servitude similar to that of topflight geishas or courtesans.

To sum up, the Bene Gesserit accept the traditional role of women as property despite their grand breeding plan, and accept the relegation of women's power to the traditional hidden kind of influence in which they must remain as shadowy (though specially trained) counselors at best. Even the eugenics plan, which might seem to give them a large say in the human future, is traditional, in that it uses and accepts the traditional role of women primarily as breeders, and aims not at the development of a superior female as its end, but at the development of a superior male. Who's fooling whom?

Lady Jessica, who comes to Duke Leto from the Bene Gesserit school on Wallach, is sold by the order as a concubine, as a part of the Bene Gesserit's secret breeding plan. She is also the most powerfully drawn of any of the female characters in this cornerstone book. Although raised in and conditioned to obedience first to the order, Jessica soon turns rebel. Acting as an even more traditional woman than the Bene Gesserit had anticipated, Jessica breaks their conditioning by falling in love with Duke Leto. She rejects his offer of marriage in order to allow him to remain free for state marriages if necessary, confident in her own natural and Bene Gesserit abilities to insure her a constant place in his life. A more important defiance is her bearing the son Leto desires when the

breeding plan calls for her to bear a daughter, the choice in this future being hers through Bene Gesserit techniques. Jessica, a natural daughter of Baron Harkonnen, carries genes whose importance have been known for two thousand years, and Leto's bloodline has been watched for over a thousand years. Jessica was to produce a daughter who would marry Feyd-Rautha Harkonnen, a nephew of the baron, with a high probability that that union would produce the Kwisatz Haderach.

When Reverend Mother Gaius Helen Mohiam comes to test Paul's "humanness," as is apparently done in all Bene Gesserit breedings, her anger at Jessica's disobedience makes her conceal in her report the fact that Paul survives more pain under the threat of the gom jabbar (a needle tipped with metacyanide) than has any other human, a fact which should have alerted her to his potential as a possible Kwisatz Haderach. What seems less explicable, given that Jessica has already disobeyed the breeding instructions, is Jessica's willingness to risk Paul's life in this test. Perhaps the answer must be sought in her Bene Gesserit conditioning, which may be more cracked than broken.

A second defiance of the order's rules is Jessica's training of Paul in the various mental techniques of the order, such as command voice. These techniques are secret to the order and have never before been taught to a male. This training, along with mentat (or human computer) training, and the ordinary arms training of the aristocrat help Paul to survive long enough to tap his deeper powers.

After Duke Leto's betrayal and death on Arrakis, Lady Jessica flees into the desert with Paul, aided by the traitor Suk doctor (another case where conditioning is broken by love) and planetary ecologist Liet Kynes. Jessica is the leader until after the first night, when Paul comes to a kind of rebirth from the still tent. Thereafter, the formidable Jessica follows, literally, in his foot-steps. When Jessica tastes the Water of Life (and of death) in the sietch, she returns to another traditional role, that of reverend mother in the Fremen religion, following a prophecy planted, as on many worlds, by the Missionaria Protectiva of her own Bene Gesserit order. Jessica accepts this role and invites the dangers of the sandworm-derived water, not primarily for her own benefit, but in order to consolidate Paul's position among the Fremen and in the protection of the order's religious legends. This very traditional move by a mother to protect the son she now follows as her duke becomes even more interesting when we realize that she does it knowing she endangers not only herself, but also her unborn girl child. To the extent that she endangers Alia in order to promote Paul's well-being, Jessica is acting out the values of the male-dominated society in which she lives. That Alia profits in some ways from this risk does not change the motivation.

Alia, after exposure to the Water of Life, can communicate with her brother Paul even from the womb. Instead of being honored, as Paul is when the same water brings him to full consciousness of his powers, she is feared among the Fremen, having stature basically through Paul and Jessica, now a Fremen reverend mother. The reaction of the Bene Gesserit to Alia's birth and powers is to name her a "monster" whom they reject and would prefer to have killed. This is the classic attitude which one too often sees in the real world, where women of intelligence and talent often find themselves attacked more viciously by members of their own sex than by men. In this first book, Alia supports Paul and is accepted rather fearfully by the Fremen because of him. In the case of both the Fremen and the Bene Gesserit, what is outside their experience is feared and at times hated. The relatively primitive Fremen seem less to blame for this than the highly educated, master-planning Bene Gesserit.

That Fremen society is male-dominated is demonstrated early and powerfully. When Paul kills Jamis, he finds that Jamis' wife and children are his by conquest, although she is relieved when he gives up his claim. Women may fight alongside men at times in Fremen culture, but there is no question of equality, except, perhaps, for Jessica in the traditionally female role of reverend mother. Chani, Paul's Fremen concubine, is a woman of great gentleness and fierce passions when the well-being of her man is at stake. She strikes the reader as the kind of frontier woman who loaded guns during an Indian attack, and when her men were dead or wounded put a gun in each window and continued fighting. But Herbert gives the reader little enough to back up this characterization except Paul's attitudes, for she is bound by the Fremen codes to be in the shadow of her man, and Usul, the desert mouse (the Fremen's name for Paul), casts a long shadow. Paul's greatest tribute to Chani is his attitude toward Princess Irulan.

As a part of his peace and consolidation-of-power agreement after his Fedaykin, or death commands, tear apart the proud Sardaukar with the help of sandworms and the family atomics, Paul agrees to marry Princess Irulan, vowing that theirs will be a "white marriage." Princess Irulan, a Bene Gesserit adept, accepts this without protest. Staying near the seat of power, linked however tenuously with the man whose Fedaykin will sweep the galaxy no matter how he tries to avoid it, is enough for her in this first book. The princess becomes, in fact, a major historian of and apologist for Paul's actions, while Chani remains the center of his emotional life. (Give a woman a hobby and keep her out of trouble. Perhaps.)

In summary, all the important women of *Dune* act within the traditional areas of female activity. Whether in the empire, on Caladan, or on Arrakis, they must operate within male-dominated societies. They express themselves as wives, mothers, sisters, and literary women, but always define themselves by male standards. If the Fremen women sometimes fight beside their men, they are also property which can be lost in a duel; if the Bene Gesserit control an ambitious, centuries-old eugenics program, they see their end result in a male form; if Jessica defies her order, she does it for her man, and if she is strong enough to lead the escape from disaster, she then turns to follow in her teenaged son's footsteps. Thus, in the novel *Dune*, the single best book of the series, one finds a male-dominated society where even the most ambitious females' responses are traditional in means and in effect.

Source: Jack Hand, "The Traditionalism of Women's Roles in Frank Herbert's *Dune*," in *Extrapolation*, Vol. 26, No. 1, Spring 1985, pp. 24–28.

John L. Grigsby

In the following essay, Grigsby identifies similarities between Herbert's "Dune" trilogy and Isaac Asimov's "Foundation" trilogy but contends that the two series lead to opposite conclusions.

Anyone at all interested in SF is probably familiar with Isaac Asimov's *Foundation* trilogy and Frank Herbert's *Dune* trilogy. Their popularity is attested to in several convincing ways. First, each series has sold millions of copies, and many other SF fans read the two when they were serialized in *Astounding Stories* and *Analog: Science Fact and Fiction* in the 1940s and 1960s, respectively. Second, both trilogies (or parts of them)

> SO, AGAIN, THE ALMOST IDENTICAL USE OF
> RELIGION IN THE TWO TRILOGIES SHOWS THAT
> HERBERT IS USING ASIMOV AS A PRIMARY SOURCE
> FOR A MAJOR ASPECT OF *DUNE*."

have been recognized as among the best of all SF by both fans and writers: Herbert's *Dune* won the Hugo award of the World Science Fiction Convention and tied for the Nebula award of the Science Fiction Writers of America in 1966, and Asimov's *Foundation* trilogy was awarded a special Hugo as best all-time series in that same year. At that point, of course, *Dune Messiah* and *Children of Dune* had not been completed, so Herbert's trilogy was not competition for Asimov's. Third, both series have been included on most lists of the important works of SF, including those by Mark Rose and James Gunn, and have been praised by many critics.

Despite the rather elaborate praise for the two trilogies by many critics, though, others have been less impressed. Sam Moskowitz, for example, doesn't particularly like *Dune*.

> The incorporation of the atmosphere of earth's medieval, political and moral climate make the plot development almost traditional by modern standards. Furthermore, the prominent use of psi phenomenon adds a note of conformity, which combined with the political climate, robs the effort of realism and transforms it into little more than a well-done adventurous romance.

Asimov's trilogy receives similar treatment by Brian Aldiss and Damon Knight. Aldiss bemoans the lack of organic unity caused, he says, by the serialization, and objects to what he sees as too much conservative faith in technology in the series. Knight attacks the *Foundation* trilogy for being too directly based on the Roman empire, saying thus it isn't speculative fiction "any more than the well-known Western with ray-guns instead of six-shooters," and he objects to sequels in general for their progressive diminution of the speculative element.

These issues touch on the subject of this investigation: the nature of the relationship between the *Foundation* and *Dune* trilogies. Robert Scholes

and Eric Rabkin note two points of similarity between them, hinting that Herbert adapted techniques and ideas from Asimov for his own use. They suggest that Herbert derived the idea for his quotation beginnings for chapters in the *Dune* series from a similar strategy used by Asimov. They also believe that the restoration of civilization idea, or theme, in *Dune* is based on Asimov's series, an adaptation they say Herbert wasn't alone in making from Asimov's influential trilogy. However, Scholes and Rabkin fail to offer an in-depth comparison. They simply curtail further inquiry with the general statement that the *Foundation* series is "a more sober affair than *Dune*, less adventurous, less swashbuckling, and in some ways less effective as fiction." Such a vague dismissal does not adequately delineate the interrelatedness of the two series.

Yet several external (non-textual) clues hint to the interconnectedness of the two series, as do numerous internal (textual) ones. The fact that Asimov's trilogy, though written in the 1940s and published as separate volumes in the early 1950s was awarded its Hugo in 1966 (the same year *Dune* was published and won the awards) seems significant as a perception of their interrelatedness. Moreover, the Asimov-to-Herbert influence relationship becomes obvious when one examines some relevant essays written by the two authors. Asimov stated in the 1960s his opinion of the new "wave" of SF writing (a "wave" which *Dune* is a product of). He objected:

> There is a growing tendency to delete the science from science fiction ... and I want to fight it. There are science fiction writers who think that science is a Bad Thing and that science fiction is a wonderful field in which to make this plain. This is part of a much more general attitude that Society is a Bad Thing and must be destroyed before a new and better system can be evolved. This may strike youngsters today as a daring and novel notion, but when great-grandfather was a boy they called it Nihilism. I'm afraid I'm too square to be a Nihilist.

With this comment on the contemporary writers who have little faith in science (Asimov doesn't name Herbert, Vonnegut, etc., but he is referring to them), Asimov begins the attacks which result in a Herbert response in "Men on Other Planets." Here Herbert praises Asimov's non-fiction, but although he concedes *Foundation* is an SF classic, he attacks the series as too firmly rooted in the B. F. Skinner-type behaviorist psychology. His opinion of such psychologists appears in more detail in "Science Fiction and A World in Crisis," where he says:

> The so-called mental sciences have been seeking political power for many years. This was to be expected as a natural outcome of their power posture. They assumed the position of all-health dealing with all-sickness. Such non-symmetrical relationships inevitably produce shattering crises.

Thus Herbert criticizes Asimov for placing his psychologists in *Foundation* in just such a position of power and then positing a healthy future. That, to Herbert's personal vision, is an invitation to chaos because of the loss of personal freedom, identity, and initiative, and because of the imposition of external, frequently misdirected control. The problem, Herbert elaborates—and the problem applies to Asimov's trilogy—is that

> the holders of power in this world have not awakened to the realization that there is no single model of a society, a species, or an individual. There are a variety of models to meet a variety of needs. They meet different expectations and have different goals. The aim of that force which impels us to live may be to produce as many different models as possible.

Asimov's society, led by hidden psychologists who control and guide human destiny, is thus a violation of the breadth and depth of human activity and existence to Herbert, and he practically confesses his plans to reverse Asimov's *Foundation* vision of the future: Asimov, in common with all the rest of us, operates within a surround of assumptions, any one (or combination) of which could serve as the jumping-off point for an entirely new series of stories. Herbert even directly recommends to other writers the reversal of such assumptions as an important, basic method he uses for discovering ideas for SF stories.

> If you want a gold mine of science fiction material, pull the assumptions out of the current best-seller list. Turn those assumptions over, look at them from every angle you can imagine. Tear them apart. Put them back together. Put your new construction on another planet (or on this planet changed) and place believable human beings into the conflict thus created.

As detailed examination of the two series will clearly illustrate, Herbert did not resist the urge to perform just such a reversal of Asimov's overall *Foundation* vision in his own trilogy while utilizing many of Asimov's specific ideas and techniques.

The restoration of civilization theme of both trilogies has been noticed, but Scholes and Rabkin missed an opportunity to point out the similarities in the way the previous civilizations fall in each story. In *Foundation*, the over-proliferation of technology, political elitism, and the federal bureaucracy result in gradual stagnation and the loss of the inventiveness which had created the Empire and made it strong. The only real difference in *Dune* is that the Butlerian Jihad (the war resulting from the overdevelopment and overuse of technology) occurred long before the novel opens; however, the political infighting and power-grabbing characteristic of the *Foundation* Empire certainly exist in *Dune*. Such a struggle precipitates the move of the Atreides family from Caladan to the desert world of Arrakis to establish an effective government there. The move to a primitive world from the center of a decaying civilization is central to *Foundation* as well; the Encyclopediasts, led by Seldon, transplant themselves to Terminus to create their encyclopedia and also a new, and better, civilization. So, though some specific motives and contexts vary, the movement in both novels from a decaying central civilization to an outlying, primitive planet for regeneration is identical. Herbert uses Asimov's future universe as his source for more than just the idea of civilization restoration. The way the restoration occurs (in terms of movement) and the similarities between the declining Empires are too great to be coincidental.

Within these large similarities of movement and design, there are also numerous specific similarities of action, setting, and character, all of which point to Herbert's adaptation of ideas from Asimov. One plot action of great significance in both trilogies is the establishment of a religious system on primitive planets which helps pave the way for the eventual ascendence of the new Empire. In *Foundation*, missionaries are sent from Terminus to the nearby primitive planets to create the "religion of science" which establishes

> the Prophet Hari Seldon and how he appointed the Foundation to carry on his commandments that there might some day be a return of the Earthly Paradise: and how anyone who disobeys his commandments will be destroyed for eternity.

A similar religious crusade is carried out in *Dune* by the *Missionaria Protectiva*, which establishes the Muad'Dib messianic legend among the Fremen on Arrakis. This paves the way for the new civilization under the leadership of Paul

Atreides. Like Seldon, Paul is seen as a Prophet who will lead the Fremen to power and a civilized existence, just as those who join with Terminus in *Foundation* are taught they are destined to lead their galaxy as the center of civilization and power. So, again, the almost identical use of religion in the two trilogies shows that Herbert is using Asimov as a primary source for a major aspect of *Dune*.

Like the missionaries, the traders in each story also play a similar role. They are independent and powerful, and at the same time highly organized, a force to be reckoned with in both series. Granted, Asimov's traders aren't addicted to melange as Herbert's are, but otherwise they are almost interchangeable. They convey missionaries, spread the new technology, and eventually, in both novels, aspire to the central position of power. One of Asimov's traders becomes the leader of Terminus, in fact, and one of Herbert's almost succeeds in replacing Paul Atreides as Emperor in *Dune Messiah*. Thus, the organized traders, or Guildsmen, are so similar as to reinforce the conclusion that Herbert is continuing to use Asimov as a source in this area, also.

A final major point of similarity between the two series is the use of advanced psychology. Although the future psychology is not used identically, it is likely (given the other similarities) that Herbert is again using Asimov as source and changing and adapting specifics for his own use. In *Foundation*, the psychohistorians have refined future prediction into an exact science and an academic discipline. Along with this mathematical-like predictive ability, though, the psychohistorians also develop the ability to communicate without words and to alter and control the minds of others. In *Dune*, prescience, or future prediction, and mental manipulation appear less as learned skills and more as personal, inherited abilities (although the Bene Cesserit of *Dune* and the psychohistorians of *Foundation* are similar, as both scheme to control history by selective breeding and special, secret training). Nevertheless, both psychohistory and prescience function in essentially the same way, enabling characters to see future probabilities and thus giving them an advantage over others in preparing for, or altering, those probabilities. The value and fate of those who engage in future prediction and thus prolonged planning and organizing is different in the two series. Yet the difference, while it seems to override specific similarities like radioactive

body shields, arranged marriages for political power, and leaders who espouse prophetic sayings with amazing regularity, is a key variation: it points to Herbert's parodying and reversing of Asimov's assumptions in the final outcome of the *Dune* series.

At the end of *Children of Dune*, Paul Atreides' son, Leto II, acts like the psychologists in *Foundation* and decides to assume sole responsibility for the future direction of mankind. Through a strange mutation, he gains great strength of mind and body and establishes himself as leader of the Empire. The normal expectation is that Paul Atreides' son takes the best course of action for all concerned. His longevity gives him ample time to plan for and place mankind on his so-called "Golden Path" which will create an ordered, planned existence for mankind like Seldon's psychologist-controlled plan. However, this greatest representative of the prescient, of the psychohistorical, becomes a domineering monster in Herbert's ironic reversal of Asimov's ordered universe. Herbert's point is that one ordered, carefully controlled universe which limits human action and arbitrarily molds human nature is not really any different from any other. This is evident in Paul Atreides' experience as Emperor. In *Dune*, he takes control of the Empire "to prevent the jihad," but the control itself, and the necessity for maintaining it, ironically takes control of him. In *Dune Messiah*, 12 years later, he explains in a moment of remorse that he has "killed sixty-one billion, sterilized ninety planets, completely demoralized five hundred others," and says that "we'll be a hundred generations recovering from Muad'Dib's Jihad." This experience with control and the "absolute power that corrupts absolutely" leads him to desert his realm and wander into the desert at the end of *Dune Messiah*. He afterwards appears in *Children of Dune* as the Preacher, a mysterious opponent of his own Empire who spreads the message that the Empire must be destroyed because

> men must want to do things out of their own innermost drives. People, not commercial organizations or chains of command, are what make great civilizations work. Every civilization depends upon the quality of the individuals it produces. If you over-organize humans, over-legalize them, suppress their urge to greatness—they cannot work and their civilization collapses.

He fails, though, because his lesson is only taught through words, and his Empire is continued by his son, Leto II, the monster-king, who will convince the people of the evils of control through himself as negative example. All the propaganda about the future benefit of man through control that Hari Seldon espouses in the *Foundation* series (primarily that the period of barbarism can be reduced from 30 thousand years to 1,000) degenerates to the *real* motive force in *Children of Dune*: the desire of one person or a group to control others and force their values and life-styles upon them. This is a parodying of *Foundation*, where psychohistorians control minds, blot out memories, and erase thoughts to keep the "normal" humans from developing in the "wrong" way or from discovering that the psychohistorians exist, and where the unbelievable assumption is that such demeaning acts are the best course for mankind, since they avoid a longer period of a very vague barbarism. Herbert reverses this situation in his ending, perceiving the planned universe and the controllers from the point of view of those who lack power and are simply led by force of one kind or another. He sees ultimate horror, horror which leads to revolt sooner or later, or a return to a sort of necessary barbarism. Herbert endorses that revolt, even has his monster-controller endorse it, because Leto II is actually, secretly trying to teach mankind a lesson. As the monster-king's sister points out:

> He'll lead humans through the cult of death into the free air of exuberant life! He speaks of death because that's necessary. . . . It's a tension by which the living know they're alive. When his Empire falls . . . when it [revolt] comes, humans will have renewed their memory of what it's like to be alive. The memory will persist as long as there's a single human living. We'll go through the crucible once more . . . and we'll come out of it. We always rise from our own ashes. Always.

That dynamic, ever redefining paradox of death and life, freedom and control, civilization and barbarism is the way Herbert sees the world, and it is the complexity of such a world that causes him to parody Asimov. Any reductionism which places the fate of the universe in the hands of a few manipulative, egomaniacal psychologists ignores the effect of that control on the people in general and is too limited to go unchallenged. The ending of *Children of Dune* directly responds to the call. Humans may make mistakes and even become a little barbaric in Herbert's world, but at least they retain their knowledge of freedom and their creative energy—their ability to respond spontaneously and completely to a complex universe in all the multitude of ways such a universe calls for.

As Herbert said in "Science Fiction and A World in Crisis," they will retain the ability to create as many different models or societies as possible and necessary. It is indeed hard to believe in the possibility that any small group of psychologists can make all the correct choices for everyone without creating the same kind of unconscious, subservient mentality created, to a large degree, by the dynasties in Earth's past. Herbert feels that all men must have the freedom to be creative and contribute to civilization in any way they can or want to if society is to avoid stagnation, a far greater danger than barbarism in the present age. Herbert's choice, in writing this ending, is clearly superior to Asimov's and is an important philosophical comment on the future, the present, and even the past.

It becomes clear, then, that both series are interrelated and similar, but also very opposite in their conclusions because of Herbert's ironic reversal of Asimov's assumptions. Both are also successful in their own special ways, though Asimov leans a bit too much on detective devices to interest his reader, and Herbert depends a bit too much on fantastic adventures for the same purpose. Though perhaps less speculative than unconnected novels, these two series also enable Asimov and Herbert to completely avoid overt moralizing, since they have the space in which to embody all their ideas and show them being worked out to their logical conclusions. Herbert's trilogy is more philosophically perceptive than Asimov's, but then Asimov must receive credit for a more probable future universe in terms of plot, character, and setting (though perhaps it is too similar to the present, given its Roman Empire basis and too-extensive fear of barbarism). Some of Herbert's characters (like face dancers, gholas, etc.) verge on the fantastic, but Asimov avoids such venturing into fantasy. But then, Asimov is the scientist and Herbert is the literary romanticist-philosopher, so the strengths and weaknesses fit logically with the authors' backgrounds. No one can deny, however, despite the limitations of the works, that the *Foundation* and *Dune* trilogies have been widely read and highly influential, and the close relationship between the two which is delineated here, when added to their generally recognized artistic merits, should guarantee both series an important place in the historical development of SF.

Source: John L. Grigsby, "Asimov's 'Foundation' Trilogy and Herbert's 'Dune' Trilogy: A Vision Reversed," in *Science Fiction Studies*, Vol. 8, No. 2, July 1981, pp. 149–55.

SOURCES

Aldiss, Brian W., *Billion Year Spree: The True History of Science Fiction*, Doubleday, 1973, pp. 274–76.

Checkland, Peter, *Systems Thinking, Systems Practice*, Wiley, 1981.

Collings, Michael R., "The Epic of *Dune*: Epic Traditions in Modern Science Fiction," in *Aspects of Fantasy: Selected Essays from the Second International Conference on the Fantastic in Literature and Film*, edited by William Coyle, Greenwood Press, 1986, pp. 131–39.

Herbert, Brian, *Dreamer of Dune: The Biography of Frank Herbert*, Tor, 2003.

Herbert, Frank, *Dune: Fortieth Anniversary Edition*, Ace Books, 2005.

———, "Dune Genesis," in *Omni* July 1980, pp. 72–75.

Killingsworth, M. Jimmie, and Jacqueline S. Palmer, "Silent Spring and Science Fiction: An Essay in the History and Rhetoric of Narrative," in *And No Birds Sing: Rhetorical Analyses of Rachel Carson's Silent Spring*, edited by Craig Waddell, University of Illinois at Carbondale Press, 2000, pp. 174–204.

List, Julia, "'Call Me a Protestant': Liberal Christianity, Individualism, and the Messiah in *Stranger in a Strange Land*, *Dune*, and *Lord of Light*," in *Science Fiction Studies*, Vol. 36, No. 1, 2009, pp. 21–47.

McNelly, Willis, E., *The Dune Encyclopedia*, Ace Books, 1984.

Miller, David M., *Frank Herbert*, Starmount House, 1980, pp. 15–26.

Minowitz, Peter, "Prince versus Prophet: Machiavellianism in Frank Herbert's *Dune* Epic," in *Political Science Fiction*, edited by Donald M. Hassler and Clyde Wilcox, University of South Carolina Press, 1997, pp. 124–47.

O'Reilly, Timothy, *Frank Herbert*, Frederick Ungar, 1981, pp. 39, 59, 166.

Roberts, Adam Charles, *Science Fiction*, Routledge, 2000, pp. 36–46.

Stratton, Susan, "The Messiah and the Greens: The Shape of Environmental Action in *Dune* and *Pacific Edge*," in *Extrapolation*, Vol. 42, 2001, pp. 303–18.

FURTHER READING

Grazier, Kevin Robert, *The Science of Dune*, BenBella Books, 2007.
> In this book, physicist Kevin Robert Grazier explores possible real-world scientific explanations for some of the technology and human transformations envisioned by Herbert.

Khazanov, Anatoly Michailovich, *Nomads and the Outside World*, translated by Julia Cookenden, 2nd ed., University of Wisconsin Press, 1994.
> Khazanov presents an illuminating study of the nomadic desert societies that were part of Herbert's inspiration for the Fremen in *Dune*.

O'Reilly, Tim, ed., *The Maker of Dune: Insights of a Master of Science Fiction*, Berkley Books, 1987.
> Shortly after Herbert's death, O'Reilly edited this collection of nonfiction essays by the author of *Dune*.

Palumbo, Donald E., *Chaos Theory, Asimov's Foundations and Robots, and Herbert's Dune: The Fractal Aesthetic of Epic Science Fiction*, Contributions to the Study of Science Fiction and Fantasy 100, Greenwood Press, 2002.
> Palumbo analyzes *Dune* in contrast to Asimov's Foundation series and in light of the recent popularity of chaos theory.

Ivanhoe

WALTER SCOTT

1819

Sir Walter Scott began his writing career as a poet, but in the early nineteenth century, he turned his talents primarily to fiction. He is generally regarded as the originator of the historical novel, a term that refers to a novel that weaves plots and characters around actual historical events. His early novels were set in Scotland and structured around events in recent Scottish history. *Ivanhoe*, published in 1819 and arguably Scott's most popular novel, differs in that it is set entirely in England, and its historical setting is the late twelfth century. It details the actions not only of the title character but also of King Richard I, known to history as Richard the Lion-Hearted for his exploits during the Crusades (a series of wars in the twelfth and thirteenth centuries between Christian Europe and Muslims in Palestine). After *Ivanhoe* became a runaway bestseller, Scott turned his attention to more English historical events.

Ivanhoe is principally an adventure tale. It contains all the trappings of a story about English knights during the medieval period, including castles, jousting, disguises, chivalry, heroes and villains, dungeons, and damsels in distress. It is also noteworthy for its heroine, Rebecca, a Jew whom Scott depicted with sympathy and admiration at a time when prejudice against Jews was commonplace in Great Britain. Because of its immense popularity over generations, the novel is widely available in paperback and hard cover, including illustrated and collectors' editions; a recent edition was published as part of the Barnes and Noble Classics series in 2005.

Sir Walter Scott (The Library of Congress)

AUTHOR BIOGRAPHY

Scott was born on August 15, 1771, in Edinburgh, Scotland, the son of a lawyer. As a child he endured a bout of polio that left him lame, though in time he largely overcame this lameness. A key event in his early life was his residence with an aunt in the Scottish Borders region (so called because it lies on the border between Scotland and England). There he was exposed to the region's colorful tales and ballads of adventure.

After completing his education at the University of Edinburgh, Scott was apprenticed to his father to become a lawyer, but his true love was literature. In the late 1700s he published English translations of literature from the European continent, and throughout his career he published collections of the poetry and plays of earlier British authors, along with historical works, biographies, and a wide range of miscellaneous writing. He also published collections of romantic tales and ballads from the Border region. Scott first made a name for himself as a poet in his own right with the 1805 publication of a long narrative poem, *The Lay of the Last Minstrel.* He followed

this successful poem with such poems as *Marmion* (1808) and "The Lady of the Lake" (1810).

Scott's career as a novelist began in 1814 with the publication of the enormously popular *Waverley.* The book was so well received that most of his subsequent novels are still referred to collectively as the "Waverley" novels. This is because these novels were published anonymously, by "The Author of Waverley," for Scott did not want to damage his reputation as a poet at a time when poetry was regarded as a higher form of literature. It was not until 1827 that he publicly acknowledged his authorship. After *Waverley,* his novels followed in rapid succession, sometimes at the rate of two a year. Among the most popular have been *Rob Roy* (1817), *The Heart of Midlothian* (1818), *Kenilworth* (1821), *Quentin Durward* (1823), *The Talisman* (1825), and of course *Ivanhoe* (1819). Scott also tried his hand at writing plays, which are generally considered less successful than his poetry and novels and are rarely performed today. During the 1820s, Scott was granted the title of baronet in recognition of his work.

In addition to writing, Scott was a businessman. He co-founded a printing business that indirectly led to his prolific output as a writer. The business was experiencing financial troubles, so Scott wrote *Waverly,* hoping that it would earn a great deal of money. Then in 1825 the firm was on the verge of having to declare bankruptcy. Scott, however, took the entire debt on himself and, in the final years of his life, worked so feverishly to repay it that his health suffered. He died on September 21, 1832, at Abbotsford House, his home in the beloved Scottish Borders region.

PLOT SUMMARY

Chapters 1–4

The opening chapters of *Ivanhoe* establish the novel's historical and social context. King Richard I has been absent fighting in the Crusades, a series of wars fought between Muslims and European Christians over the holy city of Jerusalem. On his way home from the Crusades, Richard has been captured and imprisoned by the Austrians. In his absence, tension festers between two opposing political groups, the Saxons and the Normans. The native Saxon nobles held power and influence in England until the year 1066, when England was invaded by the Normans, a French people, under the leadership of William the Conqueror. The Normans have used Richard's absence to conquer many of the Saxon nobles and reduce them to serfdom. In general, the Normans and the Saxons despise each other. The chief Saxon character in the novel, Cedric, opposed the decision of his son, Ivanhoe, to fight in the Crusades on behalf of Richard I—a Norman king—so he has disinherited Ivanhoe. Cedric also has a ward, Rowena, who is renowned for her great beauty. Cedric hopes to marry Rowena to Athelstane, a Saxon noble.

Gurth, a swineherd, and a clownish jester named Wamba are in the service of Cedric. As a storm gathers, Gurth and Wamba seek shelter, but a party of men on horseback approaches. The riders are led by Brian de Bois-Guilbert and Prior Aymer. De Bois-Guilbert is a member of the Knights Templar, a powerful religious and military organization. Prior Aymer is the head of Jorvaulx Abbey. They ask the swineherds for directions to Cedric's home, but Wamba, who resents the men's Norman arrogance, intentionally gives them false directions.

As the men ride on, they encounter a palmer (a religious pilgrim) who takes them to Cedric's castle. Although Cedric, too, is put off by their Norman haughtiness, he prepares a feast for them. When Rowena enters, de Bois-Guilbert is struck by her beauty. A page announces that a stranger has arrived at the castle gate. Cedric orders that he be admitted because of the storm.

Chapters 5–8
The page returns to inform Cedric that the stranger at the gate is a Jew named Isaac of York. Both de Bois-Guilbert and Prior Aymer are shocked that Cedric would even consider admitting a Jew to his castle, but the weather is stormy, so Cedric resolves to extend hospitality to Isaac. During the feast, the men discuss the Crusades. De Bois-Guilbert and the palmer debate the merits of Christian forces in the Holy Land.

De Bois-Guilbert and Prior Aymer are on their way to a jousting tournament at Ashby-de-la-Zouche. Isaac reveals that he, too, is going to the tournament. The palmer learns from de Bois-Guilbert's men that the Templar plans to rob Isaac. He helps Isaac avoid the robbery, and in exchange for his help, Isaac provides the palmer with a suit of armor and a horse from a friend so that he can take part in the tournament.

The day of the tournament arrives. Present is Prince John, Richard's weak and treacherous

brother. John has been able to gather power because though Richard is a Norman, the Normans distrust him because he is enemies with King Philip of France. A dispute erupts over where Isaac, who has been joined by his beautiful daughter, Rebecca, will be seated. In the end, he is forced to sit with the commoners rather than the more prominent attendees. Meanwhile, Prince John takes a purse containing gold from Isaac. The jousting begins, and the palmer, who calls himself the Disinherited Knight, defeats all his opponents, including de Bois-Guilbert. He is thus allowed to name the Queen of Love and Beauty who will reign over the next day's action.

Chapters 9–12
Attention focuses on the identity of the Disinherited Knight, who stuns the crowd by choosing Rowena, a Saxon, as the Queen of Love and Beauty. Although he is allowed to take a horse, armor, or ransom money from the knights he has defeated, he refuses to take anything from the hands of de Bois-Guilbert. He also refuses to attend a banquet hosted by Prince John.

The Disinherited Knight asks Gurth to return the horse and armor Isaac had loaned him. Isaac does not know it, but Rebecca gives Gurth money. As Gurth strolls along, dreaming of freedom, he is attacked by a band of robbers, who question him about Cedric. They tell Gurth that they will release him unharmed if he defeats a man called "the Miller" in combat. Gurth wins the contest, and to his surprise, the robbers make good on their promise and release him.

The Disinherited Knight is attacked by de Bois-Guilbert, Athelstane, and Reginald Front-de-Boeuf. He fights them off with the help of a mysterious figure called the Black Knight. Athelstane and Front-de-Boeuf are driven off, and the Knight again defeats de Bois-Guilbert. Rowena steps forward to crown him champion of the tournament. When she removes his helmet, it is revealed that the Disinherited Knight is Ivanhoe, who is badly wounded and faints.

Chapters 13–17
Attention shifts to the novel's villains. Prince John and his advisors, including Front-de-Boeuf, Maurice de Bracy, and Waldemar Fitzurse, discuss the implications of the knight's identity. John even hints that he could send his own physician to tend Ivanhoe's wounds, hinting at foul play. A messenger appears with a message suggesting that

Richard has escaped from his captors and is returning to England. The message panics John.

An archery tournament follows. A yeoman named Locksley defeats Hubert. Prince John, meanwhile, wants to firm up his support among the nobles, so he hosts a feast, but tension between the refined Normans and the coarse Saxons continues. Fitzurse talks to the nobles individually in an effort to gather support for John. When he speaks with de Bracy, he learns that de Bracy has become infatuated with Rowena. Prince John plans to marry Rowena off to de Bracy, but the knight does not want to wait, so, over Fitzurse's objections, he devises a plan to kidnap her and her party as they return home.

In the forest, the Black Knight who came to Ivanhoe's aid arrives at a hermitage, where he meets a hermit who calls himself the Clerk of Compmanhurst. The two men become friends and spend the remainder of the day singing and drinking.

Chapters 18–22
Cedric, worried about his son, sends his page to check on Ivanhoe. Cedric takes Gurth captive after discovering that the swineherd has been serving Ivanhoe in disguise, but Gurth escapes and asks Wamba to tell their master that he will never serve Cedric again. The Saxons, including Cedric and Rowena, are returning home from the tournament when they come across Isaac and Rebecca, along with a sick old man being carried on a litter. Rebecca asks the group for protection, and Rowena persuades Cedric to agree.

De Bracy and his men, disguised as outlaws, attack the party. In the confusion, Wamba escapes, but the Saxons, along with Isaac and his daughter, are captured. Wamba flees through the forest, where he encounters Locksley; they are later joined by Gurth. Locksley, along with his men and the Black Knight, agrees to help free the prisoners, who have been imprisoned in Front-de-Boeuf's castle, Torquilstone. Isaac is told that unless he pays Front-de-Boeuf a thousand pieces of silver, he will be tortured. Isaac pleads for Rebecca to be released so that she can go to York to procure the money, but he is told that Rebecca now belongs to de Bois-Guilbert. As Isaac's torture is about to begin, a bugle sounds at the gate and voices call for Front-de-Boeuf.

Chapters 23–27
At Torquilstone, Rowena and Rebecca are confronted by the men who desire them. De Bracy demands Rowena's hand in marriage, but she is in love with Ivanhoe, so she tearfully refuses. Her tears prompt a moment of human sympathy on de Bracy's part. Meanwhile, Rebecca is imprisoned with a haggard old Saxon woman named Ulrica. De Bois-Guilbert tries to force Rebecca to submit to him, but she threatens to jump over the parapet of the castle and kill herself rather than do so. De Bois-Guilbert is amazed by her strength of character.

Both men are interrupted by the bugle that sounded at the end of Chapter 22. The bugle announces the arrival of a letter from Locksley and the Black Knight, who are backed by some two hundred yeoman followers. The letter says that the men plan to free the prisoners, whether by combat or siege. Front-de-Boeuf demands that a priest be sent to hear the prisoners' confessions, though his true intention is to send the priest to bring reinforcements. Wamba poses as a priest, sneaks into the castle, and changes clothes with Cedric.

Cedric wanders about the castle, posing as a priest. He encounters Rebecca and Ulrica, who tells him that after the Normans seized the castle from her ancestors, she was forced to submit herself to them. Cedric then encounters Front-de-Boeuf, who, thinking Cedric is the priest, orders him to deliver a message to his supporter, Albert de Malvoisin. He gives Cedric a gold coin, but Cedric indignantly throws it at the feet of the Norman and leaves the castle.

Chapters 28–31
It is revealed that the sick old man on the litter in the forest before the Saxons were captured is Ivanhoe. Rebecca, who is falling in love with Ivanhoe, continues to nurse him. Meanwhile, fighting breaks out, and Rebecca stands at the window to watch, telling Ivanhoe what she sees. The bloodshed causes her to condemn the institution of knighthood, but Ivanhoe defends the code of chivalry by which knights are ruled.

During the fighting, Front-de-Boeuf is mortally wounded. Ulrica taunts him, accusing him of murdering his own father. She then sets fire to the castle. The Black Knight captures de Bracy, then runs into the burning castle to save Ivanhoe. The other prisoners escape, with the exception of Rebecca, who is carried off by de Bois-Guilbert, despite the efforts of Athelstane to stop him. The castle continues to burn as Ulrica sings an eerie death song.

Chapters 32–36

Ivanhoe is still suffering from his injuries and is being cared for in the priory of St. Botolph. The Saxons meet Locksley in the forest, where Cedric, out of gratitude, grants Gurth his freedom. The Black Knight releases de Bracy but warns him to behave with more honor in the future. The Friar, one of Locksley's men, arrives with Isaac, who learns that de Bois-Guilbert has taken his daughter captive. Prior Aymer writes a letter to de Bois-Guilbert urging him to release Rebecca. The characters then disperse. The Saxons depart for Athelstane's castle at Coningsburgh to bury him, for de Bois-Guilbert apparently killed him during their dispute in Chapter 31 by striking him on the head. Isaac, in search of his daughter, leaves for the Knights Templar stronghold at Templestowe.

De Bracy hastens to Prince John to inform him of Front-de-Boeuf's death, de Bois-Guilbert's abduction of Rebecca, and the rumored return of King Richard to England. In response, John plans an attack on Richard. Meanwhile, Isaac arrives at Templestowe, where he shows Aymer's letter to Lucas Beaumanoir, the grand master of the Knights Templar. The letter strongly suggests that Rebecca has practiced witchcraft on de Bois-Guilbert, a claim that is backed by Malvoisin. Malvoisin does not believe that Rebecca is a witch, but he and Beaumanoir are troubled by the fact that one of their own has apparently disgraced himself and the order by falling in love with a Jew. They launch plans to try her as a witch.

Chapters 37–40

The trial of Rebecca on the charge of witchcraft begins. Witnesses are brought forward to testify to her supposed supernatural powers. Ironically, her only defender is de Bois-Guilbert. As it becomes clear that Rebecca will be found guilty, de Bois-Guilbert proposes a trial by combat, with a champion who would fight for Rebecca's freedom; de Bois-Guilbert is certain that no such champion will step forward, largely because Rebecca is a Jew. Nevertheless, a message is sent to Isaac, telling him to find a champion to fight on Rebecca's behalf. De Bois-Guilbert urges Rebecca to elope with him, but she continues to resist him.

Ivanhoe leaves the priory of St. Botolph. Meanwhile, the Black Knight and Wamba are suddenly attacked by a party of men. As they defend themselves, Locksley and his men arrive and join the fray. During the battle, the attackers' leader, Waldemar Fitzurse, calls the Black Knight "Richard." The Black Knight removes his helmet and announces that indeed he is King Richard. He banishes Fitzurse from England, but he orders that his brother, Prince John, not be held accountable for the attack. As the parties are about to leave the forest, two travelers ride toward them.

Chapters 41–44

The travelers are Ivanhoe and Gurth. Ivanhoe berates the king for leaving his country to seek glory in a faraway war. Richard tells Ivanhoe that he cannot reveal his return to the country at large, for he has to raise an army to defend his throne. The men feast with Locksley and his men after it is revealed that Locksley is really Robin Hood. They then depart for Athelstane's castle to attend his funeral, but when they arrive, Athelstane mysteriously reappears, claiming that he was merely knocked unconscious by de Bois-Guilbert's blow at Torquilstone and that he had to escape from his own coffin. Athelstane persuades Cedric to give Rowena's hand in marriage to Ivanhoe. The assembled party, though, are stunned to discover that Ivanhoe and Richard have disappeared.

At Templestowe, the headquarters of the Knights Templar, a crowd has gathered to witness the trial by combat that will determine Rebecca's fate. De Bois-Guilbert, armed for combat, impatiently waits for a champion to appear. He faces a strange situation: he is forced to fight on behalf of the Knights Templar. If he wins the combat, Rebecca, whom he loves, will be found guilty and executed. If he loses, he will likely be killed. As he paces on his horse, a champion appears. The champion is Ivanhoe, but he is so exhausted by his long ride to Templestowe that he falls from his horse, apparently defeated. De Bois-Guilbert's strong emotions are so conflicted that he, too, falls from his horse and dies.

The action concludes with the marriage of Ivanhoe and Rowena, who receives a visit from Rebecca, thanking her for Ivanhoe's role in saving her life. Rowena tells Rebecca that she and her father are leaving England. In the years that follow, Ivanhoe finds distinction in serving Richard, though his career ends when the king is killed in battle in France.

CHARACTERS

Athelstane

Athelstane is a Saxon nobleman and a descendant of the last Saxon king of England. Cedric hopes to marry Rowena to Athelstane as a way of continuing the line of Saxon nobles. While Athelstane, generally a sluggish man more interested in drink and food, wants to marry Rowena, she has no interest in him.

Prior Aymer

Aymer is the prior of the monastery at Jorvaulx. He is one of de Bois-Guilbert's associates. He is more interested in the finer things in life than in religion.

Lucas Beaumanoir

Beaumanoir, a sternly moral man, is the grand master of the Knights Templar and one of the characters who orchestrates the trial of Rebecca on charges of practicing witchcraft.

Black Knight

See Richard I

Brian de Bois-Guilbert

De Bois-Guilbert is a Norman knight and the primary villain of the novel. He is a member of the Knights Templar, an order of knights originally formed to protect Christian pilgrims visiting the Holy Land during the Crusades that later acquired secular power and wealth. De Bois-Guilbert is struck by Rebecca's beauty and character, so he tries to force himself on her and, later, to persuade her to elope with him. In this way he offends his superiors in the Knights Templar, who are disgusted that he could even consider a relationship with a Jew. Although de Bois-Guilbert is a villain, he is the one character who undergoes change and development. Initially, he lusts after Rebecca and wants simply to possess her. As he gets to know her better, his love for her becomes more genuine, and he seems to care about her welfare. Nevertheless, he abducts her and carries her away to the Templar stronghold. When she is being tried for witchcraft, he is torn, knowing that her life is in danger. Though willing to take part in a trial by combat that, it is believed, would prove her guilt or innocence, de Bois-Guilbert recognizes that if he wins the combat, Rebecca will be found guilty of witchcraft and sentenced to death. If he loses, he will pay with his own life. His

MEDIA ADAPTATIONS

- *Ivanhoe* was made into a 1952 movie starring Elizabeth Taylor, Joan Fontaine, and George Sanders, directed by Joseph Barbera, Richard Thorpe, and William Hanna. The film was nominated for three Academy Awards. It was issued on DVD in 2005 by Warner Home Video.

- A television movie adaptation of *Ivanhoe*, starring Anthony Andrews, Olivia Hussey, and Sam Neill, directed by Douglas Carnfield, was produced in 1982. It was released on DVD by Sony Pictures in 2009.

- A six-part film mini-series adaptation of *Ivanhoe*, starring Steven Waddington, Ciarán Hinds, Victoria Smurfit, and Susan Lynch, directed by Stuart Orme, was released by A&E Home Video in 2002.

- Twenty-six television episodes of *Dark Knight*, a series based on *Ivanhoe* starring Ben Pullen and Charlotte Comer, were produced by the BBC's Channel 5 beginning in 2000. This series updates the story by introducing elements of fantasy and sorcery and using computer-generated special effects.

- An unabridged audiobook version of *Ivanhoe* was produced by Brilliance Audio and released in 2005.

- An operatic version of *Ivanhoe* was produced by Arthur Sullivan in 1891 and ran for an astonishing 155 consecutive performances. The opera was released as an audio CD by Pearl in 1989 and reissued in 1993.

admiration for Rebecca's strength of character in resisting him is presented as a positive trait.

Maurice de Bracy

De Bracy is a Norman knight and an ally of Prince John. He is one of the novel's villains and is attracted to Rowena, whom he abducts and carries off to Front-de-Boeuf's castle, Torquilstone. He is not entirely evil, though. When he tries to force himself on Rowena and she begins to cry, he feels sympathy for her plight and tries to give her comfort.

Cedric

Cedric, a Saxon noble, is the father of Ivanhoe and the protector of Rowena. He is representative of Saxons in general by his fierce pride and his resentment of the Normans, whom he regards as arrogant and who, in turn, regard him as coarse and unsophisticated. This resentment caused him to disinherit Ivanhoe, who serves the Norman king, Richard I. He opposes any marriage of Rowena and Ivanhoe, preferring instead to give his ward's hand to Athelstane, a Saxon, thus resurrecting the Saxon royal line. Cedric is good at heart, though, as suggested by his granting freedom to the swineherd Gurth and his eventual acceptance of Ivanhoe.

Disinherited Knight

See Ivanhoe

Waldemar Fitzurse

Fitzurse is one of Prince John's closest advisers. He has little admiration for John, but he believes it is to his advantage to connect his fortune with John's. He is calculating and calm, particularly in the face of news that panics John. He leads the raid to capture Richard in the forest, for which he is banished from England.

Reginald Front-de-Boeuf

Front-de-Boeuf is the novel's most villainous character. He is an ally of Prince John, and it is to his castle that the Saxon prisoners are taken. He threatens Isaac with torture unless his captive turns over a thousand pieces of silver. He is killed in the battle at his castle.

Gurth

Gurth is a swineherd who longs for his freedom, which he gains as a reward for helping to organize the attack on Torquilstone. Along with Wamba, he provides a note of comedy in the novel. In time, he becomes a virtual squire to Ivanhoe.

Robin Hood

See Locksley

Isaac of York

Isaac is a Jew who comes from the city of York and is the father of Rebecca. He is depicted as ultimately kind-hearted, and he deeply loves his daughter. However, he is also depicted in a way consistent with stereotypes of Jews both at the time of the novel's action and at the time when Scott wrote. The chief stereotype is that he is overly concerned with money and that he is something of a bumbler.

Ivanhoe

Ivanhoe's formal name is Wilfred of Ivanhoe. He is the son of Cedric, a Saxon noble. Before the novel begins, he joined King Richard I in fighting the Third Crusade (1189–1193), earning a reputation as a courageous and chivalric knight. Although he is the novel's title character, he plays a somewhat limited role, as he is injured for much of the time. His role is largely symbolic, for although he is a Saxon, he is loyal to the Norman king Richard. He thus represents the inevitable blending of the Norman and Saxon cultures and a bridge between England's Saxon past and its future. He also symbolizes knightly honor, in contrast to the villainy of the novel's antagonists. In the end, he marries Rowena, Cedric's ward, and continues to serve King Richard. Ivanhoe makes his first appearance in the novel disguised as a palmer, a term used to describe pilgrims who indicate that they have been to the Holy Land by wearing crossed palm leaves. Later, he competes in the tournament at Ashby as, appropriately, the Disinherited Knight.

Prince John

Prince John, brother of Richard I, occupies the throne of England while Richard is fighting in the Crusades and, later, while Richard is being held for ransom by the Austrians. He is a weak and villainous ruler so eager to retain the throne that he does all he can to ensure that Richard remains a captive. He is terrified when he learns that Richard has returned to England.

Locksley

Locksley is the name by which Robin Hood is known in the novel, possibly because some legends held that he came from the town of Loxley. He and his band of "merry men," including Friar Tuck and Alan-a-Dale, were forest outlaws who robbed from the rich and gave the money to the poor. Locksley and his men play a key role in freeing the Saxon prisoners from Front-de-Boeuf's castle, Torquilstone. Beyond that, Locksley and his band add comedy, adventure, and action to the novel by appearing at key moments, seemingly out of nowhere, to help the sympathetic characters.

Albert de Malvoisin

Malvoisin leads the Templar forces at the order's stronghold at Templestowe. He strongly opposes de Bois-Guilbert's relationship with Rebecca, arguing to the knight that such a relationship could ruin the knight's career.

Palmer

See Ivanhoe

Rebecca

Rebecca is Isaac's beautiful and strong-willed daughter, and a Jew. She was based on Rebecca Gratz, a Jewish woman from Philadelphia whom Scott briefly met. After Ivanhoe is injured during the tournament at Ashby, she nurses him, and in the process falls in love with him. She knows that they can never marry because Ivanhoe is a Christian. She plays the part of the medieval damsel in distress after she catches the attention of Brian de Bois-Guilbert, a Norman villain who initially lusts for her but in time falls in love with her and urges her to elope with him. Rebecca steadfastly resists his advances. After de Bois-Guilbert abducts her and carries her away to the stronghold of the Knights Templar, his superiors in the order, believing that he is disgracing the order by his relationship with a Jew, accuse her of witchcraft. Her guilt during her trial for witchcraft is a foregone conclusion, but she is saved when Ivanhoe arrives as her champion and fights de Bois-Guilbert. Rebecca is treated with great sympathy and thus becomes to some degree symbolic of Scott's belief that Jews in England should be treated with greater acceptance.

Richard I

Richard is the king of England and a Norman. He is at the head of the Norman royal line of succession, the Plantagenets. He won glory on the field of battle during the Third Crusade (1189–1193), but as he was returning to England, he was captured and held for ransom by the Austrians. He initially appears in the novel disguised as the Black Knight and plays a key role in defending the heroic characters against the plots of the villains. Although he is a good king who cares about his people, he is depicted as a bit of an adventurer who sometimes puts his desire for adventure and martial glory over the good of his people.

Rowena

Rowena is Cedric's ward; that is, she lives under his protection. She is depicted as the ideal of medieval womanhood by being submissive and virtuous, as well as beautiful. Her beauty attracts the unwanted attentions of Maurice de Bracy, who kidnaps her. Rowena is in love with Ivanhoe, but until the end of the novel, she cannot marry him because Cedric wants her to marry Athelstane. She stands up to Cedric on this matter, however, and ultimately gives her hand in marriage to Ivanhoe.

Ulrica

After she is captured, Rebecca is imprisoned with Ulrica, an old, haggard Saxon woman whose castle was been taken from her by the Normans. During the battle at Torquilstone, she sets the castle ablaze and sings an eerie death song as the flames surround her. Ulrica assumes the name Ulfried during part of the novel.

Wamba

Wamba represents the stock character of the jester who makes wry, witty, and sometimes wise comments about the events and people around him. Together with Gurth, he also provides comic relief in the novel.

THEMES

Culture Clash

Ivanhoe is set against the backdrop of the clash between two cultures, the Saxons and the Normans. *Saxon* is a catch-all term to refer to several Germanic tribes that migrated to the British Isles beginning in about the fifth century; often the term "Anglo-Saxons" is used. At the time of the novel, the Saxons were regarded as native Englanders. In contrast, the Normans were a French people, originating in the northern French province of Normandy. The name is derived from "Northmen," referring to the Normans' Scandinavian origins. The two cultures had considerable contact, but matters changed in 1066 when Duke William II of Normandy invaded Britain, subdued the Saxon nobles, and established the Normans as the ruling class of England. This event is generally referred to as the Norman Conquest.

The Saxon nobles, whose land was taken away and whose influence was reduced, resented the Normans. Each group held stereotypes of

TOPICS FOR FURTHER STUDY

- Compare and contrast *Ivanhoe* with a more modern novel that deals with themes of chivalry and the gender roles of men and women. Possibilities include Stephenie Meyer's *Twilight* and Beth Fantaskey's *Jessica's Guide to Dating on the Dark Side*. Both of these novels are modern-day "vampire romances," yet both depict male and female characters whose roles are similar to those of Ivanhoe, Rowena, and Rebecca. Write a review of one of these novels in which you trace its roots to *Ivanhoe*.

- Conduct research into the history of the relationship between Jews and Christians in Europe from the time of the Crusades (the late eleventh century through the late thirteenth century) up to the time when Scott wrote *Ivanhoe*. In a report, explain why Scott's depiction of Rebecca was a departure from earlier literary representations of Jews.

- Find Internet depictions of medieval European knights, particularly during the time of the Crusades. What types of weapons did they fight with? What did their armor look like? How would a Knight Templar such as Brian de Bois-Guilbert have looked and dressed? How were their horses decorated? What would a jousting tournament site have looked like? Share your findings in a PowerPoint presentation that uses as many visuals as possible.

- A prominent theme in *Ivanhoe* is the clash between two cultures, the French Normans and the English Saxons. Investigate another example of such a clash and the people who try to bridge it. One possibility is the stories surrounding Captain John Smith of the American Jamestown colony in the early seventeenth century. According to legend, Smith's life was saved by a teenage Indian girl, Pocahontas. Prepare a report in which you outline the parallels between *Ivanhoe* and the legends surrounding John Smith and his cultural clash with Pocahontas's tribe.

- The characters of Robin Hood and his band of outlaws play a prominent role in *Ivanhoe*. Trace the history of the Robin Hood legend. Focus on questions such as whether Robin Hood was a real person or a fictional creation and the nature of his relationships with King Richard and Prince John. Prepare an essay in which you report your findings.

---

the other. To the Normans, the Saxons were crude, coarse, and uneducated. To the Saxons, the Normans were haughty, arrogant, and overly sophisticated. The distinction becomes apparent in the opening scene of *Ivanhoe* when Gurth the swineherd and Wamba discuss pork. Gurth notes that pigs are referred to by their Saxon name, swine, when they are alive and being tended by Saxon laborers. When they are dead, they become pork, a dish fit for lavish Norman feasts. Later, in Chapter 27, Wamba recites to de Bracy a proverb that captures the tension between the Saxons and the Normans:

Norman saw on English oak,
On English neck a Norman yoke;
Norman spoon in English dish,

And England ruled as Normans wish;
Blythe world to England never will be more,
Till England's rid of all the four.

This culture clash motivates Cedric, a Saxon noble, to cut his son, Ivanhoe, out of his will, because Ivanhoe decided to serve the Norman king Richard I during the Third Crusade. Thematically, the character of Ivanhoe functions as a bridge between the two cultures, suggesting that in time the Saxon and Norman cultures will merge and tensions will disappear. In this way the novel reflects events in Scott's native Scotland. Historically, the English had regarded themselves as superior to the supposedly coarse and backward Scots. The two nations, though, merged in the early eighteenth century.

Religion

Ivanhoe depicts a number of religious characters: Prior Aymer, the abbot of Jorvaulx; a friar who turns out to be Friar Tuck, one of Robin Hood's men; and the palmer, who is Ivanhoe in disguise. Additionally, Isaac and his daughter Rebecca are Jewish, while all the other characters are at least nominally Christian. King Richard and Ivanhoe fought in the Crusades, a series of religious wars fought as European Christians tried to drive Muslims out of the Holy Land. Brian de Bois-Guilbert is a member of the Knights Templar, a religious-military order founded in 1119. The name of the order derived from Jerusalem's Temple of Solomon, the headquarters of the knights. They originally protected Christian pilgrims to the Holy Land, but over time the order fought many battles in the Crusades and acquired secular power and wealth.

Ivanhoe does not deal with the inner religious life of the characters. Rather, the focus is on religion as a social and cultural institution. De Bois-Guilbert holds power not because of his beliefs but because he belongs to a powerful religious order. Characters such as Prior Aymer are depicted as hypocritical and corrupt, more interested in creature comforts than in the life of the soul. Yet many of the novel's characters, including Ivanhoe, Rowena, and Rebecca, are profoundly moral, and a character such as Locksley practices a morality outside of church dogma, even though he is an outlaw. The suggestion is that true morality and religion are to be found not in titles and institutions but in having a kind and honorable heart.

Anti-Semitism

Closely related to the theme of religion is anti-Semitism, or prejudice against Jews. This prejudice was widespread both at the time of the Crusades and at the time when Scott wrote. Prior to the Crusades, Jews had established communities throughout Europe. These communities tended to remain separate from broader Christian communities. Jews were often seen as outsiders. The Crusades worsened this situation: European Christians came to regard anyone who was not Christian, both Jews and Muslims, as an enemy. During the Third Crusade, anti-Jewish riots broke out in York, the English city that was home to Isaac and Rebecca. This prejudice continued in Scott's day, and well beyond.

Scott shocked some of his readers by including sympathetic Jewish characters. While Isaac conforms to some Jewish stereotypes, primarily by being greedy, he has redeeming qualities in his love for his daughter and his kindness to Ivanhoe. Rebecca is an even more sympathetic character. Throughout, she is depicted as noble, kind, and courageous, and both her trial for witchcraft and the unwanted attentions of de Bois-Guilbert make her a character of great sympathy. Many readers expect that Ivanhoe will marry Rebecca, though such a marriage would have been impossible at the time. Again, the suggestion from Scott is that prejudice against Jews is unjust and religious dogma is less important than character.

Chivalry

The novel's two major heroes, Ivanhoe and King Richard, are brave and chivalrous knights. Chivalry was a code of conduct that knights and others aspired to. It demanded bravery, care for the weak, championship of the good and resistance to evil, loyalty to truth, generosity, and similar virtues. The novel's heroes and heroines exhibit these virtues.

Scott raises questions about the value of chivalry. In one important exchange in Chapter 29, Rebecca says to Ivanhoe, "Alas! and what is it, valiant knight, save an offering of sacrifice to a demon of vain glory . . . ? What remains to you as the prize . . . of all the tears which your deeds have caused?" Ivanhoe defends chivalry by replying, "What remains? Glory, maiden—glory! which gilds our sepulchre and embalms our name." Rebecca scoffs at the notion of glory, but Ivanhoe remains adamant:

> Chivalry! Why, maiden, she is the nurse of pure and high affection, the stay of the oppressed, the redresser of grievances, the curb of the power of the tyrant. Nobility were but an empty name without her, and liberty finds the best protection in her lance and her sword.

Scott questions the value of chivalry by suggesting that King Richard's quest for adventure comes at the expense of his people. And in the novel's climactic scene, Rebecca is saved not by heroic action on Ivanhoe's part but seemingly by fate. Ivanhoe rides in to defend Rebecca in a trial by combat, but he is so exhausted that he falls off his horse. De Bois-Guilbert is defeated not by force of arms but by his own emotions, which lead to his death.

Courtly Love

A theme related to chivalry is courtly love, the rules and conventions that governed intense love between members of the royal class, or those at court. European conventions of courtly love developed in France among poets and troubadours, though they had their origins in Muslim lands during the Crusades. While European Christians to this time had regarded women as a source of temptation into lust, based on the biblical story of Adam and Eve, Muslims regarded women more with a sense of worship. Crusaders brought this notion back from the Holy Land, and the conventions of courtly love were then celebrated in songs and poetry. Chief among these conventions was the knightly lover's belief that his lady-love was a saint, someone beyond reproach, an ideal person.

Many of the characters in *Ivanhoe* regard women as objects for their own desires. This belief is stated by Malvoisin in Chapter 36: "Women are but the toys which amuse our lighter hours." In contrast, de Bracy uses the language of courtly love when he tries to woo Rowena: "Alas! fair Rowena, you are in presence of your captive, not your jailor; and it is from your fair eyes that De Bracy must receive that doom which you fondly expect from him."

Quest

Ivanhoe is structured around three major quests. The first, which occupies roughly the first third of the novel, involves Ivanhoe's return to England in disguise and the jousting tournament at Ashby. The second involves the kidnapping of the Saxons, particularly Rowena, by de Bracy and the efforts of King Richard, aided by Locksley, to free the prisoners from de Bracy's castle. The third involves Rebecca's capture by de Bois-Guilbert, her trial for witchcraft, and Ivanhoe's heroic effort to win her freedom in trial by combat. Typically, the quest theme in literature leads to greater knowledge, wisdom, or self-awareness on the part of the character who engages in the quest. Difficulties are thrown in the hero's way, and in the process of overcoming those difficulties, the hero grows and changes. Although the characters in general, including Ivanhoe, remain fairly static, Scott depicts these quests in the context of social growth and change. The book is not a psychological portrait of characters but rather a portrait of a society that grows and changes through the actions and behaviors of its people. The quests, then, represent aspirations for a more just and equitable social order.

Elizabeth Taylor as Rebecca and Robert Taylor as Ivanhoe in the 1952 film version of the novel (*The Kobal Collection. Reproduced by permission*)

STYLE

Symbolism

One of the chief symbols in *Ivanhoe* is Front-de-Boeuf's castle at Torquilstone. The name of the castle derives from the word *torque*, which comes from the Latin word *torquere*, meaning "twist." This word is also the origin of the word *torture*. Torquilstone symbolizes some of the major themes of the novel. It is a place of corruption and lawlessness, a prison that symbolizes the oppression of Saxon culture by the Normans. It was the site of ancient evils, where Front-de-Boeuf murdered his father and, before that, Front-de-Boeuf's father murdered a Saxon noble and his sons. At the time of the novel, it is where Front-de-Boeuf imprisons the Saxons and threatens to torture Isaac, and where de Bracy tries to woo Rowena and de Bois-Guilbert attempts to subdue Rebecca. At the climax of the Torquilstone sequence, which takes up roughly the middle third of the novel, it seems appropriate that the castle is destroyed by Saxons.

COMPARE & CONTRAST

- **1100s:** Hatred and distrust of non-Christians lead the Europeans to continue the Crusades, the first of which was launched in 1095.

  1800s: Prejudice against Jews is common in Great Britain and throughout Europe. Jews are denied their civil rights.

  Today: Jews are accepted and enjoy full civil rights, but anti-Semitism still runs deep among some Europeans.

- **1100s:** The European traditions of chivalry and courtly love regard women as weak and in need of protection from men.

  1800s: Women in England and Europe are still generally regarded as weak, but Scott and other writers such as Jane Austen are depicting strong female characters.

  Today: While sexism still exists, European women's roles in politics, the professions, and the military are widely accepted.

- **1100s:** The Catholic Church is the dominant social institution throughout Europe, and in many respects it is the dominant political institution as well.

  1800s: Catholics are regarded with suspicion in largely Protestant Great Britain.

  Today: While some anti-Catholic prejudice exists, in general Catholics and Protestant Christians maintain respectful relationships.

If Torquistone represents all that is wrong with England at the time, the forest, home to Locksley and his band of men, stands in stark contrast. In the forest, Locksley leads a society that is ordered and just. Evil takes place in corrupt Norman strongholds such as Torquilstone and later, Templestowe. Good takes place in the forest, a more natural, native setting.

Foreshadowing

Scott uses foreshadowing to great effect. Early in the novel, a palmer appears. The crossed palms he wears indicate that he has made a pilgrimage to the Holy Land. The reader knows that Ivanhoe has been fighting in the Holy Land, so his appearance as a palmer foreshadows the revelation of his return to England. Similarly, he competes in the tournament at Ashby as the Disinherited Knight. The reader knows that Cedric, his father, has disinherited him, so the reader suspects that the knight is Ivanhoe in disguise. Also, King Richard's return to England is anticipated, and feared by such characters as Prince John. The appearance of the Black Knight raises anticipation that Richard has returned to England in disguise.

HISTORICAL CONTEXT

Relations between England and Scotland had long been tumultuous when Scott was born in 1771. Historically, England had dominated Scotland, regarding it as a possession rather than a partner. Throughout the sixteenth and seventeenth centuries, disputes about religion erupted, and many of these disputes continued into the eighteenth century. There was fear in England that Scotland would lead efforts to restore the Stuart line to the British throne. The Stuarts (sometimes spelled Stewarts) were the Scottish royal house that produced nine Scottish kings from 1371 to 1603. That year, James VI of Scotland laid claim to the English throne as James I after his predecessor, Queen Elizabeth I, died childless. Over the next century, England and Scotland were ruled by a total of six Stuart monarchs. In 1701, however, the Act of Settlement established the German Hanoverian line on the British throne, and in 1707 the two countries united in the Act of Union, extinguishing the line of Stuart monarchs. But in 1715 and again in 1745 Jacobite revolts in Scotland (*Jacobite* derives from the Latin version of "James" attempted to restore the descendants of King

Illustration by R. Wheelwright from the 1922 edition of Ivanhoe. *Original caption reads: "A dainty song, said Wamba."* (© Lebrecht Authors / Lebrecht Music and Arts Photo Library / Alamy)

James II of England, who was also King James VII of Scotland. English forces ended these rebellions.

In time, the relationship between England and Scotland became peaceful, but during Scott's life, many Scots looked backward to a more glorious past of Scottish nationalism. Two writers during this period became emblematic of a romantic Scottish past. One, of course, was Sir Walter Scott himself, whose early Scottish novels, including *Waverley*, *Guy Mannering*, *The Antiquary*, and *Rob Roy*, celebrated Scotland's past. The other was Robert Burns (1759–1796), whose poetry, written in Scottish dialect, was enormously popular. Further, both Scott and Burns were responsible for resurrecting Scottish folklore, particularly ballads, folktales, and folk songs. Although the setting of *Ivanhoe* is England, the "Author of Waverley," often referred to as "the Bard of the North," was, and still is, a source of enormous pride in Scotland.

The period from the mid-eighteenth century to the end of Scott's life in 1832 was one of great social upheaval and change. The Industrial Revolution was beginning, breaking down the old feudal agricultural order. The monarchy was overthrown in France with the French Revolution, and revolution created a new nation in America. Old ways of thought about science, religion, politics, and economics were being replaced by new beliefs. Scott lived at a time when old and new clashed—just as Ivanhoe stood in the middle of the clash between Saxon and Norman cultures.

CRITICAL OVERVIEW

The critical reception of *Ivanhoe* has changed over time. Throughout the nineteenth century, critics and literary historians responded with enthusiasm to the novel. The chief review of the novel was written by John Wilson shortly after the book's publication in 1819 and appeared in *Blackwood's* magazine. Wilson referred to the novel's "erudition" and "imaginative genius" and concluded that "never was the illusion of fancy so complete." (quoted in Moulton). In 1879, English novelist Anthony Trollope called *Ivanhoe* "perhaps the most favourite novel in the English language" (quoted in Moulton). Many early critics stressed the romantic adventure depicted in the novel, and in this way it achieved status as a "boy's book." In 1895, for instance, Andrew Lang wrote that "'Ivanhoe' is such a very dear and old friend that no one who has ever been a boy can pretend to apply to it any stern critical tests" (quoted in Moulton). Similarly, Leslie Stephen, writing in 1897, was willing to overlook the novel's flaws: "Its splendid audacity, its vivid presentation of mediaeval life, and the dramatic vigour of the narrative, may atone for palpable anachronisms and melodramatic impossibilities" (quoted in Moulton). (An anachronism is an error in chronology, such as mentioning an object that did not exist at the time.) In 1900, Porter Lander MacClintock too noted the novel's flaws but goes on to say, "In 'Ivanhoe' we breathe the sane and wholesome air of a heroic simple life—the life of objective deeds and sheer accomplishment.... It touches the past with a glow of poetry, lighting up situations, institutions, and men, making real and rich for us those things that in the technical records seem meagre and colorless" (quoted in Moulton).

Throughout much of the twentieth century, critics were not as kind to Scott in general and *Ivanhoe* in particular. Many critics were dismissive of the novel's romantic adventurism, in effect turning grounds of praise in the nineteenth century into grounds for disapproval. Such disapproval actually began with Mark Twain's 1883 *Life on the Mississippi*, where he writes:

> Then comes Sir Walter Scott with his enchantments, and by his single might checks this wave of progress, and even turns it back; sets the world in love with dreams and phantoms; with decayed and swinish forms of religion; with decayed and degraded systems of government; with the sillinesses and emptinesses, sham grandeurs, sham gauds, and sham chivalries of a brainless and worthless long-vanished society.

Twain even went on to blame Scott for the romantic-adventure mind-set that led the American South into the Civil War. In 1927, Herbert Grierson wrote in *Sir Walter Scott*, "The only interesting thread in the story of *Ivanhoe* is found in the fortunes and character of Rebecca and the Templar; the rest is 'tushery' and fun for boys." "Tushery" refers to writing that is of poor quality and marked by the overly self-conscious use of archaic words. It implies that the novel is fluff, not substantive. Similarly, in 1952 Alexander Gray remarked in *Sir Walter Scott* that *Ivanhoe* "has something of the unreality of a boy's adventure tale." Indeed, throughout much of the early part of the twentieth century, *Ivanhoe* was virtually ignored by critics; many studies of Scott focused on other novels, often barely mentioning *Ivanhoe*, which was dismissed as an adventure tale. Some critics who did examine the novel rejected the notion that it was chivalric and instead focused on its *anti*chivalric aspects. In *Scott's Novels*, for instance, Francis R. Hart wrote, "For generations of juvenile enthusiasts it was easy to see in *Ivanhoe* only the quintessence of chivalric adventure. The critical reader now finds it difficult to account for such blinders. Recently we have been reminded of the book's stringently anti-chivalric attitude." In a similar vein, Bruce Beiderwell, in *Power and Punishment in Scott's Novels*, faulted *Ivanhoe* for a "nostalgic medievalism" that undermines the novel's themes of justice and retribution.

Recent critics have taken a more detached approach to the novel, focusing on its themes,

> BRITISH AUTHORS CELEBRATED THE 'MERRY ENGLAND' OF THE PAST THAT SCOTT REFERS TO IN THE OPENING SENTENCE OF *IVANHOE*, WITH ITS FORESTS, GLADES, AND STANDS OF ANCIENT OAKS."

structure, imagery, and similar literary qualities. Paul J. deGategno, in *Ivanhoe: The Mask of Chivalry*, wrote:

> The spell of *Ivanhoe* becomes more evident when one accepts it as a projection of moral righteousness, an expression of how good art can rise above the merely ornamental, devising and refining an equitable system of change for the culture.

Similarly, John Lauber, in *Sir Walter Scott*, directed the reader's attention to the way in which *Ivanhoe* reflects cultural concerns at the time Scott wrote it: "Inevitably, then, *Ivanhoe* incorporates not only the language but the ideology—the racial, sexual, and historical myths and stereotypes—of the early nineteenth century."

CRITICISM

Michael J. O'Neal

O'Neal holds a Ph.D. in English literature. In this essay on Ivanhoe, *he discusses the ways in which the novel embodies some of the principles of the literary movement called Romanticism.*

Romanticism was a highly complex literary and artistic movement that began roughly in the mid-eighteenth century and reached its full flowering in the early decades of the nineteenth century. Literary historians usually distinguish between the Romantic movement or Romanticism and a more generic "romanticism" that can be found in later literature, including that written in the twenty-first century.

Defining Romanticism has been a challenge for generations of scholars, for the artists whose work embodied Romantic themes and ideals—most of them poets, including William Wordsworth, Samuel Taylor Coleridge, Percy Shelley, and John Keats—were a diverse group of

WHAT DO I READ NEXT?

- Sir Walter Scott's *The Talisman* (1825) is a novel of adventure set in the Third Crusade and features the chivalric conflict between Richard the Lion-Hearted and his Muslim counterpart, Saladin.

- Geoffrey Trease's *Bows Against the Barons*, first published in 1934 (but with new editions in 1948, 1966, and 2004), is a young-adult retelling of the Robin Hood legend from the point of view of the novel's sixteen-year-old protagonist, who joins Robin Hood and his band of outlaws.

- Esther Friesner's *The Sherwood Game* (1994) retells the Robin Hood legends through the story of a computer programmer who fulfills his dream of being a hero in the realm of artificial intelligence.

- Susanna Gregory, writing under the pen name Simon Beaufort, is the author of *A Head for Poisoning* (1999), a medieval murder mystery whose main character, like King Richard I, has just returned to Britain from the Crusades.

- Walter Noble Burns's *The Robin Hood of El Dorado: The Saga of Joaquin Murrieta, Famous Outlaw of California's Age of Gold*, first published in 1932 against the backdrop of the Great Depression and reissued in 1999, tells the story of a Hispanic social rebel at the time of the California Gold Rush.

- Michael J. O'Neal's *The Crusades: Almanac*, published in 2005, is a nonfiction introduction to the Crusades. Chapter 8 focuses on the position of Jews during the Crusades. Chapter 9 focuses on knighthood and the traditions of chivalry.

writers. Despite the difficulties, certain common characteristics can be identified, and a number of these commonalities can be found in Scott's work, including *Ivanhoe*, whose full title at the time of publication was *Ivanhoe: A Romance*.

One characteristic of Romanticism that scholars agree on is that it was a reaction to the Classicism of the work that preceded it. Classicism, so called because it was modeled on the classics of ancient Greece and Rome, valued such characteristics as order, structure, unity, and calm. Much of the literature produced during the Neoclassical period that preceded Romanticism was highly intellectual and relied on precisely defined formal structures.

Romantic literature, in contrast, was less ordered and structured. It was marked by a kind of wildness, with free rein given to the author's imagination. If Neoclassical literature was rational and sober, Romantic literature valued the irrational and the emotional. *Ivanhoe* overflows with this type of Romantic excess. It is peopled with characters from all walks of life, from King Richard I to Gurth the swineherd and Wamba, the jester; with commoners, villains, outlaws, knights, peasants, farmers, soldiers, priests—the entire range of medieval society, all driven by their passions and desires, whether for good or ill, and all speaking in their unique voices. The novel is packed less with rational wisdom than with sentimentalism, primitivism, a love of nature, and feats of derring-do. While Neoclassicists wrote about mankind in the abstract, Romantics wrote about men and women in particular. Neoclassicists wrote about the universal; Romantics wrote about the particular and the idiosyncratic.

A second feature that scholars of the Romantic movement agree on is that it often directed its attention to the medieval period, the so-called Dark Ages that ran from the fall of the Roman Empire to, roughly, the fourteenth or fifteenth century. The period of the Crusades, from the last decade of the eleventh century to the last decade of the thirteenth, represented a high point of medieval life. Romantic authors, particularly in Great Britain, reveled in the island's past. They valued the picturesque and the antique. They recreated medieval castles and ruins, moss-covered priories and monasteries, and ancient feudal architecture. British authors celebrated the "merry England" of the past that Scott refers to in the opening sentence of *Ivanhoe*, with its forests, glades, and stands of ancient oaks. All of this—the chivalric knights in shining armor, the jousting and feats of heroism, the beautiful damsels, the castles, the medieval church—were recreated through the lenses of sentimentalism and nostalgia. Among Scottish writers such as Scott, one of the goals of this effort was to assert Scottish nationalism. Scotland, these writers seem to say, is not an appendage of England but rather a nation with its own history and culture, one reflected in its folk tales, songs, ballads, and poetry, all suffused with heroism and adventure. Thus, Scott, along with many of his contemporaries, took great interest in finding and preserving Scotland's folk literature.

Scott, however, was no mere imitator of other Romantic writers. It is true that he combined some of the strands of Romanticism that preceded him. He drew on novels of sentiment published in the late 1700s. Scott admired the fiction of Ann Radcliffe and Monk Lewis, who wrote Gothic novels filled with moldy castles, mysterious villains, and extended passages celebrating the sublimity of nature. Most importantly, he reveled in the tales and ballads of adventure from the Scottish Highlands. Yet he was not a slave to history. He freely ignored or altered historical fact to suit the demands of his stories. More importantly, novels such as *Ivanhoe* were not just costume dramas. As Russell Noyes points out in *English Romantic Poetry and Prose*:

> Beneath the borrowed garments and trappings of other times and climes, his characters are true flesh and blood. Scott in fact created a new synthesis in fiction. He gathered up the threads of romance . . . and delighted his readers by giving them the same sense of real life as found in the eighteenth-century novelists but with a romantic setting of place and time. . . . Beneath a casing of romance there is a core of realism.

Yet another element of the Romantic temperament bears mentioning. Politics played a role in forging the Romantic movement. The key event was the French Revolution, which erupted in 1789 with the storming of the Bastille prison in Paris and led to the beheading of King Louis XVI, the elimination of aristocratic privilege, and reduction of the power of the church and its hierarchy. Through the ensuing ten years of violence and turmoil, the fundamental social structure of France was overturned. In the Americas, the United States was forged from revolution against Britain. In the British Isles, industrialization was altering the social structure, creating a class of city wage earners at the expense of yeoman farmers and landowners. In England there was widespread discussion about the nation's social-political structure, with

radical (for the time) proposals to extend voting rights to a much larger percentage of the population. Scott, though, was deeply conservative, and it was perhaps his conservative temperament that motivated his desire to recreate and celebrate a picturesque past.

Nevertheless, the spirit of revolt found its way into *Ivanhoe* in such characters as Locksley, or Robin Hood, and his band of "merry men." Robin Hood is a member of the supporting cast in the novel. He and his men form a counterpoint to the corruption and venality of such characters as de Bois-Guilbert and Front-de-Boeuf. As romantic revolutionaries, they do not overthrow the monarchy but work *with* the monarch in the person of King Richard to achieve a more just social order. Their headquarters are in the forests rather than in the castles at Torquilstone and Templestowe, where evil resides and corruption festers. Robin Hood, therefore, represents the superiority of nature over artificial structures of church and government—a point of view that pervades the writing of the Romantics in poetry and prose.

The conclusion of *Ivanhoe*, too, reveals Scott's Romantic temperament. Recall that Rebecca is on trial for witchcraft. In chivalric fashion, she is given hope by the possibility of a champion who will defeat de Bois-Guilbert in a trial by combat. The reader suspects that Ivanhoe will be that hero, and as Ivanhoe arrives on horseback at the Templar stronghold at Templestowe, the reader's expectations are so far fulfilled. However, Ivanhoe does not defeat his adversary by force of arms. Rather, he collapses from his horse in fatigue. Then, the modern reader is likely to be astonished by de Bois-Guilbert's death—not from a home thrust from Ivanhoe's lance or sword but from his intense emotions. This type of ending would likely not have been possible during any era other than the Romantic era. Readers at the time found the ending plausible, for it was an example of the Romantic emphasis on the power of emotion. De Bois-Guilbert is allowed to die a good death, for his genuine love for Rebecca mitigates to some degree the villainy of his character.

Although it is difficult to attach precise dates to literary movements and styles, Sir Walter Scott's death in 1832—not the death of any of the great English Romantic poets—has conventionally been used to mark the end of the Romantic movement. In this small way, literary

IN REBECCA, A NEXUS OF JEWISH AND CHRISTIAN CONCEPTIONS OF INHERITANCE CONVERGE AND CONFLICT."

historians give recognition to the firm stamp that Scott placed on the Romantic movement.

Source: Michael J. O'Neal, Critical Essay on *Ivanhoe*, in *Novels for Students*, Gale, Cengage Learning, 2010.

Judith Lewin

In the following essay, Lewin suggests that in Ivanhoe *Rebecca exemplifies the tension between conflicting Jewish and Christian notions of inheritance.*

In *Ivanhoe*, Walter Scott makes frequent use of the trope of heritage and inheritance. What inheritance and heritage mean to Jews and what they mean to the British frames one of the key tensions in the novel. Matrilineal, Jewish, sanguinary inheritance is at odds with the concept of patrilineal, Christian, nationalistic inheritance of "real property"; the two systems represent irreconcilable ways of thinking. The incompatibility of the two cultural conceptions of inheritance and the impossibility of their reconciliation is located, as I argue, in the figure of the Jewish woman, Rebecca. In this article, I read inheritance both figuratively and literally, in terms of literary inheritance or intertextuality, and inheritance based on land or blood.

I. INHERITANCE AS INTERTEXT

During the penultimate scene of *Ivanhoe*, the Jewess Rebecca offers a gift to the Saxon Rowena, who has just married the eponymous hero. The gift is symbolic—a silver casket containing diamond earrings—and the dialogue surrounding its exchange raises questions of conversion. Rebecca requests that her gift be accepted:

> "One, the most trifling part of my duty, remains undischarged. Accept this casket—startle not at its contents."

Rowena opened the small silver-chased casket, and perceived a carcanet, or necklace, with ear-jewels, of diamonds, which were visibly of immense value.

"It is impossible." [. . .]

"Yet keep it, Lady," returned Rebecca.—"You have power, rank, command, influence; we [Jews] have wealth, the source alike of our strength and weakness. [. . .] Think ye that I prize these sparkling fragments of stone above my liberty? or that my father values them in comparison to the honour of his only child? Accept them, lady—to me they are valueless. I will never wear jewels more."

"You are then unhappy," said Rowena. [. . .] "O, remain with us—the counsel of holy men will wean you from your unhappy law, and I will be a sister to you."

"No, lady. [. . .] that may not be."

Rebecca renounces her jewelry in a symbolic, covertly Christian conversion, yet rejects Rowena's offer to "wean [her] from [her] unhappy law," meaning an overt religious conversion to Christianity. The resolution of Scott's novel for Rebecca is one of redemptive resignation; symbolically converted through her renunciation of materialism (and thereby removed from its taint), she is redeemed by remaining faithful to her religion, father, and race.

Consider, however, the gift's container: a "silver-chased casket." Readers may recognize in this casket a reference to Shakespeare's *The Merchant of Venice*. Allusions to this play abound in *Ivanhoe*; they are most obvious in the chapter epigraphs that precede Rebecca's father's first appearance (chaps. 5 and 6). This allusion, however, points specifically to the Jew's daughter, Jessica, and is therefore intimately tied to Rebecca. Jessica betrays her father, Shylock, runs away with her lover, converts, and robs her father's house of jewels and money by carrying them away in a casket. Rebecca's behavior is precisely the opposite: she gives away the casket and jewels, accompanies her father into exile, and abandons her love and her country. Furthermore, Rebecca asserts not only her difference from Jessica, the materialist traitor, but also her father's difference from Shylock when she says, "'Think ye that I prize these sparkling fragments [. . .]? or that my father values them in comparison to the honour of his only child?'" This remark directly recalls and distances them from Shylock's famous remark, "'My daughter—O my ducats!'" The jewels' casket offered Rowena is silver, which recalls another aspect of *The Merchant of Venice:* the choice of the three caskets. In the play, the silver casket is engraved with the motto, "Who chooseth me shall get as much as he deserves" (II, 9). The choice of the silver casket is the choice of fools who argue that birth, property, command, and honor deserve the rewards of marriage and riches. Rowena's acceptance of this girl, in that she already possesses "power, rank, command, [and] influence," transposes the taint of the casket and the earrings onto her as a sign of worldliness. This allusion casts a skeptical shadow on the marriage of Ivanhoe and Rowena. By confronting and separating both the Jewish father and daughter from earlier, negative models and shifting his skepticism to the choices of his Christian characters, Scott effectively subverts his intertextual inheritance.

Scott and his characters confront an intertextual inheritance that Rebecca renounces through her final divestiture. Inheritance in this figurative sense refers to the absolute power of intertext, as suggested by the enormous weight exerted by Jessica and Shylock on the characters, gestures, speeches, and allusions in Scott's text. This disinheritance can be seen as paradoxical; it suggests not only a liberation (from Shakespearean prototypes) but, also, a literary disenfranchisement. In the final scene of the novel, Rebecca "divests" herself of her jewels (and Jewishness), of her dowry (and aspirations of marriage), of her personal wealth ("the source alike of our strength and weakness"), and, in a sense, of the baggage, or "literary property" of her precursor, Jessica. This figurative type of inheritance—inheritance as literary precedent—is the first of several manifestations of inheritance questions linked to Rebecca.

II. INHERITANCE AS LAND

Property is an issue central to the novel. Ivanhoe, the name that serves as the novel's title, is not only the name of the hero (in fact, this is only his name at the very end of the novel) but, also, the name of a disputed estate (Vanden Bossche 63). One common form of property is land, referred to as positive property, or "real property." Land, transmitted between fathers and sons, is a privileged possession, an idealized English inheritance that attaches one directly to a place and is also, therefore, the foundation for the concept of "a nation" associated with a specific place. Disinheritance, therefore, with regard to land, is emblematized in the novel as deracination.

In his first public appearance, Ivanhoe appropriates the theme of disinheritance by appearing in the lists bearing a shield with the Spanish motto "El Desdichado" and the emblem of an uprooted oak. Scott's own translation of the motto within the text is "Disinherited Knight," whereas the term actually means the unhappy or unfortunate one. The mistranslation of the term "disinherited" indicates the importance of inheritance, and what is more, the use of the uprooted oak as a device explicitly links disinheritance to the land. Kenneth Sroka has argued that the romance plot in *Ivanhoe* pits the "green world against the castle." Whereas the yeomen, the Saxons, and even King Richard (who uses an immense oak as a flank of defense when attacked in the forest) are at home in the green world, "the Norman castle-dwellers" are associated with the "desecration of the venerable oak" Therefore, the shield's emblem signifies Cedric's unjust disinheritance of his son, Wilfred, and associates the Saxon in "this single instance [. . .] with the Norman abusers of the oak" (Sroka 646–48). The uprooted oak, in its unnatural and inverted state, may also be related to the reversal of a knight's coat of arms, a sign of dishonor; when the Templar Knight Brian de Bois-Guilbert attempts to woo Rebecca, he swears at one point on his honor, stating that should he be found lying, "'May [his] arms be reversed.'" Therefore, the uprooted oak as a herald for the unnamed knight-errant combines many significations—dishonor, disinheritance, deracination—all of which demand remediation. The tree separated from the earth signifies a state of alienation from the land, asserting that, ideally, nature is the most natural inheritance. A "material anchor" in the shape of land guaranteed an individual "leisure, rationality, and virtue [. . .] as part of a natural order" (Pocock 111–12). This suggests an underlying theme of natural rights: inheritance as natural. Civic humanism held that virtue was only guaranteed by real property, that is, land; therefore, a relation based on exchange—such as that of commerce—would be antithetical to virtue. This variant of disinheritance is one of culture, capitalism, and cosmopolitanism, all of which are negatively associated with the Jews. Ironically, Rebecca's divestiture, examined above, partakes of a particularly Christian mode of being: the vow of poverty or renunciation of worldly goods. As an act, it relates to Ivanhoe's assumption of pilgrim's garb. Renunciation, divestiture, and disinheritance unite the heroine, Rebecca, and the hero, Ivanhoe, but it is a link that ultimately, to the chagrin of many a reader, also separates them. Although divestiture creates a parallel between the two figures, their final fates are quite different. Rebecca and Ivanhoe could each carry the shield marked El Desdichado, the Disinherited; this is Ivanhoe's initial state in the novel on his return from the Crusades as a pilgrim, and it is Rebecca's final state when she decides to leave England for safer shores. But, whereas Ivanhoe has a chance to claim his inheritance and found the British nation, Rebecca's inheritance, earned through her admirable resistance to seduction and conversion, is exile.

Isaac and Rebecca are identified with the hero as long as he remains disinherited since they belong to a "disinherited race" (Vanden Bossche 68–69). In fact, as Jews, they are disinherited many times over: traditionally, as homeless wanderers; specifically, as exiles from the Holy Land disputed between Christians and Moslems; and economically, as a displaced culture that, because of persecution, relied on mobility and portable property. In addition to the preceding three forms of disinheritance, Isaac and Rebecca are subjected to a fourth: exile from England. This exile appears as a natural, if uncomfortable, solution for the novel, since it assumes that an adopted homeland is not really a homeland at all, and thereby insures the question of the heritability of national identity against the "Other."

If *Ivanhoe* describes the founding of the British nation and investigates the constitution of national identity, the ideology of nationalism should locate the nation within the homeland. The novel suggests that those who belong to the land—or to whom the land belongs—make up the nation. Through Ivanhoe, Scott expresses a fear that national identity be linked to transmutable, heritable property, that is, a fear that "national identity is a kind of capital that exists in limited amounts and is not reproducible; hence it is vulnerable to appropriation" (Shapiro 22). National identity must be divorced from the idea of capital that can be exchanged, acquired, appropriated and thereby threatened; it must be reassociated instead with the land, or even better, with immutable terms like blood. Alexander Welsh makes clear the distinction between real property—possessed, preferred, and inherited by the fair hero and heroine—and "conveyables." Conveyables

describes the wealth for which the dark heroine no longer has any use; because her possessions are easily transferable as gifts, she gives her wealth away. Real property, however, is not given away; it is bestowed in trust: "Property not only equates itself with reality: it signifies futurity" (Welsh 116, 125). Those who can lay claim to property through inheritance possess the future.

The patriarch of the future, the founder of the nation, is the one who can reclaim his inheritance and maintain his racial integrity while having passed through the crucible of disinheritance. The state of being "El Desdichado"—voluntarily impoverished, renunciative—is ideally Christian. The son (read, both Wilfred of Ivanhoe and Jesus of Nazareth) is disinherited because of his prophetic ability. His inheritance is withheld by the generation of blind fathers (that is, both Cedric and, traditionally, the Jews). This interpretation of Ivanhoe establishes a parallel between Jews and old-time Saxons like Cedric. Both groups are out of date in terms of clothing, religion, and custom, and, therefore, both groups are fixed outside of a history in which they are non-participants. But the "real" Jews are expelled in favor of "ideal" recuperable Jews. The Saxons represent culturally assimilable Jews, with Ivanhoe as their chief success story. His loyalty to Richard and to the Crusades presents an idealized conversion of an assimilable other.

III. INHERITANCE AS BLOOD

The nation excludes the Jews when nationhood is based on an idealized attachment to the land transmitted by blood. If inheritance is also made up of heritage as blood-transmission, is that something from which one can be disinherited? The Jewish woman transmits a different sort of inheritance, in direct tension with the elective or natural inheritance transmitted from (male) citizen to (male) citizen. Rather than the patriarchal and national transmission of land or privilege, the Jewish and female locus transmits life, blood, Jewish identity, racial identity, and even secret knowledge. For example, Rebecca inherits healing techniques and medicines from her ancestor Miriam; however, the fanatical Templars and many of their followers interpret this as a cultural inheritance of mystical "powers," such as witchcraft, magic, satanic and perverse ritual, and incomprehensible language.

Part of Rebecca's Jewish inheritance is an identity inflected by preconceptions and prejudice. During Rebecca's trial, The Templars replace the signs of Rebecca's heritage, her "Oriental garments," with a plain white dress, perhaps preventing any sympathy her heritage, her inherited property, might have inspired from the inherited "prepossessions" of the crowd. [...] When Ivanhoe finally reveals his countenance at Rebecca's trial, he does so not to exchange sympathetic glances with the propertyless Rebecca, but to claim his inheritance, his heritage: "'My name,' said [Ivanhoe], raising his helmet, 'is better known, my lineage more pure, Malvoisin, than thine own. I am Wilfred of Ivanhoe.'" (Mash 58, citing Scott, ed. Wilson 499, 504) Jeffrey Mash catalogues an assortment of markers that make up inheritance in the description above—clothing, prejudice, name, and lineage—not all of which can be classified simply along the axis of autonomy and dependence, and only some of which can be claimed at all by members of a "disinherited race." Rebecca's garments are meant to represent her heritage and be inseparable outward signs of her identity (even if they are separable from her); nevertheless, inheritance is also made up of traditions (even of prejudice), lineage, and what Ivanhoe calls his "name." This type of inheritance remains out of reach of the Jewish woman. In claiming his inheritance, the hero names his land. In claiming his heritage, he unmasks himself to reveal his pure line. In declaring his "name," he claims his honor, which Jews and women, said either to have no honor or to be unable to defend it, are unable to claim at all.

In Rebecca, a nexus of Jewish and Christian conceptions of inheritance converge and conflict. Her Jewish inheritance must remain with her; she inherits prejudice, blood, and healing knowledge from her Jewish ancestors. As a Jewess, she has no access to land as property, to a name other than her father's, or to honor that she can defend without the help of a Christian man. She may, however, divest herself in an eminently Christian way: no more worldly goods, ties or desires. After doubling the exiled, impoverished, crusading pilgrim, Ivanhoe, she finally replaces him in the novel's final scene:

> "Have you then convents, to one of which you mean to retire?" asked Rowena.

"No, lady," said the Jewess; "but among our people [...] have been women who have devoted their thoughts to Heaven, and their actions to works of kindness to men, tending the sick, feeding the hungry, and relieving the distressed. Among these will Rebecca be numbered."

> WITH HIS IMMENSE POWER, HIS MORAL PERFECTION, AND HIS DEMOCRATIC SPIRIT, THE ROBIN HOOD OF *IVANHOE* DOES HAVE THE MANNERS AND SENTIMENTS TO MAKE HIM ALIVE IN THE MINDS OF SCOTT'S READERS."

Source: Judith Lewin, "Jewish Heritage and Secular Inheritance in Walter Scott's *Ivanhoe*," in *ANQ*, Vol. 19, No. 1, Winter 2006, p. 27.

William E. Simeone

In the following essay, Simeone explores the appeal of Robin Hood to Scott's readers.

In the dedicatory epistle to Dr. Jonas Dryasdust, Sir Walter Scott said that "The Kendal green...ought surely to be as dear to our feelings, as the variegated tartans of the north. The name of Robin Hood, if duly conjured with, should raise a spirit as soon as that of Rob Roy; and the patriots of England deserve no less their renown in our modern circles." Scott duly conjured, and, in *Ivanhoe*, raised a lively spirit of England's traditional hero who had not appeared in the national literature since the seventeenth century. Eighteenth century antiquarians such as Percy and especially Ritson had collected practically all of the information known about the outlaw hero, and their work prepared the way for Scott, whose novel opened a new cycle of Robin Hood fiction in the nineteenth century.

Tradition offered Scott a number of persons under the name of Robin Hood. To cite just three, there was the killer in the ballad of "Robin Hood and Guy of Gisborne," or the seaman in "The Noble Fisherman, or Robin Hood's Preferment," or the dancing partner of the Marian in the Morris Dance. Scott took none of these. From the abundance of tradition, he abstracted a figure of the hero as an outlaw archer who, after a series of adventures, makes peace with the king. Most of the Robin Hood of *Ivanhoe* Scott invented, and it is an invention made to be congenial to the sensibilities of his readers.

Scott said that the characters of his novel had manners and sentiments common to most Englishmen because he had them occupy "that extensive neutral ground, the large proportion, that is, of manners and sentiments which are common to us and to our ancestors, having been handed down unaltered from them to us, or which, arising out of the principles of our common nature, must have existed alike in either state of society." Scott made certain that under their medieval trappings, his characters were not very different from himself and his readers. The medieval trappings satisfied that interest that sent people into museums to see the artifacts of the past. But Scott knew that he could not be satisfied with a book full of artifacts. To make his reconstruction of the past alive, he had to animate his characters with manners and sentiments understood by his contemporaries. When Scott speaks of manners and sentiments being handed down unaltered or arising from the principles of our common nature, he means that his novel is an historical reconstruction of twelfth century England in the spiritual image of the nineteenth.

In this twelfth century setting, Scott reconstructed the traditional hero into the figure of a deliverer; he is an ancestral hero of superhuman power used to deliver the English people from the misrule of evil men. Resisting this misrule, perpetrated chiefly by foreigners, many men have been driven to become outlaws. The mission of the chief outlaw is to crush tyranny and to restore law and order to the unhappy country. But his mission is not just an isolated episode in the remote past. It is instead the opening chapter of the long history of the English people to wrest their liberties from tyrants. When Scott presented Robin Hood as a yeoman, as well as an outcast, he intended to show that from the beginning of the national history, ordinary men had an important role to play in the making of the nation. Scott does not speak of a dialectic of history, but his novel dramatizes an idea of history in which the lowest in the social order are as important as the highest.

In *Ivanhoe*, Robin Hood is always immersed in vital activity through which we can see the figure of the deliverer. But the figure is also defined in part by what Scott excluded from his reconstruction of it. Scott's is one of the few literary uses of the Robin Hood matter that does not make the outlaw the lover of Maid Marian. His hero is celibate. Moreover, he has no family connections. He is not distracted from his mission in the novel by any need to clear his family's name or to regain lands and a title. An outcast with no attachments to distract him, the Robin Hood of *Ivanhoe* can concentrate completely on the great mission he has in the novel, the deliverance of his country.

Robin Hood's deliverance of the country begins with a test of arms, extends through several acts of saving good people from bad situations, and ends with his feast with the king in the forest. He appears in *Ivanhoe* some time after the novel has begun. While no one has prepared the way for him, there is, before his appearance, a description of the deplorable state of the country and its citizens in the absence of King Richard and the regency of Prince John. While the King has been away, hostility has flared between the Norman conquerors, or their descendants, and the Saxon natives. The King's brother John and his marauding Norman cohorts have made no man's life or property safe. As Scott describes England, lay and clerical villains have turned it into a lawless country for their pleasure and profit. But with the coming of Robin Hood, the villains responsible for this disorder will meet a man from the people who will destroy them and restore the kingdom to its former health.

The occasion marking Robin Hood's arrival is the sport for the yeomanry following the tournament at Ashby. An unknown yeoman who calls himself Locksley turns up to take part in the shooting match. A mysterious person whom no one seems to know, he irritates his social superiors by his confident manner. He is only a yeoman; yet, he has a princely bearing and a choleric disposition, "a stout well-set yeoman, arrayed in Lincoln-green, having twelve arrows stuck in his belt, with a baldric and badge of silver, and a bow of six feet length in his hand ... his countenance, which his constant exposure to weather had rendered brown as a hazel nut, grew dark with anger." At this point, no one in the crowd knows what vast and unlikely power he has.

The stuff of many a ballad, the archery contest in *Ivanhoe* dramatizes the overwhelming superiority of the outlaw hero. "This must be the devil, and no man of flesh and blood," whispered the yeomen to each other; "such archery was never seen since a bow was first bent in Britain." In the same way, Robin Hood awes Prince John, who forgets his former annoyance with the archer to offer him a place among his soldiers. The result of this demonstration illustrates a superiority so complete that it lifts the yeoman out of the realm of ordinary mortals.

England, as Scott describes it, is ready for a deliverer. Just about everywhere in the chaotic country there are good people needing his help, and his appearance means the performance of a near miracle. There are several examples of such miraculous acts. One of them is the attack on the castle of Torquilstone, where the villains of the novel are besieged. Cedric the Saxon, the acknowledged chief of his people, declines to lead the attack on the castle gate. The outcast hero does not decline. He leads it successfully, and during the attack, manages to save the lives of Cedric and the disguised King Richard. He awes the soldiers defending the castle. "The men-at-arms were daunted, for no armour seemed proof against the shot of this tremendous archer." After Torquilstone has burned, Robin Hood's role as deliverer is still unfinished. When the King is attacked by Waldemar Fitzurse, the outlaw steps out of the forest to save him from a certain death. Now Robin Hood, who has acted through the novel more like the king of the English than the King himself, tells Richard who he is. Richard has already revealed his identity to the outlaw. With these revelations, the outlaw's role as deliverer is all but finished.

What is left is a ceremonial feast in which the King and his people are brought together. Again in the hands of its rightful master, the kingdom is restored to sound health. And eating together symbolizes the renewed oneness of the dominions of the King of the England and the king of outlaws. Whatever wrongs are implicit in the outlaws' acts the King forgives. "Your misdemeanours, whether in forest or field," the King has already remarked to Robin Hood, "have been atoned by the loyal services you rendered my distressed subjects before the walls of Torquilstone, and the rescue you have this day afforded to your sovereign."

For all of his services, Robin Hood asks for no reward for himself alone. Such selflessness reflects the Romantic idea of the nobility of the common man, personified here by the yeoman outlaw, but I think that it is also an attitude befitting the deliverer, acting through sympathy for and with people less able than he to improve upon an uncongenial world. An ordinary man could be expected to demand reward of a value proportionate to his services. But Robin Hood's reward is the noble one of having almost by his hand alone alleviated the sufferings of an oppressed people. His efforts, resulting in the harmony of Sherwood Forest, produce the nearest thing to an Eden that Scott probably could commit himself to, and this harmony is all the reward the deliverer of his country would want. Moreover, he can ask nothing of a world he has been instrumental in making. Scott mentions the death of the outlaw by betrayal, an ironic but not unusual reward for a deliverer, but this is not a part of the novel.

Robin Hood's deliverance of the country is successful because he has a massive personal power which he demonstrates for the first time at Ashby. But this power is braced by still more power whose source is the anonymous mass of common people. The power of the people, as it sustains the outlaw hero, is represented by a band of fiercely devoted men, and he emerges in the novel as a popular hero speaking and acting for the usually inarticulate and abused mass of people. In concert, they have the power and the privilege to redress their grievances. They make it clear that the chronicle of history is not the exclusive game of aristocrats and that the people are no longer a mob to be shunned or swayed.

In this game, the people have opponents. Scott does not make the opposition a class of society; he dramatizes it as a struggle between good and evil men. And in *Ivanhoe*, there are plenty of evil men. Judged by Scott's version, the history of the reign of Richard Lion Heart was a dark age full of the misdeeds of lay and clerical villains. Among them, Robin Hood is a light in the gloom.

The idea of Robin Hood as light in the gloom of history was not new with Scott. Ritson had expressed it with characteristic violence in the preface to his edition of the Robin Hood ballads. A Jacobin, Ritson described the traditional hero as a militant man of the people, a medieval Thomas Paine: "a man who, in a barbarous age, and under a complicated tyranny, displayed a freedom and independence which has endeared him to the common people, whose cause he maintained (for all opposition to tyranny is the cause of the people), and, in spite of the malicious endeavours of pitiful monks, by whom history was consecrated to the crimes and follies of titled ruffians and sainted idiots, to suppress all record of his patriotic exertions and virtuous acts, will render his name immortal."

Scott is not this violent, but his Robin Hood is drawn in the same mold. In nearly every way, he is superior to men of the highest estates of conventional society. Scott goes so far as to give him a moral perfection. This perfection, consistent with the Romantic idea of the natural nobility of the common man, glorifies the people as well as their hero. The King, perhaps thinking of such privileged ruffians as Front-de-Boeuf and Waldemar Fitzurse, praises the unbounded virtue of the low-born hero: "For he that does good, having the unlimited power to do evil, deserves praise not only for the good which he performs, but for the evil which he forbears."

In the exercise of this unlimited goodness, the Robin Hood of *Ivanhoe* is the free and generous spirit Ritson envisioned. His deportment is a paradigm of the admirable qualities of the great man of the people aware of the sinfulness as well as the dignity of all men. When Isaac of York kneels to thank Robin Hood, the benefactor is outraged. "Nay, beshrew thee, man, up with thee! I am English born, and love no such Eastern prostrations—Kneel to God, and not to a poor sinner, like me." Here the outlaw hero's impulses are democratic, but in his natural superiority over other men, he is separated from the very people whose symbol of power and goodness he is. From and of the people, he still finds it difficult to be democratic in practice. Thus, when he takes a seat equal to those of Cedric and Richard, he apologizes to them by saying that his men insist upon this democratic arrangement.

With his immense power, his moral perfection, and his democratic spirit, the Robin Hood of *Ivanhoe* does have the manners and sentiments to make him alive in the minds of Scott's readers. When Scott put Robin Hood into his novel, he knew that the outlaw hero was universally known in a tradition extending back at least as far as the fourteenth century. A thief to some, a foolish idol to others, to Scott and his generation Robin Hood was a hero of the national past. For a generation looking for the beginnings of the nation, Robin Hood became an ancestral hero fighting to establish in England the traditions by which free and democratic Englishmen thought they should be governed. Because these traditions still meet with approval, Scott's Robin Hood remains an image of the traditional hero that has not yet been put to rest.

Source: William E. Simeone, "The Robin Hood of *Ivanhoe*," in *Journal of American Folklore*, Vol. 74, No. 293, July–September 1961, pp. 230–34.

SOURCES

Beiderwell, Bruce, *Power and Punishment in Scott's Novels*, University of Georgia Press, 1992, p. 84.

deGategno, Paul J., *Ivanhoe: The Mask of Chivalry*, Twayne Publishers, 1994, p. 87.

Gray, Alexander, Speech to the Edinburgh Sir Walter Scott Club in 1952, in *Sir Walter Scott, 1771–1832: An Edinburgh Keepsake*, edited by Allan Frazer, Edinburgh University Press, 1971, p. 76.

Grierson, Herbert, Speech to the Edinburgh Sir Walter Scott Club in 1927, in *Sir Walter Scott, 1771–1832: An Edinburgh Keepsake*, edited by Allan Frazer, Edinburgh University Press, 1971, p. 13.

Hart, Francis R., *Scott's Novels: The Plotting of Historic Survival*, University Press of Virginia, 1966, p. 152.

Harvey, Paul, "Scott, Sir Walter," *Oxford Companion to English Literature*, 4th ed., Oxford University Press, 1967, pp. 735–36.

Lauber, John, *Sir Walter Scott*, rev. ed., Twayne Publishers, 1989, p. 99.

Moulton, Charles Wells, ed., *The Library of Literary Criticism of English and American Authors*, Vol. 5, Moulton Publishing, 1902, p. 153.

Noyes, Russell, ed., *English Romantic Poetry and Prose*, Oxford University Press, 1956, pp. xix–xxxiii, 518.

Scott, Walter, *Ivanhoe*, Heritage Press, 1950.

Twain, Mark, *Life on the Mississippi*, in *Mark Twain: Mississippi Writings*, Library of America, 1982, p. 500.

FURTHER READING

Brown, David, *Walter Scott and the Historical Imagination*, Routledge, 1979.

> This volume examines the historical authenticity—or sometimes the lack of historical authenticity—in Scott's Waverley novels, including *Ivanhoe*.

Hull, Anthony, "Walter Scott and Medievalism," in *English Romanticism*, Minerva, 2000, pp. 109–23.

> This essay examines the themes of chivalry, knighthood, and medieval Christianity in four of Scott's novel's, including *Ivanhoe*.

Johnson, Edgar, *Sir Walter Scott: The Great Unknown*, 2 Vols., Hamish Hamilton, 1970.

> This is widely regarded as the standard biography of Sir Walter Scott.

Lincoln, Andrew, *Walter Scott and Modernity*, Edinburgh University Press, 2007.

> Lincoln examines Scott's use of history to explore a range of problems in the modern world, including empire, relations between the West and Islam, and political reform.

Manning, Susan, "Did Mark Twain Bring down the Temple on Scott's Shoulders?" in *Special Relationships: Anglo American Affinities and Antagonisms, 1854–1936*, edited by Janet Beer and Bridget Bennett, Manchester University Press, 2002, pp. 9–27.

> The American writer Mark Twain strongly disliked Scott's novels, and his *A Connecticut Yankee in King Arthur's Court* is regarded as a satire on the type of historical fiction Scott wrote. Manning compares *Ivanhoe* and Twain's novel and explores why Scott's novels fell out of favor in the late nineteenth and early twentieth centuries.

Saul, Nigel, *The Oxford Illustrated History of Medieval England*, Oxford University Press, 2001.

> Saul's volume is a comprehensive introduction to the social, cultural, political history of England during the Middle Ages. The book is lavishly illustrated.

Sutherland, John A., *The Life of Sir Walter Scott: A Critical Biography*, Wiley-Blackwell, 1998.

> Sutherland's biography is often read as a counterpoint to Edgar Johnson's *Sir Walter Scott: The Great Unknown*. While Johnson is more laudatory, Sutherland is more critical. The biography traces the themes of Scott's novels to events in the author's life.

The Namesake

JHUMPA LAHIRI

2003

Jhumpa Lahiri's second book, *The Namesake*, was published in the United States in 2003. The book was well received by critics and highly anticipated. This anticipation was based on Lahiri's first book, the Pulitzer prize-winning collection of short stories titled *Interpreter of Maladies*. Like its predecessor, *The Namesake* explores issues of the Indian American immigrant experience and the corresponding anxieties of assimilation (conforming) and exile. From these themes of dual nationality, the question of identity arises, and this theme is further underscored by the main character's dual names. The strength of familial bonds in the midst of this cultural quandary is also addressed.

To this end, *The Namesake* portrays the Ganguli family over a course of thirty-two years. It follows Ashoke and Ashima Ganguli from shortly after their emigration from Calcutta, India, to Cambridge, Massachusetts, in the late 1960s. The story then follows the couple as their children are born and raised in the United States. It is their struggles, particularly those of the eldest son, Gogol, that comprise the bulk of the story. Notably, the novel's deft and sensitive handling of the immigrant experience has caused it to be featured in school curriculums throughout the United States.

Jhumpa Lahiri (AP Images)

AUTHOR BIOGRAPHY

Jhumpa Lahiri was born Nilanjana Sudeshna Lahiri in London, England, on July 11, 1967. However, she was raised in South Kingstown, Rhode Island. (The name under which Lahiri lives and writes was in fact a nickname bestowed upon her by a grade-school teacher). Lahiri is the eldest daughter of Amar K. Lahiri, a professor at the University of Rhode Island, and Tapati Lahiri, a teacher. Lahiri began writing stories at a young age, though she did not pursue a writing career while she was in college. Indeed, after earning her B.A. from Barnard College, she intended to continue her graduate studies. However, Lahiri's applications were not initially accepted, and she instead began working as a research assistant. It was around this time that she began writing again, before going on to study creative writing at Boston University. At that university, she earned three master's degrees, in English, creative writing, and comparative literature. She also received

her Ph.D. in Renaissance studies there. Then, rather than continue her academic career, Lahiri devoted herself to writing, publishing her work in such periodicals as the *New Yorker* and the *Harvard Review*.

Several of these early stories appear in Lahiri's first book, the 1999 collection *Interpreter of Maladies*. The volume was an instant bestseller, launching Lahiri into the international spotlight. Among several accolades, the collection won the Pulitzer Prize for fiction in 2000. The following year, Lahiri married newspaper editor Alberto Vourvoulias-Bush. (The couple has since had two children.) In 2003, Lahiri released her first novel, *The Namesake*, and in 2008, she published her second collection of short stories, *Unaccustomed Earth*. The latter was awarded the Commonwealth Writers' Prize in 2009. Indeed, with so few books to her credit, Lahiri's fame and renown are remarkable. Her work has been read the world over, and it is best known for its autobiographical nature, largely reflecting Lahiri's own Indian American heritage.

PLOT SUMMARY

1.

1968

Ashima Ganguli is nearly nine months pregnant with her first child. She is in her apartment in Cambridge, Massachusetts. Her husband, Ashoke, is studying for his doctorate in engineering in the next room. Ashima's labor begins, and the couple takes a taxi to the hospital. After Ashima has checked in, Ashoke leaves her there and promises to return. Ashima has been in the United States for a year and a half, leaving Calcutta immediately following her arranged marriage to Ashoke. Alone at the hospital, Ashima is afraid to raise her child in America. By four o'clock the following morning, Ashima has reached the final stages of her labor, and Ashoke returns to the hospital, where he sits in the waiting room.

He paces and thinks of the fateful train accident that has brought him to this moment. As an undergraduate student in India, Ashoke had been on a train on his way to visit his grandfather. There, he met a businessman who had traveled the world, returning to India only because his wife was homesick. The man told Ashoke that returning was his greatest regret, and he urged Ashoke

MEDIA ADAPTATIONS

- An unabridged audio adaptation of *The Namesake*, narrated by Sarita Choudhury, was released by Random House in 2003.
- *The Namesake* was adapted as a film with the same title in 2006. Directed by Mira Nair and produced by Fox Searchlight, this fairly literal adaptation is widely available on DVD.

to travel. Shortly afterward, while Ashoke was rereading Nikolai Gogol's "The Overcoat," a favorite short story by his favorite author, the train crashed. The businessman beside him was killed, and Ashoke lay immobile in the wreckage with the torn and crumpled pages of his book. When the rescuers arrived, they noticed him only because the pages were moving in the breeze. It was a year before he was able to walk again, and during his long recovery, Ashoke thought constantly of the businessman's advice. Seven years have passed and he still credits Nikolai Gogol for saving his life.

2.

The baby is a boy. All of the Bengali friends Ashima and Ashoke have made gather at the hospital to greet him. The baby has not been named because the Gangulis are waiting for a letter from Ashima's grandmother. The letter contains the names she has picked for her grandchild, one for a boy and one for a girl. The letter was sent over a month ago, but it still has not arrived. After three days in the hospital, Ashima and the baby are ready to go home, but they must fill out the birth certificate and choose a name before leaving. They name the baby Gogol as an homage to Ashoke's life-changing accident. The name will be a pet name, they decide, a practice common in India. Both Ashoke and Ashima have pet names. In school, at work, and in public, they are addressed by their formal names, but at home, family members call one another by their pet names. Unfortunately, the

letter never arrives. Ashima's grandmother has had a stroke, and Gogol's intended formal name has been irrevocably lost.

At first, Ashima struggles with motherhood. She is tired, sad, and homesick. However, she soon adjusts to her new routine, enjoying her renewed purpose and the attention of strangers who stop to talk to her and admire the baby. When Gogol is six months old, the Gangulis invite their Bengali friends over for his *annaprasan*, a ceremony in which Gogol is fed his first solid food. In addition, he is presented with a dollar, a pen, and soil. Whichever the baby chooses will foretell his career as either a businessman, a scholar, or a landowner. Gogol refuses all three.

3.

1971

The Gangulis have moved to a suburb just outside Boston, Massachusetts. Ashoke is working as an assistant professor at a nearby university. Although Ashoke loves his job, Ashima hates their suburban surroundings. In fact, the move from Cambridge to the suburbs was harder on her than the move from Calcutta to Cambridge. Now that Gogol is almost four years old, he is going to day care a few days a week. Without Gogol to care for, Ashima once again finds herself bored. Two years later, the family buys its first home, a newly built ranch in Pemberton, Massachusetts. The house has not yet been landscaped, and Gogol's earliest memories are of playing in the dirt.

When Gogol is five, Ashima learns she is pregnant. Now that Gogol is about to begin kindergarten, his parents finally choose a formal name for him, Nikhil. This name, too, is chosen in honor of Nikolai Gogol, the author of the short story Ashoke was reading during the accident. Gogol, however, has become accustomed to his pet name, and he does not wish to be called Nikhil. His American teachers do not understand the Indian tradition of pet and formal names; his birth certificate lists his name as Gogol and the boy refuses to answer to Nikhil. Thus, his teachers call him Gogol despite his parents' wishes.

Gogol's sister is born the following May. His parents name her Sonali, forgoing the pet and formal names because of the confusion they have caused for Gogol. Her name eventually becomes shortened to the more Americanized "Sonia." At her annaprasan, Sonia chooses the dirt and tries to eat the dollar bill. A guest at the party laughs and says, "This one is the true American."

The years go by. Ashoke is tenured and both sets of parents in India pass away one by one. Although the family visits Calcutta every few years, they have become more and more Americanized, even celebrating Easter and Christmas. The children prefer American food to Indian food. Gogol even resents taking classes in Bengali language and culture because he would rather be at his drawing class.

4.

1982

It is Gogol's fourteenth birthday. His family throws an American birthday party for him and his school friends and then a Bengali party for the family's friends. After the second party, Ashoke gives Gogol a book of Nikolai Gogol's short stories. It is the first gift the boy has ever received directly from his father (all the others having been picked by Ashima and given in Ashoke's name). Gogol feigns interest, but he has long since grown to hate his name and namesake. He resents its oddity, neither Bengali nor American. He does not know the story behind his name. In fact, Ashoke is about to tell his son the story, but something about Gogol's reticence makes him hesitate. After Ashoke leaves the room, Gogol sets the book on a shelf without even opening it.

A year later, Ashoke is up for sabbatical from his university position, and the family decides to take an extended trip to India, a trip both Gogol and Sonia resent. For them, America is their home, not Calcutta. For their parents, it is the reverse. After they return, Gogol's junior year of high school commences and he studies his namesake in English class. Though he is supposed to read "The Overcoat," Gogol does not do so. "To read the story, he believes, would mean paying tribute to his namesake, accepting it somehow." As high school wears on, Gogol does well, though he occasionally sneaks out with his friends to go to concerts in Boston. On one such outing, he attends a college party. He meets a girl there but dreads telling her his name; once again having to face the usual questions that arise from its telling. This time, he says his name is Nikhil. She comments that Nikhil is a beautiful name, and the two kiss before the night is out.

5.

Gogol is now eighteen and about to attend Yale University, a prestigious school in New Haven, Connecticut. Before doing so, he goes to the courthouse alone and has his name legally changed to Nikhil. His parents begrudgingly accept their son's decision. Gogol tells the judge that he hates his current name, that he's "always hated it." Despite his name change, everyone he knows continues to call him Gogol. It is not until he begins his new semester at Yale that he truly comes into his own as Nikhil. Nevertheless, it takes a long time for him to "feel like Nikhil." His dual names—one at school, one at home—make him feel as if "he's cast himself in a play acting the part of twins." Stranger still is when his parents visit him at school and call him Nikhil. However, when his mother forgets and calls him Gogol, her mistake also feels strange. Gogol "feels helpless, annoyed . . . caught in the mess he's made."

Gogol begins to feel more at home at school than in Pemberton. He continues to draw and begins sketching buildings, ultimately majoring in architecture. Headed home for Thanksgiving on the train during his sophomore year, Gogol meets Ruth, another Yale student. They fall in love, but Gogol does not mention her to his parents. After a year has gone by, Gogol has met Ruth's parents and been accepted by them. Ruth has not met Ashoke and Ashima. Even though Gogol's parents have since become aware of the relationship, they disapprove of it. Later, Ruth spends a year studying in England. Although the couple maintains a long-distance relationship, they ultimately grow apart and break up soon after Ruth returns.

For Thanksgiving break of his senior year, Gogol heads home on the train once more. Ashima and Sonia are in India attending a cousin's wedding, so Ashoke will pick Gogol up from the station alone. In Rhode Island, someone commits suicide by jumping in front of the train, and thus Gogol is late arriving home. Ashoke has been waiting and worrying at the station for several hours. On the drive home, Ashoke finally tells Gogol about the train accident he was in as a young man, about the true meaning of his son's name. Gogol is shocked but relieved to know the truth. When Gogol asks his father if he is a reminder of the accident, Ashoke replies, "You remind me of everything that followed."

6.

1994

Since graduating from Yale, Gogol has moved to New York City and earned his graduate degree from Columbia University. He has begun working at an architectural firm. One night at a party, he meets Maxine Ratliff. She lives with her parents in a mansion in Chelsea, a neighborhood in New York City (though she has an entire floor of the house to herself). On their first date, they have dinner at the house with Maxine's parents. The family regularly dines on fine food and wine. Their lifestyle embodies an effortless, distinctly American gentility that Gogol aspires to. As he falls in love with Maxine, he also falls in love with her family and their lifestyle.

Eventually, Maxine invites Gogol to move in with her. Gogol often thinks of the vast differences between his family and hers; "he is conscious of the fact that his immersion in Maxine's family is a betrayal of his own." As with Ruth, Gogol waits as long as possible before mentioning Maxine to his parents. He eventually introduces her, and despite Gogol's fears, the visit goes well. Maxine likes his parents and is not embarrassed by their Indian-ness, although Gogol is.

Maxine, her parents, and Gogol enjoy a summer vacation at the Ratliff's lake house in New Hampshire. Again Gogol thinks of how his parents would never fit into the genteel Ratliff family. They celebrate Gogol's twenty-seventh birthday at the lake, inviting the other families who live around the lake. One partygoer makes an ignorant remark about Gogol's heritage. He is forced to remind her and, to his surprise, Maxine's mother that he was born and raised in America. That night, Gogol is surprised that his parents have not called him to wish him a happy birthday, but later he realizes he never gave them the phone number at the lake house and that the number is not listed. Gogol feels relieved by the realization that his family cannot reach him, and that relief makes him think "that here at Maxine's side, in this cloistered wilderness, he is free."

7.

Ashoke is working as a visiting professor in Cleveland, Ohio, but Ashima has chosen to remain in Pemberton. With Sonia having long since moved to California, Ashima, for the first time in her life, is living alone. She does not like it, and she begins working part-time at the library to fill her days. Ashoke flies home for short visits every third weekend. One Sunday afternoon, Ashima is alone preparing the family Christmas cards. Ashoke calls her and says that he has driven himself to the emergency room with a stomachache; his regular doctor's office is closed. He tells her not to worry and says he will call her later.

The hours pass and Ashima grows increasingly worried. She finally calls the hospital and is told that Ashoke has died of a heart attack. Ashima is shocked. In New York, Gogol learns that his mother called while he was out but decides to call her back tomorrow. Then Sonia calls and tells him the news. Gogol flies to Cleveland the next day to retrieve his father's body, and although Maxine offers to go with him, he prefers to go alone. In Cleveland, Gogol also wraps up his father's affairs. He returns to the house in Pemberton a day later.

The surviving Gangulis are often surrounded by their Bengali friends, but they eat a mourner's diet when they are alone. That diet consists of blandly cooked vegetables and lentils. Gogol remembers being annoyed by this ritual when he was younger, but now he clings to it. This marks a major change in Gogol's outlook. On the eleventh day following Ashoke's death, a ceremony is held to mark the end of the mourning period. Maxine also attends. This time, Gogol is not embarrassed by his family or their customs. In fact, her presence there seems odd to him. Maxine wants to know when Gogol will return to the city, and she asks about a vacation they had planned. She says they need to get away, but Gogol says he does not want to escape. This also marks a major change in his outlook.

Throughout that December, Gogol, Sonia, and Ashima live together in the house in Pemberton. Sonia decides to move back from California and attend law school in Boston. Gogol returns to New York on the train, though now he returns home to visit every weekend.

8.

A year after Ashoke's death, Gogol is no longer seeing Maxine; she eventually tired of his growing attachment to his family and her exclusion from that part of his life and is engaged to another man. Gogol continues to visit Pemberton regularly, and Sonia is living with Ashima. Ashima has always been the family chef, but now Sonia now does all the cooking. Ashima has grown frail and listless. Gogol begins taking classes to prepare for his architectural licensing exam. He meets and begins an affair with Bridget, a married woman. It is a cold liaison that does not last long, ending when Gogol begins to feel guilty about the affair.

As time goes by, Ashima nags Gogol about settling down and starting a family. She finally convinces him to go on a date with Moushumi Mazoomdar, the daughter of old family friends. In fact, Gogol and Moushumi attended the same sprawling Bengali parties as children, though they never interacted. She is a doctoral student at New York University. Both are surprised by how well their first date goes, and they agree to meet again. Again to their mutual surprise, they fall in love. Their similar backgrounds bond them; both rejected their heritage, and yet they resented their American lovers for doing the same.

9.

Less than a year after their first date, Moushumi and Gogol plan to marry. Although both would prefer a small American wedding, they give in to their families and have a large Bengali ceremony. Gogol has just turned thirty, and his wedding is another reminder of his father's absence. The couple takes the money they receive as wedding gifts and puts it toward a new apartment.

The two postpone their honeymoon because of Moushumi's teaching schedule, but they travel together to Paris when Moushumi is invited to attend a conference there. She is fluent in French, having lived and studied in Paris, and the inequity between her familiarity with Paris and Gogol's unfamiliarity is starkly apparent. It seems to hint at a chasm between them.

One spring, Gogol and Moushumi are at a dinner party, one of the frequent gatherings held by Moushumi's college friends. Most of her friends are professors, artists, or editors. Gogol does not care for these affairs but goes because Moushumi cares very deeply about them. He knows she wants her life to resemble the lives of her friends (just as Gogol used to wish his family's life resembled the Ratliffs'). The party's hosts are expecting their first child, and the conversation turns to baby names. This has been a recurring conversation at almost every dinner party Gogol and Moushumi have attended lately. Gogol is exceedingly bored by the topic; however, this particular night, Moushumi reveals Gogol's given name to their friends, an act he resents. He tells

the group that he believes children should be allowed to choose their own names when they are eighteen. The other partygoers, and even his wife, stare at Gogol incredulously.

10.

1999

Gogol and Moushumi celebrate their first anniversary. Although Moushumi still loves Gogol, she has become somewhat distant. Their dinner does not go well. Moushumi finds it to be too expensive, too fussy. She leaves hungry and sad.

On her way to teach her last class before completing her doctorate, Moushumi finds herself in the university's mailroom. There, she comes across the résumé of an old flame, Dimitri Desjardins. She writes down his contact information and calls him a week later. They begin an affair, and Mousshumi spends Monday and Wednesday evening with Dimitri before returning to sleep at home with Gogol. Dimitri is middle aged, balding, and unemployed; his apartment is in disarray. Gogol does not suspect a thing.

11.

Moushumi leaves alone for a conference in Palm Beach, Florida, although Gogol would have preferred to join her. She says she will have too much work to do there, but he sees her pack a bathing suit. Gogol works through the weekend, looking forward to Moushumi's return. But he also thinks of the previous week, when he and his wife hosted Thanksgiving dinner. Sonia brought her new boyfriend, Ben, and their love presented a disappointing contrast to Gogol and Moushumi's relationship. Thinking of Moushumi's growing distance, Gogol decides they need a vacation, and he plans a trip to Italy for the coming spring. The trip will be a surprise Christmas gift.

12.

2000

A year later, Ashima is preparing to throw a Christmas party, the last that will be held in the Pemberton house. The house has just been sold, and she plans to spend six months a year in Calcutta with relatives and the other six months in the United States visiting her children and family friends. She has grown into an independent woman, no longer afraid to live and travel alone. Though she has spent over three decades missing India, she knows that she will miss

America. It has become as much a part of her as her birthplace. Sonia and Ben are engaged, and she knows that "he has brought happiness to her daughter, in a way Moushumi had never brought to her son." Ashima even feels guilty for having nagged her son to date Moushumi in the first place.

Gogol arrives on the train. He thinks of his mother's travel plans and of his parents' bravery in living so far from their home. He thinks of how little he has seen of the world, and of how he has always lived a short train ride from Pemberton. He also thinks of the same train ride a year ago, when he discovered Moushumi's affair. It was "the first time in his life [when] another man's name upset him more than his own." Moushumi moved out immediately, returning to Paris, and she and Gogol divorced a few months later. The following spring, Gogol traveled alone to Italy, taking the trip he had initially planned as a surprise for his wife.

Back at the party, Gogol breaks away and heads to his old room. He packs a few boxes of his old books. He discovers the volume of Nikolai Gogol's short stories, the long-forgotten gift from his father. Opening it for the first time, Gogol finds an inscription from Ashoke, and it causes Gogol to realize that "the name he had so detested . . . was the first thing his father had ever given him." He also thinks that there are only a few people left in his life who know him as Gogol rather than Nikhil; "yet the thought of this eventual demise provides no sense of victory, no solace. It provides no solace at all." Gogol opens the book and begins to read.

CHARACTERS

Ben

Ben is introduced in the second half of the novel as Sonia's boyfriend. He eventually becomes Sonia's husband. Ben makes Sonia happy, a fact that both Gogol and Ashima acknowledge. Ben acts as a contrast to Moushumi, who has failed to make Gogol happy.

Dimitri Desjardins

Dimitri Desjardins is the man with whom Moushumi has an affair. The two originally met when Moushumi was in high school and Dimitri was in college. At that time, the two had struck up a pseudo-romantic relationship that lasted off and

on for several years, yet that relationship was never consummated. When Moushumi later comes across Dimitri's résumé, she secretly contacts him and finds that he has become a balding, unemployed, middle-aged man with a sad apartment. Nonetheless, she begins an affair with him.

Ashima Ganguli

Ashima is Ashoke's wife and the mother of Gogol and Sonia. She represents the traditional Indian values and lifestyle that Gogol grows to resent. Indeed, Ashima adored living in India with her sprawling family. She worked as an English tutor before entering into an arranged marriage with Ashoke. In their entire married life together, Ashima never addressed her husband directly as Ashoke, a reflection of Indian tradition. After her arrival in America, Ashima is extremely homesick; she is afraid to raise her child in America without the support of her family. However, over time, she grows accustomed to her life in America, even celebrating Christmas and Easter for her children. Still, Ashima cooks predominantly Indian food and visits India every few years. She also maintains her roots by practicing Hindu rituals and making predominantly Bengali friends. These Bengali friends become something of a surrogate extended family for Ashima. The raucous parties she throws for her Bengali friends punctuate the Ganguli family's life over the course of three decades.

When Ashoke is working in Cleveland, Ashima lives alone for the first time in her life, a frightening experience for her. Once again, though, she shows her inner strength and adaptability by getting a part-time job, her first job since before she was married. Through this job, Ashima makes the first truly American friends she has ever had. When Ashoke suddenly dies, Ashima grows frail and listless, and it is a long while before she adjusts to her widowhood. By the story's end, however, Ashima has grown independent enough to sell the family home and travel back and forth between India and America. The latter country, she knows, has become as much a part of her now as her birthplace.

Ashoke Ganguli

Ashoke is Ashima's husband and the father of Gogol and Sonia. Ashoke is a rather stoic and reserved individual who plays the traditional role of distant father and breadwinner. In most cases in the book, he is referred to as being at work. Ashoke's deeper nature, however, is revealed through his love of Russian literature. His deeper nature is also revealed through his life-changing encounter with the businessman who urges him to travel and the subsequent train accident. It is further revealed through Ashoke's subsequent rescue, a rescue that hinges on the crumpled pages of a story by Nikolai Gogol. This incident influences Ashoke's life and the name he chooses for his son. Although Ashoke is a rather static (unchanging) character, he features in some of the most poignant moments in the book, such as his gift of Nikolai Gogol's stories to his son and the late-discovered inscription in that book. In another poignant moment, Ashoke finally reveals the true meaning behind Gogol's name. When Gogol asks his father if he is a reminder of the accident, Ashoke replies, "You remind me of everything that followed."

The adult Gogol also fondly recalls a time when he was around five and he and his father walked alone to the very tip of Cape Cod. Ashoke's sudden death also acts as a catalyst for his son. Indeed, losing his father causes Gogol to finally appreciate his family and heritage.

Gogol Ganguli

Gogol is the novel's protagonist. He struggles with his identity as both an Indian and an American. As a child, he does not wish to be called by his formal name of Nikhil, but by the time he reaches adolescence, he resents his odd name so much that he legally changes his name to Nikhil when he turns eighteen. He tells the judge he has "always hated" the name. Throughout his life, Gogol had avoided reading the work of Nikolai Gogol: "To read the story, he believed, would mean paying tribute to his namesake, accepting it somehow." Now that Gogol has changed his name, however, he must struggle not only with the duality of his cultural identity but with the duality of his two names. It takes some time for Gogol to "feel like Nikhil." His dual names—one at school, one at home—make him feel like "he's cast himself in a play acting the part of twins." It is also odd to him when his parents visit him at school and call him Nikhil, but it is equally odd when his mother forgets and calls him Gogol. He "feels helpless, annoyed... caught in the mess he's made."

As Gogol matures, he distances himself more and more from his family; he resents their Indian-

ness and provincial lifestyle. He dates Maxine Ratliff, a woman whose family he admires and whose lifestyle he aspires to, yet "he is conscious of the fact that his immersion in Maxine's family is a betrayal of his own," though he is untroubled, even relieved, by this acknowledgment. His seemingly preposterous relief is evident when his parents are unable to reach him at the Ratliff family lake house. This realization makes Gogol feel "that here at Maxine's side, in this cloistered wilderness, he is free."

However, after his father's death, Gogol experiences a change of heart. He breaks up with Maxine, is closer to his family, and makes peace with his heritage. He ultimately marries an Indian American woman. Sadly, Gogol's wife, Moushumi, has not made the same peace with her background that Gogol has, and her constant dissatisfaction destroys their marriage. When he learns of her affair it is "the first time in his life [when] another man's name upset him more than his own." Moreover, the peace that Gogol has made with himself is underscored at the end of the novel when he realizes that "the name he had so detested... was the first thing his father had ever given him." He also thinks that there are only a few people left in his life that know him as Gogol, and "yet the thought of this eventual demise provides no sense of victory, no solace. It provides no solace at all."

Nikhil Ganguli
See Gogol Ganguli

Sonali Ganguli
See Sonia Ganguli

Sonia Ganguli

Sonia is Gogol's sister. She does not appear much in the story, but when she does, she often serves as a contrast to Gogol. As a baby, she is given only one name and is labeled the "true American." Also unlike Gogol, she moves rather far away from her family. However, like Gogol, she returns after Ashoke's death. Sonia marries Ben, an American who makes her very happy.

Moushumi Mazoomdar

Moushumi becomes Gogol's wife. Like Gogol, she is an Indian American. In fact, they attended the same large Bengali parties as children, but they never interacted and only vaguely remember one another. The two are chosen as romantic possibilities by their mothers; to their mutual surprise, they fall in love. Notably, both rejected backgrounds, and both nevertheless resented their American lovers for doing the same. Moushumi, unlike Gogol, has not truly made peace with her background. She still aspires to be like her American college friends. Her disappointment at her failure to achieve that ideal keeps her largely dissatisfied with her life. In fact, it is this dissatisfaction that drives her into the arms of an idealized old flame who has aged badly.

Maxine Ratliff

Maxine is one of Gogol's girlfriends. She lives on a private floor in her parents' mansion in Chelsea (in New York City), and dines with them regularly. Maxine and her family represent the fine American lifestyle to which Gogol aspires. He is comfortable in her world in a way his parents never could be. On the other hand, Maxine is comfortable around Gogol's parents despite Gogol's own embarrassment. Eventually, Maxine's charm wears thin when Gogol becomes more attached to his family. Gogol prefers to retrieve his father's body alone and to mourn with his mother and sister alone. When Maxine urges him to take a vacation and get away from his family's grief, Gogol says that he does not wish to do so. Indeed, Gogol's growing attachment to his family and his exclusion of Maxine lead to the end of their relationship.

Ruth

Ruth is Gogol's first love. He is introduced to her parents and accepted by them, but he does not introduce Ruth to his parents. This is because he knows his parents would rather he date a Bengali girl—or rather, they want him to focus on his studies and date Bengali girls after he graduates. Ruth dates Gogol for a couple of years, even maintaining a long-distance relationship with him while she is studying abroad in England. However, when she returns, she and Gogol agree that they have grown apart, and they break up shortly thereafter.

THEMES

Immigrant Experience

One of the main themes in the novel is that of the immigrant experience. Ashoke and Ashima are immigrants traveling from the country they have always known to make their life in a vastly foreign land. While Ashoke is able to throw himself

TOPICS FOR FURTHER STUDY

- Read a short story by Lahiri and compare it to *The Namesake*. In an essay, discuss the similarities and differences in theme and tone between the two works. Lahiri's writing is known for its portrayal of the Indian American experience. How does your reading add to your understanding of that experience?

- Conduct an Internet research project on immigration in the United States during the twentieth century. What statistics can you uncover regarding the immigration rates of Indians over that period? How do the Gangulis' experiences correlate with those statistics? Present your findings to the class using charts and graphs.

- Read "The Overcoat," a short story by Nikolai Gogol, and give an oral book report relating your impressions of it. Be sure to discuss any added insights the story has lent to your reading of *The Namesake*.

- Which character in the novel did you identify with most (or least)? Why? Write a brief essay answering these questions. In the essay, give specific examples from the text showing what makes that character most (or least) like you.

into his work, through Ashima readers catch a glimpse of the anxiety and alienation of foreigners. In the first sentence of the novel, Ashima is attempting to make a snack resembling her favorite food back home. However, the attempt is an inexact copy; the original ingredients are unavailable in Cambridge, and Ashima can only effect an approximation. This first image applies to much of Ashoke and Ashima's lives. Their Bengali friends are an approximation of the extended family they left behind. Their attempts to name Gogol according to the Indian tradition of pet names and formal names are misconstrued and ultimately abandoned, another failed approximation. Indeed, even as the years go on, Ashoke and Ashima remain tied to India, visiting it every few years. No matter how

Kal Penn as Gogol, Irrfan Khan as Ashoke, Sahira Nair as Sonia, and Tabu as Ashima in the 2006 film version of the novel (© *Fox Searchlight Pictures | The Kobal Collection | The Picture Desk, Inc.*)

long they live in America, they will always be living in a foreign land. This is an essential aspect of Ashoke and Ashima's experience.

The process of assimilation, in which immigrants take on the mannerisms and customs of their new country, is also evident in *The Namesake*. For instance, Ashoke and Ashima begin celebrating Christmas and Easter, though they do so mainly for their children. In fact, Gogol and Sonia, as first-generation Americans, also demonstrate an important aspect of the immigrant experience. As first-generation Americans, they are not living in a foreign land; they are not pulled between two countries in the way that their parents are, but they are pulled between two *cultures* in a way that their parents are not. Indeed, Ashoke and Ashima do not feel the need to conform to American ideals and traditions, yet their children, especially Gogol, do. As children, Gogol and Sonia urge their parents to celebrate Christian holidays, they prefer

American food to Indian food, and they resent the long family trips to India. Where their parents entered into an arranged marriage, Gogol and Sonia date Americans freely. Even when Gogol and Moushumi eventually marry, they still prefer an American wedding. Instead, they have a Bengali ceremony to please their families. Gogol, Sonia, and even Moushumi must balance two heritages, the American one they grew up with and the Indian one they inherited. Each does so with varying degrees of success.

Identity

While *The Namesake* largely explores the immigrant experience, it cannot help but touch upon the closely related theme of identity. Indeed, the dual heritages that Gogol, Sonia, and Moushumi carry are essentially two cultural identities. The unasked question that haunts their lives is whether they are Indian or American. The answer is that they are simultaneously both and neither. It would be an oversimplification to say that they are Indian Americans, but this nevertheless speaks not only to the trouble that first-generation immigrants have identifying themselves but also the trouble that outsiders have in identifying bicultural individuals. This quandary is largely represented in Gogol's two names. In fact, Gogol's changing feelings regarding his name correspond to his feelings about his cultural identity. When Gogol accepts the name given him by his parents, it is as if he is accepting them. Notably, when he attempts to create himself anew as Nikhil, he feels torn between two identities, but when he fully embraces his name and his Indian heritage, he does not feel any anxiety. His two names—one at school, one at home—make him feel as if "he's cast himself in a play acting the part of twins." Amidst the confusion he has caused, Gogol "feels helpless, annoyed . . . caught in the mess he's made."

As the novel progresses, Gogol becomes more comfortable with his Indian identity, with the rituals and customs that connect him to his family. This change enables him to marry Moushumi, to ungrudgingly do so in a ceremony contrary to his personal tastes. By the novel's end, Gogol realizes that "the name he had so detested . . . was the first thing his father had ever given him." Indeed, by rejecting his name, Gogol had rejected his father, his parents, his roots, and his identity—all things he no longer rejects. Now, having all but succeeded in obliterating his original name, "the thought of this eventual demise provides no sense of victory, no solace. It provides no solace at all."

STYLE

Omniscient Third-Person Narrator

The use an omniscient third-person narrator in *The Namesake* gives the reader insight into the private thoughts of each of the novel's characters. This narrative device allows the reader to observe both the outer and inner realities of each character. In this way, the reader truly understands the angst and anxiety that are experienced by Ashima, Gogol, and Moushumi, as well as their perceived reasons for those feelings. On the other hand, the omniscient narrator simultaneously acts as a distancing device. If the novel were told from a first-person point of view, particularly from Gogol's perspective, then the reader would identify directly with the narrator's actions. The book would also take on a more conversational tone, as if the reader and the first-person narrator were interacting directly. Instead, the narration becomes somewhat static, matter-of-factly relating Gogol's actions and thoughts over the course of thirty years. Indeed, this approach leaves the reader with a greater awareness of the fact that a story is being told. Thus, the reader becomes somewhat more distanced from the characters' lives and realities, as they are being held at arm's length by the book's narrative approach.

Motif

Originally a musical term, a motif is a thought or idea that appears repeatedly throughout a work. The importance of names and their origins is one of many motifs in *The Namesake*. In fact, it is the force that drives and informs the entire narrative. Indeed, while Gogol's name is a particularly strong motif, motifs in general act to bind together a work, adding continuity and thematic resonance. Another important motif in the novel is that of the train, and even of the train's odd pairing with love and death. For instance, Ashoke's train accident is of obvious significance, and that significance is underscored by Gogol's frequent use of the train to visit with his family. Indeed, Gogol meets his first love on the train, and his marriage also falls apart on the train. When Gogol and his family are traveling by train through India, a man is murdered in another car. When Gogol heads home on the train Thanksgiving break of his senior year, someone commits suicide by jumping on the tracks. This latter incident causes Gogol to be late, and Ashoke sits alone at the station, worrying that the same fate that once befell him may have befallen his son. Indeed, it is Ashoke's relief following this worry that spurs him to reveal the true meaning behind his son's name.

HISTORICAL CONTEXT

Nikolai Gogol

Russian author Nikolai Gogol was born in Velikie Sorochintsy, in what is now Ukraine, on March 20, 1809. His parents, Maria Ivanovna and Vasilii Afanas'evich Gogol-Ianovsky owned land; though the family was not rich, they were relatively well off. Gogol was the first infant in

Indian couple exchanging wedding rings (*Image copyright Nick Vangopoulos, 2009. Used under license from Shutterstock.com*)

the family to survive, though Maria Ivanovna and Vasilii Afanas'evich went on to have five more children. Gogol began writing satirical poetry in high school, though he was not a good student. However, after his father died in 1825, Gogol pursued his studies with greater dedication. It was around this time that he began writing longer poems, but few, if any, have survived. In 1828, Gogol moved to St. Petersburg in the hopes of securing employment, but he was sorely disappointed by the low-level civil service positions available to him. He eventually took a poorly paying job that left him with enough time to pursue his writing. In 1829 he self-published the poetry collection *Gants Kiukhel'garten* under the name V. Alov. It received such bad reviews that Gogol burned all of his remaining copies.

That same year, Gogol traveled to Germany for six weeks before returning to St. Petersburg and taking a job in the ministry of the interior. He also resumed his literary career, publishing essays, poems, and historical chapters in various periodicals. Almost all were written under various pseudonyms. He eventually began to attract the attention of literary patrons, including the great Russian writer Alexander Pushkin. Through these connections, Gogol secured a job as a history teacher at the Patriotic Institute for the daughters of the nobility in 1831. At this time, Gogol began collecting family anecdotes related to the Ukraine, most of which comprise his earliest short stories, first published in *Vechera na khutore bliz Dikan'ki* in two volumes in 1831 and 1832. The work established Gogol's reputation as a writer of note.

In 1834, Gogol joined the University of St. Petersburg as an assistant professor in history, but he left in 1835. He also published his second and third story collections that year, *Arabeski* and *Mirgorod*. Both were well received by critics. Over the course of the 1830s and early 1840s, Gogol also wrote several plays, with mixed success. In 1842, Gogol achieved his greatest literary success, releasing the short story collection *Sochineniia*, which includes "The Overcoat," his best-known story. He also published his first and only novel, *Mertvye dushi*, which is best known in English translation as *Dead Souls*. Both works represent Gogol at the height of his prowess. Afterwards, he struggled to write a sequel to his novel and destroyed several versions.

By the late 1840s, Gogol had befriended Father Matvei Konstantinovsky. The priest lambasted the author's work as vain and sinful. Believing Konstantinovsky and fearing for his soul, Gogol stopped writing in 1852. He also began fasting, ultimately starving himself. Despite the efforts of friends and other clergy, Gogol refused to eat, and he died February 21, 1952.

Indian American Immigration in the Late Twentieth Century

Until 1946, Indian and other Asian immigrants experienced greater difficulty entering the United States than their European and Latin American counterparts. This changed to some extent with the signing of the Luce-Cellar Bill by President Harry S. Truman in 1946. The bill was incorporated into the Immigration Act of 1946; it allowed Indians the ability to gain citizenship to the United States. The bill also allowed Indian immigrants to travel back and forth between India and America more freely. At the time, however, only 100 Indian citizens per year were able to immigrate legally to the United States. With the passage of the Immigration Act of 1965, however, this number was expanded to 20,000. This change led to a marked influx in the Indian population in America. Indeed, *The Namesake* begins in 1968, three years after the act was passed. The Gangulis' presence in America, as well as that of the myriad Bengali friends they make, is attributable to this act.

CRITICAL OVERVIEW

Given the remarkable success of Jhumpa Lahiri's first book, *Interpreter of Maladies*, the author's follow-up publication was highly anticipated. For the most part, *The Namesake* did not disappoint; like its predecessor, the volume met with wide critical approval. For instance, Michiko Kakutani states in the *New York Times* that the novel "is that rare thing: an intimate, closely observed family portrait that effortlessly and discreetly unfolds to disclose a capacious social vision." Proffering further praise, Kakutani declares that "Lahiri has not only given us a wonderfully intimate and knowing family portrait, she has also taken the haunting chamber music of her first collection of stories and reorchestrated its themes of exile and identity to create a symphonic work, a debut novel that is as

assured and eloquent as the work of a longtime master of the craft."

On the other hand, *Commentary* reviewer Sam Munson was less impressed. In his article, he remarks that the tone features "an excess of dispassionateness: Lahiri's novel is linear to the point of monotony." He adds that the book "does occasionally rise to the level of which Lahiri is manifestly capable," but he ultimately finds that "these moments only serve in the end to underline the flatness of the whole." Nevertheless, Munson's opinion is decidedly in the minority. Indeed, *Kenyon Review* contributor David H. Lynn notes that "what Lahiri aspires to is considerably grander than whether readers become emotionally engaged with her characters. Her ambition is to play in the literary big leagues." Mandira Sen, writing in the *Women's Review of Books*, also gives a glowing assessment in her critique. She comments that "Lahiri's beautifully crafted and elegantly written novel will speak to many. It is as different as it can be from the exotic outpourings of Indian immigrants writing in English for whom the home country provides a canvas for their magical interpretations." Furthermore, Sen observes, Lahiri "steers away from providing easy answers, offering readers a complex look into the immigrant experience."

CRITICISM

Leah Tieger

Tieger is a freelance writer and editor. In the following essay, she discusses Gogol's changing feelings toward his name, his family, and his heritage in The Namesake. *In particular, she looks at Gogol's relationship with his father and his relationships with women as a means of tracing Gogol's evolving emotions.*

Jhumpa Lahiri's *The Namesake* opens with a pregnant Ashima attempting to recreate a favorite snack from India. This image, of a woman clearly homesick and disconnected from her roots, sets the tone for Gogol's birth shortly thereafter. When the infant Gogol is named, a further disconnection is underlined in the form of a lost letter from India, one containing the boy's intended formal name. This twist of fate leaves Gogol with no more than a pet name, albeit one with great significance. Despite this, his parents Ashoke and Ashima hope to replace the name when Gogol

WHAT DO I READ NEXT?

- Kashmira Sheth's *Blue Jasmine*, published in 2004, is the story of twelve-year-old Seema, who moves from India to Iowa City, Iowa, with her family and struggles to adjust to her new home. This young adult novel presents a another aspect of immigrant experience, this time from the point of view of a young girl.

- For another fictional look at an Indian American who must come to terms with her heritage, read Anjali Banerjee's *Maya Running* (2005). This young adult novel features Maya, a Canadian whose parents are Bengali. Maya experiences the normal teenage angst that accompanies first crushes, but she also must compete with her beautiful cousin Pinky, who is visiting from India.

- Edwidge Danticat's *Behind the Mountains* (2002) also looks at the immigrant experience, this time from the viewpoint of a Haitian refugee. This young adult novel is written as the journal of Celiane, a thirteen-year-old girl who writes about her and her mother and brother's lives in Haiti. Celiane also discusses her new life in Brooklyn, New York, as she and her family travel to join her father there.

- Lahiri's Pulitzer Prize-winning collection of short stories, *Interpreter of Maladies* launched the author to international fame in 1999. The book will add much to any reading of *The Namesake*, as both volumes explore the Indian American immigrant experience. Both books are also largely autobiographical.

- For more insight into the works of Nikolai Gogol, read his *Collected Tales*. The volume, published in 2008, was translated into English by Richard Pevear and Larissa Volokhonsky. The collection also features the Russian writer's best-known story, "The Overcoat."

- The anonymously authored *India*, released by DK Publishing in 2008, presents a pictorial survey of the country that informs Lahiri's novel. The book also includes text on the customs, religions, and history of India.

- While the Gangulis are not particularly religious, or even identified as Hindus, the rituals they take part in are indeed Hindu customs. For more insight into this fascinating and ancient religion, read *The Essentials of Hinduism: A Comprehensive Overview of the World's Oldest Religion* (2002), by Swami Bhaskarananda.

---

begins his formal education. However, the five-year-old Gogol, too young to question who he is, accepts only his pet name, rejecting his formal name, Nikhil. Here, another twist of fate, again underlying the Gangulis' foreignness, occurs. Gogol's American teachers, unfamiliar with the Indian tradition of pet and formal names, accept Gogol's birth certificate and his wishes.

As Gogol grows up, however, he becomes more and more aware of his dual heritage and of the pitfalls inherent in navigating it. To him, his name has grown to embody these pitfalls, and he resents it accordingly. He is unaware of the true meaning behind his name, and Gogol overlooks the gift of Nikolai Gogol's short stories

given to him by his father on his fourteenth birthday. This willful ignorance continues throughout his life, as Gogol studiously avoids reading the Russian author's works. To do so, he feels, would be to accept a name he in no way accepts. Later, though, when Gogol legally changes his name, he only complicates matters. He does not want to be Gogol, and yet he does not "feel like Nikhil." His dual names—one at school, one at home—make him feel as if "he's cast himself in a play acting the part of twins." Trapped between his two names, Gogol "feels helpless, annoyed . . . caught in the mess he's made." Although this feeling subsides as Gogol makes his way in college, his feelings toward his dual heritage have grown no less accepting. In fact the opposite occurs. Even when Gogol learns the truth behind the meaning of his name during his senior year at Yale, his ambivalence toward his Indian heritage remains unabated.

Gogol's two girlfriends are perfect examples of this pattern. The first, Ruth, will surely bring his parents' disapproval. Gogol is well aware of this, and he avoids mentioning her for as long as possible. Even though he and Ruth date for almost two years, Gogol never introduces her to his family. The relationship, like most college liaisons, ends when both Ruth and Gogol grow apart. Gogol again rejects his Indian heritage, to an even greater degree, when he dates Maxine Ratliff. Both she and her family are the direct opposites of the Ganguli clan, a fact of which Gogol is acutely aware. He constantly makes comparisons between the two families, all of which cast the Gangulis in an unflattering light. Indeed, "he is conscious of the fact that his immersion in Maxine's family is a betrayal of his own."

However, the death of Gogol's father sparks a deep change in his view of himself and his family. Indeed, when Ashoke dies, Gogol insists on traveling to Cleveland without Maxine, and he does not invite her to join his family in the initial mourning period. Indeed, for the first time in his life, Gogol finds himself clinging to the Bengali rituals that follow in the wake of his father's death. According to Natalie Friedman in *Critique: Studies in Contemporary Fiction*, Gogol "desires a 'return' to his Indian-inflected parental home and his Indian community in Massachusetts after the death of his father, which awakens in him a sudden need to reconnect with lost Bengali rituals." Gogol's desire to embrace his Indian heritage is, unsurprisingly, matched by his failing desire to actively reject it—especially in the form of his girlfriend. Friedman observes:

> Gogol recognizes his romance with Maxine for what it was: a temporary experience, a diversion. The return to his family and to Bengali rituals serves to reinstate for Gogol the importance of his ethnic difference, and he loses interest in Maxine.

Friedman adds that "his return to his parents' house in Massachusetts is a physical and metaphoric return to his Indian roots; it is the first time in the novel that Gogol acknowledges that he is Indian and not simply another American suburban boy."

Gogol's next girlfriend underscores his closer ties to his family and heritage. Indeed, while Gogol is surprised by his love for Moushumi Mazoomdar, it hardly comes as a surprise to the reader. Gogol's weekly visits home, an acquiescence to his mother's nagging, are in line with the changed Gogol. Moushumi, who has shared a similar distaste for her background, is motivated to return to tradition following a broken engagement to an American. Gogol and Moushumi marry as expected, and they hold a traditional Bengali ceremony only to please their families. The irony, of course, is that Moushumi remains dissatisfied with her roots in a way that Gogol no longer shares. That dissatisfaction ultimately sows the seeds of discontent that will destroy their marriage. The irony, of course, is readily apparent: while Gogol chases his perceived American ideal before growing disenchanted with it, he unwittingly marries a Bengali woman who is still actively chasing that ideal.

Despite his acceptance of his cultural identity, Gogol still struggles to accept his given name. This is evidenced in two events that occur with Moushumi. In the first, Moushumi reveals Gogol's birth name at a dinner party, and Gogol can barely conceal his anger and resentment. Indeed, his unresolved feelings toward his name are revealed again only a moment later when he tells the shocked partygoers that children should go only by pronouns until they name themselves at the age of eighteen. In the second instance, when Gogol learns the name of Moushumi's lover, it is "the first time in his life, [when] another man's name upset him more than his own." Nevertheless, only a year later, Gogol finally accepts his name. In doing so, he finally accepts himself, and his father (who named him) as well.

In fact, it is Gogol's discovery of his father's long-ago gift—a book of Nikolai Gogol's short stories—that triggers this epiphany. Gogol discovers an inscription from Ashoke inside the book and realizes that "the name he had so detested ... was the first thing his father had ever given him." He also thinks that there are only a few people left in his life who know him as Gogol, and "yet the thought of this eventual demise provides no sense of victory, no solace. It provides no solace at all." Still, Gogol's final epiphany has been brewing for some time. Earlier that day, he thinks of the bravery required of his parents to live so far from their homes, and of how he has never lived farther than a quick train ride away from his own. This line of

The Taj Mahal palace in Agra, India (*Image copyright Kharidehal Abhirama Ashwin, 2009. Used under license from Shutterstock.com*)

thought is brought on by the knowledge that Ashima will spend half the year in Calcutta and that his childhood home has been sold. Indeed, as Friedman states, "with Ashima's retirement to India, Gogol will be, effectively, without a home." And so, in the face of that loss, he chooses no longer to be without a name.

Source: Leah Tieger, Critical Essay on *The Namesake*, in *Novels for Students*, Gale, Cengage Learning, 2010.

Natalie Friedman

In the following excerpt, Friedman considers The Namesake *as a contemporary immigrant narrative and as a travel narrative.*

CHILDREN, COSMOPOLITANISM, AND THE NEW IMMIGRANT NOVEL

When Jhumpa Lahiri's first novel, *The Namesake*, appeared in 2003, critics such as David Kipen, Gail Caldwell, and Stephen Metcalf hailed it as a richly detailed exploration of the immigrant family. Lahiri's work is still relatively new, and the corpus of criticism about it still small (a search for Lahiri in the MLA International Bibliography yields only sixteen articles); the majority of writing on Lahiri has focused on her first collection of short stories *Interpreter of Maladies*, and scholars and critics have dubbed her a documentalist of the immigrant experience (see Goldblatt; Dubey). *Interpreter* does include a few short stories about immigrants who travel from India to America, and the last story in particular, "The Third and Final Continent," is based loosely on the experiences of Lahiri's parents.

Her novel, although it does revisit the themes of immigration and acculturation that she introduced in her collection, cannot be called only an immigrant narrative. Michiko Kakutani said that Lahiri's novel is "[...] about exile and its discontents, a novel that is as affecting in its Chekhovian exploration of fathers and sons, parents and children, as it is resonant in its exploration of what is acquired and lost by immigrants and their children in pursuit of the American Dream" (El). The first part of Kakutani's quotation is correct—the novel is an exploration of intergenerational differences as well as the losses and acquisitions of an immigrant American family. But she oversimplifies the idea that the book is an immigrant narrative

> LAHIRI'S NOVEL ALSO SUGGESTS ANOTHER POSSIBILITY, ONE THAT SHE DOES NOT SHARE WITH SOME OF HER CONTEMPORARIES: THAT THE IMMIGRANT OR CHILD OF IMMIGRANTS DOES NOT BECOME DISILLUSIONED WITH AMERICA BECAUSE AMERICA IS NOT THE ENDPOINT OF HIS OR HER TRAVELS."

about the pursuit of the "American Dream"—a cliche of immigration on par with that of "the melting pot." This dream has its roots in Western Christian models of pilgrims seeking a "beacon on a hill," a "New Jerusalem"; as Cynthia Sanling Wong says in writing about Asian American literature—non-European, non-Christian immigrant autobiographies are "indifferent" to the concept of a "dream" that is saturated with Christian symbolism of seeking and finding Eden. I claim that Lahiri, as part of this growing Asian American author group, is less interested in the pursuit of the American Dream as it was traditionally rendered in older immigrant narratives than she is in focusing on what happens once that dream (in its variety of incarnations) is achieved, not only by the generation of immigrants but also by its children.

This difference between the immigrant generation and its children is important in understanding how the immigrant novel has changed. Lahiri is part of a vanguard of young, contemporary ethnic American writers whose novels, short fiction, and memoirs suggest that assimilation—cleaving to the hope of an "American Dream"—is no longer at the heart of the immigrant story. Instead of shedding the trappings of the home culture and throwing himself headlong into the work of Americanizing, the protagonist of the contemporary immigrant novel—whether an immigrant or a child born to immigrants—is more concerned with his or her dual identity as it manifests itself in America and in the shrinking global community. Lahiri's depictions of the elite class of Western-educated Indians and their children's relationship to both India and America dismantle the stereotype of brown-skinned immigrant families that are always outsiders to American culture and recasts them as cosmopolites, members of a shifting network of global travelers whose national loyalties are flexible. In so doing, she correctly depicts the new generation of immigrants in literature as moving beyond the cliche of the "American Dream," and she takes her place among contemporary novelists such as Gish Jen and Bharati Mukherjee from Asia, but also European and Caribbean authors who challenge the Western Christian notion of the search for Edenic America, such as Gary Shteyngart and Julia Alvarez. Lahiri, in her attempt to portray an immigrant family that is not beset by poverty or persecution, blatant racism, or a punishing quest for economic success, remains true to the complexities of earlier immigrant novels while also differentiating herself from that literary precedent and aligning herself with other contemporary immigrant authors.

In *The Namesake*, Lahiri's immigrant family challenges the stereotypes of the disenfranchised immigrant who remains in one place once he or she reaches America's shores, trapped by poverty or political and legal restrictions. As Zygmunt Bauman writes (89), immigrants and their children have ceased to be "locally tied" and have entered what Arjun Appadurai calls the world of "global flows" (30), or what Kwame Anthony Appiah calls "cosmopolitanism" in the book of the same name. Today's immigrant characters, particularly the children of immigrants, like their creators, belong to a world of cosmopolites that Tim Brennan described as "exempt from national belonging" and who are perennial migrants "valorized by a rhetoric of wandering" (2).

This rhetoric of wandering pervades Lahiri's novel and is evident in the novel's recursive structure, third-person narration, and character development. The novel's narration opens from the perspective of Ashima Ganguli, the mother of the protagonist Gogol, the "namesake" of the novel's title. The novel eventually breaks off from Ashima's perspective to follow the life, travails, and innermost thoughts of Gogol, Ashima's child, but then transfers briefly to the interests of Gogol's wife, Moushumi, an Indian American woman who was born, like Lahiri herself, in London. The novel then returns to Ashima and ends with her widowhood and her plans to return to India, where she will spend part of each year in her retirement. This wandering narrative structure, which allows the reader access to the emotional lives of several characters while still focusing mainly on Gogol, reflects the unfixed sensibility shared by all of the characters, whether immigrant or native-born American.

The narration, shared by two generations of Gangulis, also speaks to the contemporary fact that even the older generation of immigrants is beginning to see America not as a newly adopted homeland, but as an option—Ashima does not feel bound to stay in America, nor does she feel nostalgically driven to return to India, but rather, seeks to divide her time between the two countries. Conventional wisdom seems to suggest that immigrants are just as Emma Lazarus's 1883 poem "The New Colossus" describes them: "the huddled masses" who are "yearning to breathe free" and who, once they reach "the golden door," will have been fulfilled (203). Immigrant literature often represents immigrant characters as such: poor, disenfranchised people coming to America in search of opportunity, seen in novels such as Abraham Cahan's *The Rise of David Levinsky* (1917), Anzia Yezierska's *Bread Givers* (1925), and O. E. Rolvaag's *Giants in the Earth* (1927). These novels focus on a central immigrant character whose trials and tribulations are often rewarded by economic or educational success. Rolvaag's characters find their piece of the American Dream in the parcels of land available to homesteaders out west at the close of the nineteenth century; in the case of Cahan, David Levinsky becomes a rich businessman, while in Yezierska's novel, the protagonist Sara Smolinsky achieves her dream of becoming an English teacher.

These immigrant characters are typical of many novels about immigration, across ethnicities and nationalities. In fact, most immigrant narratives share themes and tropes, and Lahiri's novel bears many marks of earlier immigrant narratives. William Boelhower, in writing about Italian immigrant narratives, attempted to codify the narratological devices of immigrant writings. He found that immigrant autobiographies had three narrative constants: anticipation, contact, and contrast (14, 15). I mention Boelhower here because his troika of tropes is present not only in autobiography but also in immigrant fiction, which is often at least semi-autobiographical (as in the case of, for example, Yezierska).

Lahiri's novel also describes the anticipation of the parental immigrant generation to make a new life in America (which is bound up, for mother figure Ashima Ganguli, in the birth of her child on American soil); her novel also describes the awkwardness of the contact with America (in terms of linguistic and cultural mistakes that Ashima makes), and she explores the contrasts between the old and new worlds. One thing that Boelhower elides, however, is the more complex themes within immigrant novels, which often center on the disillusionment that immigrants experienced once they landed on American soil: that America was not a land ready to accept them (as in Rolvaag's novel, where the Norwegian immigrants encounter xenophobia, but also face a literal rejection by the land as they struggle to farm it); that America required hard labor of its newest residents (as in Yezierska's novel, where the heroine must work in a sweatshop to pay for her education); that assimilation asked the immigrant to shed his or her ethnic particularities (as in Cahan's novel, where the protagonist divests himself of the garb of Orthodox European Judaism). Despite their disillusionment, these older immigrant characters did not, or could not, leave their adopted home or return to their native lands; in contrast, the disillusioned or disappointed ethnic Americans in Lahiri's novel and the novels of her multicultural contemporaries can and do leave America—some return to their countries of origin, while others divide their time between countries. Lahiri's novel also suggests another possibility, one that she does not share with some of her contemporaries: that the immigrant or child of immigrants does not become disillusioned with America because America is not the endpoint of his or her travels. America becomes a stop on the voyage to discover a better life, a more fulfilling career, or a more interesting lover; and this voyage is no longer unidirectional, or even bidirectional, but is continuous and global.

LAHIRI'S RHETORIC OF WANDERING AND THE TRAVEL NARRATIVE

In *The Namesake*, Gogol, the child of immigrants, does not feel dislocated, because he is at home in America. Nevertheless, the constant flux of travel in his life and the unsettled feeling that accompanies his parents' immigration creates, out of necessity, a desire to travel, to discover a place from which to leave and to which to return. For the immigrant generation, the return is always to India: Gogol's parents go back to their home again and again for funerals, vacations, and other family functions. America, for them, is not entirely a new adopted home, and India is never completely forsaken. For the children (namely, Gogol, his sister, and his wife), it is not India to which they turn for comfort or to reinforce any nascent nationalist impulse; for them, the return must be to their parental home in America, a place where India is re-created, albeit in a diluted form. These children do not see India as their country of origin or as a putative homeland, and they can only define home as the place where their two cultures merge—the literal and metaphysical location is in their parents' house.

Gogol, whose life resembles that of other American children of a certain class—he eats hamburgers instead of traditional Indian foods, grows up to attend Yale, and acquires multiple girlfriends before marriage—spends most of his life traveling away from his Cambridge home, either to India with his parents or to less "exotic" locales such as New Haven and New York. But he desires a "return" to his Indian-inflected parental home and his Indian community in Massachusetts after the death of his father, which awakens in him a sudden need to reconnect with lost Bengali rituals; this desire to return culminates in marriage to an Indian American woman, who is an immigrant born in London but feels that her spiritual home is Paris. The novel, therefore, suggests that to the American-born second generation from India, the idea of a "home country"—a desh, as Lahiri calls it—is fallacious; but the idea of a community of conationals or ethnically and religiously bound expatriates is a reality that permeates their experience, and that inspires in them a sense of pluralist identity.

The perspective of the child of immigrants in Lahiri's novel illustrates the position in American culture that he occupies. It is a unique position: on one hand, the child born in America is unequivocally American; on the other hand, he is visibly different from his Caucasian conationals. Lahiri herself has articulated this notion in an interview:

> I think that for immigrants, the challenges of exile, the loneliness, the constant sense of alienation, the knowledge of and longing for a lost world, are more explicit and distressing than for their children. On the other hand, the problem for the children of immigrants—those with strong ties to their country of origin—is that they feel neither one thing nor the other. (Readers 2003)

Lahiri's novel examines this existential confusion, but it also complicates it: children of immigrants do not always feel closely tied to their country of origin, but rather, they feel American. They move fluidly between the private sphere of their Indian home life and the public sphere of their American experience. Their behavior is akin to that of tourists in their home countries; tourism, therefore, becomes a useful way of examining the psychic condition of the cosmopolitan children of immigrants in Lahiri's novel. In fusing two closely related literary traditions—the immigrant narrative and the travel narrative—Lahiri enables readers to understand that a novel about an immigrant family can also focus on how the children of immigrants have gained a certain kind of power. Their power comes from economic and class ease, not from a sense of ethnic identity that is part of some mythic melting pot. Lahiri values the entitlement that American-born children feel to the goods and experiences that surround them.

Michael W. Cox states that Lahiri's youngest characters provide her readers with "a more probing insight, perhaps, than her adult characters might allow into cultural difference and cultural accommodation, and in particular, into the not uncommon impulse to exaggerate or exoticize distinctions" (120). According to Cox, children do not come with the same emotional or cultural baggage as their adult counterparts and therefore are "largely judgment-free" (121), allowing them to act as translators between American culture and Indian culture (or Indian American culture). To expand on Cox's notion, children in Lahiri's novel are not only observers and translators of two worlds that encounter each other on American soil but also are conduits of change, importing American culture into their Indian homes and creating a kind of metissage that does not threaten their ethnic or cultural identity, but that enriches their experience.

Like his mother's, Gogol's sense of tourism emerges from his navigation of multiple cultures at once: his parental home, his American public sphere, his distant land of origin, the upper class he ascends to as he moves from his Ivy League school to his adult life. Lahiri deliberately plays up the idea of Gogol-as-tourist by combining her contemporary take on the immigrant-ethnic narrative with some of the tropes and themes of nineteenth- and twentieth-century travel writing. Gogol is constantly traveling, whether it be from his home to college, from Boston to New York, or from America to India; he also "travels" the terrain of a few failed romances and one doomed marriage, reinforcing the notion that travel and return are metaphors as much as physical realities in the lives of contemporary ethnic cosmopolites.

The term travel narrative covers an immense literary field, and there are hundreds of variations of the genre, including utopic meditations, such as Sir Thomas More's *Utopia*, and empirical explorations, such as the writings of Richard Hakluyt (Hulme and Youngs 3). James Buzard writes that the history of "traveling" in Europe corresponds roughly to the period of the Restoration in Britain in 1660 to the accession of Queen Victoria to the throne in 1837 (38); with the growth of mass tourism, the tourist-as-writer inaugurated a new travel-writing paradigm that Buzard calls "the picturesque" (38). Nigel Leask expands on the notion of the "picturesque," explaining that it rejected British "georgic conventions of prosperous husbandry" in favor of an exotic landscape that gave the reader a sense of arrest in history and in narrative (169).

As a young boy navigating his native Massachusetts, Gogol sees his surroundings as might a tourist seeking the picturesque—the language of the narrator, written in the present tense and in the third person, lends an air of detachment and neutrality to the narrative, as if Gogol is not experiencing his own life, but is watching himself travel through it. Part of his detachment might be a result of his youth; the novel follows Gogol from birth through the age of thirty-two, and it is not until he reaches adulthood that his perspective on his Indian family and his own ethnic difference changes. The majority of the novel focuses on his feelings as a child and teenager, thereby lending Gogol an air of immaturity, even into adulthood.

The narration emphasizes this notion when Gogol—who has visited India three times by the age of ten—travels to Calcutta with his family for an extended stay. When Gogol is fourteen, his father earns a sabbatical from his job and decides to move the family to Calcutta. Gogol's eight-month trip with his parents feels like a forced exile; he "dreads the thought of eight months without a room of his own, without his records, his stereo, without friends." Gogol, like any American boy, feels the lack of his middle-class accessories, and Lahiri gently mocks his love of these objects, but eventually takes

Gogol's side, as if to say that American life is indeed more comfortable than Indian life.

Gogol indulges in the pastimes of a colonial-era traveler, visiting the famous sites, such as the Taj Mahal, and looking for the "picturesque." As if to underscore Gogol's role as a tourist, the narrator describes him participating in one of his favorite hobbies: sketching. Like a young John Ruskin in Italy, Gogol attempts to sketch the facade of the grand edifice, but "the building's grace eludes him and he throws his attempt away. Instead, he immerses himself in the guidebook." Like characters in E. M. Forster's *A Room with a View*, Gogol increasingly relies on his guidebook to tell him about his country's history; after all, he is not really of that country, as he was born in America.

As if to underscore Gogol's status as tourist in India, Lahiri abandons the picturesque mode and writes what Mary Louise Pratt calls "sentimental plot lines of hard luck and victimization" (85). According to Pratt, several British imperialist travel narratives contain such plot lines to emphasize the ruggedness and shortcomings of the exotic locale and to prove the hardiness and pluckiness of the traveler, thereby assuring the British reader safe at home of his or her own physical and moral superiority (85). Gogol and his family encounter a series of unfortunate events on their way back from their excursion to Agra: Gogol's sister has an allergic reaction to jackfruit; someone is stabbed in a compartment of their train; and after their return to Calcutta, Gogol and his sister become ill with a stomach ailment (Lahiri, *Namesake*). None of these experiences is life threatening to Gogol, but they increase his desire to return home. His stay in India becomes a mere sojourn in his life as a traveler, and he remains firm in his belief that the cultural goods available to him in America are superior to those of India, the grandeur of the Taj Mahal notwithstanding. He would trade in the Taj Mahal for the relief he finds when he returns home to his cupboards filled with familiar labels: Skippy, Hood, Bumble Bee, Land O'Lakes.

Such cultural relativism was common to colonial travel narratives. Gogol's participation in such relativism, as well as his view of his parents' homeland and his own presumed land of origin as lacking in comforts and corporeally rejecting him, signifies his own desire to be what he is: a slightly spoiled, middle-class American boy. His desire for the consumer goods of America, however, also marks him as a contemporary cosmopolite—someone who can claim to have lived in at least two countries and who has an appreciation for the goods that both can offer. His slight preference for American foods is, in fact, prescient—it is a sign of the "Coca-Colonization" of South Asia and the blend of Asian and American cultures that Gogol's peers will enjoy. Lahiri writes of Gogol's childhood in the 1970s and 1980s with the advantage of hindsight; her description of Gogol's love of peanut butter is her way of saying that Gogol's behavior—that is to say, his appreciation of American goods over Indian goods—heralds the change in tastes that will sweep India in the twenty-first century, when young Indians in Kolkata will eat paneer tikka masala wraps as well as fried chicken at the local Kentucky Fried Chicken (see Roy).

Lahiri, however, resists the desire to attach the label hybrid to her characters. Had this novel been published ten years ago, it may have been read as an examination of hybridity, an exploration of what Homi Bhabha saw as the outcome of global diaspora and migration: "Hybridity is a problematic of colonial representation and individuation that reverses the effects of the colonialist disavowal, so that other 'denied' knowledges enter upon the dominant discourse and estrange the basis of its authority—its rules of recognition" (114). Bhabha's words—"disavowal," "denied," "estrange"—suggest a kind of violence and dislocation, as if the blending of cultures needs to be attended by attack, war, and domination.

Appiah offers an alternative; he writes that globalization can produce homogeneity through the proliferation of similar products, but that the erasure of distinctions among certain cultures can be beneficial these days:

> It's true that the enclaves of homogeneity you find these days—in Asante as in Pennsylvania—are less distinctive than they were a century ago, but mostly in good ways. More of them have access to effective medicines. More of them have access to clean drinking water, and more of them have schools. Where, as is still too common, they don't have these things, it's something not to celebrate but to deplore. And whatever loss of difference there has been, they are constantly inventing new forms of difference: new hairstyles, new slang, even, from time to time, new religions. No one could say that the world's villages are becoming anything like the same. ("Contamination")

Appiah's description of capitalism-induced global changes is largely positive, and he argues that they have less to do with people's cultural or national identity (or loss thereof) but rather with individual demands for a better moral and physical lifestyle. His arguments also suggest that the kinds of hybridization brought on by economic growth and the spreading of global capital are not threatening to traditional cultures, but rather inaugurate changes that are progressive.

Appiah's description of the discernment among consumers is a refreshing departure from the image of hybridization that Bhabha suggested, in which hybridity is the outcome of the violence of colonization: Appiah gives credit and agency to the traditional cultures that are experiencing a nonviolent "invasion" by Western products. He also suggests that America, as representative of the West, is not the dominating and invading nation that is spreading its capitalist power all over, but that America is itself not immune to the effects of global capital flows.

Lahiri's story is really one of Appiah-style cosmopolitanism, in which Indian and American cultures bleed into one another when they encounter each other on American soil and Indian immigrants are open to Americanization and cosmopolitanism because of the postcolonial, and therefore necessarily cosmopolitan, history of India itself. Lahiri's novel, in its digressions into the past that feature an India prior to Gogol's birth, underscores the idea that internal Indian class differences conferred an almost predetermined elitism on the children of the upper classes. In other words, those Indians of privilege migrated to America under auspicious conditions, which in turn enabled their children to succeed quickly in America. Ashima and Ashoke do not come to America to escape penury or persecution, as do so many immigrant protagonists from the early period; their journey to America is enabled by Ashoke's middle-class upbringing in Calcutta.

The Ganguli men occupy a long-standing position of privilege in India, one that allows them the pleasures of reading foreign literatures, travel across India and to points abroad, and foreign study. Gogol's great-grandfather is described as a great lover of Russian literature, who passes on his love for Nikolai Gogol to Gogol's father, Ashoke (Lahiri, *Namesake*); this love of foreign literatures is a legacy of British colonial rule, and as a functionary in the British government,

Ashoke's grandfather benefited from this literary import. Ashoke nicknames his son Gogol, partly out of a sense of filial love and partly because of a specific incident that leads him to invest the name with superstitious power. Ashoke had traveled to America to study fiber optics at MIT. Clearly, the idea of a fixed, poor, disenfranchised Indian who comes to America to better his life through the discovery of some ineffable "dream" does not apply to Lahiri's characters; the history of colonization in India creates a cosmopolitan culture and a "rhetoric of wandering" that even the immigrant generation recognizes. Gogol's tourism, therefore, although particular to his Indian American experience, is somewhat inherited; the legacy of colonization cannot be seen as only violent, coercive, and destructive, but also, for the Gangulis, positive, in that it enables them—as members of an elite class—to acquire a Western education and to travel abroad. Gogol's love for all things American and his tourist sensibility can be read in multiple ways: as a result of Americanization, as a legacy of colonialism, or as evidence of what Appiah would call a healthy "cross-contamination" of cultures that reaches back in history and continues today. . . .

Source: Natalie Friedman, "From Hybrids to Tourists: Children of Immigrants in Jhumpa Lahiri's *The Namesake*," in *CRITIQUE: Studies in Contemporary Fiction*, Vol. 50, No. 11, Fall 2008, p. 111.

Benjamin Austen

In the following mixed review, Austen contends that The Namesake *lacks the subtlety and resonance of Lahiri's short fiction but nevertheless displays her promising talent.*

"We all came out from under Gogol's 'Overcoat.'" That tip of the *shapka* to a fellow writer's brief masterpiece has been variously attributed to Fyodor Dostoyevsky, Leo Tolstoy and Ivan Turgenev. Jhumpa Lahiri—winner of the 2000 Pulitzer Prize for fiction with her first collection of stories, *Interpreter of Maladies*—goes the Russian greats one better by offering a full-length homage to Nikolai Gogol in her debut novel.

In "The Overcoat," when the beleaguered copying clerk Akaky Akakievich seeks out a tailor to mend his shabby cloak, Gogol reflects on his own obligations: "Of this tailor I ought not, of course, say much, but since it is now the rule that the character of every person . . . must be completely described, well, there's nothing I

> WITH RESERVE AND PRECISION, SHE ALTERNATES BETWEEN INTIMATE SHOTS OF ASHOKE AND A NEWSPAPER-STYLE ACCOUNT OF THE CRASH, ELEVATING THE EPISODE'S ELEMENTS TO AN AFFECTING PITCH."

can do but describe Petrovich too. . . . He was true to the customs of his forefathers, and when he quarreled with his wife he used to call her a worldly woman and a German. Since we have now mentioned the wife, it will be necessary to say a few words about her, too."

In *The Namesake* Lahiri, whose short fiction success is in large part due to a fastidious preciseness, succumbs to the rules Gogol was mocking. Both her stories and the novel recount the lives of Bengali immigrants and their American-reared children (like the author herself), and are composed in an understated, plain style. Yet as Lahiri weaves together numerous narrative threads in the novel her ambitions crowd out the subtlety, structural intricacy and thematic resonance that garnered her short work so much praise.

Nevertheless, a good story lies within the pages of *The Namesake*. Several months ago, a tightly focused and graceful excerpt appeared in the *New Yorker*. Each of its scenes emanated from the book's central event, the naming of the son of Ashoke and Ashima Ganguli, recent arrivals to Cambridge, Massachusetts, from India. The child is born two weeks early, and the parents are pressured by their American doctors to fill out the birth certificate, even though the traditional Hindu "good name" for their child has failed to reach them from Ashima's grandmother in Calcutta. Reluctantly, they break with custom and name their son Gogol—in gratefulness for Ashoke's surviving a catastrophic train wreck years before because rescuers spotted a page of "The Overcoat" falling from his fingers.

The decision, like many of Ashoke and Ashima's daily experiences in America, illuminates their disconnection from their family, native country and traditions. Their existence as foreigners, is a "perpetual wait, a constant burden, a continuous feeling out of sorts." In the early sections of the novel, Lahiri artfully illustrates the extent of this displacement as the Gangulis conduct their everyday affairs and slowly cobble together new lives as he settles into his academic career. They purchase a rake and shovel, shop for rice, walk laps daily around a manmade pond. Their pride stirs at the sight of Ashoke's name printed in a faculty directory.

Tensions between cultural sacrifice and hard-earned material gain, restraint and perpetual adjustment, are familiar themes of immigrant tales. The very ordinariness of the challenges and achievements Lahiri outlines makes *The Namesake* a fresh and worthy contribution to this literature. But she fails to deliver on her promise to show how different Ashoke and Ashima would have been if they had never left Calcutta. Scenes of their yearly trips to India fall flat, and the goings on of the surrogate family they form with fellow Bengalis in the suburbs of Boston pale in comparison to relations between parents and children.

Lahiri's meticulous chronicling of Ashima and Ashoke's relocation is a prelude to Gogol's own cultural identity crisis. The assimilated son attends public schools and then Yale, works as an architect in Manhattan, falls in and out of love with women who are not of Indian descent. He is an "American-born confused deshi"—a phrase he hears from a sociologist at a college lecture. "Teleologically speaking," the professor declares, "ABCDs are unable to answer the question 'Where are you from?'" In his very name, Gogol sees all his parents' awkwardness, their otherness, and the limits he believes they place on him.

Soon after he legally changes his name to Nikhil, Ashoke tells him how he came to be named Gogol. Here is Lahiri's account of the father riding a train to visit his grandfather and rereading the copy of Gogol's stories he had given him:

"Ashoke was still reading at two-thirty in the morning, one of the few passengers on the train who was awake, when the locomotive engine and seven bogies derailed from the broad-gauge line. The sound was like a bomb exploding. The first four bogies capsized into a depression alongside the track. The fifth and sixth, containing the first-class and air-conditioned passengers, telescoped into each other, killing the passengers in their sleep. The seventh, where Ashoke was sitting, capsized as well, flung by the speed of the crash farther into the field. The accident occurred 209 kilometers from Calcutta, between the Ghatshila and Dhalbumgarh stations."

This is Lahiri's writing at its finest. With reserve and precision, she alternates between intimate shots of Ashoke and a newspaper-style account of the crash, elevating the episode's elements to an affecting pitch.

In the best stories in *Interpreter of Maladies*, unexceptional events and actions subtly acquire meaning for Lahiri's characters, whose lives are transformed by encounters that initially seem commonplace. *The Namesake*, by contrast, is too often heavy-handed and haphazard. Symbolic weight is arbitrarily ascribed to a flock of low flying pigeons, a square of sunlight, a robe "a size too small" that "is a comfort all the same." As Lahiri repeats Gogol's gripes about his name and parents, once sharp and convincing emotional tangents become strained and less credible. This isn't *Oedipus*, or even Johnny Cash's "A Boy Named Sue." Gogol's conflict with his parents gradually comes off as an extended adolescent phase, a self-centered expression of individual uncertainty: "The only person who didn't take Gogol seriously, the only person who tormented him, the only person chronically aware of and afflicted by the embarrassment of his name... was Gogol."

Lahiri also devotes many pages to Gogol's failed romances, each a predictable lesson in his cultural education. One of his lovers, for example, is simplistically presented as his WASP opposite: A wealthy New Yorker who "has never wished she were anyone other than herself," she "emulates her parents... respects their tastes and their ways." They, in turn, "are secure in a way his parents will never be." His eventual marriage to one of the Bengalis who used to attend birthdays and holidays at his parents' home, and his subsequent acceptance of all things Indian, reads like an unearned form of redemption, the answer to an equation.

None of Gogol's failed relationships is rendered as effectively as those in Lahiri's earlier work. Moreover, even as the novel progresses the writing becomes increasingly unpolished. Over and over Gogol "realizes" one thing or another about his parent; an entire chapter is told, jarringly and inconsistently, from the vantage point of his soon-to-be ex-wife; and there are numerous descriptions ("wearing jeans and flip-flops and a paprika-colored shirt") that pile on the type of surplus information the Gogol of "The Overcoat" sends up.

Despite the shortcomings of this novel, though, Jhumpa Lahiri remains one of today's most promising young talents. Unlike many contemporaries who have won quick renown, she does not strive for cleverness, or promote quirky ventures for their sheer novelty. Nor does she peddle personal tragedy, hipness or exoticism, let alone insulate herself with alternating blasts of irony and earnestness. Where Zadie Smith's chaotic romps through multicultural England teem with sketched characters and abundant wackiness, Lahiri's realism aims for the human and avoids easy cultural comedy.

Indeed, there are instance of muted poignancy in *The Namesake* as memorable as any in Lahiri's first book. After Ashoke explains the history behind his son's name. Gogol responds with tears and anger.

"Why haven't you told me this until now? Is that what you think of me? Do I remind you of that night?"

"Not at all," Ashoke says. "You remind me of everything that followed."

This is a powerful exchange, a moment of intimacy that reveals its limitation. The name cannot mean the same thing to father and son, nor can it eclipse the distance between the two.

Source: Benjamin Austen, "In the Shadow of Gogol," in *New Leader*, September/October 2003, pp. 31–32.

SOURCES

Adams, Amy Singleton, "Nikolai Vasil'evich Gogol," in *Dictionary of Literary Biography*, Vol. 198, *Russian Literature in the Age of Pushkin and Gogol: Prose*, edited by Christine A. Rydel, The Gale Group, 1999, pp. 137–66.

Friedman, Natalie, "From Hybrids to Tourists: Children of Immigrants in Jhumpa Lahiri's *The Namesake*," in *Critique: Studies in Contemporary Fiction*, Vol. 50, No. 1, Fall 2008, p. 111.

Kakutani, Michiko, "From Calcutta to Suburbia: A Family's Perplexing Journey," in *New York Times*, September 2, 2003, p. E8.

Lahiri, Jhumpa, *The Namesake*, Houghton Mifflin, 2003.

Lynn, David H., "Virtues of Ambition," in *Kenyon Review*, Vol. 26, No. 3, Summer 2004, p. 160.

Munson, Sam, "Born in the U.S.A.," in *Commentary*, Vol. 116, November 2003, p. 68.

Rezaul Karim, "Jhumpa Lahiri," in *Dictionary of Literary Biography*, Vol. 323, *South Asian Writers in English*, edited by Fakrul Alam, Thomson Gale, 2006, pp. 205–210.

Sen, Mandira, "Names and Nicknames," in *Women's Review of Books*, Vol. 21, No. 6, March 2004, p. 9.

Singh, Inder, "Struggle of Indians for US Citizenship," in *Guyana Journal*, July 2006.

FURTHER READING

Khandelwal, Madhulika S., *Becoming American, Being Indian: An Immigrant Community in New York City*, Cornell University Press, 2002.
    This book, a nonfiction, anthropological account, provides an excellent overview of the Indian immigrant experience from the 1960s to 2000.

Lahiri, Jhumpa, *Unaccustomed Earth*, Knopf, 2008.
    As of 2009, Lahiri had written only three books. All three explore the Indian American experience, and while they are stand-alone works, their unifying subject matter makes it worth reading them together.

Nabokov, Vladimir, *Nikolai Gogol*, New Directions, corrected edition, 1961.
    This volume is a classic biography of the Russian writer, written by another famous Russian author. It has remained in print for over forty years.

Roy, Arundhati, *The God of Small Things*, Random House, 1997.
    Roy portrays an Indian family living in India during the 1960s in this contemporary classic novel. The volume provides a nice contrast to Lahiri's portrayal of Indian Americans living in the United Sates.

The Power and the Glory

GRAHAM GREENE

1940

Graham Greene's novel *The Power and the Glory* concerns a Catholic priest's struggle for survival in postrevolutionary Mexico, where priests are marked for death. This "whiskey priest" has not been a good clergyman, but his trip through the jungle, to another state where the laws against religious worship are less strict, is blocked at every turn by devout people who have not seen a priest in years and beg for his attention.

The idea of this novel came when Greene traveled through southern Mexico, in Tabasco and other states that provided the framework for the story. Greene, a devout Catholic, was appalled by the Mexican laws suppressing religious worship. The story came into shape when he heard a tale about a priest who arrived at a christening so drunk that he baptized the infant boy with the name of a girl, Brigida; in the novel, Brigida is the illegitimate daughter of the whiskey priest.

The Power and the Glory was first published in the United States in 1940 under the difficult title *The Labyrinthine Ways* because there already existed another book with the other title. Neither that book nor Greene's sold well, but eight years later, when it was selling well in Europe, Greene rereleased *The Power and the Glory* under the title it had been using in Europe all along. It has stayed in print ever since then and is considered one of Graham Greene's most moving and personal novels.

Graham Greene (*AP Images*)

AUTHOR BIOGRAPHY

Graham Greene was born in Berkhamsted, Hertfordshire, England, on October 2, 1904. He was the fourth of six children. His father, Charles, was a professor of history and classic literature and headmaster at Berkhamsted School. Graham secretly became a prodigious reader at a young age. In 1912 he enrolled in Berkhamsted, where he was miserable: bullied and alienated, he attempted suicide several times. His parents put him under the care of a psychoanalyst at age sixteen, and when he returned to Berkhamsted he felt more calm and made friends more easily.

In 1922 Greene enrolled in history at Oxford. There, his life was defined by the manic-depressive (bipolar) disorder that troubled him his whole life. He was not a notable student, but while at school he did publish a volume of poetry, *Babbling April*. After graduation, he worked for the British Tobacco Company and began writing fiction. He eventually decided to concentrate on journalism, and in 1926 he moved to Nottingham, England.

A young woman named Vivien Dayrell-Browning wrote to correct him about a factual error about Catholicism in one of his film reviews for the *Nottingham Times*, and they struck up a correspondence. They were married in 1927 after Greene had converted to Catholicism, which was to be a passion throughout his life.

Greene worked as a subeditor for the *London Times* until the 1929 publication of his first novel, *The Man Within*. The book was a critical success, leading to a publishing contract that offered financial independence. The three weak, awkward action stories that he wrote under that contract damaged his reputation and left him destitute. He then took to writing for popular audiences, having success when *Stambul Train* sold ten thousand copies in 1932. He became an ardent traveler, alternating between writing fiction and travelogues. His trip to Mexico, which led to *The Power and the Glory* (1940), was begun in order to get out of England to avoid prosecution on libel charges after his review of a Shirley Temple movie was found to insinuate that the filmmakers were exploiting the young star's sexuality. Several of his books were adapted by movie studios.

Throughout the 1940s, 1950s, and 1960s, Greene continued to travel to increasingly dangerous locations, going to Vietnam four years in a row; writing dispatches from Stalinist Russia, Haiti, Cuba, and the Belgian Congo; and writing about his journeys, often in fictionalized form. He was appointed to the board of the Bodley Head publishing firm and read hundreds of manuscripts. His many awards included Honorary Associate of the American Academy of Arts and Letters in 1961, the Shakespeare Prize in 1968, and the Chevalier de la Légion d'Honneur in 1969. In 1966 he left England for good, moving to Antebes, an island off the coast of France, for sixteen years and then spending his final years in Vevey, Switzerland, where he died in 1991.

PLOT SUMMARY

I

Chapter One of the first part of *The Power and the Glory* begins with Mr. Tench, a British dentist who is hoping to make enough money some day to go home. He strikes up a conversation with an educated stranger who he assumes is a doctor; this is the man referred to in the novel as the priest or the whiskey priest, who has come to the capital city to meet a man named Lopez, hoping that Lopez will be able to get him out of the country. They have a drink together, and Tench tells him that Lopez was shot the week before by the chief of police, who wanted Lopez's girlfriend. A boy comes to Tench's office

MEDIA ADAPTATIONS

- Director John Ford adapted this novel as a movie, *The Fugitive*, in 1947. The action of the film has been moved to an anonymous South American country. It was written by Dudley Nichols and stars Henry Fonda, Dolores del Rio, Pedro Armendáriz, and J. Carroll Naish. It is not available on DVD, but it was released on videocassette by Turner Home Entertainment in 1990.

- An unabridged sound recording of this book, read by John Aulicino, was released in 1990 by Recorded Books of Prince Frederick, Maryland.

- Also in 1990, Blackstone Audio released an unabridged recording of the book on seven cassettes, read by Bernard Mayes.

- Andrew Sachs read an unabridged audiocassette version of the book that was released by Sterling Audio of Bath, England, in 1991.

- *The Power and the Glory* was adapted to a television movie that was broadcast on CBS in 1961. It starred Laurence Olivier as the priest, Julie Harris as Maria, George C. Scott as the lieutenant, and Patty Duke as Coral.

and says that he needs help because his mother is sick, and Tench tells the priest to go, still thinking he is a doctor. The priest objects, but Tench tells him that the boat he wants to leave the country on will not leave for hours or days. Following the boy into the jungle, the priest prays that he will be caught soon.

Chapter Two follows the police squad that is run by the lieutenant. The chief of police enters with news that the governor of the province wants them to capture the one remaining priest rumored to still be alive, though the lieutenant believes that the final priest has been caught and killed. The chief of police, referred to as "el jefe," has a bad toothache and gives the lieutenant the responsibility of capturing the priest and James

Calver, a notorious criminal from the United States who is hiding out in their district. The narrative follows the lieutenant to the small furnished room where he lives alone; he has heavy thoughts about the priests whom the government has executed. Nearby is the home of Padre José, a priest who has avoided persecution by renouncing his vows and marrying a woman.

Chapter Three introduces Captain Fellows, who runs the Central American Banana Company plantation. The Captain's wife, Trixy, is bedridden with a terrible headache, and his teenaged daughter Coral, who runs the plantation in his absence, takes him aside to talk to him. The police lieutenant wants to search the plantation, she says, looking for the fugitive priest. Fellows thinks that there is nothing to fear, but Coral explains that they are in fact harboring the priest, who is hidden in a barn. Fellows refuses the lieutenant's request and sends him away, and Coral speaks to the priest to let him know it is safe to go. Traveling through the jungle again, the whiskey priest comes upon a small village, a collection of huts; he tells the inhabitants that he must leave, but they implore him to stay and hear the confession of a dying man. The priest knows that the police are nearby, but he allows the villagers to talk him into staying to hear confessions from all of the Catholics in the village.

Chapter Four of this section provides glimpses of the lives of various characters who have already been introduced. Tench, the dentist, has gotten a letter from the wife he left behind in England fifteen years earlier, and he intends to write back but instead allows himself to be distracted by a patient. Padre José walks through a cemetery and is approached by a family who wants him to say a prayer for their five-year-old daughter who has died, but he refuses to do so because prayers are against the law. Luis, whose mother earlier read to her children from a book about a martyred Mexican child, tells his mother that the story is silly and unbelievable: when he and his friends play, he says, they idolize revolutionary figures. Coral Fellows, on the other hand, is curious about Catholic doctrine after her encounter with the priest and asks her mother about it, even though her parents are Protestants. The police lieutenant is skeptical about the jefe's order to kill civilians in order to bring the fugitive priest out of hiding. Walking across the square, the lieutenant runs into young Luis playing a violent game, and he indulges the boy's fantasy by letting him examine his gun.

II

Chapter One of the second section is about the fugitive whiskey priest riding into the village where his parish once was. He encounters Maria, whom he does not recognize because he has not seen her in six years, although she is the mother of his child. She agrees to hide him at her home, but the other people of the village, thrilled to have a priest among them, implore him to hear their confessions and say Mass. The priest tries to talk with his young daughter, Brigida, but she is cynical and uninterested. In the morning, as he is saying Mass, soldiers invade the village. The whiskey priest is nearly found out, but Maria asks Brigida who her father is, and when she points to the whiskey priest they leave, first taking a young man from the village as a hostage. As the priest leaves the village, he comes across Brigida playing by the garbage dump, and she curses and says she's ashamed that he is her father. He moves along to La Candelaria, a village where he hopes to hire a boat to take him across the river, but there is no boat. A poor "half-caste" person (that is, a person of mixed Mexican and Indian ethnicity) talks to him and gives him directions, and it dawns on him that this is the priest who has a bounty on his head. The half-caste catches up with him up the road and offers to be his guide, but the priest refuses to admit who he is. When they stop for the night, the half-caste is sick with a fever, and the priest tries to sneak away, but the other man catches up with him. The priest pulls away from the weakened man and insists that he tell the police that he never entered the village of Carmen, so that they will not take any hostages there.

Chapter Two opens in the capital city, where the book began. The priest approaches a stranger as a beggar. To save him from being found out by the police, Maria poured out the small cache of wine he needs to say Mass, and the priest needs it replaced. He strikes up a conversation with a stranger; after some questions, the stranger offers to take him to the Governor's cousin, who can sell him some wine. They go to the man's room, but the Governor's cousin will only sell him the necessary grape wine if he also buys some brandy, and then the two other men insist that he drink it with them. They are joined by the chief of police, and the priest is forced to drink the brandy and all of his wine with them, leaving him drunk, penniless, and without the wine he came for. He has a little brandy in the bottle in his pocket when he enters a cantina and bumps across a soldier,

ruining the man's billiards shot. When the soldiers chase him, he runs to the home of Padre José for sanctuary, but Padre José refuses to help him. The whiskey priest is arrested for having forbidden alcohol and put in jail.

Chapter Three is about the priest's night in jail. There are people there who blame the country's troubles on the church and people who are devout Catholics. Hoping that his long journey will be over, the priest tells them who he is, but although he is locked up with criminals, none of them turns him in for the reward. In the morning, he is made to clean out the buckets that serve as toilets. He runs into the half-caste, who recognizes him, but he convinces the man that the only way to continue the kind treatment the police have been giving him is to keep the hunt for the priest alive. Later, he is brought before the police lieutenant, who does not know that this is the priest he has been hunting for. The lieutenant looks at the pathetic figure standing before him and feels mercy, giving the man some money from his pocket. The priest tells the lieutenant that he is a good man.

In Chapter Four, the whiskey priest returns to the Central American Banana Company plantation, hoping to find Coral Fellows, remembering her kindness to him. The plantation is empty, though, with no sign of people and all of the Fellows's belongings removed. He is so hungry that he fights to take a bone out of the mouth of a starving, crippled dog. Later, he is approached by an Indian woman who shows him her child, who has been shot. To gain her confidence so that she will help him bandage the child, he tells her he is a priest, but it is too late, and the child dies. The only word she recognizes is "Americano," so the priest assumes that her child was killed by the American gangster that the police are seeking. When she is not looking, he steals the little piece of sugar that she left on the dead child's mouth as part of the burial ritual, and the sugar gives him the energy to ride on through the forest. After a time, he comes to a town where, to his surprise, the church still stands, and where the arrival of a priest is an occasion for rejoicing.

III

At the start of Chapter One of the third section, the priest has been a guest in the home of Miss Lehr and her brother, Mr. Lehr, for a while. The Lehrs are from Germany, and they are wealthy. They are not Catholics, but they are tolerant of the priest's faith and enjoy having philosophical conversations with him. Their town is in a more relaxed state, where priests are not executed for celebrating Mass but are only forced to pay a small fine. When the local people come to ask him to baptize their children, the priest tells them that they must pay him for the service; every amount that he quotes is considered too high, but he remembers having been trained to insist that the peasants must pay if they are to value the privilege. In the back of his head, he calculates how much he is going to make in order to buy a new suit and move on to the safety of the big city, Las Casas, with a comfortable amount in his pocket. A local man, recognizing that the whiskey priest likes to drink, convinces him to buy some bottles of brandy for his upcoming trip. He has conducted the baptisms and the final mass and is ready to leave town a wealthy man when he is approached by the half-caste, who has come to tell him that the American gangster has been shot and wants the priest to come and hear his confession. The priest knows that it is a trap, to lure him back over the border to the state where Catholicism is severely punished, but the story that the half-caste told him about the gangster shielding himself with a boy is confirmed by the bullet-ridden Indian boy whom he buried. Driven by a sense of duty and disbelieving the good luck that almost let him escape, he relents and agrees to go.

In Chapter Two, the priest is certain that he has ridden into a trap, but he shows compassion for the half-caste who tried to trick him, giving him his brandy and his money before he enters the hut to which the man leads him. As soon as he enters, the American tells him that he must leave. He denies that he wanted to see a priest. When he reaches for his gun and finds it gone, it becomes certain that someone set him up as a trap; still, the priest stays with him and prays over him until he dies.

In Chapter Three, the police lieutenant enters the hut to arrest the priest, and the priest recounts the two times they have been face-to-face before: in his village, when Brigida identified him as her father, and at the jail, when the lieutenant gave him money. A sudden downpour forces them to take refuge in a hut, where they talk about their similarities and differences. The police bring the priest back to the capital city, and there he asks for just one favor, to be able to say his confession before his execution. The lieutenant agrees to bring the defamed priest, Padre José.

He arrives at Padre José's home in Chapter Four, but suspecting that he is being tricked into

performing a Catholic rite, Padre José refuses to go to the jail. He nearly succumbs, but his wife resolutely refuses to let him go, and Padre José is left listening to the mocking children who line up outside his fence and tauntingly shout his name. The lieutenant returns to the jail with a flask of brandy and tries to console the whiskey priest that there will be no pain when he is shot. The priest spends his last night saying his confession to himself.

IV

There is only one chapter in Section IV. It begins with Captain and Mrs. Fellows in a hotel room, having abandoned the banana plantation; Mrs. Fellows assumes that they will be leaving the country, but Captain Fellows tells her that whether she goes or not, he is going to stay. Nothing is said about their daughter, who is not with them. Mr. Tench, the dentist, finally has time to work on the chief of police, the jefe. When they hear shots fired, the jefe explains that a man is being executed. Tench watches out the window and recognizes the priest, whom he took to be a doctor in the book's first chapter. He remembers the bond that he made with the man during their conversation while the jefe complains about the pain of his untended tooth. The book ends with Luis, who is listening again to his mother read about the young martyr. The martyr's execution is like the execution of the whiskey priest, except that the martyr, Juan, is noble in his death. For the first time, Luis asks questions about the story and shows signs that he believes it. Later, when he has gone to bed, a stranger arrives at their home, a man who identifies himself as a priest. Instead of turning him away or running to tell the police, Luis lets him in and motions for him to be quiet.

CHARACTERS

Brigida

Brigida is the whiskey priest's child, born from his one night of drunken passion with Maria more than six years earlier. In his absence, she has grown to be steely and unsentimental, a child of poverty who seems to have no interest in religion. She has adult features, and her face and her cynicism haunt the priest throughout his escape.

James Carver

Carver is an infamous American gangster who has escaped to Mexico to evade the law. He is often referred to in the novel as "the Gringo," an ethnic slur Mexicans in this novel use to describe Americans. The same policemen who are charged with capturing the whiskey priest are after him, and their photos are hung side-by-side over the desk of the police lieutenant. The priest is captured when he hears that the gangster, who has held an innocent young child in front of him to shield himself from bullets, is dying and wants to say confession. When the priest does show up, Carver denies asking for him, and he tries to chase the priest away before he can be trapped. Because he is a man of violence, he offers the priest his gun and knife with which to fight the law.

Captain Fellows

Captain Fellows runs the Central American Banana Company plantation. The whiskey priest hides out at his plantation for an evening while the Captain is away, having been invited by Captain Fellows's daughter Coral. Later, when the plantation has been closed down and Coral has disappeared, Captain Fellows disagrees with his wife, who would like to go back to England, and wants to stay in Mexico instead.

Coral Fellows

Coral Fellows is a thirteen-year-old girl from England who is being raised in the Mexican jungle by her father, who runs a banana plantation, and her mother, who is chronically ill. Although she is a Protestant, not a Catholic, she has compassion for the whiskey priest when she finds him running from the law, and she lets him hide on the plantation. She teaches him a small amount of Morse code, which becomes a symbol for religious understanding between them. At the end of the novel, the plantation is deserted and her parents are living in a hotel. There is no mention of Coral's fate, whether she has been arrested for aiding the priest or has run away.

Trixy Fellows

Captain Fellows's wife, Trixy, is presented as a coddled Englishwoman, taking to her bed for days at a time because of her headaches while around her the people of Mexico are dying of starvation.

The Half-Caste

As he is being pursued by the police, the whiskey priest is recognized by a half-caste, also referred to as a mestizo, a person of mixed racial background. This man rides beside the priest, asking leading questions intended to make the priest confess his identity. In crossing a river to catch up with him, the half-caste catches a fever, and the priest is able to leave him behind. Later, when the priest enters the capital city, he sees the half-caste in the company of police officers and finds out that they need him because he is the only person who can identify the priest. When he is in jail, the half-caste recognizes him but decides that the priest must continue to be hunted if the police are going to keep treating him as their honored guest, and so he says nothing. Later, when the priest has escaped across the border and is safe, the half-caste comes to him and says that the American gangster is dying and has requested a priest for confession. The priest knows that it is a trap, but he goes with the half-caste, giving the man who has led him to his doom his money and his brandy before the trap is set, and telling him to ride away before he is caught in the gunfire that is to come.

The Jefe

The jefe is the chief of police in the capital city. When the governor of the state orders that the last remaining priest must be caught and executed, the jefe turns the responsibility over to his lieutenant, not wanting to be responsible for the consequences if the political situation ever shifts back in the other direction.

Padre José

When the law declared that priests had to renounce their priesthood or be executed, Padre José renounced his vows. To prove it, he married his housekeeper, which canceled his vow of celibacy. It is a loveless marriage, and Padre José avoids going to bed at night when his wife calls for him. Sitting in the darkness, he hears the neighborhood children mocking him from outside the gates of his home. When the whiskey priest comes to him for help with hiding from the police, Padre José refuses to take the chance because he is afraid of prosecution. At the end, the police lieutenant comes to Padre José with the whiskey priest's request to say his confession, but Padre José, fearing that it is just a trap to catch him participating in a Catholic rite, refuses to accompany the lieutenant to the jail.

Miss Lehr

Miss Lehr once lived in Pittsburgh, where she ran a hotel for musicians. She moved to Mexico to run her brother's household after his wife died. She is not a Catholic, but she had a revelation once when she saw atrocities in a newspaper, and she seems to be on the verge of some religious revelation. Miss Lehr has aided another priest in his flight out of the state and tries to be helpful to this priest as well. She tells him thoughts and fears that she would not share even with her brother, indicating her loneliness.

Mr. Lehr

Mr. Lehr is a German man who owns the plantation where the priest takes refuge when he crosses the border. He is a pacifist who left Germany when he was just a boy in order to avoid mandatory service in the military. Mr. Lehr does not believe in Catholicism. He is a businessman. Still, he is a congenial man who is glad to have the company of an intelligent person, and he allows the priest to stay in his house and even use his stables to conduct Mass, even though it is illegal.

The Lieutenant

The lieutenant is the police official in charge of capturing two wanted men, the American gangster and the fugitive whiskey priest. He is a devoted public servant: when the jefe suggests that he should take hostages from among the peasants to find the priest, he is personally opposed to the tactic, although he goes along with it. Readers can see that the lieutenant is actually a good man in the scene in which he releases the priest, who has been held in jail overnight: he does not recognize the priest from the old picture that is tacked to the wall behind him; taking him for a poor beggar, the lieutenant takes a coin out of his pocket to give to him. Later, when the lieutenant traps the priest and arrests him, the two of them have a philosophical discussion about the nature of goodness and government, and it becomes clear that the lieutenant sincerely feels that the government treats the people better than the church ever did. The lieutenant does what he can to make the priest's last hours on earth bearable, going so far as to try to bring another priest in to hear his confession, although it is illegal and he himself does not believe in its redemptive powers.

Luis

Luis is a little boy who, along with his sisters, is read an inspirational story about a boy who was martyred. Although he is young, he is cynical and rejects the message that his mother is trying to impress on her children. At the end of the book, however, it becomes clear that the story his mother told him has in fact had an effect on Luis, as he invites a priest to hide in his house.

Maria

Maria is the mother of the whiskey priest's daughter. When he returns to her village for the first time in six years, he does not recognize Maria, partly because of how she has changed and partly because they had little to do with each other, despite their brief affair. She is hard and cynical toward him when he comes back to the village to hide, but she helps him evade capture by pretending to be his wife. To save his life, she destroys the bottle of grape wine that he needs to conduct Mass and throws away his religious paraphernalia.

Miguel

Miguel is the innocent hostage taken away from the small village in the jungle. He is taken by the police to force the priest to identify himself or to encourage one of his neighbors to turn the priest in, but no one speaks up. Later, when he is in jail in the capital, the priest sees Miguel, who has been beaten.

Mr. Tench

Mr. Tench is an alcoholic dentist who came to Mexico fifteen years ago, leaving his family behind in England. As the economy worsened, he gave up the idea of being able to send any usable money home. One of his two sons has died while he has been gone. He is stranded and miserable, despairing, in part because all alcohol stronger than beer has been outlawed by the revolution. When Tench tries to write a letter to his wife, Sylvia, he has to address it to Sylvia's mother's home because he does not know where his wife currently lives. At the end of the novel, Tench is working on the teeth of the chief of police when he hears the whiskey priest being executed outside; he is drawn to the window, recognizing the priest as someone he once talked to, and finds himself thinking about the political situation, which is something he has avoided for a long time.

The Whiskey Priest

The priest who is the protagonist of this novel is given no name, and is referred to only as "the priest" or "the whiskey priest." The latter expression is a common one in the culture described in the story, used to describe a priest who has let himself fall into alcoholism. In the story, he avoids alcohol, mostly because it is unavailable. When he has a little money and finds someone who sells alcohol illegally, he tries to buy grape wine, which he can use for saying Mass. When he arrives in a safe haven, though, and he is able to charge the peasants for performing his priestly duties, he lets a seller of brandy talk him into buying three bottles, proving that his abstinence from liquor was driven by necessity and not by a desire to lead a cleaner life.

He is the last priest surviving in the southern Mexican state where religious practice has been outlawed. The authorities are hunting him with the same techniques they are using to hunt down a legendary thief and bandit who has come to their state to hide. His flight to the border, to another state where he might be able to live freely, is hindered throughout the novel when people beg him to perform sacraments for them with the power invested in him as a priest: he is asked to say Mass, hear confessions, and perform baptisms. Although doing so puts him at risk of exposure, he feels duty bound to comply.

His flight through the jungle takes the priest to the small village where he once had a church. It is there that he meets Brigida, his illegitimate child. Although he abandoned her long ago and finds that she has come to despise him in his absence, his thoughts constantly go back to her. The night before his death, when he finds himself locked in a cell and unable to clear his sins through confession, he thinks of her as a true reason for his life.

The whiskey priest makes no pretense of being a good man or motivated by his faith. He does not think much of the good things that he does, but only of his race to save his own life because he fears the pain of being shot.

THEMES

Catholicism

The priest in *The Power and the Glory* finds his plans for escape foiled on several occasions because he feels that it is his responsibility to perform certain functions. Several times, for instance, he is asked to put his flight on hold because people need him to stay with them and

TOPICS FOR FURTHER STUDY

- Alan Moore and David Lloyd's graphic novel *V for Vendetta* takes place in an alternative version of England, ruled by a totalitarian government that is like the one Mexico tried to establish in the 1930s. Pick one episode from the book and rewrite it with illustrations, inserting Greene's whiskey priest into the story.

- There are several places in the world where specific religious groups are outlawed, such as Falun Gong in the People's Republic of China or Baha'i in Iran. Study a case of a contemporary religion that is outlawed and use your results to write a short story that illustrates the political situation.

- Interview a member of the clergy or some other person who is educated in the traditions of a religion that you are not familiar with to find out what sacred items he or she feels would need to be saved in the event of a catastrophe. Create a PowerPoint presentation that illustrates how these items support the religious tradition.

- Explore the life of one of the more prominent figures from the Mexican revolution, such as Pancho Villa, Emiliano Zapata, or Venustiano Carranza. Write an essay that explains what that person's position on the Catholic Church would be, and a response that shows whether you would agree or disagree with them.

- Often, during times of religious persecution, people use artistic works to carry on forbidden traditions. Make and perform a song that you think could be legally sung in the Mexico that the book portrays, but that would still communicate a message of hope to people who feel that their religion is being repressed.

hear their confessions. According to Catholic doctrine, Jesus conferred upon his disciples the power to forgive sins that were committed after baptism under certain conditions, and the same power was passed on to all ordained priests. In the sacrament of penance, a sinner who says confession to a priest and performs the penance that the priest assigns can be absolved of her or his sins. The importance of having sins absolved through this sacrament is shown in the novel when the priest knowingly walks into a trap set by the police because he is required by his oath to hear the confession of the American gangster, James Carver, who has expressed the desire to confess; under other circumstances a person might ignores such a request, coming from a criminal, and say that he deserves whatever fate awaits him, but the truly devoted Catholic priest cannot turn his back on such a request.

Another church doctrine that complicates the priest's escape from the authorities is the necessity for grape wine in performing the sacrament of Holy Communion. In this sacrament, bread and wine are blessed and thereafter stand for the body and blood of Jesus. When he can find none of the unleavened wafers traditionally used for Holy Communion while saying Mass, the priest is able to substitute bread from Maria's oven, but church doctrine requires him to use grape wine. This is why Maria pours out the wine he has left, because a man caught in possession of wine will easily be recognized as a priest. It is also why the priest puts himself in danger in the capital: his pretense of having a thirst that will not be quenched by wine made from quinces or by brandy does not fool the governor's cousin or the chief of police, and so they prevent him from taking the wine with him to someplace where he could use it for Communion.

Class Conflict

In the end, the priest's moral position is balanced in this novel by the secular morality of the lieutenant who is charged with capturing him. Greene establishes that the lieutenant is a decent man when, faced with a penniless beggar, he takes money from his own pocket to help the man. Although he could present this agent of the law as being heartless or evil, Greene instead makes it clear that he does care about the poor people he watches over. The lieutenant is frustrated; he knows that the peasants are helping the priest in his escape, and he cannot understand why they would choose to side with the church when, in his view, it is the government that really looks after the interests of the poor.

To the revolutionaries who fought against the status quo in Mexico in the 1910s and 1920s, the church was considered a tool for keeping the poor oppressed. As the lieutenant points out, the promise of a better life in the afterworld can be used to make people accept suffering in this world. The lieutenant's skepticism is confirmed in the novel, to some degree, when the priest considers how much he should charge for saying Mass and performing baptisms: he tells himself that it would be better for the peasants to pay more than they think they can afford, to make them suffer for it and therefore appreciate the sacraments more, but it is clear that he is also driven by thoughts of how much he stands to profit. In the priest's greed, Greene tacitly shows how the church could actually have a hand in keeping the poor of the country oppressed.

Sin

The protagonist of this novel is a priest, but he is clearly not free of sin. He has allowed his addiction to alcohol to become so powerful that his drunkenness is obvious, and people refer to him as a "whiskey priest," a condition so common that a phrase has been coined for it. Even worse than his drinking is that he has given in to lust and fathered a child. The priest is well aware of his moral shortcomings, his human frailties; he does not feel that he is a pious man, even though he risks his life several times to give religious comfort to those who need it. Faced with death, he is anxious to have his sins absolved through confession.

Green shows moral ambiguity in several other characters as well. Padre José, the priest who broke his vow of celibacy by marrying his housekeeper, earned the acceptance of the government, but he suffers from a guilty conscience, which is brought to life in the novel by the taunts of the children outside his gate. The American gangster is reputed to be a thief and a murderer and clearly commits a venial sin by holding a young Indian boy to shield himself from the policemen's bullets, but he does show remorse, asking for a priest to hear his confession, and when he realizes that he is being used as a trap he does what he can to chase the priest away. Even the lieutenant who is killing innocent hostages in order to bring the priest out into the open is not simply the sinner that circumstances seem to imply: not only does he give money to a poor man whom the legal system abuses but he sees the goodness in the priest after they have had a chance to talk. He follows his duty to the law, but is also willing to bend the law to bring him a bottle of brandy or a priest to hear his confession.

Henry Fonda as "A Fugitive" and Pedro Armendariz "A Lieutenant of Police" in the 1947 film The Fugitive, *based on* The Power and the Glory *(© Photos 12 | Alamy)*

STYLE

Nameless Characters

Graham Greene does not give names to several of the key characters in this novel. Readers never even find out the name of the book's protagonist, who is identified only as "the priest" or "the whiskey priest." To retain his anonymity, Greene must resort to such obvious omission as having him tell a man he runs into in the jungle his name, but only relating it in the book as "Father So-and-so." Obviously, the priest has spoken his name in the story, but that information is withheld from the reader by the narrator.

Other key characters who do not have names are the lieutenant, the half-caste (who is also referred to sometimes by the alternate description "the mestizo"), and the chief of police (the jefe). There are also named characters, such as Maria, Brigida, Luis, and Mr. Trent.

Identifying characters by descriptions rather than names serves to keep readers' minds on their social functions. Greene uses these characters as examples of how this society is run and how people interact with each other. Even when the setting is not in a social situation, there are characters who are defined by the roles that other people project upon them: for instance, the Indian woman whom the priest runs into in the jungle has no other name because all that he knows about her is that she is an Indian woman. Because readers are not given a name for the priest, they constantly think of him as a priest, regardless of how much they come to understand how he feels. Likewise, the lieutenant shows himself to have several dimensions, but his military rank is always foremost in the reader's mind. Readers are not, however, constantly reminded that Mr. Tench is a dentist, that Maria is an ex-lover, or that Brigida is a daughter; Greene grants these characters internal personalities that are independent of their social functions.

COMPARE & CONTRAST

- **1940:** A criminal on the run from the U.S. government can disappear into the depths of southern Mexico, where the government is unlikely to find him or her and would have a difficult time securing extradition if it did.

  Today: Under the many treaties passed since the United States began its international offensive against terrorism, criminals worldwide find it harder to escape the long arm of foreign law enforcement.

- **1940:** Many readers in the United States view Mexico as a backwards country of poverty and illiteracy.

  Today: Until the global financial crisis of 2008, the Mexican economy was making substantial gains. Additionally, the Internet

  and a push in U.S. schools toward multiculturalism have helped Americans dispel many of the cultural stereotypes held by earlier generations.

- **1940:** Catholicism is very centered on the priest, who says Mass and administers sacraments. Lay Catholics turn to him for all matters concerning their religious faith. Priesthood is limited to males.

  Today: The Catholic priesthood is still limited to males, but after the reforms of the Second Vatican Council in the early 1960s there has been a push to make the Mass more inclusive, with roles for parishioners to participate in readings, in music, and even in distributing the blessed Eucharist.

Historical Novel

By the time Graham Greene wrote *The Power and the Glory*, the anti-Catholic sentiment in Mexico had begun to soften, even in the hardline southern provinces where the book is set. Still, people who lived through the situation Greene described recognize his novel as an accurate portrayal of what it felt like to be present at that time and place.

For many novelists, character development is such an important focus that the setting is hardly noticeable, mentioned only in passing; it could be replaced with another setting without substantially altering the impact of the book. Other novels are set in a specific, recognizable time and place, like the Boston of George V. Higgins or Chicago in Saul Bellows's stories, but the location is not the author's main concern. Some writers, such as Gabriel Garcia Marquez or Sherwood Anderson, choose to make up entirely imaginary settings for their fiction. *The Power and the Glory*, however, is so inexorably bound to its setting that it could not work as a story if it took place anywhere else. Although the whiskey priest and the other characters are

products of the author's imagination, the situation Greene puts them in is a matter of verifiable, historical fact. Readers can confirm the truth of Greene's descriptions or point to evidence that refutes it.

HISTORICAL CONTEXT

This novel takes place in Tabasco, a state in Mexico, during the 1930s. Tabasco was the state where the most extreme ideas of the Mexican Revolution were implemented, where intense poverty caused a backlash against the social order that had oppressed the peasantry for more than a century.

In the early years of the twentieth century, Mexico's dictator, Porfirio Díaz, ran a corrupt government that suppressed the rights of the poor and the middle class. In the election of 1910, Díaz was announced the winner by an overwhelming majority, but his opponent, Francisco Madero, who was living in the United States, declared that the election was illegitimate and that he was the true president. The question over the election riled the population to armed revolt: followers of Madero, as well as revolutionaries following Pascual Orozco and Pancho Villa, rose up against the government. Díaz resigned as president in May of 1911, and after a brief rule by an interim president, Madero was inaugurated in November of that year. After fifteen months, Madero was in turn overthrown by one of his generals, Victoriano Huerta, a cruel and violent man who drew the enmity of the United States. Between 1910 and 1920, Mexico was in a constant state of revolt, with between 1 and 2 million people out of a population of 15 million dying violently, and hundreds of thousands fleeing the country over the United States border.

One result of the revolution was the constitution of 1917. The constitution, which is still the ruling document of Mexican politics to this day, provided political reforms and land distribution rights that gave the country's millions of poor a voice in their political system. It created a modern social democracy, a system that was new to that part of the world and provided a model for countries throughout Latin America. With a constitution that was generally agreed upon by several of the revolutionary factions, violence fell off during the 1920s, though there were still scattered outbreaks against the government. By the end of that decade, the government's control of the country was secure under a one-party system. The Institutional Revolutionary Party ruled Mexico from 1929 to 2000.

One result of the national constitution was the suppression of Catholicism. The Catholic Church had been established in Mexico for centuries, going back to the arrival of the Spanish adventurer Hernán Cortés, who was accompanied on his expedition by several members of the Roman Catholic clergy. In the 1800s, the government feared that the church was becoming a rival in power and made several moves to limit it. Measures were passed in 1833 and 1857 that were designed to confiscate the property of the Catholic Church in the name of the government, leading to a civil war in 1857–1860 to support the Church's right to exist. By the period of Porfirio Díaz, Catholicism was accepted and encouraged, and so it was natural that the revolutionary forces that overthrew Díaz would view religion as a tool to suppress the rights of the poor. The 1917 constitution includes several statements about religious reform. Article 3, for instance, forbids church activity in elections, and Article 5 prohibits the establishment of new religious orders. Article 24 forbids religious

Paul Schofield in a scene from the play The Power and the Glory, *adapted from the novel, at the Phoenix Theatre in London* (© Hulton-Deutsch Collection / Corbis)

ceremonies from taking place outside religious buildings, and Article 27 turns the ownership of all religious buildings over to the government. Article 130 gives individual state governments the authority to determine how many clergy members are allowed to function within the state and strips the church of any authority in the social sphere, such as the power to wed people or the power to criticize the government.

The Cristero Rebellion of 1926–1929 was a violent uprising on behalf of religious freedom that eventually ended with even greater repression. After the rebellion was quelled, the state of Tabasco outlawed Catholic worship except in cases where priests were willing to break their vows of celibacy and marry. In Sonora, all churches were closed, and in Chihuahua only one priest was permitted to remain to serve the entire population.

CRITICAL OVERVIEW

When it was first published in 1940, *The Power and the Glory* suffered from very low sales. One reason was the confusion that arose when the book was, for copyright reasons, published in the United States under a title different from the one it bore in Europe. Another reason was that it was published just a month before Adolf Hitler's Nazi forces invaded England, and the novel was overlooked in the ensuing social upheaval. The main reason that it failed to find an audience, though, was that it is a book with strong Catholic themes, focused on a Catholic priest, but it was denounced by the Catholic Church upon its publication. The "whiskey priest" at the center of the novel was taken to be a heretic, and Catholics avoided the book until the French edition, for which French Catholic novelist Francois Mauriac provides a thoughtful introduction that explains the book's piety. As A. A. DeVitis explains in the book *Graham Greene*, critics who rejected the book because they could see the whiskey priest only in terms of his Catholic faith failed to do justice to Greene's work. As DeVitis puts it,

> The whiskey priest may be a Roman Catholic, but what he represents transcends the narrow limits of any one religious belief. The fact that he is a Catholic merely intensifies the conflict of the novel and lends dignity to the action.... Through the character of the priest, Greene approaches the precincts of myth.

After the novel's original weak reception, critics generally agreed that it represents an admirable achievement on Greene's part. "*The Power and the Glory* is one of the most powerful of Greene's novels," Richard Kelly wrote in his book *Graham Greene* (1984), "and the one considered by most critics to be his finest." Though not all critics agree with this assessment, most have agreed that it is worth serious consideration. Neil McEwan, notably, finds an element of humor in Greene's tale of desperation: "Much of the novel shows what is not funny about being a sinful priest in desperate circumstances," he writes in yet another work titled *Graham Greene*. "But it has its own sense of humour, and the clue to the priest's endurance is his frightened giggle." The most resilient criticism of the book has been that it is too unpolished as fiction, and instead functions as a lecture by Greene, who speaks his views too directly to the reader. Addressing this

issue, Frank Kermode notes in his essay "Mr. Greene's Eggs and Crosses," published in *Puzzles & Epiphanies*, that the book has been subject to some "damaging criticism," and that some critics feel that it amounts to "a ventriloquial performance with an interesting dummy."

CRITICISM

David Kelly

Kelly is a writer and an instructor of creative writing and literature. In the following essay on The Power and the Glory, *he examines the ways in which Greene uses two-dimensional characters to highlight aspects of his protagonist, and the questions raised by one unusual scene at the end.*

Graham Greene has been called a theoretical or automatic writer, in that he uses the objective perspective, with his narrative point of view roaming around from one image to another and one scene to the next without much commentary. In *The Power and the Glory*, for example, he presents a man on the run from both the law and his own uneasy lack of connection to the world. The narration does not need to dig deeply into the man's thoughts to establish what is awry in his view of the world, though. How can readers be shown that he ruminates about his existence without going into his thoughts? Simple—the man is a priest. And how do readers know that he is more than just a living embodiment of the spirituality that priests aspire to? Because he is often referred to as a "whiskey priest," which shows his understanding of what the world thinks of him. Oh, and any doubt about his moral complexity can be settled by the fact that he has fathered a child after giving in to his drunken lust one night, which is certainly not something that a Roman Catholic clergyman is supposed to do. The point is that Greene knows how to tell a lot about this character from his external circumstances, and he can tell a lot about the society that is persecuting the man by giving detailed accounts of his actions.

There are several characters in the novel who, though they are rendered with precision, are also functional, revealing what it meant to be a priest in Mexico in the early to middle twentieth century. Almost all of the children are used for pathos, as examples of innocence either lost or found. Coral Fellows, the daughter of the

WHAT DO I READ NEXT?

- Mike Hayes's 2007 book *Googling God: The Religious Landscape of People in Their 20s and 30s* explores the many ways that contemporary young adults experience the Catholic faith. The book's emphasis is on exploring how Catholicism has evolved to maintain relevance in the quickly changing world.

- The Chinese Cultural Revolution is said to have been just as repressive regarding religion as the Mexican revolution tried to be. Ji-li Jiang's memoir *Red Scarf Girl: A Memoir of the Cultural Revolution* chronicles what it was like to be a child during the Cultural Revolution and to observe murders and beatings doled out by the state for ideological purposes. This book, aimed at readers of middle and high school age, was published by HarperTeen in 2008.

- Greene went to Mexico in 1937 and 1938 to avoid a lawsuit that was brought against him. His trip provided the inspiration for *The Power and the Glory*. After the novel was published, his notes from that trip were published in 1939 as *The Lawless Roads*; this book is currently available from Penguin Classics.

- Critics often associate this book with Greene's next novel, *The Heart of the Matter*, published in 1948. That book concerns a police inspector in a British colonial town in West Africa who has his Catholic faith questioned as he feels himself drawn into the decadent, lawless world around him. It is also available from Penguin Classics, in a 2004 edition.

- *The Power and the Glory* was rescued from its initial obscurity when French Catholic novelist François Mauriac wrote a persuasive introduction for its 1948 reissue. Mauriac, the 1952 winner of the Nobel Prize, is best known for his novels about the character Therese Desqueyroux, which have been compiled into one volume by Penguin Classics, called *Therese*, published in 1995.

- Norman Sherry, Graham Greene's official biographer, completed an extensive three-volume study of the author's life. *The Life of Graham Greene: Volume I: 1904–1939*, published in 1989, covers Greene's time in Mexico; *Volume II: 1939–1955*, published in 1994, covers the publication of this book and the ways that Greene's life changed as his career took off. All three volumes are published by Penguin Non-Classics.

- American author Katherine Anne Porter's short story "Flowering Judas" is set in Mexico in the same time period as this novel and concerns an American tourist who has to keep her Catholic faith a secret. Readers can compare Porter's perspective to Greene's: the story is included in the Harvest Books edition of *The Collected Stories of Katherine Anne Porter*, published in 1979.

English plantation owners, is a good example. She has been raised a Protestant, and readers might expect her to follow her upbringing, but her imagination wanders toward Catholicism after she meets the fugitive priest; she represents the kind of clean-slate, childlike curiosity that only the wealthy can afford. Pedro, the boy who is the priest's emissary to the people of the village where he finds himself finally able to operate in the open after months underground, is the conscience that keeps him tethered to the deep faith that has gotten him through his ordeal, as he finds himself thinking of squeezing the village's peasants for greater and greater payment for his services.

Brigida, his illegitimate daughter, is also easily recognized as a force of conscience for the whiskey priest, though she has a dour, adult look in her eyes that makes the priest fear that his sins are out in the open for everyone to see;

> **IF EXECUTION IS THE CULMINATION OF THE STRUGGLE THAT HAS BEEN GOING ON BETWEEN THE HUNTED AND HUNTER, PRIEST AND POLICEMAN, SPIRITUAL AND WORLDLY REPRESENTATIVES, THEN ONE WOULD EXPECT THAT THE JEFE'S TRIP TO THE DENTIST IS MEANT TO PROVIDE A PARALLEL-WORLD INTERPRETATION OF THAT STRUGGLE, A PARODY OF IT."**

she stands in contrast to Pedro, whose trust in the priest projects a reputation that he feels he must live up to. In addition, the young boy Luis serves such a symbolic function that he does not even interact with the priest: his story runs through the novel on a parallel track, as he grows from a sadistic little cynic, a totalitarian tool in training, into a proreligion revolutionary after the story read to him by his mother teaches him about a child like himself who stood up against religious persecution.

It is not only the young characters who function as symbolic objects in the novel. Green provides a range of characters who clearly have little purpose in the story except for their symbolic significance. Those are the characters who do not seem very bright, who do not appear to have much going on beneath their surface: the Lehrs, for instance, or the half-caste, or Padre José.

Mr. Lehr's function in the novel is fairly obvious. He is the man who comes from a traditional, calcified old European culture where religion is not a sentiment or a way to understand man's place in the universe; it is nothing more than a cultural habit. This is driven home by the Gideon Bible that the priest finds in Mr. Lehr's house: in a country where Bibles are forbidden texts and people are literally dying to get their hands on one, this particular version aims to sell its scripture to jaded travelers with the cheerful message that it is all about "Good News." Mr. Lehr's sister, Miss Lehr, has a little more complexity, but not much: She is the Lutheran who is broad-minded and good natured enough to wish well to anyone of any faith, charmingly

naïve in the way that she pines for her lost life in Pittsburgh while she sends the priest off to his death with sandwiches for the trip.

In another situation, the half-caste might seem to have a hidden personality, as he proves to be very clever for an uneducated man, with the constant evasions and protestations that he uses to hide his true intentions. In this book, though, his ruses only serve to show that the priest himself is too cynical about the world to let himself be fooled. In another context, the tragedy of Padre José, who has saved his own life at the expense of any sliver of self-respect, could have borne enough weight in itself to carry the whole novel, but in *The Power and the Glory* his story just serves to highlight one facet of the whiskey priest's complex psyche.

In light of all of these easily identifiable character functions, it may surprise the critics who call Greene cold, methodical, and impersonal that he would relate the book's moment of high drama, the actual death of the character who has been running for his life, through a scene with two characters whose function is not all that clear. When the actual execution takes place, Greene's narration is with neither the priest nor his philosophical counterpart, the police lieutenant: the shot that ends the priest's life is heard from within the office of Mr. Tench, the alcoholic dentist, as he is working on the tooth that has been bothering the chief of police throughout the entire novel.

On one level, it is easy to see how these two characters function in the book. They have the same duty that Padre José has: showing limited versions of characters more complex than themselves. When Mr. Tench ushers the book through its first few pages, he establishes a lower standard for behavior than readers are probably used to in their own lives. He drinks whatever he can get his hands on and he has no aspiration beyond drunkenness. Even his name prepares readers for the hopelessness that they are going to encounter in the coming pages: he is called "Mr." and not "Dr.," while "Tench," used in a dentist office, is an echo of trench mouth, an oral infection that was prevalent throughout World War I. This dentist is neither accredited nor sanitary. When he meets the priest, their alcoholism forms a bond between them. Tench mistaking the priest for a doctor has a dual function. On the one hand, it is as careless to call him a doctor as it would be to call Tench one, showing that this is a place where formality is irrelevant, but readers soon learn that the priest is just as conscientious in his duty to care for people's souls as a doctor is sworn to be about caring for their bodies.

The chief of police, the jefe, is of course used to throw light on the lieutenant who serves under him. The lieutenant follows through with capturing the priest for a number of reasons, ranging from a sense of duty to a sense of solidarity with the peasants, who he feels are being exploited by religion. The jefe has no such high-minded motives. His only concern is his toothache. He is below ideology; his only enemy is his own body.

These two characters are significant for what they can show readers about the book's two main characters. Even so, it is strange that Greene should put them into such an important strategic position in the book. If execution is the culmination of the struggle that has been going on between the hunted and hunter, priest and policeman, spiritual and worldly representatives, then one would expect that the jefe's trip to the dentist is meant to provide a parallel-world interpretation of that struggle, a parody of it.

In fact, that is exactly what it does. In the main story, bureaucratic efficiency triumphs over religious sentiment. The fugitive priest is captured and almost immediately executed, in part because the lives of innocent hostages have been taken. In the office of the shabby pseudo-dentist, however, the authority figure is at the mercy of the same entropy that is pulling Mexican society apart. Focusing on this scene allows Greene to show that it is not a land of efficient lawmen who enforce constitutional mandates against the clergy after all. It is a land of drunken priests and married priests, of police informants who delay their informing in order to enjoy the good life in jail, and where hopeless refugees are the best available practitioners when dental work needs to be done. One reading of this scene could be that the jefe treats his toothache as more important than the death of a good man, but Greene makes it clear that, the physical world being what it is, so long as men like Mr. Tench have even the slightest glimmer of what it used to be like to have a conscience, the totalitarian government will always be vulnerable.

Source: David Kelly, Critical Essay on *The Power and the Glory*, in *Novels for Students*, Gale, Cengage Learning, 2010.

> IN CONTRAST, THE LIEUTENANT IN *THE POWER AND THE GLORY* LONGED TO BE POPULAR WITH THE CHILDREN, BUT SUCCEEDED ONLY IN HAVING THEM SPIT AT HIM."

Stephen Benz

In the following excerpt, Benz examines Greene's views on militarism in Latin America as evidenced in his writings, including The Power and the Glory.

"If one takes a side, one takes a side, come what may," Graham Greene wrote in his memoir *Getting to Know the General*. He was speaking about what he called his "involvement" with Panama's General Omar Torrijos, but his comment applies equally well to his general involvement with the politics of Latin America. By the time of his death in 1989, Greene's long-standing, ever-deepening interest in Latin America had developed from the touristic to the analytical to the polemical. It was an interest that had begun with a 1938 visit to Mexico that resulted in a travel narrative and a novel. In the 1950s and 1960s, his visits to Haiti, Cuba, and Paraguay produced four novels and several essays. Finally, his trips to Chile (1972), to Panama (1976 to 1983), and to Nicaragua (1980 to 1986) culminated in one more novel (his last), a series of articles, a book-length memoir, and several letters to *The Times* arguing for the support of governments and causes that he found admirable in Latin America. His visits to Latin America, he said in an interview, "brought with them a political commitment in a number of ways." In his later years, Greene had indeed taken a side.

In his work on Latin America, Greene revisited and reworked four major themes: religion, politics, anti-American sentiment, and militarism. A review of these themes reveals the insistent and yet elusive sensibility that informed Greene's interest in the region. Once taken into account, this sensibility necessarily alters some of the more extreme assumptions of those critics who find in Greene's fiction a generic, savage landscape (sometimes referred to as "Greeneland") that is more imaginary than real. Rejecting the implication that his settings were purely fictional, Greene insisted that the world he wrote about was "carefully and accurately described." . . .

There are as many military men in Graham Greene's fiction as there are priests, but for whatever reason, Greene's colonels, lieutenants, and captains have not received as much critical attention as his religious characters. Perhaps it is too easy to assume that these military men are the villains of Greene's novels and to leave it at that. For example, in the film version of *The Power and the Glory* (John Ford's *The Fugitive*), the lieutenant is portrayed as completely dissolute—to the extent that the lieutenant is even made the father of the priest's child. But Greene clearly intends these characters to be more than two-dimensional villains. In fact, Greene's use of military men as characters in his fiction and his frequent analysis of militarism in his nonfiction makes this one of his major themes. He first addressed this theme in *The Lawless Roads*, in an account of his meeting with General Saturnino Cedillo, a minor force in Mexican politics who interested Greene because he had managed to resist the authority of the central government in allowing churches and parochial schools to operate in spite of laws prohibiting their existence. The theme of militarism was then developed in characters such as the lieutenant in *The Power and the Glory*, Captain Concasseur in *The Comedians*, and Colonel Perez in *The Honorary Consul*. Greene's nonfiction about Latin America provided a coda for this theme in its depiction of generals who have ruled Latin America as dictators.

More than anything else, Greene's military men were typified by their commitment to violence, to "useless cruelty," to an "ideal lost and the violence just going on" (*Lawless*, p. 47). The best example of a military man losing idealism is the lieutenant in *The Power and the Glory*. He engages in the "mysticism" of an atheistic revolution: "He was a mystic, too, and what he had experienced was vacancy—a complete certainty in the existence of a dying, cooling world, of human beings who had evolved from animals for no purpose at all." But this purposelessness renders null the ideals of the revolution. He tries to convince himself that the violence of his office is for a cause:

> . . . it was for [the children] he was fighting. He would eliminate from their childhood everything which had made him miserable, all that was poor, superstitious, and corrupt. They deserved nothing less than the truth—a vacant universe and a cooling world, the right to be

happy in any way they chose. He was quite prepared to make a massacre for their sakes—first the Church and then the foreigner and then the politician—even his own chief would one day have to go. He wanted to begin the world again with them, in a desert.

The lieutenant is not troubled by the likelihood that in a moral desert the children would have a hard time exercising their "right to be happy in any way they chose." But even if his ideals made sense, the violence he perceives as necessary to effect those ideals does not accomplish what he thinks it will. The killing of the whiskey priest proves unsatisfying to him. The child who earlier had admired his gun now feels deceived and sees the priest and not the lieutenant as the hero. Dedication to violence, Greene suggests, becomes an end in itself—a dead end predicated on false ideals.

The lieutenant's motives were at least rooted in a revolution, albeit a now corrupt revolution. In Captain Concasseur of *The Comedians*, on the other hand, we encounter a representative of the military who rules by a violence that is rooted in nothing so rational. Concasseur, perhaps the cruelest character in all of Greene's Latin American work, emerged from Greene's own experiences in Haiti. Greene had observed officers in Mexico, and he knew of the "notorious police chief Captain Ventura" in Cuba, but not until Greene experienced the terror of having a Tonton Macoute (Duvalier's military police) stare at him through dark glasses while Greene waited for hours at a police station could he conceive of a cruelty and violence so pure. Unlike the Mexican lieutenant, Concasseur has no ideals whatsoever. Describing the Tonton Macoute in "Nightmare Republic," Greene wrote: " . . . never has terror had so bare and ignoble an object as here—the protection of a few tough men's pockets."

Despite the captain's evil, Greene saw the same pathos in Concasseur that he saw in the lieutenant of *The Power and the Glory*. There comes an inevitable moment in Greene's fiction when the military man exposes this pathos. In one of his confrontations with Concasseur, Brown observes "a hint of weakness. I could understand why it was these men wore dark glasses—they were human, but they musn't show fear; it might be the end of terror in others" (*Comedians*, p. 125). Greene suggests that the attempt to frighten and terrorize others is really an indication of weakness on the part of the military.

In his nonfiction, Greene turned his attention to the generals who ruled Latin America and submitted them to a scathing critique. In "The Great Spectacular," for example, he observed the generals gathered in one room for the signing of the Panama Canal Treaty:

> The real character actors were all up on the platform—an unpleasant sight but more impressive than the stars below: General Stroessner of Paraguay whom I had last seen in uniform one National Day in Asunción saluting the cripples of the Bolivian war as they wheeled by and the colonels stood stiffly upright in their cars like ninepins in a bowling alley (he had reminded me then of some flushed owner of a German *Bierstrube*, and in civilian clothes he looked more than ever the part); General Videla of Argentina with a face squashed so flat there was hardly room for his two foxy eyes; General Banzer of Bolivia a little frightened man with a small agitated mustache—he would have looked more like a dictator if he had worn a uniform, he had been miscast and misdressed; there too was the greatest character actor of them all—General Pinochet himself, the man you love to hate.

In an article that satirized everyone (except Torrijos), Greene saved his most brutal sarcasm for Pinochet, who "like Boris Karloff" had "really attained the status of instant recognition." At the treaty ceremony, Pinochet so dominated the scene, in Greene's view, that "he didn't need to have a speaking part—he didn't even need to grunt." Greene was sure that Pinochet "knew that he dominated the scene—he was the only one people were protesting about with banners in the streets of Washington." Despite the satire, Greene saw real, Concasseur-type evil in Pinochet....

Although Pinochet dominated the scene in one sense, the general who was at the center of the treaty ceremony was Torrijos of Panama. If Pinochet represented one extreme of militarism, Torrijos was the rare exception representing the opposite extreme. Truly a "lone wolf" among generals, Torrijos had "no political prisoners and unobtrusively ... [gave] aid to many political refugees from Chile and Argentina." Furthermore, this general was "popular in the countryside (especially with the children)." In contrast, the lieutenant in *The Power and the Glory* longed to be popular with the children, but succeeded only in having them spit at him. Torrijos was the kind of military man not found in Greene's fiction; the lieutenant (*Power and the Glory*), Concasseur (*The Comedians*), Segura (*Our Man in Havana*), and Perez (*The Honorary Consul*) all

had more in common with Pinochet than with Torrijos.

It is noteworthy, therefore, that in this last article Greene brought together these two generals who stood at opposite ends of a spectrum. The article ended, in fact, with the curious image, no doubt disappointing to Greene, of the two generals caught in an embrace:

> After the signing of the treaty Carter and Torrijos set off down the platform in opposite directions to greet the heads of state. An embrace is the usual greeting in the southern hemisphere, and I noticed how Torrijos embraced the leaders of Colombia, Venezuela, and Peru ["the more reputable leaders"] and confined himself to a formal handshake with Bolivia and Argentina as he worked his way down the row toward Pinochet. But Pinochet noticed that, and his eyes gleamed with amusement. When his turn came he grasped the hand of Torrijos and flung his arm around his shoulder. If any journalist's camera had clicked at that moment it would be thought that Torrijos had embraced Pinochet.

Choosing to end the article with this image, Greene clearly saw this as a symbolic moment. He seemed to be suggesting the power of Pinochet-style militarism, a power so overwhelming that it dominated those who attempted to rule differently. As Greene's last comment on the military in Latin America, it is an intriguing, disturbing image....

Source: Stephen Benz, "Taking Sides: Graham Greene and Latin America," in *Journal of Modern Literature*, Vol. 26, No. 2, Winter 2003, pp. 113–28.

Thomas A. Wendorf

In the following excerpt, Wendorf compares The Power and the Glory *and J. R. R. Tolkien's* The Lord of the Rings, *arguing that the author's use of myth and religious mystery unite these works of seemingly disparate genres.*

If realist Graham Greene could draw criticism that his works were products of his own psychological distortion, a projected "Greeneland" (*Ways of Escape* 60), it is no wonder that, as Tom Shippey has recently pointed out, J.R.R. Tolkien's fantasy *The Lord of the Rings* has provoked shrill criticism from the literary academy because, as a work of fantasy, it is "intrinsically less truthful than realistic fiction," and so presumably forfeits serious critical consideration (327). Writing in 1961, C.S. Lewis zeroes in on the problem: "The dominant taste at present demands realism of content" (*Experiment*

GRAHAM GREENE, IN FACT, COULD IMAGINE PURE EVIL IN THE WORLD, ALTHOUGH HIS FICTION HAS ALWAYS PROVED MORE AMBIGUOUS AND COMPLEX HERE THAN HIS EXTRA-FICTIONAL COMMENTARY MIGHT SUGGEST."

60). Lewis helpfully distinguishes between "Realism of Presentation—the art of bringing something close to us, making it palpable and vivid, by sharply observed or sharply imagined detail" (57)—and "realism of content," which demands that fiction be "probable or 'true to life'" (59). As Lewis and Shippey rightly imply, there's something mistaken in upholding strict realism of content as the test for literary worth, particularly since such realism is a relatively recent development in literary history. There is also something mistaken in denying fantasy any claims to truthfulness.

Writing such different kinds of fiction, Greene and Tolkien might seem odd literary bedfellows. However—both English, both Roman Catholic, both writing over long careers during the 20th century—Greene and Tolkien, in their fiction and other writing, suggest that realism and fantasy, often contentiously opposed in critical debate, have more complex relations and can effect similar truths. Because Greene's *The Power and the Glory* and Tolkien's *The Lord of the Rings* both effect a vision of the world governed by divine imperatives, the divide they might represent between realism and fantasy becomes less precise, insofar as both works embody mythic dimensions, both suggesting the kind of revelatory power that theologian David Tracy ascribes to religious classics:

> To enter the conversation of religious classics through real interpretation, therefore, is to enter a disclosure of a world of meaning and truth offering no certainty but promising some realized experience of the whole by the power of the whole. That world affords no technically controlled comprehensibility yet it does release the self to the uncontrollable incomprehensibility of an experience of radical mystery. (177)

The Power and the Glory and *The Lord of the Rings*, the masterpieces of their respective authors, arguably suggest in their different literary approaches the kind of paradoxical disclosing and concealing "of the whole of reality by the power of the whole" and that essential oneness of morality, mystery, and reality that Tracy attributes to religious classics (163). As Greene and Tolkien together suggest, placing realism and fantasy on opposite ends of a continuum of truthfulness (and by direct implication, on a similar continuum of literary merit) is a move that ignores realism's relations with fantasy and downplays fiction's power to reveal mystery through a mythic dimension.

The surface similarities between Tolkien's trilogy and Greene's novel are striking, and here for a moment we take that view from a distance that Northrop Frye describes as the vantage point from which we can best see the archetypal organization of a work (140). Both the whisky priest and the ring-bearer are reluctant heroes whose journeys lead them where they had not intended to go but where they find they are compelled to go by their sense of calling, the priest because he is a priest, Frodo because he is the ring-bearer. Frodo often moves forward, particularly in the realms of Mount Doom, without hope, and the whisky priest, even when he has accepted martyrdom over escape, has little hope for his own salvation or much conviction that his death will prove honorable in the eyes of God or others.

Both journeyers also become swallowed in landscapes marked by heat, filth, desolation, and danger (Frodo through the marshes and vast, decimated territory of Mordor, the whisky priest in the harsh land of Tabasco and amid human squalor—a trash heap where he encounters his daughter, the jail where he finds communion with fellow sinners, among the great crosses and in the bitter rain as he approaches the state border). Both are pursued, Frodo by every power allied with Sauron, the whisky priest by the lieutenant and soldiers. Both with some reluctance show mercy to figures who betray them (Frodo to Smeagol/Gollum and the whisky priest to the yellow-fanged mestizo), and this mercy proves crucial in both stories to the success of the journeyers (Smeagol/Gollum completes the destruction of the ring when Frodo wavers; the whisky priest makes his extraordinary decision to give up his life only after receiving the Yankee fugitive's scrawled note from the mestizo). Finally, both of their journeys involve a renunciation of power—Frodo gives up the Ring, and the whisky priest gives up his life. Within the narratives both become a part of stories foretold and told later (Frodo's role is prophesied, and his providential success becomes the stuff of Middle-Earth history and song; the whisky priest's life ironically becomes the story of a Catholic martyr/saint).

These parallels of their journeys, of course, exist amid great conceptual and aesthetic differences. Greene's priest is a figure living very much in what Tolkien calls the "Primary" or actual world, and this is the most crucial difference between the two works; it marks the aesthetic divide between realism of content and fantasy. Even if Green creates what some critics have, in various ways, called "Greeneland," even if he unavoidably projects his own psychology onto his scene, he is still representing early twentieth-century Mexico. Greene's represented world is also explicitly and historically shaped by Christianity. His whisky priest is, as R. W. B. Lewis puts it, a rogue whose particular sins as a priest (habitual drinking, begetting a child) emerge in all their mundane humanity amid other sins equally human but more theological (pride, Despair). As such, he is unlike the Halfling Frodo whose moral character is more exclusively figured in terms of how he deals with the Ring and his role as ring-bearer. The whisky priest journeys mostly alone while Frodo almost always has a companion. The sacraments of the Catholic Church have an explicit place in Greene's novel, as does worship and a more general sense that God works through nature; Tolkien's creatures in *The Lord of the Rings*, while the most noble among them allude to the presence of a benevolent and omnipotent Providence and sometimes show prayer-like reverence, are not religious in any modern sense of the word and do not engage in explicit worship.

Clearly there is no magic in Greene's novel, nothing fantastic in the sense of overt supernatural action, though the sacraments are certainly fantastic to those who don't believe in them; the lieutenant certainly sees them as bogus. The evil the priest encounters is always ordinary human evil—use of power to dominate others, egotism, lust, gluttony, nihilism, merciless accusation, pride, greed, sensuality—and Greene represents all of these with his characteristic ambiguity. The nihilistic lieutenant is motivated by a desire to help the poor and sometimes shows mercy to match that of the whisky priest; the pious woman in prison judges the sexual

intercourse of the inmates, while the whisky priest recognizes a possible goodness in it and the worse sin in her pious judgments. On the other hand, Tolkien's most evil creatures in *The Lord of the Rings*—Sauron, the Orcs, the Nazgul—seem more purely and irredeemably so, though Elrond, implying the goodness of creation and the larger mythic history out of which the trilogy grows, emphasizes that "nothing is evil in the beginning. Even Sauron was not so" (261).

Graham Greene, in fact, could imagine pure evil in the world, although his fiction has always proved more ambiguous and complex here than his extra-fictional commentary might suggest. By his own account, he first experienced literature's power to reveal the nature of reality and particularly the mystery of evil in a historical romance, Marjorie Bowen's *The Viper of Milan* (1906). Greene famously claims, "[Bowen] had given me my pattern—religion might later explain it to me in other terms, but the pattern was already there—perfect evil walking the world where perfect good can never walk again, and only the pendulum ensures that after all in the end justice is done" ("The Lost Childhood." *Essays* 17). Greene found Bowen's historical romance true to life because it mirrored his already acute sense of the human capacity for evil.

In Greene's earliest sense of realism, mystery and fantastic were already important. Biographer Norman Sherry has well noted Greene's early attraction to fantasy not only in his reading but also in his writing (*Volume I* 113). In 1992 Greene wrote a story for the school newspaper *The Berkhamstedian* tellingly titled "The Tyranny of Realism," an allegorical story that suggests a reconciliation between "Fantasie" and "Realism." In it a boy, bound before the throne of King Realism, sees a sad maiden named "Fantasie" at the King's feet. After bewailing the King for taking away his "unknown country of dark caves and hidden ways, and sun-splashed woods" and for keeping the boy's love, "Fantasie," a slave, the King, with a "little, whimsical smile" instructs the boy to try his bonds. The bonds disappear, the King takes him to the throne, and the walls around them disappear, exposing "great, dark rolling plains, and the star-encrusted sky." In the final moment of the story, the boy sinks to his knees before the King, whose face is "the face of a God," and the boy sees that King Realism looks not at him but at Fantasie, who has taken her place on a throne beside the king. Realism and Fantasie kiss "in a long passion of joy" (2–3). Sherry perceptively suggests that "the allegory is probably a pointer to Graham's hope that because he felt he must in the future write in a more realistic vein it did not mean (as clearly he had feared) that his fantastic imaginings could not also flourish" (*Volume I* 114). Greene's boyhood story reflects not only a reluctance to sacrifice fantasy to realism but also a desire to unite them.

Greene continued to dabble with fantasy during his long literary career. Characters recalling haunting childhood memories often provided the realistic frame for such forays. In the short story "The Hint of an Explanation" (1948), a provocative childhood encounter with a pitiful, evil-bent, anti-Catholic baker changes the life of the story's central figure. In "Under the Garden" (1963), a childhood "fantasy" narrative, a "memory" of a visit to two strange people living underground becomes a compelling, if ambiguous, reflection of truth and mystery for the terminally ill main character Wilditch. Even in his last novel *The Captain and the Enemy* (1988), Greene teases us with an ambiguously allegorical father figure dubbed "the Devil," suggesting that Greene's interest in the fantastic never died, even if he would only present these dimensions under the garb of irony and in a realistic frame, leaving the nature and imperatives of mystery ambiguous.

Graham Greene, of course, is not primarily a fantasy writer, but he did have a religious vision that found literary expression after his conversion to Roman Catholicism in 1926, particularly in the string of novels explicitly dealing with Catholic themes of sin and salvation, good and evil—*Brighton Rock* (1938), *The Power and the Glory* (1940), *The Heart of the Matter* (1948), and *The End of the Affair* (1951). Because Greene's realism here includes that wider reality embraced by Catholic belief, involving both the natural and the supernatural, the seen and the unseen, it already exceeds the limits of naturalism or radical realism. Given its theological dimension, Greene's explicitly religious fiction might seem fantastic, might even seem to fit C.S. Lewis's broad definition of literary fantasy: "any narrative that deals with impossibles and preternaturals" (*Experiment* 50).

But Greene's commitment to referential narrative placed even his explicitly religious fiction in a more realistic mode with its own challenges. Catholic writer Flannery O'Connor recognized well the difficulty that Christian writers like Green and herself faced in writing for an increasingly secular audience:

> The problem of the novelist who wishes to write about a man's encounter with . . . God is how he shall make the experience—which is both natural and supernatural—understandable, and credible, to his reader. In any age this would be a problem, but in our own, it is a well-nigh insurmountable one. (*Mystery and Manners* 161)

In his realism of content, Greene rises to the challenge that O'Connor describes. Though always heterodox and doubtful in a way that O'Connor was not (Greene's fiction and life, even by his own account, attest to this), Greene still reveals in his explicitly Catholic fiction a similar gritty sacramentality, a stubborn sense that nature and human nature are the privileged sites in which and through which any kind of divine grace works. Indeed, he was rarely heavy-handed in his narration, rarely overleapt the human and the natural to get to the divine dimension. His works often suggest, amid great suffering and absurdities, eternal possibilities and consequences for human action, a dramatic effect he praised in Henry James and found lacking in Virginia Woolf and Somerset Maugham. But as it was with Henry James, Greene's treatment of the spiritual dimension is subtle and grounded in the physical and psychological dimensions of character and place. Few would mistake Greene for a fantasy writer even in C.S. Lewis's terms—indeed the "preternatural" is rarely laid bare in his fiction and virtually all that he represents is wonderfully and terribly possible in the actual world. . . .

The Power and the Glory is not a fairy-tale in the way that *The Lord of the Rings* is, but the two works converge in their different evocations of myth and mystery, particularly the mystery of Christ. The whisky priest's life and death and the ripple of transforming effects that emerge from them are invested with mystery and power because they explicitly evoke and participate in the eucatastrophe of Christ's Incarnation and Resurrection. While the integrity of Tolkien's mythic dimension, like Greene's, demanded distance between his belief and his representations, he nonetheless recognized that his belief ennobled and gave meaning to his art. Referring to the Gospel of Christ and emphasizing the charmed analogical relations of art and life, of God and human being, Tolkien might have spoken for the albeit more skeptical Graham Greene, too, when he wrote in his poignant Epilogue to "On Fairy-Stories,"

> Redeemed Man is still man. Story, fantasy, still go on, and should go on. The Evangelium has not abrogated legends; it has hallowed them, especially the "happy ending" ... All tales may come true; and yet, at he last, redeemed, they may be as like and as unlike the forms that we give them as Man, finally redeemed, will be like and unlike the fallen that we know. (84)

Christian hope, with its companion respect for mystery, informs and finally unites the aesthetics of both Tolkien and Greene, for their respective works of fantasy and realism both reach haltingly toward such an ultimate future.

Source: Thomas A. Wendorf, "Greene, Tolkien, and the Mysterious Relations of Realism and Fantasy," in *Renascence*, Vol. 55, No. 1, Fall 2002, pp. 79–100.

Bruce Bawer

In the following excerpt, Bawer explores Greene's attraction to Catholicism and critiques The Power and the Glory.

In his long and celebrated literary career—which I began to examine in the last issue of *The New Criterion*—Graham Greene has written some three dozen novels, "entertainments," plays, essays, memoirs, short story collections, and travel books. But it is those books which, for want of a better term, we may call his Catholic novels (*The Power and the Glory, The Heart of the Matter, The End of the Affair*, and *A Burnt-Out Case*) and his later political novels (*The Quiet American, The Comedians, The Honorary Consul*, and *The Human Factor*) that are generally acknowledged, for better or worse, to comprise the nucleus of his oeuvre. Though there are other works by Greene that have scattered and enthusiastic support, critics who speak of Greene's literary mastery tend almost exclusively to cite some or all of the books on this list as evidence of that mastery; and it is the Catholic novels that are mentioned most frequently of all. This being the case, it seems necessary to devote special attention to those books, and to ask certain questions in connection with them, namely: How did Greene come to Catholicism? In what form did Catholicism, in turn, come to enter his work? What does religious faith mean to him, and what role does it play in his fiction?

Considering that Graham Green is one of the world's most respected Catholic writers, the story of his introduction to the Roman Catholic faith is

> PATENTLY, GREENE SEEKS TO CONVEY IN THIS NOVEL A SOLEMN, INTENSE VISION OF THE HUMAN CONDITION—A VISION IN WHICH THERE WOULD APPEAR TO BE LITTLE ROOM FOR THE HUMOR THAT HELPS (OCCASIONALLY, AT LEAST) TO RELIEVE THE DARKNESS OF HIS EARLIER BOOKS."

somewhat less than inspiring. In 1925 Greene met and fell in love with a Catholic girl named Vivien Dayrell-Browning, who declared that she would not marry him unless he converted to her faith. He did so within the year, although Norman Sherry's account, in his recent biography of Greene, shows no evidence of a real conversion, and Greene (in his memoir *A Sort of Life*) is oddly vague and noncommittal: "I can only remember that in January 1926 I became convinced of the probable existence of something we call God, though I now dislike the word with all its anthropomorphic associations and prefer Chardin's 'Omega Point.'" Greene's references to Catholicism in his letters of the period are flippant, as is his reminiscence of his Catholic instruction: "Now it occurred to me, during the long empty mornings, that if I were to marry a Catholic I ought at least to learn the nature and limits of the beliefs she held. It was only fair, since she knew what I believed—in nothing supernatural. Besides, I thought, it would kill the time." (To "kill the time" has, of course, always been an important end for Greene.) For the most part, then, Greene seems to have looked upon his conversion to Catholicism in the same way that he looked upon his youthful association with the German embassy and his entry into the Communist Party—namely, as a means to other ends, in this case marriage to Vivien.

Though the time came when Greene found it useful to place Catholic doctrines and characters at the center of his work, true Catholic piety and reflectiveness have continued to seem alien to him. He has often described himself, paradoxically, as a "Catholic agnostic." Certainly he has never made any bones about his distrust of orthodox Catholic theology, his utter lack of curiosity about the intellectual underpinnings of the Church. One cannot help but connect him, in this regard, with Henry Pulling's dotty, lawless Aunt Augusta in *Travels with My Aunt*, who, upon being asked if she is really a Roman Catholic, replies, "Yes, my dear, only I just don't believe in all the things they believe in." For Greene, intellectual assent to a set of doctrines prescribed by somebody else has little or nothing to do with being a Catholic; he has always felt free to accept or discard various elements of Roman dogma as he sees fit, and to contort Catholic precepts beyond recognition in order to suit his own psychological needs.

At times, indeed, Greene seems to have disposed of so much of Catholicism that there would appear to be no particular reason to call it Catholicism and not something else. Like Maurice, his protagonist in *The End of the Affair*, he "find[s] it hard to conceive of any God who is not as simple as a perfect equation, as clear as air." Greene much prefers a primitive religion to a doctrinaire, over intellectualized one; he obviously shares the feeling of Dr. Colin, the African-based leprosy specialist in *A Burnt-Out Case*, when he comments that "it's a strange Christianity we have here, but I wonder whether the Apostles would find it as difficult to recognize as the collected works of Thomas Aquinas. If Peter could have understood those, it would have been an even greater miracle than Pentecost, don't you think? Even the Nicaean Creed—it has the flavour of higher mathematics to me." At one point Querry, the book's protagonist, goes so far as to say that "it would be a good thing for all of us if we were even more superficial."

In this connection, it should be observed that Catholicism served Greene for many years as the locus—the essentially arbitrary locus—of something that he called "faith." A remark that Greene made in a 1986 interview with the *Literaturnaya Gazeta* is of interest. In the interview, he nonchalantly politicized the story of his conversion for the Soviet editors: "The nearer fascism came to us, and the more it spread all over the world, the more necessary it was to oppose it by building moral obstacles to it in the consciousness of the masses. It is here that I opted for faith.... I felt it necessary to make faith the symbol of resistance." Patently dishonest though this anti-fascist version of Greene's conversion may be, there is a truth at its center: namely, that Catholicism has generally functioned, in

Greene's personal metaphysics, as a sort of escape hatch from the cold-eyed realism of which he is so proud; despite his professed loathing of romanticism, and his much-vaunted "realistic" attitude toward the Western world, the capitalistic system, and the United States, Greene's "faith" has provided him with a means of holding what are basically romantic views of certain aspects of life—in particular of Marxist ideas, exploits, and leaders. As the narrator remarks in *The Heart of the Matter*, "[I]f romance is what one lives by, one must never be cured of it. The world has too many spoilt priests of this faith or that: better surely to pretend a belief than wander in that vicious vacuum of cruelty and despair."

In its emphasis on faith, on the individual's personal relationship with God, and on a vigorous suspicion of prescribed doctrine, Greene's personal version of Christianity might seem to some observers more Protestant (if anything) than Catholic. Yet time and again Greene has gone out of his way to belittle Protestantism in general and the Anglicanism of his birth in particular. At times, indeed, he writes as if it were agreed by the whole world that Catholicism were the only real religion—the only one, that is to say, which can truly inhabit a soul and bring a communicant closer to God—and Anglicanism nothing more than a social club, a collection of pompous, empty rituals whose participants give no thought to virtue or sin or the deity. "You are an Englishman," a Portuguese captain says to Scobie, a colonial policeman, in *The Heart of the Matter*. "You wouldn't believe in prayer." Scobie counters, "I'm a Catholic, too." Later in the novel, Scobie reflects that his mistress, Helen, has it good: since she's not a Catholic, "[s]he's lucky. She's free." The implication here—and elsewhere in Greene's oeuvre—is that non-Catholics are innocents of a sort, bound by no moral code and free of the dark and difficult knowledge that Catholics share. Catholicism, in short, is serious; Anglicanism is vain and frivolous. And yet Greene's easy dismissal of orthodox Catholic thought, his audacious distortion of its precepts to suit his own purposes, and his facile fictional use of such concepts as eternal damnation may well strike some readers—Catholic, Anglican, or otherwise—as the very height of vanity and frivolity.

How did a young man who had been brought up in the Church of England end up such a fervent—if iconoclastic—Catholic? The question brings us back, I think, to Greene's childhood at the Berkhamsted School and to his headmaster father's stern sexual precepts; for the more closely one examines Greene's attitude toward religion, the more strongly one feels that conversion to Catholicism must have seemed, to the young Greene, a perfect way of rejecting his Anglican father, even while, in a sense, he was (consciously or not) perpetuating the old man's moral domination over him. For however much of Catholic doctrine Greene chose to leave out of his personal version of the religion, he certainly retained—and, it might be argued, blew out of all proportion—Catholicism's strict views on sex and marriage. In the process he managed to make of the Catholic Church (at least in terms of its sexual teachings) a veritable replica of the Berkhamsted of his youth. The Catholic protagonists in several of his novels, after all, agonize over the sin of fornication in a way that would have been far more familiar to a tormented Victorian (or, in Greene's case, Georgian) public school boy than it would be to even an unusually devout modern-day Catholic. And so many of his autobiographical protagonists prove to have been educated at seminaries or Jesuit schools that one gets the impression Greene regards such institutions as rough equivalents of Berkhamsted—at least, that is, when it comes to the attitudes toward sex and sin that these schools have inculcated into the souls of their alumni. It is almost as if the young Greene, feeling irrationally guilty as he broke his childhood ties to family and school, found it necessary to replace Berkhamsted with the Catholic Church, and his father with God—and, in the process, also found it necessary to make certain adjustments in Catholicism so that it might more nearly approximate, in temper and teachings, the institution in which he had been raised.

There are other likely reasons for his attraction to Catholicism. Given the fact that Greene, even in his early youth, was a master of suicidal boredom and misanthropic despair, he must surely have seen Roman Catholicism, with its reverence for suffering, as a way of legitimizing his veritable fetishization of misery. Time and again, his Catholic novels equate suffering with life, seriousness, wisdom. "As long as one suffers," he writes in *The End of the Affair*, "one lives." And in *The Heart of the Matter* "Despair is the price one pays for setting oneself an impossible aim. It is, one is told, the unforgivable sin,

but it is a sin the corrupt or evil man never practices. He always has hope. He never reaches the freezing point of knowing absolute failure. Only the man of good will carries always in his heart this capacity for damnation." The epigraph to *The End of the Affair* is from Léon Bloy: "Man has places in his heart which do not yet exist, and into them enters suffering in order that they may have existence." Too often, alas, Greene's fixation on suffering seems masochistic, morbid; certainly the notion that religion should be nothing but suffering is as distasteful as the notion that it should be nothing but sweetness and light.

There is one additional factor in Greene's attraction to Catholicism whose importance cannot be underestimated. Norman Sherry's biography mentions only one aspect of Catholicism that genuinely appealed to Greene at the time of his conversion: the belief in hell. As Greene said at the time, "It gives something hard, non-sentimental and exciting." . . . And indeed it seems to have been not so much hell itself but the *melodrama* of hell, and of Catholicism in general, that captivated the young man. To the thoroughly English Greene, Catholicism must have seemed exotic and Latin, must have appealed not only to his personal sense of alienation but to the thrill-ermeister's love of the sensational. His Catholic novels, in any event, make it clear that Greene cherishes the drama of sin and eternal damnation; one thinks, for example, of the scene in *The Heart of the Matter* in which Scobie, taking communion in a state of mortal sin, is "aware of the pale papery taste of his eternal sentence on the tongue." What other religion could provide higher drama?

Traces of Greene's distinctive view of Catholicism—or of its development—appear in virtually all of Greene's novels. But it reaches its apotheosis in four of them: *The Power and the Glory, The Heart of the Matter, The End of the Affair,* and *A Burnt-Out Case.* Taken together, these books almost seem to have been designed as a set of Greenian Articles of Faith. The chief tenets of this faith—among them the notion of experience as the road to metaphysical knowledge, of prodigious sin as the path to saintliness—are explored tirelessly in these books; if various other Greene novels convey the idea that it is important to have some kind of faith or to take a stand on one side or the other of a given contest, these four novels spell out Greene's specific brand of faith with considerable precision. Each of them contains a major character who is a sinner, whose central conflict is his struggle with faith, and whose struggle ends in death; invariably, the assumptions upon which the conflict takes place, the terms in which it is presented, and the conclusions which are drawn from its outcome derive entirely from Greene's own iconoclastic version of Catholicism.

For instance, *The Power and the Glory* (1940), set in socialist Mexico in the 1930s, takes as its protagonist a cowardly alcoholic priest who has married one woman and fathered a child by another. This "whiskey priest" (whose name we never learn) is the last Roman Catholic cleric remaining in a province where it's been declared a crime to say Mass; like many a Greene hero, he spends much of the book on the lam from the authorities. This simply structured novel is dense with evocations of rural poverty and with pronouncements about various spiritual topics— good and evil, love and lust, experience and innocence—from which Greene typically doesn't distance himself at all. "[O]ur sins have so much beauty," the whiskey priest declares at one point. "I'm a bad priest, you see. I know—from experience—how much beauty Satan carried down with him when he fell. Nobody ever said the fallen angels were the ugly ones." It is his corruption, the priest says, that has brought him close to God: as a "comparatively innocent" young man, he was "unbearable." (In Greene's novels, of course, innocent men are invariably unbearable.) And indeed we are meant to understand, at the book's conclusion, that for all his sin the priest may well be something of a saint.

Though Greene does not depart radically here from the brisk, lucid manner of his early novels and entertainments, he does—rather like Hemingway in *For Whom the Bell Tolls*—attempt to modify his characteristic precision and simplicity in the direction of a certain austere stateliness, and thereby to give his "whiskey priest" a magnitude, and even a kind of coarse nobility, that his previous heroes didn't have. As in Hemingway's novel, however, the results of this stylistic modification are questionable. For one thing, the frequent appearance of colons between strings of independent clauses ("The squad of police made their way back to the station: they walked raggedly with rifles slung anyhow: ends of cotton where buttons should have been: a puttee slipping down over the ankle: small men with black secret Indian eyes") seems to have no *raison d'être*

other than the author's affectation; for another, the novel's plainness of style ("He hustled them out: one by one they picked their way across the clearing towards the hut: and the old man set off down the path toward the river to take the place of the boy who watched the ford for soldiers") feels strained and phony in the way of the most self-parodic Hemingway.

Patently, Greene seeks to convey in this novel a solemn, intense vision of the human condition—a vision in which there would appear to be little room for the humor that helps (occasionally, at least) to relieve the darkness of his earlier books. But it's less a vision, really, than a contrivance, a repetitive and deliberate hammering away at the irony of the priest's position as "a damned man putting God into the mouths of men." The priest constantly flagellates himself, and we're plainly meant to be moved by his distress; but because that supposed distress is, for the most part, simply reiterated, rather than being reflected in a serious effort to change his ways, it's hard to take it very seriously. It's hard, for that matter, to believe that *Greene* takes it seriously: for the novel shows every sign of having been built less upon a passionate devotion to the idea of God than upon a view—at once glib, sentimental, patronizing, and uppercrust-Protestant—of swarthy, dirt-poor, Romance-language-speaking Catholics as close to the earth and, *ipso facto*, close to the Almighty....

Source: Bruce Bawer, "Graham Greene: The Catholic Novels," in *New Criterion*, Vol. 8, No. 2, October 1989, pp. 24–32.

SOURCES

DeVitis, A. A., *Graham Greene*, rev. ed., Twayne Publishers, 1986, pp. 83–4.

Greene, Graham, *The Power and the Glory*, introduction by John Updike, Penguin Classics, 1991.

Kelly, Richard, "The Man and His Work," in *Graham Greene*, Frederick Ungar, 1984, pp. 1–23.

———, "Novels," in *Graham Greene*, Frederick Ungar, 1984, p. 46.

Kermode, Frank, "Mr. Greene's Eggs and Crosses," in *Graham Greene: A Collection of Critical Essays*, edited by Samuel Hynes, Prentice-Hall, 1973, p. 134.

———, *Puzzles & Epiphanies*, Chilmark Press, 1963.

McEwan, Neil, *Graham Greene*, St. Martin's Press, 1988, p. 58.

"Mexican Revolution," in *The Concise Oxford Dictionary of Politics*, edited by Iain McLean and Alistair McMillan, Oxford University Press, 2009.

"Mexico—A Country Study," in *Encyclopedia of the Nations*, edited by Tim L. Merrill and Ramón Miró, Federal Research Division, Library of Congress, http://www. country-data.com/cgi-bin/query/r-8728.html (accessed May 18, 2009).

Pohle, Joseph, "The Blessed Eucharist as a Sacrament," in *The Catholic Encyclopedia*, Vol. 5, Robert Appleton, 1909, http://www.newadvent.org/cathen/05584a.htm (accessed May 19, 2009).

Schroeder, Michael J., "Mexican Revolution," in *Encyclopedia of World History: Crisis and Achievement, 1900 to 1950*, Vol. 5, Facts On File, 2008.

FURTHER READING

Hahn, Scott, *Lord, Have Mercy: The Healing Power of Confession*, Doubleday Religion, 2003.

> Much of the plot of Greene's novel hinges upon the priest's ability to give, and finally to receive, the sacrament of confession. In this book Hahn explains in clear terms the ideas behind confession, which has declined in significance among Catholics since Greene's time.

Hesla, David H., "Theological Ambiguity in the 'Catholic Novels,'" in *Graham Greene: Some Critical Considerations*, edited by Robert O. Evans, University of Kentucky Press, 1963, pp. 96–111.

> Although critics often associate Greene with his Catholicism, especially for the important emphasis he gives religion in his novels, Hesla looks at the ways in which religious faith is presented in unclear or uneven ways.

Knight, Alan, "The Mentality and Modus Operandi of Revolutionary Anticlericism," in *Faith and Impiety in Revolutionary Mexico*, edited by Matthew Butler, Palgrave Macmillan, 2007, pp. 1–20.

> This scholarly analysis gives a rare look at the philosophy of the years of religious repression in Mexico, focusing on the 1910–1940 period.

Kunkel, Francis L., *The Labyrinthine Ways of Graham Greene*, Paul P. Appel, 1973.

> This book, first published in 1960 and then in a revised edition in 1973, is an interesting commentary on Greene's career as it was still developing. The fact that Kunkel's title was based on the title used for the American publication of *The Power and the Glory* indicates his focus and thoroughness.

Lewis, R. W. B., "The 'Trilogy,'" in *The Picaresque Saint*, J. B. Lippincott, 1959, pp. 239–64.

> Lewis examines the interconnecting themes of a cluster of Greene's novels—*Brighton Rock*, *The Power and the Glory*, and *The Heart of the Matter*—written in the late 1930s through the late 1940s.

The Princess Bride

WILLIAM GOLDMAN

1973

The Princess Bride is a fantasy romance and adventure novel by William Goldman, first published in 1973 under the full title *The Princess Bride: S. Morgenstern's Classic Tale of True Love and High Adventure, the "Good Parts" Version, Abridged by William Goldman.* Throughout the book, Goldman pretends he is writing an abridgement of a classic work by a writer named S. Morgenstern from the European country of Florin. This is a fictional device; there is no S. Morgenstern, no country called Florin, and no original work called *The Princess Bride* that Goldman is abridging. The entire work is Goldman's and his alone. He invents the fictional author Morgenstern for a variety of reasons, including humor and satire and the desire to create different ways in which the story may be understood. He frames the main story, about a beautiful girl called Buttercup and her true love, Westley, with another story in which he as an adult looks back on his first encounter with "Morgenstern's" work as a child, when his father read the book to him aloud. As he writes of this childhood encounter with the book, Goldman creates a persona for himself that is equal parts truth and fiction. He presents himself as William Goldman, the author of novels and screenplays (true) who is married to a psychiatrist named Helen with whom he has a ten-year-old son named Jason (fiction). The story itself is an amusing parody of an old-fashioned tale of love and adventure. Goldman tells it with a modern twist, since he refuses to guarantee a happy ending for

William Goldman *(© Will Ragozzino/Getty Images)*

his two fairy-tale lovers. He also intersperses sections in which he comments about the "original" he is abridging. The result is a comedic satire that also embraces serious themes about love and life.

A thirtieth anniversary edition of *The Princess Bride* was published in 2007 by Houghton Mifflin Harcourt.

AUTHOR BIOGRAPHY

Goldman, a novelist and screenwriter, was born on August 12, 1931, in Chicago, Illinois. In 1952, he graduated from Oberlin College with a B.A. in English and then served in the U.S. Army until 1954. He entered Columbia University and received an M.A. in theater in 1956. Goldman always wanted to become a writer, even though he had not excelled at the creative writing classes he took in college. In 1957, he wrote his first novel, *The Temple of Gold*, which was published by Alfred K. Knopf. After that initial success, Goldman never looked back, although he admitted in

an interview with Richard Andersen, published in *William Goldman*, that he did not much enjoy writing and did not consider himself a good writer. He wrote his next novel, *Your Turn to Curtsy, My Turn to Bow* (1958), in seven days, and followed that with several other novels. In 1973, Goldman wrote *The Princess Bride: S. Morgenstern's Classic Tale of True Love and High Adventure, the "Good Parts" Version, Abridged by William Goldman.* He told Andersen that this is the only novel he enjoyed writing and of which he was proud. Goldman used the authorial voice of S. Morgenstern once again when he penned *The Silent Gondoliers*, published in 1983. He has written seventeen novels over the course of his career.

Despite his prolific output as a novelist, Goldman is perhaps best known for his screenplays. These include *Butch Cassidy and the Sundance Kid* (produced 1969; published 1971); *The Stepford Wives* (1974); *All the President's Men* (1976), based on the book by Bob Woodward and Carl Bernstein (1976); *The Chamber* (1996), written with Chris Reese and adapted from the novel by John Grisham; *Absolute Power* (1997), based on the novel by David Baldacci; and *Dreamcatcher* (2003), written with Lawrence Kasdan and based on the novel by Stephen King.

Goldman also adapted many of his own novels for the screen, including *Marathon Man* (1976), *A Bridge Too Far* (produced in 1977, published as *William Goldman's Story of a Bridge Too Far*, 1977), *Magic* (1978), and *Heat* (1987). Goldman also wrote the screenplay for the movie adaptation of *The Princess Bride* (1987).

During his long career as a writer Goldman has received a number of awards, including the Academy of Motion Picture Arts and Sciences Award (Oscar) for Best Original Screenplay in 1970 for *Butch Cassidy and the Sundance Kid* and a Laurel Award in 1983 for lifetime achievement in screenwriting.

Goldman married Ilene Jones in 1961, and they had two daughters. The marriage ended in divorce. In the early 2000s, he continued to write books of essays and memoirs about his experiences working in Hollywood while continuing his work as a screenwriter.

PLOT SUMMARY

Introduction

The Princess Bride begins with an introduction in which Goldman explains the (fictional) origin of

MEDIA ADAPTATIONS

- An abridged version of *The Princess Bride* was released on audio cassette by Dove Audio in 1987. It is read by Rob Reiner, who directed the film version of the book.

- The novel was directed for film by Rob Reiner, with a screenplay written by Goldman. Robin Wright Penn (Buttercup) and Cary Elwes (Westley) starred as the two young lovers. The movie was applauded by critics and audiences for its fidelity to the spirit of the book. It was made by the Twentieth Century-Fox Film Corporation in 1987 and is currently available on DVD and Blu-ray disc.

- *The Princess Bride* was also adapted as a video game, *The Official Princess Bride Game*, by Worldwide Biggies in 2008. It is available for PC, Mac, and Linux computers.

- Though not directly the inspiration, *The Princess Bride* has paved the way for many movies of swashbuckling and romance, including the extremely popular *The Pirates of the Caribbean* movie trilogy, released by Disney from 2003 through 2007, and *Stardust*, a 2007 film produced by Paramount, based on the 1999 Neil Gaiman novel of the same title.

the book. At ten years old, William is lying in bed recuperating from pneumonia, and his immigrant father reads to him from a book called *The Princess Bride*, written by S. Morgenstern, a great author. Like Goldman's father, Morgenstern came from a country called Florin. Young William is too sleepy to take much of it in, but the story sticks in his mind and for the first time in his life he becomes interested in a book. His father reads the entire book to him twice over a month. William then develops a keen interest in adventure stories of all kinds, to the surprise of Miss Roginski, his schoolteacher. Looking back as an adult, Goldman identifies this encounter with *The Princess Bride* to be the best thing that ever happened to him. While in California working on

a screenplay, he arranges with a bookstore to deliver a copy of the *The Princess Bride*, in the original Florinese and in an English translation, to his home in New York. He wants Jason, his ten-year-old son, to read it. He returns in two weeks, and when he is having dinner with his wife, Helen, and Jason, the boy says he loved the book, but Goldman soon finds out that Jason read only the first chapter and did not like it. Goldman consults the book himself and finds that it is long and much of it tedious. He realizes that his father only read him the good parts, the sections with all the action. He decides to abridge the book and republish it, the text of which follows.

Chapter 1: The Bride

In Florin, a country between what would later become Sweden and Germany, a beautiful young woman named Buttercup is growing up on the family farm. She is so attractive that all the village boys follow her around, but she is not interested in them. Nor is she interested in the hired hand, whom she simply calls Farm Boy, who lives in a hovel on the farm. She orders him around and he does what he is told.

One day, Buttercup's parents, who are always quarreling, see Count and Countess Rugen passing by with an entourage of servants. To the surprise of the farm couple, the procession enters the farm. The Count tells Buttercup's parents that he wants to consult them about their cows, since he has heard they are the best in the land. Buttercup's father is astonished, because he knows their cows are nothing of the kind. In truth, the Count has come just to see the seventeen-year-old Buttercup, since he has heard how beautiful she is. When he sees her, he cannot stop looking at her. Meanwhile, the Countess is quite taken by the appearance of Farm Boy, whose name turns out to be Westley, and she watches him milk the cows as if the secret of how great they are must be in his milking technique. That night, Buttercup reflects on the strange incident. She realizes that the Countess was interested in Westley, and he was interested in her. Then Buttercup realizes that she is jealous. Before dawn she goes to Westley's hovel and declares her eternal love for him. He shuts the door on her without saying a word. Buttercup runs away weeping, but at dusk, Westley comes to her door. She pretends that what she said earlier was a joke, but he cuts her off and says he is leaving for America to make his fortune. He declares his love for Buttercup and wants her to join him when he is rich. Buttercup can hardly believe it, but they soon fall into each other's arms. Over the next few weeks she receives letters from Westley, but then the letters stop. One day her parents tell her that Westley has been killed by pirates off the Carolina coast. Buttercup swears never to love again.

Chapter 2: The Groom

The chapter opens with a section by Goldman explaining that he has cut most of Morgenstern's original chapter because it was mostly about Florinese history. He takes up the story only when it becomes interesting.

Prince Humperdinck, the son of King Lotharon, loves war but loves hunting even more. He likes to kill something every day and has built an underground Zoo of Death, stocked with all kinds of beasts that he can kill. One day he is about to finish off a monkey when Count Rugen brings him the news that his father, King Lotharon, is dying. The Prince is displeased. The death of his father means that he will have to get married so he can produce an heir.

Chapter 3: The Courtship

Humperdinck, Count Rugen, the King, and Queen Bella (Humperdinck's stepmother) agree that Princess Noreena from the neighboring country of Guilder would be a good choice of a bride, and arrangements are made for the Princess to visit. (In one of Goldman's explanatory passages, he notes that he has cut the details of how the visit was arranged because it consisted of over fifty pages detailing the packing and unpacking of clothes and hats). The state dinner for Princess Noreena is a disaster. A fire breaks out, and because the doors are open, there are huge gusts of wind, one of which blows the Princess's hat off, revealing her to be bald. This ensures that the wedding is called off. Prince Humperdinck says he would not mind a commoner as a bride as long as she is beautiful. The Count suggests Buttercup, and the two men go to see her. Humperdinck proposes but she only agrees to marry him when he assures her she will not be required to love him.

Chapter 4: The Preparations

This chapter consists of a half-page note by Goldman saying that the original chapter by Morgenstern goes on at great length about how Buttercup is made a princess and trained to behave like one, and the King's health improves. This all takes three years, but nothing really happens.

Chapter 5: The Announcement

Prince Humperdinck introduces the twenty-one-year old Princess Buttercup to a cheering crowd in the great square of Florin City. Later that day, as Buttercup is riding alone, she is kidnapped by three paid assassins: a humpback Sicilian named Vizzini, a Spaniard named Inigo, and a huge Turk named Fezzik. They plan to kill her at the Guilder frontier and make it look like the Guilders are responsible. The purpose is to start a war between Florin and Guilder. The assassins take Buttercup away in a boat; she jumps overboard and swims but is pulled back into the boat before the sharks get her. They reach huge cliffs that they must cross, and they fear they are being followed by another boat. The Sicilian throws a rope that holds fast at the top of the cliff. Fezzik, sinks the boat and carries the other three up the cliff. They are followed by a masked man in black from the boat that followed them. They reach the top and cut the rope, leaving their pursuer hanging from a rock. However, the man keeps climbing. As the others move on, Inigo remains behind to deal with him, and his back story is revealed.

Inigo's father Domingo Montoya was a great sword maker in Spain. One day a nobleman came to him who had six fingers, and he asked Domingo to make him a six-fingered sword. It took Domingo a year of hard work to make the sword. When he returned the nobleman did not like the sword, and when Domingo gave the sword instead to ten-year-old Inigo, the nobleman killed Domingo. Inigo challenged the nobleman, who cut Inigo's face and left. Inigo went to Madrid, Spain, where for two years he was looked after by Yeste, a friend of his father and a famous sword maker. Inigo departed and returned ten years later. He spent the entire time mastering the art of swordsmanship, with the aim of getting revenge on the six-fingered man. He asked Yeste if he was up to the task. Yeste indicated that he was, so Inigo traveled the world for five years in search of his enemy but failed to find him. He started to drink too much and his life went downhill before he was rescued by the Sicilian who recruited him for his criminal activities.

When the man in black reaches the top of the cliff, he and Inigo fight a duel. The advantage swings back and forth but eventually the masked man wins. Because he respects Inigo too much as a swordsman to kill him, the masked man knocks

Inigo unconscious and follows the other two assassins. On seeing the man in black coming after them, the Sicilian leaves Fezzik behind to kill him. Fezzik has always been huge, even as a child, but he was also gentle, and his father had to train him to defend himself. He became a fighter and easily defeated all his opponents, even when he was only eleven. When his parents died he joined a traveling circus, but he was too big and too good and the crowds booed him. After he was fired by the circus, Vizzini found him in Greenland and recruited him.

Fezzik and the man in black fight. After a long struggle, the man in black wins, leaves Fezzik exhausted on the ground, and continues the chase. The masked man reaches Vizzini, who is holding a knife at Buttercup's throat. Vizzini boasts about how smart he is, and the man in black challenges him to a battle of wits. The man in black produces some poisonous powder and, out of Vizzini's sight, puts it in one of the two goblets of wine Vizzini has laid out. Vizzini has to choose which glass contains the poison. He guesses wrong, drinks the poisoned goblet and dies. The man in black unties Buttercup and tells her that both glasses were poisoned; he spent years building up his immunity to the poison.

The mysterious man forces the frightened Buttercup to run behind him across the mountainous terrain. They reach a ravine and see below them, in Florin Channel, an armada that Prince Humperdinck has sent to rescue her. Buttercup pushes the man in black down the ravine, from where he removes his mask, revealing himself to be Westley. She tumbles down after him.

At the head of the armada, Prince Humperdinck gazes at the cliff, plotting his next move. He gives instructions to the Count, and the armada splits up, leaving Humperdinck's as the sole ship approaching the coastline. In less than an hour the Prince is on horseback at the top of the cliff, where the Count and a hundred men soon join him. The Prince uses his skill as a hunter to interpret the tracks left by the sword fight and the hand-to-hand fight. He comes upon the dead Vizzini and deduces that two people fell down the ravine. He tells the Count that the ravine opens into the fire swamp.

Westley and Buttercup enter the fire swamp. Westley leads the way, but soon Buttercup disappears in the Snow Sand, a kind of quicksand. Westley dives into it and saves her. He explains to Buttercup how he came to survive: the Dread

Pirate Roberts spared his life because Westley made himself so useful. He became Roberts's valet and then second in command. Eventually, Roberts retired and let Westley adopt his name, and Westley is now a feared pirate. His ship is anchored in the bay, and he tells Buttercup that they must reach it. Westley fights off an attack by giant rats, but when they reach the edge of the fire swamp, the Prince and all his forces confront them. Buttercup gets the Prince to promise he will not hurt Westley, and then she leaves Westley behind. Westley accepts his defeat and is captured. He notices that one of the Count's hands has six fingers.

Chapter 6: The Festivities

Goldman notes that the next section in Morgenstern is boring, since it deals at length with all the festivities leading up to the wedding of Buttercup and the Prince that is to take place in three months. Goldman skips forward a month and returns to the story of Inigo, who regains consciousness and makes his way to the Thieves Quarter in Florin City, hoping to meet up with Vizzini. Meanwhile Fezzik finds Vizzini dead and goes searching for Inigo. He ends up at a village being taunted by the local boys.

Westley awakes in an underground cage in the Zoo of Death, guessing that he will be tortured. Meanwhile, the King dies and the Prince ascends to the throne. He is very busy learning how to conduct affairs of state so the wedding to Buttercup is not as big as planned. As the couple stands on the balcony, an old woman boos the new queen for choosing gold over love. Then Buttercup awakes from a nightmare; she is not in fact married yet. She has a series of nightmares, all related to her choice to walk away from Westley in the fire swamp. She tells the Prince she made a mistake and she really loves Westley. The Prince appears to be sympathetic and says he will allow her to marry Westley if he still wants to marry her. In truth, it is the Prince who hired the assassins and he now plans to kill Buttercup on their wedding night, blame it on the Guilders, and start a war.

Count Rugen tortures Westley while the Prince questions him, trying to get him to say who hired him to kidnap Buttercup. Westley truthfully denies that anyone hired him. He resists the pain by thinking of Buttercup. The Prince helps Buttercup write to Westley, and she lets slip the information that Westley is frightened of Spinning Ticks. That night Westley is tortured by having Spinning Ticks placed on his skin. Next, the Count tortures him with a fiendish device called the Machine.

Meanwhile, the Prince orders the Thieves Quarter to be cleared out by his thugs, the Brute Squad, since he fears the Guilders are there, plotting a covert attack on his kingdom. One of the Brutes turns out to be Fezzik, who was hired for his strength. Fezzik finds Inigo, and together they take refuge in an alehouse in the now empty quarter. Inigo wants to kill the Count to avenge his father, but he needs the help of the man in black, so Inigo and Fezzik seek him out. Meanwhile Buttercup has found out that the Prince never sent her letter to Westley asking if he still wished to marry her. She calls him a coward. Outraged, the Prince goes to the Zoo of Death and murders Westley.

Chapter 7: The Wedding

Fezzik and Inigo enter the Zoo of Death. They go past caged animals down to the third level, where they beat off an attack by snakes. At level four, Fezzik is terrified by bats, but Inigo kills them with his sword. At the fifth level they find Westley's body, which they take to Miracle Max, a healer who used to be employed by the king. They tell Max they need a miracle. After much argument and negotiation, which also involves Max's wife Valerie, Max agrees to bring Westley back to life. Inigo and Fezzik gather ingredients for a resurrection pill that will work for only one hour.

It is the day of the wedding, and the Prince is still plotting to murder Buttercup that night and frame the Guilderians for the crime. Fifty minutes before the wedding, Inigo and Fezzik feed Westley the pill and he revives. The wedding ceremony has begun as the three men advance on the castle guard. Fezzik terrifies the guards by claiming to be the Dread Pirate Roberts and appearing to burst into flames, although only his coat is on fire.

Chapter 8: The Honeymoon

Fezzik, Inigo, and Westley enter the castle, although unknown to them they are too late to stop the wedding. Inigo confronts the Count, who runs away. Buttercup goes to the Prince's chamber, intent on suicide. Fezzik, Inigo, and Westley get separated, and Inigo pursues the Count. When Inigo catches him, the Count stabs him with a dagger. However, Inigo fights on, and eventually the Count dies of fright when he realizes that Inigo will cut his heart out. Meanwhile, Westley has made it to Buttercup, but they are found by the Prince. Westley threatens to mutilate him, which frightens the Prince. Buttercup then ties up Humperdinck. Inigo and Fezzik arrive, and the four make their escape on horseback to the Florin Channel.

Goldman comments that when his father read him the story, he ended it there, but Morgenstern made the ending more ambiguous. The four are pursued by the Prince, and each meets with a setback. The final outcome of their escape is unstated.

CHARACTERS

Queen Bella

Queen Bella is King Lotharon's wife and Prince Humperdinck's stepmother. He calls her the evil stepmother, but actually she is sweet and considerate and much beloved in the kingdom.

Buttercup

Buttercup grows up on a farm and at the age of fifteen is potentially one of the most beautiful women in the world. However, she does not care about beauty or about the hired hand she calls Farm Boy who works on her family's farm. When she is nearly seventeen she falls in love with the Farm Boy, Westley, and starts to take some trouble with her appearance. Within a few weeks she goes from being the twentieth most beautiful woman in the world to ninth, and is still rising. She is happy to wait while Westley makes his fortune in America and is devastated when she hears about Westley's death at the hands of pirates. She vows never to love again. When Prince Humperdinck, seeking a beautiful bride, asks her to marry him, she agrees only on the condition that she will not be required to love him. When Westley rescues her from kidnappers, she once more expresses her love for him. When they are cornered by Prince Humperdinck she surrenders to the Prince rather than dying with Westley, admitting that she can live without love. She later has nightmares in which she regrets her choice, and she remains calm as her wedding to Prince Humperdinck takes place, knowing that Westley will come to save her.

Buttercup's Father

Buttercup's father is a farmer who is not good at anything. He is neither a good farmer nor a good husband. He and his wife spend much of their time squabbling, each trying to score points in a running argument.

Buttercup's Mother

Buttercup's mother worries a lot and is a bad cook. She always wanted to be popular, but it never happened. What keeps her alive is her endless fighting with her husband. When he dies, she dies soon after, as if she could not live without him.

Falkbridge

Falkbridge owns an alehouse in the Thieves Quarter. He practically runs the Thieves Quarter and has a hand in almost every crime that goes on there. To escape jail he regularly pays a bribe to Yellin.

Farm Boy

See Westley

Fezzik

Fezzik is a huge, gentle Turk who is recruited by Vizzini to help kidnap Buttercup. When Fezzik was one year old, he already weighed eighty-five pounds, and he started shaving when he was in kindergarten. Fezzik is incredibly strong. He once held up an elephant using only the muscles in his back, and his arms are tireless. However, he is not very bright and always has to be told what to do. Even so, he is fascinated by words and loves to make rhymes. When Fezzik is put to the test in the fight with Westley, he comes up short; Westley is the first person to beat him. However, Fezzik proves his worth later on, terrifying the guards outside the castle and allowing Buttercup's rescuers to enter.

Billy Goldman

See William Goldman

Helen Goldman

Helen Goldman is the author's fictional wife. She has a brilliant intellect and is a child psychiatrist. However, she does not seem to be very skillful in handling people, and her marriage to William seems unhappy. He thinks she lacks a sense of humor.

Jason Goldman

Jason Goldman is the ten-year-old son of William and Helen Goldman. He is an overweight boy who eats too much, and his father thinks that, like his mother, Jason lacks a sense of humor. His father gives him an unabridged copy of *The Princess Bride* to read but Jason finds it boring. This gives William the idea to abridge the book to include only the interesting parts.

William Goldman

William Goldman is the author of the novel in which he also appears as a character. The character is a careful mixture of fact and fiction. In the novel, Goldman is, as in real life, the successful author of screenplays such as *Butch Cassidy and the Sundance Kid* and *The Stepford Wives*, and the novel *The Temple of Gold*, which was published when he was twenty-six. However, most of the rest is a fictional creation. Goldman the fictional character is married to a child psychiatrist and has an overweight son. He also remembers hearing his father read *The Princess Bride* to him when he was ten, an experience that was instrumental in giving him a love of literature that no doubt contributed to his career as a writer. His wife thinks he is emotionally needy, and he admits that he does not love her. In spite of this, when he is away they talk to each other every day on the phone.

William Goldman's Father

The fictional William Goldman's father was a nearly illiterate immigrant from Florin who worked as a barber in Highland Park, Illinois. With great difficulty, and in a tongue that was foreign to him, he reads *The Princess Bride* to his ten-year-old son, but he skips through the boring parts. He also shows a sensitivity to his son's feelings. He wants to skip the part where Wesley dies and he omits the ambiguous ending so that Billy (as he called his son) would think the story ended happily.

Hiram Haydn

Hiram Haydn is Goldman's editor at Harcourt Brace Jovanovich. Goldman calls him in the middle of the night to suggest an abridgement of Morgenstern's classic story.

Prince Humperdinck

Prince Humperdinck is the son of King Lotharon and the heir to the throne. He is a huge, barrel-chested man who weighs about 250 pounds. He likes war but loves hunting so much he builds an underground Zoo of Death that contains all varieties of creatures, so he can amuse himself by hunting and killing them. He has no friends and confides only in Count Rugen. It soon becomes apparent that Humperdinck is a villain of the highest order. After he gets Buttercup to marry him he hires some assassins to kidnap her and dump her on the frontier of Guilder, the neighboring country, so he can blame Guilder for her death and start a war. He has wanted to conquer Guilder since he was a boy. When his first plan is foiled by Westley's rescue of Buttercup he devises another one, in which he will personally kill Buttercup on her wedding night and blame her death on soldiers from Guilder. Humperdinck's true nature is fully revealed when Buttercup calls him a coward. Outraged, he throws her into her room and locks the door, then goes to the Zoo of Death where he murders Westley.

King Lotharon

King Lotharon is the king of Florin. He is very old and sick and can speak only by muttering and mumbling.

The Man in Black

See Westley

Miracle Max

Miracle Max is a healer who tended the king but was fired by Prince Humperdinck. This caused him to lose all his patients, and he now lives in a hut with his wife, Valerie. When Inigo and Fezzik bring the dead Westley to him, saying they need a miracle, Max at first refuses, saying he is retired. He agrees to bring Westley back from the dead only when he learns that Westley will stop Humperdinck's marriage.

Domingo Montoya

Domingo Montoya was Inigo's father. He was a master sword maker from the village of Arabella in the mountains of northern Spain who met his death when a nobleman for whom he had made a six-fingered sword was dissatisfied with the product and, after an argument, killed him. His son Inigo has sworn to avenge his father's death.

Inigo Montoya

Inigo Montoya is a Spaniard who is a master swordsman. He developed his skills over many years of study and travel because he wanted to avenge his father's death at the hands of a six-fingered nobleman. He witnessed this event when he was ten years old. After traveling the world for five years but failing to find his enemy, Inigo starts to drink and lose his purpose in life. He is rescued by Vizzini and recovers his sword fighting skills as a member of Vizzini's criminal gang. He is bested by Westley in a sword fight but teams up with him to confront and kill Count Rugen, the six-fingered man, in the castle.

Edith Neisser

Edith Neisser wrote books about the psychology of human relationships. The fictional Goldman writes that he knew Neisser (a real person) when he was in his teens because they lived in the same town. It was Neisser who first told him that life is not fair.

Dread Pirate Roberts

See Westley

Miss Roginksi

Miss Roginksi is Goldman's teacher from third to fifth grade at Highland Park Grammar School. She calls him a late bloomer because he is not good at academic subjects. When he later sends her a copy of his first novel, he is relieved to find that she remembers him.

Count Rugen

Count Rugen is a big man with black hair and six fingers on his right hand. He is the only Count in Florin and is a confidant of Prince Humperdinck. The Count is an accomplished man and Humperdinck depends on him for his skills as an architect and inventor. The Count designed crucial elements of the Zoo of Death and invented the torture device known as the Machine. He is interested in pain and is writing a book about it. Many years ago he murdered Domingo Montoya, and he eventually gets his comeuppance when Inigo tracks him down. They engage in a sword fight, but the Count dies of fright when he realizes that Inigo is about to cut his heart out.

Countess Rugen

The Countess is the wife of the Count and is much admired, and also feared, in Florin. She is much younger than her husband and is considered to embody the height of taste and fashion. She acquires her clothes from Paris and eventually settles there.

Sandy Sterling

Sandy Sterling is a Hollywood starlet. Goldman meets her at the hotel swimming pool when he is in California. She tells him that *The Stepford Wives* is one of her favorite books and that she would do anything to be in the movie.

Six-fingered Man

See Count Rugen

Valerie

Valerie is Miracle Max's wife. She encourages him to come to an agreement with Inigo and resurrect Westley because she and Max need the money.

Vizzini

The hunchback Vizzini is a Sicilian criminal who is hired by Humperdinck to kidnap and kill Buttercup. Vizzini recruits Inigo and Fezzik to help him do the job. Vizzini is the undisputed leader of the group and he prides himself on his intelligence and cunning. He tells Westley that he is "the slickest, sleekest, sliest and wiliest fellow who has yet come down the pike." But this formidable assembly of qualities does not enable him to outwit Westley, who tricks him into drinking a poisoned goblet of wine.

Westley

Westley is an orphan who was taken on by Buttercup's father to work on the farm. He lives in a hovel but keeps it clean and reads by candlelight. Buttercup, however, thinks he is stupid and treats him with contempt as her virtual slave. She calls him Farm Boy. Westley is in fact handsome, muscular, and intelligent, and he has already fallen in love with Buttercup. After Buttercup finally realizes that she is in love with him too, he goes to America to make his fortune so that she can come and join him later. Within a few months, Westley is reputed to have been killed by pirates; but this is not so: he has become the Dread Pirate Roberts. He returns to Florin to save Buttercup from her abductors and then rescue her from Prince Humperdinck. Westley is the ideal hero throughout the story. He is a better fighter than either Inigo or Fezzik, and he cannot be forced by torture into lying. He never stops loving Buttercup and is brought back from the dead solely because his love is true. Also, he lives for longer than the resurrection pill should allow because he asks the "Lord of Permanent Affection" for the strength to stay alive for the entire day.

Yellin

Yellin is the head of law enforcement in Florin City. He is a crafty man who takes bribes.

Yeste

Yeste was a rich, fat master sword maker from Madrid who was a friend of Domingo Montoya. After Domingo was killed, Yeste looked after his son Inigo for two years.

THEMES

The Unfairness of Life

The reader might expect this fantasy romantic/adventure novel to follow the usual pattern of such stories: good is always rewarded, evil perishes, and the good characters live happily ever after. But this is not entirely the case in *The Princess Bride*. The author is at pains to show that life is not fair, that it can be disappointing and not measure up to one's hopes and dreams. In this sense he introduces a strong note of realism into the tale. The theme that life is not fair occurs both in the passages Goldman inserts where he comments on his own life and the "original" Morgenstern story, as well as in the tale itself. In the introduction, in which Goldman describes how he came to write the book, he explains that he once thought his life would follow the subtitle of the story and be all about "true love and high adventure," but it did not happen. In particular, his fictional self admits that he is not especially happy in his marriage, and he adds, "I don't know if I love anything truly any more beyond the porterhouse at Peter Luger's and the cheese enchilada at El Parador's." It is a light-hearted comment with serious undertones, and it is relevant for the story that follows, since it serves as ironic, real-life commentary (although of course the real-life element is also a fiction) on the romance and future prospects of Buttercup and Westley. The theme of the unfairness of life is stated explicitly in the section in which Goldman comments on his own reaction when as a boy his father read to him the part about Buttercup marrying Humperdinck. Even a ten-year-old knows that in stories like *The Princess Bride* such things do not happen. Yet they do. This leaves the young boy with the disappointed feeling that something is not right, both in the story and in life, and this feeling remains with him even as an adult. He recalls

TOPICS FOR FURTHER STUDY

- Read *Stardust* (1999), a fairy tale about a prince and his adventures on behalf of his beloved, by Neil Gaiman. In a written report, compare this book to *The Princess Bride*. What do the two books have in common in terms of theme and style, and how do they differ? Wherein lies their appeal? As an alternative to *Stardust*, you may choose *The Neverending Story* (1983) by Michael Ende.

- Watch the movie version of *The Princess Bride*. Working with another student, analyze how the film compares to the book. What elements are changed? In what sense is it true to the original? Are the actors well cast in their roles? Give a class presentation in which you discuss your findings, using Power-Point and images to support your argument. Also include clips from the film if possible.

- Write a short romantic fable, fantasy, or fairy tale in which you mix the traditional and the modern to create an amusing effect. Read folktales and fairy tales from other cultures to support your new story. Does your story express fairy-tale ideals, remote from the way real life happens, or does it also, like *The Princess Bride*, have a serious message? Using your design skills, add some pictures that contribute to the story's appeal and create an appealing page layout.

- Research the current divorce rate in the United States. Is it going up or down? Why do so many marriages fail? Is there any connection between a high divorce rate and our society's acceptance of romantic love as the main basis for marriage? How would you describe romantic love? With another student, lead a class discussion on this topic, using *The Princess Bride* as a way of introducing and commenting on it.

that when he was in his teens, an acquaintance of his named Edith Neisser (who was a real-life author of books on psychology) explained to him:

Life isn't fair, Bill. We tell our children that it is, but it's a terrible thing to do. It's not only a lie, it's a cruel lie. Life is not fair, and it never has been, and it's never going to be.

The theme of the unfairness of life continues when the young William Goldman's father does not want to read him the chapter in which Westley dies. Young William is horrified when he learns that the hero dies, and also that no one kills the evil Prince Humperdinck. This little episode enacts exactly what Edith later explained. The story being read reflects the unfairness of life, but the parent is very reluctant for the child to discover this distressing fact.

True Love versus Love of Power

Although the author keeps reminding the reader that life is unfair, this does not stop him from writing a story which shows the enduring power of love and its capacity to defeat evil. Buttercup and Westley genuinely love each other and prove it again and again. Westley overcomes everything in his path to claim Buttercup as his bride. Buttercup never for a moment betrays Westley by loving Prince Humperdinck; she surrenders to the Prince only when she has made him promise that he will not hurt Westley. She cannot bear that Westley should suffer.

The story also shows that love has the capacity to enhance and prolong life. When, for example, Westley asks the "Lord of Permanent Affection" to extend the efficacy of the resurrection pill for the rest of the day, his wish is granted. In contrast, the torture machine has the effect of subtracting life. The machine sucks ten years from Westley's life in just a week. This neatly shows what Prince Humperdinck and the Count represent: they are the anti-life forces; they exist only to dominate others, to revel in their own power and cruelty. Humperdinck is the classic evil character. He has no tender feelings for Buttercup; he only loves war and hunting. Buttercup is just another form of prey for him, since he plots to kill her so he can create a pretext that will allow him to indulge his other love—he wants to make war with Guilder. As for the Count, his only interest is in pain, and he has the coldheartedness to inflict it on others without a qualm. When he is finally killed by Inigo and is forced to suffer the same fear that he liked to inflict, this is also an illustration of the power of love: the love of a son for his murdered father.

The struggle between the power of love and the love of power is illustrated in one of the most

Cary Elwes as Westley and Mandy Patinkin as Inigo Montoya in the 1987 film The Princess Bride *(© Photos 12 | Alamy)*

STYLE

Parody

The novel is part fairy tale, part fantasy, part adventure, and part romance, but it is all these things only with a twist. The author is familiar with these genres and is determined to parody them. A parody is a spoof in which something—a style, a genre—is imitated only to make fun of it.

The fairy-tale element includes the beautiful girl who becomes a princess and marries a prince. Fantasy literature often includes events, creatures, and situations that could not happen in real life, such as the climbing of the Cliffs of Insanity, fighting giant snakes and rodents, and making the resurrection pill. The adventure story is all action, including the kind of fights and chases that take place in *The Princess Bride*. The presentation of Inigo as the greatest swordsman in the world is a nod to *The Three Musketeers* (1844), the adventure novel by Alexandre Dumas that the fictional Goldman mentions reading as a boy in the introduction. The romantic element in the novel is obvious: the love of Westley and Buttercup is the central fabric around which the story is woven.

However, the elements of parody are not difficult to spot. In the first chapter the fairy-tale cliché of the most beautiful woman of the world is parodied in the figure of Buttercup, who has potential but has to work her way up into the top ten rankings. Inspired by her love for Westley, she races up the charts, moving from twentieth, to fifteenth and then up to ninth, and is still on the rise. The humor works by anachronism (being chronologically out of place): the modern concept of the Top Ten ranking list for this or that is juxtaposed with a fable set mostly in medieval times, and this makes it stand out as funny.

The fairy-tale element, as well as the conventions of the popular romance, are parodied in the exaggerated language with which Buttercup and Westley first declare their love for each other. They go completely overboard, as this quotation, spoken by Buttercup, shows:

> I have loved you for several hours now, and every second, more. I thought an hour ago that I loved you more than any woman has ever loved a man, but a half hour after that I knew that what I felt before was nothing compared to what I felt then.

And so on.

The description of Westley as handsome, tanned, and muscular is a parody of the bare-chested hero who appears on the covers of countless romance novels that adorn the

dramatic moments in the novel, the long scream that Westley utters as he dies, which is heard all over Florin City. Inigo recognizes it as "the sound of Ultimate Suffering." The scream expresses the terrible pain that occurs when a genuine and deep love is sundered by the cruel murder of one of the lovers. It represents the apparent triumph of evil over good, the anguish of life when love is extinguished. But, significantly, this scream is not the last sound in the novel, and nor is it without positive effect. It inspires Inigo to find Westley quickly, and when he and Fezzik take the dead man to Miracle Max, it is because Westley, thanks to Max's ingenious use of the bellows, says that he wants to live because of true love that Max (with a little prodding from his wife) agrees to bring him back. There is something about love that will not be defeated despite all the forces arrayed against it.

supermarket racks. However, there is an extra joke there too, because at the time Buttercup is so naive she does not yet perceive Westley as the attractive man he obviously is. Puzzled by the Countess's interest in him, she concludes that the noble lady must be attracted to him because he has good teeth, although this explanation does not end her puzzlement.

Another parody is that the prince whom the princess marries is not her true love (as in a fairy tale) but rather the evil Prince Humperdinck. The parody shows up in the title of the second chapter. Having introduced the bride in chapter 1, and the apparent groom, Westley, the author then kills off Westley (or so it seems) and devotes chapter 2, "The Groom," to Prince Humperdinck. Clearly, this is no ordinary romance, and certainly in no traditional romance would the hero die by torture at the hands of his enemy. Just in case the reader should miss these obvious parodies, Goldman draws attention to them through the device of his ten-year-old fictional self, who is hearing the story read by his father.

Symbolism

Recurring symbolism of rebirth enhances the theme of the power of love and the capacity of life to renew itself in the name of good. The first examples are Inigo and Fezzik. They are both "good" characters but when they are first introduced they are rather less than that. Allowing their own failures and disappointments in life to obscure their true natures, they have been recruited by Vizzini for his criminal gang. However, both undergo a kind of rebirth when they are defeated and knocked unconscious by the man in black (Westley). This breaks their attachment to criminality, and when they recover they eventually find their way back to more positive endeavors. Instead of being part of a three-member criminal enterprise, they form another gang of three, with Westley replacing Vizzini, dedicated to ensuring the triumph of love and goodness.

Westley is also the agent of another symbolic rebirth when Buttercup falls into the snow sand in the fire swamp. She goes through a near death experience: "She was just falling, gently, through this soft, powdery mass, falling farther and farther from anything resembling life." She would have died had it not been for Westley coming to the rescue. The incident shows that there is nothing that Westley cannot or will not do for her. He is like Orpheus, the hero in the ancient Greek myth who goes down to Hades (the underworld) to recover his bride Euridice.

Westley undergoes the most dramatic rebirth of them all, but even before Miracle Max's resurrection pill is forced down his throat, he has already been symbolically reborn twice. After all, Buttercup is informed that Westley has been killed by pirates, and the reader knows no better until the man in black reveals in the ravine that he is Westley. Later, Westley explains that he eventually took on the identity of the Dread Pirate Roberts, which is another symbolic rebirth. This shows that he was able to do what he had to do in order to survive. Finally, Westley's literal resurrection from the dead shows the power of love to triumph even over death itself.

HISTORICAL CONTEXT

The Fantasy Novel

Goldman published *The Princess Bride* at a time when the fantasy novel was gaining popularity. Much of the new interest in fantasy was fueled by the success of J. R. R. Tolkien's *The Hobbit* (1937) and the *Lord of the Rings* trilogy (1954–55), which became extremely popular in the United States in the late 1960s. C. S. Lewis's seven-volume *Chronicles of Narnia* (1950–56), written for children but also read by adults, also contributed to the growing interest in fantasy literature. The first great fantasy work to be published in the United States following the wave of interest in Tolkien was Ursula K. Le Guin's *Earthsea Trilogy* (1968–72), written for young adults but read by a far wider group for its psychological insight. The trilogy is set in the fantasy islands of Earthsea and shows the coming of age of a young wizard. Another of the most popular fantasy writers of the period was Terry Brooks, whose first book, *The Sword of Shannara* (1977) reached the *New York Times* best-seller list. Brooks followed this with many other books during the 1980s and 1990s, making him one of the most successful fantasy writers of all time. He had, and still has, a large following among young-adult readers.

With the growth of fantasy literature, a scholarly interest in defining and categorizing it also began to grow. For Ann Swinfen, in *In Defense of Fantasy: A Study of the Genre in English and American Literature since 1945*, "The essential ingredient of all fantasy is 'the marvellous'... anything outside the normal space-time continuum of the everyday world." Brian Attebery, in *The Fantasy Tradition in American Literature: From Irving to Le Guin*, offered another

COMPARE
&
CONTRAST

- **Medieval Era:** This is the age of chivalric romance, in which many popular stories feature brave knights who fight for justice in battles between good and evil. People believe in great heroes and their exploits.

  1970s: At the height of the difficult and unpopular Vietnam War, and with the Watergate scandal in Washington politics, there are few heroes to be found. War is no longer perceived as glamorous and exciting but as a last resort in settling disputes between nations.

  Today: Heroes are less often found in military or political figures, but instead are often ordinary people who show great bravery in unexpected, dangerous situations. An example is Wesley Autrey, a construction worker in Harlem, New York, who is a Vietnam War veteran. Autrey jumps down onto the subway tracks to save a man who has had a seizure and fallen on the tracks. Autrey lies on top of the man in the ditch between the rails as the train passes over both of them. Then-President George W. Bush later acknowledges Autrey's bravery during his State of the Union address.

- **Medieval Era:** This era produces two of the great love stories of all time. Gottfried von Strassburg writes his poem "Tristan and Iseult" (first transcribed in 1210), and the real-life Abelard and Heloise live out a romance in the twelfth century that, through

  their letters to each other, becomes famous through the ages. Abelard is a philosopher and theologian, and Heloise is also an accomplished scholar.

  1970s: Love stories still have the power to entrance and delight. Eric Segal's *Love Story* (1970), which tells the story of a tragic love, becomes a bestseller and is made into the equally popular movie of the same name starring Ryan O'Neal and Ali MacGraw.

  Today: In the age of short attention spans and 140-character messages on the social networking and micro-blogging service Twitter, love stories are much shorter. Harper Perennial publishes *Six-Word Memoirs on Love & Heartbreak: By Writers Famous and Obscure* (2009), in which people sum up their experience of love in just six words.

- **Medieval Era:** In war and battle, combat is often hand-to-hand; there are few weapons that can kill at a distance.

  1970s: Nuclear weapons are capable of traveling across continents, and a nuclear war could annihilate human civilization in a matter of hours.

  Today: One of the chief threats to world peace is nuclear weapons in the hands of terrorists or so-called rogue states.

---

broad definition of fantasy: a story that "treat[s] an impossibility as if it were true." He suggested that fantasy can then be further defined into subcategories based on elements such as "the marvelous within the story, the orientation of the tale toward wonder or its obverse, horror, the location of the supernatural in another world or in this," and other elements.

Among the subcategories of fantasy, many of which overlap, are high fantasy, such as Tolkien, in which there is a titanic moral struggle between

good and evil; animal fantasy, which features talking animals, as in Richard Adams's *Watership Down*, published in 1972; heroic fantasy, sometimes also called "sword and sorcery," which focuses on action and adventure; historical fantasy; time travel fantasy; romantic fantasy; and others.

The Princess Bride is hard to place in any one fantasy category. With its vaguely medieval setting and battle between good and evil, it resembles high fantasy, and there are also elements in the story of heroic and romantic fantasy. But often these kinds

Robin Wright Penn as Buttercup and Cary Elwes as Westley in the 1987 film The Princess Bride
(© Photos 12 / Alamy)

of fantasies are serious works, in the sense that they do not contain much humor. In contrast, Goldman's book bubbles over with humorous characters, dialogue, and scenes. This aligns him most closely with other fantasies from the same period that employ liberal doses of humor. One example is *Bored of the Rings* (1969), by Henry N. Beard and Douglas C. Kenney, a comic parody of Tolkien's *Lord of the Rings*. The popular "Xanth" books by Piers Anthony, beginning with *A Spell for Chameleon* (1977), provide more examples of comic fantasy, as do British author Terry Pratchett's "Discworld" series, beginning with *The Color of Magic* in 1983.

CRITICAL OVERVIEW

The Princess Bride garnered several positive reviews when it was first published in 1973. In *Newsweek*, S. K. Oberbeck recommends it as a "charming hoax" and a "ridiculously swashbuckling fable" that "sounds like all the Saturday serials you ever saw feverishly reworked by the Marx brothers." In the *New York Times Book Review*, Gerald Walker shows a similar appreciation, commenting on the "witty, affectionate send-up of the adventure-yarn form." Walker also notes the effect of the passages in which Goldman interrupts the narrative to explain what he is doing, commenting that this introduces "a kind of comedic extension of Brecht's distancing effect, alienation to provoke not an intellectual response, but an *entertained* response. And it works." Walker is referring to the German dramatist Bertolt Brecht (1898–1956), whose "distancing effect" was aimed at preventing an audience from identifying too strongly with the characters and encouraging them to remain aware that they were watching a play, an artificial construct designed so that the audience would be better able to reflect on and evaluate the play. The novel is also positively evaluated by Liz Holliday in *St. James Guide to Fantasy Writers*. She admires Goldman's storytelling skills and calls the novel an "immensely enjoyable romp." She further comments, "As with all the best fairy tales, the characters are cardboard cutouts—but Goldman pulls off a real trick by making us care for them all."

CRITICISM

Bryan Aubrey

Aubrey holds a Ph.D. in English. In this essay on The Princess Bride, *he discusses the novel in terms of how the father-son and husband-wife relationships are presented.*

In *The Princess Bride* Goldman managed to produce a fantasy novel that parodies the genre in a consistently amusing manner, yet also reveals an underlying seriousness of purpose. It is a fine balancing act, successfully accomplished, which is why *The Princess Bride* is usually regarded as Goldman's best novel. Rob Reiner's excellent film adaptation of the novel to the screen has added to the popularity of the book, giving it a new generation of readers both young and old.

In many ways, although the romance between Buttercup and Westley takes center stage, *The Princess Bride* is the story of three pairs of fathers and sons, with some glancing insight into two marriages and the prospects for a third. The fathers and sons are the fictional William Goldman's father and the author's fictional ten-year-old self; the fictional Goldman and his ten-year-old son, Jason; and Domingo Montoya and his ten-year-old son Inigo. The fact that all three boys are ten years old suggests a thematic link between them. The relationship between the young Goldman and his immigrant father is a particularly tender story within a story. The boy is in bed at home recovering from pneumonia, and his father, lovingly portrayed, reads to him from Morgenstern's original story. The father, whose life in America has not been successful, is almost illiterate, and it is hard for him to read the book to his son. Goldman gives a sympathetic portrait of the man, "slumped and squinting and halting over words, giving me Morgenstern's masterpiece as best he could."

The father is very protective of his son's innocence. He tries to skip reading the chapter in which Westley is killed by Prince Humperdinck; young William knows something is amiss but his father simply says, "Trust me," although he also wants reassurance that his son accepts his judgment. However, Billy, as his father sometimes calls him, will not take no for an answer, and his father relents. When his father tells him what happens Billy starts to cry, and his father, saddened, starts to leave the room. It is a touching moment. The father is ever anxious for his young son's happiness, but he cannot shield him

> THERE ARE NO GOOD MARRIAGES IN THIS STORY, WHICH SERVES AS IRONIC COMMENTARY ON WHAT THE LOVELY BUTTERCUP AND HANDSOME WESTLEY MIGHT EXPECT WHEN IT COMES DOWN TO DOING THE DISHES AND HAULING OUT THE TRASH."

against the knowledge that life contains tragedy, and that not everything works out the way we would like it to. From that point on, Billy's innocence is lost: "Like Buttercup's, my heart was now a secret garden and the walls were very high." Goldman later commented in an interview with Richard Andersen, published in Anderson's *William Goldman*, that this was the scene that had most moved him when he was writing the book, and had even made him cry.

The same thing happens at the end of the story, when the father pretends that the novel ends with the lovers living happily ever after. Goldman explains that Morgenstern's tale ends far more ominously, with Westley having a relapse, Buttercup's horse throwing a shoe, and the sounds of the Prince and his men in hot pursuit. Goldman in his fictional guise says that he did not find this out until he read the book for himself as an adult.

It is clear that Goldman the author, though writing a fantasy, refused to follow the conventions of the genre by providing an unambiguous, fairy-tale ending. He relented, however, when it came to the movie, for which he wrote the screenplay. Bowing to the demands of a Hollywood ending, he allowed the film to close with the lovers kissing, without a trace of the vengeful Prince Humperdinck in pursuit.

The story of Inigo also contains a traumatic event that happens when the boy is ten. Inigo is an only child, and his mother died in childbirth, so the bond between him and his father Domingo is especially strong. He takes on a responsibility older than his years as he comforts his emotional father, who doubts whether he will be able to succeed in the very difficult task of making a sword for the six-fingered man. When Inigo watches his father being murdered in front

WHAT DO I READ NEXT?

- *The Silent Gondoliers* (1983) is another work by the great S. Morgenstern (a pseudonym for Goldman) about why the famous gondoliers of Venice no longer sing. Told with Goldman's typical humor, it is the story of Luigi, an aspiring gondolier.

- In 1998, a twenty-fifth anniversary edition of *The Princess Bride* was published. It includes not only a new introduction by Goldman, in which he discusses the film version, it also includes a the first chapter of a sequel to *The Princess Bride* titled "Buttercup's Baby," and an introductory "explanation" by Goldman as to how this new "abridgement" of "Morgenstern" came about.

- *Like Water for Chocolate* (1995) is a first novel by Mexican writer Laura Esquivel. Set in Mexico about a hundred years ago, it tells the story of life in a Mexican family. The main character is Tita, the youngest daughter, who falls in love with Pedro but is not allowed to marry him because she must take care of her aging mother. The novel was a bestseller in Mexico and the United States.

- British fantasy author Diana Wynne Jones writes for young-adult readers. She is noted for her excellent plotting and well-realized fantasy worlds. *Howl's Moving Castle* (1986) was one of five Jones novels to be named by the American Library Association as one of the Best Books for Young Adults. The story focuses on Sophie, a teenage girl who must lift the curse that has turned her into an old woman. Jones tells the tale with plenty of humor.

- *The Three Musketeers* is a famous adventure story by Alexandre Dumas, first published in France in 1844 and available in translation in many modern editions. Set in seventeenth-century France, it features the adventures of three of the king's musketeers, Athos, Porthos, and Aramis, and their friend, d'Artagnan, as they defend the interests of the king and queen against the schemes of Cardinal Richelieu.

- *On a Pale Horse* (1983), by prolific fantasy writer Piers Anthony, appeared on the American Library Association list of Best Books for Young Adults in 1984. The book is the first in Anthony's popular series "Incarnations of Immortality," in which abstract concepts such as death, fate, and time are personified. In this book, the hero, Zane, and other powerful figures, such as a magician, must stop Satan from starting World War III.

- Some readers may prefer their romantic tales without the ironies and parodies that Goldman embeds in *The Princess Bride*. For such readers Nicholas Sparks's bestseller, *A Walk to Remember* (1999), might make a good choice. This story about two young people in North Carolina in the 1950s is as romantic as it gets, and Sparks's unadorned style and storytelling skills make it hard to put down. Oddly enough, like *The Princess Bride*, it also has a rather ambiguous ending, and readers are free to interpret it in an optimistic or a pessimistic light.

---

of his eyes by the nobleman, he screams. "He could not believe it; it had not happened. He screamed again. His father was fine; soon they would have tea. He could not stop screaming." This terrifying experience is the equivalent for Inigo of young Billy's tears. At the age of ten, both boys have learned a hard lesson—Billy through fiction, Inigo through real life—about the power of evil, and they will carry it with them for the rest of their lives.

When he writes of these two father-son relationships, Goldman is in earnest. He is very serious indeed, and no one laughs. However, when it comes to the third father-son relationship—between the fictional Goldman and his ten-year-old son Jason—he takes a very different tack. This relationship is almost a satire on the tenderness of the other two. It is as if the author is saying, *It is not always like that*, which is thoroughly in keeping with his desire to infuse his fantasy tale with a dose of realism about what life may in fact offer. The fictional Goldman and Jason are not close. The boy is overweight, and he and his father squabble over the fact that he eats too much. His father also thinks the boy is fat and spoiled (by his mother) and possesses no sense of humor: "I don't know; maybe he's funny and I'm not. We just don't laugh much together is all I can say for sure." In a contrast with Goldman's experience at ten, Jason is bored by *The Princess Bride*, although this may be because Goldman expects him to read it on his own rather than have it read to him.

The problematic aspect of relationships, rather than the ways in which they work, is also the focus of the author's presentation of marriage. There are no good marriages in this story, which serves as ironic commentary on what the lovely Buttercup and handsome Westley might expect when it comes down to doing the dishes and hauling out the trash. Buttercup does not have good role models for marriage. Her parents are always at each other's throats: "All they ever dreamed of was leaving each other." On what sounds like a pretty average day, by dinner time they have had thirty-three spats, and they keep score as to who is ahead. Given the parents she has, it is a miracle that Buttercup turned out as well as she did.

The second marriage depicted is between the fictional Goldman and his wife Helen. This relationship is painted in quite dark colors. These two do not seem to get along. "Helen wasn't ever understanding," Goldman complains, stung into the comment by the sympathetic ear of the gorgeous starlet Sandy Sterling as they sit together by the pool in California. "I got a cold wife," he writes later, adding, "She's brilliant, she's stimulating, she's terrific; there's no love; that's okay too, just so long as we don't keep expecting everything to somehow even out for us before we die." Some readers might feel that a loveless marriage is rather less than okay. Goldman knows what he is doing, though; he is presenting a romantic story that keeps undermining its own reason for being.

For her part, Buttercup shows more awareness than your average fairy-tale princess that the course of true love never does run smooth.

When Westley gives her an evasive answer after they have both fallen to the bottom of the ravine, Buttercup says, "We must not begin with secrets from each other." When she and Westley are cornered by the Prince and his men at the edge of the fire swamp, Goldman the author allows Buttercup to undercut the romantic cliché of dying for love, like lovers (Antony and Cleopatra, Romeo and Juliet, even Jack Dawson, the character played by Leonardo DiCaprio in the 1997 movie *Titanic*) are supposed to do. Buttercup says, devastatingly for the romantic theme of the story, "I can live without love." In the seesaw ending of the novel—now they are happy; now they may not be—Goldman manages to get in one more jab that knocks down the notion of romantic love and "happy ever after." Looking to the future, he expects that Buttercup and Westley "squabbled a lot," like (the unstated connection looms large) Buttercup's parents, like Goldman and Helen, and like . . . all couples everywhere? This appears to be what Goldman is suggesting to his readers. When innocence passes over into experience, love is never quite the same. It begins in adoration and ends in irritation, or so *The Princess Bride* would have readers believe.

Source: Bryan Aubrey, Critical Essay on *The Princess Bride* in *Novels for Students*, Gale, Cengage Learning, 2010.

SOURCES

Andersen, Richard, *William Goldman*, Twayne's United States Author Series, No. 326, Twayne Publishers, 1979, pp. 16, 82.

Attebery, Brian, *The Fantasy Tradition in American Literature: From Irving to Le Guin*, Indiana University Press, 1980, pp. 2–3.

Buckley, Cara, "Man Is Rescued by Stranger on Subway Tracks," in *New York Times*, January 3, 2007, http://www.nytimes.com/2007/01/03/nyregion/03life.html?_r=2&ref=nyregion&oref=slogin (accessed April 20, 2009).

Goldman, William, *The Princess Bride: S. Morgenstern's Classic Tale of True Love and High Adventure, The "Good Parts" Version, Abridged by William Goldman*, Harcourt Brace, 1973.

Holliday, Liz, "The Princess Bride," in *St. James Guide to Fantasy Writers*, edited by David Pringle, St. James Press, 1996, p. 235.

MacRae, Cathi Dunn, *Presenting Young Adult Fantasy Fiction*, Twayne's United States Authors Series, No. 699, Twayne Publishers, 1998.

Oberbeck, S. K., "Shaggy Dog," in *Newsweek*, Vol. 82, No. 12, September 17, 1973, p. 98.

Swinfen, Ann, *In Defense of Fantasy: A Study of the Genre in English and American Literature since 1945*, Routledge & Kegan Paul, 1984, p. 5.

Walker, Gerald, "The Princess Bride," in the *New York Times Book Review*, December 23, 1973, p. 14.

FURTHER READING

Armitt, Lucie, *Fantasy Fiction: An Introduction*, Continuum, 2005.

    This is an introduction to a wide range of fantasy fiction, including the work of Jonathan Swift, J. R. R. Tolkien, George Orwell, H. G. Wells, J. K. Rowling, and many others. The book includes a useful introduction defining the genre and a chapter on the origins of modern fantasy, as well as a glossary of terms.

Brady, John, *The Craft of the Screenwriter*, Touchstone, 1982.

    Brady includes interviews with many of the most successful screenwriters of the 1970s, including Goldman, Robert Towne, and Paul Schrader.

Goldman, William, *Adventures in the Screen Trade: A Personal View of Hollywood and Screenwriting*, Warner, 1983.

    This book will be useful for those who have enjoyed the films for which Goldman wrote the screenplays. He reflects on his twenty-year involvement with Hollywood, gives his views on the film industry, and provides individual chapters on some of his most well-known films, including *Butch Cassidy and the Sundance Kid*, *The Stepford Wives*, and *All the President's Men*.

Le Guin, Ursula K., *The Language of the Night: Essays on Fantasy and Science Fiction*, rev. ed., Perennial, 1993.

    Goldman once commented that he felt very close to his subconscious mind during the writing of *The Princess Bride*, but he said nothing further about it. In the essays that make up this book, one of the greatest writers of fantasy explores, among many other things, the creative process and how it taps into dreams and archetypes.

The Prince and the Pauper

MARK TWAIN

1881

The only one of Mark Twain's novels written specifically for children, *The Prince and the Pauper* was published in 1881. A historical novel set in sixteenth-century England, *The Prince and the Pauper* appropriates some historical facts, such as those relating to the Tudors, the family of King Henry VIII, in order to tell a tale of mistaken identity. When the young and impoverished Tom Canty, who is fascinated by the king's son, Prince Edward, is treated rudely by one of the king's soldiers, Prince Edward defends Tom and invites him into his personal chambers inside the palace. There, the two young boys compare the details of their very different lives and also discover the similarity in their appearances. After the prince rushes out, wearing Tom's clothes, to admonish the soldier who injured Tom, the prince is assumed to be a poor beggar and is barred from the palace. Throughout the remainder of the novel, Edward attempts to survive on the streets of London and beyond, while Tom muddles his way through affairs of state, attempting to play the role of the prince since no one believes his claim that he is not Edward. Likewise, Edward asserts his name and station, but he is laughed at and treated rudely for claiming to be royalty. The class differences between the two boys and the inequalities inherent in such a class system are a main focus of the novel, as are such themes as religious intolerance and the notion of personal identity. In the end, the matter of mistaken identity is resolved and all wrongs made right.

Mark Twain (AP Images)

Originally published in 1881, *The Prince and the Pauper* is available in numerous modern editions, including the 2003 edition published by The Modern Library.

AUTHOR BIOGRAPHY

When Twain was born on November 30, 1835, in Florida, Missouri, he was named Samuel Langhorne Clemens. The pseudonym "Mark Twain" was one he adopted later in life. His parents were John Marshall Clemens and Jane Clemens, and they and Samuel's five siblings had just moved to Missouri from Tennessee when he was born. When Samuel was about four years old, the family moved to Hannibal, Missouri, the town where Samuel would spend his youth and that consequently became the setting of two of Twain's most well-known novels, *The Adventures of Tom Sawyer* (1876) and its sequel, *The Adventures of Huckleberry Finn* (1884). Samuel attended school until his father died in 1847. He now needed to

help support the nearly destitute family, which had been left impoverished by John Clemens's failed business ventures. Samuel worked as an apprentice and typesetter for Hannibal newspapers, some of which were owned by his brother. In 1853, when he was eighteen, Samuel Clemens left home, traveling to St. Louis, New York, and Philadelphia. He later spent time in Washington, D.C., and lived briefly in St. Louis, Missouri, and Cincinnati, Ohio. His brother, Orion, published his travel writings in the newspapers he owned (including the *Hannibal Western Union and Journal* and the *Muscatine Journal*). In 1857, Clemens secured a position as a cub pilot on a steamboat that traveled the Mississippi River. He received his own pilot's license two years later. The outbreak of the Civil War in 1861 shut down the river traffic, however. That same year, he and Orion traveled to Nevada, where Orion had been appointed secretary to the governor of the Territory of Nevada. Clemens wandered, speculating in silver and writing correspondence pieces for the *Virginia City Territorial Enterprise*. In 1862, he was hired as a regular reporter for that same paper and worked there for two years. It was here, in 1863, that he first used the pseudonym (or pen name) Mark Twain. He later moved to California, where he wrote humorous sketches for various papers. In 1865, his story "The Celebrated Jumping Frog of Calaveras County" was published in the *New York Saturday Press*. The work catapulted Twain to fame and solidified his reputation as a humorist. His career then became one in which he was paid to travel and write about his adventures. In 1867, Clemens met Olivia Langdon, the sister of his friend Charles Langdon. Twain and Olivia were married in 1870. During their courtship, Twain published his first novel, *The Innocents Abroad* (1869), which became a best-seller. For the next several years, Twain continued to write novels, and his family continued to grow. Their firstborn, a son, died in 1872 at the age of two; the Clemenses had three daughters. Twain published *The Prince and the Pauper* in 1881. The work did not greatly impress the critics, and the archaic language of the historical novel disappointed readers who were accustomed to a more casual, humorous tone. Despite some later successes, the cost of his wife and daughters' living in Europe (due to Olivia's heart condition), along with a national financial crisis in 1893 and 1894, resulted in Twain's approaching poverty at the age of sixty. Further health issues followed, with one daughter, Susy, dying of meningitis in 1896, and another, Jean, being diagnosed with epilepsy. Olivia died in 1904, and Jean in 1909. Twain's later years were occupied with continual writing in order to support his family. After his wife's death, he focused on an autobiography; he died of a heart attack in Redding, Connecticut, on April 21, 1910.

PLOT SUMMARY

Chapter 1

The first chapter of *The Prince and the Pauper* announces the birth of Edward Tudor, Prince of Wales, and that of Tom Canty, a pauper.

Chapter 2

In this chapter, the narrator tells of Tom's poverty, recounting the deprivations of Tom's formative years in Offal Court, the part of London where Tom and his family live. Tom lives with his mother, his father, his fifteen-year-old twin sisters Nan and Bet, and his grandmother. The narrator tells of the drunkenness, violence, and hunger that plague this poor area. Father Andrew, a kindly old priest who teaches an eager Tom reading, Latin, and writing, is also introduced. Tom gradually becomes fixated on the idea of seeing a prince; he is also increasingly aware of the "sordidness of his surroundings."

Chapter 3

Tom wanders around London and finds himself at the palace, where carriages are arriving and departing. Prince Edward is among the nobles in the carriages, and Tom is lucky enough to be able to peer through the bars of the gate to catch a glimpse. He is knocked back roughly by one of the soldiers. The prince happens to notice the incident; he chastises the soldier and asks that Tom be brought inside. After the two are alone in Edward's private chamber, the boys exchange descriptions of their lives and circumstances. Tom is in awe of the luxury in which Edward lives, and Edward longs for the freedom to play that Tom possesses. Out of curiosity, the two exchange clothing and notice that they bear a striking resemblance to each other. Edward sees the wound the soldier inflicted on Tom; he runs from the palace to admonish the soldier. But, dressed in Tom's ragged clothing,

MEDIA ADAPTATIONS

- The 1937 film *The Prince and the Pauper* stars Errol Flynn and Claude Rains. Directed by William Dieterle and William Keighley, it is available on DVD through Warner Home Video (2003).

- The 1977 film adaptation of Twain's *The Prince and the Pauper* titled *Crossed Swords* stars Oliver Reed, Raquel Welch, and Ernest Borgnine. The same film was released in the United Kingdom under Twain's original title. The DVD is available through Lion's Gate (2007).

- The 2000 television movie *The Prince and the Pauper*, directed by Giles Foster, was aired in the United Kingdom in 2000. The adaptation of Twain's novel was written by Duke Fenady, and the production starred Aidan Quinn as Miles Hendon. It was produced by HCC Happy Crew and distributed by the Hallmark Channel in the United States in 2000.

- *The Prince and the Pauper* audio CD (2006) is available through Greenbrier International.

- *A Modern Twain Story: The Prince and the Pauper* (2007) is a modern adaptation of Twain's novel in which two boys—a "normal" boy and a movie star—trade places. It was produced by Moresco Productions and distributed by Sony Pictures. The film was directed by James Quattrochi, and the screenplay written by Amanda Moresco. It starred Cole and Dylan Sprouse as the boys who trade places.

- An animated version of Twain's story, *Disney Animation Collection 3: The Prince & The Pauper*, is available through Walt Disney Video (2009).

he is mistaken by the soldier for a common beggar and is thrown into the street, despite his insistence that he is the prince.

Chapter 4

Edward is lost and alone in London, mocked and abused each time he insists he is the prince. He becomes aware of the injustices in his kingdom with each new indignation done to him. He is found by Tom's drunken father. John Canty, assuming the boy is Tom, thinks he is mad when he says that he is Prince Edward.

Chapter 5

Tom, not having any idea what has happened, begins to grow uneasy when he realizes how long the prince has been gone. When other members of the royal household see what appears to be Prince Edward claiming to be but a poor beggar named Tom Canty, they assume he is mad. The king, Henry VIII, instructs everyone to ignore his protestations, and insists that the prince's madness is temporary. Tom's previous mimicry of royalty in the games he used to play and his knowledge of reading and Latin contribute to the misunderstanding that he is Edward. Tom is uneasy, but he cannot find a way to escape.

Chapter 6

Tom is instructed by two of the king's trusted nobles, the Earl of Hertford (Prince Edward's uncle) and Lord St. John, on how to conduct himself in the presence of others. Thinking Tom is a very ill Edward, everyone treats him with the utmost kindness, gentleness, and respect. Tom's discomfort begins to lessen.

Chapter 7

Tom is served his first royal dinner, alone save for his attendants, who ignore his crude manners. When he is finally left alone, he discovers a book on courtly etiquette and manners, with which he begins to instruct himself.

Chapter 8

Tom is questioned about the location of an official seal of the king, but he does not know what object he is being asked about. The king needs the seal in order to command the beheading of the Duke of Norfolk.

Chapter 9

The narrator describes a grand pageant on the river, a parade of lavishly decorated boats and barges, presided over by Tom.

Chapter 10

Prince Edward is about to be beaten by Tom's father when a man steps in to protect the boy. With his cudgel (a short stick used as a weapon), John Canty knocks the man to the ground. Edward is then brought to the Canty home, where he encounters Tom's sisters, mother, and grandmother. He asserts that he is Prince Edward, and they think him mad. Canty hits Edward. Tom's mother steps between Edward and Canty and receives the remainder of the blows herself. When all settle down to sleep, she considers the possibility that the boy is in fact someone else and attempts to contrive a test to determine whether or not the boy is actually her son, who has gone mad. Edward fails her test, but Tom's mother is nevertheless certain the boy is her own son.

This test becomes important later in the story. Tom's mother describes the way her son, once startled by fireworks, always brought his hand to his face to cover his eyes, palm out, rather than shielding his eyes with the palm of his hand inward, the way most people do. She shines a candle in Edward's face to see which way his hand will shield his eyes, and it is not Tom's way.

During the night, Canty is awakened and told that the man he struck in the street earlier was Father Andrew, and that he has died as a result of the blow. Canty rouses his family, fleeing the house and the authorities who will soon be after him. The escape is hampered by the festive atmosphere along the river, where people have gathered to watch the river pageant. Edward manages to run off when Canty finally unhands him. Edward believes Tom has usurped him. He vows to have Tom hanged for high treason.

Chapter 11

Tom is enjoying the luxury of the royal barge. After the journey down the river, he presides over a celebration in his first public experience as the prince. From the crowd, Edward sees Tom, and he begins to shout that he is the prince. The crowd mocks him cruelly. A man named Miles Hendon sees Edward and takes pity on him, saving him as he is about to be physically attacked. Soon afterward, a bugle is heard, and a messenger from the palace announces that King Henry VIII has just died. Edward becomes King Edward VI in that moment, although it is Tom who is now looked to as the king.

Chapter 12

Being pulled along by Hendon, Edward grieves his dead father and wonders at the notion that he is now the King of England. Hendon takes Edward to London Bridge, where the pair encounter John Canty, who claims Edward is his son. Seeing that the man appears to be violent, and that Edward insists the man is not his father, Hendon continues to protect Edward, and takes him to the inn where he is staying. He is impressed by Edward's persistence in asserting that he is royalty and by his regal nature. Hendon humors what he believes to be the boy's false notions and treats him as if he is in fact the recent prince, now king.

Chapter 13

Hendon lets Edward sleep while he goes out to purchase better clothing for him. When Hendon returns, he finds that the boy is gone. He questions a servant and is told that a youth came to the inn, saying that Hendon wanted the boy Edward to meet him. Edward then departed with the youth.

Chapter 14

At the palace, Tom is dealing with the notion that he has become the King of England. He has more duties to attend to than he did as prince, most of which he does not fully understand. He finds the talk of money, petitions, and proclamations to be tedious and dull. He also discovers he has a "whipping boy," a youth who is paid to receive any lashes that Edward would have for misbehavior, such as failure to attend to his lessons. Tom finds the boy a useful source of information about the royal family and all the activities of the palace. With the whipping boy's help, Tom appears to everyone else to be Edward (once again sane) rising admirably to his new role as monarch, although when asked about the location of the official seal, he still can offer no information.

Chapter 15

Several days pass with Tom as king. He is dreading his first public meal, and as the hour approaches, he feels "the sense of captivity heavy upon him." When Tom looks out a window and spies a mob of approaching people, he wonders aloud what is happening. The Earl of Hertford orders a messenger to discover the source of the commotion. It is announced that three people from the crowd are to be executed, and Tom demands that they be brought before him. He hears their stories, assesses the facts, and eventually sets them all free. Everyone is impressed with his intelligence and his kindness, for the former king was known to be cruel and punishing, prone to sentencing people to torture and death.

Chapter 16

Tom's confidence is growing and he no longer dreads the upcoming dinner. He begins to feel comfortable and confident and bears himself like royalty. The dinner he dreading is endured without any mistakes on Tom's part.

Chapter 17

Miles Hendon searches for Edward, who is being dragged along by Tom's father, John Canty. Canty has joined up with his band of petty thieves and criminals, and Edward is forced to travel among them and live as one of them. His insistence that he is King Edward is mocked.

Chapter 18

Edward travels with Canty's "troop of vagabonds." When Edward has a chance at escape, he takes it. He finds a barn to sleep in and after a fearful moment of realizing he is not alone in the stall, he discovers a young calf next to him. He huddles against the animal for warmth, and is grateful just to be warm and sheltered. Having these two things, he finds that he is actually happy.

Chapter 19

Stepping out of the stall the next morning, Edward encounters two little girls. When they ask who he is, Edward says he is the king, and they believe him. Edward is relieved to be able to tell them his story, and they listen attentively. The girls bring Edward to their mother, who pities him, but of course does not believe him. Edward speaks comfortably and knowledgeably about matters of the court, so the mother, thinking Edward must have worked in a noble household or even the palace, questions him subtly about a variety of occupations. Edward is allowed by the mother to sit at the table and eat with the family, and he agrees to eat with them, owing to her kindness toward him. The woman finds a number of chores for Edward, and he does them, but he eventually abandons the family when he finds that John Canty and Hugo, one of his men, are approaching.

Chapter 20

Edward travels onward, and discovers a hermit, who welcomes him into his home. The hermit claims to be an archangel, and Edward becomes fearful that he is the prisoner of someone truly insane. The hermit, however, begins to chat in a friendly way and feeds Edward supper, and Edward's fear begins to lessen. When Edward falls asleep, the hermit binds him and ties a cloth around under his chin and atop his head so he cannot open his mouth. He sharpens his knife and says that he blames Edward's father for preventing him from becoming Pope, and that he therefore intends to kill Edward.

Chapter 21

Edward wakes up in terror but is unable to move or cry out. The hermit rants and is about to kill Edward, but voices are heard outside the cabin. The hermit drops his knife, and leaving Edward alone in the room, goes to see who is at his door. It is Miles Hendon, who has been tracking Edward. The hermit tells Hendon that Edward has been here and that he will shortly return. Meanwhile, Edward is attempting to draw attention to himself with as much noise as he can make. To get Hendon out of the cabin, the hermit tells Hendon that together the two of them will go look for the boy. While they are gone, John Canty and Hugo find Edward, untie him, and take him.

Chapter 22

Rejoined with Canty's band of vagabonds, Edward is now placed in Hugo's care. While the group attempts to make some use of Edward, he refuses to beg by the roadside for money for them, or to play any role in their treachery. Several days go by. Hugo, seeking to rid himself of the troublesome boy, finds a way to make it appear as though Edward has stolen a woman's parcel. Edward is captured. Hendon arrives, and his presence ensures that Edward will at least be tried in a court of law rather than being treated roughly by the crowd.

Chapter 23

Hendon accompanies Edward, along with the wronged woman, to the judge. When the woman tells the judge what her parcel was worth (the parcel contained a butchered pig) the judge informs her that the penalty for the theft of an item of that value would be hanging. The woman becomes upset and asserts that she certainly does not want Edward hanged. The value of the parcel is subsequently adjusted so that Edward can avoid such severe punishment. Hendon next overhears the constable who had witnessed these proceedings offering to buy the pig for the adjusted, lower value. She exclaims that she would not sell it for such a low price, as it cost her much more. He threatens to have her charged with lying under oath and says that this will also result in Edward's being hanged. She sells him the pig for the lower price and goes off in tears. The judge sentences Edward to a short imprisonment and public flogging.

Chapter 24

Hendon arranges for Edward to escape his prison sentence. He approaches the constable and tells him that he overheard the way the constable tricked the woman. Hendon knows the constable fears that the judge will learn this information, and he also senses that the judge was reluctant to sentence Edward at all and would not pursue him if he escaped. Hendon also convinces the constable to return the pig to the woman.

Chapter 25

Hendon and Edward embark for Hendon Hall, Hendon's family home. Hendon has previously recounted the tale of his brothers and his own exile, and he anticipates being welcomed warmly and being hopefully reunited with his love, Lady Edith. Upon his return, however, Hendon's brother Hugh, who is now married to Edith, acts as if he does not recognize Miles at all; nor does Edith.

Chapter 26

Hendon contemplates how he can regain his former life and assert the truth of his identity. Edith appears and tells him to flee for his life, for Hugh is ruthless. She continues to claim that she does not recognize him. Officers enter and, overpowering Hendon, take both Hendon and Edward to prison.

Chapter 27

Days pass in the squalor of the prison. Various men are brought before Hendon and are asked to identify him. All claim not to recognize him. Finally, an old man who has claimed not to know Hendon approaches when he has the chance and acknowledges Hendon as his former master. The old servant brings food and information to Hendon and Edward during the coming days. When the servant reveals the rumors that King Edward (Tom) is mad, the real Edward begins to wonder whether the pauper boy he left in his chambers has been impersonating him all this time and is acting as king. Hendon and Edward are befriended by two women being held in the prison for their religious beliefs. Soon afterward, the women are burned at the stake for their beliefs while the other prisoners and a crowd watch. They discovered other prisoners who were destined to receive cruel punishments. Edward is desperate to break out of prison and reclaim the crown.

Chapter 28

Hendon learns that his punishment is to stand in the pillory for two hours. (The pillory was a wooden frame through which the head, hands, and feet were held in place. It was erected in a public place, and punishment included having various objects thrown at the prisoner by a crowd.) When Hendon is secured in the pillory, a member of the crowd throws an egg at Hendon's face. Edward rises to Hendon's defense and is consequently ordered to be whipped. Hendon insists on taking Edward's lashings himself. Edward quietly makes Hendon an earl as a show of gratitude and respect.

Chapter 29

Hendon is released from the pillory, and he and Edward depart for London. They arrive on the eve of the coronation of the new king. Hendon and Edward are separated.

Chapter 30

Tom is about to be crowned King of England. He admits to feeling guilty and ashamed when he thinks of Edward. He has also grown increasingly regal and dignified, while retaining his kindness and gentleness. He falls asleep happy the night before Coronation Day, looking forward to the official ceremony in which the kingship will be bestowed upon him. Edward himself has just arrived outside Westminster Palace, where the coronation is to take place.

Chapter 31

A procession, known as the "Recognition Procession," begins. It is a grand parade through the streets of London in which Tom, mounted on a war house, gazes upon his royal subjects. He sees two old friends from Offal Court but turns away

from them. Tom's excitement, despite this glimpse of his past, increases. Soon, however, he recognizes his own mother staring up at him. Startled, he raises his hand to his face, palm facing outward, and in so doing reveals his true identity to his mother. As he passes, she grasps his leg and calls out to him, but an officer snatches her away and he denies knowing her. Tom's shame is so great he can barely continue. His excitement has evaporated, along with his confidence and regal bearing. With some encouragement he makes it through the procession, but his transformation does not go unnoticed by his closest advisors.

Chapter 32

At the coronation, just as the Archbishop of Canterbury is about to place the crown on Tom's head, Edward appears, announcing that he is the true king. As Edward is about to be seized, Tom orders him not to be touched. He claims that Edward is indeed the king. Panic and chaos ensue momentarily. Edward's uncle, the former Earl of Hertford, whom Tom has made the Duke of Somerset and who is also now the Lord Protector (the chief representative of an underage king), examines Edward in his vagabond's clothes with "an expression of wondering surprise." The resemblance between Tom and Edward is noted, and as both boys insist Edward is the true king, the nobleman attempts to find ways to confirm Edward's true identity. It is the location of the official seal that is determined to be the one thing that only the real Edward would know. Once the object is finally described to Tom, he is able to help Edward remember precisely what Edward did with the seal just prior to leaving the palace in Tom's clothes. The whole story comes out, and Edward is at last proved to be king.

Chapter 33

In the final chapter, Hendon's true identity is also confirmed. King Edward bestows on Tom the title of "King's Ward," and he and his mother and sisters are provided for. Edward reveals how he stole into the palace with a group of workmen and hid until the coronation.

Conclusion

The confession of Miles Hendon's brother Hugh is revealed, as is Hugh's manipulation of Edith. Hugh abandoned his wife, left for the Continent, and shortly died, whereupon Hendon, now Earl of Kent, married Edith. We also learn that John

Canty, Tom's father, disappeared and was not heard from again, and that King Edward attempted to save all the people wrongly sentenced to punishment or death that he had encountered during his travels. Edward's reign is described as short but merciful.

CHARACTERS

Father Andrew

Father Andrew is the kindly priest who instructs the pauper Tom. He teaches him reading, writing, and some Latin. He shares with Tom stories of castles and kings and princes, encouraging in Tom the boy's yearning toward nobility. When Edward is captured by John Canty and taken to be his own son, Father Andrew rises to the boy's defense as Canty is about to beat Edward. Father Andrew receives a blow to the head from Canty's cudgel, a blow that later kills him.

Bet Canty

Bet is one of Tom's fifteen-year-old twin sisters. Bet and her twin Nan are portrayed as kind and comforting toward Tom.

Grandmother Canty

Grandmother Canty is Tom's paternal grandmother. She is prone to drunkenness and often abuses Tom and presumably his sisters as well.

John Canty

John Canty is Tom's poor, abusive, drunken father. After beating Father Andrew, who later dies, Canty forces his family to flee their home. Separated from his wife and daughters, he clings to Edward, thinking he is Tom. Canty hopes to be able to use the boy, as he has always used Tom, as a source of meager income from the boy's begging. After Edward escapes him, Canty continues his pursuit. He treats his son, or the person he thinks is his son, like a possession, something to be utilized for his personal gain. Canty and his band of vagabonds and thieves catch up with Edward, who is able to escape again. After Edward is restored to his throne, John Canty disappears.

Mrs. Canty

Tom's mother, Mrs. Canty, is depicted as an abused, impoverished woman who tries to protect her children from her husband and mother-in-law's abuse. When Edward appears in Tom's stead, she fears that he is mad and wonders if he can in fact be someone else, but is so desperate for her son not to have disappeared that she convinces herself that Edward is Tom. She refuses to "give him up," and asserts that "he *must* be my boy!" Near the novel's end, she becomes convinced that Tom, about to be crowned as King Edward, is her lost son. In his surprise at seeing her in the crowd, the startled Tom raises his hand to his face, but in his characteristic, and unusual, way: palm outward. Her son denies that he knows her, but it is his shame at having treated his mother so that makes him so willing to relinquish the kingship when Edward attempts to reclaim the crown. She and her children are provided for financially by Edward after his coronation.

Nan Canty

Nan is one of Tom's fifteen-year-old twin sisters. Nan and her twin Bet are portrayed as kind and comforting toward Tom.

Tom Canty

As the novel opens, Tom's birth is announced following the discussion of Edward's birth. Tom has been born into a family of paupers. He is educated by a priest, Father Andrew, who teaches him reading, writing, and Latin, and gives Tom a taste for stories about princes and kings. As a youth Tom desires nothing more than to see a real prince. When he finally makes his way to Westminster Palace, the residence of the royal family, Tom presses his face to the gate and spies Edward. After Tom is shoved back by a soldier, Edward sees the treatment Tom is receiving and invites him into the palace. He and Prince Edward discuss his life, his poverty, his family, and the freedom Tom possesses to do such things as play in the mud and have races with his friends. Edward listens with interest and genuine curiosity, and claims that to him, Tom's life sounds "glorious." After the two boys inadvertently trade places, Tom is initially impressed by the luxury in which Edward lives but he is soon intimidated by the formal court manners of the people around him. He is not used to being served and dressed and bowed to. He strongly feels that he is being held captive, and he cannot convince anyone that he is not the prince. He reflects that while his dreams of living life as a prince had been happy ones, "this reality was so dreary!" However, Tom gradually gains confidence in his new role and enjoys the kindnesses extended to him by Edward's family as well as the new luxuries and entertainments available to him. When Henry VIII dies, Tom realizes he has inherited the role of ruler that was Edward's right. His first act is to pardon the Duke of Norfolk, whom he knew Henry had intended to execute. He decrees, almost upon the instant of gaining the kingship, that "then shall the king's law be law of mercy, from this day, and never more be law of blood!" His inherent kindness rebelled at the often cruel rule of Henry, and his first act as king transforms the monarchy. Tom continues to show mercy, interceding on behalf of individuals sentenced to death, after hearing their cases. The admiration he receives for his intelligent and judicious decisions bolsters Tom's confidence. He continues to dismantle unjust laws. In short, he becomes kingly, and yet he is ashamed when he thinks of Edward and what the true king must be enduring. He feels similarly wretched when contemplating his mother and sisters, who must surely be as miserable as when he left them. Yet thoughts of Edward and his family recede, and he anticipates the coronation with excitement. When Tom spies his mother in the crowd during the procession preceding his coronation and denies he knows her, however, the shameful and guilty thoughts he has suppressed rise uncontrollably within him. The confidence he has been gaining and gradually turning to an arrogance common among royalty begins to fade: "A shame fell upon him which consumed his pride to ashes and withered his stolen royalty." Tom's journey is a complex one. He learns first the confidence he never had. His new power to make positive changes in his kingdom fuels this confidence and the praise he receives inflates his attitude toward one of prideful arrogance. When he denounces his mother, his shame consumes him, and reshapes his sense of self once again. He is now ready to do everything in his power to restore Edward to the throne. When Edward praises Tom and bestows the title and responsibilities of the King's Ward upon Tom, he feels a sense of worthiness and happiness.

Lady Jane Grey

Lady Jane Grey is a nine-year-old cousin of Prince Edward. Edward's description of her to Tom is laden with praise. Jane Grey is the first to encounter Tom dressed in Edward's clothes and is concerned when he denies he is the prince. She sounds the alarm that something is not quite right, and the rumor spreads through the palace that Edward is mad. Jane and Elizabeth, as Edward's companions, become Tom's as well.

Arthur Hendon

Arthur Hendon does not appear in the story but is mentioned by Miles Hendon. Arthur is Miles Hendon's older brother. Arthur was betrothed to Edith, whom Miles loved. Arthur loved another woman, but he was unhealthy and died, presumably before he married Edith. With Arthur dead and Miles in exile at his brother Hugh's contrivance, Hugh marries Edith.

Edith Hendon

Edith Hendon is the wife of Miles Hendon's brother Hugh. We learn her story when Miles recounts the tale of his past life to Edward. Edith was betrothed to another of the Hendon brothers (Arthur), who does not appear in the story. Arthur, however, was not in the best health, and also loved another woman. Miles always loved Edith, but Hugh wanted her, or at least her fortune, for himself. Hugh contrived to make it appear as though Miles intended to run off with Edith; Miles was consequently banished for three years. When Miles and Edward appear at Hendon Hall, the rest of the story unfolds. Hugh falsified documents in order to convince his family that Miles had died. When Arthur died, Hugh married Edith. Upon Miles's return, Hugh orders Edith to pretend she does not know who Miles is. Edith complies only because the abusive Hugh has threatened to kill Miles. Following Hugh's departure and subsequent death, the novel's conclusion informs us that Miles and Edith are finally married.

Hugh Hendon

Hugh Hendon is Miles Hendon's younger brother. Miles describes him to Edward as "a mean spirit, covetous, treacherous, vicious, underhanded—a reptile." Hugh's actions prove this assessment accurate. In an effort to gain lands, wealth, and a noble title, he contrived to have Miles exiled and then later asserted that Miles was dead. When Miles returns, he has him arrested. In the end, after Edward is restored to the throne, Miles's status as the rightful heir to the Hendon's land, wealth, and title is reinstated. Hugh deserts his wife, Edith, and leaves for Europe, where he soon dies.

Miles Hendon

Miles Hendon is Prince Edward's rescuer. Hendon finds Edward during the celebration of the river pageant presided over by the false prince Tom. In the crowd, as he is being jostled and roughly treated, Edward asserts that he is Edward, Prince of Wales. As he is being mocked, Hendon, who has been watching Edward, steps in to defend him. Hendon too is attacked by the mob. The attack ceases when the king's messenger announces that King Henry VIII has died and Edward is now the King of England. Hendon retreats with Edward, tends to him, and out of pity (thinking the boy is mad), indulges Edward's assertions of his royal status. When Edward is tricked into leaving Hendon's protection and is forced by John Canty into the band of homeless beggars and thieves, Hendon persistently pursues Edward. Hendon finally catches up with Edward when Hugo has framed Edward with the theft of a woman's butchered pig. Hendon aids in rescuing Edward from being hanged for the theft. When Hendon is sent to jail by his brother Hugh, Edward remains with him until Hendon is sentenced to two hours in the pillory. Edward rises to Hendon's defense when the angry crowd begins to pelt Hendon with rotten food, and is ordered to be whipped for this action. But Hendon insists on taking the blows himself, an act that inspires Edward to make Hendon an earl. In the end, Edward, restored to the throne, is instrumental in returning to Hendon all that he is rightfully due. Despite Hendon's private belief throughout the novel that Edward is mad, he continues to treat him with the reverence due to royalty, and Edward generously rewards Hendon's kindness and noble behavior.

Henry VIII

Henry VIII is the King of England when the novel opens. The father of Prince Edward, and the Princesses Elizabeth and Mary (who historically all have different mothers), King Henry possesses a reputation for brutality and cruelty toward his subjects. Edward is aware of this reputation, but he notes on more than one occasion that as a father, Henry always treated him gently and lovingly. This is demonstrated through Henry's behavior toward Tom, who he believes is his son Edward. When Tom is brought before Henry, Henry shows concern for what appears to be his son Edward's madness. Tom (as Edward) does not recognize the king as his father. Yet Henry, convinced by Tom's appearance and by his knowledge of Latin, is certain that Tom is Edward, and he assures him that he is his "loving father." Soon after, Henry dies and Edward becomes king.

Hermit

The Hermit is a man Edward encounters after he escapes John Canty. The Hermit announces to Edward that he is an archangel, and Edward is initially fearful, for the man appears to be insane. The Hermit does not doubt Edward's assertion that he is now the King of England (for at this point in the story Henry VIII has died). Rather, he welcomes Edward to dinner

and treats him kindly. Edward's feeling of fear changes to affection. But once he has drifted off to sleep, the Hermit binds him and intends to kill him, claiming that if it were not for Edward's father, the Hermit would have been made Pope. Hendon's arrival distracts the Hermit, who leads Hendon away from the cabin where Edward is being held. Edward is then recaptured by John Canty.

Earl of Hertford (later Duke of Somerset, the Lord Protector)

The Earl of Hertford is Edward's uncle. After Tom and Edward inadvertently switch places, Hertford is one of the men placed in charge of aiding the apparently insane prince in conducting himself in the proper manner. Hertford and St. John become the guardians of Tom (as Edward). When St. John expresses some doubt that Tom is in fact Edward, Hertford passionately defends the boy, saying that the child has been known to him since he was a baby. After King Henry's death, Hertford is chosen to ascend to the office of Lord Protector (the chief representative of an underage ruler). Tom additionally makes Hertford a duke, the Duke of Somerset.

Hugo

Hugo is a member of John Canty's band of thieves, beggars, and vagabonds. He dislikes Edward for his grand assertions, his obvious nobility, and his refusal to do anything (begging, stealing) that will bring money to the group. After Edward is recaptured by Canty and Hugo (when they free him from the Hermit's cabin), Canty puts Hugo in charge of Edward; he is to prevent Edward's escape. Yet Hugo is eager to be rid of the boy. He creates a situation in which it appears that Edward has stolen a woman's parcel, and he abandons Edward to the authorities.

Margery and Prissy

These two peasant girls encounter Edward, dressed in rags, in their barn, where he has just slumbered peacefully with their calf. They are the only people who truly believe Edward is the king. Feeling sorry for him, after hearing his story, they take him to their mother.

Margery and Prissy's Mother

This peasant woman is moved to pity when her daughters bring her the bedraggled and starving Edward. She feeds him and treats him with kindness. She does not believe him but allows Edward to eat with the family before finding chores for him to do.

Humphrey Marlow

Humphrey Marlow is Prince Edward's whipping boy. As Humphrey explains to Tom (whom he obviously believes to be Edward), his job is to receive any lashings with which Edward would have been punished for transgressions such as inattentiveness to his lessons. Humphrey becomes very useful to Tom, as he has extensive knowledge of the royal court and its members and practices.

Duke of Somerset

See Earl of Hertford

Lord St. John

Lord St. John is one of the men, along with the Earl of Hertford, who is placed in charge of Tom when everyone believes him to be Edward gone mad. Speaking with Hertford, his fellow keeper of Edward, St. John tentatively conveys his doubt that Tom is indeed the king, explaining that the way the madness afflicts Edward seems inconsistent. He claims to have felt haunted by Tom's assertion that he was not the prince. Hertford denounces St. John's thoughts as treasonous, and St. John immediately begs forgiveness. Along with Hertford, St. John continues to guard, monitor, and advise Tom throughout the course of the novel.

Edward Tudor

Edward Tudor is the adolescent son of King Henry VIII and his now-dead wife Jane Seymour. Historically, Edward was nearly ten years old when he became king. In Twain's novel, Edward and Tom are fifteen years old. Edward is depicted as a kindly boy, quick to rise to Tom's defense. Throughout his adventures, after he is dressed as a pauper, he demonstrates his truthfulness, honor, and bravery. He never wavers from the truth of his story and is only occasionally convinced to remain silent about his identity by his protector Miles Hendon. He recognizes the sacrifices others make to protect him, as when Father Andrew and Tom Canty's mother receive the blows John Canty intended for him. He faces his new hardships without panic, seeking ways to escape Canty and, with Hendon's help, to return to London. Edward is observant, commenting on the harshness of the laws and punishments of his country and vowing to improve things when he returns to

the throne. From the very beginning of his adventures as a pauper, Edward diligently strives to remember the details of the journey in order to make positive changes in the future. Treated roughly by a group of boys, Edward vows to make learning, not just food and shelter, an integral part of the charity offered at Christ's Hospital. Loyal to those who helped him, Edward rewards Hendon, as well as Tom and his family, after he has been recognized once again as the rightful ruler. Edward initially shows an arrogant and vengeful streak as well. His arrogance is born of his station; he has always been waited upon and has always been treated as though his person were sacred. Yet during his travels, he finds he is happy snuggled with a calf in a barn stall and awaking with a rat on his chest. His initial desire is to seek revenge on Tom when he realizes Tom must be impersonating him in the palace; he vows that Tom will hang for treason. However, when he interrupts Tom's coronation, he is moved by Tom's own honesty in acknowledging Edward as king. Rather than punishing Tom after he has proved his identity, he rewards Tom and his family. His adventures as a pauper teach him both humility and mercy.

Elizabeth Tudor

Elizabeth, who will later become Queen Elizabeth I, is Edward's fourteen-year-old sister. She and Lady Jane Grey are Edward's most frequent and favorite companions. He speaks fondly of them to Tom and they become Tom's companions as well, thinking him, of course, to be Edward gone mad. Elizabeth is quick to notice when, in social and courtly settings, Tom (as Edward) is in need of assistance. She intuitively and gracefully smoothes over any awkwardness Tom's ignorance creates in her presence.

Mary Tudor

Mary, who will later become Queen Mary I, is only mentioned periodically by Edward during the course of the novel. He describes her as his "gloomy" sister when he and Tom discuss their families; she does not appear in the story.

THEMES

Social and Economic Inequality

Twain's novel demonstrates the stark contrast between two social classes in sixteenth-century

TOPICS FOR FURTHER STUDY

- In *The Prince and the Pauper*, Twain paints a distinct portrait of the English monarchy under Henry VIII and includes in his novel a number of other historical figures in addition to the king. Using print and electronic resources, research the history of the English monarchy from Henry VIII's immediate predecessor (Henry VII) through the reigns of his children (Edward, Mary, and Elizabeth). Create an online interactive timeline of this time period and these rulers. Be sure to provide birth and death information for each individual, as well as important information about each ruler's particular reign.

- Twain's book *The Tragedy of Pudd'nhead Wilson* (1894) also features two boys from very different backgrounds (one is a slave baby, one is the master's baby) who switch places. Read *The Tragedy of Pudd'nhead Wilson* and compare it with *The Prince and the Pauper*. How are the books similar? Do the plots proceed along similar lines? Does the story end with each individual returned to his "rightful" place? How do the experiences of the characters in *The Prince and the Pauper* shape their identities? Write an essay in which you compare the two novels. Does the racial difference in *The Tragedy of Pudd'nhead Wilson* carry more weight in establishing the contrast between the boys' lives than the class difference does in *The Prince and the Pauper*? Discuss in an essay which book, in your opinion, uses the switching technique most effectively, and define your notion of "effectively." (For example, is the technique more believable in one story or the other, or is it used more convincingly in one of the stories as an instrument of character development?)

- From his nineteenth-century perspective, Twain wrote for young readers about England in the 1500s, and about the beginning of the short reign of King Edward VI. From a twenty-first century perspective, Ann Rinaldi writes for young-adult readers about the same time period. Her novel *Nine Days a Queen: The Short Life and Reign of Lady Jane Grey* (published in 2006 by HarperTeen) focuses on the life and experiences of the successor King Edward (under the influence of one his advisors) selected: Lady Jane Grey. Read Rinaldi's novel. How do Twain's and Rinaldi's approaches to historical fiction differ? Are there similarities? Does each author make a different set of assumptions about his or her audience? What do the novels convey about the attitudes of these American authors regarding England and its monarchial system? Present your findings in the form of an oral or written report.

- When Tom Canty and Prince Edward first meet, they spend some time discussing one another's life and families. Despite the fact that their speech reflects Twain's version of sixteenth-century vernacular, their conversation, in terms of content, could easily take place today, if one sees them as two boys from different backgrounds sharing their stories. Rewrite this scene from a modern perspective. Establish the difference in the boys' backgrounds by giving them modern personal histories that would reflect the same economic and class differences as found in Twain's story. Change the dialogue to reflect these differences, and act out the scene for your class, or digitally record the scene as a short film and present it to the class.

England. The society of the day is organized around the idea of a class system. The noble class is a group of people who inherit titles and the corresponding wealth, and usually lands, as well. One is born into this class of status and privilege; such a designation cannot be earned through the accumulation of wealth. On the opposite end of the spectrum is the lowest class of society, that of paupers and peasants. These are individuals who usually have no education or even access to it. They typically manage to acquire a few coins by begging but often have no regular income. The prince's world, that of the noble class, is associated with luxury, ease, and comfort, while Tom's world is filled with drunkenness, violence, and ignorance. However, the noble class has its cruelties as well. The torturous punishments endorsed by King Henry are discussed in Twain's novel, as is the frequency with which executions are ordered. In the violent world of the lower class, there are also kind and gentle people, such as Father Andrew, Tom's mother, and the unnamed peasant woman who takes Edward in. In the world Twain portrays, members of the lower class are viewed by the noble class as inhuman and are readily disposed of (executed) for the smallest of crimes. The nobles are viewed by the lower class as objects of reverence and awe. They too are seen as barely human, but because of their elevated status rather than their degraded one. A smaller, third class is presented in the novel as well, though not discussed in detail. This class consists of business owners (such as innkeepers and merchants) who are neither wealthy nobles nor ignorant beggars. Through the adventures of both Edward and Tom, Twain portrays the best and worst of both the highest and lowest classes of this sixteenth-century society.

Closely linked with the social inequalities represented in Twain's novel are the attendant economic disparities. The class differences discussed above provide the overarching structure of the society, and many of the other examples of prejudice and intolerance grow out of this structure. The economic disparities are strongly related to the class structure of society. Typically, the noble class is wealthy; although a nobleman may squander his wealth, he cannot lose the title to which he was born. By the same token, the lowest class is one marked by dire poverty, but someone from the lowest class might find a way to provide a living for himself. Yet no amount of wealth can make him a noble. The poorest of the poor are treated by everyone else with extreme derision. Edward, dressed in Tom's beggar's rags, is verbally and physically abused by his own soldier, who calls him "rubbish." Simply having the appearance of someone who is poor (for the prince maintains his regal bearing and insists on his true identity) results in inhumane treatment.

Religious Conflict and Intolerance

In addition to the prejudicial treatment the lower class receives, religious conflict leads to injustices inflicted on various groups as well. A great deal of religious intolerance pervaded England during Henry VIII's rule, stemming largely from the king's break with the Roman Catholic Church and the resultant conflicts between Catholics and Protestant groups. Twain portrays some of this tension in his novel, as when Edward is imprisoned with Miles Hendon. Hendon and Edward watch two women, women who have demonstrated their kind and gentle natures in dealing with Edward in prison, being burned at the stake for their religious beliefs, which conflicted with those of the Church of England. Edward's own prejudices against Roman Catholicism are hinted at in his comments about his half-sister Mary, who would later, as queen, repair the bond with the Roman Catholic Church that Edward, as king before her, would continue to sever, following his father's lead. The young Edward speaks derisively of Mary's dour and disapproving attitude and of her constant talk of sin. Another example of the religious conflict simmering in the country is embodied in the odd character of the Hermit. The Hermit claims to be an archangel and is devoured by his thwarted ambition to be appointed Pope. He blames King Henry, who, in severing England's official ties to the Roman Catholic Church, essentially (in the Hermit's thinking) prevented his rise to this powerful Catholic position. The king's actions left the Hermit a "poor obscure unfriended monk." While the Hermit is clearly depicted as suffering from insanity, his feelings, as a Catholic, of being abandoned and rejected by his king must surely have been felt among the country's Catholic population as a whole.

Errol Flynn as Miles in the 1937 film version of the novel (© INTERFOTO | *Alamy*)

STYLE

Nineteenth-Century Historical Romance

The Prince and the Pauper was labeled upon publication a "historical romance." As a genre, nineteenth-century historical romances did not necessarily feature a romantic relationship between two individuals. Rather, the term *historical romance* was used to characterize books that looked back to an earlier time in European history and focused on the adventurous aspects of that earlier time period. These books featured knights and kings, princes and peasants. The genre was popularized in England before crossing the Atlantic to become a significant literary genre in America as well. Twain's foray into this genre—*The Prince and the Pauper*—was seen by many critics as serious and well mannered, as opposed to Twain's more overtly humorous and boisterous tales, such as *The Adventures of Tom Sawyer* (which is a combination of several genres, featuring aspects of the coming-of-age novel, the American frontier novel, and the satirical novel).

Social Satire

Although *The Prince and the Pauper* is not an overtly humorous tale of the type Twain was known for, the work is one in which the author employs adventure and more subtle humor to entertain young readers. Yet this story is also filled with social commentary, and the author's lighthearted tone may be seen as somewhat deceptive, for the entertaining story also highlights certain negative aspects of both sixteenth-century English society and nineteenth-century American society. Satire is a means by which humor is used to subtly criticize, in this case to criticize the inequalities in the society in which Edward and Tom live. Twain depicts the enormous disparities between the prince's way of life and that of the pauper.

Tom's foibles are often a source of humor in the book, and they frequently disguise deeper issues. For example, when Tom meets Edward's whipping boy, his instinct is to protect the boy from further harm, but the whipping boy insists that taking the prince's beatings is how he earns his living. (As the prince's body is viewed as sacred, he is not allowed to physically receive such a degrading punishment on his own. Hence the need for a whipping boy.) Tom therefore assures him that he will "study so ill" that the whipping boy's wages will have to be tripled. The whipping boy is grateful, and the incident can easily be taken as a source of humor, until one considers that for the boy's wages to be tripled, he will have to endure three times the number of beatings; the greater sadness is that he is grateful to Tom for promising this. The humor disguises the wretchedness of a society in which a boy's wages are earned for being beaten, and the fact that his body is viewed as somehow less valuable or more disposable than that of another, simply because the other was born to a higher station.

This incident also highlights the social issues of Twain's day; the book was written in the aftermath of the Civil War. The United States was still rife with social and racial injustices and Twain's social satire was just as applicable to the contemporary society of the United States as it was to the society of sixteenth-century England.

Third-Person Narration with First-Person Commentary

Twain relates most of the story of *The Prince and the Pauper* in the past tense and in the third person (in which the author uses "he" or "she" in reference to the characters). Yet he additionally intersperses commentary in the first person plural (using "us" and "we" instead of "I" as one would do in the first person singular). By using this method, Twain lends a sense of immediacy to his storytelling. Readers hear the related tale interrupted by a narrator saying such things as, "Let us skip a number of years" or "We left John Canty dragging the rightful prince into Offal Court." Twain's purpose in interrupting his narrative in this way is to subtly remind the reader of the presence of the storyteller. The method lends the story a casual, comfortable nature that stands in contrast to the affected, sixteenth-century speech of the characters, perhaps making the tale more approachable for the younger audience to whom it was originally directed.

HISTORICAL CONTEXT

The Monarchy of Henry VIII

As a historical novel, *The Prince and the Pauper* is inspired by the general history of the time period in which the novel is set. (Like any historical novel, it does not claim to be wholly accurate factually. For example, historically Prince Edward was only nine when he became King of England, but in the novel he and Tom Canty are fifteen.) During this period in English history, Henry VIII ruled as king from 1509 until 1547. Over the course of his controversial reign, he had six wives. The children (Mary, Elizabeth, and Edward) of these wives are mentioned in or appear in Twain's novel. The first wife was Catherine of Aragon, whom Henry married in 1509. The couple had one daughter, Mary, who would later become Queen Mary I and reign from 1553 to 1558. Henry wanted a male heir and when Catherine did not produce one, Henry decided to divorce her. The Pope refused to allow the divorce, but Henry proceeded with it anyway in 1533 and passed an act that declared him the head of the English Church. In addition to the matter of the divorce, Henry had long objected to the power the Roman Church held over the English monarchy. The separation of the English Church from Rome is known as the English Reformation.

King Henry married the already-pregnant Anne Boleyn in 1533. Their daughter, Elizabeth, would later enjoy a lengthy reign (from 1588 to 1603) as Queen Elizabeth I. Anne was executed for infidelity to the king in 1536. King Henry's third wife was Jane Seymour, whom he married the same month that Anne was executed. Jane died shortly after giving birth to Edward in 1537. Edward was Henry's only male heir; he died in 1553. King Henry had three other wives with whom he had no children. Lady Jane Grey, one of Edward's companions in the novel, was a cousin of Edward and a descendant of King Henry's sister Mary. Jane Grey ruled as queen for just over a week, after Edward's death, but when the popularity of Mary Tudor (daughter of Henry and Catherine of Aragon) was established, she became queen instead. Jane Grey was executed in 1554 on Queen Mary I's orders.

Henry VIII's reign was also noted for the extreme nature of the punishments of various crimes. Some of these are discussed in Twain's novel. Physical punishments (such as time in the pillory or whipping) along with jail time

COMPARE
&
CONTRAST

- **1500s:** In the late 1500s, the relationship between England and what would become America is in the earliest of stages. In 1584, Richard Hakluyt writes a paper called *A Discourse Concerning Western Planting* advocating to Queen Elizabeth I (King Henry VIII's daughter) the importance of English settlements in North American lands for the purposes of agricultural development.

  1800s: Relations between the United States and Great Britain are strained during the time period of Twain's writing career. One indicator of their current relationship is the 1871 Treaty of Washington, in which the two countries attempt to resolve differences that arose between them during the Civil War (1861–1865).

  Today: Relations between the United States and Great Britain today are undergoing a transformation with the recent transfer of power from former President George W. Bush to President Barack Obama. Obama meets British Prime Minister Gordon Brown in London, along with other world leaders, for an economic summit in 2009. Previously there has been some tension between the two nations over the U.S. handling of the war in Iraq. Both countries are extracting themselves from Iraq and focusing on the great economic challenges facing the United States and Great Britain. Despite differences, the two nations are very close allies and friends.

- **1500s:** English literary works with both fictional and historical content take the form of lengthy poems and plays, such as Shakespeare's plays on the history of the English monarchy, which are written during the reign of Elizabeth I (King Henry VIII's daughter).

  1800s: The historical novel is emerging as a popular genre in both England and America; some examples of the genre at this time are characterized as "historical romance," though this designation does not typically refer to the prominence of romantic relationships in the books. American historical novels include Nathaniel Hawthorne's *The Scarlet Letter* (set in seventeenth-century Boston) and Mark Twain's *The Prince and the Pauper* (set in sixteenth-century England). English historical novels include Walter Scott's *Waverly* (set in eighteenth-century Scotland).

  Today: Modern historical novels may take the form of romantic historical mass market fiction or more serious literary historical fiction. Historical fiction of the romantic variety, such as Philippa Gregory's *The Boleyn Inheritance* (set in sixteenth-century England) is a genre featuring romantic relationships within a historical setting. Literary historical fiction, such as Umberto Eco's *Baudolino* (set in twelfth-century Europe) typically is arguably more serious in nature than the modern historical romance and explores literary themes within a historical setting.

- **1500s:** English society is structured by a strict class system in which nobles, with their inherited wealth and titles, are respected, revered, and powerful. Peasants and working-class individuals have few rights guaranteed them. Peasants in particular, with little or no means to provide for themselves, are often treated as objects by their superiors.

  1800s: The class system is still a prominent feature in English society, yet with the rise in industrialization, the working class is able to establish itself as a powerful group. Additionally, slavery was abolished in the British Empire in 1833, although it would be many years before all British citizens were truly treated equally.

  Today: Despite the persistence of the monarchy, class divisions in Great Britain are no longer institutionalized as they have been in the past. The society is a democratic one, with representatives elected by the people in Parliament's House of Commons. Class divisions within the nation are now largely the result of economic status rather than inherited titles.

Charlton Heston as Henry VIII in the 1977 film Crossed Swords, *based on* The Prince and the Pauper
(© Photos 12 / Alamy)

were often ordered for more minor offences. Executions included hanging, which could be ordered even for stealing, and beheading, often reserved for treasonous offences.

Post–Civil War America

At the time Twain wrote *The Prince and the Pauper*, the United States was still recovering from the aftermath of the Civil War. In the South, an agricultural society previously dependent on slavery for profit was finding a new way to function. The second half of the nineteenth century was one of increasing reliance on industrial development. Twain, who for a time grew wealthy from his success as a writer, was also an investor in many of the new technologies. Yet, as Larzer Ziff observes in his 2004 biography (titled simply *Mark Twain*), Twain appeared to possess a "genius for miscalculation," and was known to lose large sums of money on technological innovations (such as a mechanical typesetter) that were soon improved upon by other, more profitable models.

Twain's immediate literary predecessors were those who had risen to prominence in the first half of the nineteenth century, writers such as Henry David Thoreau, Ralph Waldo Emerson, and Nathaniel Hawthorne. These writers were known for their social commentary and literary style. In contrast, Twain wrote in the vernacular of everyday Americans, in a boisterous and humorous style. Yet Twain had much to say about society and morality as well, and his ability to do this in a less formal way "revolutionized American literary expression," according to Ziff. Walt Whitman, writing at the same time as Twain, was also part of this relaxed, sometimes bawdy, approach to literature, and he too tackled such weighty philosophical issues as morality, identity, and freedom. This revolutionary, realistic, down-to-earth, lively approach of American writers such as Twain and Whitman was influenced by the significant changes in America at the time, an America whose western frontier was still being populated, and that was fresh from a war that had torn the country in half.

CRITICAL OVERVIEW

Twain published *The Prince and the Pauper* with a reputation as a frontier writer and a humorist, and shortly following the publication of the spirited tale *The Adventures of Tom Sawyer*. His contemporary reviewers were not sure what to make of it. Ron Powers says in his 2005 critical biography *Mark Twain: A Life*, "The reviewers cogitated, decided that they liked it—most of them—and struggled to explain why." Powers goes on to say that, in general, they found it likably "polite." The lukewarm reviews influenced the novel's tepid popular reception, and even modern critics have little that is positive to say about the work. Powers himself finds that for the most part, the vibrant qualities to be admired in Tom and Edward "are heavily muffled under the novel's artifices." Larzer Ziff, in his 2004 critical biography, states that "Critics from Twain's day to this have been too hard" on the novel. Yet Ziff additionally comments that the novel "falls well below" the "level of achievement" of either *The Adventures of Tom Sawyer* or *The Adventures of Huckleberry Finn*. Ziff faults, in part, Twain's use of the affected speech of the boys and comments on the way the narrator at times slips into the same vernacular.

Everett Emerson, in his afterword to the 2002 Signet Classic edition of *The Prince and the Pauper*, claims that the book has risen above the spotty reviews it received initially, noting that it is now considered a classic and is counted among the most popular of Twain's novels. Taking another approach in his assessment of the novel, Christopher Paul Curtis, in his introduction to the 2003 Modern Library edition of *The Prince and the Pauper*, explores the way Twain's book reshaped the American understanding of children's books. He contends that until Twain's novel was published, books geared toward children tended to be dull and overly moralistic. But Twain's book combined fun and adventure with "things that will make you think and give you great insights into Twain's opinion of what was going on in the world."

CRITICISM

Catherine Dominic

Dominic is a novelist, freelance writer, and editor. In the following essay, she explores the ways in

> THROUGH THE EXPERIENCE OF MISTAKEN OR LOST IDENTITY, TWAIN DEPICTS ONE'S PERSONAL IDENTITY AS SOMETHING WITH A DUALISTIC NATURE. FOR TWAIN, AS THESE CHARACTERS' EXPERIENCES DEMONSTRATE, IDENTITY EXISTS AS A COMPOSITE OF HOW WE VIEW OURSELVES AND HOW WE ARE VIEWED BY OTHERS. "

which Twain emphasizes the duality within the concept of individual identity in The Prince and the Pauper.

Twain's *The Prince and the Pauper* contains several instances of mistaken identity, the most obvious cases being those of Prince Edward and Tom Canty. Through the experience of mistaken or lost identity, Twain depicts one's personal identity as something with a dualistic nature. For Twain, as these characters' experiences demonstrate, identity exists as a composite of how we view ourselves and how we are viewed by others. Additionally, the author's creation of his own overtly dual identity—that of Samuel Langhorne Clemens and that of Mark Twain—underscores the significance to Twain of this conception of identity and selfhood.

From the moment Edward realizes that, after he has changed clothes with Tom Canty, no one recognizes him as his true self, he continues to insist on who he truly is. His personal sense of self is strong, as he has been nurtured from the time he was an infant to believe his physical person is sacred. He has been told from the time he was born of his superiority, as heir apparent, to all others. This strong sense of self lends Edward a confidence that never appears to wane. Edward endures nearly constant struggle throughout the novel—he is beaten, pursued relentlessly by John Canty, half-starved, and called a variety of degrading names. Such trials, such certain perception on the part of so many people that he is only a poor pauper and not a prince at all, would seem sufficient to shake even the most confident youth. But Edward does not demur. He does not deny who he is, and he almost defiantly continues to insist upon his true identity. Yet he is humbled enough to

WHAT DO I READ NEXT?

- Twain's *The Adventures of Tom Sawyer*, originally published in 1876, and available in a 2006 Penguin Classics edition, is one of Twain's most well-known and best-loved works and is characteristic of the rollicking style with which Twain is typically associated.

- Originally published in 1889, Twain's *A Connecticut Yankee in King Arthur's Court* places a nineteenth-century protagonist in medieval England. The work reflects Twain's interest in historical fiction and is regarded as more intentionally satirical and humorous than *The Prince and the Pauper*. It is available in a 2009 edition through BookSurge Classics.

- *Grant and Twain: The Story of a Friendship That Changed America* by Mark Perr, published in 2004 by Random House, offers insights into the relationship between Twain and Ulysses S. Grant, and additionally provides the political and cultural context within which Twain's writings may be better understood.

- Jessica Wollman's young-adult novel *Switched*, published in 2007 by Delacorte Books for Young Readers, follows a premise similar to that of *The Prince and the Pauper*. In this modern day story, two look-a-like teenage girls, one from a working class family and one from a rich family, switch places and for a time live the life of the other girl.

- The works of Charles Dickens and Mark Twain are often compared to one another, as both authors share an interest in capturing the details of everyday life in their novels' settings. Dickens's 1861 coming-of-age novel, *Great Expectations* (Penguin Classics, 2002), is one of his best known works.

- *Let the Circle Be Unbroken*, written by Mildred D. Taylor and published by Puffin Teenage Fiction in 1995, is a young-adult historical novel that takes place during the Great Depression. Just as Twain explores class prejudices in *The Prince and the Pauper*, Taylor examines racial intolerance, as well as the nature of identity, particularly through the character of an African American girl who attempts to pass for white.

enjoy the warmth of a barn stall shared with a calf, and to accept the charity of others, and to willingly perform chores in exchange for the supper and shelter shared with him. His fatigue shows particularly in the "tears of mortification" he sheds when he is insulted and abused by the mob, in his impatience to escape prison, and in his desperation to return to London.

Edward's clearly weary but persistent confidence is bolstered in two significant ways. Miles Hendon does not truly believe Edward is a Tudor, a prince who becomes a king while in his care. But Hendon, out of a combination of pity and the perceived strength of Edward's character, treats Edward as royalty. Additionally, Hendon is not the only person on Edward's side through the course of his trials. The two

peasant children—Margery and Prissy—he encounters after escaping John Canty believe Edward is their king, on the strength of his word alone. The value to Edward of their belief in him cannot be overstated. He states that once he has been restored to the throne he will "always honor little children," and remember the way these girls "trusted me and believed in me in my time of trouble, whilst they that were older, and thought themselves wiser, mocked at me and held me for a liar." Edward's notion of who he is becomes strengthened by the true belief the peasant girls have in him, as well as by Hendon's fealty.

Tom Canty has the opposite experience of Edward in many ways. Tom enters into a more appealing situation than the one Edward finds himself in, and he enters it from a much weaker position than Edward. Having experienced a childhood of having nothing and of being treated as if he were nothing, Tom does not have a strong or confident view of himself. Unlike Edward, Tom is rather quick to stop asserting his true identity once he finds himself being taken for the prince. Before entering the palace, Tom allows other people's views of him to shape who he is, and that does not change once he arrives at the palace. In his life before he enters the palace, Tom is beaten regularly by his father and his grandmother. From John Canty's first words to Edward, who he believes is Tom, we learn that Tom is only a source of revenue for John. What little Tom begs, the father takes, and he is beaten whether or not he has acquired any money. It is no wonder Tom fantasizes about life as a prince and possesses almost no sense of identity of his own. However, the noble people who surround him in the palace do not, like Tom's abusive father and grandmother, belittle him. Rather, they fill him with a sense of self-worth and importance. Despite his initial nervousness and anxiety, Tom relaxes into the role of prince almost with a sense of relief. Tom, with little identity of his own, becomes what others perceive him to be: prince-like. Yet it is clear also that he has some true strength already residing within him, for as king Tom excels; he is decisive and merciful without being coached. The confidence he gains through the nobles' kindness to him, and through his initial success in masquerading as prince, becomes his own as king.

While the dual nature of personal identity is demonstrated through Tom and Edward's experiences of mistaken identity, for two other characters, it is demonstrated through their loss of identity. Both Miles Hendon and Tom's mother are denied, by people whom they love dearly, recognition of who they are. Both Hendon and Mrs. Canty also demonstrate a strong sense of self. Hendon repeatedly asserts his identity when his brother denies knowing him. When Miles's brother Hugh tries to turn him out of Hendon Hall, Miles says that "Miles Hendon is master of Hendon Hall and all its belongings. He will remain—doubt it not." When his long-lost love, now married to his brother, refuses also to acknowledge Miles's identity, he utters his disbelief. Likewise, Mrs. Canty insists that Tom, about to be crowned as King Edward, is her son, that she is his mother. Tom denies knowing her. The effect on both Hendon and Mrs. Canty on being denied recognition by people they love is devastating. Hendon cannot decide if what has happened to him should be considered "most tragic or most grotesque." He feels both confusion and torment. Mrs. Canty, Tom observes, appears "wounded" and "broken-hearted" by what he has done to her.

When denied the confirmation of identity by others, a confirmation that balances one's own sense of self, the result is pain and confusion, as in the cases of Hendon and Mrs. Canty. When the balance between what we know of ourselves and what we know of others' perceptions of us is skewed, a sense of desperation to restore the balance is triggered. Edward is desperate to return to London and make his presence known. While his confidence in his true identity remains strong, the weight of constantly having that identity questioned is wearying for the young king. When Tom allows the truth of his own identity to pervade his thoughts again, after he had so willingly and thoroughly allowed the perception that he was king to take hold, he is shaken to the core. At the coronation, Tom, like Edward, is eager for everyone to take their proper places.

Twain takes pains to show that peoples' identities are predicated both on who they believe themselves to be and on who others perceive them to be. At the same time, he demonstrates the consequences of these two positions being out of balance. Particularly in the cases of Edward and Tom, there is discomfort and anxiety in the out-of-balance state. But in this state, as when Edward and Tom are living each other's lives, the weight of what others think of them is suddenly extraordinarily great. In this state there is opportunity for self-improvement. Edward is able to grow in humility by experiencing life as a peasant, while Tom is able to grow in self-worth and confidence by experiencing life as prince. Hendon and Mrs. Canty's opportunities for growth, however, are cut short when they are once again recognized for who they are. Hendon does not need to contemplate who he is, if not the master of Hendon Hall. Mrs. Canty no longer needs to reshape her identity as someone other than the mother of Tom.

Twain appears to have been intrigued by this notion of identity. *The Prince and the Pauper* is not his only story in which two unlikely individuals take each other's place. He uses the same technique in *The Tragedy of Pudd'nhead Wilson* (1894), in which a slave's baby and the master's

"THE TWO WENT AND STOOD SIDE BY SIDE BEFORE A GREAT MIRROR"

Illustration from The Prince and the Pauper
(© Mary Evans Picture Library / Alamy)

baby are switched. As a writer, Twain also created for himself a dual identity, adopting the pen name Mark Twain at the age of twenty-eight, just as he began to become well known as an author. His given name of Samuel Langhorne Clemens was reserved for friends and family, for his personal life, for the person he understood himself to be. The public figure, the author, the object of other people's perceptions, went by the name of Mark Twain.

Source: Catherine Dominic, Critical Essay on *The Prince and the Pauper*, in *Novels for Students*, Gale, Cengage Learning, 2010.

Bradford Smith

In the following essay, Smith explores Twain's preoccupation with identity and disguise in his writings, including The Prince and the Pauper, *and suggests sources for this fascination in Twain's life.*

The key to Mark Twain's mind is the concept of identity. In every one of his important books it is the identity of the individual on which his attention focuses. And on the mystery of

> HIS HUMOR THEREFORE IS A PHILOSOPHY AND AN ACT OF FAITH. THE DROLL COMEDIAN IN HIM AS WELL AS THE ROMANCER SERVED THE INDIGNANT MORALIST WHO COULD NOT ABIDE ANY SIGN OF CRUELTY, INGRATITUDE, SHAM OR DISLOYALTY."

identity. The quest for identity is central to both his writing and his personality. Its importance in his works can be traced to its importance in his life. The devices that recur in his stories—disguise, deception, self-deception and make-believe—all grow out of this concern with identity.

Nearly everyone in Mark Twain's books, consciously or unconsciously, is playing a part. Colonel Mulberry Sellers pretends to be a successful businessman and political power instead of the conspicuous failure he is. The Yankee plays at being a knight, a ruler, a magician. Sally Sellers, to humor her father, has to be the Lady Gwendolen. Miles Herndon gracefully pretends to believe in the royalty of his little pauper.

Disguise is often a way of exposing either the "real" identity or the essential mystery of all identity. In *The Prince and the Pauper* Prince Edward, shorn of his fine clothes, is no better than the boy whose rags he wears. He merely makes himself ridiculous when he tries to be the king he really is (his father having just died), while Tom Canty quickly takes on kingly qualities and is soon able to rule as well as Edward. King Arthur (in *A Connecticut Yankee*) without his royal accoutrements cannot be recognized as a king. So he wanders through his own kingdom, shorn of his identity as surely as of his royal clothes. Huck's king and duke make a mockery of the whole sham and pretense of royalty.

This brings us to the central problem of identity. A king is not a king unless he possesses the innate traits that prove him. The common man with his sufferings, his ability to work and endure, is not only equal to kings but superior to them. The Yankee proves this by becoming The Boss—superior of kings and knights and of the wastrels and crooks spawned by poverty and the class system. The classes man has set up and rigidified by custom and prerogative go against nature and result in false identifications. Good men and bad are found in all walks of life. The mystery of identity therefore becomes a matter of seeking out the true character beneath the social disguise.

Roxana can change the two babies about so that her Chambers becomes the young master Tom Driscoll. But she cannot change the characters they were born with. The false Tom grows up to be a crook and a murderer. A man's true identity has nothing to do with crowns and class and wealth. It is a mystery—something rooted deep in the unknown past.

Because the idea fascinates him, Mark plays with it in many ways, trying every approach from romance to burlesque, from detective story to allegory. It is the basis for much of his humor, and one of the reasons why this humor is great and lasting is that it fools around with an idea that has serious and even tragic implications.

In *Pudd'nhead Wilson* a pair of noble Italian twins turn up in the inconsequential river town of Dawson's Landing for no apparent reason. Any stranger would have done as well and would have been more plausible.

Mark's own explanation of them is very funny; it forms the preface to *Those Extraordinary Twins*. He tells how, seeing a poster advertising a set of two-headed Italian twins, he started to write a "fantastic little story" about them. But the tale kept spreading, other people got into it, and finally he discovered that he had two stories on his hands, one a farce, the other a tragedy.

"So I pulled out the farce and left the tragedy," he explained. "Also I took those twins apart and made two separate men of them. They had no occasion to have foreign names now, but it was too much trouble to remove them all through, so I left them christened as they were and made no explanation." An interesting method of composition!

Yet why did Mark Twain want to write about twins in the first place? Why did he instinctively make one light and the other dark? Why does the idea of twins fascinate him, so that he introduces them even in books which have no apparent need of them?

Twins dramatize the mystery of identity. Even when he makes a burlesque of the whole affair in *Those Extraordinary Twins* his mind is at work upon this mystery. How can two men be virtually the same? Or rather, how can two such separate characters manage to dwell in one body? Angelo is fair, dainty, delicate, easily upset. Luigi is dark, bold, masculine, hearty, rough. He drinks, and Angelo gets drunk. He smokes, and Angelo gets dizzy.

Behind the fooling lies the recognition that one man in himself can contain opposites—can drink though he knows he will suffer for it, can be part Free Thinker and part Baptist, can will to go in one direction and find himself walking in the other, can even hold two separate views of what is good and evil at the same time. For while Luigi considers duelling honorable, Angelo abominates it; while Luigi would stand and fight it out, Angelo runs away.

Mark keeps returning to the theme of identity in various ways. In *The Mysterious Stranger* and *The Man That Corrupted Hadleyburg* the identity of the chief person is a mystery, and the effect he works upon people raises a still deeper question of identity: can we know ourselves? Is there an incorruptible self which never changes, or can identity be completely changed if the temptation is strong enough?

When kindly old Uncle Silas (*Tom Sawyer, Detective*) is mistakenly seized as a murderer, he himself is so unsure of his identity that he believes himself guilty. We cannot count on society to tell us who and what a man is—*The Prince and the Pauper* and *A Connecticut Yankee* make this clear—for the truth is written only in his heart. Yet possibly man cannot even know himself whether he is good or bad, noble or ignoble. This is the final mystery of identity. What we see of Jim, Tom Canty, The Boss, Huck, King Arthur, and the people of Hadleyburg leads us to conclude that society's rating of men is mostly phony. Society, and especially monarchy, is a vast joke surpassed only by the trick God plays on men by giving them qualities which chain them to an identity they cannot escape.

Identity begins in comedy and ends in tragedy—the human tragedy of failing to live up to ideals. Was it only an amateurish failure which led Mark to confuse the two stories of *Pudd'nhead Wilson* and *Those Extraordinary Twins*? Or did the thing happen because his vision of life was broad enough to embrace both the tragic and the farcical? Nothing that a writer does is pure accident. What happens,

happens as a result of all that he is. Mark got the tragedy and the farce mixed up because these two aspects of human experience kept intermingling in his experience, and because his humor was a deceptively pleasant palace built over a dungeon from which there was no escape.

Separating farce and tragedy, as he did with these two stories, was really no solution, and the stories show the weakness of that attempt. In *Huck* and *Tom Sawyer* he did better; he fused them together in a way which gave breadth and life. Tom changed his identity for fun and Huck changed his out of desperation, to save himself from his father and from one impending catastrophe after another. In either case the fun arises out of this artificial twinning—this separation of the true and the assumed identity.

Best of all disguises are those that a boy puts on. For a boy is a realist who knows the uses of make-believe. Poised in a middle world between the primitive and the civilized, he can be what he wants to be—a pirate, a riverboat pilot, Robin Hood, a detective—without ever losing his grip on reality. This is his victory over the adult world which has forsaken the glorious realm of let's pretend for its shabby aftermath, self-deception.

Neither Tom nor Mark Twain, in all likelihood, ever heard of the *eiron*, the character in Greek comedy who gains his ends by seeming innocence and deep guile. But in the scene where he successfully whitewashes the nature of work itself, Tom is as authentic an eiron as any in Aristophanes. Mark's books are full of such people. As for Huck, deception is his rhetoric. He uses it as an orator would use words to persuade and control an audience. So the liberties he takes with his own identity are not carefree make-believe, but a desperate strategy for survival.

Mark Twain found in himself both the Tom Sawyer whose deceptions were pure fun and the Huck Finn whose deceptions were necessary for the preservation of self and freedom. We shall soon see why.

Since identity is part mystery and mostly chance, it follows that a man's greatest freedom would be in escaping it. Perhaps this is why disguise and prevarication are so frequent in Mark's books.

Is there also a connection with the flight from home and parents which is so recurrent a theme?

Huck had no mother—we know nothing about her—and a father whom he could only reject and evade, even to the point of destroying his own identity and taking up a new and pseudonymous existence. Tom Sawyer is an orphan, raised by an aunt and with no father substitute. Tom Canty's father is a villain, intent only on harming him. Tom Driscoll hates his father and ends by murdering the father substitute, his kindly uncle. The parenthood of the two children in *Pudd'nhead Wilson* is the crux of the whole book. We are never told who the father of Chambers really is, though presumably he was Percy Driscoll, father of the other boy. There is a similar mystery about the parents of Laura Hawkins in *The Gilded Age*—a mystery Mark never felt able to clear up, and left hanging at the book's end.

The mystery of identity is apparently related in some way to the mystery of parenthood—that is, to the childhood fantasy of not knowing who one's parents are. There are also hints in *Tom Sawyer* that Sam Clemens as a boy had experienced rejection, had contemplated running away from home so as to make his parents feel sorry for their mistreatment of him, and longed like Tom to sneak back and find them mourning him.

Sam Clemens was only twelve when his father died. Perhaps deprivation by death felt like rejection to the boy.

It was through his brother Henry that Mark came closest to grasping the mystery of identity. He felt very close to Henry, and in fact dreamed of his death a few weeks before Henry was wounded in a steamboat explosion and then killed by an overdose of morphine. Every detail of the funeral corresponded with Mark's dream.

This was evidence enough to convince Mark—and he was to have other experiences equally compelling—that there was another self within him which could sense the shape of things to come. There was also, it seems, a feeling that Henry had been his *alter ego*. He was the good boy of the family while Sam was bad. Sam, having got his brother the steamboat job, was even responsible for his death, and thus for the death of the person to whom he was so close that they were indeed a part of each other, as the dream had proved.

The frequent recurrence to the theme of twin brothers, one good, the other bad, has obvious parallels with Sam and Henry Clemens. In his *Autobiography* Mark identifies a number of the incidents in *Tom Sawyer* in which Sid does things

Henry Clemens actually did—calling his mother's attention to the black thread with which Sam had sewed his collar back on after swimming, breaking a sugar bowl for which Sam was blamed.

"But Sid was not Henry. Henry was a very much finer and better boy than ever Sid was." The close relationship between the two brothers is evident in all Mark's allusions to Henry. Was this the origin of the fantasy of twin brothers which was continuously present in Mark's mind since it came out so often in his books?

Twins are dragged into *The American Claimant* where they are not needed at all. But questions of identity are the core of the story, and the twins appear as a sort of leit-motif to put us on notice.

It would be impossible to describe without confusion the various complications of this story, all of them invented as ways of exploring the mystery of identity which is the real theme of the book. To look at just one of them: Sally Sellers confesses to Berkeley (in his disguise as Tracy) that she has almost fallen in love with Berkeley, presumed dead, for his heroism in the hotel fire. Tracy finds himself jealous of his own true self.

"In a sense the dead man was himself; in that case compliments and affection lavished upon that corpse went into his own till and were clear profit. But in another sense the dead man was not himself; and in that case all compliments and affection lavished there were wasted, and a sufficient basis for jealousy."

Identity was a compelling topic to the man who, not content to be Sam Clemens and Mark Twain, tried to be many other things too. He had tried several trades and professions, moving from one city to another, always seeking some acceptable image of himself. He played at soldier for a few weeks and escaped from that, for it failed to furnish him with the self-image he was seeking. He went west and became a rough-and-ready miner, then a newspaperman, a humorist, a lecturer. He traveled to Hawaii and back, then to Europe and the Holy Land. He began to find himself in the role of humorist. But then, in a sudden burst of respectability born of love, he married a rich girl and tried to settle down as part owner of a newspaper. It stifled him—he needed to be somebody different, larger, more unique. He needed a role in which his personality, his identity would be the public thing—

would be recognized and admired. So he became a writer and lecturer in the way that would take him closest to the lively admiration of the largest audience—through humor.

Still he liked to experiment with his identity. He went back to the Mississippi where he had once worked as a steamboat pilot, boarded a boat without revealing his name, and had that experience in the pilot house which he has told in *Life on the Mississippi*. Of course he was delighted to be recognized immediately. It confirmed his identity.

Still he kept on trying to be other persons. He tried to be a businessman, and after making large sums lost even larger. So it became necessary to take on another part—that of the ruined but noble writer who, like the very man whose works he had loved and ridiculed, Walter Scott, set himself the huge task of paying off every penny of debts which he could legally have avoided. It was truly a grand role, but does it not remind one of Tom Sawyer playing at Robin Hood?

Then there was the Mark Twain who loved to dress up in his Oxford gown—still in love with brilliant reds, with medieval trappings; still romancing, still seeking a role glamorous and colorful enough to satisfy his large thirst for identity.

For it was not enough to be only Sam Clemens. He had to be Mark Twain too. And Mark was the superego, under the broad license of whose fictitious name and imaginary identity he could be all the things he could never dare be as plain Sam Clemens.

Mark *Twain*. He was not one, but two. He himself was the extraordinary twins—dark and light, brave and shy, realist and romanticist, businessman and literary genius, tough man of the world and dreaming romantic, companion of mining camp and steamboat toughs and a lion in polite society, tender father and husband but a man who still loved profanity.

What but a surpassing sense of humor could blend these opposites into one identity? Through humor he could present himself both as the coward who deserted the army and as the successful pilot, as the skillful silver miner (which he was not) and as the fool who lost a fortune. And soon, in role after role, Mark Twain as jester could be a hundred people, a hundred personalities. That he relished them all is one of the secrets of the durability of his humor.

In the name of Mark Twain there is not only a fond recollection of the river days when the leadsman called out "Mark twain" to Sam Clemens up in the pilot house, guiding his boat through bars and reefs. There is also an obvious pun which asks us to mark the twain in man—the mystery of identity.

In Mark Twain's books a consistent pattern emerges. The hero, faced with some problem of choice or duality, solves or attempts to solve it by two responses: a change of identity and a change of place. So had Sam Clemens done in his own life. So, taught by the ever-moving river, he gets motion into his books—by moving relentlessly, endlessly, restlessly from place to place. Even in his platform appearances he moved back and forth from chair to lectern to table, trying to recapture that vital, essential motion.

In his books a trip or voyage permits the hero to sink, disguise or change his identity. The trip, itself symbolic of the onward thrust of time or the life passage, helps to accelerate or emphasize the nature of that passage by heightening the colors of experience, by opening up new locales, conditions, personalities. It also allows the hero to appear unknown, unidentified, in new communities where he can test himself among strangers, thus trying out his identity, and where he may present himself in new roles.

To travel is therefore to expand one's identity. It is to accelerate experience by going out to meet it in all its variety. On a deeper level it is to be reborn. The road, the river are symbols of that passage we all take on our way into the world, or through it. We emerge to new life. That is what Mark's books are about.

But travel also helped him to resolve the conflict between realism and romance, for by change of place one can make even the common romantic by continuous change and novelty. Travel makes even the debasing qualities of man quaint and comic by mere transiency; they never come to have the tragic consequences they would have in a static community. The road, the disguise—these were the means by which Mark Twain converted into humor what would otherwise have been unendurable. For he knew, as he finally expressed it in *The Mysterious Stranger*, that the dark dungeon undergirded the palace of pleasure.

His humor therefore is a philosophy and an act of faith. The droll comedian in him as well as the romancer served the indignant moralist who could not abide any sign of cruelty, ingratitude, sham or disloyalty. Tom and Huck both lived in him. The romanticist in him made him yearn toward perfection, but the realist in him said it was unattainable. Humor was the governor which kept the fire of romance and the steam of indignation from running away with the machine.

No more than Chaucer could Mark Twain look at man without seeing the comedy. He was not a funny man, building laughs with a series of disconnected wisecracks. He saw that humor was in life, and with his superb plain American frontier voice he drew it out, as one may draw sap from the maple. But then of course he had to boil it down to get the flavor.

The flavor is unmistakably American—not only in the ring of voices and the recognizable scenes but in that search for our identity which, three hundred and fifty years since we began to separate ourselves from the culture of Europe, is still going on.

Source: Bradford Smith, "Mark Twain and the Mystery of Identity," in *College English*, Vol. 24, No. 6, March 1963, pp. 425–30.

Leon T. Dickinson

In the following article, Dickinson examines how and why Twain borrowed from other books in constructing The Prince and the Pauper.

Mark Twain, we usually say, was a remarkably independent writer, one who wrote primarily from experience and was anything but bookish. Such a view has, of course, much truth in it. And yet he did refer to books in his writing. We know that he read about foreign countries before and during the writing of the travel books. He read widely, also, in preparing to write his historical books. Of these, *The Prince and the Pauper* offers some interesting problems. It is clear what the sources are, for Clemens acknowledges his indebtedness in notes appearing at the end of the volume. I am concerned with how he used the sources and why he admitted dependence on them.

The work most frequently cited in connection with Clemens' book is Charlotte M. Yonge's juvenile, *The Prince and the Page* (1865). No critic, however, points to similarities in the two books, for they are entirely different. Clemens' biographer believed that the earlier story, an historical romance laid in the thirteenth century, might have "inspired" the later tale; but he concludes, rightly, that "no comparison of any sort is possible between them."

He did borrow from books, however, in writing *The Prince and the Pauper*, as can be seen from his appended notes. Some of these refer to the book of his Hartford friend, J. Hammond Trumbull, entitled *The True-Blue Laws of Connecticut and New Haven and the False Blue-Laws*. Trumbull's book was written to show that the laws of seventeenth-century Connecticut were not so foolish or so severe as were commonly supposed, and that compared to the English statutes of the same period, the Connecticut laws were humane and enlightened, a point that Mark Twain makes in a "General Note" at the end of his volume. In order to show that what was harsh in the Connecticut laws was of English origin, Trumbull included in his introduction several cases involving infringement of the severe laws in England during the sixteenth and seventeenth centuries. It was from these cases, as his notes show, that Mark Twain borrowed for his story—borrowed accounts of persons losing their ears, being branded, being burned to death, boiled to death (sometimes in oil), hanged for such offenses as larceny above twelve pence, stealing a horse, a hawk, and so on.

Another source which he used in much the same way was *The English Rogue*, a seventeenth-century English book by Richard Head and Francis Kirkman. Several details in Chapters 17 and 18 of *The Prince and the Pauper* he took, sometimes without acknowledgment, from Chapters 5, 6, and 7 of the English tale. Clemens' chapters treating the low life of London include canting terms, a snatch of song, dialogue, description, and episodes, all of which are to be found in *The English Rogue*. At times he sticks close to his original, as is evident from the following passages, dealing with the set speech of beggars asking for coins:

The English Rogue

For Gods sake some tender hearted Christians, cast through your merciful eyes one pittiful look upon a sore, lame, and miserable wretch: Bestow one penny or half-penny upon him that is ready to perish, &c.

The Prince and the Pauper

"...o' God's name cast through your merciful eyes one pitiful look upon a sick, forsaken, and most miserable wretch; bestow one little penny out of thy riches upon one smitten of God and ready to perish!"

At other times Mark Twain elaborates on his original, as, for instance, when he takes an episode, treated in two pages in the source, and expands it to fill six pages, adding detail and dialogue that make the incident more dramatic. But whether he followed his source closely or whether he elaborated on it, he borrowed for the same purpose: to give an air of authenticity to his book. He read a good deal to prepare himself for writing the book, and he was interested not only in making it authentic, but in making it *appear* authentic.

Several points are clear regarding Clemens' use of sources in *The Prince and the Pauper*: (1) he used source material to acquaint himself with the period he was writing about; (2) for the most part he followed his sources quite closely, taking specific things from them; (3) usually, but not always, he acknowledged his debt to a source, either in a footnote or in a note at the end of the volume. This last point calls for comment.

Granted that he had a respect for facts, why did Clemens want to document a work of fiction? Two explanations seem likely. One has to do with his purpose in writing the book. He wrote with serious intent, trying to give his readers "a realizing sense of the exceeding severity of the laws of that day by inflicting some of their penalties upon the King himself and allowing him a chance to see the rest of them applied to others." So anxious was he for the book to be taken seriously, that he considered publishing it anonymously. Regarded at the time strictly as a funny man, he feared that the name Mark Twain on the title page would inevitably suggest humor. If the documentation were missing, certainly some of the details of the story would seem, to one unacquainted with Tudor history, to be Mark Twain "whoppers." It was precisely this that Clemens wanted to avoid.

The other explanation concerns Mark's theory of fiction. Fiction based on fact, he seemed to think, was superior to purely imaginative writing. We are told in *The Gilded Age*, for instance, that "The incidents of the explosion [of a steamboat] are not invented. They happened just as they are told." Similarly, in the preface to *Tom Sawyer*, Clemens writes: "Most of the adventures recorded in this book really occurred." He makes the same point in the preface to *A Connecticut Yankee*: "The ungentle laws and customs touched upon in this tale are historical, and the episodes which are used to illustrate them are also historical." Again, a footnote at the beginning of Chapter I in *Tom Sawyer, Detective* is to the same effect: "Strange as the incidents of this story are, they are not inventions, but facts—even to the public confession of the accused." If the story is true, Clemens thought, if it is based on fact, it is somehow better than if it were wholly imaginary. Such a theory of fiction, common enough in the West of his day, would go far toward explaining the presence of documentation in *The Prince and the Pauper*.

Source: Leon T. Dickinson, "The Sources of *The Prince and the Pauper*," in *Modern Language Notes*, Vol. 64, No. 2, February 1949, pp. 103–106.

Arthur Lawrence Vogelback

In the following essay, Vogelback examines the critical response to The Prince and the Pauper *upon its publication, in order to illuminate the critical standards of the day.*

With the appearance in 1869 of *Innocents Abroad*, Mark Twain established himself as a "funny man," and it was as the work of a funny man that each new book of his was interpreted. While there were occasional comments along the way which revealed a growing appreciation of abilities in Clemens other than that of mere humorist, for the most part there appeared little disposition by critics to take him seriously. But with the publication of *The Prince and the Pauper* in 1881, there sprang up sudden and widespread recognition of unusual qualities in Clemens the writer, qualities which caused many reviewers to express astonishment that such a work could have been written by Mark Twain. Remarked the Boston *Transcript:* "There is little in the book to remind one . . . of the author," and the *Atlantic Monthly* significantly titled its review: "Mark Twain's New Departure." Howells summarized this attitude when, after dealing with the fictional elements in Clemens's story, he stated: " . . . we have indicated its power in this direction rather than in its humorous side, because this has struck us as peculiarly interesting in the work of a man who has hitherto been known only as a humorist—a mere farceur—to most people."

It will be profitable as a study in the critical standards of the day to inquire what were these "new" qualities in *The Prince and the Pauper* which so pleased the critics, and why the critics liked them. This will be best shown by a consideration of the critical reaction to Mark Twain, not only as

> THE CHARACTERS, TOO, IN *THE PRINCE AND THE PAUPER* WERE SWEETER AND MORE GENTLE THAN SUCH ROUGH-AND-TUMBLE FELLOWS AS TOM SAWYER AND HUCK FINN. THE BOOK DEALT PLEASANTLY WITH A FARAWAY PLACE AND EPOCH, NOT WITH THE RUDE, EXUBERANT FRONTIERLAND OF THEIR OWN TIMES."

fictionist—that is, as writer of description, stylist, architect of plot, and depicter of character—but also as "philosopher."

I

Previous to the publication of *The Prince and the Pauper*, there had been little recognition of Mark's talents as a descriptive writer. Occasionally there occurred an appreciative comment, but for the most part attention remained incidental. When some clearer-visioned critic like Howells insisted upon unusual descriptive talents in Twain, his voice rarely found echoes in other reviews. But with the publication of *The Prince and the Pauper*, the majority of critics awoke to a sharp realization of Twain's powerful descriptive gifts. This was reflected not only in the increased attention given in reviews to the descriptive portions of the book, but in the importance accorded those portions. Thus the *Transcript* took note of Twain's "vivid descriptive powers," and another critic, praising "the skilfully painted background of more subdued and often delicate description," belatedly called the attention of the reader to "the many picturesque passages in *Innocents Abroad* and *A Tramp Abroad*." At the same time the accuracy of Clemens's description was commented on. Said the *Critic:* "It is obvious that Mark Twain has taken considerable pains in bringing the local color of his story into harmony with the historic period in which the action is laid," and the reviewer in the *Transcript* acknowledged that "the local coloring of the time in which [the story] is laid—that of Edward VI—is carefully studied," a judgment that was echoed by *Harper's*, which found in the story "a careful regard for the historical accessories." One of the most flattering observations on this aspect of Clemens's writing came from the *Atlantic Monthly:*

> However skillful in invention a writer may be, it is certain that his work loses nothing of effect from a studious harmonization with the period in which it is placed. In *The Prince and the Pauper* this requirement has been scrupulously observed. The details are never made obtrusive, and the "local color" is never laid on with excess; but the spirit of the age preceding that of Elizabeth is maintained with just the proper degree of art to avoid artfulness. Critical examination shows that no inconsiderable labor has been given to the preservation of this air of authenticity. . . . It is in every way satisfactory to observe that the material accessories are brought into view with an accuracy that coherently supports the veracity of the narrative. Dresses, scenery, architecture, manners and customs suffer no deviation from historical propriety.

II

It is notable, too, that *The Prince and the Pauper* was the first work of Clemens's in which his ability as a stylist received attention. Most of the reviewers registered not a little surprise at the difference between the former style of Clemens and that exhibited in the new book. The *Transcript*, for example, remarked: "There is little in the book to remind one of the individual style of the author," and the *Atlantic Monthly* commented similarly: "There is nothing in . . . its style of treatment that corresponds with any of the numerous works by the same hand. It is no doubt possible to find certain terms of phraseology, here and there, which belong to Mark Twain . . . but these are few. . . . "

Many were the complimentary things said about this aspect of Twain's writing. The *New York Herald* praised the "plastic and finished" style of the book; another journal wrote that "all the charm is owing to the sincerity, the delicacy, and the true feeling with which the story is told . . . ;" and the *Transcript*, seeking to describe the style, used the adjectives "vivid" and "natural."

III

Again, *The Prince and the Pauper* was the one book on which most critics were agreed that Twain demonstrated outstanding powers as a constructor of plot. There were, of course, dissenting reviewers. The *Transcript*, for example, remarked that "the highly improbable plot will . . . task the credulity of the most imaginative reader," but the larger number praised

Clemens's achievement. To Howells, *The Prince and the Pauper* was definite confirmation of Clemens's ability as plot architect. He prophesied that the book would come in this respect as a surprise to many:

> Like all other romances, it asks that the reader shall take its possibility for granted, but this once granted, its events follow each other not only with probability but with realistic force. The fascination of the narrative . . . [is] felt at once, and increase[s] . . . to the end in a degree which will surprise those who have found nothing but drollery in Mark Twain's books, and have not perceived his artistic sense. . . .

The critic for the *Atlantic Monthly* was inspired by the construction of the tale to point out how remarkably Mark had developed in stature as a writer:

> It will be interesting to watch for the popular estimate of this fascinating book. . . . It has qualities of excellence which [the author] has so long held in reserve that their revelation now will naturally cause surprise. Undoubtedly the plan upon which most of his works have been framed called for neither symmetry, nor synthetic development, nor any of the finer devices of composition. Generally speaking, they serve their purpose without the least reference to the manner in which they were thrown together. . . . Notwithstanding [their merits], they remain the most heterogeneous accumulation of ill-assorted material that ever defied the laws of literature, and kept the country contentedly captive for half a score of years. Now the same public is called upon to welcome its old favorite in a new guise—as author of a tale ingenious in conception . . . artistic in method, and, with barely a flaw, refined in execution.

The *Century Magazine* praised the structure as "an ingeniously formed chain of circumstances," and the *Critic* pointed out that Clemens deserved commendation for the development of a plot which must have "at every step impressed the author as a fertile theme for extravaganza."

IV

In the same fashion, with the publication of *The Prince and the Pauper* Clemens came newly, as it were, to the attention of critics as a gifted depicter of character. The reviewer in the *Atlantic Monthly* warmly praised Clemens for the latter's achievement in this regard. After describing the two little boys in the story as "one, a bright figure in history, the other a gem of fiction," the critic made these appreciative comments in which he compared Twain's work with that of a pair of famous English novelists:

The characters come and go, live and breathe, suffer and rejoice, in an atmosphere of perfect reality, and with a vivid identity rarely to be found in fictions set in medieval days. The same life-like verisimilitude that is manifest in many pages of Scott, and throughout Reade's *Cloister and the Hearth*, glows in every chapter of this briefer chronicle of a real prince's fancied griefs and perils. To preserve an illusion so consistently, it would seem that the author's own faith in the beings of his creation must have been firm, from beginning to end of their recorded career.... The big-hearted protector of guileless childhood is as palpable to our senses as to the grateful touch of the prince's accolade. The one soft spot in the hard old monarch's nature reveals itself to our apprehension as clearly as to the privileged courtiers at Westminster. The burly ruffian of the gutters, the patient, sore-afflicted mother, the gracious damsels of pure estate and breeding, the motley vagabonds of the highway, the crafty and disciplined councilors of the realm, the mad ascetic, and the varied throng of participants in the busy scenes portrayed—all these take to themselves the shape and substance of genuine humanity, and stamp themselves to our perceptions as creatures too vital and real to be credited to fable land.

Howells, in his review, likewise pointed out the unusual merits of the character portrayal:

> The author has respected his material ... and has made us feel its finer charm in the delicacy and subtlety with which he has indicated Tom Canty's lapse from lively rebellion at his false position to appreciation of its comforts and splendors, and, finally, to a sort of corrupt resignation in which he is almost willing to deny his poor old mother, when she recognizes him in one of his public progresses.... The character of Miles Hendon is dashed in with a rich and bold humor that gives its color to all the incidents of their association.... The whimsical devotion with which he humors the boy's royal exactions is charmingly studied ... amidst the multitude of types with which the story deals, he is realized the best; he is first of all thoroughly recognizable as a man; and then as a man of his own time and country—the adventurous and generous Englishman of the continent-hunting age.... The effect of prosperity on the mock Prince is, perhaps, more subtly studied than that of adversity on the real Prince ... but ... it is this [latter] phase, apparently ... which the author most wishes [the reader] to remember....

Perhaps no higher commendation was possible than the remark of the *New York Herald:* "The character of [the] two boys, twins in spirit, will rank with the purest and loveliest creations of child-life in the realm of fiction."

V

Finally, not only were reviewers enthusiastic about *The Prince and the Pauper* as Clemens's first artistic work, but they found in the book even more unusual revelations. They discovered that it demonstrated a philosophical side to Twain. The author had proved himself quite capable of dealing with a profound and serious theme. In almost every review one detects the note of surprise over this aspect of the book. The *Transcript* found "a quality so refined and so searching as to excite wonder that it should flow from the same pen as that which wrote *The Innocents Abroad....*" *Harper's* spoke of the tale as being "charged with a generous and ennobling moral." The critic in the *Atlantic Monthly* found the story "pure and humane in purpose"; and the *Century* called the writer of *The Prince and the Pauper* "a satirist and ... true philosopher." Howells, likewise, found *The Prince and the Pauper* evidence of growth in Clemens:

> The strength of the implied moral [is] felt at once and increase[s] ... to the end in a degree which will surprise those who have found nothing but drollery in Mark Twain's books, and have not perceived ... the strain of deep earnestness underlying his humor. Those even who have read him with this perception will recognize an intensified purpose in the human sympathies which have hitherto expressed themselves in some ironical form. The book is in this way an interesting evidence of growth in a man who ought to have his best work before him. The calm of a profound ideal ... make[s] this a very remarkable book.

And the reviewer in the *Critic* decided with satisfaction that the "finer element" in Mark Twain's nature had at last "hid[den] ... the humorous vein out of sight."

VI

It appears that the first work on which critics generally agreed that Mark Twain displayed notable abilities as a serious writer and literary artist was *The Prince and the Pauper*. They found the book a praiseworthy departure from his former writing, and they regarded its publication as heralding the advent of a new Clemens. It is time now to ask why this book created such a stir. What were these "new" qualities that so appealed to the critics? Why was it that they ignored a work like *Tom Sawyer* (1876), and poured critical abuse upon the head of Twain when, three years after *The Prince and the Pauper*, his *Huckleberry Finn* (generally acknowledged now as Clemens's finest book) appeared? The answer to these questions may be found in the prevailing critical standards of the day. Reviewers liked the description in *The Prince and the Pauper* because it was "delicate" and "subdued." Even the structure was praised on the ground of being "refined in execution." The characters, too, in *The Prince and the Pauper* were sweeter and more gentle than such rough-and-tumble fellows as Tom Sawyer and Huck Finn. The book dealt pleasantly with a faraway place and epoch, not with the rude, exuberant frontierland of their own times. The story was charged with a "pure" and "ennobling" moral; it might be introduced to any classroom or household without fear of its consequences to the gentle reader, an advantage which could not be held out for either *Tom Sawyer* or *Huckleberry Finn*. In short, critics approved of *The Prince and the Pauper* because, more than any other of Mark Twain's books up to that time, it complied with conventional literary ideals. Works like *Tom Sawyer* or *Huckleberry Finn* puzzled and disturbed the critics; therefore they ignored or denounced them. But *The Prince and the Pauper* was a work reviewers could understand; it fitted in perfectly with the tradition of correctness and imitation—with the genteel tradition; and therefore the critics acclaimed as "new" those qualities in *The Prince and the Pauper* which were actually least original.

Source: Arthur Lawrence Vogelback, "*The Prince and the Pauper*: A Study in Critical Standards," in *American Literature*, Vol. 14, No. 1, March 1942, pp. 48–54.

SOURCES

Bly, Marjie, "The Anti-Slavery Campaign in Britain," in *Victorian Web: Literature, History, and Culture in the Age of Victoria*, http://www.victorianweb.org/history/antislavery.html (accessed May 18, 2009).

Brown, Everit, "Alabama Claims," and "Treaty of Washington," in *A Dictionary of American Politics*, A. L. Burt, 1892, pp. 12–13, 517–18.

Curtis, Christopher Paul, "Introduction," in *The Prince and the Pauper*, The Modern Library, 2003, pp. xi–xvi.

Emerson, Everett, "Afterword," in *The Prince and the Pauper*, Signet Classic, 2002, pp. 211–18.

"Fight Class Divide, Says Phillips," in *BBC News*, July 21, 2008, http://news.bbc.co.uk/go/pr/fr/-/2/hi/uk_news/politics/7518207.stm (accessed May 18, 2009).

Hill, Hamlin, "Samuel Langhorne Clemens," in *Dictionary of Literary Biography*, Vol. 12, *American Realists and Naturalists*, edited by Donald Pizer and Earl N. Harbert, Gale Research, 1982, pp. 71–94.

Lye, John, "Romance as a Genre: Some Notes," Brock University's Department of English Language and Literature Web site, http://www.brocku.ca/english/courses/2F55/romance.php (accessed May 16, 2009).

"Monarchs of Britain," in *Britannia History*, http://www.britannia.com/history/h6f.html (accessed May 14, 2009).

Pike, Luke Owen, "Chapter VI: From the Ascension of Henry VI through the Death of Elizabeth," in *A History of Crime in England*, Vol. II, Kessinger, 1876, pp. 1–112.

Powers, Ron, "'A Powerful Good Time' (1888–1882)," in *Mark Twain: A Life*, Free Press, 2005, pp. 448–64.

Sacks, David Harris, "Discourses of Western Planting: Richard Hakluyt and the Making of the Atlantic World," *The Atlantic World and Virginia: 1550–1624*, edited by Peter C. Mancall, University of North Carolina Press, 2007, pp. 410–53.

"The Sixteenth Century: Introduction," in *Norton Anthology of English Literature*, http://www.wwnorton.com/college/english/nael/16century/welcome.htm (accessed May 18, 2009).

"*Telegraph* View: Barack Obama's Chance to Don Mantle of a Statesman," in *Telegraph* (London), March 31, 2009, http://www.telegraph.co.uk/comment/telegraph-view/5084978/Barack-Obamas-chance-to-don-the-mantle-of-a-statesman.html (accessed May 18, 2009).

Twain, Mark, *The Prince and the Pauper*, The Modern Library, 2003.

Ziff, Larzer, "Celebrity," and "Novelist," in *Mark Twain*, Oxford University Press, 2004, pp. 1–29, 58–88.

FURTHER READING

Cannadine, David, "The Nineteenth Century: A Viable Hierarchical Society," in *The Rise and Fall of Class in Britain*, Columbia University Press, 1999, pp. 59–108.
    Cannadine explores the dynamics of the British class system during the nineteenth century, observing the ways in which, over time, historians have tended to ignore class distinctions despite the pervasiveness of the idea of class consciousness in British culture.

Twain, Mark, *The Autobiography of Mark Twain*, edited by Charles Neider, Harper Perennial Modern Classics, 2000.
    Completed on his deathbed, Twain's autobiography is among the most highly regarded pieces of his writing. Its often humorous style is reflective of his popular novels, and at the same time it has been praised as both candid and deeply insightful.

Vogel, Todd, *Rewriting White: Race, Class, and Cultural Capital in Nineteenth-Century America*, Rutgers University Press, 2004.

> Vogel studies the ways in which African American, Native American, and Chinese American writers in the nineteenth century approached the issue of racial awareness and prejudice in their literary works. Vogel's analysis is divided into pre–Civil War and post–Civil War sections, in order to more precisely understand the social, cultural, and political atmosphere within which nonwhite writers attempted to practice their craft.

Weir, Alison, *Henry VIII: The King and His Court*, Ballantine Books, 2002.

> Weir, a highly regarded historian, provides an accessible biography of Henry VIII, examining his court and reign in detail. Her approach challenges the modern stereotypes that surround a king known largely as womanizer.

Reservation Blues

SHERMAN ALEXIE

1995

Sherman Alexie published *Reservation Blues* (1995), his first novel, after appearing on the literary scene to much acclaim several years earlier. He had published half a dozen books of verse and short fiction, including *The Lone Ranger and Tonto Fistfight in Heaven*, about life on Washington State's Spokane reservation, where Alexie was born and raised. He then signed a deal to write a novel on the strength of a single-sentence description of "an all-Indian Catholic rock-and-roll band," as noted in an interview with Tomson Highway, quoted by Daniel Grassian in *Understanding Sherman Alexie*. But after the pitch, Alexie changed his focus: the novel features characters from his earlier stories, forming Coyote Springs, a blues band rather than a rock-and-roll group. While the religious circumstances and conversations give *Reservation Blues* greater moral and philosophical weight, the novel's most singular aspect may be the fusion of cultures signified in the title, with the musical histories of Native Americans and African Americans presented as intertwined.

Although some critics—such as Gloria Bird, a fellow Spokane Indian—have questioned Alexie's presentation of Indians who seem stereotypical, such as in their apathy or drunkenness, most have effusively praised Alexie's first work of long fiction. Blythe Tellefsen explains that while Alexie himself rates the novel an aesthetic "C+," *Reservation Blues* is widely taught and highly regarded in high schools and colleges, attesting to the extent

Sherman Alexie *(© Christopher Felver / Documentary / Corbis)*

to which Alexie has succeeded in communicating an essential version—even if not a definitive one—of life on a reservation in the modern United States.

AUTHOR BIOGRAPHY

Alexie was born Sherman Joseph Alexie, Jr., on October 7, 1966, in Spokane, Washington, and grew up in the town of Wellpinit, Washington, on the state's Spokane Indian Reservation. His father, a Coeur d'Alene Indian, sometimes logged and drove trucks but was a heavy drinker; his mother, Lillian, who was Spokane, sewed and worked odd jobs to support the family. Alexie was born with a life-threatening ailment, hydrocephalus, a condition marked by excess fluid around the brain. He underwent surgery at six months and defied doctors' expectations by both surviving and ultimately thriving, although the first seven years of his life were marked by seizures and other conditions. Teased in school, he took refuge in educating himself, and he developed a keen sense of humor, largely as a measure of social defense.

Alexie excelled in high school and attended Gonzaga University—but he grew disillusioned by the ivory-tower ambience of the small liberal arts school and developed a drinking habit. Dropping out and finding work as a busboy, he was robbed at knifepoint on his twenty-first birthday; he then decided to regain his direction, enrolling at Washington State University. Fainting often in anatomy class, he balked at a career in medicine and ended up in a poetry workshop instructed by Alex Kuo, also of American Indian descent, who encouraged his inspired student to pursue a career in writing. Shortly after graduating in 1991, Alexie published *The Business of Fancydancing: Stories and Poems* (1992), which earned him immediate recognition as a significant new literary voice. His ensuing publications earned various awards, with *Reservation Blues* earning the Before Columbus Foundation American Book Award in 1996.

Alexie has continued to evolve in terms of both literary strategies and professional roles. His controversial novel *Indian Killer* (1996) features a boy of Indian blood who is raised by white people and grows up to self-destruct. Alexie wrote the screenplay for *Smoke Signals* (1998), a film adapted from his story collection *The Lone Ranger and Tonto Fistfight in Heaven* (1993), and he both wrote and directed the 2002 film *The Business of Fancydancing*. Alexie has continued to produce well-regarded work while living in Seattle with his wife, Diane, and two sons.

PLOT SUMMARY

Chapter 1: Reservation Blues

As *Reservation Blues* begins, jazz musician Robert Johnson shows up at the reservation crossroads in Wellpinit, Washington, looking for a woman on a hill. Thomas Builds-the-Fire kindly drives Johnson toward the mountain home of Big Mom—who generations ago witnessed a tragic slaughter of horses by U.S. troops—but the van dies en route. Johnson must walk up, and he leaves behind his guitar, which Thomas adopts. In front of the Trading Post, Victor Joseph finds Thomas and smashes the guitar before leaving with Junior Polatkin to deliver water and then go drinking. Meaning to burn the guitar, Thomas wakes up to find it healed; he converses with it while it intermittently plays itself. Summoned by the music, Victor and Junior arrive and agree to join Thomas's band.

MEDIA ADAPTATIONS

- Alexie collaborated with the musician Jim Boyd, a Colville Indian, to produce *Reservation Blues: The Soundtrack* (1995), which puts to music the lyrics that open each chapter of the novel and includes several additional songs as well.

- The film *Smoke Signals* (1998) is based on Alexie's story collection *The Lone Ranger and Tonto Fistfight in Heaven* and features the characters of Thomas and Victor as young men, who in the film have slightly different biographies from those presented in *Reservation Blues*.

Chapter 2: Treaties

Rehearsing at an abandoned grocery store, Thomas, Victor, and Junior's band starts drawing crowds. Father Arnold—who had arrived years back naively expecting buffalo in the Pacific Northwest—quells the fears of the local Catholic community. David WalksAlong, the tribal council head whose nephew is just returning from two years in prison, tells the band they're too loud. The white New Age bookstore owners Betty and Veronica become devoted fans. Naming themselves Coyote Springs, the band travels to a gig in Arlee, Montana, that starts promisingly.

Chapter 3: Indian Boy Love Song

At the show at the Tipi Pole Tavern, Chess and Checkers Warm Water make their way to the front of the crowd. Victor and Junior are playing drunkenly, but Chess and Thomas share looks, and he dedicates a song to her, performing several versions. She then joins him onstage to sing along. Afterward, Chess invites him back to their house, and the two chat over coffee about her family's tragic stories while the others sleep. In the morning, Victor impresses them with his sober guitar playing, and the women join the band. The Arlee tavern again hosts Coyote Springs, and they earn much admiration. They

all then go to Spokane, where Thomas and Chess become more intimate. Later they drive to a non-reservation show at a cowboy bar, getting towed there after their van breaks down, and earn a warm newspaper review.

Chapter 4: Father and Further

Back at the Spokane reservation, Thomas's father is asleep on the lawn. Chess and Checkers help Thomas carry Samuel inside and lay him on the kitchen table. Thomas tells of how his father excelled at basketball; one time, having committed an infraction, he challenged the tribal cops to a six-on-two game, with Lester FallsApart as his only teammate. The two women brush Samuel's hair and sing old choir songs as he sleeps, while Thomas stands outside. Victor and Junior dream of their deceased parents; Junior's parents died in a car accident after a party at Samuel's house. In that basketball game, though Officer Wilson broke Lester's nose, Samuel kept the score close with dazzling play—but the cops prevailed. Victor speaks ill of the dozing Samuel, and Checkers rages at him. Coyote Springs is invited to Seattle to play for a thousand dollars, but Checkers will not go anywhere with Victor and stays behind.

Chapter 5: My God Has Dark Skin

In Seattle, the band stops at a motel hoping the Backboard club will pay for rooms, but Thomas calls to find out the event is actually a contest; they get cheap food and sleep in the van instead. In Wellpinit, Checkers goes to the Catholic Church and takes a liking to the sympathetic Father Arnold. The band members go to Pike Place Market and lose themselves in the scene; Victor chats with drunks and then plays guitar while an old Indian man sings beautifully—and listeners drop much money in his hat—and though they may be late for the contest, Thomas cannot interrupt. Finally, they rush off; after they win, Thomas gives a radio interview. At church, Checkers sings in the choir. With Betty and Veronica, now backup singers, riding in the back, Thomas and Chess drive the van home and discuss faith, God, and the fates of America's Indians.

Chapter 6: Falling Down and Falling Apart

David WalksAlong writes an open letter to the Spokanes denouncing Coyote Springs as unworthy of the tribe. Nervously accompanying Chess and Checkers to church, Thomas feels faint and dreams of a sweat lodge. An old woman then relates the people's hostility toward the band for leaving the reservation and for adopting white women. Outside the Trading Post, Michael White Hawk clobbers the drunken Victor and Junior until the-man-who-was-probably-Lakota knocks White Hawk out with a two-by-four. Caught in the scuffle, Betty and Veronica, bruised and disillusioned, head back to Seattle. Sheridan and Wright, two white men, arrive in a Cadillac to check out the band; they offer to fly Coyote Springs to New York City to try rehearsing in a studio. Checkers rejoins the group; she kisses Father Arnold.

Chapter 7: Big Mom

Honored to be invited, Thomas leads the band members up to see Big Mom, who is said to have schooled many a renowned musician. She counsels forgiveness to Victor, gives Junior heavy drumsticks, and takes the Warm Water sisters to her sweat lodge. Victor, disbelieving any Indian magic, resists Big Mom's education. Fearing his old guitar, Robert Johnson hides in the woods. Thomas shares his fears and ambitions with Chess. After a week they leave for the airport, where Victor is almost too afraid to board. Thomas gives everyone eagle feathers.

Chapter 8: Urban Indian Blues

In the Cavalry Records studio, Victor fumbles with the guitar while Checkers forgets her chords; Mr. lArmstrong, the CEO, declares Coyote Springs unfit and promptly dismisses them. Victor rages, and Sheridan and Wright have them ejected by security. Junior and Victor then disappear into the masses of people to go drink. Checkers stays at the hotel while Chess and Thomas, fearful for the others, set off to search for them at bars. With Victor toppling over drunk, Junior reminisces about his college romance with Lynn, a white woman. Checkers has a nightmare in which Sheridan chastens her—and her whole race—and then assaults her; Wright, concerned for the band, happens to wake her up by knocking. Close to dawn, Thomas and Chess return to find Junior and Victor in the lobby and Checkers asleep upstairs, watched over by Wright.

Chapter 9: Small World

Coyote Springs returns to Wellpinit, and a week later Junior commits suicide atop the water tower. The night before, Checkers sneaks out of Thomas's house to visit Father Arnold, who says he must leave the reservation. The day before that, in a dream, Victor tells his guitar he would give up Junior, whom he loves most, to get it back. Thomas and Chess talk about leaving for Arlee or elsewhere. The day before that, Robert Johnson watches as White Hawk walks and mumbles around the softball diamond. Back in 1930, Johnson surrendered his freedom to the Gentleman to play the best guitar ever. At Cavalry, Sheridan tells Betty and Veronica they can play for the company as Indians or not at all. Wright objects and goes back home—to his grave in Sacramento; he was the one who ordered the slaughter of the horses.

Chapter 10: Wake

Coyote Springs holds a wake for Junior in Thomas's house; Lester FallsApart gives them three dogs. Giving Robert Johnson the cedar harmonica she made, Big Mom descends and gets Father Arnold to help at the burial. Victor tells everyone Junior had a kid, and Chess imagines the difficult lives of half-blood Indians; she tells Thomas she wants to have full-blood children with him. Checkers, who is leaving for Spokane with Thomas and Chess, reconciles with Father Arnold, who will stay. Victor talks to Junior's ghost, swearing off alcohol and tossing silver flasks into Turtle Lake. He seeks a job but is denied by David WalksAlong and starts drinking again. Receiving a demo cassette of Betty and Veronica's quasi-Indian music, Thomas smashes it. Before they leave, Thomas and the sisters go along with Big Mom to a feast, where she breaks all the fry bread in halves to feed everyone, and a collection hat yields a couple hundred dollars for the three departing. When they drive off, shadow horses race alongside the van.

CHARACTERS

Mr. Armstrong

The head of Cavalry Records, Armstrong quickly concludes that Coyote Springs does not have what it takes, and he agrees to promote two white women, Betty and Veronica, dressed up like Indians instead.

Father Arnold

A onetime rock singer who heard his calling to the Catholic priesthood in a McDonald's, Father Arnold is devoted to his Indian congregation and admiring of both their defiantly cheery nature and their physical beauty. When Checkers develops a crush on him, he has a crisis of faith and nearly leaves the reservation, but Big Mom brings him to his Christian senses.

Betty

Along with Veronica, Betty becomes a Coyote Springs groupie who later joins the band, but quits after the scuffle outside the Trading Post. The two white women later sign up with Cavalry Records as pseudo-Indians.

Big Mom

A sort of goddess-like matriarch of the Spokane tribe, Big Mom has lived atop her mountain for many generations; the horse slaughter she witnessed happened in 1858. According to legend, she schooled many famous—and ill-fated—musicians, such as Jimi Hendrix and Janis Joplin. She invites Coyote Springs up for a week of intensive training and, like an oracle, seems to already know what is inside and what is needed by each of their hearts. At the feast, in a practical miracle reminiscent of one of Jesus', she doubles the quantity of fry bread by splitting it in halves. She then reconciles the tribe with the departing Thomas and Warm Water sisters.

Samuel Builds-the-Fire

Thomas's father, Samuel, has earned himself the Indian name of Drunk and Disorderly. He was state basketball player of the year in high school—and a proficient trash-talker—but afterward declined into alcoholism. He is found passed out on Thomas's lawn and is laid on the kitchen table inside. When they leave the reservation, Thomas says Samuel has "Indian father radar" and will find them wherever they go.

Thomas Builds-the-Fire

Thomas is the central protagonist and hero of the novel. A lonesome, awkward man, he has a heartfelt belief in the power of stories and tells them compulsively to anyone who will listen, and even to those who do not. His mother died of cancer when he was ten, and he fondly remembers her "rocking him into sleep with stories and songs." Where Junior and Victor are driven more by fame, Thomas wants to help his people rise up out of the emotional desolation so many are stricken with. On the other hand, he also confesses more selfish motivations to Chess, saying, "I want all kinds of strangers to love me." In general, he acts virtuously, not drinking and rarely speaking ill of others—except his father and the Christian Americans who have wrought havoc on his people—leading Coyote Springs through thick and thin. He is unfailingly forthright; even when Victor ridicules him or asks mocking questions, he does not trade insults but speaks openly and sincerely. When he trades looks with Chess at the Tipi Pole Tavern, far from playing it cool, he devotes a song to her and repeats it so many times, in various versions, that Chess is able to come on stage and sing along. While Thomas's singing is said to be good but not remarkably so, his lyrics, which open each chapter, resound with the spirit of the blues, evoking the sorrows of generations of Indians. Powerful in his heart and in his mind but practically powerless in the context of the American world created by white people, Thomas stoically but faithfully clings to traditional Indian ways, and he ultimately finds peace and solace in the love he shares with Chess and the promise of a stable, happy, full-blood Indian family.

Lester FallsApart

A beloved local drunk, Lester materializes throughout the book "like a reservation magician" at pivotal moments, such as showing up to cast the deciding vote not to kick Chess and Checkers off the reservation. Picked up by Samuel as a hitchhiker long ago, he joined his friend in the game against the tribal cops and had his nose broken.

The Gentleman

The Gentleman, who as "a handsome white man" can be understood to represent the devil, met the young Robert Johnson at a crossroads and offered him the ability to play guitar better than anyone in exchange for what he loves most—his freedom. Thenceforth, the guitar becomes like Johnson's cruel master.

The Guitar

A character in its own right, Robert Johnson's old guitar heals itself, has conversations, and seems to get around independently. Johnson could never lose it, Victor's smashing of it proves only temporary, and the guitar ultimately possesses Victor. The guitar may represent the notions of fame and ego, having been effectively cursed by the Gentleman when Johnson wanted to be the best player ever. It may also be understood to have become Johnson's, and later Victor's, cruel master.

Thomas is infatuated with the instrument for a time but, unlike the others—perhaps reflecting his more virtuous storytelling aims—relinquishes it without serious torment.

Robert Johnson

Actually a jazz musician who died in 1938, Robert Johnson is imagined by Alexie to have faked his death and wandered onto the Spokane Indian Reservation in 1992, "old and tired." His role is reminiscent of a Greek mythic hero: an agent of supernatural phenomena who fulfills a fantastic destiny. Having surrendered his freedom to the Gentleman in order to play guitar better than anyone ever, he could never manage to escape his now mystical instrument—until, desperately following a dream, he finds his way to Big Mom's mountain and leaves the guitar with Thomas. He hides out there, fearful the guitar or the Gentleman will find him, until Big Mom gives him a cedar harmonica, and he comes down to live with the tribe.

Victor Joseph

Victor seems to be the most psychologically troubled of all the members of Coyote Springs, drinking too much and angering easily. At first little more than a bully, upon gaining Robert Johnson's guitar, he becomes the creative musical force that drives the band's success; his playing sends off sparks and is portrayed as transcendent. Feeling allied with the drunks in Seattle, he self-lessly joins an old man for a magical duet that rakes in money. Imagining himself as a rock star, he favors white women, to the disgust of his fellow Indians. Big Mom recognizes that he is captive to his anger toward the priest who abused him as a boy. Victor seizes up when auditioning for Cavalry Records and so smashes the guitar, only to mourn it afterward. He then betrays the person he loves most to the guitar in his dream, and he feels responsible for Junior's death.

The-man-who-was-probably-Lakota

Always hanging around outside the Trading Post and shouting that the end is near, the tall old Indian, suspected to be Lakota, develops a sort of outcast partnership with Thomas, extending sympathy and some assistance. He seems to join forces with Robert Johnson in the end.

Junior Polatkin

Junior is presented as an intelligent yet simple man; he made it to college but now seems content to drive a water truck and see his earnings drunk through by his questionable friend Victor. Junior's parents' death by car accident and Victor's consequent befriending of the boy explain their lasting affection for each other. Junior had a college romance with a white woman, Lynn, that ended with her abortion of their child, and he saved her parting note in his wallet ever since; the absence of that child in Junior's life seems to correspond to the absence of his creative spirit. He believes in the power of dreams and music, but after Coyote Springs fails—as he tells Victor as a sort of ghost—he chose to kill himself because when he closed his eyes, he envisioned nothing at all.

Phil Sheridan

After bringing Coyote Springs to New York, Sheridan tries to show them sympathy when they fail to impress, but driven by the bottom line, he ultimately dismisses them; he later orchestrates the farcical signing of Betty and Veronica. He haunts Checkers in her dreams.

Simon

Simon drives his truck backwards only, for reasons unclear. After he picks up the hitchhiking Coyote Springs from near the airport, Junior uses one of his rifles to commit suicide. Simon then leaves the reservation forever.

Veronica

Along with Betty, Veronica becomes a Coyote Springs groupie who later joins the band but quits after the Trading Post scuffle. The two white women leave behind their New Age bookstore to sign up with Cavalry Records as pseudo-Indians.

David WalksAlong

The chairman of the Spokane Tribal Council, WalksAlong stokes animosity toward the dangerously unwholesome Coyote Springs. He does not wield his authority as chief objectively. When he was police chief, WalksAlong joined five fellow cops to play a dirty game against Samuel and Lester.

Checkers Warm Water

Chess's younger sister, Checkers (actually named Gladys) joins the band to sing but quits to sing in the choir at the Catholic Church. Perhaps owing to her fraught relationship with her own father, Luke, Checkers has long demonstrated interest in older men; she quickly grows infatuated with the sympathetic Father Arnold and feels compelled to stay in Wellpinit. Nonetheless, her bond with her sister, forged through the family's several tragedies (including their baby brother's death and mother Linda's disappearance), proves primary, and she leaves for Spokane with Chess and Thomas.

Chess Warm Water

The older sister of Checkers, Chess (actually named Eunice) takes a liking to Thomas at their first show and eventually falls in love with him. Chess is perhaps the most powerful voice of reason in the novel, often giving advice to the visionary but hesitant Thomas. She and her sister have been working as firefighters on their Flathead Reservation, and Chess in particular sustains this role of being a cooling or pacifying influence. She tries to counsel Thomas toward Catholicism, but he is too disillusioned by past injustices. In the end, Chess tries to lead Thomas and her sister to a better life by accepting a telephone operator job in Spokane.

Michael White Hawk

WalksAlong's nephew, White Hawk is a would-be warrior who has trouble negotiating the rules of society, going to jail for clouting someone with a saxophone. He pounds Victor and Junior, incidentally injuring Betty and Veronica, until the-man-who-was-probably-Lakota knocks him out. He then takes to erratic circling behavior on the softball diamond.

Officer Wilson

Wilson, mostly white, pulls Samuel over and then plays in the basketball game against him.

George Wright

Unlike his partner, Sheridan, Wright feels guilty for the failure and self-destruction of Coyote Springs, and in seeking the band out he wakes Checkers from her nightmare. Though a modern music producer, Wright is also the general who ordered the horse massacre in 1858.

THEMES

The Power of Music

Alexie has much to say in *Reservation Blues* about the power of music to inspire, heal, and unite listeners. Thomas professes to have been inspired by music from an early age, as his mother sang not only traditional Spokane songs but also Broadway numbers and Catholic hymns. When the enchanted guitar suggests, "Y'all need to play songs for your people," Thomas, a storyteller, is immediately open to the idea. The music that the guitar plays of its own accord, as heard by Victor and Junior, is said to have "worked its way into their skins," and when it rises to the clouds and rains down, the reservation "arched its back, opened its mouth, and drank deeply." In a magic realist style, the music is made palpable, given a physical presence that affects people and even the land in an insistent way, whether they wish it to or not.

The spiritual nature of music is emphasized particularly through the character of Big Mom, a goddess-like matriarch of the tribe with remarkable powers. Though her powers are not typically miraculous, she is especially gifted at reading people's thoughts and at hearing, playing, and teaching music. When she plays "the loneliest chord that the band had ever heard," it crawls up their clothes and makes Junior faint; she later declares that it is "the chord created especially for us," for American Indians. The fantastic notion that a single chord could carry such extraordinary emotional weight is indicative of the degree to which the novel presents how music can and should touch people's souls.

While the band is largely rejected by the other Spokanes, a woman in church informs Thomas that not the quality but the genre of the sound is the issue: "The Christians don't like your devil's music. The traditionals don't like your white man's music." In turn, the band ultimately fails, but this is portrayed as a fate determined by the white hierarchy overseeing the recording industry, which overlooks the band's artistry as well as its local success. Despite the demise of Coyote Springs, the novel's conclusion leaves no doubt as to the power inherent in music. After Big Mom sings a powerful "protection song" for all Indians, in a collective dream she teaches a new "shadow horses' song," "a song of mourning that would become a song of celebration." And as they drive to Spokane and the future, Thomas, Chess, and Checkers sing together, and it means nothing less than that "they were alive; they'd keep living."

Dreams, Visions, and Television

Dreams of the major characters, including the five members of Coyote Springs as well as Father

TOPICS FOR FURTHER STUDY

- Keep a dream journal for a week, writing down whatever you can remember from your dreams upon waking up. Then pick one of your dreams and consult Sigmund Freud's *The Interpretation of Dreams*, M. J. Abadie's *Teen Dream Power: Unlock the Meaning of Your Dreams*, or any other such text to analyze your dream. Write a paper discussing the relevance of the dream to your life as you see it, addressing conflicts and agreements between the text you consulted and your own opinions.

- Read one or more stories from Alexie's *The Lone Ranger and Tonto Fistfight in Heaven*. Then write an essay comparing and contrasting the story or stories you read with *Reservation Blues*, considering Alexie's skills as an author, the development of the characters, and the arcs of the plots.

- Put together a PowerPoint presentation in which you chart the trajectory of your life thus far as framed by the music that you have listened to regularly and have found influential. Include graphics representing relevant songs or groups who have been meaningful to you.

- Pick one of the songs that open each chapter and put the lyrics to music. Then play for your class, first your song—live or recorded—and then the version of the song found on *Reservation Blues: The Soundtrack* (which you should not listen to until you have completed your own version). Lead a class discussion on the two songs.

- In some American Indian cultures before the arrival of Europeans, boys would typically grow up to become warriors. In modern America, warrior culture has largely been replaced by sports culture. Pick one popular American sport and examine it in this context, reading articles comparing sports culture and warrior culture, then considering perceptions of those who play the sport, cultural expectations within the sport, attitudes of spectators, and any other relevant aspects. Present your findings in a written or oral report.

- Read Alexie's young-adult novel, *The Absolutely True Diary of a Part Time Indian*. Compare life on the reservation as it is depicted in the two novels. Draw cartoon images, like the ones Arnold Spirit draws in *The Absolutely True Diary of a Part Time Indian*, that depict scenes in *Reservation Blues*. Present these to your class, explaining why you chose the moments you did, and how the images relate to both novels.

Arnold, are integral to the text of *Reservation Blues*. Early on, Alexie signals the relevance dreams should be assigned through the character of Junior, who learned in college psychology classes that, according to Sigmund Freud and Carl Jung, "dreams decided everything," a perspective that aligns with traditional Indian views of dreams. While the characters' dreams generally do not determine their fates—excluding the dream in which Victor sacrifices Junior to the will of the guitar, prefiguring Junior's suicide—the dreams reveal much about their inner lives, particularly their fears and the memories that haunt

them. In Victor's dream of his deceased parents, the boldface names stress the impact their repeated imagining would have on a man who has determined never again to utter the names while awake. Checkers's nightmare about Sheridan, while very personal, could also be any Indian's nightmare, with a reincarnated murderous white military officer insisting that he will keep waging war on native peoples no matter how defeated they already are.

Beyond dreams, television gives Junior the impression that Indians should even have visions. Yet Junior's dreams tell him little more than to

A male member of the Spokane Indian tribe, c. 1900-1910 *(© Michael Maslan Historic Photographs / Corbis)*

eat peanut butter and onion sandwiches, and his lack of visions is what leaves him feeling spiritually bereft enough to commit suicide (as his ghost tells Victor). Alexie hints that television may in fact deserve some blame for supplanting not only Junior's visions but also Thomas's. In the first discussion of Junior's dreams, his watching television and his wanting more material comforts are closely linked. Later, one of Junior's nightmares features narration in the style of a television sportscaster. Thomas, in turn, has a dream marked precisely by television and wanting; he is hungry and is reminded by television of all he does not own. What both Junior and Thomas end up seeing in their mind's eye, then, are the images of the material riches of the lives of white people as seen on television. Whether Junior might have been blessed with life-affirming visions had he ceased watching television is a question the text does not address.

Masculinity

Alexie portrays the modern Indian male as facing a particularly poignant version of the broader American dilemma of masculinity. If an Indian man tries to fulfill his masculine instinct—or televised ideals—and become a warrior, he risks a fate like that of Michael White Hawk, who through impulsive violence gains first a trip to prison and then a destabilizing concussion. Yet being a warrior also has the connotations of resistance. Checkers recognizes in both Samuel and Thomas "that warrior desperation and the need to be superhuman in the poverty of a reservation." Samuel is presented in his youth as a proud modern Indian warrior, channeling aggression as well as finding physical fulfillment through the sport of basketball. Yet his success in high school only sets him up for the inevitable defeat that will come at the hands of white society—as represented by the authority-wielding tribal cops—and his ultimate fate is despairing alcoholism. Victor aspires to warrior status, wishfully calling Coyote Springs "a warrior band," but when he fails to play under pressure at the Cavalry studio, his unchanneled aggression leaves him wanting "to steal a New York cop's horse and go on the warpath," "to scalp stockbrokers," and "shoot flaming arrows into the Museum of Modern Art." Instead, he gets drunk.

Regardless of Victor's self-destruction, Alexie suggests that resolution for the Indian's dilemma of masculinity may be best found through music. In many ways, Thomas is presented as the antithesis of the warrior, being physically weak and virtually never rising to anger or aggression. His preferred occupation is that of the storyteller, an artist, as he wishes to create, not destroy. And while other characters are resigned primarily to the fates of death and drink, Thomas will not only survive but will also raise a family with Chess, gaining the fulfillment of fatherhood. Big Mom, speaking to White Hawk, affirms that the musician provides what the warrior cannot: "Don't you understand that the musical instrument is not to be used in the same way that a bow and arrow is? Music is supposed to heal."

STYLE

American Indian Literature

Works that would be classified as Native American fiction, as put forth by Daniel Grassian in *Understanding Sherman Alexie*, are often marked by a return journey of sorts, where an Indian protagonist ventures out into the world fashioned by whites and, eventually disillusioned or disheartened, returns to reconnect with his tribe. Such a work cannot be properly examined through the lens of white individualism—a motivating factor in many Western works—as the concept of belonging to a tribe cannot apply to members of modern white society in the same way. Necessarily, then, American Indian writers must be conscious of two or even three audiences who will perceive their work differently: their own tribe, other tribes, and the remainder of contemporary society, which happens to be the portion whose appreciation for a novel will largely determine its degree of success. Yet if an Indian writer believes in and is motivated by the healing power of his stories, as with Alexie's character Thomas, then his own tribe may very well be his most important

audience. Among the most highly esteemed Native American authors are N. Scott Momaday, Leslie Marmon Silko, Louise Erdrich, and James Welch.

The place of *Reservation Blues* within the expanding canon of American Indian literature has been a source of some critical debate. Perhaps most notably, Gloria Bird, Spokane herself, in "The Exaggeration of Despair in *Reservation Blues*," suggests that Alexie's novel does a disservice to American Indians in that it ultimately supports stereotypical representations of Indians from popular culture. She does make clear, however, that she is examining the novel specifically for its implications for the Indian reader, and from a traditionalist perspective. It has been soundly argued, by Stephen Evans among others, that for his adroit use of ironic and satiric techniques in examining modern Indian culture, Alexie should be seen as a "consciously moral satirist rather than as a 'cultural traitor.'" Regardless of critical perspectives, Alexie himself has asserted (as quoted in Grassian) that his novels could not be considered anything but American Indian literature: "If I write it, it's an Indian novel.... That's who I am."

Magic Realism

The modern literary strategy of "magic realism" has fascinated critics into the twenty-first century. While certain western European and American texts may demonstrate magic-realist elements, the style is recognized as having blossomed particularly among Latin American authors like Gabriel Garcia Marquez and Isabel Allende. In her essay on magic realism in *Reservation Blues*, Wendy Belcher concisely posits, "Critics identify a text as magic realist if it treats the extraordinary as real." In Alexie's novel, much of the extraordinary revolves around the guitar, which fixes itself, talks, plays itself, and even moves around; when it sets off sparks that start a small fire, Chess and Checkers put it out without much ado, and when a chord Victor plays knocks out people's fillings, the dentist simply puts them back in. Another fantastic occurrence comes when Coyote punishes Junior by stealing his truck and putting it in the dance hall, where it couldn't have fit through the doors; Junior has to disassemble the truck and loses his job. The narrator relates all of these episodes as if they are legitimate happenings.

Belcher notes that magic realism is often discussed in political terms as "a literary form of the colonized," and that often the magical occurrences are linked to the indigenous, traditional culture in opposition to the modern, rational colonizer. Thus, a wizened elder would be expected to be an agent of magic, while a white businessman would not. Belcher observes that the opposite is the case in *Reservation Blues*. Modern American objects, like the enchanted guitar, and people, like the Cavalry Records executives who were also nineteenth-century military officers, are agents of the magical. Meanwhile, Big Mom, the long-lived Spokane matriarch who carves a humble harmonica and praises mathematics, largely does not accomplish the magical, although she does boast a mythical past and exhibits extraordinary empathy and musical ability. Belcher concludes that Alexie's use of magic realist elements reflects the notion that for American Indians, products and people of modern American culture are what function in such fantastic ways as to be represented in fiction as magical.

HISTORICAL CONTEXT

Robert Johnson and the Blues

Although during his short lifetime his reputation reached not far beyond the bars and roadhouses of the Deep South where his music evolved, Robert Johnson, after his death, as noted by Barry Lee Pearson and Bill McCulloch in their biography, "rose from obscurity to become an all-American musical icon, the best-known although least understood exemplar of the Mississippi Delta blues tradition." The blues developed early in the twentieth century from African American musical traditions such as spirituals and work songs, incorporating particular guitar chord progressions, call-and-response patterns, and lyrical lamentations, with the resulting music serving to both express and purge worldly sorrows. Born in 1911, Johnson flourished in the 1930s, when he traveled and played constantly and recorded a couple of records that sold modestly. He died a mysterious death, presumably poisoned, in 1938. As noted by Pearson and McCulloch, music historians came to recognize his recordings as "the last and most highly evolved example of an older style—a dying echo of one of the primitive building blocks from which jazz was constructed," while also representing "the first faint rumblings of the rock-and-roll revolution."

In *Reservation Blues*, Alexie hypothesizes the injection of the blues into modern American

Indian culture through the person of an aged Johnson, and he adapts the myth about Johnson having sold his soul to the devil to gain otherworldly musical skill. On the one hand Alexie portrays the pairing of Indians and the blues as a perfect fit, the blues being "ancient, aboriginal, indigenous;" they "created memories" and "lit up a new road" for the Spokanes. And yet on the other hand Alexie's Spokanes as a community reject the blues, from both Catholic and traditional perspectives, and Coyote Springs proves to fail ingloriously, as if fate wished to have it that way. This failure is especially interesting in light of Alexie's suggestions of a persistent Native American influence on popular musical traditions, as personified by Big Mom, gifted teacher of a variety of revolutionary musicians. In *When Brer Rabbit Meets Coyote*, Paul Pasquaretta asserts that musicologists have indeed recognized that Indian musical traditions were influential on the early development of African American forms, and many renowned black artists, including Lena Horn and, perhaps most significantly, Jimi Hendrix, have degrees of Native American ancestry. Alexie might have cemented the musical link between black and Indian cultures by blessing Coyote Springs with success—or at least by saving them from failure—but his more tragic conclusion, in which white oppressors persist as white oppressors, may be more reflective of the modern music industry.

Spokane Indians and Faiths

The Spokane Indians have long resided in the region of the Spokane River in eastern Washington, historically being a people whose livelihood revolved around salmon fishing. Like many other tribes, the Spokane suffered from imported diseases and saw their land usurped by white settlers supported by the U.S. government. The construction of the Grand Coulee Dam on the Columbia River, into which the Spokane River flows, was a catastrophic event for many tribes in the region, as it forever cut off salmon migrations farther east, in addition to flooding hallowed grounds. While Alexie was raised on the Spokane reservation, the primary setting of *Reservation Blues* as well as other stories of his, he does not infuse the novel with tribal history or cultural practices. Although readers and critics would likely respond positively to a more intimate portrayal of lives of traditional Spokanes, Alexie has stated that he does not believe it appropriate to delve fictionally into his tribe's traditions,

Playing guitar *(Image copyright Silver-John, 2009. Used under license from Shutterstock.com)*

particularly spiritual ones, because doing so would open the door for the sort of cultural theft exemplified by Betty and Veronica in his novel.

Instead, Alexie deals with the faith that has become a great influence on modern Spokanes, namely, Catholicism. As throughout much of the United States, missionaries came to Spokane territory in the mid-nineteenth century, to endeavor to convert the tribe away from traditional practices in favor of Christian ones, with mixed success. Accordingly, Alexie gives his characters a variety of relationships with Christianity: Thomas cannot forget that the U.S. soldiers who murdered so many Indians were God-fearing Christians; Victor was abused by a priest; Junior demonstrates no faith at all; and Chess and Checkers are devout Catholics. Out of these clashing modes of experience, Alexie perhaps presents an ideal resolution for Catholic and traditional Indian faiths on a modern reservation when he has Big Mom and Father Arnold join forces in the closing chapter to mourn for Junior.

CRITICAL OVERVIEW

The critical response to *Reservation Blues*, as with much of Alexie's work, has been primarily favorable. In the *Bloomsbury Review*, Abigail Davis asserts that the novel is an exceptional effort to convey the modern Indian experience to non-Indian readers, such that one "closes the book feeling troubled, hurt, hopeful, profoundly thoughtful, and somehow exhausted, as if the quest of the characters had been a personal experience." She notes that Alexie's singular narrative voice "is laced with humor and anger and driven by great intelligence." In the *Los Angeles Times*, Verlyn Klinkenborg observes that Alexie "is willing to risk didacticism" to explain Indian experiences but "never sounds didactic. His timing is too good for that. *Reservation Blues* never misses a beat, never sounds a false note." Klinkenborg likewise praises Alexie for being "scathingly funny. His sense of humor ignores every cultural boundary, and its frankness is amiable and appealing." In *World Literature Today*, Howard Meredith remarks, "The art of

Sherman Alexie surprises and delights the reader," as "form and content act in unity to provide a captivating story of the tragic sense of life within a Spokane frame of reference."

Following the initial reviews, numerous critics delved into the particular themes and stylistic approaches in Alexie's first novel. The Winter 1997 issue of *Studies in American Indian Literatures* was devoted to Alexie, with essays addressing the roles of doppelgängers, magic, memory, popular culture, and music in *Reservation Blues*. There has been debate over the presence of stereotypical characters in the novel and its virtues as a work of American Indian literature, but the resulting consensus has affirmed that Alexie's portrayal of modern Spokane reservation life, as infused with the spirit of the blues, is honorable in its humor as well as in its tragedy, in its joys as well as in its sorrows. As the renowned Native American author Leslie Marmon Silko asserts in a review in *Nation*, "Alexie's talent is immense and genuine, and needs no Devil's typewriter.... On this big Indian reservation we call 'the United States,' Sherman Alexie is one of the best writers we have."

CRITICISM

Michael Allen Holmes

Holmes is a writer and editor. In this essay, he contemplates the impressionistic effects of magic realism in Reservation Blues.

In *Reservation Blues*, Alexie has scattered magical occurrences throughout his otherwise perfectly realistic fictional world, an approach critics refer to as magic realism. In her essay "Conjuring the Colonizer: Alternative Readings of Magic Realism in Sherman Alexie's *Reservation Blues*," Wendy Belcher discusses how the association of magic with the guitar, a secular Western object, inverts the critically recognized paradigm whereby indigenous or mythical objects are usually sources of magic. While she astutely concludes that in this novel, "Indian culture and people frequently embody rationality while the West spews easy, dangerous magic," she concedes that Alexie may not have intended to address this critical paradigm at all. As Belcher notes, "In interviews, Alexie rarely talks about magic realism but emphasizes his own interest in the real, the everyday, and the human." This almost seems contradictory, as the author's inclusion of magical elements partly

> THUS, IT MAY BE USEFUL TO CONSIDER THE 'MAGIC REALISM' IN ALEXIE'S NOVEL LESS AS A LITERARY STRATEGY THAT DEPARTS FROM THE EVERYDAY AND MORE AS IMPRESSIONISTIC REFLECTIONS OF THE EVERYDAY."

withdraws his novel from the realm of the everyday, and yet the novel offers much commentary on the daily lives of modern Spokane Indians. Thus, it may be useful to consider the "magic realism" in Alexie's novel less as a literary strategy that departs from the everyday and more as impressionistic reflections of the everyday.

The average American reader approaching *Reservation Blues* may be caught off guard by the first few magical occurrences in the novel. In British and American literature, the inclusion of such extraordinary or impossible events usually places a work in the genres of fantasy or science fiction, but few serious critics would classify Alexie's work as such. The appearance of the renowned—and actually long deceased—jazz musician Robert Johnson at the opening of the novel sets the stylistic tone. Alexie accounts for this plot device with the statement that Johnson actually faked his death (in 1938) and has been on the run ever since. On the one hand, this hypothetical situation is highly unlikely but at least feasible. On the other hand, the image of Johnson having wandered from crossroads to crossroads for over fifty years, perhaps in the same suit, looking for an "old woman lives on a hill" whom he has been dreaming about, with his guitar alone as his "best friend," may strike the reader as ridiculous. Thomas Builds-the-Fire sees nothing wrong with the situation, however, and so Johnson hops in his van—as does the complicit reader—to head toward Big Mom's home on Wellpinit Mountain. Thus, the reader is made open to the idea of suspending disbelief and accepting the fantastic as truth in the context of the novel.

Alexie soon demonstrates that his narrator will indeed take certain liberties with the truth, if perhaps in the name of humor rather than magic. The old man who hangs around the Trading

WHAT DO I READ NEXT?

- *The Business of Fancydancing: Stories and Poems* (1991) was Alexie's breakthrough work and was recognized as a notable book of the year by the *New York Times Book Review*; it was also adapted by Alexie as a film, *The Business of Fancydancing* (2002), which he wrote and directed.

- Alexie's first young-adult novel is *The Absolutely True Diary of a Part-Time Indian* (2007), a first-person narrative by an American Indian teenager who is raised on Washington's Spokane reservation but transfers to an all-white high school, as did Alexie himself.

- Louise Erdrich, a member of the Ojibwe (or Chippewa) nation, also focuses on a tribe's relationship and conflicts with Western religion in *The Last Report on the Miracles at Little No Horse* (2001), set in North Dakota.

- In contrast to the minor role of traditional Indian ways in *Reservation Blues*, Leslie Marmon Silko's *Ceremony* (1977) portrays a half-white, half-Laguna Indian who suffers emotional instability after surviving World War II and ultimately finds redemption in the spiritual traditions of his people.

- Alexie professed to be deeply moved and originally inspired to write by *Songs from This Earth on Turtle's Back* (1983), a volume of American Indian poetry edited by Joseph Bruchac.

- The German author Hermann Hesse presents a man's struggle to reconcile his inner animalistic self with his civilized self, a struggle reminiscent of Victor's compulsion to be a warrior, in his renowned novel *Steppenwolf* (1927).

- The central character in the Nobel Prizewinning author Toni Morrison's novel *Song of Solomon*, Macon "Milkman" Dead, has drawn comparison to Thomas Builds-the-Fire; the story addresses his understanding of his African American and Native American heritage as he matures to adulthood.

- David Foster Wallace's *Infinite Jest* (1996) is an epic-length postmodern novel that conveys the compelling and disturbing thesis that the American addiction to entertainment, especially in the form of television, is tantamount to spiritual death.

- In *Woman Warrior: A Girlhood among Ghosts* (1975), a work of semiautobiographical fiction presented as memoirs, Maxine Hong Kingston details the experiences and trials endured by a young Chinese American woman through her adolescence.

- One of the most highly regarded works making extensive use of magic realism is the Colombian author Gabriel Garcia Marquez's *One Hundred Years of Solitude* (1967), which draws connections between the lives and decisions of different generations within a family.

Post and is presumed to be Lakota "had cheekbones so big that he knocked people over when he moved his head from side to side." This image, which the open-minded reader will duly envision, is intentionally ridiculous. Alexie is known for giving readings of his work that come across like stand-up comedy, and critics have hailed the skill with which he uses humor in this novel. Indeed, the reader who finds himself laughing at this image—even if it may be

considered offensively stereotypical of Lakota Sioux Indians—has been rewarded for reading with an open mind, as willing to absorb whatever impressions Alexie wishes to make. The act of laughter, in turn, serves to dissipate bodily tension, likely leaving the reader able to sustain an open-minded approach to the text.

Magic is introduced explicitly when Johnson's guitar, which Victor smashed but Thomas has kept, repairs itself and proceeds to have a conversation with Thomas, even playing some music that serves to summon Victor and Junior. At this point, the reader has no choice but to continue with an open mind toward the fantastic because the plot now depends upon it. The aggressively deductive reader might yet conceive that Alexie is actually framing circumstances in such a way that the novel's events can be legitimately explained, just not as the narrator explains them. For example, such a reader might imagine that Thomas, who is described as "pretty goofy," perhaps repaired the guitar himself at night but does not remember, and perhaps the conversation with the guitar could be understood as a hallucination. Victor and Junior's hearing guitar music in their dreams, then, could just be coincidental. But Alexie even insists that the reader accept these magical incidents not as some literary device but as truth of a sort. After the oft-quoted passage in which the guitar's music is said to rise to the clouds and rain down on the reservation, a page later Alexie's narrator asserts, "The music did rise into the clouds. It did rain down on the reservation, which arched its back and drank deeply. It did fall on the roof of the water truck, disturbing Junior's and Victor's sleep." In effect, then, the narrator, as the storyteller, is engaging in dialogue with the reader about the truth of his story.

Alexie proceeds to pepper his novel with both humor and magic, often coincidentally. By the time Coyote punishes the blaspheming Junior by hiding the water truck in the old dance hall, where "the truck was too big for the doors, so nobody was sure how that truck fit in there," and Junior has to disassemble the truck and loses his job, the reader is likely to take such plot-hinging magical events in stride. In terms of the impression it makes, this particular event may lead the reader to conceive that there is indeed a sort of moral justice to the world, something like karma or fate, which brings negative consequences to those who act or speak immorally. Alexie does not state such a notion, of course, but rather presents magical circumstances that leave the impression of that notion in the reader's mind.

Other magical events likewise leave particular impressions about the circumstances involved. The magic of the guitar is evil magic, which hollows out Robert Johnson until he is left to cower in the forest at Big Mom's house in fear of it, and which so possesses Victor that he sacrifices his best friend in a dream because of it. Both the guitar and its magic, then, can be understood to represent the ideas of fame or prideful individualism, and indeed, the motivation to become a star, shared by Robert Johnson and Victor, can perhaps best be understood as a sort of magic that twists one's mind, shifting priorities away from friends and community and toward things like material goods and admiration from strangers. That is, Alexie might have forgone magic and, with strictly rational narration, told the same story and communicated the same ideas; but if the self-consuming drive for fame is irrational, perhaps no arrangement of rational ideas can do it justice. The motif of a cursed guitar, on the other hand, leaves the reader with an emotional—and nonrational—impression as to the perils of the idea of fame.

Collectively, the magical events as well as the humorous asides in *Reservation Blues* may be understood to covertly direct the reader into a mode of feeling rather than thinking, a mode of absorbing images, however fantastic, and allowing them to make an emotional impression, rather than simply absorbing words and sentences and the sum of their rational constructions. The necessity that the reader be open-minded would indeed seem a hallmark of the fantasy and science-fiction genres, genres from which the reader who is unwilling to suspend disbelief, who is constantly judging the verisimilitude of a text, will undoubtedly shy away. In his first novel, Alexie demonstrates that magic realism can serve to accomplish the same end—forcing the reader to remain open-minded toward the text—in the context of a literary work. As such, beyond the humor and magic, the reader has no choice but to absorb and feel the tragedy as well. And this may be Alexie's ultimate aim, as his readers, no matter their race, are immersed in the daily joys as well as the centuries of sorrows of the American Indians he portrays. Thus, when at the end of the novel the smoke of Alexie's humor and magic has cleared, the fires of his people's tragedies—the slaughtered horses, the suicides, the terminal alcoholism—are left to blaze, and the reader's tears may flow like musical rain, which and might one day, over the centuries to come, even redeem the irrevocable sins of the American nation against this continent's first peoples.

Source: Michael Allen Holmes, Critical Essay on *Reservation Blues*, in *Novels for Students*, Gale, Cengage Learning, 2010.

AT LEAST IN FICTION YOU CAN LIE AND SORT OF JUSTIFY YOUR DELUSION ABOUT YOUR "EPICNESS." BUT WHEN YOU'RE WRITING A MEMOIR, YOU'RE TRYING TO MAKE YOUR LIFE EPIC AND IT'S NOT— NOBODY'S LIFE IS...."

Joelle Fraser

In the following excerpt from an interview with Fraser, Alexie shares his perspectives on issues of race, gender, society, and the media and discusses his writing process and preferred genres.

On a rare sunny Seattle day, Sherman Alexie's manager offered me my choice of soda or bottled water and gave me a tour of Alexie's three-room office, a good-looking rooftop space with a deck that overlooks the tony community of Bellevue. Some worlds may contrast more starkly with Alexie's boyhood home on the Coeur d'Alene Indian Reservation, but not many.

Alexie arrived late, comfortable in cotton, hair pulled back in a loose ponytail. As we introduced ourselves his smile hid a sense of weary obligation—this poet, fiction writer and filmmaker has many projects to promote. Though he became quite friendly after a few questions, at first his manner seemed to suggest, "Let's get to it."

[Fraser]: You're called "the future of American fiction" by the New Yorker.

[*Alexie*]: It's because they needed a brown guy. They had five of us I think. A guy asked me how do you feel about there being so few white men on the (1996) *Granta* list. I said there were 11 out of 20: how could that be 'few'? And 16 overall were white! I got all sorts of grief for being on the *Granta* list by the way. Like I didn't belong on it—

You only had Reservation Blues *then. What about the response to the* New Yorker *list?*

Everybody's really happy with it.

You've earned your place?

Yeah I guess. I'm an important brown guy now. (Laughs). Being different helps. I'm not going to deny that it helps a lot. I mean the work has to be good, but the fact that I'm different makes it more attractive to magazines.

So you grant that?

Oh yeah. I'm a firm believer in affirmative action—nobody unqualified ever gets a job through affirmative action. Maybe less qualified, but not unqualified. Certainly I might get on lists or get opportunities because I'm different, because I'm Indian.

And it doesn't bother you?

No! Hell no! Reparation. (Laughs). Nobody white is getting anything because they're white. It doesn't happen in the literary world, never, never once has a white guy gotten more because he's white. But then you have that cabal of New York writers, young good-looking New York literary boys, and they have their own sense of entitlement. I'm not anywhere near that stuff....

You've said of writers who aren't Indian, like McMurtry, that they shouldn't write about Indians.

Not exactly.

Clarify that.

At the beginning it was probably that but it's changed. People can write whatever they want—people accuse me of censorship when I say these things. But what I really want to say is that we should be talking about these books, written about Indians by non-Indians, honestly and accurately. I mean, they're outsider books. They're colonial books. Barbara Kingsolver's novels are colonial literature. Larry McMurtry's books are colonial literature. These are books by members of the privileged, of the powerful, writing about the culture that has been colonized. This is no different than Nadine Gordimer, who's a colonial writer, and she would call herself that.

So I think this illusion of democracy in the country—it's the best country in the world—but this illusion allows artists to believe that it isn't a colony. When it still is. The United States and South Africa: the only difference is about 50 years, not even that much. And people forget that. So when McMurtry does what he does, he thinks he's being democratic, but he's actually being colonial. I wish we could talk about the literature in those terms, beyond the quality of it, but actually talking about in terms of "hey this person doesn't know this—it's completely a work of imagination."

How does this compare to, say, occupying the other gender?

(Laughs). Oh that's the same thing.

You've done that, and written from a white person's view, too.

Well, I know a lot more about being white—because I have to, I live in the white world. A white person doesn't live in the Indian world. I have to be white every day.

What about your female characters?

I'm not a woman. (Laughs). Never was. I think often my characters, outside of Spokane Indian guys, are often a little bit thin because I have a difficult time getting into them and getting to know them. My white people often end up being sort of "cardboardy"—which is thematically all right—but it isn't necessarily my original purpose. I just get uncomfortable writing about them.

Really. Is that something you're trying to develop and work on?

Yeah, I'm trying to become a better writer. I think in the end I'll get closer to that. . . .

You've said having come from a matriarchal culture gives you more insight.

I think it helps. And I give my stuff to the women around me. 'Does this work?' I spend my whole life around women—I should know something. If I don't know it, I ask. It has to be a conscious effort. It's too easy to fall back on stereotypes and myths, and I think that's what most writers do about Indians and what most men do when they write about women.

So you're conscious of it. . . .

I'm conscious of the fact that I mythologize. (Laughs). I'm still a caveman. I just like to think of myself as a sensitive caveman.

Going back to your growth as a writer, as you develop and gain facility—you're getting better technically, for example—do you fear that you'll lose some of that tension that comes from being a struggling new writer?

My friend Donna, who helps me edit, we talk about this. When I first started, my grammar was atrocious, but she said that often people don't care when so-called "unprivileged people's" grammar is atrocious because it's part of the "voice." And they account for it in that way.

In fact readers might think it's "appropriate."

When in fact it's just bad grammar. It's the result of a poor education. But I'm better now. Most of my sentence fragments now are intentional. (Laughs).

What did your parents expect you to be?

Oh God. Alive. In their fondest hopes. I'm the first member of my family—that's extended—who's graduated from college. No one else has since. I was a very bright kid; I was a little prodigy in all sorts of ways. There were friends and family telling me I was going to be a doctor or a lawyer. Nobody predicted I would be doing this, including me.

So you didn't have a sense of yourself as a writer until college?

Right. I wrote and I loved reading, and brown guys—you're supposed to be Jesus, saving the world with law or medicine.

And with writing can you save the world?

You can do more than a doctor or a lawyer can. If I were a doctor nobody would be inviting me to talk to reservations. I'd be a different person. Writers can influence more people.

Can poetry change the direction of society?

I don't know. A lot of people are reading my poems and other people's poems because of me. This 55-year-old white guy at a reading said, 'I never got poems, I hated them, and then I read your book and liked them, and now I'm reading all sorts of poems.' And that's great. If I can be a doorway. . . .

Paula Gunn Allen says of Native Americans, "We are the land." What do you think of that?

I don't buy it. For one thing, environmentalism is a luxury. Just like being a vegetarian is a luxury. When you have to worry about eating—you're not going to be worried about where the food's coming from, or who made your shoes. Poverty, whether planned or not planned, is a way of making environmentalism moot. Even this discussion is a luxury.

This interview.

You and me—doing this. Besides, Indians have no monopoly on environmentalism. That's one of the great myths. But we were subsistence livers. They're two different things. Environmentalism is a conscious choice and subsistence is the absence of choice. We had to use everything to survive. And now that we've been assimilated and colonized and we have luxuries and excesses, we're just as wasteful as other people.

But the myth persists with contemporary Indians.

Part of it is that we had a land-based theology, but all theologies are land-based. Christianity is land-based in its beginnings. I think in some ways Indians embrace it because it's a cultural or racial self-esteem issue. We're trying to find something positive that differentiates us from the dominant culture. And the best way to do that—because the US is so industrial and so wasteful—is to say, 'OK we're environmentalists' and that separates us. When in fact, we're just a part of the US as well, and the wastefulness. The average everyday Indian—he's not an environmentalist—he could give a shit. Just like the average white American. I grew up with my aunts and uncles and cousins throwing their cans out the window.

How does this tie in with literature?

You throw in a couple of birds and four directions and corn pollen and it's Native American literature, when it has nothing to do with the day-to-day lives of Indians. I want my literature to concern the daily lives of Indians. I think most Native American literature is so obsessed with nature that I don't think it has any useful purpose. It has more to do with the lyric tradition of European Americans than it does with indigenous cultures. So when an Indian writes a poem about a tree, I think: 'It's already been done!' And those white guys are going to do it better than you. Nobody can write about a tree like a white guy.

Now why is that?

I don't know. They've been doing it longer.

I'd like to see what you'd write about a tree.

I'm not even interested! I'm interested in people. I think most native literature is concerned with place because they tell us to be. That's the myth. I think it's detrimental. I think most Native American literature is unreadable by the vast majority of Native Americans.

It's not reaching the people.

If it's not tribal, if it's not accessible to Indians, then how can it be Native American literature? I think about it all the time. Tonight I'll look up from the reading and 95% of the people in the crowd will be white. There's something wrong with my not reaching Indians.

But there's the ratio of whites to Indians.

Yeah. But I factor that in and realize there still should be more Indians. I always think that. Generally speaking Indians don't read books. It's not a book culture. That's why I'm trying to make movies. Indians go to movies; Indians own VCRs.

And maybe they'll read your books after.

I'm trying to do that—sneak up on them.

This is what your purpose is—to reach Indian people?

It's selfish in the sense that we haven't had our Emily Dickinson or Walt Whitman; we haven't had our Shakespeare or Denis Johnson or James Wright. We haven't written a book that can compare to the best white novel. But they're out there. There's a kid out there, some boy or girl who will be that great writer, and hopefully they'll see what I do and get inspired by that.

There are many celebrated Indian writers—

But we haven't written anything even close to Faulkner or Hemingway or Jane Austen. Not yet. Of course, white people are about 30, 40 generations ahead in terms of writing. It'll happen. I meet young people all the time, email a lot of kids. The percentage of Indian kids doing some sort of artistic work is much higher than in the general population—painting, drawing, dancing, singing. The creation of art is still an everyday part of our culture, unlike the dominant culture, where art is sort of peripheral. It's not a big leap from a kid who dances to a kid who writes poems. It's the same impulse. It just needs a little push.

What about writing programs, teaching? You don't teach college students, but do you have opinions on MFA programs, on artists' colonies?

I think the summer stuff is just the place where writers go to get laid. You can't teach anything in a week or two.

What about a writing program like Iowa?

Yeah, that's fine. That's dedicated internship. But a summer thing? I've done two, both for friends. People do them because they need the money, and/or to get laid—because they will. Dedicated writers don't go—they're in MFA programs or they already have books. These people who attend the conferences and colonies are very privileged, mostly women, groupie types. They exist so ugly white guys get laid. (Laughs).

Ouch. You don't mind this going out?

No! It's true! Only in rock music and the literary world do you see so many ugly white guys with beautiful women. That says a lot about the women, their character. They're attracted to more than surface.

Will you ever get an academic position?

I hope not. I don't want a real job of any variety. I don't want to have to get up in the morning, that's what it comes down to. Work is not the issue; I don't want the structure.

Is it hard for you to switch hats, from poetry to screenplays to fiction? Some people might say you're trying to find your genre.

It's all the same. It's just telling stories. It's not like I think about it separately. . . .

So what's the future for you?

I don't know. I know I'll keep writing poems. That's the constant. I don't know about novels. They're hard. It takes so much concentrated effort. When I'm writing a novel it's pretty much all I can do. I get bored. It takes months. I wrote *Res Blues* in about 4 months, *Indian Killer* in about 6. Movies do the same thing. *Smoke Signals* was 14 months, and that's quick. It's all-encompassing. It feels like I'm going to end up writing poems, short stories and screenplays. I'll continue to work for studios, honestly because it's enormous sums of money and I'll use one project to finance the other. Some people teach; I write screenplays. One's a lot more lucrative.

What about memoir?

In the end you are sort of responsible to the truth, and I like to lie. (Laughs). I'm 33, and as much as I talked about it, it doesn't matter whether you're 25 or 45, not a whole lot has gone on; the journey I'm on is pretty young. And I've rarely read a memoir that wasn't masturbatory. In a sense, you're always mythologizing your life; it's always an effort to make yourself epic. At least in fiction you can lie and sort of justify your delusion about your "epicness." But when you're writing a memoir, you're trying to make your life epic and it's not—nobody's life is. . . .

In your poem, "Capital Punishment," the refrain is "I am not a witness"—but it seems like you are.

I guess a witness is all I am. I think as a writer, you're pretty removed. As much as I talk about tribe or belonging—you don't, really. Writing is a very selfish, individualistic pursuit. So in that sense I'm a witness because I'm not participating.

And literally, you're in Seattle and you're a witness on your old life on the reservation, on the other side of the state.

Yes, I'm not there. And I'm not in the writing world; I'm outside a lot of circles.

Whom do you connect with?

With young people—one of the things I like to do is watch MTV, even though I don't like much of the music, I try to pay attention to what's in their lives.

What's your take on TV?

They've been screaming about the death of literacy for years, but I think TV is the Gutenberg press. I think TV is the only thing that keeps us vaguely in democracy even if it's in the hands of the corporate culture. If you're an artist you write in your time. Moaning about the fact that maybe people read more books a hundred years ago—that's not true. I think the same percentage has always read.

So you're not worried about the culture. You're not worried about video games—

No. Not at all. (Laughs).

A lot of people are, it seems . . .

People also thought Elvis Presley was the end of the world. (Laughs).

You do use a lot of pop cultural references in your work.

It's the cultural currency. Superman means something different to me than it does to a white guy from Ames, Iowa or New York City or L.A. It's a way for us to sit at the same table. I use pop culture like most poets use Latin. (Laughs). They want to find out how smart they are—or, they think they're being "universal."

You said once that universality is a misnomer, that it's really a Western sense of the word.

Well, when people say universal they mean white people get it.

What about Smoke Signals' universal themes of grief, and loss and coming to terms with death?

That's an appropriate way to talk about it, saying universal themes. But some people call the whole work universal. That's wrong. And even if there are universal themes, it's within a very specific experience and character. And that's what made it good. It was promoted as the first feature film written, directed and produced by Native Americans to ever receive distribution, and reviewers would fall all over themselves trying to discount that, saying 'that doesn't really matter. Who cares.' Of course it matters. It matters, and it's good, and it is what it is precisely because of that specificity. So "universal" is often a way to negate the particularity of a project, of an art. I hate that term; it's insulting. I don't want to be universal.

But do you want to touch people who will say, "I've felt that too"?

Yeah, but the thing is, people always told me their story. They didn't say, 'This made me feel like 100 other people.' The creation is specific and the response is specific. Good art is specific. Godzilla is universal. A piece [. . .] like that plays all over the world. Then you know you got a problem.

Along those lines, I'm wondering about a seeming paradox. You often say during readings and talks that you want to honor your culture's privacy, and yet your work is so public. It seems like you protect it and expose it at the same time. There's a tension created.

Yes, of course there is. One of the ways I've dealt with it is that I don't write about anything sacred. I don't write about any ceremonies; I don't use any Indian songs.

True. You mention sweat lodges but only obliquely. I'm thinking of the image of the old woman in the poem who emerges from the sweat lodge.

Yes, I'm outside the sweat lodge. In *Reservation Blues* I'm in it and I realized I didn't like it. I approach my writing the same way I approach my life. It's what I've been taught and how I behave with regard to my spirituality.

How do you draw the line as to what is off limits?

My tribe drew that line for me a long time ago. It's not written down, but I know it. If you're Catholic you wouldn't tell anybody about the confessional. I feel a heavy personal responsibility, and I accept it, and I honor it. It's part of the beauty of my culture. I've been called fascist a couple of times, at panels. I've censored myself. I've written things that I have since known to be wrong.

What kind of things . . . I guess you can't say.

(Laughs). All I can say is that I've written about cultural events inappropriately.

How did you know?

The people involved told me. After considering it, I realized they were right. In a few instances. Not every instance, but in a few. I can't take them out of what they're in, but I'm not going to republish them, or perform them in public, no anthologizing: they've died for me. There are Indian writers who write about things they aren't supposed to. They know. They'll pay for it. I'm a firm believer in what people call 'karma.' Even some of the writing I really admire, like Leslie Silko's *Ceremony*, steps on all sorts of sacred toes. I wouldn't go near that kind of writing. I'd be afraid of the repercussions. I write about a drunk in a bar, or a guy who plays basketball.

So the only flak you get is from individuals who say, "I think you're making fun of me." Do you try to soothe things over?

Some people are unsoothable. But I'm a nice enough guy, and I think people know that. If I weren't pissing people off I wouldn't be doing my job. I just want to piss off the right people. I try not to pick on the people who have less power than I. It's one of the guidelines of my life. And if I have, then I feel badly about it. I try to make amends.

You're only in your early thirties—and you have 12 books and two screenplays behind you. What was it like to have written so much so young and yet feel like you need to be a better writer? Do you feel like some work came out too soon?

Everything, everything! *Reservation Blues*— ooh, ooh. I'm working on the screenplay now, and I see where I could be so much better. What I could have done. I can tell you what happened. In *Reservation Blues*, the original impulse was that I can't sing, and I wanted to write a novel about somebody who could. Everyone wants to be a rock star. You get to date supermodels (it's a joke!) . . .

One of the things you said is that poetry equals anger and imagination. Do you feel like a lot of the power of your earlier work came from being a younger man full of passion and anger, and do you ever worry about that lessening as you get older and things get easier for you? That is, are you still angry, and has it changed if you are?

I could respond to that in two ways: the richest black man in the country still has a hard time getting a taxi in New York at midnight. But for me, personal success or personal privilege—I have a tremendous amount of it now—I mean I have my own [. . .] office. How many writers have that? Just to manage my life I had to hire somebody. And I'm rich. Not by Steve Forbes standards, but by Indian standards I'm the Indian Steve Forbes. I bought a TV last night because I wanted one for the office.

Are you still amazed by that?

Oh yeah. I just laugh. When I had no money, and a great book came out, I couldn't get it. I had to wait. I love the idea that I have hardcover books here and at home that I haven't read yet. That's how I view that I'm rich. I have hardcover books I may never read. (Laughs).

But even though I have success and privilege, my cousins don't. My tribe doesn't. I still get phone calls in the middle of the night—about deaths and car wrecks. I've lost uncles and cousins to violence or to slow deaths by neglect and abuse and poverty. I could try to walk away from that, to separate, but I don't. Every time I drive downtown Seattle I see dozens of homeless Indians. I would be callous beyond belief not to feel that, not to know I have cousins who are homeless in cities out there. So even if it's not happening to me directly, it's certainly happening to my family, and I have to pick up the phone. I'm incredibly privileged when I'm sitting at a typewriter, but once I get up and out of that role, I'm an Indian.

Source: Sherman Alexie and Joelle Fraser, "An Interview with Sherman Alexie," in *Iowa Review*, Vol. 30, No. 3, Winter 2000–01, pp. 59–70.

Leslie Marmon Silko

In the following essay, acclaimed author Silko examines the characters in Reservation Blues *and contends that "Alexie's talent is immense and genuine."*

When N. Scott Momaday won the Pulitzer Prize for his novel *House Made of Dawn* in 1969, book reviewers fretted that the experience of Indian reservations was too far out of the "American mainstream" for most readers; by now, such expressions of concern should seem quaint. Since 1969, the "global economy" has brought changes; now a good deal of urban and suburban United States has begun to resemble one giant government reservation—clear-cut, strip-mined then abandoned not just by Peabody Coal and General Motors but by Wal-Mart too—where massive unemployment and hopelessness trigger suicide and murder. As the good jobs have gone

> THE POWER OF HIS WRITING RISES OUT OF THE SPOKANE RIVER AND THE SPOKANE EARTH WHERE IT IS SWEETENED WITH THE MUSIC OF ROBERT JOHNSON, HANK WILLIAMS, ELVIS PRESLEY, JANIS JOPLIN AND JIMI HENDRIX."

the way of the great herds of buffalo, the United States has become a nation of gamblers. Suddenly Indian writers are not "writing from the margins" of U.S. culture, they are writing from the center of the front page.

Thanks to Bishop Landa and his thugs, who burned the great libraries of the Americas in 1540, we know very little about the early literatures of the Americas. But it is clear from oral narratives that lengthy "fictions" of interlinked characters and events were commonplace. So it should come as no surprise that voices such as Linda Hogan, Betty Louise Bell, Ray Young Bear, Greg Sarris and Adrian C. Louis are emerging.

Another of these writers, Sherman Alexie, has swept onto the publishing scene with poems and short stories that dazzle with wicked humor, lean, fresh language and deep affection for his characters. His collection of interlinked short stories, *The Lone Ranger and Tonto Fist Fight in Heaven*, won a number of prizes, including the PEN/Hemingway Award for best first book. My favorite story in that collection is titled "Because My Father Always Said He Was the Only Indian Who Saw Jimi Hendrix Play 'The Star-Spangled Banner' at Woodstock." In *The Business of Fancydancing*, Alexie's characters from the Spokane reservation stop off in Reno. With their last dollars they hit the jackpot and live it up for about twenty-four hours before they lose it all again. The old American Dream: Hit the jackpot, win the lottery, bingo big.

Now Alexie's first novel, *Reservation Blues*, focuses on the American Dream and the price of success. All over the world in rural communities, young people share similar dreams, stirred by the same images beamed in by satellite TV and by the same lyrics of rock and roll music. Youth in this "global village" share similar discouragement too—unemployment, hunger and aborted attempts to escape their hopeless situation.

The characters in *Reservation Blues* have been out of high school for a few years. Their home is a small Indian town on the Spokane reservation with dead-end jobs and shared poverty and sadness to look forward to. The Spokane people still watch out for one another like one big family, except sometimes this big family seems a bit dysfunctional. (Of course, a dysfunctional family is still better than no family at all.) But for the rural landscape and the strong sense of tribal identity, Alexie's Spokane Indian town of Wellpinit could be a neighborhood in East L.A. or the Bronx; except the Spokane people use car wrecks and cheap wine, not drive-by shootings and crack, to make their escape. Reservation housing and inner-city housing are quite similar:

> Thomas still lived in the government HUD house where he had grown up. It was a huge house by reservation standards...however, the house had never really been finished because the Bureau of Indian Affairs cut off the building money halfway through construction. The water pipes froze every winter, and windows warped in the hot summer heat.

So while Alexie writes about the "Spokane Indian reservation," the reader begins to realize that poverty in the United States has common denominators. Take the powdered milk that connects poor rural communities and poor urban areas all over the country:

> No matter how long an Indian stirred her commodity milk, it always came out with those lumps of coagulated powder. There was nothing worse. Those lumps were like bombs, moist on the outside with an inner core of dry powdered milk. An Indian would take a big swig of milk, and one of those coagulated powder bombs would drop into her mouth and explode when she bit it. She'd be coughing little puffs of powdered milk for an hour.

But Sherman Alexie doesn't limit his world to a single, corporeal dimension; Shakespeare and Henry James use ghosts, and he does too. Blues guitarist Robert Johnson walks into Wellpinit, having faked his death by poison years before so he could find out how to undo the deal he made with the old "Gentleman," the Devil got up as a well-dressed white man. He's been told there is a large woman on a mountaintop somewhere who can help him. Thomas Builds-the-Fire gives Johnson a ride up the sacred mountain where Big Mom lives; Big Mom is part of God but she's not God herself.

Later, Thomas notices that Johnson left behind his guitar in the van. When his friend Victor touches the guitar, it makes wonderful music despite his lack of skill. Victor "wanted to resist all of it, but the guitar moved in his hands, whispered his name. Victor closed his eyes and found himself in a dark place. 'Don't play for them. Play for me,' said a strange voice." This is the Devil's guitar; by the time Victor stopped playing, "his hair stood on end, his shirt pitted with burn holes and his hands blistered."

The Devil guitar seduces them, and Thomas, Victor and Junior, with Chess and Checkers as backup, form a rock and roll band named Coyote Springs. They dream of modest success—to open for Aerosmith at Madison Square Garden and make a little money; here the "American Dream" has been downscaled. This being an Indian reservation, everyone has an opinion about Coyote Springs: Christian churchgoers call their efforts Devil music (which in this case is literally true); the tribal chairman is jealous and yearns to find any excuse to arrest them. But "gossip about the band spread from reservation to reservation. All kinds of Indians showed up: Yakima, Lummi, Makah, Snohomish, Coeur d'Alene. Thomas and his band had developed a small following before they ever played a gig."

With the sounds from the Devil guitar, Coyote Springs wins a battle of the bands in Seattle, and record company executives pounce on them with a recording contract and studio time in New York City. These New York record company executives are named Sheridan and Wright—names of the two U.S. Army generals who fought the Spokane people and slaughtered thousands of Spokane horses in cold blood. Chess and Checkers, the young backup singers from the Flathead reservation, begin to have their doubts about the price Coyote Springs may have to pay for success, but Thomas, Victor and Junior know only that rock and roll stardom is calling them. They've got only one more number to go and they'll "bingo big"; all they have to do is make the demo tape in New York! Suddenly the pressure is on:

> We have to come back as heroes. They won't let us back on this reservation if we ain't heroes. Unless we're rock stars. We already left once, and all the Spokanes hate us for it.... What if we screw up in New York and every Indian everywhere hates us? What if they won't let us on any reservation in the country?

Alexie may use an image from Indian culture, the gambler's sticks, but the meaning is clear: "If an Indian chose the correct hand, he won everything, he won all the sticks. If an Indian chose wrong, he never got to play again. Coyote Springs had only one dream, one chance to choose the correct hand."

The atmosphere of the recording studio, however, leaves a lot to be desired. The fiery Sheridan says of Coyote Springs and their music: "They don't need to be good. They just need to make money. I don't give a fuck if they're artists. Where are all the executives who signed artists? They're working at radio stations now, right?" Not even the Devil guitar can endure this. Coyote Springs is playing along just fine when suddenly Robert Johnson's haunted guitar twists itself out of Victor's hands and spoils the take. Victor loses his temper and tears apart the recording studio. Coyote Springs is finished and so is the dream.

With guys like Sheridan and Wright running the music business, the Devil guitar probably does these young Indians a favor by breaking up the recording session. But this is one area of the novel that is a bit fuzzy. There is ambivalence throughout toward the guitar, toward a talent or gift that consumes individuals and calls them away from the community. Alexie's version of Robert Johnson, on the run to escape the music, his hands burned and scarred by the guitar, casts an ominous light on talent. A gift for making music or for writing sets you apart from others, family and friends, whether you want this distance or not. Alexie wrestles with the conundrum: Did their gift for music kill Jimi Hendrix and Janis Joplin or did the music sustain them and lengthen their time in this world? Is it better to throw away your guitar or word processor and live an ordinary life? Will you be happier?

Coyote Springs' members return to the Spokane reservation, but everything has been changed by their brush with success. Junior commits suicide, as he probably always meant to. His ghost visits Victor and says he just got tired of living. The ghost helps Victor throw away the liquor bottle, but when Victor tries to get a job to save himself, his own uncle, the pompous tribal chairman, writes him off. Victor seems bound to join Junior in the other world. Only Thomas and Chess, who are in love, and Checkers, who loves them, survive the crushed dream. Again there is a whiff of ambivalence about success in the "mainstream" world. Big Mom hadn't wanted them to go to New York

in the first place—the implication being that music should be made for people, for the community, not for record companies.

Yet it is clear that having a shot at success means a great deal. Thomas is infuriated when he learns that the only musicians who get a big recording contract and realize the American Dream are the two young white women, Betty and Veronica, who once sang backup for Coyote Springs. The record company executives Sheridan and Wright decided they needed "a more reliable kind" of Indian. "Basically, we need Indians such as yourselves," they tell the two young white women, who reply, "But we ain't that much Indian." "You're Indian enough, right? I mean, all it takes is a little bit, right? Who's to say you are not Indian enough? . . . What it comes down to is this. You play for this company as Indians. Or you don't play at all. I mean, who needs another white-girl folk group?" When Betty and Veronica send Thomas a copy of their first album, he furiously destroys the tape.

Yet Alexie's characters are young, still learning; with the blessing of Big Mom and the citizens of Wellpinit, the remaining former members of the rock band decide to leave the reservation for a while. The town of Spokane isn't far from the reservation, and the phone company is hiring—just as it might be. If we Indians do not "represent" our communities as we see them, then others, the likes of Sheridan and Wright, will concoct fantasies that pass for truth. Unlike the bucolic idylls of small-town America pawned off by, say, Garrison Keillor, Alexie's portrayal of the reservation town of Wellpinit and its people is in the tradition of communities evoked in *The Scarlet Letter*, *Babbitt*, *Sanctuary* and *The Last Picture Show*. These small towns are like the old cat who eats her kittens.

It is difficult not to imagine *Reservation Blues* as a reflection of the ambivalence that a young, gifted author might have about "success" in the ruthless, greed-driven world of big publishing, where executives very much resemble cavalry generals. He may feel the same pressure the members of Coyote Springs felt to come home to the reservation a "hero." At the same time, small communities, Indian and non-Indian alike, are ambivalent about the success of one of their own. There is bound to be a bit of jealousy, and maybe even those who mutter that they prefer anonymity for their community.

Make no mistake: Alexie's talent is immense and genuine, and needs no Devil's typewriter. The power of his writing rises out of the Spokane River and the Spokane earth where it is sweetened with the music of Robert Johnson, Hank Williams, Elvis Presley, Janis Joplin and Jimi Hendrix. On this big Indian reservation we call "the United States," Sherman Alexie is one of the best writers we have.

Source: Leslie Marmon Silko, "Big Bingo," in *Nation*, Vol. 260, No. 23, June 12, 1995, pp. 856–58, 860.

Abigail Davis

In the following review, Davis praises Reservation Blues *for its masterful plot and effective narrative style.*

This first novel by Sherman Alexie [*Reservation Blues*] comes as close to helping a non-Native American understand the modern Indian experience as any attempt in current literature. The reader closes the book feeling troubled, hurt, hopeful, profoundly thoughtful, and somehow exhausted, as if the quest of the characters had been a personal experience.

Alexie, a 28-year-old Spokane/Coeur d'Alene Indian raised on the Spokane Indian Reservation, is a powerfully prolific writer whose earlier works have received much attention. *The Business of Fancydancing* (1992), a collection of poems and stories, was named a *New York Times* Notable Book for 1992; Alexie is a citation winner for the PEN/Hemingway Award for Best First Book of Fiction and winner of the 1994 Lila Wallace-Reader's Digest Writers' Award.

Reservation Blues chronicles the career of an Indian rock group called Coyote Springs. The three male members, Thomas Builds-the-Fire, Junior Polatkin, and Victor Joseph, are from the Spokane Indian Reservation in Wellpinit; two women vocalists, Chess and Checkers Warm Water, are members of the Flathead tribe. When, for a brief time, two white groupies (who are into Indian men rather than musicians) join the band as backup singers, all [. . .] breaks loose. The group evolves rather than forms, and with little or no direction or planning moves from playing reservation bars to a club in Seattle to a potential recording contract in New York. Readers of Alexie's previous collections of poems and stories—*The Lone Ranger and Tonto Fistfight in Heaven* (1994), *First Indian on the Moon* (1994), and *The Business of Fancydancing* (1992)—will recognize some familiar characters, and will most significantly be alert to Alexie's unmistakable narrative voice, which, as always, is laced with humor and anger and driven by great intelligence.

As musicians, Coyote Springs puts the "a" in amateur. Their burgeoning skills and subsequent success are due to a mystical guitar—clearly a tool of the devil—that was once owned by blues legend Robert Johnson, who was said to be murdered in 1938. Johnson allegedly sold his soul Faust-style for his talent, and his appearance as a living character in Alexie's story is significant. Johnson is still trying to "lose" the guitar and escape its grip. In Alexie's version of the Faust legend, the devil tells Johnson that he has to give up "whatever you love the most" in exchange for superhuman musical ability. Johnson sacrifices his freedom (*not* his soul), and until the guitar finds a new "owner" (in this case, Victor Joseph, lead guitarist for Coyote Springs), Johnson is trapped. Alexie gives the theme of evil as a pandemic and enduring force a new twist when Victor cuts his own deal with the devil and, presented with the same choice as Johnson, sacrifices his best friend. Unlike those who addressed the theme before him—authors Marlowe and Goethe, composers Berlioz and Liszt—Alexie seems to find the loss of freedom and friendship more serious and dangerous than the loss of one's own soul; or perhaps we are meant to understand that the three are intrinsically interconnected, symbiotic, and that the human experience is more complex than even Goethe thought.

Alexie is a plot magician, and the actual story of the musical escapades of Coyote Springs is but a fraction of this complex book. The narrative contains traditional dialogue along with songs and poems, dreams, visions, newspaper excerpts, charismatic characters, an Indian (and, to my mind, improved) version of the Faust legend, several well-placed whacks at missionary and Catholic Christianity, as well as some riotously funny scenes. The collective impact of these various narrative devices is startling; layer after layer, we are pulled into the fractured experiences and spiritual lives of the characters. We (and here I speak as an outsider to the experiences that Alexie writes about so vividly) are jarred into any number of acknowledgments: that reservation life includes a cruel Catch-22, whereby the people who leave the reservation to break the cycle of dependency on the U.S. government are considered traitors by those who stay; that prejudices between tribes are just as virulent and hostile as the racist attitudes that infect other areas of American society; that life for mixed-blood children is the same hell on the reservation as it is in most other places for most races. "*Your son will be beaten because he's a half-breed*," Chess says to a vision of a white woman and half-Indian child.

> No matter what he does, he'll never be Indian enough. Other Indians won't accept him.... Don't you see?...Those quarter-blood and eighth-blood grandchildren will find out they're Indian and torment the rest of us real Indians.... [They] will get all the Indian jobs, all the Indian chances, because they look white. Because they're safer.

Alexie casts a wide net, and in *Reservation Blues* his narrative style is a highly effective combination of all the prose forms. In chronicling the pain and progress of one five-person, mixed-tribe rock band, Alexie has, miraculously, managed to speak to all of us.

Source: Abigail Davis, "Review of *Reservation Blues*," in *Bloomsbury Review*, Vol. 15, No. 4, July–August 1995, p. 16.

SOURCES

Alexie, Sherman, *Reservation Blues*, Grove Press, 1995.

Belcher, Wendy, "Conjuring the Colonizer: Alternative Readings of Magic Realism in Sherman Alexie's *Reservation Blues*," in *American Indian Culture and Research Journal*, Vol. 31, No. 2, 2007, pp. 87–101.

Bird, Gloria, "The Exaggeration of Despair in Sherman Alexie's *Reservation Blues*," in *Wicazo Sa Review*, Vol. 11, No. 2, Fall 1995, pp. 47–52.

Cox, James, "Muting White Noise: The Subversion of Popular Culture Narratives of Conquest in Sherman Alexie's Fiction," in *Studies in American Indian Literatures*, Vol. 9, No. 4, Winter 1997, pp. 52–70.

Cutter, Martha J., *Lost and Found in Translation: Contemporary Ethnic American Writing and the Politics of Language Diversity*, University of North Carolina Press, 2005, pp. 124–130.

Davis, Abigail, Review of *Reservation Blues*, in *Bloomsbury Review*, Vol. 15, No. 4, July-August 1995, p. 16.

Evans, Stephen F., "'Open Containers': Sherman Alexie's Drunken Indians," in *American Indian Quarterly*, Vol. 25, No. 1, Winter 2001, pp. 46–73.

Grassian, Daniel, *Understanding Sherman Alexie*, University of South Carolina Press, 2005.

Highway, Tomson, and Sherman Alexie, "Spokane Words," in *Aboriginal Voices*, January-March 1997, http://www.fallsapart.com/art-av.html (accessed May 24, 2009).

Klinkenborg, Verlyn, "America at the Crossroads: Life on the Spokane Reservation," Review of *Reservation Blues*, in *Los Angeles Times Book Review*, June 18, 1995.

Meredith, Howard, "Review of *Reservation Blues*," in *World Literature Today*, Vol. 70, No. 2, Spring 1996, p. 446.

Pasquaretta, Paul, "African-Native American Subjectivity and the Blues Voice in the Writings of Toni Morrison and Sherman Alexie," in *When Brer Rabbit Meets Coyote: African-Native American Literature*, edited by Jonathan Brennan, University of Illinois Press, 2003, pp. 278–91.

Pearson, Barry Lee, and Bill McCulloch, *Robert Johnson: Lost and Found*, University of Illinois Press, 2003, pp. 1–4.

Quirk, Sarah A., "Sherman Alexie," in *Dictionary of Literary Biography*, Vol. 278, *American Novelists since World War II, Seventh Series*, edited by James R. Giles and Wanda H. Giles, Thomson Gale, 2003, pp. 3–10.

Ruby, Robert H., and John A. Brown, *The Spokane Indians: Children of the Sun*, University of Oklahoma Press, 2006.

Schroeder, Patricia R., *Robert Johnson, Mythmaking, and Contemporary American Culture*, University of Illinois Press, 2004, pp. 121–27.

Silko, Leslie Marmon, "Big Bingo," Review of *Reservation Blues*, in *Nation*, Vol. 260, No. 23, June 12, 1995, pp. 856–58, 860.

Tellefsen, Blythe, "America Is a Diet Pepsi: Sherman Alexie's *Reservation Blues*," in *Western American Literature*, Vol. 40, No. 2, Summer 2005, pp. 125–47.

FURTHER READING

Crisp, Tony, *Dream Dictionary: An A to Z Guide to Understanding Your Unconscious Mind*, Gramercy Books, 2005.
> In this recently revised work, Crisp, a dream therapist, draws on more than twenty years of dream research to help the reader understand his or her own dreams.

Palmer, Robert, *Deep Blues: A Musical and Cultural History of the Mississippi Delta*, Penguin, 1982.
> Palmer focuses on the roots of the blues as it was played by the earliest African American practitioners, including Robert Johnson, in the Mississippi Delta region.

Ratliff, Ben, *The Jazz Ear: Conversations over Music*, Times Books, 2008.
> This volume contains interviews by Ratliff with famous jazz artists in which they listen to songs and discuss their appreciation for the music.

Zinn, Howard, *A People's History of the United States: 1492–Present*, HarperCollins, 2003.
> In this extraordinarily honest and comprehensive volume, Zinn presents the history of America largely from the perspective of the oppressed, including African Americans and American Indians.

The Scarlet Pimpernel

EMMUSKA ORCZY

1905

The Scarlet Pimpernel, an archetypal adventure tale by Baroness Emmuska Orczy set in the period leading up to the French Revolution's Reign of Terror, was produced as a play before being published as a novel in 1905, with resounding success. Capturing the popular imagination, the work spawned a successful series for its author and has been repeatedly adapted for film and television—also recently becoming a Broadway musical—in the century since its publication. The story's renown can be attributed to its highly original notion of a superhero with a secret identity, adapted by many later writers; its well choreographed dialogue and plot, reflecting Orczy's greater critical success as an author of detective fiction; and the suspenseful pace, fueled by the ever-present urgency and danger characteristic of revolution.

In contrast to the swordplay and violence of the film versions, the novel features little actual action and derives much of its power from the theatrical strength of the characters. The Scarlet Pimpernel, the character for whom the work is named, is of course designed to be the source of most of the intrigue; his identity is revealed halfway through the novel, under circumstances that allow for a strikingly gradual revelation on the part of both his wife, Lady Blakeney (Marguerite), and the reader. Percy Blakeney's classical heroic qualities are well masked by seeming laziness, foolishness, and even stupidity. Marguerite, in turn, not only provides the eyes and ears

Baroness Emmuska Orczy (© Hulton-Deutsch Collection / Corbis)

through which the reader follows most of the plot but also serves as a primary agent of narrative action. Her decisions, which are comprehensively examined under a moral lens, are what drive the tale. By the end of the novel, only a cynically detached reader could fail to feel sympathy for the hero and heroine and to rejoice in their ethical and humanitarian success.

AUTHOR BIOGRAPHY

Emmuska Magdalena Rosalia Maria Josefa Barbara Orczy was born on September 23, 1865, in Tarna-Örs, Hungary. Her father, Baron Felix Orczy, was a conductor and composer and owned a significant estate, worked by peasants. Baron Orczy sought to modernize his farming operations by introducing machinery, but the peasants resisted, out of both superstition and concern for their livelihood. When Emmuska (also called Emma) was only three, during a party for her five-year-old sister, the peasants burned down the estate, inducing the family to leave the estate. Drifting through western Europe over the years, they stayed in Budapest, Brussels, and Paris before ending up in London when Orczy was fifteen.

Through her schooling, Orczy found herself leaning toward the arts, in part because her father's aristocratic standards did not leave much room for his daughters to pursue other sorts of careers. Her father encouraged interest in music, but she did not have a gifted ear; she instead developed a love for painting and

drawing but eventually focused professionally on writing. As she details in her autobiography, *Links in the Chain of Life* (1947), Orczy learned much about the craft of storytelling through her devotion to attending the theater. As noted by Sarah Juliette Sasson in her introduction to *The Scarlet Pimpernel*, Orczy professes being especially fond of the "unsophisticated productions," at which crowds tended to be more casually and honestly responsive to the onstage action—often quite vocally—allowing her to study the effects of the various turns of tales on audiences.

In the early stages of her career, Orczy penned detective stories, some published in *Royal Magazine*, and a pair of novels. The first, *The Emperor's Candlesticks* (1899), being received poorly and the next, *In Mary's Reign* (1901), faring decently. Then, one day while waiting for an underground train, Orczy found herself clearly visualizing the character of Percy Blakeney, from his fashionable garments to his thin hands to his lazy manner of speech. It took quite a bit of effort to find a publisher willing to take a risk on what would become her most famous work; only after Orczy and her husband, Montague Barstow, adapted the work as a play and saw it brought to the stage in London, in 1905, did *The Scarlet Pimpernel* finally get published in book form, also in 1905. The stage version was critically panned but eventually became a success with audiences, while the novel was immediately popular.

Orczy went on to write more than a dozen Scarlet Pimpernel stories, as well as a tale of an adventurous ancestor of Blakeney's, *The Laughing Cavalier* (1913). She gained greater critical appreciation for her detective stories, particularly those featuring the title character of the 1909 collection *The Old Man in the Corner*. The old man, who reads about cases in newspapers and gets additional clues from a journalist friend, is recognized as one of literature's earliest "armchair detectives," never leaving his seat to solve mysteries. Orczy also created a similarly pioneering but less popular female detective in *Lady Molly of Scotland Yard* (1910). After a long and prolific career, having lived her last few years in her villa in Monte Carlo, Orczy died in London in 1947.

PLOT SUMMARY

Chapter I: Paris: September, 1792

As *The Scarlet Pimpernel* opens, the French Revolution's Reign of Terror is imminent, with dozens

MEDIA ADAPTATIONS

- *The Scarlet Pimpernel* was produced as a film by London Film Productions in 1934, with Harold Young directing and Leslie Howard and Merle Oberon in the lead roles.

- A television movie version of *The Scarlet Pimpernel* was produced in 1982 by Edgar J. Scherick Associates, starring Anthony Andrews and Jane Seymour, as well as Ian McKellen as Chauvelin.

- *The Scarlet Pimpernel* was produced as a television series by A&E Television starting in 1999, featuring Richard E. Grant and Elizabeth McGovern. It aired for two seasons.

- Michael Page reads an audiobook version of *The Scarlet Pimpernel* (2005), produced by Brilliance Audio.

- Another audiobook version of *The Scarlet Pimpernel*, produced by Blackstone Audio in 2007, is read by Ralph Cosham.

- The latest audiobook version of *The Scarlet Pimpernel* (2009), published by Tantor Media, is read by Wanda McCaddon.

of aristocrats being guillotined daily. Sergeant Bibot ridicules the executed Grospierre, who allowed the daring, disguised Scarlet Pimpernel to slip an aristocrat family past his watch, but then Bibot lets a frightful hag drive a covered cart through his gate—and it is the rescuer himself.

Chapter II: Dover: "The Fisherman's Rest"
In his hostel on the southeast coast of England, Jellyband discusses the turmoil in France and the effects on Britain with his patrons, including two strangers in the corner, while preparing for the arrival of nobility from across the English Channel.

Chapter III: The Refugees
After Lord Antony arrives by horse, Sir Andrew Ffoulkes escorts the comtesse de Tournay and her son and daughter into the hostel. The locals clear out, and Sir Andrew and the young Suzanne flirt while supper is prepared.

Chapter IV: The League of the Scarlet Pimpernel
One of the strangers ducks under a bench, and the other leaves; imagining themselves alone, the Englishmen and the French aristocrats freely discuss their escape and the league of the Scarlet Pimpernel, to which the two men belong. Marguerite St. Just, known to the comtesse for having denounced the executed marquis de St. Cyr, arrives by coach with her husband, Sir Percy Blakeney.

Chapter V: Marguerite
As Lady Blakeney is fairly worshipped in England, although she is hated by French aristocrats, Jellyband and the others are stunned when the comtesse insults her. Though Marguerite and Suzanne were girlhood friends, the comtesse insists that her daughter follow her out.

Chapter VI: An Exquisite of '92
Though Sir Percy is rich and irreproachable in fashion, his dull wits and lazy manner are known to be hardly worthy of his brilliant wife. The vicomte de Tournay challenges Percy to a duel over the women's discord, but Percy mocks the young man, to the others' amusement, until he stands down.

Chapter VII: The Secret Orchard
Out by the cliffs, Marguerite shares parting words with her brother, Armand St. Just, before he returns by schooner to the republican government in Paris. She reveals her estrangement from Percy, whose honor was compromised by the rumors of her denouncement of the marquis de St. Cyr.

Chapter VIII: The Accredited Agent
After watching Armand sail away, Marguerite returns toward the hostel, to be approached outside by an agent of the French government, Chauvelin. They exchange pleasantries, but then Chauvelin tries to persuade her, as a French citizen, to seek out the identity of the Scarlet Pimpernel, whom she esteems as a romantic hero. Marguerite refuses to help, despising the vicious French government's slaughter of the aristocracy.

Chapter IX: The Outrage

Lord Tony and Sir Andrew are drinking wine, seemingly alone after Jellyband and all others have gone to bed, and start discussing plans for their league to rescue next the comte de Tournay. A noise startles them, and the hidden stranger and others appear and seize the two Englishmen. Papers they are carrying reveal that Armand St. Just is a traitor to France.

Chapter X: In the Opera Box

In London, the city's most important personages are gathered at the opera. The comtesse de Tournay is advised not to quarrel with the widely respected Lady Blakeney. Arriving late, Lady Blakeney is left alone by Percy to be visited by the many who wish to see him—including Chauvelin, who relates that he has evidence against Armand that will condemn him as a traitor. He wants her to help identify the Scarlet Pimpernel at Lord Grenville's ball that evening.

Chapter XI: Lord Grenville's Ball

At the magnificent ball, Chauvelin is shunned by the royalist British high society, including the Prince of Wales, who praises Lady Blakeney before the comtesse. A laughable comment by Percy eases the tension.

Chapter XII: The Scrap of Paper

With a few lines of petty verse by Percy being echoed around the room, Marguerite notices a note being passed to Sir Andrew. She follows him into the boudoir (his private room), where he is reading the note by candlelight. She sneaks behind him, and when he turns she pretends to swoon—then swipes the note as he is burning it, as if the burnt-paper odor is a remedy. As he tries to retrieve the note she knocks the candles over and then reads the note as he quickly puts out the fire. She pretends to believe the note an illicit love missive.

Chapter XIII: Either—Or?

Having seen that the Scarlet Pimpernel should be in the supper-room at one o'clock, Marguerite dances with Sir Andrew before being escorted to dinner by the Prince of Wales, who has been losing at dice to Sir Percy.

Chapter XIV: One o'Clock Precisely!

Marguerite speaks with Chauvelin in the boudoir, informing him of the contents of the note and asking for assurance that Armand will be spared. In the otherwise deserted supper-room, Chauvelin finds Sir Percy snoozing and lies down himself to pretend to sleep while waiting to see what will happen.

Chapter XV: Doubt

Marguerite regrets her decision to betray the Scarlet Pimpernel yet still values foremost her own brother's life. She is told by Lord Fancourt that Percy and their coach are waiting. In departing she meets Chauvelin, who relates that he saw only Sir Percy in the supper-room.

Chapter XVI: Richmond

The Blakeneys ride home in the dark, which they both much enjoy. Feeling pitiable and lonely, Marguerite meets her husband on the lawn and tries to bridge the gap of misunderstanding between them. She expresses how she aches for the happy times they once had, but Sir Percy will not put aside his resentment for her recent callous treatment; regarding her role in the death of St. Cyr, he feels that she forced him to choose between his honor and her love. Finally, though he remains cold, she begs him to keep Armand from harm—but she cannot go as far as to fully explain and confess her shameful deed of that night. He gives his word to protect Armand, and after she slips into the house, he kisses the ground she walked on.

Chapter XVII: Farewell

Marguerite retires to her chamber as dawn breaks, vowing to win back her husband's love. She nods off but is awakened by footsteps; Percy has left a note saying he is leaving for the north to deal with pressing business. She rushes out to bid him farewell as he gallops off on horseback, after which she returns inside and sleeps.

Chapter XVIII: The Mysterious Device

Awakening midday, Marguerite wanders into Percy's private office, which is surprisingly orderly. Baffled by the French maps, she finds on the floor a seal ring bearing the insignia of the Scarlet Pimpernel.

Chapter XIX: The Scarlet Pimpernel

Marguerite is dumbfounded and distracted when Suzanne arrives for the day. Finally, she realizes the truth of the situation—that her husband is indeed the daring rescuer, and that he is now in grave danger—especially since the arrival by runner of the letter revealing Armand's guilt indicates that Chauvelin is hot on Percy's trail. She bids Suzanne farewell before determining to seek Sir Andrew's aid and intercept her husband in Calais, France.

Chapter XX: The Friend

Marguerite confesses everything to the hesitant Sir Andrew, who at last agrees to offer whatever assistance she needs. They will travel separately to the Fisherman's Rest in Dover, thence to charter a schooner and cross the English Channel to France.

Chapter XXI: Suspense

Jellyband and Sally are confounded by the midnight arrival of first Lady Blakeney and then Sir Andrew dressed as a servant, but Andrew assures them of the honesty of their travel together. Meanwhile, a storm coming from the south will prevent them—as well as Chauvelin, who is traveling the same route—from setting sail until the following day.

Chapter XXII: Calais

Not until late in the day are Marguerite and Sir Andrew able to cast off and reach France, which has the feel of a nation in turmoil. They are shunned as aristocrats, even if English, around town as well as at the filthy Chat Gris tavern. At great length, the innkeeper, Brogard, serves food that is at least palatable and reveals that Percy is expected to have supper there that evening.

Chapter XXIII: Hope

Knowing that Chauvelin is on their trail less than an hour behind them, and hoping to save both Sir Percy and the men he has come to rescue, Sir Andrew steps out to seek Percy in the town while Marguerite conceals herself in the loft behind a curtain.

Chapter XXIV: The Death-Trap

Marguerite is optimistic until Chauvelin himself walks in the door, dressed as a churchman. She overhears that French patrols are everywhere about town and the beachfront is being closely watched. Wishing now above all to tell Percy how much she loves him, she hears him singing as he approaches the inn.

Chapter XXV: The Eagle and the Fox

Percy enters and quickly throws Chauvelin off guard by identifying the disguised agent even before seeing his face. Playing dumb, Percy

chats idly with Chauvelin, who anxiously awaits the return of his secretary, Desgas, with soldiers. As distant footsteps are heard, Percy fools Chauvelin into inhaling pepper; while the Frenchman suffers a sneezing fit, the Englishman slips out.

Chapter XXVI: The Jew

The enraged Chauvelin sends the arriving soldiers back out to find Percy; they locate instead an elderly Jewish man who claims that a tall Englishman rented a horse and cart from one Reuben Goldstein. Not hiding his contempt for the miserable old man, Chauvelin hires him to trail the others over the few leagues to the Père Blanchard's hut, the reported meeting place for the fugitives.

Chapter XXVII: On the Track

When the Jew and Chauvelin rumble off, Marguerite descends from the loft and trails them on foot, weary but determined. Along the road, two soldiers on horseback arrive from ahead to report that they have not seen the tall Englishman but have located the hut, where two men have arrived to wait for their rescuer. The cart rumbles onward.

Chapter XXVIII: The Père Blanchard's Hut

The cart stops at the start of the footpath leading to the hut, some eight hundred meters toward the cliffs and shore. Marguerite crawls alongside the path to hear Chauvelin instruct the many soldiers to await the tall Englishman's arrival. The Jew (whose name, Chauvelin now learns, is Benjamin Rosenbaum) protests that if left alone on the road he might ruin their plan out of fright; therefore, he is gagged and taken along. Panicking as they approach the hut, Marguerite rushes ahead intending to warn whoever is inside, but she is caught and gagged by Chauvelin.

Chapter XXIX: Trapped

With the Englishman's schooner in sight on the sea, the French soldiers wait. Chauvelin removes Marguerite's gag to allow her the choice of letting the Scarlet Pimpernel be caught, thus securing Armand's release, or warning her husband, in which case all four men now in the hut will be slain. Percy's singing voice is heard once more.

Chapter XXX: The Schooner

Unable to restrain herself, Marguerite rushes to the hut, shrieking for Armand to act and for

Percy to flee. Chauvelin's men then seize her and storm the hut—but no one is inside. A soldier confesses that they had witnessed the men in the hut escaping but did nothing—in accord with their orders to await the Englishman. The four fugitives are already out at sea, having rowed to the schooner, meaning that Percy must still be ashore. In the hut, a note indicates that Percy expects to be picked up back near Calais and the Chat Gris. Chauvelin orders the beating of the Jew, who failed to properly assist them, then leaves the Jew and Marguerite behind as he and his soldiers head back toward Calais.

Chapter XXXI: The Escape

Suddenly, Percy's voice is there with her—and Marguerite at last discovers that the Jew is none other than her husband in disguise. Having met Sir Andrew in town, he devised the plan to disguise himself so as to reach the hut, where he managed to slip instructions—and a false note to be left behind—in to the fugitives. Sir Andrew arrives on foot, and Percy carries his wife along to meet the boat that they take to board the schooner.

CHARACTERS

Sergeant Bibot

Brash and overconfident, Bibot lets a filthy hag drive her cart unchecked through the Paris gates—but the woman is the Scarlet Pimpernel, and Bibot will surely be executed for his folly.

Marguerite Blakeney

The plot revolves around the actions of Marguerite, the central protagonist. A clever French actress with Bohemian leanings, Marguerite St. Just became Lady Blakeney in marrying Sir Percy. The two grew quickly estranged, however, when Percy learned from others of her denouncement of the executed marquis de St. Cyr; she chose to test Percy's love rather than explain the circumstances and her lack of ill intent, but he felt his aristocratic British honor to be compromised. Thenceforth, he could only tepidly serve her, leaving her resentful and inclined to exploit his eccentricities to sharpen her wits. She laments her increasingly lonely marriage before Armand when he leaves for France after a few weeks' stay with her.

After Chauvelin presents Marguerite with the dilemma of either helping him find the Scarlet Pimpernel, whom she reveres (especially as a

contrast to her idle husband), or leaving Armand to be executed as a traitor to France, she can find no peace of mind. She holds her brother too dear to imagine losing him, and so she regretfully settles on aiding the conniving Chauvelin, making use of her impeccable acting skills to dupe Sir Andrew. When she realizes that she has in fact betrayed her husband, she can think only of tracking him down in France so as to warn him of his grave danger as well as to profess her undying love. Riding sentimental waves, she becomes a nervous wreck and loses sleep while waiting out the storm in Dover, then feels effusive optimism upon hearing Percy should be supping at the Chat Gris in Calais, and then despairs again when Chauvelin arrives first. Indeed, Marguerite's perspective is the perfect one to be offered the reader in the narration of the tale, as her full emotional engagement and limited knowledge of circumstances allow the reader to experience the utmost sympathetic emotion and suspense.

Marguerite's sentimental priorities can be understood as her primary weakness, as her romantic notions led her to refuse to offer Percy the rational explanation about St. Cyr that he needed to hear, while, as she admits, the more virtuous choice would have been to sacrifice her brother's life so as to allow the Scarlet Pimpernel to continue saving others. However, her heroic efforts to make up for her unwitting betrayal of her husband redeem her by the novel's end. She demonstrates extraordinary courage and determination in first trailing, on foot, the cart Chauvelin hires for over a dozen miles on a muddy road and then crawling on her hands and knees through prickly brush in hopes of somehow warning the fugitives and her husband. She is caught by Chauvelin, but he leaves her ungagged, and her last crucial decision is to cry out in warning upon hearing Percy's singing voice. Percy perhaps expected her to take this action, which sets in motion the final stage of his impromptu plan to save the French fugitives as well as himself and his wife.

Sir Percy Blakeney

On the surface, Sir Percy seems a laconic, dim-witted dandy, excelling mostly at appearing fashionable and laughing inanely at his own jokes. However, he has an impressive physique, is among the richest men in England, and has somehow managed to charm the brilliant Marguerite St. Just. As do many men of his class, he values his honor perhaps above all—such that the rumors of Lady Blakeney's role in the execution of the marquis de St. Cyr's family sting him so severely that he finds himself unable to continue showing the same affection and devotion that he extended to Marguerite when courting her. When she comes to treat him with condescension, he resigns himself to perfunctorily serving her. When, after Lord Grenville's ball, she pleads with him to try to feel as he felt when they first fell in love, his honor yet keeps his passion in check. Only his occasional yearning glances and his kissing of the ground where she walked reveal his persisting love for her.

As it turns out, Percy's vacant appearance is largely intended to conceal his secret identity as the Scarlet Pimpernel. Marguerite only realizes this truth after entering his unexpectedly pristine study and finding the ring with the seal of the red flower (a pimpernel). His strength and wealth alike—as well as his fondness for driving his coach at a gallop in the middle of the night—certainly serve the activities of the rescuers' league well, and he is a master of disguise. He fools Bibot by dressing as an ugly old woman, and later, taking advantage of the French people's supposed low opinion of Jewish people, dupes Chauvelin by playing the part of the sniveling Benjamin Rosenbaum. Percy's flair for the dramatic is also in evidence when he twice alerts Chauvelin to his presence by heartily singing "God save the King!" Proving a true romantic hero, Percy rises with great effort after suffering a sound beating at the hands of Chauvelin's soldiers to then carry his stunned, exhausted, beloved Marguerite to the safety of the schooner's boat.

Briggs
Briggs is the skipper of Percy's schooner, the *Day Dream*.

Brogard
As the innkeeper at the filthy Chat Gris in Calais, Brogard is a caricature of the utterly free postrevolutionary Frenchman: he spits on the ground before the cursed aristocrats, serves them with exaggerated indifference and deliberation, smokes in their faces (rudely asserting his equality to them), and answers their questions as curtly as possible.

Chauvelin
The official representative of the French government in Britain and a French spy, Chauvelin's primary goal is to uncover the identity of the Scarlet Pimpernel and capture him on French soil. He uses the incriminating letter from Armand St. Just to blackmail Marguerite into assisting him. At Lord Grenville's ball, he concludes that Sir Percy must be the daring rescuer, and he tracks Sir Percy to Calais, just across the channel from Dover, dressed as a churchman. At the Chat Gris, he is startled when Sir Percy walks in and chats with him; outraged after Percy leaves him in a sneezing fit, he fails to realize that the haggard Jew who professes to be a witness is Sir Percy in disguise. Ever calculating as he tracks his prey, Chauvelin is often characterized as a fox. His downfall is his obsessive need to capture the Scarlet Pimpernel. At the Père Blanchard's hut, his soldiers, fearing retribution, follow his strict orders to await the Englishman even when the fugitives slip out on their own. Chauvelin then leaves the cruelly beaten Jew and Marguerite behind because he wants all his men available to capture the Scarlet Pimpernel back toward Calais—and he thus unwittingly allows Marguerite and the disguised Percy to escape.

Desgas
Chauvelin's secretary and servant, Desgas helps coordinate the soldiers' tracking of the Scarlet Pimpernel and the French fugitives.

Lord Antony Dewhurst
A member of the league of the Scarlet Pimpernel, Lord Antony welcomes the comtesse's family at the Fisherman's Rest. When he later meets privately with Sir Andrew, the two are seized by the French agents directed by Chauvelin, who thus gains the letter that compromises Armand St. Just.

Lord Fancourt
A cabinet minister, Lord Fancourt kindly helps Marguerite locate her husband when she wishes to leave Lord Grenville's ball.

Sir Andrew Ffoulkes
As a member of the Scarlet Pimpernel's league, Sir Andrew escorts the comtesse's family over the channel to Dover, taking a liking to the young Suzanne along the way. He and Lord Antony are later attacked by Chauvelin's men, giving up the letter from Armand St. Just. At Lord Grenville's party, Sir Andrew fails to prevent Marguerite from reading a note from the Scarlet Pimpernel, but she seemingly dupes him into thinking she misunderstood its contents. When Marguerite later confesses her errant actions and begs his help in reaching her husband, he affirms his

loyalty to Percy Blakeney and gallantly plays the role of her servant to guide her to the Chat Gris in Calais. There, he manages to warn Percy and later meets up with the couple by the Père Blanchard's hut.

Reuben Goldstein

Reuben Goldstein lives in Calais and has a horse and cart available for hire. Sir Percy pays him to disappear for the day so as to trick Chauvelin into thinking Goldstein has driven the Scarlet Pimpernel to the Père Blanchard's hut.

Lord Grenville

The English secretary of state for foreign affairs, Lord Grenville hosts the magnificent ball at which Chauvelin identifies Sir Percy as the Scarlet Pimpernel. As his office demands, he treats Chauvelin with dignity even though others would rather not.

Lord Hastings

A member of the Scarlet Pimpernel's league of rescuers, Lord Hastings hands Sir Andrew the note that Marguerite later reads.

Mr. Hempseed

Locally respected for his knowledge of the Scriptures, Hempseed frequents The Fisherman's Rest.

Mr. Jellyband

Ever ready to serve his customers, especially the high-society ones, Jellyband has proud royalist leanings and applauds the efforts of the Scarlet Pimpernel's league, which he supports by allowing the use of his hostel as a meeting place.

Louise

Louise is Marguerite's helpful personal maid.

Lady Portarles

Lady Portarles shrewdly advises the comtesse about navigating English high society.

Benjamin Rosenbaum

See Sir Percy Blakeney

Sally

The young and pretty daughter of Mr. Jellyband, Sally serves and flirts with customers at the Fisherman's Rest.

The Scarlet Pimpernel

See Sir Percy Blakeney

Armand St. Just

A rare humanitarian member of the new republican French government, Armand finds himself unable to support the mass slaughter of the aristocracy. Soon after he sails from Dover to France via Sir Percy's schooner, the French agent Chauvelin obtains a letter signed by Armand indicating that he has been aiding the Scarlet Pimpernel's league. Armand's extremely close relationship with his sister accounts for much of Marguerite's uncertainty about how to resolve her dilemma of whether to help Chauvelin find the Scarlet Pimpernel or allow Armand to be condemned to death. The elder sibling by eight years, Armand effectively raised Marguerite after their parents died while she was still a child. Armand escapes France after taking shelter in the Père Blanchard's hut along with the comte de Tournay.

Marguerite St. Just

See Marguerite Blakeney

Comte de Tournay de Basserive

The comte huddles in the Père Blanchard's hut with Armand St. Just and two others, awaiting rescue. They slip out while the soldiers stick to orders and keep waiting.

Comtesse de Tournay de Basserive

The comtesse is grateful when she and her children are rescued by the league, but she fears for her husband's life. She distrusts and insults Marguerite, who is known to her as a betrayer of aristocrats, and tries to prevent Suzanne from associating with Marguerite. However, she is advised not to shun the most fashionable woman in England, and she later allows the two former classmates to meet with each other.

Suzanne de Tournay de Basserive

Suzanne, the daughter of the comtesse de Tournay, develops a fondness for one of her family's rescuers, Sir Andrew. She visits Marguerite, her old schoolmate, at the Blakeney estate, but Marguerite is just realizing that she must pursue her husband to warn him of his peril. Suzanne marries Sir Andrew after her father escapes from France.

Vicomte de Tournay de Basserive

In accord with French etiquette, the young vicomte invites Sir Percy to a duel after the indignities between the comtesse and Lady Blakeney at the Fisherman's Rest. Sir Percy refuses, being a genteel Englishman, and belittles the lad.

Harry Waite

A local patron of the Fisherman's Rest in Dover, Waite grows quickly jealous when Lord Antony dotes on Sally.

Prince of Wales

At Lord Grenville's ball, the Prince of Wales (the next in line for the British throne) escorts Lady Blakeney in and praises her before the stewing comtesse. He also proudly tells Chauvelin of the profound esteem that the British have for the Scarlet Pimpernel, the daring, selfless English rescuer of French aristocrats. (This Prince of Wales is the future King George IV.)

THEMES

Conflicting Loyalties and Moralities

The most prominent theme in *The Scarlet Pimpernel* is that of conflicting loyalties and moralities, a theme that is explored through both individual relationships and interpretation of the broader events of the French Revolution. Those broader events, though historically significant, are given far less consideration than are Marguerite's particular dilemmas. This is partly because Orczy was clearly condemning the horrific actions of the French proletariat; she did not mean to present a balanced perspective.

The context of the revolution, nonetheless, is what gives rise to the several dilemmas faced by Marguerite in the course of her life, each of which forces her to choose between loyalties or moralities. Her central dilemma is whether to refuse to help Chauvelin and thus allow her brother's execution or to help reveal the identity of the Scarlet Pimpernel. An unbiased philosophy would suggest that the most ethical action would be to allow her brother's death so as to prevent the deaths not only of the English rescuer but of the many aristocrats he might still save. But Marguerite is swayed by her love for her brother, imagining him saying, "You might have saved me, Margot!" when she seeks to read Sir Andrew's note. She later feels that "she had not been strong enough to do right for right's sake, and to sacrifice her brother to the dictates of her conscience." When she learns that the Scarlet Pimpernel is her husband, she notes

TOPICS FOR FURTHER STUDY

- In a pair, choose one of the two-person conversations from Orczy's novel to act out, such as Marguerite and Chauvelin's first meeting or Marguerite and Percy's conversation on their lawn. You may either stage the scene precisely as found in the novel or adjust dialogue and gestures as you see fit. After playing the scene, interview one audience member with regard to ways the staging could have been improved, and then write a reflection paper on what you learned from the theatrical experience.

- In an essay, compare and contrast the French Revolution with the American Revolution. Consider the overarching political ideals, military conflicts, resulting governments, and any other relevant aspects of the two major historical events.

- Carol Gilligan and Lawrence Kohlberg are two theorists who have established moral frameworks in which people's actions can be assessed. Research the work of both theorists, then write an essay discussing what each would have to say about Marguerite's decision to aid Chauvelin so as to save her brother, Armand.

- Read *League of Superheroes*, by Stephen Rice, or another young-adult novel featuring a character with superhero qualities. Write a paper comparing and contrasting the Scarlet Pimpernel with the hero or heroes in the novel you choose.

- Research the cities of Dover, England, and Calais, France, using the Internet. Then imagine you are a travel agent and create on the computer two brochures, with pictures, advertising each city as a vacation destination.

- Invent your own superhero, detailing an ordinary identity, a secret identity, special powers or abilities, and a costume. Then write a short story or draw an episode in comic-book form that depicts your superhero using his or her powers for good.

Leslie Howard as Sir Percy Blakeney in a scene from the 1934 film version of the novel (© *Bettmann / Corbis*)

that had she known, her love for her husband would have outweighed her love for her brother, who in signing his name to a treasonous letter did compromise himself. Thenceforth, Marguerite's determination to right her wrong by pursuing Sir Percy to the end is what drives the novel's action—and allows the reader to witness the Scarlet Pimpernel's final ingenious escape.

Two other choices made by Marguerite in the past shape the course of events throughout the novel. In the distant past, she chose to speak of the marquis de St. Cyr's treasonous correspondence with the Austrian emperor in front of friends who then reported the information. The text says that Marguerite was "impulsive, thoughtless, not calculating the purport of her words"—which might be understood to mean that she in fact believed that the marquis would deserve whatever fate he had earned with his treason. In other words, she perhaps spoke freely of the marquis' plotting because as a plebeian (that is, not an aristocrat), and because her

brother had been ordered beaten by the marquis, her loyalty at that time was to the common people and to Republican France. Although this might be called a subconscious choice, she professes to have made the conscious choice not to explain to her husband the exact circumstances surrounding her denouncement of the marquis. Early on she recalls having "made full confession" of the incident, but when she and Percy meet on their lawn, he remarks, "I fancy that you refused me *all* explanation then, and demanded of my love a humiliating allegiance it was not prepared to give." She responds, "I wished to test your love for me, and it did not bear the test." Thus, in these circumstances, Marguerite prioritizes the dictates of romantic love—unquestioning devotion—over the perhaps more modern notion of complete truthfulness between two people who are romantically involved. Percy, in turn, chose to defer to his injured pride—and to the loyalties of the British aristocracy, which lay with their embattled peers across the channel—and position himself at an emotional distance from Marguerite. As such, together their choices led to their estrangement.

Tides of Emotion

An aspect of *The Scarlet Pimpernel* that relates to its classification as a sort of romance is the manner in which the narrative follows the tides of Marguerite's emotions. She is the one character who is given a narrative voice; when she finds herself alone, such as on the Dover cliffs after Armand has departed and in her room in Richmond after Lord Grenville's ball, the narration follows the train of her sentiments. As such, the reader is immersed in Marguerite's mindset, perceiving what she perceives and considering what she considers. In this regard, analyst Gary Hoppenstand goes as far as to declare that the novel is "obviously misnamed," in that the true hero of the book is "the heroine, Lady Blakeney." He notes that readers "feel her anguish when she is blackmailed," "celebrate with her triumph" in discovering Percy's secret, and "experience the catharsis of her passion" when she and her husband unite in the end. Some critics have this emotional trajectory in mind when dismissively classifying the popular novel in the genres of adventure or romance. However, in linking Marguerite's emotional states not just to the plot turns but also to her moral choices, Orczy demonstrates that a novel that focuses on sentiment can be just as enlightening with regard to human nature as any more dispassionate literary work.

STYLE

Superhero in Disguise Character

Orczy's most famous work is often cited for giving rise to the genre of the superhero with an alter ego or secret identity. As Sarah Juliette Sasson notes, "Superheroes had not been invented when the baroness wrote her novel, but the Scarlet Pimpernel's chivalry, courage, and impressive powers make him, in certain respects, their ancestor." Johnston McCulley presented his character of Zorro, who dons a black mask and costume to fight evildoers, in 1919 in *The Curse of Capistrano*. Other characters written in the mode of the Scarlet Pimpernel can be found primarily in comic books, as with Superman and Batman, characters who have received increased attention in modern films.

Indeed, stories of superheroes have become a veritable obsession with modern popular audiences. Some commentators have noted that during trying or fearful times—such as an economic recession—moviegoers may be more likely to desire to escape into adventurous tales with fantastic saviors or heroes.

Some of the superheroes of popular literature and film, such as the X-Men, have extraordinary powers, whereas others are ordinary humans who by experience and circumstance find themselves in the role of do-gooder or rescuer. The Scarlet Pimpernel, a character who has exceptional skills but is grounded in reality, is the latter sort of hero. Orczy endows him, though, with such impressive abilities that he leaves the French soldiers and peasants alike wondering whether or not he is merely human. The tales of his escapes "certainly savoured of the supernatural, and though the Republic had abolished God, it had not quite succeeded in killing the fear of the supernatural in the hearts of the people." When Sergeant Bibot realizes that the disguised Englishman has slipped past him, "a superstitious shudder ran down his spine"—and the Scarlet Pimpernel's identity as an archetypal larger-than-life superhero is firmly established.

Adventure/Historical Romance

In accord with the focus on Marguerite's emotions and her climactic reunion with her husband, Orczy herself (as noted by Sasson) referred to *The Scarlet Pimpernel* as a "historical romance." In keeping with a narrative based on intrigue and action, the work is also often classified as an adventure novel. Sasson thoroughly explores the ways in which the novel exhibits the features of these genres, accounting for both limitations and strengths. With regard to the historical aspects, the setting of the French Revolution provides appropriate circumstances for endangered lives and acts of heroism, but it is not treated as cause for extensive philosophical inquiry. Orczy certainly demonstrates a philosophical perspective, but it is an unquestioning one: whatever the initial aims or virtues of the revolution, the slaughtering of the aristocracy and the people responsible for that slaughter can only be deemed evil. Sasson considers this one-sided view to be appropriate for Orczy's purposes: "Adventure novels require dramatic simplicities, not historical subtleties; historical truth is always secondary to fictional invention." She adds, "The efficacy of this type of text relies on an obvious conflict and a chivalric, courageous, and clear-headed hero." Indeed, as befits this romantic work, the Scarlet Pimpernel is portrayed in only the most admiring light. Tension is derived instead from the questions of the hero's identity, of the course of action Marguerite should take, and of whether Percy will be caught.

Theatricality

Orczy was a devoted theatergoer, and she developed *The Scarlet Pimpernel* both as a novel and as a play. Unsurprisingly, then, the novel bears many hallmarks of theatricality. On the level of the structure of the tale, the typical chapter is set as a self-contained scene, taking place in a single (stageable) locale—such as the Fisherman's Rest, the opera box, the yard at Richmond, the Père Blanchard's hut—and its immediate (offstage) surroundings. The plot, in turn, revolves more around the interactions of the characters than around actual action; aside from the opening chapter, when the Scarlet Pimpernel slips out of Paris disguised as the old hag, the reader is not treated to the adrenaline rush of his daring escapes—which would have certainly been complicated to stage. The final escape hinges not on Percy's prowess or strength at all but on his ability to act the part of the obsequious Jew. Indeed, the roles of Marguerite and Percy are both characterized by their acting abilities. Marguerite is an actress by profession, and she spends the first half of the novel playing different parts, depending upon the company she finds herself in: parrying with the comtesse, receiving admirers' attention at the opera, trying to ward off Chauvelin, feigning illness with Sir Andrew, or revealing her passion for her husband. Percy, in turn, is shown at first to be a sort of buffoon but is later revealed to be only acting that part, while his heroics as the Scarlet Pimpernel are dependent on his knack for fooling even those with whom he is well acquainted into thinking he is someone else entirely.

HISTORICAL CONTEXT

The French Revolution

Within the greater setting of the French Revolution, which began in 1789, *The Scarlet Pimpernel* takes place beginning in September 1792, a month marked by what became known as the September Massacres, in which raging mobs murdered more than a thousand suspected criminals—many of whom were innocent—held at five different prisons. Orczy establishes the horrors of this period of time in the opening chapter, the only one that takes place in Paris, the heart of the nation's violence. Every day, condemned aristocrats—men, women, and children alike—would be wheeled to the guillotine and executed, before enthusiastic audiences of commoners. Renowned were the *tricoteuses*, old ladies who passed the time knitting just beneath the platform where victims were beheaded; the Scarlet Pimpernel successfully poses as one of these chilling women.

Thus, Orczy plunges the reader into the most sickening violence of the period leading up to the Reign of Terror, which began in September 1793 (when official decree allowed the Republican government to convict and execute, with much greater ease, those suspected of treasonous acts). As such, the reader is left largely uninformed regarding the foundations and initial phases of the French Revolution. The peasant class had been oppressed by the aristocracy and the government for centuries, and conditions had worsened substantially in recent years. Famine was widespread, and with the added burden of heavy taxes (which were levied to account for the various wars fought by Louis XV and the grand consumption of the court of Louis XVI) on top of rent owed to noble lords and tithes owed to the Catholic Church, many of the poorest people were left to starve. Under the royal government, the common people were simply not represented. The spark for revolution came on July 14, 1789, when a mob stormed and seized the Bastille, an infamous prison. In the ensuing months, unrest spread through the country, as mobs seized aristocrats' castles and sometimes murdered the inhabitants. Peasants pressured the king, and in July 1791 some fifty protesters were slain by royal troops; the next year, a peasant force overran the royal palace, killing some six hundred royal guards and then imprisoning the king. By this time, politicians representing France's commoners had established governmental authority through various legislative maneuvers, and in the next few years, power would fall into the hands of ever more ruthless and even bloodthirsty governors, such as Maximilien Robespierre, of the Committee of Public Safety, who spearheaded the Reign of Terror.

COMPARE & CONTRAST

- **1790s:** In the course of the French Revolution, legislative acts discontinue the authority of the Roman Catholic Church to levy tithes, withdraw special privileges previously granted to the clergy, and confiscate church property in the name of the state.

  1900s: Legislation passed in 1905 establishes separation of church and state in France, reversing Napoleon's 1801 establishment of the Church of France.

  Today: A 2004 law bans the wearing of conspicuous religious garments in schools, applying most notably to head scarves worn by Muslims.

- **1790s:** By and large, British citizens are appalled at the murderous turns taken by the French Revolution, but the nation proves unwilling to declare war against France—until France declares war first in January 1793.

  1900s: In 1904, a series of agreements known as the Entente Cordiale is signed between France and Great Britain, with the two nations compromising to resolve outstanding colonial disputes and establish peaceful relations.

  Today: Although their two nations have been drifting apart, Prime Minister Gordon Brown of England and President Nicolas Sarkozy of France both call for a strengthening of the relationship with their neighbors across the channel.

- **1790s:** Despite his nation's defeat in the American Revolution, King George III enjoys a high degree of popularity.

  1900s: King Edward VII is greatly respected for his diplomatic skill and for maintaining peaceful relations with Europe.

  Today: With the British Empire dissolved and most power in the hands of Parliament and the prime minister, Queen Elizabeth II is popular but wields little influence over the government.

What little attention Orczy pays to these greater events relates primarily to how they were understood from Great Britain, where her sympathies naturally lay (being a longtime resident). By and large, her novel's citizens of England, from the ale drinkers at the Fisherman's Rest to the uppermost echelons of high society at Lord Grenville's ball, express horror at the extreme violence that the revolution has brought. At that time, under the influence of the hesitant Prime Minister William Pitt, the British government had no intention of intervening with military force, even though the legislator Edmund Burke argued convincingly for action. In *The Scarlet Pimpernel*, then, on the tip of everyone's tongue is the name of the dashing rescuer of the imperiled French aristocrats. However they managed to escape, the aristocratic French emigrants were welcomed warmly—and in the course of the revolution some 120,000 people fled France, with many crossing the English Channel. Orczy's portrayal of this era focuses on the indisputable notion that innocent people, including women and children, were being murdered by a vindictive government; the author thus ensures that virtually all sensible readers will find themselves sympathetically allied with the cause of the Scarlet Pimpernel.

Anti-Semitism

Perhaps the most unfortunate feature of Orczy's novel is the vein of anti-Semitism that characterizes the portrayal of Sir Percy disguised as Benjamin Rosenbaum. On the one hand, the fact that Percy casts himself as an especially despicable person arguably serves his purpose; he asserts in the end that Frenchmen are so prejudiced against Jews that such a disguise ensured that they would give him as

The Reign of Terror during the French Revolution (© *Bettmann / Corbis*)

little direct attention as possible. Indeed, in terms of the greater narrative, in which all agents of the Republican French cause are portrayed negatively, whether as foolhardy braggarts, loathsome witches, vile oafs, or amoral predators, the portrayal of the French as prejudiced against Jews can be understood as a condemnation of such anti-Semitism. Nonetheless, rather than acting merely as a Jewish person with a loathsome appearance, Percy as Rosenbaum acts in ways that are without doubt offensively stereotypical of Jews. Orczy's narrator, in turn, gives an egregious verbal flourish to certain descriptions of Rosenbaum's actions and character, such as when he is first introduced to Chauvelin. Unfortunately, negative feelings toward Jews were common in parts of Europe, including France, throughout recent centuries, especially among those dogmatically religious Christians who held Jews accountable for the death of Jesus, and among lower-class citizens and ethnic nationalists who resented Jewish immigrants who happened to be financially successful. Most of Orczy's turn-of-the-twentieth-century readers (excluding Jews, of course) would have been unlikely to object to her disguising Sir Percy as a pathetic older Jewish man.

Readers may choose, then, whether to hold Orczy only to the lower moral standards of her own era and not let their appreciation for the book be compromised, or whether to let the stereotypical depiction cloud their perception of Orczy as an artist.

CRITICAL OVERVIEW

The sort of attention given to *The Scarlet Pimpernel* in the *New York Times Book Review* in 1905 is perhaps emblematic of how critics received the work generally. Evidently considering the novel a prime example of the popular (that is, nonliterary) press, the anonymous reviewer cannot help but address its workings with wry condescension. After labeling it a "thrilling story," the reviewer snidely observes that "it was first written as a play, and one can imagine it being better for acting purposes than for reading." The reviewer proceeds to assert that "from the very first, of course, the reader recognizes the hero," demonstrating the reviewer's own priorities as a reader, and yet Percy is simplistically described as "apparently indifferent" to his wife's beauty and appeal, revealing that the reviewer failed to appreciate the ideological standoff (of, say, pride versus romance) in which Percy and Marguerite are engaged and which accounts for the essential tension between the two protagonists.

Other scholars, not necessarily being dismissive of *The Scarlet Pimpernel*, have focused rather on Orczy's pioneering detective stories. In *Great Women Mystery Writers* (1994), Barrie Hayne finds Orczy's generally simplistic views of the social order, which are also demonstrated in her most famous novel, to be grounds for criticism: "Baroness Orczy's stories embody an aristocratic superiority that brings the lower orders to justice but often allows the upper classes to hush up their crimes." Hayne concedes that this outlook was fairly widespread in detective fiction of her era. Gillian Mary Hanson includes a discussion of Orczy's *The Old Man in the Corner* in her study *City and Shore: The Function of Setting in the British Mystery* (2004), noting the author's apt contrast of open spaces such as forests with enclosed settings such as cafés and rooms; similar strategic use of setting can be found in *The Scarlet Pimpernel*, such as the contrast of the stifling Chat Gris and the sea exposure of the Père Blanchard's hut. Len Platt discusses Orczy's novel extensively in his *Aristocracies of Fiction* (2001), viewing the novel less as mere popular fiction and more as a critique of the mediocre values of the middle and lower classes. All in all, the indisputable success of *The Scarlet Pimpernel*, as novel, play, and film alike, perhaps says more about the quality of the story than could critics' assessments of it.

CRITICISM

Michael Allen Holmes

Holmes is a writer and editor. In this essay on The Scarlet Pimpernel, *he considers the qualities that make the Scarlet Pimpernel not just a superhero archetype but also unique among literary and motion-picture superheroes.*

Baroness Orczy is generally credited with creating the literary figure of the disguised superhero in 1905 with *The Scarlet Pimpernel*. The character of Zorro was created some fourteen years later, Superman was introduced in 1938, and before long an entire genre was flourishing. The comic book proved the favored medium for superhero stories, which mostly featured impressively

> THE MOST APPARENT REASON FOR SIR PERCY'S CHARACTERIZATION AS BOTH MASCULINE AND FEMININE MAY BE THAT, UNLIKE MOST LITERARY AND MOTION-PICTURE SUPERHEROES, THE SCARLET PIMPERNEL WAS CREATED BY A WOMAN."

masculine figures and so were naturally enjoyed in particular by boys, who would be drawn to the fantastic action and, perhaps less consciously, the dramatic depictions of how to be a man. In his introduction to Orczy's novel, Gary Hoppenstand notes that the heroic qualities of the Scarlet Pimpernel can be traced to a variety of later fictional figures. For example, the "hedonistic protagonist who knows his wine and clothes" can be found reincarnated in Ian Fleming's James Bond, who debuted in the novel *Casino Royale* in 1953. The "trickster hero who is able to readily escape any life-and-death trap" can be found in the adventure fiction of Edgar Rice Burrroughs. And "the wealthy do-gooder who uses his riches to help those less fortunate than himself" can be seen in pulp-fiction characters such as the Shadow and Doc Savage.

However, although the Scarlet Pimpernel was a forerunner to these heroic do-gooders, he should be recognized as distinct from most of them by virtue of certain qualities. To begin with, the orientation between his ordinary self and his secret identity is less strictly defined than is the case with most other dual-identity heroes. That is, he does not put on a recognizable costume and then, upon meeting a villain, interact in that guise, as do figures such as Batman and Captain Marvel. In *Super/Heroes: From Hercules to Superman*, Peter Coogan observes that such heroes benefit from their costumes because the distinct garb communicates to any onlookers that, even if engaged in destructive behavior, they are acting in the name of good to defeat some evil. The Scarlet Pimpernel, on the other hand, benefits from having no recognizable costume; rather, he successfully uses unlimited alternate identities to smuggle aristocrats out of France. Coogan also notes that whereas most superheroes have adopted a name and

WHAT DO I READ NEXT?

- *The Triumph of the Scarlet Pimpernel* (1922) centered around the Thermidorian Reaction of July 1794, is one of the many sequels to the original tale written by Orczy.

- *The Old Man in the Corner* (1909), a collection of short stories by Orczy, features her pioneering armchair detective, Bill Owen.

- Orczy provides much detail about the conception and development of the Scarlet Pimpernel stories, as well as her writing and life in general, in her autobiography, *Links in the Chain of Life* (1947).

- *A Tale of Two Cities* (1859), by Charles Dickens, is perhaps the best known novel set during the French Revolution, contrasting scenes of the era and fates of people in London and Paris.

- Victor Hugo, one of France's most cherished novelists, finally addressed the French Revolution in his last work, *Ninety-Three* (1874), which concerns the counterrevolutionary uprising of 1793.

- An adventure novel set in France 150 years before the revolution, *The Three Musketeers* (1844), by Alexandre Dumas tells of swashbuckling exploits of the musketeers (soldiers) of the title and their friend d'Artagnan.

- In *The Amazing Adventures of Kavalier & Clay* (2000), by Michael Chabon, the title characters develop an anti-fascist comic-book superhero called the Escapist, who bears certain similarities to the Scarlet Pimpernel.

- Many throughout history have needed to escape their circumstances for political, social, or personal reasons. *Copper Sun* (2006), a novel by Sharon M. Draper, tells the story of a fifteen-year-old African girl named Amari who is abducted by slave traders and who seeks to escape her life on a plantation in the Carolinas. The book won the Coretta Scott King Award.

- Sally Gardner uses the context of the French Revolution in her young-adult novel, *The Red Necklace: A Story of the French Revolution* (2008), about a magician's assistant whose employer dies.

---

appearance that reflect their identity and powers—Spider-Man shoots webs from his wrists and wears a webbed costume—the Scarlet Pimpernel's name reflects no more than the symbol he uses on his calling cards.

Whereas these differences relate mostly to the mechanics of being a superhero, other differences can be seen as intrinsic to the character of the man who is that hero, Sir Percy Blakeney. The typical male superhero, whether disguised or not, has a definitively masculine bearing, if perhaps a self-effacing one, so as not to draw excessive attention to himself. This bearing often reflects the physical prowess of the character; Clark Kent can hide his superior physique beneath a business suit, but to go so far as to be unmasculine would not befit the man who is Superman. In *Action Figures: Men, Action Films, and Contemporary Adventure Narratives*, Mark Gallagher observes that iconic constructions of masculinity serve psychological purposes for the modern male: "Cinematic and literary representations of male action compensate for threats to stable, traditional masculinity, threats posed by economic and cultural changes affecting men's roles in the workplace and in the domestic space." In other words, as men (especially middle- and upper-class men) have lost opportunities to engage in physical work that is done more efficiently by machines, instead sitting before computers in offices, and as women have gradually assumed the roles of co-breadwinners, rather than being constricted domestic figures, men have found themselves more and more drawn to and comforted by portrayals of ultramasculinity that connote ultimate control. The muscle-bound heroes played by the likes of Sylvester Stallone and Bruce Willis may or may not succeed in their ventures, but whether they are soldiers, police officers, or men on the street, their physical engagement with their surroundings is exemplary (inevitably provoking adrenaline rushes in viewers) and their masculine honor is rarely, if ever, compromised. Divergence from this formula is typically associated with comedy or farce, as with Arnold Schwarzenegger's *Kindergarten Cop*, where the hero's actions are dictated not by his macho self but by five-year-olds.

Sir Percy Blakeney, on the other hand, is perhaps less masculine than any male superhero who has succeeded him in literature or in films. In *Heroes, Antiheroes, and Dolts: Portrayals of Masculinity in American Popular Films, 1921–1999*, Ashton Trice and Samuel Holland describe Leslie Howard's Scarlet Pimpernel, of the 1934 film, as being an "alternatively virile/effete hero." Indeed, Orczy presents a character who is decidedly unmasculine in a number of respects. On the one hand, he is introduced as "massively built," tall with broad shoulders. On the other hand, he pays exquisite attention to fashion; despite arriving in poor weather, "his hands looked almost femininely white, as they emerged through billowy frills of finest Mechlin lace." Gallagher points out that James Bond exhibits fashion sense without sacrificing masculinity: "Bond's concern with personal grooming and luxuries recuperates fashion and consumerism from the realm of the feminine, promoting the ideology of male style"; Sir Percy, on the other hand, pairs his fashion sense with daintiness. He greets the vicomte's invitation to duel, which would at least rouse the dignity of most men, with clear distaste and indifference. This unmasculine laziness is targeted by Marguerite when she pokes fun at her husband. In turn, Percy generally subjugates himself before his exceedingly clever wife. While his character through most of the novel is understood to be a self-effacing act of sorts, he does not suddenly become more masculine even when alone with Marguerite at the Père Blanchard's hut. He rests his head on her shoulder, rather than vice versa, speaks but "tenderly," and still laughs "that funny, half-shy, half-inane laugh of his." Even after his beating, he is not bristling with manly anger but has a "good-humoured twinkle in his blue eyes" as he envisions exacting revenge. And yet, still a masculine hero, as he

carries his beloved the few miles to safety, "his muscles seemed made of steel, and his energy was almost supernatural."

The most apparent reason for Sir Percy's characterization as both masculine and feminine may be that, unlike most literary and motion-picture superheroes, the Scarlet Pimpernel was created by a woman. Interestingly, Orczy claimed not to have consciously designed Sir Percy; rather, standing on a platform waiting for an underground train, she found herself suddenly envisioning him. As she states in her autobiography, *Links in the Chain of Life* (quoted by Hoppenstand), "I saw him in his exquisite clothes, his slender hands holding up his spy-glass: I heard his lazy drawling speech, his quaint laugh." Thus, rather than directly creating the character to appeal to the public, she simply derived the image of this idealized gentleman from her own preconceived notions about who such a gentleman would be. As such, he is a character who perhaps appeals, on the surface, more to female readers or viewers than to males. And for this very reason, aspiring gentlemen would perhaps be wise to learn from Sir Percy—from his gallantry, devotion, and humanitarianism, as well as from his poise, strength, and bravery. For while the ultramasculine hero may serve as inspiration to other men, the hero who successfully unites masculine and feminine qualities in himself is perhaps more likely to be the one carrying in his arms the cleverest woman in all of Europe.

Source: Michael Allen Holmes, Critical Essay on *The Scarlet Pimpernel*, in *Novels for Students*, Gale, Cengage Learning, 2010.

Billie Melman

In the following excerpt, Melman explores how Orczy popularized the aristocratic romance through her "Scarlet Pimpernel" novels.

The thriving new genre and the wider bonanza of Revolution narratives have been contemptuously denigrated by students of popular literature and virtually ignored by historians. There is not a single monograph on it and the few references that we do have are mainly taxonomic. Yet contemporaries, most notably lexicographers and bibliographers of popular historical fiction, were quick to note the phenomenal popularity of all forms of fiction to do with the Revolution. The wealth of revolution fiction is recorded in the first to do with the

> THE BARONESS, WITH REMARKABLE BUSINESS ACUMEN, RESPONDED TO POPULAR DEMAND AND PRODUCED A SEQUEL OF TEN PIMPERNEL NOVELS AND TWO COLLECTIONS OF SHORT STORIES, APPEARING IN THREE SEQUENCES."

Revolution. The wealth of Revolution fiction is recorded in the first two English bibliographies of historical fiction by Jonathan Nield (1902, 1911, and 1927) and Ernest A. Baker (1914), probably the first bibliographies of a popular genre. Their appearance itself testifies to the renewed and unprecedented popularity of the historical novel at the turn of the century. The sheer quantity of novels in English and of translations from French and German necessitated not only listing and citation of prices, but also classification, according to subgenres, periods, settings, and the geography of the events described. Of the 254 novels Baker lists in the 1914 edition, some 141 are on the extended era of the Revolution (1789–1814) in France, and 113 on its impact on Britain and Ireland (there is an entire section on the 1798 rebellion of the United Irishmen), and these figures do not include many more novels on Spain and Portugal, mainly during the period of the Peninsular Wars, or novels set in central Europe.

Certain themes were not novel and present continuities with the older, mid-century Revolution novel and, more broadly, with the sensationalist, cross-culture Revolution lore, with the Terror and guillotine as its central subjects and metaphors (see Chs. 1–3). Additionally, there is a great curiosity about the military aspects of the Revolutionary Wars, most notably about maritime battles, which proves a gold mine for authors specializing in juvenile fiction. Examples abound and include Gordon Stables's tale of the Battle of the Nile, *As We Sweep through the Deep* (1893), G. A. Henty, *At Aboukir and Acre* (1899), H. G. Hutchinson, *A Friend of Nelson* (1902), and Poynter H. May, *Scarlet Town: A Conceit*, published in 1894 by the Society for the Propagation of Christian Knowledge (SPCK). Of course, the maritime

revolutionary tale had a precursor in early nineteenth-century panoramic spectacle, genre painting, and drawing, but came into its own after the 1870s with the rise of popular interest in the new Empire. The plethora of narratives of a threatened French invasion, hindered by a combined British naval and civilian effort, also reflects the periodic invasion scares which punctuated the period directly leading to the outbreak of the First World War and responding to the international (and mainly British–German) naval competition. Examples include R. D. Blackmore (known for his regional historical novel *Lorna Doon*), *Springhaven: A Tale of the Great War* (1887), and Avery Harold, *In Days of Danger: A Tale of the Threatened French Invasion* (1909).

Novels featuring aristocrats, the dispersed court at Versailles, and émigrés are legion and form an easily definable category of romance cum adventure. Molly Elliot Seawell, *The Last Duchess of Belgrade* (1908) is a lugubrious tale of imprisonment in the Temple Prison and the noble death of the scions of an aristocratic house. Stanley Weyman, *The Red Cockade* (1895) narrates the misfortunes and downfall of a Republican aristocrat, and P. A. Sheehan, *The Queen's Fillet* (1911) represents the Thermidorian backlash following the fall of Robespierre and the Jacobin Republic. A. H. Biggs, *The Marquis' Heir*, Mary C. Rowsell, *Monsieur de Paris*, and Mrs E. M. Field, *Little Count Paul: A Story of Troublesome Times* (1895), all featuring the doom of aristocrats, catered for the expanding juvenile market. Quite a few novelists tapped into the theme of Royalist landed revolts against the centralist Jacobin Republic to portray an aristocratic–plebeian alliance targeting the metropolitan middle and lower classes. Such an alliance could be taken to have duplicated the Tory ideal of a bond between the landed classes and the rural and urban lower classes. The war at the Vendée in Brittany in 1793 came to be seen as the epitome of such an alliance. Discovered in 1850 by Anthony Trollope in his failed novel *La Vendée*, dropped and taken up again by the novelists of the 1890s, the *petite guerre* of the Vendée and its aristocratic leadership were embraced by writers for adolescent readers, notably G. A. Henty (*No Surrender! A Tale of the Rising in La Vendée*, 1899); Hubert Rendel (*The King's Cockade*, 1903), D. K. Broster and G. W. Taylor, *Chantemerle: A Romance of the Vendean War* (1911); H. C. Bailey, *Storm and Treasure* (1910); and F. S. Brereton, *Foes of the Red Cockade* (1903). Victor Hugo's 1872 account of the rebellion, *Quatrevingt-treize*, inspired a number of translations and adaptations, and translations of French and German novels on the court and nobility during the *ancien régime* (by Alexandre Dumas and the popular German historical novelist specializing in fiction on aristocracies, Louise Mulbach) had a good run. The royalist rebellion's status as a domestically consumable story, easy to digest by both adults and juveniles and thus constituting 'family reading', was affirmed when the SPCK began to bring out novels on it like *Duchenier, or The Revolt of La Vendée* by J. M. Neale (1905).

To be sure, the Revolution's assault on privilege, the downfall of the monarchy, and the plight of the aristocracy had all been amply covered before the end of the nineteenth century in the historical novel, in historiography, and in painting, not to mention theatrical realizations, panoramas, and popular shows like the Tussaud collection. But characteristically in the earlier fiction and spectacle, the French aristocracy of the *ancien régime* and its British counterpart had been constantly vilified. One has only to recall Dickens's account of the Marquis St Évremonde in *A Tale of Two Cities*. To middle-class early and mid-Victorian novelists and their readers, these aristocrats and their English analogues were as corrupt and pernicious as their plebeian persecutors. Recall Dickens's and Thackeray's popular depiction of aristocratic renegades and louts. Mainstream historians too regarded the French nobility and the world of privilege as a major cause for the outbreak of the Revolution. Where the French royal family and aristocracy had been favourably depicted in hagiographies and in Madame Tussaud's shrine to the *ancien régime*, they had been cast as victims. And either as victims or as villains, the nobility had been marginalized. One important innovation of the new popular histories was their removal to the centre of action and the plot: aristocrats 'move' the narrative, that is history. Another innovation is the introduction of the English aristocrat as, on the one hand, a mediator of style and the good life and, on the other, as a superhero whose adventures are the main feature of historical romance. The battle to preserve a kind of leadership based on privilege, hierarchy, and a distinct lifestyle is presented as a defence of English liberties. Put differently, the defence of liberty is pitted against the excesses of popular democracy. No less important than his agenda and deeds is the formulaic hero's masked identity: his swift change from a man of fashion, a

Georgian or Regency 'beau' and dandy, to a redeemer of lives, limbs, and good causes.

The formula was hit upon in 1900 by Emma Magdalena Rosalia Maria Josefa Barbara Orczy, known to her millions-strong audience as Baroness Orczy, and slowly worked by her into *The Scarlet Pimpernel*. Rejected by a dozen publishers (including Macmillan, Murray, and Hutchinson), she adapted the novel to the stage, with the collaboration of her husband Montague Barstow, a fairly well-known illustrator and watercolourist. It was first staged by Fred Terry and Julia Neilson, one of the theatre's leading romantic couples (on stage and off it), in Nottingham; it toured the provinces, then, revamped, finally made its way to a London West End debut almost two years later, together with the novel, which was finally published by Greening, owners of *Picture Play* and with an interest in theatrical materials. Killed by the critics, the play was nevertheless a smash hit. It had a run of over 2,000 performances by the mid-thirties and was constantly revived. The novel instantaneously became a publishing phenomenon. Standard six-shilling editions and cheap editions were followed by American editions and translations into twelve languages (including one into Russian made after the outbreak of the October Revolution) and a number of Indian dialects, French, Italian, Spanish, and German adaptations for the stage followed rapidly, with the French version bowdlerizing the original and substituting a bourgeois hero for the aristocrat. Stage versions were marketed to the Empire and enjoyed a good run in South Africa, before and after the First World War, and in the Far East. Matheson Lang's version, performed by him in all major South African towns (the rights for which had been bought from Orczy) and by subcontractors in small towns, proved a steady success. The baroness, with remarkable business acumen, responded to popular demand and produced a sequel of ten Pimpernel novels and two collections of short stories, appearing in three sequences. *I Will Repay* and *The Elusive Pimpernel* appeared in 1906 and 1908 respectively and *Eldorado* saw publication in 1913. After an interim of about a decade appeared *The League of the Scarlet Pimpernel* (1919), *The First Sir Percy* (1920), *Pimpernel and Rosemary* (1924), and *Sir Percy Hits Back: An Adventure of the Scarlet Pimpernel* (1927). The third crop of Pimpernel adventures overlaps the 1930s vogue for films on high society and the aristocracy with the film adaptation of

Orczy's own original, an overlap that presents and accretion of production of historical genres and artefacts and their chain consumption, which were such staples of the culture of history. *A Child of the Revolution, The Way of the Scarlet Pimpernel*, and *A Spy of Napoleon* saw publication in 1932, 1933, and 1934, and a related, fictive, biography of the Duchess de Barry, *The Turbulent Duchess*, followed in 1935, *Mam'zelle Guillotine* brought up the rear in 1940.

The Pimpernel sequel offered readers an endless variety of the formula crystallized between 1903 and 1905. Sir Percy Blakeney Bt., a super-rich and useless fop, the husband of an ardent French Republican with Jacobin leanings (she is, it transpires in the 1922 sequence, *Triumph of the Scarlet Pimpernel*, the cousin of St Just, the Jacobin leader with a near Communist agenda and Robespierre's right hand), leads a double life as the 'Scarlet Pimpernel'. In this life, which becomes the stuff of nationalist legend in his home country and a rabid Anglophobe myth in France, he leads the clandestine 'League of the Scarlet Pimpernel,' an organization of young aristocrats set on rescuing the lives of their counterparts during the reign of Terror. By 1922, the Pimpernel and his acolytes had become such familiar characters that *Punch*, which stated that Orczy no longer invented 'any very thrilling new situations or introduced us to any very lifelike new acquaintances', acknowledged readers' comfort at finding out that these 'old friends are there' for them. The phenomenal appeal of the aristocrat adventurer-trickster is demonstrated by the success of the two subgenres of historical novels featuring an aristocrat posing as a useless fop to conceal his 'real' life as a masked avenger: the Scaramouche and Zorro tales. In the former, inaugurated in Sabatini's eponymous novel (1922), Andre-Louis Moreau is not an aristocrat by birth, but he is (metaphorically) 'fathered' by an aristocrat, the Marquis de Gravillac. An espouser of some revolutionary ideas and at one time a deputy of the People at the National Assembly, he is in fact an avenger of 'real' aristocratic and chivalric values under his disguise as Scaramouche, the master manipulator of commedia dell'arte, played by Moreau as a popular actor. Pimpernel's other successor, Zorro, constituting another deviation from Orczy's historical model, is an Americanized and republican version of the aristocratic hero. Transferred by McCulley from France and England to Spanish California, Zorro made an American Pimpernel, more suited to a republican US readership: by day a phlegmatic and useless Latin dandy, Don Diego Vegas, by night the black-masked 'Zorro', the Fox, a social anarchist, righter of wrongs.

Orcyz's blueprint and its emulations were given new lease of life by film. Even more than the writer of Tudor and Elizabethan best-sellers, whose fiction was adapted to the screen, the three churners of aristocratic romance were aware of the new medium and produced high-velocity action adapted to modern readers/spectators and the generic modern form of telling about the past. Orczy especially, with her knowledge of the stage, appreciated the power of film as a mediator of history. Since non-fiction rights on the original were held by Terry, early film adaptations drew on sequels. *The Elusive Pimpernel*, a Stoll Pictures production directed by Maurice Elvey, who also played Sir Percy, was released in 1919, and *I Will Repay*—produced by Henry Kolker—in 1923. The best of this early batch, *The Triumph of the Scarlet Pimpernel*, starring Matheson Lang and directed by T. Hayes Hunter, was released in 1928. But undoubtedly the definitive, most popular, and most enduring film version was London Films' Alexander Korda's production, with Leslie Howard as its millions of spectators' ultimate Sir Percy. Follow-ups included BFP's *The Return of the Scarlet Pimpernel*, produced in 1938 with Barry K. Barnes in the title role. A colour version of the original, directed in 1950 by Michael Powell and starring David Niven in the title role, proved a disaster. Both the 1905 novel and its sequel are still 'steady sellers', inspiring film, television, and theatre productions (lately music-hall productions)....

Source: Billie Melman, "The Revolution, Aristocrats, and the People: The Returns of the Scarlet Pimpernel, 1990–1935," in *The Culture of History: English Uses of the Past 1800–1953*, Oxford University Press, 2006, pp. 247–280.

Janice Rossen

In the following excerpt, Rossen examines the protagonists of The Scarlet Pimpernel *in the context of the "world gone mad" portrayed in the novel.*

... Baroness Orczy, in contrast to Bowen and Manning, takes her story to the extreme of melodrama. Anthea Trodd points out that *The Scarlet Pimpernel* is a successful melding of two different genres: 'a hybrid based on the two major contesting definitions of romance of the period,' in other words, adventure fiction which was 'set in the more dangerous past or on the

THE EXTREME CLEVERNESS OF ORCZY'S PLOT, HOWEVER, LIES IN THE FACT THAT THE NOVELIST BRINGS ABOUT THE TOTAL DEFEAT (THROUGH AUDACITY AND DECEPTION) OF THE VILLAIN—AT THE SAME TIME THAT LADY BLAKENEY BECOMES HEROIC."

frontiers of empire' and the traditional female version of romantic fiction. I think that it is also interesting to show it in contrast with these other, contemporary, self-consciously modern novels, because its enduring popularity shows the hunger for heroic tales which a sentimental public still holds. Yet it is escapist in a way that both distances it from and relates it to the twentieth century.

Set in 1792, the novel was published in 1905. It has a very simple plot, centering on a marriage (the couple are estranged, when the novel opens) and a crafty villain, the arch-spy for the French revolutionaries, M. de Chauvelin. By threatening the life of her brother, he blackmails Lady Blakeney into discovering for him the identity of the Scarlet Pimpernel, leader of the band of English aristocrats who are rescuing doomed French noblemen sent to the guillotine. Predictably, the Pimpernel is her husband, Sir Percy Blakeney, whom she does betray; but Chauvelin's plan is altogether foiled, as the two lovers escape together and are reunited in perfect accord.

Both main characters are lavishly idealized figures. Before her marriage, Lady Blakeney, née Marguerite St. Just, was a young Parisian actress described as being 'lavishly gifted with beauty and talent,' and able to gather around her in her Parisian flat 'a côterie which was as brilliant as it was exclusive.' Superlatives abound in the narrator's description of her position as hostess of a salon:

> Clever men, distinguished men, and even men of exalted station formed a perpetual and brilliant court round the fascinating young actress of the Comédie Française, and she glided through republican, revolutionary, bloodthirsty Paris like a shining comet with a trail behind her of all that was most distinguished, most interesting in intellectual Europe.

Not only is Marguerite able to command admiration from the most discerning, she is herself exalted with the title of 'the cleverest woman in Europe.'

Because of the extreme political tenor of the times—and the shocking and violent behavior of some of the French aristocracy she is in contact with—she betrays two different men at two different times. First, she denounces St. Cyr, a nobleman who has caused her brother to be harmed ('thrashed like a dog within an inch of his life,' for daring to write a love sonnet to St. Cyr's daughter). Second, she betrays the identity of the masked Pimpernel to Chauvelin, this time to protect rather than to avenge her brother. The narrator goes to great lengths to explain the background of the various pressures brought to bear upon Lady Blakeney, and the many sources of her unhappiness, so that we will not condemn her, but acquit her—at least, to some extent. Further, she is shown to be penitent for her denunciation of St. Cyr, and is punished (indirectly) for this error by the withdrawal of her husband's love. This isolates her in her plight, alone with her blackmailer.

As for Sir Percy Blakeney, Orczy goes to the same trouble to give an elaborate explanation of the complex forces which affect his emotional state. It cannot be claimed that she is conscious!y trying to give a psychological profile of him, but she does allow the reader to delve to the roots of her character's motivations by way of his childhood history. This, in its way, is as melodramatic as the dazzling career of Marguerite. Sir Percy's mother has been utterly unable to tend to her son's needs, as she had

> become hopelessly insane after two years of happy married life. Percy had just been born when the late Lady Blakeney fell a prey to the terrible malady which in those days was looked upon as hopelessly incurable and nothing short of a curse of God on the entire family.

Percy has spent his youth abroad, by his father's arrangement, where he 'grew up between an imbecile mother and a distracted father.'

Since the romantic reconciliation of the two main characters forms a major part of the plot, it is important to know why and how their estrangement has occurred. The civil violence in France is a vital background to this, as it provides the pretext for a fundamental misunderstanding between the two spouses: Sir Percy cannot trust his wife with the secret of his aid to the threatened aristocrats, as he believes she is in sympathy with the Jacobins. And this problem derives from another, more basic, one, which is that the two are hiding their essential characters from each other. Sir Percy affects nonchalance and even stupidity, to preserve his secret; but this underscores the fact that he is a master of disguise. Her exposure of him to Chauvelin is ironic, since in his Sir Percy persona she dislikes him, while she admires the Scarlet Pimpernel identity which he has constructed.

To the extent that this is a romantic novel, the great drama is her reconciliation with her husband, and this involves three things: thinking and detective work on her part, penance and forgiveness, and active adventure. Once she has handed Chauvelin the vital piece of information about the secret band of rescuers, this sparks the departure of Sir Percy for France, and she begins to notice clues in the house around her which point to her husband's secret identity. Looking at his private study, which bespeaks the authority with which he administers a vast family estate, she goes through a rapid intuitive thought process which first divines the fact that he is hiding his abilities:

> this obvious proof of her husband's strong business capacities did not cause her more than a passing thought of wonder. But it also strengthened her in the now certain knowledge that with his worldly inanities, his foppish ways, and foolish talk, he was not only wearing a mask, but was playing a deliberate and studied part.

This leads to a chain of intuitive reasoning, where she assumes the role of detective: 'At what particular moment the strange doubt first crept into Marguerite's mind, she could not herself afterward have said.' Yet it is a tribute to her much acclaimed brilliance and cleverness that she does reach the correct conclusion, and takes immediate action.

The novel then becomes pure adventure story, as she sets off in pursuit of her wronged husband, collecting a minor character along the way to escort her to France. This constitutes the active penance, as she suffers physical discomfort and anxiety on the journey, and she formalizes this by asking Sir Percy's forgiveness. Her explanation of the urgency of her quest to Sir Andrew, Percy's associate in his small band of heroes, expresses passionate regret: '"I *must* get to him! I *must*," she repeated with savage energy, "to warn him that that man [Chauvelin] is on his track!"' Her penance also includes her determination to perish with him, if necessary; 'Can't you see—can't you see that I *must* get

to him...even...even if it be too late to save him...at least...to be by his side...at the last.'

The extreme cleverness of Orczy's plot, however, lies in the fact that the novelist brings about the total defeat (through audacity and deception) of the villain—at the same time that Lady Blakeney becomes heroic. Lady Blakeney remains suitably feminine—in one sense entirely passive, as she must look on helplessly at what she believes to be the inevitable demise of Sir Percy. When he appears at the French farmhouse where Chauvelin has expected him, she realizes that her proposed warning or aid would be useless: 'The trap was closing in, and Marguerite could do nothing but watch and wonder.' None the less, her determination emphasizes her penance, as she decides—should Percy be surrounded by soldiers, as she expects—to 'rush down and help Percy to sell his life dearly.'

Percy's confrontation with Chauvelin, and Marguerite's covert observation of it, brings together both of Percy's roles in his wife's perception, as she 'indulged in the luxury, dear to every tender woman's heart, of looking at the man she loved.' For her own perception has now been sufficiently sharpened that she can easily pierce his assumed disguise:

> She looked through the tattered curtain across at the handsome face of her husband, in whose lazy blue eyes and behind whose inane smile she could now so plainly see the strength, energy, and resourcefulness which had caused the Scarlet Pimpernel to be reverenced and trusted by his followers.

This reflection brings the reader back to recalling the civil violence which first caused the Pimpernel to don his mask—a mask which he must wear with humility (as the rest of the world believes him to be a fool), yet also with secret pride at the cleverness of deceptions. Wartime, in this novel, serves to highlight the dashing heroism of its major characters—especially when it is conveniently located in another country, from which they themselves can escape. (Sir Percy's yacht, used for these purposes, is named—probably without irony—the *Day Dream*.)

As a heroine, Marguerite retains old-fashioned ideas of femininity, in the novel's climactic crisis. Nonetheless, despite her enforced passivity as an onlooker, she plays a heroic role, in the sense that she is an active presence in the final drama. Since women are not expected to participate in such affairs, in this historical context, Lady Blakeney has all the glory of being heroic in an unlikely setting. She can also be allowed to be traditionally feminine, in that she is passionately devoted to her husband; and she achieves a happy ending. She does prove herself to be self-consciously brave, and Orczy emphasizes this, unlike Bowen and Manning, whose heroines are invariably seen to be deliberately cool and calm.

For all three authors, it is crucial that it be seen by the readers that the *world* has gone mad—not the heroines themselves. It is a way of justifying their actions, or their moral characters, to insist that *they* are all thinking rationally—or at least attempting to do this—under the most trying of circumstances. With the exception of the stereotypically passionate Lady Blakeney, all of the other heroines are cool and detached, even when in the proximity of physical and emotional violence and danger. Bowen's and Manning's heroines all keep their heads, though it is hardly a matter of pleasure. Facing down their grim, sadistic blackmailers, or puzzling over the inexplicable behavior of their lovers, they bring their minds to bear upon difficult problems, and under the most wearisome of circumstances. Wartime poses a special challenge to purely personal dilemmas because it polarizes beliefs and also intensifies powerlessness in individuals. As Bowen's Harrison aptly puts it, war causes everyone to be on 'one side or the other.' Accordingly, it can become a matter of life and death to determine which side one's friends and lovers are, in fact, on. Reason is portrayed as a high value, in each of these novels, as it aids in discernment. To be the 'cleverest woman in Europe' is no mean advantage to Lady Blakeney. Yet it is not this which renders her, at the close of the novel, 'the most beautiful woman' present at the society wedding which rounds out the amazing adventures of the Scarlet Pimpernel and his adoring consort.

Source: Janice Rossen, "The World Gone Mad in Wartime," in *Women Writing Modern Fiction: A Passion for Ideas*, Palgrave Macmillan, 2003, pp. 11–33.

SOURCES

Coogan, Peter, "The Definition of the Superhero," in *Super/Heroes: From Hercules to Superman*, edited by Wendy Haslem, Angela Ndalianis, and Chris Mackie, New Academia, 2007, pp. 21–36.

Craciun, Adriana, *British Women Writers and the French Revolution: Citizens of the World*, Palgrave Macmillan, 2005, p. 146.

Gallagher, Mark, *Action Figures: Men, Action Films, and Contemporary Adventure Narratives*, Palgrave Macmillan, 2006, pp. 3, 9.

Hancock, Ralph C., and L. Gary Lambert, eds., *The Legacy of the French Revolution*, Rowman & Littlefield, 1996.

Hanson, Gillian Mary, *City and Shore: The Function of Setting in the British Mystery*, McFarland, 2004, pp. 13–17.

Hayne, Barrie, "Emmuska Orczy (1865–1947)," in *Great Women Mystery Writers: Classic to Contemporary*, edited by Kathleen Gregory Klein, Greenwood Press, 1994, pp. 259–61.

"A Hero in Disguise," Review of *The Scarlet Pimpernel*, in *New York Times Book Review*, October 14, 1905.

Hoppenstand, Gary, Introduction to *The Scarlet Pimpernel*, by Baroness Orczy, Signet Classics, 2000, pp. ix–xviii.

Huet, Marie-Hélène, "Performing Arts: Theatricality and the Terror," in *Representing the French Revolution: Literature, Historiography, and Art*, University Press of New England, 1992, pp. 135–49.

Orczy, Baroness, *The Scarlet Pimpernel*, Barnes & Noble Classics, 2005.

Platt, Len, *Aristocracies of Fiction: The Idea of Aristocracy in Late-Nineteenth-Century and Early-Twentieth-Century Literary Culture*, Greenwood Press, 2001.

Sasson, Sarah Juliette, Introduction to *The Scarlet Pimpernel*, by Baroness Orczy, Barnes & Noble Classics, 2005, pp. xiii–xxx.

Trice, Ashton D., and Samuel A. Holland, *Heroes, Antiheroes, and Dolts: Portrayals of Masculinity in American Popular Films, 1921–1999*, McFarland, 2001, p. 20.

FURTHER READING

Hibbert, Christopher, *The Days of the French Revolution*, Harper Perennial, 1999.

This is a thorough, highly readable historical narrative of the multifaceted French Revolution.

Kaveney, Roz, *Superheroes! Capes and Crusaders in Comics and Films*, I. B. Tauris, 2008.

Kaveney offers a thorough and engaging examination of the popular mythology of superheroes, especially as developed in the comic book genre.

Landau, Elaine, *Fleeing to Freedom on the Underground Railroad: The Courageous Slaves, Agents, and Conductors*, Twenty-First Century Books, 2006.

Whereas the Scarlet Pimpernel is an entirely fictional rescuer, countless real-life heroes were involved in helping American slaves escape servitude through the Underground Railroad; Landau's volume offers excellent portraits of some of those heroes.

Parker, Noel, *Portrayals of Revolution: Images, Debates and Patterns of Thought on the French Revolution*, Southern Illinois University Press, 1990.

In this academic volume, Parker investigates how the greatest turning point in France's history is portrayed in many settings, from festivals to fashion to fiction to philosophy.

Speak

LAURIE HALSE ANDERSON
1999

Melinda Sordino is about to begin her first day of senior high school in Laurie Halse Anderson's 1999 novel *Speak*. Melinda cowers on the bus as she sits alone. She refers to herself as an outcast while she stands in the gym during freshman orientation. She sees her friends from middle school, and they see her. But no one speaks to her. When they laugh, Melinda senses they are laughing at her. Her ex-friends do not know what happened to her the night of the summer party. All they know is that Melinda ruined the party and got many of them in trouble when she called the police.

Melinda's experience is revealed very slowly in Anderson's provocative and touching novel. The book has won the praise of educators and critics for Anderson's ability to tell a disturbing story with irony, humor, and frankness. *Speak* was named a 2000 Printz Honor Book and was a finalist for both the 1999 National Book Award and Edgar Allan Poe Award.

In a voice that is well tuned to high school life in the 1990s, Anderson has created a character whose first year at Merryweather High is anything but merry. Melinda is psychologically tortured by her memories of having been raped. Those memories, which she refers to as the beast, lock her voice inside of her. She has no one she can trust to share her story with. When she finally gains the courage to speak, her ex-best friend calls her a liar. The only person

Janitor's closet *(Image copyright Andrew Gentry, 2009. Used under license from Shutterstock.com)*

since. The first book she wrote was *Ndito Runs*, a picture book published in 1996. Her next two books, both featuring the same characters, were *Turkey Pox* (1996) and *No Time for Mother's Day* (1999).

Speak (1999) was Anderson's first young adult novel. Her 2002 novel *Catalyst* is set in the same high school as *Speak* and even contains some of the same characters. Anderson's more recent titles include *Wintergirls* (2009), about a girl suffering from anorexia, and *Chains* (2008), about the eighteenth-century lives of teenage slaves. The award-winning author's books frequently appear on the *New York Times Best Seller List*. Anderson stated in an interview with Julie Prince in *Teacher Librarian*, "I've never worried about trends or trying to catch the next big thing. I write the stories that I can hear in my heart. It seems to be an effective strategy." Anderson then added, "I had my own struggles as an adolescent and I remember what it feels like to be lost and overwhelmed."

After college, the author married Greg Anderson. The couple had two daughters. The Andersons later divorced. She has since married Scot Larrabee and lives in upper state New York. Anderson writes a blog called *Mad Woman in the Forest* at http://halseanderson.livejournal.com to keep her reader fans up-to-date on her travels as she journeys around the nation on speaking tours.

who knows about that night is the student who raped her. It is not until he tries to do it again that Melinda finds the strength to speak and to stop him.

AUTHOR BIOGRAPHY

Anderson was born on October 23, 1961, in Potsdam, New York. After high school, Anderson attended Onondaga Community College in Syracuse, New York, the setting of her novel. Later she transferred to Georgetown University in Washington, D.C., where she earned a bachelor's degree in languages and linguistics.

From 1989 until 1992, Anderson worked as a reporter for two newspapers in Philadelphia, the *Record* and the *Inquirer*. Between 1992 and 1998, she turned to freelancing, writing articles for various trade journals. Later, she decided to write children's books and has not turned back

PLOT SUMMARY

First Marking Period

Anderson's novel *Speak* begins with the protagonist, Melinda Sordino, on her way to the first day of high school. Melinda is very nervous about boarding the bus, though the reason for her tension is not provided. The school bus is empty when she gets on, but she carefully contemplates where she will sit. Although sitting in the front of the bus reminds her of being in elementary school, she decides sitting close to the front door is her best choice. By the time the bus arrives at school, Melinda is the only student who sits alone. All her old friends have shunned her.

Inside the school gym, Melinda looks to find someone to stand with. She recognizes the different groups by types, such as the athletes, the cheerleaders, the Plain Janes. Her middle-school friends look her way and laugh. Melinda assumes they are laughing at her. No one motions for her to join

MEDIA ADAPTATIONS

- In 2003, *Speak* was adapted to film, starring Kristen Stewart as Melinda. The movie was produced by Speak Film Inc., and directed by Jessica Sharzer. The film was released as a DVD in 2005.
- *Speak* is available on CD, read by Mandy Siegfried, at audiobooks.com and published in 2008 by Listening Library.

them. When she spots Rachel Bruin, who used to be her best friend, Melinda sees Rachel mouth the words "I hate you." Melinda turns away and remains in her group of one. She names her group the Outcast.

Melinda wanders from class to class, offering a cynical view of her teachers. Her English teacher is dubbed Hairwoman, because of the woman's long black hair that is tinged in neon orange at the tips. Melinda refers to her social studies teacher as Mr. Neck, because of the thickness of his neck. Mr. Freeman, her art teacher, retains his name. He makes her feel relaxed and appears, to Melinda, to be more sane than most other adults in her life. Mr. Freeman tells his students that in his class they will discover their souls. For their first assignment, students pull pieces of paper out of an old globe. On the papers are names of objects. Melinda's paper contains the word *tree*. Mr. Freeman says that they will use this object as their model for all the art work they will complete that year. They may paint, sketch, sculpt, or use any other medium they choose. However, all their work will focus on their selected object. Their grades will be based on how well they express an emotion through their finished pieces.

Later, Melinda thinks about her mother, with whom she has a strained relationship. Her mother manages a clothing store in downtown Syracuse. Most clothing stores that Melinda is familiar with and where her friends shop are located in the suburban malls. Downtown

stores are considered dangerous. Melinda believes her mother likes the challenge. Her mother thrives on doing things that scare other people. Melinda demonstrates, as the novel progresses, that, unlike her mother, her most dominant emotion is fear.

The only student willing to associate with Melinda is a new girl named Heather. She is very unlike Melinda. She is very attentive to her clothes and her grooming, wants to be popular, and seeks ways to insert herself in the middle of school activities. Heather dominates Melinda, telling her how and what to eat at lunchtime and criticizing Melinda's negative outlook about socializing, exercising, and attending classes. However, Heather is better than nothing. Melinda goes along with Heather's plans and accepts her evaluations because Melinda also feels that having at least one friend is better than being alone.

One day, while Melinda is attempting to avoid Mr. Neck, who is trailing her because she has not turned in her assignments, Melinda ducks into a janitor closet to hide. In the back of the closet she discovers an overstuffed chair and decides this will be the perfect place to get away if the pressure of school becomes too intense. Eventually, she hangs up posters and some of her art projects, claiming the space as her personal lounge.

At a pep rally before a football game, a student Melinda does not know asks, "Aren't you the one who called the cops at Kyle Rodger's party?" Another student adds, "My brother got arrested at that party." Then the student says, "I can't believe you did that." It is through these statements that readers gain further insights into Melinda's social problems.

Melinda receives her report card, and her parents explode. She gets an A in art, a B in biology, and Cs in everything else. Previously, she received straight As.

Second Marking Period

Melinda begins to show physical symptoms of her stress. She chews on her lips hard enough to draw blood and scabs have formed around her mouth. Her throat is always sore, which she believes is from having to hold back screams. She says she has a beast that is locked inside her. The beast represents the memories of what happened to her on the night of the summer party. She seldom speaks to anyone, even when they ask questions. Her thoughts are so disoriented that she cannot manage words. She has headaches and rarely sleeps.

In her biology class, David Petrakis sits next to her. Melinda believes that he has the potential to be cute one day. She also fantasizes about being friends with him. David is also in her social studies class. One day after Mr. Neck cuts off a spontaneous classroom debate about immigrants, David stands up to him and demands a right to speak. A few days later, David brings a video recorder to class to gather information about Mr. Neck's teaching performance. Rumors are that David is working to gather evidence for a suit against Mr. Neck. Melinda is impressed. David becomes her hero.

On Thanksgiving Day, Melinda's mother is called to the store on an emergency. So Melinda's father must cook the turkey. Her dad makes a mess and has to throw the turkey away. Melinda gets an idea to use the turkey bones for an art project. She rescues the carcass. Mr. Freeman is impressed with the sculpture that Melinda creates from the bones and other found objects. When Melinda finds a doll's head, she seals the doll's mouth with tape. From this, Mr. Freeman senses Melinda is in pain. When he acknowledges this, Melinda runs from the classroom.

On Christmas Day, Melinda is touched emotionally when her parents give her art supplies. They have noticed she has taken an interest in drawing. The fact that they have noticed her is what impresses Melinda. This makes her want to tell them what happened to her, but she quickly changes her mind.

Back at school in her biology class, Melinda and her partner David must dissect a frog. David places the frog on its back and pins its feet to the dissecting board. Melinda raises the knife to make a cut down the length of the frog's belly when her mind is flooded with a flashback to that summer night. She hears a scream deep inside her and feels a pain. Then she passes out. As she falls, she hits her head against the table and must go to the hospital. As a doctor flashes a light into her eyes, checking for signs of a concussion, Melinda wonders if the doctor can see her thoughts. She wishes he could cut out all her memories.

A few days later, Andy Evans comes to the table where Melinda is sitting, eating her lunch. Some of Melinda's former friends are sitting at the other end. Andy stops behind Melinda and plays with her ponytail. She runs to the bathroom and pukes. Andy is the boy who raped her. It worries Melinda that her ex-best friend flirts with Andy.

Report cards come out. Melinda's grades are getting worse.

Third Marking Period

Melinda misses the school bus and must walk to school. She passes a bakery. Just as she approaches the front door, Andy walks out. She freezes in fright. Andy asks if she wants a bite of his donut. She cannot speak, but she does run. As she escapes, she wonders why she did not run that summer night when he attacked her. Why did she stay and take his punishment?

In Hairwoman's English class, the students are reading *The Scarlet Letter*. The story is about a woman who has committed adultery and is forced to wear a red letter *A* on her chest. Melinda thinks that she and this woman would have been good friends. She thinks she should wear the letter *S* on her clothes. The *S* would stand for "silent, for stupid, for scared. S for silly. For shame."

The tree Melinda is working on in art class is frustrating her. She has tried to paint a tree, to sketch a tree, and to carve a tree out of a linoleum tile. None have worked.

Melinda's relationship with Heather is, at best, strained. Heather has joined a group called The Marthas. One of the rules of this group is that they buy similar clothes and wear coordinated outfits to school. They also do charitable work. Heather always enlists Melinda's help. Heather, being the newest member, is given all the grunt work, which she then passes on to Melinda. Melinda always caves in, as Heather is her only friend. At lunch one day, Heather tells Melinda that the two of them have nothing in common. She thanks Melinda for being nice to her when school first started, but it is now time to cut their ties. She also says Melinda is depressed and should seek help.

A white envelope is taped to Melinda's locker on Valentine's Day. She does not know how to react to it. She has a glimmer of hope that it might be from David, but she does not want to get too excited. The envelope could also be a cruel joke. So she does not open it right away. After her next class, she comes back to her locker and opens the envelope. It is from Heather. Besides the card, the friendship necklace that Melinda gave Heather is inside. Heather thanks Melinda for understanding. Melinda is crushed.

Mr. Freeman hands Melinda a book on the artist Pablo Picasso in art class. He thinks it will give her some ideas. After reading it, Melinda draws a tree in cubist form, with lots of geometric shapes. Mr. Freeman is impressed. After school, he sees Melinda walking toward town and offers a ride. Before he drops her off, he tells her he is available at any time if she needs to talk.

A few days later, Melinda runs into David at a basketball game. He invites her to a party at his house. She refuses the invitation. She is afraid that he might be lying about his parents being there. She thinks he might be luring her into a position where she cannot defend herself. She cannot stand the thought of his touching her. Later, she gets angry with herself for refusing to go. She then thinks back on the events of that summer party. She went with a group of her girlfriends. Most of the kids there were older and were drinking. Melinda drank beer for the first time in her life and got sick. She went outside, fearing she might vomit. Andy followed her. She was amazed that he paid attention to her. He pulled her into him and started kissing her. All she could think was how amazed her girlfriends would be if they could see her in Andy's arms. But things went too far, and Melinda struggled to get free. Andy covered her mouth with his hand and forced her to the ground. He hurt her. Then he left her lying there.

Melinda was only thirteen. She had no experience with other boys. She did not know what to do next. She could only think of calling the police. When they came, Melinda had run away. She did not want to tell anyone.

The third report card comes out. Melinda gets an A in art, but all the other grades are Ds and Fs.

Fourth Marking Period

Ivy is in Melinda's art class. Ivy is the first not to shun her. Ivy knows nothing of what happened at the summer party, but she appreciates the art projects that Melinda creates. She praises Melinda, telling her she is better than she realizes. She encourages Melinda when she shows signs of giving up. Ivy and Mr. Freeman help to rebuild Melinda's self-confidence.

When Melinda notices how attached Rachel is to Andy, she tries to warn her. She senses that she cannot come right out and tell her what happened, but she does send her an anonymous note telling Rachel to be careful. When Melinda's note to Rachel does not appear to affect her, Melinda

finally tells Rachel that Andy raped her. Rachel is furious with Melinda, telling her she is just jealous because Andy has asked Rachel to the prom.

While at home, sick with the flu, Melinda again reflects on the summer party. It is the first time that she is able to see that she did nothing wrong. She did not entice Andy. She even told him to stop. She did not want to have sex with him. She was raped. Up until then she was too overcome with shame to acknowledge this. Now, as she is able to more fully grasp what actually happened, she knows that what Andy did was wrong.

Rachel breaks up with Andy. Apparently, Andy became too aggressive, and Rachel fought him off. Andy is furious about this. When he learns that Melinda warned Rachel, he follows Melinda to the janitor's closet and traps her. He is harsh with her both verbally and physically and tries to rape her again. This time, Melinda screams out and tries to push him away. She makes it out of the closet unscathed. At the end of the story, Melinda creates the perfect tree in art class, a tree that opens up all her emotions, and Melinda begins to tell Mr. Freeman what happened to her.

CHARACTERS

Rachel Bruin

Rachel was the protagonist's best friend from elementary school through middle school. She is the one person that Melinda wishes she could talk to. However, Rachel believes that Melinda ruined her summer because of the police raid on the last party before school resumed.

Rachel hangs out with foreign exchange students at school. She takes up the habit of pretending to smoke candy cigarettes to give her a more European flair. When Melinda runs into Rachel in the girls' bathroom, Rachel responds to Melinda's statements with grunts or foreign phrases. Melinda learns that Rachel changes the spelling and pronunciation of her name to Rachelle, to sound more French.

When Melinda sees Rachel falling for Andy, Melinda wants to warn her. Melinda finally gets up the courage to do so, but Rachel thinks Melinda is jealous. However, it is because of Melinda's warning that Rachel finally sees who Andy really is. When he becomes to sexually aggressive at the prom, Rachel is strong enough to resist him. There is no statement in the novel that Rachel and Melinda mend their relationship, but Melinda does notice that after the prom, Rachel has taken an interest in one of the male foreign exchange students, which Melinda applauds.

Dad

Melinda has only a surface relationship with both her parents. However, she appears to be closer to her father. They have an unspoken understanding of one another, which usually means they leave one another alone. Melinda often comes home to an empty house, eats her dinner alone, and then retreats upstairs to her room. Later, when her father returns home, Melinda listens to the sounds he makes and tries to guess what he is doing, such as microwaving his dinner, pouring himself a drink, turning on the television. They seldom speak to one another. Melinda's attitude toward life, in many ways, mimics her father's style. This is exposed on Thanksgiving when after Melinda's mother must abandon dinner plans to go to work, her father throws the turkey in the trash after unsuccessful attempts at cooking it. They order pizza instead of eating the traditional meal, which pleases both of them. It appears that her father is only vaguely aware of who Melinda is, what she is doing with her life, and what she is feeling. Her father is oblivious to the signs of her depression.

Andy Evans

Andy Evans is a handsome, well dressed senior at Merryweather High School. Girls are very much aware of him and would give anything to go out with him. At least this is true in the beginning of the year, especially among the freshmen girls. Andy appears to enjoy hanging with the freshmen, and one can assume that he is preying on their innocence.

Melinda, in her secret thoughts, refers to Andy as *It*. She is very reluctant to say his name. Andy comes up to her, at one point in the story, and plays with her ponytail as he talks to some of the other freshmen girls. He appears unaware that he has done anything damaging to Melinda. He eventually latches on to Rachel, Melinda's ex-best friend. When he discovers that Melinda has told Rachel about what he did to her, Andy corners her in the janitor's closet. He tells her that she wanted to have sexual relations with him at that summer party and should not be spreading rumors otherwise. He then tries to force himself on Melinda

again. When Melinda fights back, Andy gets angry. Melinda yells out for help and is able to escape from Andy. Nothing is said, however, about what happens to Andy after that. Readers are left in the dark in reference to whether Andy is punished for his crime.

Mr. Freeman

Mr. Freeman is an art teacher at Merryweather High School. Melinda initially describes Mr. Freeman as being ugly. He reminds her of a grasshopper or a circus entertainer walking on stilts. He has a big nose and talks a lot. As the story progresses, though, Mr. Freeman becomes Melinda's favorite teacher. She cannot believe he can get away with teaching his class the way he does because it is so much fun. Mr. Freeman encourages his students to reach down deep inside of themselves to find secrets they have never before realized they possess.

Mr. Freeman is also a father figure for Melinda. Throughout the story, it is Mr. Freeman who notices that Melinda is troubled and attempts to get her to open up. He encourages her art and praises her for her attempts. He tells her that he is always available should she want to talk. When words fail Melinda, Mr. Freeman implies that her emotions can be expressed through her projects. At the end of the story, in the final lines, the author suggests that Melinda goes to Mr. Freeman and begins to tell him her story.

Hairwoman

Hairwoman is the nickname that Melinda gives to her English teacher. Hairwoman is so named because she uses her dark, long hair, whose ends are dyed bright orange, to hide behind. She seldom gives her students eye contact. When she talks to them, her head is often bowed toward her desk, or she is turned toward the blackboard or the flag.

Heather

Heather is a new student at Merryweather High School. When she finds Melinda sitting alone, she assumes that Melinda is also new at the school. Melinda describes Heather as having a mouth full of braces, being in good physical shape, and talking way too much. However, Melinda welcomes Heather's company, at first. It is better than standing alone.

Heather needs to set goals for her future life in school. Melinda tolerates Heather, which makes Heather believe that Melinda agrees with her.

Heather chooses the best clubs at school and makes every effort to be accepted. She takes on projects that are too big for her and then drags Melinda in on them, insisting that Melinda do some of the dirty work. In the end, after Melinda refuses to do any more work for her, Heather comes to Melinda and says that their relationship is not working out and should end. They have little in common, Heather says, and besides, Melinda's attitude is too negative. Heather returns a friendship necklace Melinda gave her and thanks Melinda for being so understanding.

Ivy

Ivy was not one of Melinda's close friends in middle school, but they did hang out from time to time. When Melinda finds Ivy in her art class, she tries to make contact with her, but Ivy does not notice. It is not until Melinda brings to class her unusual sculpture made with turkey bones that Ivy takes an interest. Ivy praises Melinda for her creativity and tells her, when Melinda becomes frustrated with her projects, that she is a good artist and should continue with her work.

Melinda believes that Ivy is the better artist, and she remarks on Ivy's good personality, a trait that makes it easy for Melinda to like her. Ivy goes looking for Melinda one day when Melinda abruptly leaves class. She finds Melinda in the girls' bathroom. While there, Melinda opens up a little about her feelings about Andy. Ivy joins in the conversation, telling Melinda that she is disgusted about how Rachel is falling all over Andy. Melinda is impressed that Ivy has noted the flaws in Andy's personality. She is also moved that Ivy was concerned enough to come looking for her, making sure that Melinda was all right.

Ms. Keen

Ms. Keen is Melinda's biology teacher. Very little is said about this particular teacher except for the strange clothes she wears. Melinda does not complain very much about Ms. Keen's teaching methods or the subject matter. In other ways, Ms. Keen is a nondescript teacher whom Melinda does not despise.

Mother

Melinda's mother is just the opposite of her daughter. Melinda states that her mother not only is fearless, she goes out of her way to confront dangerous situations. Her mother manages a store downtown in a dangerous district. She is often called away from her family to confront ongoing challenges and thus is seldom home. Melinda's mother is different in other ways too. She wants Melinda to buy clothes that Melinda does not feel comfortable with. The two of them have little in common. Melinda's mother is so busy, she hardly notices that Melinda is in emotional pain. She thinks that Melinda is rebelling against some unknown cause. She does not understand why Melinda is so quiet and why she is doing so poorly at school. Her solution is punishment, which does not work. Melinda is impressed, though, when her mother buys her art supplies for Christmas. She is pleased that her mother at least took a little time to notice her.

Mr. Neck

Mr. Neck, so called because Melinda sees him as a jock with a neck thicker than his head, is her social studies teacher. Mr. Neck makes statements about how well he knows students. When he first sees Melinda, he dubs her a troublemaker and pursues her in the halls, handing out demerits and other punishments when she fails to turn in a pass. Melinda paints Mr. Neck as arrogant and hypocritical. She also praises her fellow student, David Petrakis, for standing up to Mr. Neck's hypocrisy in class.

Nicole

Nicole is briefly mentioned as another of Melinda's former friends. Nicole is an excellent athlete, the opposite of Melinda. She is a star soccer player, looked up to by even the male athletes. Gym teachers praise Nicole for her gifts. Nicole is neutral as far as friendship with Melinda is concerned. She neither shuns her nor goes out of her way to communicate.

David Petrakis

David Petrakis shares a lab table with Melinda in biology class. He shows signs that he is unaffected by the gossip that surrounds Melinda. Meanwhile, Melinda sometimes finds herself daydreaming about David as a potential boyfriend. One day, David invites Melinda to a pizza party at his house. Melinda is flattered, but she is also frightened by the proposal. She refuses the invitation because she is concerned he might merely want to lure her into another bad situation in which she might not be able to defend herself. David thus portrays some of the difficulties that Melinda faces in developing future intimate male relationships. As the story progresses, David grows on Melinda. He becomes her hero after he stands up to Mr. Neck's insulting behavior.

Melinda Sordino

Melinda is the protagonist of this story. She was thirteen years old when she was sexually attacked at a summer party. She has kept this a secret from everyone, and it is eating her up inside. All that her parents know about this is that Melinda has suddenly become very quiet and her interest in school has begun a huge downward spiral. Melinda's friends only know that Melinda was at the party and while there called the cops. This caused trouble for many of the students who were there. Many were underage drinkers. Some lost their jobs because of this. Now, everyone at school shuns her.

Melinda has kept the attack a secret because she is ashamed. She feels she brought it on herself, even though she tried to fight the boy off. Much of the story is told from inside Melinda's head. There is very little dialogue with friends or family. Melinda lives through her feelings of self-doubt and the forced isolation that her secret has brought on.

Melinda's grades disintegrate as she cannot focus on her schoolwork and often skips class. All her energies are focused on keeping her emotions from exploding out of her. An abandoned janitor's closet becomes her refuge when she senses she is losing control of her fears and anxieties. She often wishes she could talk to someone, but she does not know how to start. She fears that other people will think she is despicable. Her parents are always too busy. Her friends have made it clear they already hate her. In the end, she finds her voice. She is able to refuse Heather's demands. This gives her the courage to stand up to Andy when he tries a second attack. Then she is ready to talk, to tell someone what really happened that night.

THEMES

Trauma and the Restorative Power of Speech

The trauma of the rape that Melinda experiences before Anderson's novel *Speak* even begins influences the entire story. Because of that trauma, Melinda's mental state continues to deteriorate as the story progresses. As she attempts to find, within herself as well as in the world around her, places in which to hide, she sinks deeper into silence. So many people disallow her a chance to reveal her inner fears, shame, and confusion. Her peers have already judged her and decide to ban her from their groups. Her parents do not have time or patience to encourage her to open up to them. Only Melinda's art teacher perceives that something is troubling her. He is the only one who understands that sometimes words are either too difficult or too inadequate to express the deepest emotions. However, he also understands that in order for Melinda to heal, she must find a way to articulate her feelings. That is why he encourages her to speak symbolically through an art form. It is through art, the author suggests, that Melinda begins to unravel all the emotions that have entangled her mind. By working on her art project, Melinda begins to understand that she has no reason to feel guilty for what happened to her. Once she clears her mind, she is then able to think more clearly and in the process she informs herself of the truth of the rape. When she begins to speak out, she realizes that her role in the rape was that of victim not that of perpetrator, and thus the healing begins.

Friendship

The theme of friendship runs throughout Anderson's novel *Speak*. It is as if the author were posing questions about what true friendship is. Melinda, the protagonist, was once a fairly popular young girl. She had maintained friendships from elementary and middle school. However, because of one incident, she appears to have lost every friend she ever had. It was a big incident, but even still, why did no one bother to ask her side of the story? Why did everyone turn on her with one ex-friend going so far as stating that she hated her?

With friendship playing such an important role in high school, the loss of it, as portrayed in this novel, is almost as tragic as the rape that Melinda suffered. Melinda has no one to talk to, no one to sit with at lunch, no one to help her unravel the consequences of the terrible crime committed against her. The character Heather steps in as a pseudofriend, but Melinda soon discovers that there is no authenticity involved. Heather, like Melinda, is lonesome. She is the new kid in town and finds that breaking in with a crowd is very difficult. Heather uses Melinda to develop her plan to become popular. When Heather believes she has succeeded, she tells Melinda the two of them have nothing in common. Later, Heather returns the friendship necklace that Melinda gave her, thus making the break very clear.

The closest Melinda comes to having a true friend is in her relationship with Ivy, who is in Melinda's art class. The development of their

TOPICS FOR FURTHER STUDY

- Research cubism, especially as Pablo Picasso developed it through his paintings. At one point in Anderson's story, Melinda's creativity is reawakened by studying Picasso's art. She draws a tree reflecting the concepts of cubism. Imagine what that tree might have looked like. Produce several samples of your own, using various media, such as charcoal, oil paints, and linoleum tiles, as Melinda did. Display your artwork for your class to see and explain what cubism is.

- What are the legal standards established by the U.S. Equal Employment Opportunity Commission and the U.S. Supreme Court that define sexual harassment? After researching this on the Internet and in your library, take a survey of students at your school, asking them how they define sexual harassment. Are there gaps between what students know and what the law is? After compiling your results, create a presentation for your class. Be ready to present your facts as well as answer questions.

- Interview your school counselors, asking them for advice about what a student should do if she thinks she is the victim of date rape. Then create a script that will be turned into a short film with student actors playing the roles of victim and counselor. The aim of this film should be to educate students on how to avoid this situation as well as what they should do if they find themselves a victim.

- Read Heidi Ayarbe's novel *Freeze Frame* (2008) about a teenage boy who accidentally shoots his friend. Kyle Carroll is the protagonist of this story, and like Melinda in *Speak*, Kyle is ostracized by his fellow students. Compare the two stories. How do the two authors depict the psychological struggles that each protagonist goes through? How do the protagonists deal with the challenges they experience? How are those challenges resolved? Present your findings in an essay.

---

friendship signals a turning point in the story. It is with Ivy that Melinda begins to express her fear and hatred of Andy, the boy who raped her. Melinda's steps toward being David's friend show signs of developing, but she is fearful of the thought of him touching her because of the rape. It is easier for her to start a friendship with Mr. Freeman, her art teacher. He is safer, in Melinda's judgment, because he is like a father figure. It is with Mr. Freeman, at the very end of the story, that Melinda begins to open up. And with this her healing begins, signaling the possibility of new friendships.

Identity

Another important theme is that of identity. The author takes readers into the lives of teens who are developing a sense of who they are outside of definitions of who their parents and teachers believe them to be. There are many struggles in the process. These struggles are playfully exaggerated in the constant changing of the school's mascot. As the school board tries on various rallying names for the school, from hornets to blue devils, so too the high school students try on different definitions of themselves. Rachel changes the sound of her name to Rachelle, making her appear more European. Heather joins a club whose identity is established through its members wearing matching outfits.

Melinda's struggle for identity is more serious. She calls herself an outcast in the beginning of the story. She does this for two reasons. First, her friends have shunned her. More critically, Melinda has shunned herself. She is ashamed about what happened to her, believing that she was at fault. Because of this, she has a constant struggle to keep her real self buried deep inside of her. She does not want to consider how she truly feels because she believes she is a monster. She refers to her reactions to the rape as the beast. There once was the sweet girl, the good student, the young girl with a lot of friends. And then there was the rape. Melinda's former identity no longer exists. What identity she claims now is uncertain. She cannot think straight. She would rather hide. It is not so much that she is hiding from the truth of who she is, but rather that she is hiding because she does not know the truth. To protect herself, Melinda has become a blank.

The lack of identity that Melinda experiences is exposed in her relationship with Heather. Melinda knows she has nothing in common with Heather. She dislikes the chores that Heather continues to talk her into doing. But Heather gives Melinda a hint of identity, so she clings to her. It is not until Melinda finally gains the courage to say "No" to Heather that she begins to reclaim her real identity. After that step, Melinda knows she must warn her ex-best friend Rachel about Andy, a step that exposes what has happened to her. Finally, Melinda also realizes that Andy was the culprit in the rape. She has nothing to be ashamed of. Once she begins to reclaim her identity, she is able to tell the whole story to Mr. Freeman and thus begin to heal.

Alienation

Despite the silence Melinda displays by either never talking to anyone or having great difficulty in sorting through her thoughts inside her head in order to speak, Melinda has a lot to say. Many of her thoughts reflect the alienation that she feels from her fellow students, her teachers, and her parents. For instance, she gives her least favorite teachers unflattering names. This name-calling makes Melinda's teachers a little less human in her mind. She can then create a bigger distance between them and her, which is what alienation is all about.

Melinda also creates a gap between herself and her fellow students. One way she does this is to put them down. In particular, she chooses the cheerleaders. She lumps the individuals together as a group and then tears into them. They all sleep with the football players, she states, and then come Monday morning they play their roles as goddesses. Melinda is obviously jealous of them, but rather than admit this human emotion, she alienates herself from them.

Melinda's parents are often not at home. When they are, Melinda rarely talks to them. Both parents are very busy and never seem to notice that Melinda is suffering. They know she is quiet and is not doing well in school, but they take

Tree and hands (*Image copyright Elena Ray, 2009. Used under license from Shutterstock.com*)

that as a sign of disobedience rather than asking what is troubling her.

STYLE

Suspense

Anderson does not reveal what is bothering her protagonist until well into the story. This creates suspense, which keeps her readers turning the pages to find out what is going to happen next and why Melinda is acting so strangely. Authors tend to use various forms of suspense to keep their readers engaged in the story. Suspense can also put readers in an active, rather than passive state, as they attempt to guess what happened by putting together the clues the author provides. Not all novels have to be classified as mysteries in order to create suspense. Most good novels have some element of suspense. Some are more subtle than others. Suspense is most obvious in crime novels and psychological thrillers. However, all well-written novels will provide enough unanswered questions to sustain the reader's curiosity and thus offer suspense.

Narrative Sequence

Throughout Anderson's novel, the narrative follows a certain path for only a short period. Rather than having long chapters devoted to a particular scene, Anderson hops from one short scene to another with little transition between them. This can be a little confusing at first, but by doing so, the author reflects the state of the protagonist's mind. Melinda admits that she has trouble sorting through her thoughts. For this reason, she has difficulty speaking. Her focus is on keeping her emotions buried, and this takes a lot of concentration. She sometimes loses control over her emotions and must run away. By jumping from one topic to another, the author recreates that same feeling in the reader's mind. For a few paragraphs, the reader follows the activities in Melinda's art class, for example. Then without any forewarning, Melinda might next be at home, in another class, or in the halls. The reader follows along, symbolically sharing the protagonist's unstable psychological state of mind, switching from one short thought to another.

HISTORICAL CONTEXT

Date Rape

According to the U.S. Department of Health and Human Services, the definition of *date rape* is when "forced sex occurs between two people who already know each other." Date rape occurs in about half of all rape cases reported. "Even if the two people know each other well, and even if they were intimate or had sex before, no one has the right to force a sexual act on another person against his or her will." The Department goes on to state that rape should not be confused with passion or love: "Rape is an act of aggression and violence." Another major point that the Department clarifies is that the victim of a rape should not feel that he or she brought it on by the clothes they were wearing or how they might have been acting: "Rape is always the fault of the rapist."

In a report offered by the U.S. Department of Justice, the number of incidents of date rape has slowly declined. In the 1990s, the time period for Anderson's novel, 1.1 million women reported intimate violence in 1993 as compared with 900,000 female victims in 1998. Of the female victims, women between the ages of sixteen and twenty-four were more likely to experience intimate violence than any other age group. The statistics for men, however, remained the same

with about 160,000 violent crimes reported by an intimate partner both in 1993 and in 1998.

The Federal Government Source for Women's Health Information provides suggestions concerning how to avoid date rape and how to report an assault.

Development of the Young Adult Novel, 1960s to 2000s

Young Adult literature usually implies stories written for a teenage audience, roughly ninth through twelfth graders, though the age range can vary. Before the 1960s, Young Adult literature often meant romantic stories for girls and adventure books for boys. The material in Young Adult (YA) books rarely touched on controversial topics. Rather, the stories glossed over topics that were considered too involved with adult situations. However, with the 1960s, Young Adult literature began to change.

S. E. Hinton's novel, *The Outsiders* (1967), was one of the first to tackle teenage problems that had not previously been written about in literature for the young adult market. Hinton, only sixteen years old when she wrote the story, took on topics such as teen violence, drug and alcohol abuse, and dysfunctional family relationships. In the 1990s, the American Library Association (ALA) still listed this book as one of the most frequently challenged books by various adult groups wanting to ban the book from school libraries. Young Adult author Judy Blume raised eyebrows when she published her 1975 novel *Forever*, which included a discussion of teenage sex. Though the novel found its way into high school libraries, it too remains on the ALA's list of most challenged books. *The Chocolate War* (1974) by Robert Cormier is another Young Adult title that is often challenged because of its language and sexual content.

Despite the challenges some YA titles have received in the past, the popularity of novels both written for and read by teens has grown. According to Cecilia Goodnow, a writer for the *Seattle Post-Intelligencer*, not only are sales increasing but the quality of the material has significantly improved. The subject matter is becoming more sophisticated. For instance, one of the more popular teenage books is *The Book Thief* (2005) by Markus Zusak. This story is set in Nazi Germany and deals with the Holocaust.

Goodnow also points out that some of the most prestigious national book awards are reflecting the growing market as well as the improved

High school hallway (*Image copyright Matty Symons, 2009. Used under license from Shutterstock.com*)

quality of writing in the Young Adult field. In 1996, the National Book Foundation decided to include a Young Adult literature section to its considerations for annual awards. The ALA also expanded their annual awards to include the Michael L. Printz Award for Excellence in Young Adult Literature. *Speak* was named a Michael L. Printz Honor Book in 2000.

CRITICAL OVERVIEW

Anderson's award-winning novel *Speak* attracted many teenage readers when it first came out in 1999, thus placing the novel on the *New York Times* best-seller list. Reviewers enjoyed the book as well. One critic, Casey Casias, writing for the *Santa Fe New Mexican*, states that *Speak* is a "truly enjoyable novel." Although Casias says books with depressing topics were not his usual fare, this one is "told with such dry wit and believable voice that it is impossible to put aside." Though the topic might be depressing, a reviewer

for *Horn Book* calls the novel "an uncannily funny book" due to the witty observations that the protagonist uses. Debbie Carton, of *Booklist*, uses similar words to describe the novel. Carton writes that Melinda "recounts her past and present experiences in bitterly ironic, occasionally even amusing vignettes."

Another element that is often pointed out is the authenticity of the author's voice and her characters. Chris Liska Carger, writing for *Book Links*, refers to the "realistic picture" of high school that Anderson creates. A reviewer for *Publishers Weekly* points out Anderson's "gritty realism" and predicts that "Melinda's hard-won metamorphosis will leave readers touched and inspired."

CRITICISM

Joyce Hart

Hart is a published author and a creative writing teacher. In the following essay, she examines the symbolism in Speak.

WHAT DO I READ NEXT?

- Anderson's novel *Catalyst* (2002) takes place at Merryweather High, the same setting in which *Speak* is set, but the focus in this novel is on different students. The novel's protagonist is Kate Malone, an honors student who pushes herself relentlessly to be her very best. Besides the good grades she makes, she runs cross country, takes care of her widower father and her brother, and works hard to stay out of trouble. When a neighbor's house burns down, she offers to share her bedroom with a teenager who once used to be her archenemy. These are not Kate's only challenges. She has applied to only one college, Massachusetts Institute of Technology, a school with difficult admissions standards. As other students receive acceptance letters, Kate nervously waits to see if she made a big miscalculation.

- Anderson has received praise for her novel *Twisted* (2008), which focuses on the mental anguish of a teenage boy, Tyler Miller. Tyler was a computer nerd for most of his high school years. That is, until he pulled a graffiti prank that boosted his popularity but landed him a community service sentence doing physical labor all summer long. The punishment built his muscles as well as his character. When the new Tyler Miller enters his senior year, he is pleased with all the attention he receives, especially from Bethany Milbury. Tyler develops a big crush on Bethany, which infuriates her brother, Chip. Conflicts between Tyler and Chip keep the tension high at school, while fights with Tyler's alcoholic father provide anxious moments at home.

- Anderson's 2009 novel *Wintergirls* has received praise from several reviewers. The young protagonist, Lia, faces the problems of anorexia in what has been described as a very realistic portrayal. Anderson's writing skills makes this novel hard to put down despite the difficult topic of teenage self-destruction caused by a debilitating eating disorder.

- Melinda in Anderson's novel *Speak* finds solace in a janitor's closet at school, a place where she can hide. Keeping her company is a poster of author and poet Maya Angelou. Angelou is an African American writer who first came to fame through her book *I Know Why the Caged Bird Sings* (1970). Though written in the form of a novel, this book is actually the autobiography of Angelou's challenging childhood. The story is powerfully written and has become an inspiration for many teenage girls because of the strong emotions and courage that are displayed.

- *If I Stay* (2009) by Gayle Forman takes a different perspective on teenage life. In this story, the protagonist, Mia, has been in a car accident and is in a coma. As she lies in her hospital bed, her mind wanders back through her life, focusing on her relationships with her family and friends, with a special focus on her boyfriend. Should she fight to regain consciousness? In this novel, the protagonist digs down into her life to find the things that are most important to her.

- Sherman Alexie's *The Absolutely True Diary of a Part-Time Indian* (2007) is a story of the trials and tribulations of a tribal youth, Arnold Spirit, who tries to spread his wings. Arnold, known as Junior throughout most of the novel, is awkward in many different ways. Only his brain is perfectly coordinated. But when he decides to better his education by attending the public high school off-reservation, he finds trouble on both sides of the boundary lines. The story is told with humor, but the challenges Junior faces are emotional and trying.

> **MELINDA WOULD LIKE TO RETURN TO THAT PLACE WHERE SHE WAS STILL INNOCENT. THE SEXUAL ASSAULT, HOWEVER, WILL NOT ALLOW THIS."**

In Anderson's novel *Speak*, the protagonist's English teacher remarks: "It's all about SYMBOLISM." The teacher is referring to Nathaniel Hawthorne's work. However, because of the stress placed on the word *symbolism* (placing the word in all capitals), one might question whether Anderson is referring to her own writing as well. If she is, what symbols does she create and how does she use them?

Literary symbolism is the use of a person, object, image, word, or event that suggests a deeper meaning beyond its literal one. For example, the snowstorms through which the protagonist of this novel must walk are both literal storms and a symbol of conditions in Melinda's life. The snow blots out much of the landscape, exemplifying Melinda's feelings of isolation. The harsh coldness of the blizzard symbolizes Melinda's struggle to find warmth in her personal relationships. The snowstorm is just one of the many symbols that the author uses to give more depth to her story. Symbols help readers to become more involved in what the characters are experiencing emotionally. The word *isolation*, for instance, is very abstract or intangible. Readers might grasp the meaning on a rational level but not know what it feels like to be isolated. The symbol of a person walking through ice and blowing snow provides a more physical expression, something the reader can latch on to.

As readers examine the text of Anderson's novel, they will come across many symbols, but three stand out. First, there is the animal symbol. A turkey appears on Thanksgiving Day. The Thanksgiving holiday itself is a symbol. In American culture, Thanksgiving is a day of family reunions. For Melinda, though, the day is anything but. For this family, whose normal mode of daily communication consists of notes to one another left in the kitchen, Thanksgiving is much like any other day. Mother is called away in the middle of preparing the meal and abandons the family. Dad steps in as cook but botches the meal so badly that the turkey must be thrown in the trash. All of this symbolizes the dysfunction of Melinda's family.

However disastrous Thanksgiving Day is, Melinda attempts to salvage a part of it. She gathers the bones from the trash and takes them into her art class. She wants to make something out of the carcass, the main structure of the turkey. She also finds a small doll and pops the head off. She smacks a piece of tape across the doll's mouth and places the head on top of the bones. She attaches a plastic knife and fork to the doll's head to make them look like legs. With the tape across the mouth, the doll obviously is a symbol of Melinda. She feels she cannot speak about what has happened to her. Does she also feel that her flesh has been stripped away as the turkey's has? She has been raped, which means her body has been violated. She might also be feeling that she has little protection between her outer and inner self. Her emotions are so strong that she is constantly feeling like she might burst open. So the turkey skeleton could be a reflection of how she sees herself emotionally. It is through this symbol of the bones and the doll head that the author expresses Melinda's pain. Using this symbol, readers can grasp a better understanding of how that pain feels.

A second strong symbol in this story is the abandoned janitor's closet. Melinda needs a refuge, a place to hide, a tiny room where she does not have to be anyone. She does not have to be a student, a daughter, or an ex-friend. She can just be a nobody. She does not have to define herself for those few minutes or hours that she hides in the closet. She does not have to think. The closet symbolizes a space between her present mental anguish as she faces the world and her memories of what happened to her. Or it might be a respite between who she was and who she is yet to be. It is a place void of anything that is Melinda except for the things she chooses to bring into that place.

Melinda claims this small space by cleaning out the cobwebs and bringing in some personal objects. One of the main objects is a poster of the author and poet Maya Angelou. But there may be something other than Angelou's literary accomplishments that attracts Melinda to her. There also may be a symbolic reason why the author chose Angelou over so many other female authors. The reason could be something that Melinda and Angelou have in common. In 1970, Angelou published her autobiography *I Know*

Why the Caged Bird Sings. In this book, Angelou recounts the rape that occurred when she was eight years old. The rapist was an acquaintance, who was later murdered by a gang of men. The effect of the rape and the murder, which Angelou felt she had caused, led to the author's inability to speak. Thus Angelou is likely to have become a symbol of the terror Melinda is experiencing. Melinda might be using the poster of Angelou to give her hope. Angelou, despite the trauma in her early life, was able to not only move past the experience but to excel in life. Angelou could be Melinda's symbol of inspiration.

Into this closet, Melinda also brings her art pieces. It is through her art that Melinda attempts to reclaim herself. As her art teacher has expressed it, his students have the opportunity to find their souls through art. Melinda has so many questions about herself that she no longer knows who she is. Did she do something wrong to bring on the sexual assault? Why did she not run away? Why did she not scream? Is she just as guilty as her assailant is? Was she misguided when she called the police? Should she tell someone what really happened? Would they believe her? The creation of art and the source of emotions both come from the same place, the subconscious. Though she might not consciously understand how her art projects are helping her, her teacher does. He continues to encourage her. Slowly she begins to feel an emotional reaction to the art pieces she creates and starts gaining confidence. She brings these works into the closet so she can look at them, as if to read them. It is possible that there in the closet, where she does not have to define herself through other people's perceptions, she can see her art more clearly. She is free to explore her artistic expressions with new eyes.

The third major symbol in this novel is the tree. In art class, Mr. Freeman has told his students that each must blindly pull a piece of paper out of a container. On the pieces of paper are the names of some random objects. The paper that Melinda chooses has the word *tree* on it. She believes, at first, that this object is too simple. But when she tries to draw a tree, to make a work of art that stirs the emotions, it is not as easy as she first perceived. Her initial attempts at drawing a tree remind her of how she drew in elementary school. Regressing into an earlier, more innocent time of her life, she draws stick-figure type trees, which Mr. Freeman criticizes for not being very realistic. Melinda's trees are too

perfect, he tells her. Real trees have crooked limbs, blemished leaves, and decayed spots on them. The difference between Melinda's perception of a tree and Mr. Freeman's creates part of the meaning behind this symbol. Melinda is trying to live in a fantasy world, drawing perfectly formed trees, as a child imagines them. Like her trees, Melinda would like to return to that place where she was still innocent. The sexual assault, however, will not allow this. Her innocence has been stolen. Mr. Freeman is telling her that she must draw a tree from the place where she is now. She must look at trees from a different, more realistic place. She is moving into an adult space and must no longer look at things so naively.

As Melinda ponders this, she notices a tree in her front yard. A portion of the tree is rotting. If the rot is not cut out, the tree could die. A tree doctor is called in, and the diseased portion of the tree is removed. At another point in the novel, Melinda wishes that a doctor could go into her brain and cut out her memories, her damaged parts. So it is through the tree in her yard that Melinda realizes that she must cut out her memories by facing them rather than trying to repress them or run away from them.

In the end, after many attempts at creating an emotionally moving depiction of a tree, Melinda finds success. "My tree is definitely breathing," she says. "This one is not perfectly symmetrical. The bark is rough." She adds, "One of the lower branches is sick." She tells herself that the sick branch will have to drop some day in order for the rest of the tree to get stronger. Then she continues, "The new growth is the best part." It is obvious, with these statements, that the author has used the tree to symbolize her protagonist. Melinda has faced her demons in her confrontation with her assailant. She fought him off. Afterward, she senses her own new growth through the tree she is creating. "And I'm not going to let it kill me," she says, referring to the rape. "I can grow."

The author has created symbols for her protagonist to learn from. In the process, readers will learn from them too. Anderson has thus created depth, enabling readers to relate more closely to Melinda and giving them something to take with them. The story therefore becomes more than just words on a page. Through the use of symbolism, readers feel as if they take away a shared experience.

" I KNOW THAT BOOKS SAVE LIVES BECAUSE MY READERS TELL ME SO."

Source: Joyce M. Hart, Critical Essay on *Speak*, in *Novels for Students*, Gale, Cengage Learning, 2010.

Joan F. Kaywell

In the following excerpt from an interview with Kaywell, Anderson identifies Speak *as one of the works she's most proud of and discusses her writing process, influences, and life principles.*

. . . *Joan: First* Speak *hit the shelves and flew off with gusto, and now* Twisted *is on* The New York Times *Best Seller List. My first question is, How do you do it? I often compare you to Chris Crutcher because he writes about such serious topics while getting readers to laugh out loud. Publishers Weekly aptly described* Twisted *as "a dark comedy." There's a real artistry behind weaving comedy with tragedy, and I wonder if you attribute your skill to anyone in particular.*

Laurie: I come from a fairly messed-up family with a dark and twisted sense of humor. As a kid, we went through some ugly things, but my parents and other relatives were always quick with a witty observation or wry remark. Laughter fights off the darkness and keeps you warm until dawn . . . .

Joan: You've written eight books by my last count, ranging from children's picture books to young adult novels, but you are still best known for Speak. *Do you have a preference for what kind of books you write? What appeals to you about writing novels? Picture books? What appeals to you about writing for kids?*

Laurie: By the end of this year, the count will be up to 26: 6 picture books (4 fiction, 2 nonfiction); 12 books in the series (originally published as *Wild at Heart* by American Girl and being reissued as *Vet Volunteers* by Penguin); 2 nonfiction books for kids about Saudi Arabia; and 6 novels, including *Chains*, my historical that comes out in September. Oh, and I was the ghost-writer for a psychiatrist who "wrote" a book about introverted kids. So I guess that makes a total of 27.

I think kids are a more important audience than adults, that's why I write for them.

Joan: Of all of the books you've written, which one is your favorite? The best? The one that makes you most proud? Why?

Laurie: I don't know how to judge them. They are all my favorites, the way that all of my children are my favorites. I think I am most proud of the writing in *Twisted*, because that was from a male point of view; I'm most proud of the storytelling in *Chains*, because there is important and meaty stuff in there; and I am most proud of the impact of *Speak*, because it has helped so many survivors find the courage to talk about what happened and start to heal and grow.

Joan: Is there a particular moment in your life that confirmed for you that becoming a writer was the absolute best decision you ever made? Or the worst?

Laurie: Every time I lose myself in a story, I come our knowing that this is what I was put on the planet to do. Deadline pressure makes me doubt myself in a nasty way. My mother was not convinced that being a writer was a useful or good thing for years. She kept pushing me to go to nursing school and get a degree that would translate into a "real job." When she found out that my agent also represents Nora Roberts (her favorite author) she said. "Well, maybe it will work out."

Joan: Have you ever had a direct experience with a censorship attack? Do you ever write with censorship in mind?

Laurie: I don't worry about censorship when I'm writing. It's hard enough trying to tell a good story. I've had people write to me—and yell at me—a few times because they think that by reflecting reality in my books, I am warping young people and encouraging readers to experiment with unhealthy behaviors. This is, of course, absolutely ridiculous.

I used to get defensive and angry. Now I try to be patient with my attackers and remember that their confusion comes out of their own pain and fear. These kinds of attacks make me more committed than ever to be honest in my stories, because kids need to see the real world if they are ever going to learn how to survive in it.

But I won't lie; it really hurts my feelings when people yell at me.

Joan: What is your writing process like, and what is the most difficult aspect of the process? Do you draft the before and after of each story in your mind or do you just start and let the story take on its own life?

Laurie: My writing process is mostly a muddle. I start with a character or a slice of life that keeps bugging me. I ponder it for a year or two while I'm working on another project. I start to jot down thoughts and whispers, and then the jottings get longer . . . and longer . . . until I wind up with a first draft that is a confusing horror. Most of my writing is done in revision—the significant structural work and character development happen in drafts two through five. My editor usually sees draft five. Then I tinker with the finer story threads and language and image systems and consistency issues, until the editor finally peels my fingers off the manuscript and takes it away to be published.

I often feel that I have no idea what I'm doing and that I'll wind up milking cows for a living again.

Joan: Do you write every day, or do you fit it in when you can?

Laurie: I used to wait for the "right writing moment" and fuss if I couldn't find a big chunk of time. Now I have sucked it up and I write every single day, including holidays and weekends. If I'm on the road, I wake up early or I write on the plane. This helps me keep my momentum going, and it is not nearly as arduous as it sounds . . . .

Joan: Is there a particular novelist or literary work you admire? Do you have a writers' group that you converse with as you're working on a piece? How does that help you as a writer?

Laurie: I admire the work of Francesca Lia Block and Neil Gaiman above all others, because of their use of the mythic. I had a lovely writer's group when I lived in Philly, but now that I live out on the tundra I don't get to meet with them. I do have a core group of early readers: dear friends and my oldest daughter. They know how to be honest, yet gentle, with me when I ask them to read a draft. Their insights are very useful—the hardest thing in the world is for a writer to have perspective on her own work.

Joan: Do you do workshops for teachers or students? If so, I'd be interested to learn about the kinds of instruction you provide.

Laurie: I have spoken at a number of Society of Children's Book Writers and Illustrators conferences (SCBWI, www.scbwi.org) and recently gave a three-part lecture at the Kindling Words retreat, an annual retreat for published authors and illustrators (www.kindlingwords.org).

I am beginning to think about teaching—I really like working with people as they unpeel the layers around their stories. But I have a number of books I want to write before I pursue this. Maybe I'll write a book about writing. That would serve both purposes!

Joan: What advice can you offer to an aspiring writer of any age?

Laurie: Read every single day, write every single day, and learn how to live frugally.

Joan: Do you think writers have a different way of seeing the world? Do you think that you have the ability to "see" details, the small things that provide you with a glimpse into a larger world?

Laurie: I'm pretty sure that I see the world differently than most people. I suspect that other writers and artists feel the same way. If I am in "observant" mode, I pick up on behavior patterns and small details that can be used to illustrate larger points . . . .

Joan: Please describe a typical day in your life. Do you have a typical day?

Laurie: Typical day, the good kind: Up at 6:00 a.m., breakfast while answering e-mail and posting a blog entry. Work starts at 7:00 a.m.— writing new stuff first, then moving to revising and research as my brain shifts gears. Somewhere between 3:00–4:00 p.m. I go to the gym to run or lift weights. After that, it's dinner with my husband. Evenings can be spent reading or answering e-mail and fan mail, or if it's summertime, working in the garden. (If I'm on deadline, it's back to writing after dinner. This can make me cranky, but it is unavoidable.) I rarely watch television except for sports.

There are also those days filled with interruptions and the travel days, but I don't like thinking about those.

I write every day and I connect with my family every day. As long as those two pieces of my life are in place, I'm a happy camper.

Joan: If you had to identify a principle or tenet that you live by, what would it be? Who taught it to you, and could you give an example of a time when you applied it?

Laurie: (1) Be kind. (This is from Jesus and Dr. Martin Luther King Jr. and my grandparents.) (2) Put your best effort into everything you do. (Grandpa Halse) (3) Live like you're going to die tomorrow. (I figured out this one by myself when I found out I had melanoma in 2002. So far, I haven't died; but it's still good advice.)

I use these principles many times every day.

Joan: Some people believe that books save lives. What do you think?

Laurie: I know that books save lives because my readers tell me so.

Joan: You've had Speak made into a movie. How was that process? Did you have much input? Would you do it again?

Laurie: I had very little to do with the movie, and it turned out just fine. I think it's hard enough to write books—I'll leave the movies up to people who sort of know what they're doing.

Joan: My last question. Is there anything else you'd like to share with JAAL readers?

Laurie: Thanks for your incredible (and much appreciated) support of my books. More important, thank you for caring so much about your students! When you hand good books to kids, you give hope to a generation. I cannot think of a finer thing than that.

Source: Laurie Halse Anderson and Joan F. Kaywell, "A Conversation with Laurie Halse Anderson," in *Journal of Adolescent & Adult Literacy*, Vol. 52, No. 1, September 2008, pp. 78–83.

Janet Alsup

In the following excerpt, Alsup argues that Speak *is a valuable work for promoting critical literacy among high school students, as the text presents difficult real-world issues that many teens face.*

As I write this article, the television news blares details about the latest school shooting in the United States, this time in California. Another adolescent boy managed to kill two fellow students and injure 11 others before he was taken into custody. By now, this scene is eerily familiar. We have seen similar pictures from Colorado, Mississippi, Kentucky, and Arkansas, and we have heard about numerous other potential shootings that have been stopped in the nick of time.

This latest school shooting brings to our attention yet again that something is wrong in our schools and perhaps within the psyches of our teenagers. The perpetrators of these shootings share certain characteristics: they are adolescent white boys from suburban, middle-class families who, for whatever reason, were bullied,

> ONE OF THE THINGS I LIKE BEST ABOUT *SPEAK* IS HOW ITS THEME OF FINDING VOICE (AND HENCE IDENTITY AND PERSONAL POWER) IS ONE THAT IS MIRRORED EVERY DAY IN REAL TEENAGERS' LIVES AS THEY SEEK TO BECOME INDEPENDENT, YET INTEGRATED, MEMBERS OF THEIR SCHOOL AND HOME COMMUNITIES."

teased, and ostracized by schoolmates until they finally "cracked." What is perhaps most important is that they rarely talked to anyone about their feelings of isolation and emotional pain. Peers describe them as loners, without many friends, and uninvolved in extracurricular activities.

If we can identify these characteristics and create profiles of these violent teens, why can't we change their behavior before they act out? Teachers and administrators, parents, and university teacher educators have asked themselves this question many times, but there appears to be no simple answer. So we keep asking: Why can't we help these students? How can we help them?

It is a common assumption that adolescence is a very difficult time of life. Psychologists have long described the confusion and self-doubt that accompany puberty. Young people have to face raging hormones and changing bodies that they are not yet comfortable inhabiting. Hall (1904) characterized this time as one of "storm and stress" as teenagers try to understand their new biological urges and emotional needs. The difficulties and stresses adolescents face are not surprising to high school or middle school teachers. They interact with adolescents every day and often watch them grow emotionally. But what happens when students cannot quite seem to make this transition from child to adult? What happens when adolescents, dependent on peer acceptance, feel like outsiders in their schools? What happens when self-esteem is not nurtured, and teens come to dislike themselves and hence others around them? I do not want to imply that these difficulties, however painful, necessarily result in violence. On the contrary, most young people, with the support of friends, relatives, and teachers, are able to make it through this stage of life and grow into well-adjusted adults. However, in the past few years, it seems that feelings of isolation and frustration long associated with adolescence have erupted more and more often into violence, and not just schoolyard fights.

English and reading teachers, like teachers of every discipline, have their own strategies for easing students through this time of "storm and stress," and their tool is often books. A recent novel by Todd Strasser, *Give a Boy a Gun* (2002), tells the story of a school shooting at fictional Middletown High. The two young, male perpetrators end up dying (one shoots himself and another is beaten to death by fellow students who finally overtake him), but only after shooting a fellow student and the school principal. Strasser narrates the events through a series of quotes from various characters who were witnesses to the shooting. He also includes several footnoted descriptions of real school shootings since the mid-1970s along with saddening statistics about gun deaths and the prevalence of teasing in U.S. schools. In this book Strasser makes a definite and powerful point about the seriousness of teen violence. However, I do not want to imply that asking students to read and respond to a book such as Strasser's can stop school shootings from occurring. Although this is a wonderful thought, it would be far too idealistic. There are clearly other issues that must be addressed in order to stop the problem, including the trivializing of peer teasing and the resulting humiliation that often leads to depression and anger. But what I do want to suggest is that reading literature can be an ethical as well as an intellectual process, and as such it can assist adolescents in coping with their tumultuous lives.

THE POWER OF LITERATURE

Reading and English teachers understand the power of literature. They can remember reading novels, poems, or stories and feeling as if the author had a window into their souls, understanding and counseling them from afar. They have experienced variously [*sic*] what a book's narrator experienced, and they believe they have grown as people because of it. They have managed to learn about various kinds of people and places through literature, and, consequently, they have become more empathetic and educated human beings. Such teachers believe in the positive effects literature can have on readers, even if

their beliefs come off sounding like clichés. They want their students to read literature and other texts not only to become "critical thinkers" and do well on standardized tests, but also to become "critical feelers." Rosenblatt (1938) made this point when she wrote, "As the student shares through literary experience the emotions and aspirations of other human beings, he can gain heightened sensitivity to the needs and problems of those remote from him in temperament, in space, or in social environment" (p. 261). In short, many teachers tend to see reading and responding to literature as a pathway to becoming more human.

Nussbaum (1997) explained this function of literature by defining the concept of "world citizenship" as

[cultivating] in ourselves a capacity for sympathetic imagination that will enable us to comprehend the motives and choices of people different from ourselves, seeing them not as forbiddingly alien and other, but as sharing many problems and possibilities with us. (p. 85)

Nussbaum saw literature as one way to teach this "world citizenship." "In a curriculum for world citizenship, literature, with its ability to represent the specific circumstances and problems of people of many different sorts, makes an especially rich contribution" (p. 86). Nussbaum also viewed literature as more than a text to be "analyzed" for symbols, figurative language, or character development. She saw it as a way for readers to develop a "narrative imagination" and become more caring people.

I agree with Nussbaum, and I can think of no other time of life when such an education is more important than adolescence. Sometimes adults see adolescents as hedonistic and cruel to their peers. Under the most trying of circumstances, they can see them as materialistic, selfish, mouthy, and sometimes just plain mean. Often adults do not understand that these negative characteristics stem from frustration and sadness, and, frankly, sometimes it is just hard to remember when they are so upset with an adolescent's behavior.

Literature can be a way for teens to release these tensions, and the literature class can become a forum for talking about issues adolescents want and need to talk about but are often too shy or embarrassed to address. Students can read a book, for example, about a teenager reaching puberty and can talk about what the character is feeling in the third person, not the first. They can say "she felt" instead of "I felt." While they might actually share many of these feelings, they do not have to admit this fact in order to have frank conversation about an issue.

Young adult literature seems to have special potential to help students understand their tumultuous time of life. Donelson and Nilsen (1997) defined young adult literature as "anything that readers between the approximate ages of 12 and 20 choose to read" (p. 6), and in their textbook they discuss how YA literature often mirrors adolescent problems. Bushman and Bushman (1993) defined young adult literature as "literature written for or about young adults" having themes and conflicts of interest to young people (p. 2). Both texts recognize that above all, YA literature is something that adolescents want to read, as opposed to being forced to read by teachers. Why do they want to read it? Perhaps because it helps them feel as if they are not alone.

While there are young adult books being published for a high school or upper adolescent audience (for example, many books by Chris Crutcher and Robert Cormier), I believe that the majority of young adult books recently published in the United States are written for a middle school or early adolescent audience. For example recent Newbery Award winners include Karen Hesse's *Out of the Dust* (1997), Louis Sachar's *Holes* (1998), Christopher Paul Custis's *Bud, Not Buddy* (1999), Richard Peck's *A Year Down Yonder* (2000) Linda Sue Park's *A Single Shard* (2001), and Avi's *Crispin: The Cross of Lead* (2002). While these are all wonderful books, they were written primarily for an audience of 9- to 12-year-olds, and, with the possible exception of *Out of the Dust* (which seems ageless), they often read that way. For example, *Holes* tells an almost fable-like story of a boy's discovery of hidden treasure, and *Bud, Not Buddy* is a rather innocent story about a young boy running away from home to find his musician father. Even though *Holes* has a fairly complex plot that takes many twists and turns before the novel's end, including a subplot about an interracial romance, and *Bud, Not Buddy* takes place during the difficult years of the Great Depression, both books focus on conflicts that are either somewhat fantastical or that end happily. For example, in *Holes* a 100-year-old stash of preserved peaches ends up saving a character from dehydration and serving as a

remedy for foot odor, and in *Bud, Not Buddy* the orphaned main character almost effortlessly finds a loving extended family by the end of the book. The conflicts are relatively straightforward and easily solved, and therefore seem more appropriate for younger adolescents who are just beginning to experience the difficulty of the teenage years.

One possible reason young adult authors might focus on a middle school-aged audience is because this age group is where publishing companies have identified the greatest potential for sales. Donelson and Nilsen (1997) proposed several reasons for this belief, ranging from demographics (e.g., there are currently fewer children of high school age in the United States, and more middle school teachers are implementing whole language or "immersion" approaches to reading instruction and hence buying more books for classrooms) to more negative pronouncements about today's youth (e.g., older teens are spending more time watching television and playing video games than reading). Regardless of the reasons, as one scans the bookstore shelves there appear to be a greater number of YA books with middle school age protagonists that address the concerns of early adolescence. Much young adult literature meant for the middle school or junior high student avoids issues especially relevant and traumatic for older students, such as drugs, alcohol, violence, and sex. While such issues, of course, are also of concern to many younger adolescents, I believe that high school teens confront them on a more consistent and persistent basis; therefore, high school teachers often find themselves seeking out texts that explore these so-called "controversial" issues. However, high school teachers of English and reading may have difficulty finding contemporary, high-interest books for their students that are written at an appropriate level of difficulty and with age-relevant content. Because of this difficulty, many teachers find themselves reverting to traditional canonical texts that have a long history of use in high schools but at times also a long history of eliciting student apathy and disinterest.

While we may have to look harder to find them, there are high-quality young adult novels being published that are written for a senior high (14- to 18-year-old) audience. Many of these books address difficult or explosive issues that, whether we like it or not, are real in students' lives. I have found that when YA books are directed to the older teen reader, they tend to be about issues like violence, drug use, and sexuality; therefore, they sometimes make teachers, parents, and administrators nervous or uncomfortable.

In the rest of this article, I focus on one of these books, *Speak* (1999) by Laurie Halse Anderson. Through analysis of this book, I argue that as a critical young adult text it can help us redefine and broaden the use of young adult literature in the high school classroom. While sometimes teachers are understandably hesitant to teach such books because of possible resistance from administrators and parents. I argue that such books should be made available to students as often as possible because they may be a first, small step toward helping teenagers find their voices and come to terms with an intensely difficult phase of life.

SPEAK

There is an inherent contradiction evident in some high school classrooms. The same young girls who often claim they are not "feminists," because of the erroneous connotations with radical bra burning and man hating, desire equal opportunity and a chance at happy, fulfilling lives as adult women. Sometimes they are even victimized in an abusive or violent relationship with a boyfriend or a male relative, yet they lack the emotional maturity or knowledge necessary to seek help. *Speak* a is about a girl named Melinda who is raped at a beer party the summer before her first year of high school. As a result she becomes depressed and alienated, retreating into silence throughout most of the book. The novel is written in an unconventional style including short, vignette-like chapters and life-like visual representations of Melinda's report cards (her grades steadily fall throughout her freshman year).

Speak begins this way: "It is my first morning of high school. I have seven new notebooks, a skirt I hate, and a stomachache." This is the first time the reader hears Melinda's voice, which is consistently sincere and engaging throughout the book. The emotional and psychological effects of Melinda's rape are devastating, not only because of her personal trauma but also because none of her girlfriends know or understand what happened. The reader does not even learn about the rape until the very end of the novel (although there is much foreshadowing of it). We simply know that Melinda is intensely unhappy, none of her former friends will talk to

her, she is failing in school, and she cannot talk to anyone about it, not even her parents. At one point Melinda says, "I open up a paper clip and scratch it across the inside of my left wrist. Pitiful. If a suicide attempt is a cry for help, then what is this? A whimper, a peep?" Melinda does not attempt suicide, but this scene demonstrates the depth of her emotional pain and also reveals the likability of Melinda, who despite her difficulties, displays an ironic, subtle humor throughout the book. But Melinda cannot "speak" about her pain, and, consequently, the adults in the novel tend to see her as arrogant and apathetic and angry at her lack of participation in class, her failing grades, and her all-around "bad" attitude. Only Melinda and her rapist, a high school boy named Andrew, truly know why she is so quiet.

The end of the book is positive as Melinda begins to come to terms with her trauma and regains her dignity (and her voice) with the help, in part, of a supportive art teacher. In fact, there is a wonderful ending scene where Melinda fights back against her attacker and overpowers him. However, this "happy" ending to her teen angst is one of the few similarities between this book and some more traditional young adult novels. *Speak* tackles issues that many other YA books will not touch due to publisher constraints or a preoccupation with marketability. But *Speak*, in addition to being a skillfully written novel, is a book that might "speak" to teen readers and help them cope with problems such as dating violence, divisive peer groups and cliques, and feelings of isolation and alienation from school.

TEACHING *SPEAK* IN THE CRITICAL CLASSROOM...

Critical pedagogues following Freire (1970) have written about the "critical classroom" in which teachers encourage student "liberation" and "critical consciousness" through dialogue and student-centered curricula. In such classrooms, students are asked to read, write, talk, and think about social-cultural issues permeating their world and then critically analyze these realities. As Applebee (1993) wrote, "Instruction becomes less a matter of transmittal of an objective and culturally sanctioned body of knowledge, and more a matter of helping individual learners learn to construct and interpret for themselves" (p. 200). School in general (and English and reading classrooms are no exception) does not often seek to be critical but instead encourages students to be quiet and conform to the status quo. Consequently, as Bleich (1988) wrote,

> We—teachers and students—have learned not to name or identify in school most of the consequential things in our lives, and we have few ways of teaching others a literacy that shows conviction, motivation, and social and political discourse. (p. 329)

In the face of recent problems, such critical literacy instruction seems a necessity—a course of action that can help students become more critically literate and self-aware in an increasingly dangerous and unpredictable world.

Young adult books like *Speak* can provide opportunities for writing activities or conversation about teenage problems in an attempt to achieve such critical literacy. Imagine a class in which students are having a discussion about *Speak*, and the issue of "speaking out" or "having a voice," a major theme in the novel, comes up. Students may raise the point that if Melinda had spoken about her rape earlier, she might have received help sooner and hence avoided some pain. They might also mention that her peers, her supposed friends, did not try very hard to talk to her or understand her plight. They might also discuss whether they have ever seen anything violent occur at parties, and if so, whether alcohol was a factor.

These discussions could have direct implications for real experiences the students have had and might have in the future. However, they might never have felt comfortable discussing these issues openly in class or with teachers when they would have had to implicate themselves directly in such behavior. But they do feel comfortable talking about Melinda, a fictional character, and her experience. They can talk or write about real problems vicariously and with little personal risk. They can try out certain responses to Melinda's situation, certain suggestions for what she might have done, with no fear that the teacher or peers will think they are talking about themselves. Consequently, in the words of critical pedagogues, students might become more "critically conscious" of their social and cultural realities, and hence better able to deal with them in real-life situations. They are using literature as a tool for thinking about their world. In addition, I would argue that they are simultaneously becoming better readers, thinkers, and communicators.

Trites (1997) described voice as "essential to a girl's subjectivity" and stated that "those who are denied speech, denied language, are also denied their full potential as humans; they are denied community" (p. 62). One of the things I like best about *Speak* is how its theme of finding voice (and hence identity and personal power) is one that is mirrored every day in real teenagers' lives as they seek to become independent, yet integrated, members of their school and home communities. Any adult who has lived with or taught a teenager knows how difficult it can be to have an open conversation with him or her. While this lack of speech can just be an annoyance to adults, it can become a much more serious situation when students do not tell about potentially dangerous experiences with violence, sex, drugs, or alcohol. In the most extreme of situations, silence not only isolates adolescents, it can actually put their lives at risk. One of the facts that has recently emerged about the California school shooting is that the young perpetrator apparently told several peers, and even adults, about his plan, yet no one took him seriously or reported his threats to school officials. They kept silent out of fear or apathy or perhaps a failure to believe what they could say would be heard.

Women and girls are often afraid to tell that they were raped because they believe they will be blamed or they could be seen as "defiled" and untouchable by other males. When rape stories are told, either verbally or through a written or visual text, the narrative tale of rape has certain features—certain characteristics that define it as a female cultural genre. These characteristics often include guilt and self-blame on the part of the victim. The rape survivor has to justify why it was preferable to be raped and live rather than to fight back and die. This cultural narrative has become so pervasive that it is seen as the "truth" about rape. Books are written with "10-step plans" for surviving rape, and victims appear on talk shows to tell their "rape stories" in relatively predictable ways. The narratives begin to seem identical, and it is assumed that every rape survivor's experience has a kind of sameness. Consequently, the stories become easy to ignore, and they blend into the cultural landscape. Rape is just something that happens to some girls and women. We learn the "story" of the rape survivor, just as we know the "story" of the victim of domestic violence, the alcoholic, or the addict. The viewer or listener who is not a rape survivor thinks she has heard it all before, and in the event that she is ever raped, she will know almost subconsciously how to respond, or at least how she has been taught to respond.

However, some testimonies by rape survivors can break the silence and disrupt dominant, oppressive discourse. Hooks (1989) wrote, "True speaking is not solely an expression of creative power; it is an act of resistance, a political gesture that challenges politics of domination that would render us nameless and voiceless" (p. 8). In other words, speaking out can be an action in its own right. Discourse of resistance, such as Melinda's loud "NNNOOO!!!" as she fights off Andrew Evans at the end of *Speak*, as well as her eventual decision to narrate her story to her art teacher ("Me: Let me tell you about it," p. 198) has power and can have a positive effect on material reality. In addition, because *Speak* tells this story of rape in an unconventional way, using a nontraditional narrative structure that includes lists, multiple subheadings, extended spacing between paragraphs, and script-like dialogue introduced by names followed by colons, the effect of the discourse is magnified. *Speak* does not tell the "rape story" in a way that is identical to others readers have heard or in a way that is easy to ignore. Anderson narrates Melinda's story so that adolescent readers are compelled to pay attention instead of dismissing it as yet another example of a sad story like so many others they have heard in the past.

To sum up, Champagne (1996) stated that the difference between a survivor of violence and a victim of violence is the "political meaning made" of the experience. She writes, "Survivors move to a place where they reject the demand to remain politely silent. Polite silence condones the social order of the law of heteropatriarchy" (pp. 2–3). By speaking up, by deciding to no longer be silent and polite, the survivor takes a sort of control over her story and her experience. Only through this kind of resistant testimony, as exemplified by Melinda in *Speak*, can the oppressive cultural scripts be exposed and subverted.

CAN YA LITERATURE REALLY BE AN ANSWER FOR TROUBLED TEENS?

A critical text is a text that confronts difficult issues in society—a text that does not break down into meaningless clichés and predictable plot patterns. A critical text could also be called a resistant text, because it not only resists some of the "rules" of its genre but also encourages its readers to resist the "rules" for mindless, complacent reading. Such books have found their way into classrooms, before (e.g., J.D. Salinger's *The Catcher in the Rye*), but now without controversy. However, these books are almost universally loved by students and often become cult classics, read under the sheets at night or stuck inside a math book propped on a desk. Why can't we bring such resistant texts into the open? Why don't we allow students to read them within our sight and then talk to us about them? If we did so, the critical text could be addressed in the critical classroom and consequently opened up to critical reflection in a supportive environment containing an adult voice.

Yagelski (2000) wrote about the importance of "local literacies" if students are to become truly literate readers and writers. Students need to read, write, and talk about issues that are relevant and real to them and that have immediate meaning for them in their lives. This is not to say that students should never read about people or places to which they cannot easily relate, but first they have to discover that books are places to see themselves, to re-experience and rethink their lives. Carey-Webb's *Literature and Lives: A Response-Based, Cultural Studies Approach to Teaching English* (2001) provided an accessible introduction to teaching literature through critical theoretical lenses, such as feminist, Marxist, and postcolonial theories, that encourage such reflexive thought. Carey-Webb argued that such a cultural studies approach may not only help students see the relevance of literature but also encourage them to experience it as a catalyst for social activism or personal change.

Reading a novel such as *Speak* could be personally relevant for most U.S. teens. Critical pedagogues have consistently asserted that asking students to critique dominant ideologies and their own role in such configurations of power can be quite unsettling to students who are thinking critically about themselves and their culture for the first time; however, such an experience is often essential for intellectual and emotional growth. While reading *Speak*, perhaps students will see a little of themselves in Melinda or in her friends, and after reading, writing about, and discussing the book in a classroom, they might act a little differently the next time a classmate seems unnaturally withdrawn or when they witness violence at a weekend party—or even at school. They might even begin to acquire a mature "narrative imagination" that will help them be better citizens and more emphatic human beings.

Source: Janet Alsup, "Politicizing Young Adult Literature: Reading Anderson's *Speak* as a Critical Text," in *Journal of Adolescent & Adult Literacy*, Vol. 47, No. 2, October 2003, pp. 158–66.

Sally Smith

In the following review, Smith characterizes Speak *as "an alternative narrative, an irreverent struggle to resist and connect in the face of loss of self-esteem."*

The novel's title is *Speak*, but the silence of the main character predominates. Melinda, a ninth grader whose early silence about an unspeakable act turns her toward harmful isolation and self-hatred, narrates the story. As the school year progresses, Melinda finds it harder and harder to speak up for herself, to connect to her anger and fear or to anyone who can help her. Her silence is almost palpable. It stands between this adolescent girl and any useful, caring contact with those who inhabit her world of school and family. Her silence, while extreme, is emblematic of the silence that often afflicts girls—particularly middle class girls—as they enter adolescence and the comparatively impersonal, competitive atmosphere of secondary school.

The author gives a bitterly humorous tone to Melinda's narrative, revealing that the girl is aware of cultural expectations for femininity, the rigid prescriptions for female attractiveness, for female friendship and gossip, for being a "good" girl. She might once have been able to negotiate her way through these expectations, with her obvious understanding of the discourses of power and with her own rich and cynical inner voice, like the girls described in many studies of early and middle adolescence (Brown, 1998; Brown & Gilligan, 1992; Finders, 1997; Fine & MacPherson, 1993; Pastor, McCormick, & Fine, 1996). However, these resources betray the unsuspecting 14-year-old, causing her to lose confidence in herself as a person, a female, a student. The complicity of her social and school environments in her situation forces her to blame herself and detach from all that she has known and valued.

Gradually it is revealed that a male classmate has raped her at an illicit end-of-year party, and that in panic and fear she called for help via 911. Her panicked phone call resulted in arrests, and she has been identified as a snitch, a traitor. Melinda is forced to experience her freshman year as an outsider, one who unbelievingly lives through the personal hostility of former friends and classmates and the impersonal hostility of the school bureaucracy. The sadness, anger, and sense of betrayal that girls often feel entering this transitional period in their lives is increased by this shocking and demeaning experience. Melinda's responses—anger at the powerlessness and inability of parents and close friends to help and protect her, and her closing off—are consistent with psychological accounts of adolescents (Pipher, 1995). They also represent the phenomenon of "going underground" documented by researchers. Melinda's harming of herself physically, biting her lips till they bleed and cutting herself, is also congruent with research on girls in adolescence (Steiner-Adair, 1990). Anderson contrasts Melinda's awareness of and resistance to pressures to learn the correct, feminine, sanctioned ways of speaking with the behavior of her one friend Heather, whose pathetic attempts to please and be attractive come at great personal cost.

The novel positions the protagonist's struggle as an individual against the gender and sexual stereotypes and pressures of the adolescent world. But in the end, her struggle is connected to that of other girls who have also silently borne sexual harassment and abuse. In moving to the wider environment of the school and the female community, the story begins to connect to the concept of "hardiness" (Ouellette, 1993). This concept describes the stance of an individual in relation to a stressful context, and provides a framework for identifying developmental experiences girls may need to resist racism and sexism (DeBold, Brown, Weseen, & Brookins, 1999). Girls' anger, their understanding and use of the discourses of power, their attempts to connect with one another, can be seen as strategies used by both working class and middle class girls to resist and subvert the stress of adolescence.

Recent research on adolescent female development explores the adaptive strategies of girls during this developmental phase. Earlier studies have portrayed white, middle class adolescents as helpless in the face of societal expectations and stereotypes. Lyn Mikel Brown's study contrasting two groups of girls from different communities, working class and middle class, details the harmful effects of societal expectations and limiting stereotypes, but also documents strikingly different but useful strategies both groups of girls developed to maintain a sense of whole-ness and self-worth (Brown, 1998).

Anderson shapes her character's inner dia-logue so that it reveals her resistance as she questions and rages at her plight:

> I don't want to be cool. I want to grab her by the neck and shake her and scream at her to stop treating me like dirt. She didn't even bother to find out the truth—what kind of a friend is that?

Melinda's acerbic commentary on school, the behavior of her former friends, and family dynamics, is used to confirm the young teenager's mastery of a lucid and critical discourse, a dis-course that helps her maintain her sanity in the face of overwhelming pressures. To the outside world, however, her only resistance is silence:

> You don't understand, my headvoice answers. Too bad she can't hear it. My throat squeezes shut, as if two hands of black fingernails are clamped on my windpipe. I have worked so hard to forget every second of that stupid party, and here I am in the middle of a hostile crowd that hates me for what I had to do. I can't even tell them what really happened.
>
> It's getting harder to talk. My throat is always sore, my lips raw. When I wake up in the morn-ing, my jaws are clenched so tight I have a headache. . . . Every time I try to talk to my parents or a teacher, I sputter or freeze. What is wrong with me?

Anderson uses Melinda's inner monologue to move her from disbelief and pain and almost total withdrawal toward a final encounter with her rapist that forces her to emerge from hiding and to speak.

For girls like Melinda, whom Brown describes as "those educated into the culture of power, and thus comfortable enough to reappropriate the meanings of unjust or divisive words and actions" (1998, p. 222), language can be transformative. It enables them to find ways to express their anger, disbelief, and pain, and to connect with female peers and caring adults. When Melinda makes her anger and knowledge visible, she has not only found her voice, but finds that she has released the voices of other girls also, enabling them to con-front male predatory acts.

Young adult novels such as *Speak* are important for adolescent readers. They docu-ment an experience that is all too common to girls entering adolescence and the treacherous paths of acceptable femininity. This novel illu-minates the experiences of adolescent girls with

its portrait of hardiness and resistance, and in its urgent resolution, which focuses on the need to take the struggle away from the individual girl and locate it in the school and community. The author recognizes the potential power of anger, an anger that is heard, understood, and engaged in dialogue. *Speak* is an alternative narrative, an irreverent struggle to resist and connect in the face of loss of self-esteem.

Source: Sally Smith, "Review of *Speak* by Laurie Halse Anderson," in *Journal of Adolescent & Adult Literacy*, Vol. 43, No. 6, March 2000, pp. 585–86.

Jennifer M. Brown
In the following excerpt, Brown and Anderson discuss how the author conceived of and composed Speak.

One night, Laurie Halse Anderson awoke to the sound of a child crying. After checking on her own two children and finding them asleep, she realized that what she had heard was a night-mare in her own head. She picked up a notebook and began writing to make 'sense of the dream. That's when Melinda Sordino, the magnetic nar-rator of *Speak* (Farrar, Straus & Giroux/Foster, Oct.), took over. Anderson describes Melinda stepping up to the microphone, blowing on it (as if to test that it was on) and announcing, "I have a story to tell you." The author wrote a first draft that night, from start to finish.

Speak is narrated by Melinda, an alienated girl who, during the course of her freshman year of high school, harbors a terrible secret and is ostracized by her peers. The novel, which was a finalist for the National Book Award this fall, is remarkable for both Melinda's strong voice—an ironic twist for a character who rarely speaks but has a pungent internal monologue—and for its taut structure.

Anderson's nightmare may have been the catalyst for the book, but its themes had been brewing in the author's head for a while. Her daughters are both teenagers and Anderson had been reading Mary Pipher's *Reviving Ophe-lia* at the time. "I had been processing all this information about adolescence and girls, and remembered all too vividly what it was like. When I sat down ready to write, [the story] was waiting. *Speak* is the least deliberately written book I've ever done."

The author admits that she "wrote some bad novels before this one that no one will ever see, and that taught me a lot about writing novels." While the first draft for *Speak* came easily, Anderson revised it twice before submitting the manuscript. She decided to send it to FSG because she had previously received nice rejections from Frances Foster for some picture book manuscripts (Anderson went on to publish several picture books elsewhere); it was Foster's assistant, Elizabeth Mikesell, who first read the new manuscript, asked Anderson to revise it one more time, then accepted it.

Anderson keeps a rigorous work schedule. She wakes up at 4:30 a.m. to write in her journal before her family wakes up, getting one daughter off to high school, the other off to middle school, and her husband off to work before settling in to write until noon; she uses her afternoons for research and reading. She is currently revising a middle-grade historical novel due out next year from Simon & Schuster, called *Fever 1793*, which is set in Philadelphia during the Yellow Fever epidemic. She is also working on another YA novel for FSG.

Anderson insists that the starred reviews *Speak* has received, and the NBA attention, have not changed her life: "I have two kids who do a great job of keeping me grounded, and a cat who gnaws my ankles if I don't feed her." But she does concede that her writing life has changed. At first her goal was to get one starred review, now she has four of them. "I had to change my expectations of myself. No matter how long you've been writing, I think all writers think, 'Oh, God, can I do it again?' Now I think, 'I want to do it again, but I want to do it better.'" She recalls an analogous time when she was training for a half-marathon. "If I could train without collapsing, I felt good. Then I got up to running eight to [sic] miles a day. Then I wanted to run faster, further." Her newfound fans will want to meet her at each new milestone.

Source: Jennifer M. Brown, "Flying Starts," in *Publishers Weekly*, Vol. 246, No. 51, December 20, 1999, p. 24.

SOURCES

Anderson, Laurie Halse, *Speak*, Farrar, Straus and Giroux, 1999.

Carger, Chris Liska, Review of *Speak*, in *Book Links*, January 2007, Vol. 16, No. 3, p. 38.

Carton, Debbie, Review of *Speak*, in *Booklist*, September 15, 1999, Vol. 96, No. 2, p. 247.

Casias, Casey, "Young Woman Finds Her Voice in *Speak*," in *Santa Fe New Mexican*, July 28, 2006, p. D3.

"The Federal Government Source for Women's Health Information," in U.S. Department of Health and Human Services Web site, http://www.womenshealth.gov/faq/date-rape-drugs.cfm (accessed April 25, 2009).

Goodnow, Cecilia, "Teens Buying Books at Fastest Rate in Decades—New 'Golden Age of Young Adult Literature' Declared," in *Seattle Post-Intelligencer*, March 7, 2007, http://www.seattlepi.com/books/306531_teenlit08.html (accessed April 25, 2009).

Laurie Halse Anderson Home Page, http://www.writerlady.com/ (accessed April 25, 2009).

"The 100 Most Frequently Challenged Books of 1990–2000," in American Library Association Web site, http://www.ala.org/ala/issuesadvocacy/banned/frequentlychallenged/challengedbydecade/100mostfrequently.cfm (accessed April 25, 2009).

Prince, Julie, "Writing from the Heart: An Interview with Laurie Halse Anderson," in *Teacher Librarian*, December 2008, Vol. 36, No. 2, pp. 70–1.

Rennison, Callie Marie, and Sarah Welchans, "Intimate Partner Violence," January 31, 2002, in U.S. Department of Justice Web site, http://www.ojp.usdoj.gov/bjs/pub/pdf/ipv.pdf (accessed April 25, 2009).

Review of *Speak*, in *Horn Book Magazine*, September 1999, Vol. 75, No. 5, p. 605.

Review of *Speak*, in *Publishers Weekly*, September 13, 1999, Vol. 246, No. 37, p. 85.

FURTHER READING

Covey, Sean, *The 6 Most Important Decisions You'll Ever Make: A Guide for Teens*, Fireside, 2006.

> Covey believes that teens have six very important decisions to make that will affect their entire future. He begins with the importance of a good education and continues through developing good relationships with parents, choosing whom to date, staying away from drugs, and developing self-confidence.

Ford, Amanda, *Be True to Your Self: A Daily Guide for Teenage Girls*, Conari Press, 2000.

> Written by a young author whose memories of teenage years were still fresh in her mind, Ford explores the challenges young girls face. She explores stories and advice about some of the most important issues facing young teenage girls, such as dating, drinking, self-esteem, relationships, dealing with parents, and building confidence.

Fox, Annie, *The Teen Survival Guide to Dating and Relating: Real-World Advice on Guys, Girls, Growing Up, and Getting Along*, Free Spirit Publishing, 2005.

> Working from letters she received from teenagers, author Annie Fox gives advice about

dating and relationships as well as about sexual identity and a sense of self.

Muhlberger, Richard, *What Makes a Picasso a Picasso?* Viking Juvenile, 1994.

Picasso's cubist paintings helped open up new ways to look at objects (and helped protagonist Melinda, too). This book offers an introduction to the famed artist, exploring what he painted and why.

Nikkah, John, *Our Boys Speak: Adolescent Boys Write About Their Inner Lives*, St. Martin's Griffin, 2000.

Nikkah was a graduate student in psychology when he gathered information from 600 teenage boys and wrote this book. Each chapter is a combination of the author's own recollections on the subject, followed by responses from the male teens. Topics range from sports to sex and include teenage angst, drugs, and death.

Simmons, Rachel, *Odd Girl Out: The Hidden Culture of Aggression in Girls*, Harcourt, 2003.

Girls are often raised in a culture that insists that they be nice. They should not express anger or acknowledge conflict. Instead, they turn to silence and passive aggression, the author concludes. After interviewing 300 girls, the author came up with specific acts, such as gossiping, note passing, and exclusion that young girls use to get back at someone they do not like. Simmons offers guidance and ways to increase better communication between girls and their friends and parents.

Warshaw, Robin, *I Never Called It Rape: The Ms. Report on Recognizing, Fighting, and Surviving Date and Acquaintance Rape*, Harper Paperbacks, 1994.

Writing for a young adult audience, a freelance journalist interviewed hundreds of male and female college students to put together his study of incidents of date rape. Warshaw also offers advice on how women can protect themselves and how men can avoid such situations.

A Tree Grows in Brooklyn

BETTY SMITH

1943

A Tree Grows in Brooklyn, by Betty Smith, is the coming-of-age story of Francie Nolan, who is eleven years old when the story begins in 1912. Smith's novel was published in 1943 and became an immediate hit. It was quickly purchased by Twentieth Century Fox, and a film version was released in 1945. *A Tree Grows in Brooklyn* was also the basis of a Broadway musical in 1951. Smith's first novel is a semiautobiographical story of her early life as the child of first-generation Americans. Its themes include the problems that many new immigrants face, including the often overwhelming poverty that they must overcome in their effort to achieve the American dream; overcrowded schools; the importance of education in achieving success; and the need to be loved. The book is also rich in symbolism, including the Tree of Heaven, which symbolizes the tenacity of the poorest immigrants, and the tin can bank, in which the family places all its hopes for the future.

Smith's novel is difficult to summarize briefly because it is autobiographical and thus lacks a clear plot. Instead, its fifty-six chapters relate the life of Francie Nolan. This is a story that unfolds in a succession of small episodes in this girl's life. The novel is divided into five books, loosely defined by either events or periods of time. Book 1 is a brief introduction to the protagonist, Francie Nolan, and her family and neighborhood. Book 2 provides essential background information about Francie's parents and her very early childhood. Book 3 relates

Betty Smith (© *Ann Rosener | Time & Life Pictures | Getty Images*)

Francie's experiences in school and how hard life was for her family. Book 4 explains what happens to Francie after she is forced to go to work at age fourteen and is unable to enroll in high school. All of the novel's themes come together in Book 5, as Francie prepares to leave for college. By the end of Smith's novel, readers have vicariously experienced many of the trials that the Nolan family faced. Because the novel is told in the third person, readers know the inner thoughts of each character and are better able to appreciate the struggles that each endures.

AUTHOR BIOGRAPHY

Elizabeth Lillian Wehner, better known as Betty Smith, was born December 15, 1896, in Williamsburg, a neighborhood of Brooklyn, New York. She was one of three children born to German immigrants John and Catherine Wehner. Smith attended school through the eighth grade at Public School 23 in the Brooklyn neighborhood of Greenpoint, but her family was poor, and in 1910, she left school and began working to help support the

family. In 1915, Smith was able to return to school and enrolled at Girl's High School, which she attended from 1915 to 1917 and where she was editor of the school newspaper. She also volunteered at the Jackson Street Settlement House, where she met George Smith. The couple eloped on June 6, 1919, to Ann Arbor, Michigan, where Smith was able to attend Ann Arbor High School. Smith's first child, a girl, was born in November 1922. A second daughter was born in 1924.

From 1927 to 1930, Smith was enrolled at the University of Michigan, auditing classes as a special student. Beginning in 1928, Smith had weekly articles accepted for publication by the Newspaper Enterprise Association, which helped to support the family. While enrolled in the university, Smith began taking playwriting classes. When she and her husband separated in 1929, their two daughters were sent to stay with an aunt in Queens, New York. Smith spent the next year writing, and in 1930, she was awarded the Avery Hopwood Award for her play *Jonica Starrs*. The award included a $1,000 prize, which Smith used to enroll at Yale University in New Haven, Connecticut. After Smith and her husband reconciled, she continued to study at Yale University Drama School. While at Yale, Smith had two one-act plays produced, *Mannequin's Maid* and *Blind Alley*, in 1932. By 1933, Smith's marriage was no longer working, and although she tried to continue as a student at Yale, eventually she and her daughters moved to Queens to stay with her mother.

In 1935, the Federal Theatre Project hired Smith as a play reader. The following year, the Federal Theatre Project moved Smith, Bob Finch (a fellow student at Yale with whom Smith was romantically involved), and two other playwrights to Chapel Hill, North Carolina, to join the Carolina Playmakers. In 1937, Smith won a Berkeley Playmakers award for her play *So Gracious in the Time*. She would win the same award in 1938 for *Three Comments on a Martyr*. In 1939, Smith received a $1,200 Rockefeller Fellowship. In 1940, she received a $1,000 Rockefeller & Dramatist Guild Award. Despite these awards, Smith was able to earn very little money, although she continued to write plays and to collaborate with other playwrights. During this period, many of Smith's plays were written in collaboration with Bob Finch before his job with the Federal Theatre Project ended in 1941 and he left Chapel Hill.

Smith began writing an autobiographical novel in the late 1930s. The novel would eventually become *A Tree Grows in Brooklyn*, which was accepted for publication in 1942 and published in 1943. By the time the novel was published, Smith and her family were living in poverty. Twentieth Century Fox soon purchased the film rights, but half the money went to the publisher, Harper & Brothers. In 1943, Smith married Joe Jones, a soldier in the army, stationed in Virginia. The film of her book, *A Tree Grows in Brooklyn*, was released in 1945, and by the end of that year, Smith had earned nearly $110,000 from the sale of more than 3 million copies of the book. Her second novel, *Tomorrow Will Be Better*, was published in August 1948. In 1951, *A Tree Grows in Brooklyn* opened as a musical comedy at the Alvin Theater on Broadway. The same year, Smith divorced her second husband and reconnected with Bob Finch, who had become an alcoholic in the years that he and Smith had been apart. They finally married in 1957, after his previous wife agreed to a divorce. Smith's third book, *Maggie-Now* was published in 1958. Early in 1959, while Smith was away from Chapel Hill publicizing the new book, Finch died. Smith's last novel, *Joy in the Morning*, an autobiographical novel of her marriage to George Smith, was published in 1963. Smith died of pneumonia on January 17, 1972, in Shelton, Connecticut. She was buried in Chapel Hill at the Legion Street Cemetery, next to Bob Finch.

MEDIA ADAPTATIONS

- *A Tree Grows in Brooklyn* was filmed by Twentieth Century Fox and directed by Elia Kazan. The film was released in 1945 and is now available on DVD. It starred Dorothy McGuire, Joan Blondell, James Dunn, Lloyd Nolan, and Peggy Ann Garner. Louis D. Lighton was the producer.

- An audio CD recording, produced by Sony, of the 1951 Broadway musical production of *A Tree Grows in Brooklyn* is available. The cast included Arthur Schwartz, Dorothy Fields, Nathaniel Frey, Delbert Anderson, Albert Linville, Johnny Johnston, and Shirley Booth.

- The 1945 screenplay was also used in the made-for-television version of *A Tree Grows in Brooklyn* in 1974. The film was directed by Joseph Hardy and starred Cliff Robertson, Diane Baker, Pamelyn Ferdin, and Nancy Malone.

PLOT SUMMARY

Book 1

Book 1 includes the first six chapters of *A Tree Grows in Brooklyn* and provides background information about the Nolan family and specifically Francie Nolan, the novel's protagonist. The setting is a poor immigrant area of Brooklyn called Williamsburg. There is a tree growing in the area that survives no matter how poor the soil or water. The tree is called the Tree of Heaven by some of the residents; it grows only in the neighborhood where the poorest people live.

The book opens on a typical Saturday. Francie and her younger brother, Neeley, spend part of the morning collecting metal scraps to sell to the junk man. The children keep half the money, and half is put in the tin can bank at home. Francie's mother, Katie, works as a janitor cleaning three buildings.

Francie's father, Johnny, drinks and does not support the family. He is charming but irresponsible. His job is singing at weddings and in restaurants. He earns good tips but uses the money to buy alcohol. Francie loves her father, in spite of the fact that he tells Francie that he never wanted a family. He has told her this many times and she is always hurt, but she quickly forgives him. Francie describes one of her aunts to readers. Aunt Sissy is funny and vivacious. She works in a condom factory, although the actual product made there is not discussed. Instead, Francie knows that this factory makes rubber toys and other rubber articles that are never described.

In these first six chapters, Francie describes several trips to buy food, so readers know that food is important in the story. Later Saturday evening, Francie's Aunt Evy and Uncle Willie Flittman visit. Uncle Willie complains about his horse, Drummer, who urinates on him. Willie also complains that he is a failure, since even the horse does not respect him. His self-esteem is poor and so he is similar to Johnny, who also knows he is a failure. As Neeley and Francie prepare for bed, they read one page from the Bible and one page from Shakespeare, as they have done since they were old enough to read.

Book 2

Book 2 consists of chapters 7–14. In the first two chapters of this section, which jumps back in time to begin in 1900, readers learn the story of Katie and Johnny's courtship and wedding. This chapter also provides background information about Katie and Johnny Nolan's family. Katie's father, Thomas Rommely, hates Katie's marriage because he wanted all four of his daughters to work their entire lives to support him. Sissy, the oldest of Katie's sisters, did not attend school and cannot read or write. Katie's second sister, Eliza, was encouraged to become a nun. The third sister, Evy, married Willie, with whom she has two sons and a daughter. Johnny is also one of four children, all boys. All of Johnny's brothers died by age thirty, which suggests to readers that Johnny is also destined to die young. Johnny's parents, Ruthie and Mickey Nolan, were immigrants from Ireland. All four of the Nolan boys have worked as singing waiters.

Katie and Johnny are happy when they are first married, but by the time that Katie discovers she is pregnant, she already knows that Johnny cannot be relied upon. While Katie is giving birth to Francie, Johnny gets drunk and loses his job. After the baby is born, Katie's mother, Mary, visits with good advice for her daughter, including the advice to begin saving money so that she can buy land; Mary believes that owning land is the only way that poor people can escape poverty. Mary also tells Katie that she must read to her children and they must read Shakespeare and the Bible every day, since these are the most important books ever written.

When Francie is three months old, Katie discovers that she is pregnant again. Francie is not a healthy baby, but Katie compares her daughter to the Tree of Heaven, which survives no matter what happens. The second child is a big healthy boy, Neeley. Katie loves Neeley more than anyone, although she vows that Francie will never know her mother loves her brother more. After Johnny celebrates his twenty-first birthday by staying drunk for three days, Sissy tells Katie that everyone has something about them that

must be tolerated. Drinking is Johnny's weakness, and Katie must learn to live with his weakness. Katie knows that Johnny is not dependable and that he will not be able to support his family. She decides that the family must move where no one will know that Johnny is a drunk. Katie moves the family to the outskirts of Williamsburg, and in exchange for janitorial work, the house will be rent-free.

After the move, things continued as they had before. Johnny still drinks, and Katie works. When not in the apartment, Francie watches the other children play games, but she is not invited to play with them. As a result, she is very lonely. She speaks like Shakespeare or in the antique language of the Bible–the only speech she has learned at home. The family has to move a second time after Sissy flirts with a policeman and then creates a small scandal with some condoms that Francie and Neeley find and blow up into balloons. The family moves to a new apartment in Williamsburg. Francie is six and could start school, but Katie makes her wait a year for Neeley so that they can go together.

Book 3

Book 3 consists of chapters 15–42. The first few chapters of this book describe the apartment and the neighborhood where Francie will grow up. She is six years old and it is 1907. The kitchen looks out over a courtyard, where the Tree of Heaven grows out of the cement. Neeley will soon be old enough to start school, and so in chapter 18, Katie tells Francie and Neeley that they must walk to the health department clinic by themselves, where they will receive their school vaccinations. Francie tries to distract her brother, who is afraid of the shot, by helping him make mud pies before they leave. When they arrive at the clinic looking very dirty, the doctor sees the dirt on Francie and begins complaining that the poor are filthy and not even capable of using soap and water, and the nurse agrees.

Francie has been looking forward to school, but she learns right away that the teacher likes only the rich children. Bullies rule recess and do not allow the poor children to use the bathroom, but the teachers will not allow them to use the bathroom at other times. After Francie wets her pants, Sissy goes to Francie's teacher and tells her that she is Francie's mother and that her husband is a cop. The teacher is sufficiently intimidated that in the future she allows Francie to use the bathroom when she raises her hand. Because of overcrowding, many children at school have lice, which creates embarrassment within the community. When Katie learns of the epidemic of lice, she scrubs Francie's head with the harsh soap that she uses to clean the floors and then combs kerosene through Francie's hair. Katie combats a mumps epidemic by tying garlic around the children's necks. The kerosene and garlic further isolate Francie, who still has no friends.

One day Francie walks beyond the borders of her neighborhood and ends up in a neighborhood where there are no large apartments, which means the population is not as densely packed together. She sees a lovely brick school building and wants to attend. When Francie asks her father, he agrees that she can change schools. Francie does not mind that she must walk twenty-four blocks each way to the new school. The school is much nicer, perhaps because all the students are the children of parents who have lived in the United States for many generations. These parents understand the system better and have a clearer sense of their rights than immigrant parents.

By chapter 25, readers learn that Johnny has begun to drink even more, but on those occasions when he is sober, he tries to be a better father to his children. One day, he takes Francie and Neeley to the elegant Bushwick Avenue to show them what they can achieve living in a democracy. Anything is possible in the United States. At Thanksgiving, one of the children brings a small five-cent pumpkin pie from home. Francie's teacher asks the children if someone wants to take it home but no one wants to accept charity. Francie says she will take it and give it to a poor family. Instead, Francie eats the pie as she walks home. The next day when the teacher asks about the pie, Francie lies but finally admits the truth. The teacher tells Francie that she should always tell the truth, but that she can write down stories as they should have happened. Francie's teacher provides an important first step toward turning Francie into a writer.

It is Christmas in chapter 27, and the children go to a tree lot, where they hope to get a free Christmas tree. At midnight, the tree lot owner always throws the leftover trees into the crowd. When the man throws the first tree, which is always the largest tree left on the lot, no one thinks the children can possibly catch this giant

tree. The tree is ten feet tall and the children are very small. For a moment, the tree lot owner feels a twinge of guilt about throwing such a large tree to the children, but then he reasons that if he gives it to them, everyone will expect the same treatment. The children do catch it, although Francie is hit on the head by the tree trunk and Neeley receives some scrapes. On Christmas Day, Katie makes a huge fuss over Neeley's gift, calling it the best gift she has ever received. Francie is hurt because her mother pays little attention to the gift that Francie gives her. Francie begins to realize that her mother is not always right about everything, but she also learns that her father's drinking is a problem for the family. As she gets older, Francie is less able to be distracted from her hunger and the family's poverty.

In the opening chapters of the novel, Willie has said how much his horse hates him and that Drummer urinates on him while he washes the horse's belly. Willie is mean and abusive to the horse, which finally retaliates by kicking Willie in the head and knocking him out. Since Willie must stay in the hospital, Evy begins to deliver the milk to Willie's customers. Drummer loves Evy because she heats his oats and feeds him carrots and sugar cubes. She also warms up the water to wash him each day, and when it is cold, she puts a warm blanket over him. In response, the horse works hard and helps Evy with the milk route. Women are not permitted to work these kinds of jobs, though, and so as soon as Willie is well, he returns to work. Drummer, however, refuses to work for Willie, and eventually Willie is given another horse.

In chapter 32, Francie is fourteen. She began writing in a diary when she was thirteen. When Katie finds the diary, she insists that Francie change the entries in which she wrote that her father was drunk to read that her father was sick. When a seven-year-old child in the neighborhood is sexually attacked and murdered, Johnny borrows a gun from a friend. One day, as Francie enters her apartment building, the prowler is hiding under the stairs and grabs her. Katie sees the man attacking her daughter; she quickly goes back to the apartment and grabs the gun. Katie shoots him in the stomach, and Francie is unharmed. The police doctor gives Francie a sedative and tells Katie and Johnny that when Francie wakes up they are to tell her that it was just a bad dream.

Sissy, whose pregnancies have all ended in the death of her babies, wants a baby desperately. She learns of a young girl who is unmarried and pregnant, and Sissy visits her family one day. Sissy offers to adopt the baby and to provide food for the family during the pregnancy. When the baby girl is ten days old, Sissy brings her new daughter home. She convinces her husband that she has given birth to the baby and that he is the father. Only Katie, Johnny, and Francie know that the baby is not really Sissy's. Katie is pregnant with their third child, and Johnny is once again not happy at the news.

It is almost Christmas again in chapter 35, and there is even less money than normal and the family is living on oatmeal. One day Johnny comes home crying hysterically because the Waiters' Union has kicked him out and is demanding that their union pin be returned. Johnny is extraordinarily proud of his union pin and the thought of not having it makes him fall to pieces. Johnny has not worked or contributed money to the support of the family in a very long time. He leaves the apartment the next day and disappears for two days. Finally, police sergeant McShane appears at the door to tell Katie that Johnny has been found unconscious in the street and is dying. The next morning Katie tells the children that their father has died and not to cry. Johnny had $200 in insurance, and the undertaker charges $175, leaving Katie barely enough money to buy mourning clothing for the family. The money from the tin can bank is used to buy Johnny's burial plot, so the family now owns a tiny plot of land as Katie's mother has advised.

The doctor at the hospital wants to list alcoholism and pneumonia as the causes of death, but Katie insists that alcoholism not be listed on Johnny's death certificate. The priest supports Katie, and the doctor lists only pneumonia. When Neeley and Francie refuse to enter the living room of the apartment, where their father's body is laid out in a casket, Katie tells the children that everyone thinks that they are refusing to see the body because Johnny was not a good father. When Francie goes into the room and views her father's body, she is surprised at how young and at peace he looks. At the funeral service, Katie is unable to weep, but once they return home Katie begins to weep uncontrollably. Sissy tells her she must stop crying to avoid harming her unborn child.

Johnny's death is very hard on Francie and Neeley, but Katie says that the family needs to return to their usual customs and so that night

they will read a story from the Bible. She chooses the birth of Jesus for that evening's reading. The new baby is due in May, and Katie is worried about how she can earn enough money to feed the family when she is unable to work as hard as she usually does. She prays to Johnny and asks him to help her. That day, McGarrity, who owns the saloon where Johnny most often did his drinking, offers Francie and Neeley jobs after school.

In chapter 39, the narrative returns to Francie's schooling. She has been doing poorly in her composition class since the death of her father. After Johnny died, Francie began writing about poverty, drunkenness, and death. The teacher does not like these topics and wants Francie to write about beautiful and nice things, but Francie realizes that all the writing that earned her good grades was about things that she had never experienced. Francie burns all her A compositions, but she keeps the failing papers that her teacher did not like.

When Katie goes into labor, she tells Francie to send Neeley for Evy. When Evy and Sissy arrive, they learn there is no money for a midwife; they will need to deliver the baby. As the birth becomes imminent, Katie insists that Francie be sent from the house to buy food. Katie does not want Francie to hear the sounds of a painful childbirth. The new baby is named Annie Laurie.

Chapter 42, the last chapter in book 3, ends with both Francie and Neeley graduating from elementary school and receiving their diplomas. Their two graduation ceremonies are on the same night, and Katie chooses to attend Neeley's. Aunt Sissy attends Francie's graduation. Francie dreads entering her classroom, since each girl receives flowers for graduation, and Francie knows that she will not receive flowers. When she looks at her desk, however, there is a large bouquet of roses on the top of the desk. The card says they are from her father, and it is written in her father's neat handwriting. For a moment, Francie thinks that the past six months have been a bad dream and that her father did not die, but Sissy explains that Johnny signed the card a year ago and that he gave her the money to buy the roses before he died. At home Katie is pleased with Neeley's grades, which are Bs and Cs. She ignores all of Francie's As and focuses only on the one C-minus, in composition.

Book 4

Book 4 consists of chapters 43–54. These chapters tell of Francie's teenage years and growing into young adulthood. After graduation, Francie and Neeley both get jobs. Francie wants to work in an office but needs to be sixteen years old to do so. After she buys more grown-up clothing and puts her braids up, Francie looks old enough to pass for sixteen, although she is only fourteen. She gets a job as a reader at the Model Press Clipping Bureau in Manhattan. Francie is very good at her job and is given a large raise. Francie does not want to tell her mother about the raise, since she knows that her mother will want her to keep working instead of returning to school. Although Neeley does not want to go to high school, Katie decides that he is the one who will attend school. Katie claims that Neeley will need to be pushed into school, but Francie will find a way to attend even if she must also work to support the family.

It is now 1917, and Neeley has been playing the piano and singing at the ice cream shop. Unlike his father, who was forced to sing what people requested, Neeley plays only what he wants. Francie is sixteen years old and is still lonely, as she has been all her life. Aunt Sissy finally tells her husband, Steve, that she adopted their baby girl, but he is not upset. It was Steve who told Sissy about the unmarried pregnant girl, who had an affair with a married man. Coincidentally, the baby looks just like Steve.

One of the clipping bureau's biggest clients turns out to be a German spy, and soon the business is shut down and Francie is out of a job. Francie's new job pays less money, but it is enough to support the family. Francie knows she will never go to high school, but she wants to sign up for summer college courses. Francie loves college, and a boy she meets in the bookstore, Ben Blake, helps Francie fit in and get used to college. Francie is in love with Ben, but he does not have time for a girlfriend since he takes care of his mother.

The only way Francie can enroll in college for regular classes is to pass the entrance exams, so she begins to study for them. She meets a young soldier, Lee Rhynor, who is about to ship overseas to the war. He tells Francie that he is engaged to a girl back home, but Lee asks Francie to pretend that she is his girl just for the evening. Lee kisses Francie good night. The next day, she and Lee go dancing, and Francie falls in love with Lee as they dance. Lee asks Francie to spend the night with him and says he will not marry his fiancée

back home. Francie refuses, but she agrees to Lee's request that she write a letter telling him that she loves him. Within a few days, a letter from Lee's bride arrives thanking Francie for entertaining her fiancée while he was in New York. The new Mrs. Rhynor says that it was cruel of Lee to pretend to be love with Francie. Francie is brokenhearted. Book 4 ends with the reappearance of Sergeant McShane, who comes to visit the Nolan family. He asks Katie to marry him, and she accepts; he is a good man. McShane asks whether he can adopt Laurie and give her his name, and Katie agrees to this also.

Book 5

Book 5 consists of chapters 55 and 56 and concludes the novel. As soon as her mother is married, Francie, who has passed her college entrance exams with Ben's help, will be leaving Brooklyn to attend the University of Michigan. Ben has given Francie a ring, with their two sets of initials engraved on the inside, but he is not pressuring her to make a decision about loving him. He loves her, and he will wait for her to decide. He has another five years before he can finish law school and marry and he is willing to give Francie that long to know what she wants.

In the final chapter of the novel, Francie says goodbye to her neighborhood and to the life the family lived in their apartment. The next day, Katie and Mr. McShane will marry and leave the apartment for good. Francie visits many of the neighborhood stores that she visited in the opening pages of the novel. She also visits her old school and is surprised at how tiny it looks. Francie returns to the apartment, and Neeley comes in looking for a clean shirt to wear to work. He calls her Prima Donna, as Johnny used to, and sings, also just as their father once did. He hugs her goodbye and kisses her. Francie thinks that Neeley is very much like Johnny in appearance and voice. When she is finished packing, Francie prepares for her date with Ben that evening. She admits to herself that she does not love him, but she is willing to give it time and perhaps she will learn to love him. It is the end of her old life and the beginning of a new one.

CHARACTERS

Ben Blake

Ben is the young man Francie meets on her first day at her summer college classes. He is practical and a careful planner, who also helps care for his mother. He helps Francie study for her classes. Ben plans to attend college and law school. He loves Francie and is willing to give her the time she needs to learn to love him.

Doctor and Nurse

The doctor and nurse have only a brief role; they administer the vaccinations that Francie and Neeley need to begin school. The doctor shows no compassion or understanding about what it means to live in poverty. Although the nurse grew up in the neighborhood, she has managed to escape the poverty of her childhood and seems to have forgotten its lessons.

Evy Rommely Flittman

Aunt Evy is Katie's older sister. Like all of the sisters, Evy is a practical woman, willing to work hard for her family. She is married to Willie Flittman, who is a failure at everything he attempts. When Willie cannot work, Evy takes over his job. When Willie disappears one day, Evy again takes over Willie's job and supports the family. Evy tells good stories: when she recounts Willie's experiences with his horse, Drummer, she is able to imitate both Willie and the horse and bring the stories to life.

Willie Flittman

Uncle Willie is Evy's husband. Willie believes he is a failure, since even his horse does not respect him. He never understands that his abuse of the horse is why the horse urinates him. Willie does not drink, but like Johnny, Willie is also a dreamer who wants to escape from his everyday life. After Willie becomes a one-man band, he disappears from his family and the novel.

Miss Garnder

Miss Garnder is Francie's eighth grade English teacher. She believes that Francie's writing should only be about pretty things. Miss Garnder gives Francie's papers failing marks when they do not reflect her own ideas about what constitutes a proper topic for a paper.

John

John is Sissy's third husband. His real name is Steve, although readers do not learn his name until near the end of the novel. Like all of Sissy's husbands, Steve lets Sissy call him John. But at the end of the novel, he finally asserts himself and insists that his name is Steve. He also insists that Sissy marry him in a church, since he knows that this the only way she will consider their marriage real.

Lucia

Lucia is a Sicilian girl who is unmarried and pregnant. Sissy helps Lucia and adopts her baby. There is a suggestion that Lucia had an affair with Sissy's husband and that the baby Sissy adopts is actually his.

Mr. McGarrity

Mr. McGarrity owns the bar where Johnny drinks. McGarrity's wife and children never talk to him, but Johnny knows how to have a real conversation, and McGarrity loves him for this. After Johnny dies, McGarrity helps Katie by giving after-school jobs to Francie and Neeley.

Sergeant Michael McShane

McShane is a retired policeman and a successful politician. He asks Katie to marry him after the proper mourning period to honor his first wife is ended. McShane is a good and kind man who married a young, unmarried, pregnant girl to save her and her family from shame. He was a faithful husband until his wife's death. He is wealthy, and so readers know that Katie and her youngest child, Laurie, will not have to struggle to survive. He offers to pay for Francie and Neeley's college educations.

Annie Laurie Nolan

Laurie is Francie's new baby sister. Laurie is born five months after her father, Johnny, dies. Her birth creates even more problems for the family, since Katie has less time to work. She is named after a song Johnny used to sing. McShane promises to adopt Laurie and give her his last name after he and Katie marry.

Francie Nolan

Mary Frances Nolan is the central character. She was named Frances after the fiancée of her father's brother Andy, who is dead. Her personality is a combination of her father's romantic nature and her mother's pragmatism. Like her father, she dreams of the world beyond their neighborhood, but like her mother, Francie knows that if she wants her dreams to be real, she has to make them real through hard work. Francie is often alone and often very lonely, and so she escapes into reading. Francie has a rich imagination that is sometimes frightening to her, as when she imagines the loneliness of old age; however, her imagination also allows her to imagine a better life, as when she sees that attending a school outside her neighborhood will give her a better education. Although Francie grows up in terrible poverty, she never feels like she is poor. Francie is a storyteller who makes up stories to entertain herself. She loves her father deeply, even though she knows that his drinking is responsible for the family's poverty. Francie understands that her mother loves Neeley more than she loves her daughter. Francie is a complex character who grows and matures throughout the novel. By the end of the novel, it is clear that Francie has inherited her mother's strength.

Johnny Nolan

Johnny is Francie's father. Johnny is weak; he is unable to survive the poverty in which the family lives. He is a dreamer and a romantic who does not have either the ability or the incentive to make his dreams come true. When faced with the need to support his family, Johnny escapes into alcohol. Johnny loves his wife and his children, but he is unable to be the kind of husband and father they deserve. Johnny earns his living as a singing waiter, but the work is inconsistent. The tips he earns are used to buy alcohol, and performing provides the instant applause he desires. Johnny knows that Katie, his wife, can always be depended upon to support the family, so her reliability allows him to continue drinking. Johnny does understand that an education is the way for his children to escape from the family's poverty. He also tries to provide Francie with extra love to make up for her mother's lack of attention. Johnny is charming and handsome, but he has no depth of character. Johnny is a static character who neither grows nor changes during the novel.

Katie Rommely Nolan

Katie is Francie's mother. Katie comes from a family of strong women. When she needs to accomplish something, Katie always finds the strength to succeed. She learns after Francie's birth that her husband, Johnny, cannot be depended on to support the family. When her second child is born, Katie admits that she loves her son more than her daughter. He is a strong, healthy baby, but Francie was small and frail. Katie knows that Francie is a survivor who can manage without her mother's help, but Neeley, who was born strong and did not have to struggle to survive, will need his mother's help to overcome the hardships of life.

Although she wants to treat the children equally, Katie cannot do so. Her love for Neeley is more intense than her love for Francie. Katie works hard to support her family, but no matter how poor they become, her pride will not allow her to accept any charity. Katie's efforts to survive sometimes make her hard, but there is no doubt that she loves her family. She wants her children to have a better life and feels that education is the key to escaping poverty. Katie never questions her decisions and thinks that she is always right. When the family can only afford to send one child to high school, Katie chooses to send Neeley, reasoning that Francie is determined enough to continue her schooling no matter how hard she must struggle.

Neeley Nolan

Cornelius "Neeley" Nolan is Francie's brother. He is a year younger than his sister. The two children are close friends, as well as siblings, who share the poverty of their childhoods. As he grows up, Neeley begins to resemble his father physically and even has his father's singing voice. However, Neeley is not like his father. He has inherited his mother's work ethic and he dislikes alcohol. Neeley is obedient and loving, a good son and brother.

Ruthie Nolan

Ruthie is Johnny's mother. She did not want Johnny to marry Katie and leave his mother's home. At Johnny's funeral, she never speaks to his widow or her grandchildren.

Lee Rhynor

Lee is a young soldier who is about to leave for Europe when Francie is introduced to him by a friend at work. At first, Lee seems to be genuinely sweet and caring. He easily convinces Francie that he loves her, and she falls in love with him. Lee tries to convince Francie to spend the night with him, but she refuses. He returns to his hometown to see his mother, and two days later, he marries his fiancée. The novel never makes it clear whether he was just lonely and caught up in the romanticism of going off to war or whether he deliberately tried to seduce Francie to take advantage of her youth and inexperience.

Mary Rommely

Mary Rommely is the mother of Katie, Sissy, Evy, and Eliza; she is Francie's maternal grandmother. She and her husband immigrated to the United States from Austria. She insists that her four daughters learn to speak only English so that they will not understand their father's abuse, since he speaks only German. Mary is a strong woman who believes that getting an education and owning a plot of land are the ways to escape poverty and succeed in their new land. Mary is very religious and tells Katie after Francie is born that she must teach her child about the supernatural, including ghosts and fairy tales. Mary also tells Katie that her children must read every day from the two most important books published, the Bible and the collected works of Shakespeare. Mary insists that Katie make a tin can bank and begin saving money to buy land.

Sissy Rommely

Aunt Sissy is Katie's oldest sister. Sissy is the only sister who did not attend school, and thus, she cannot read and write. Sissy is generous and loving and longs for motherhood. She gives birth to ten babies, all of whom die at birth. Sissy has been married three times; all her husbands are called John because that is a name she loves. After her first four children die, she leaves that husband, who she thinks is responsible for the babies' deaths, and marries again. She repeats this pattern with her second husband. Sissy does not bother divorcing her husbands because she was not married to them in the church. Because she is a Catholic, she does not consider herself married to these men in God's eyes. She also has many lovers, trying to fill the emptiness of her heart, which longs for a baby. Sissy uses her sexuality to attract men, and this causes her trouble, especially after she embarrasses Katie in front of the neighbors. Sissy also has a giving and compassionate heart, and this is seen as more important than her promiscuity. After she finally adopts the baby she longs to mother, Sissy becomes a loyal and loving wife. She is finally able to give birth to a baby who lives when she rebels against the tradition that only women can be present at a birth; the male doctor saves the baby's life. In choosing the doctor rather than a midwife, Sissy breaks with tradition, just as she has all her life.

Thomas Rommely

Rommely is Mary's husband and Katie's father. He is Francie's maternal grandfather. He is a cruel and selfish man who never forgives Katie for marrying Johnny, since he thought that she should work and support her father.

Steve

See John

THEMES

Education

At Francie's birth in chapter 9, Mary Rommely tells her daughter, Katie, that it is important that she read to her children every night, because education is a way to escape poverty. Katie reads a page from the Bible and a page from Shakespeare, and this bedtime reading is the start of the children's education. Learning to play the piano and learning to love music are also a part of an education, so the piano lessons in chapter 17 also emphasize Katie's commitment to her children. When Francie starts school in chapter 19, it is an important event for the family. Although Francie is thrilled to finally learn how to read, her first school is a terrible place, where the children are beaten and mistreated. It is Francie who finds a school where she thinks she can get a better education. In chapter 27, as Katie watches her children struggle to drag a large Christmas tree up the steps to their apartment, she suddenly realizes that education will be the only way for her children to have a better life. When Johnny dies in chapter 36, it is more difficult for Francie and Neeley to continue in school, since the family desperately needs the children to work; however, Katie insists that they stay in school and graduate from eighth grade. Because they need the money from Francie's job, only Neeley is sent to high school, but Francie is able to enroll in college summer school in chapter 48 because of her determination to get an education. In chapter 55, Francie is accepted by the University of Michigan. Through the education won for Francie by the determination of her grandmother and her mother, as well as her own tenacity and hard work, Francie is finally able to escape the poverty of her parents' lives.

Love

When Neeley is born in chapter 10, Katie admits to herself that she will always love Neeley more than Francie. Katie thinks that she can treat the children the same and that Francie will never know that she is loved less. Of course, Katie is unable to treat the children the same. In chapter 3, Francie wonders why she likes her father best, but the reason is revealed in several chapters of

TOPICS FOR FURTHER STUDY

- Francie's experiences as the child of immigrants include several difficulties that she and her parents have in adapting to a new culture. In a well-developed essay, compare Francie's experience with that of the Chinese child depicted in Laurence Yep's novel, *The Dragon's Child: A Story of Angel Island*.

- Research the immigration experience in the early twentieth-century United States. Choose one immigrant group from this period, such as Italian, Irish, or Jewish, and prepare an oral presentation describing the experience.

- It is always easier to write about familiar objects and places. Smith uses events and people from her past as a way to create characters and plots in her novel. Choose one of your own memories and use it as the basis of a short story that you will write about your life. Smith makes little effort to disguise the story of her life, changing only names and small details. You should change names and locations slightly and try to disguise some of the details so that people will not recognize themselves.

- An important theme in Smith's novel is the importance of education. Research the kind of education that most new immigrant children received during the years 1900–1915. In a carefully written essay, compare what you have learned about education at the turn of the twentieth century with the kind of education that you have received thus far.

- Find some photos that depict Brooklyn in the first two decades of the twentieth century. Use them to create a poster or PowerPoint presentation for your classmates. Be sure that you thoroughly understand the context and history for each photo so that you can provide background information when you review the images for your classmates.

- With two or three other classmates, create a multimedia group presentation in which you report on the ways in which immigration has changed in the past two hundred years. Have one member of your group research immigration laws, while another researches immigration from the mid- nineteenth century through the mid-twentieth century. A third person should research illegal immigration in the later part of the twentieth century. If you have a fourth member of your group, that person should look for a documentary about immigration that your group might use as part of your presentation on how immigration has changed. Good group presentations involve many ways of presenting information, so take the time to prepare graphs and handouts that will help your classmates follow the presentation. Be sure to prepare a bibliography of your sources, as well.

---

the novel. For example, in chapter 27, Francie makes an elaborate hat pin holder for her mother for Christmas, and Neeley gives each member of the family a candy cane that he bought. Katie makes a greater fuss over Neeley's gift than Francie's. Johnny tries to makes up for the lack of extra attention from Francie's mother. His death in chapter 36 leaves Francie without the one person who has always loved her. In chapter 42, Katie chooses to attend Neeley's graduation, while Francie attends her graduation with her Aunt Sissy. In one instance, although Francie's grades are much better than Neeley's, Katie makes a fuss over Neeley's grades and chastises Francie for the one grade that is not an A. Katie cannot help loving one child more than the other, but Francie's knowledge that she is loved less by her mother will affect Francie's life and the choices that she makes.

After Johnny's death, Francie is desperately lonely and needs someone to love her. Her need for love results in her falling in love with Lee Rhynor,

Dorothy McGuire as Katie, James Dunn as Johnny, Peggy Ann Garner as Francie, and Ted Donaldson as Neeley in the 1945 film version of the novel (© *John Springer Collection | Corbis*)

a young soldier, who tells her that he loves her after knowing her less than two days. Because she is desperate to be loved, Francie gives Lee her heart and a promise that she will wait for him to return from the war. Even after he betrays her, Francie continues to think about him. In chapter 56, Francie sums up her great need for love in her assessment of Ben Blake, who has given her a ring. He loves her, but he does not need her, and Francie has learned throughout her life that she must be needed as well as loved.

Survival

The opening chapter of *A Tree Grows in Brooklyn* explains that the tree growing out of the cement in the Nolan's' courtyard is a Tree of Heaven. This tree symbolizes the family's ability to survive all that threatens to tear it apart. This tree grows only in the poorest of neighborhoods and it grows no matter how poor the circumstances. It can thrive in cement and without water or fertilizer; it represents the tenacity and strength of the poor inhabitants of the neighborhood, who survive with little food or money. Like the tree that receives so little care and nourishment, the Nolan family survives and eventually thrives, emerging from extreme poverty to achieve success. Although Johnny does not survive, his widow and his three children survive the most desperate of circumstances. Although they do not always have much food and are often forced to work backbreaking, menial jobs, the family eventually overcomes adversity. In the final chapter of the novel, Francie observes that the Tree of Heaven is still alive. It has been chopped down and the stump has been set on fire, but the tree is not dead. It has sent out a new branch and is surviving. Like the tree, the Nolan family has survived poverty and death and has worked hard to continue to grow.

STYLE

Autobiographical Fiction

Fiction refers to any story that is created out of the author's imagination, rather than factual events. Sometimes the characters in a fictional piece are based on real people, but their ultimate form and the way they respond to events are solely the creation of the author. In *A Tree Grows in Brooklyn*, the characters are fictional, but they are based on people or character types from Smith's life. This inclusion of facts from the author's own life is the defining element of autobiography, the biography of oneself. For instance, many of the details and locations in *A Tree Grows in Brooklyn* mirror Smith's own life. Examples include Smith's own love of reading and writing, which Francie also loves, and the jobs that Smith held after finishing elementary school, which are the same kinds of work that Francie does. *A Tree Grows in Brooklyn* is a work of autobiographical fiction because it is a fictional story that contains elements of autobiographical fact.

Characterization

Characterization is the process by which the author creates a lifelike person from his or her imagination. To accomplish this, the author provides the character with personality traits that help define who the character will be and how he or she will behave in a given situation. Katie, for example, is a complex character whose inability to love both her children equally leaves Francie always hungry for love. Characters can range from simple, stereotypical figures to more complex, multifaceted ones, and they may also be stock characters defined by personality traits, such as the rogue or the damsel in distress. Although Francie's father, Johnny, is a stereotypical Irishman who drinks too much, in general, Smith portrays her characters with a great deal of depth. This may be because they are loosely based on people she has known in her own life.

Coming-of-Age Novel

A Tree Grows in Brooklyn can be described as a coming-of-age story. Typically, in a coming-of-age novel, the protagonist endures great trials and difficulty, at the end of which he or she has matured and grown stronger. It is common for the character to suffer and undergo hardships that test his or her strength and will to succeed.

The heroine of *A Tree Grows in Brooklyn* is Francie Nolan, who undergoes many difficulties and endures many hardships in her attempt to survive the devastating poverty of her childhood. Francie grows from an innocent child into a confident young woman, who has learned that she is smart, tenacious, strong, and brave. Other coming-of-age novels include Mark Twain's *Adventures of Huckleberry Finn* and Charles Dickens's *Great Expectations*.

Symbolism

Symbolism is the use of a concrete object to represent an abstract concept. In *A Tree Grows in Brooklyn*, the Tree of Heaven symbolizes the family's ability to survive the terrible poverty that threatens to destroy it. The tin can bank, in which the family members save extra pennies, represents the hope that they can somehow escape the poverty of their neighborhood and start a new life in a home they will own. Finally, the pearl studs that Katie gives to Johnny on their wedding day symbolize Katie's love for Johnny, but they also symbolize her expectation that he will be deserving of such a financial sacrifice. When he dies, Johnny is buried with the pearl studs. The promise of a better life that the studs symbolized died with Johnny and was buried with him.

HISTORICAL CONTEXT

The Irish and German Immigration Experiences

Francie Nolan is of Irish and Austrian origin. Her parents were first-generation Americans, and as new immigrants they faced many problems in their effort to be successful. The Nolans were Irish, a group that was a huge force in immigration. Between 1820 and 1860, it is estimated that anywhere from a third to half of all new immigrants were Irish. Many were fleeing the potato famine that enveloped Ireland in the 1840s. Even in the years after 1860, when Irish immigration slowed, their numbers hovered at about 15 percent of new immigrants. By 1900, there were 10 million foreign-born people living in the United States; of those, 15.7 percent were Irish. Since most Irish immigrants were Catholic, a group that had been both religiously and economically oppressed in Ireland, their influx also changed the religious dynamics in the

COMPARE & CONTRAST

- **1910s:** By 1910, it is not unusual for eleven thousand new immigrants a day to pass through the center at Ellis Island in New York City. New York residents become used to seeing many ocean liners lined up alongside the piers of the Hudson River, along Manhattan's West Side.

  1940s: The Port of New York becomes the point of departure for much of the European campaign of World War II, with troops and supplies leaving from the city. It is feared that New York City will be a target for German bombings. Every day the sky is filled with fighter planes searching the skies for German bombers, which never materialize.

  Today: After the terrorist attacks on lower Manhattan on September 11, 2001, the air over the city and the piers along the Hudson River are patrolled and guarded more closely than ever before. Because of shipping methods that use standardized containers, the Port Newark–Elizabeth Marine Terminal in Newark Bay becomes the principal facility for shipment of goods entering or leaving the United States.

- **1910s:** In the years from 1904 to 1912, more than four thousand new apartment buildings are built in New York City to house many of the new immigrants pouring into the city. As the new immigrants move away from the Lower East Side and out toward the five boroughs, including Brooklyn, the building of new apartments to house them quickly follows.

  1940s: Mayor Fiorello LaGuardia begins work on a program to tear down slum housing and replace it with better quality housing for low-income residents.

  Today: The New York City Housing Authority continues to work to create more affordable housing for lower income residents. In Brooklyn, empty parking lots are targeted to be replaced with new, more affordable town houses.

- **1910s:** A series of new bridges and the new subway system link Manhattan to Brooklyn and the other boroughs, allowing people to move easily from one neighborhood to another.

  1940s: Under Mayor LaGuardia, the subways are expanded to include more of the outlying areas; the fare remains just a nickel.

  Today: Transportation in New York consists of a complex web of subways, railroad lines, buses, taxis, and automobiles, as well as several bridges, tunnels, and airports, all of which connect the island of New York City to the rest of the United States and the world. The goal of the New York City Transit Authority is to keep people moving around and in and out of the city smoothly.

United States. Much of the anti-Irish fervor that greeted the new immigrants came from hostility to their Catholic religion. Like most new immigrants, the Irish filled a need for laborers. They helped build the infrastructure—canals, railways, streets, and sewers—of their new country.

The few Austrians who immigrated to the United States were usually grouped together with the German immigrants, since they came with similar backgrounds and with similar expectations. In many ways, German immigration paralleled Irish immigration, with similar numbers over peak years during the nineteenth century. Katie Nolan's parents came to the United States during what would be the peak decade for Austrian and German immigration, the years between 1881 and 1890, when nearly 1.5 million Germans immigrated. Unlike the Irish, who immigrated for political, economic, and religious reasons, German immigrants were largely motivated by a desire for economic prosperity. Unlike the Irish, who were largely laborers, German immigrants tended to be involved in skilled trades and they expected to be successful. This can be seen in Thomas Rommely's insistence that his four daughters must sacrifice their lives to work and make him wealthy. He is unable to forgive his daughters for leaving him, either for the nunnery or to marry. Thomas embodies many of the symptoms common to new immigrants. These include failed dreams, nostalgia for a homeland that exists only in memory, and intergenerational conflict, as children grow up assimilated into the new culture and reject, in anger, frustration, embarrassment, and humiliation, the attempts by their parents to preserve a connection to them through common cultural practices and assumptions. The children of immigrants want independence, but they also want their own identity and the opportunity to make their own choices. They choose their own spouses, as Johnny Nolan and Katie Rommely did. As a result, Johnny Nolan's mother refuses to speak to or acknowledge Johnny's wife, even at his funeral. Other problems that the first generations of new immigrants may face include increasing marital conflict, as spouses adapt differently to the new or imagined standards of the new culture and as spouses attempt to assert their identity by acts that are destructive to their relationship. This is seen in the marriage of Mary and Thomas Rommely. The relationships that Smith depicts in the Nolan and Rommely families, in *A Tree Grows in Brooklyn*, provide a useful way to learn about the immigration experience during the first decades of the twentieth century.

Life in Williamsburg, Brooklyn

The setting for *A Tree Grows in Brooklyn* is very important in understanding Francie's life. The opening chapters of the novel are spent describing the neighborhood and the small businesses that surround the apartment in which Francie lives. During the 1830s, Irish and German immigrants settled in Williamsburg, which for much of the rest of the nineteenth century projected a genteel, almost resort-like atmosphere of comfortable living, and in fact, Williamsburg served as a getaway for people who worked in Manhattan. However, by 1912, when Francie's story begins, Williamsburg was undergoing tremendous change. Brooklyn had become one of the five boroughs within the city of New York in 1898, a move that linked Brooklyn neighborhoods more closely to the greater city of New York. In 1903, the new Williamsburg Bridge opened the neighborhood to an influx of new

A family living in a dilapidated New York tenement building, ca. 1910 (© Bettmann / Corbis)

immigrants and second-generation Americans, who crossed over from the slum tenements of Manhattan's Lower East Side. As a result, Williamsburg became a densely populated neighborhood, with crowded tenement housing and crowded schools, in which several children were forced to share the same desks and books—something that Smith describes in *A Tree Grows in Brooklyn*. Between 1900 and 1920, the population of Williamsburg doubled. Many of the new residents in Williamsburg were Eastern European Jews. In the opening chapters of her novel, Smith mentions the uneasy relationship between the Catholic children in Francie's neighborhood and the Jewish children. In addition to the Jewish immigrants, others from Italy and Poland poured into Williamsburg. By 1917, when Francie is sixteen years old, Williamsburg is the most densely packed neighborhood in New York City.

CRITICAL OVERVIEW

One of the first reviews of *A Tree Grows in Brooklyn* was published in the journal *Social Forces*, published by the University of North Carolina Department of Sociology in 1943. This is a journal with a focus on social research, which suggests that the editors saw Smith's novel as an important means of studying the transmission of stories from one generation to the next and of understanding the legacy of family and neighborhood in forming personalities. In her review of *A Tree Grows in Brooklyn*, Katharine Jocher singles out Smith's "penetrating interpretation" of her Brooklyn neighborhood and the people who live there. Jocher notes that Smith writes "earnestly and sympathetically, as well as poignantly," creating a "folk portraiture" of the inhabitants. It is the set of relationships between family members, between generations, and between suffering and hope that creates characters who might live in any large city, not just Brooklyn. Jocher argues that *A Tree Grows in Brooklyn* is sociology and that it "should be read by every sociologist and every social worker, for its clear and understanding interpretation" of why people behave the way they do. Smith does so, according to Jocher, "in simple rhythmic prose that is frequently of the essence of poetry."

It is worth noting that *A Tree Grows in Brooklyn* has an appeal to readers that extends far beyond that of the sociologist. In his 1943 review for the *New York Times*, Meyer Berger also refers to Smith's writing as poetic, but without limiting the audience as Jocher does in her review. Berger observes that the novel has little plot and, in fact, is not really a novel at all, but is instead "a stringing together of memory's beads." Calling Smith's book an autobiography, Berger says that as autobiography, "the workmanship is extraordinarily good." Berger claims that the fact that Smith is a woman provides for a "gentler woman's viewpoint" that softens the harshness of poverty and the misery of the slums that Smith describes. Lest it seem that *A Tree Grows in Brooklyn* lacks power beyond its 1943 audience, a 1999 review, also published in the *New York Times*, makes clear that Smith's autobiographical novel remains a favorite of readers. Robert Cornfield calls the book "a treasured rite of passage" for its many devoted readers. More importantly, Cornfield finds that Smith's book is also a history of Williamsburg in the first two decades of the twentieth century. In a sense, then, Cornfield finds both the sociology that Jocher thought so important and the autobiography that captivated Berger blended together in Smith's novel. Cornfield calls the book a "social document" that "illuminates the past," but he says that *A Tree Grows in Brooklyn* is more than those things. It has an "emotional life" that ensures that

the book will remain in print. Williamsburg's history is intrinsically linked with Smith's novel. The book's lasting appeal is in the history the writer paints of a time nearly a century ago, but what keeps readers going back to the novel are the characters, who bring that history to life.

CRITICISM

Sheri Metzger Karmiol

Karmiol has a Ph.D. in English Renaissance literature. She teaches literature and drama at the University of New Mexico, where she is a lecturer in the University Honors Program. She is also a professional writer and the author of several reference texts on poetry and drama. In this essay, she discusses the role of imagination in achieving the American dream in A Tree Grows in Brooklyn.

The American dream was an important motivating factor in the immigrant experience. Immigrants left their homes, families, friends— indeed all that was familiar and comfortable about their old lives—to move to the United States in search of a better life. Both Johnny and Katie Nolan are the children of immigrants, and like most first-generation Americans, they hope they will be more successful than their parents. They also hope that their children will be able to achieve even more of the American dream. The desire for each generation to achieve more than the previous is an essential feature of the quest to possess a share of the American dream. In *A Tree Grows in Brooklyn*, Francie is able to fulfill the family's goal of achieving the American dream, a goal that eluded her father. Unlike Johnny, who was a dreamer, Francie possesses the determination, the strength, and especially the imagination necessary to escape the poverty of her childhood.

In chapter 25, when Johnny takes Francie to Bushwick Avenue and shows her the mansions and the opportunities for wealth that await all immigrants, he implants in his daughter the knowledge and desire to achieve a similar level of success. Johnny suggests to Francie that in a democracy like America, anything is possible. Whether success means living in mansions or riding in fancy carriages, Francie glimpses all that is possible for the children of immigrants and imagines that she can accomplish a similar result. Francie is ten years old on that day on Bushwick Avenue, but the seeds of the American dream were actually planted much

WHAT DO I READ NEXT?

- Betty Smith's second novel, *Tomorrow Will be Better* (1948), also takes place in Brooklyn and is a coming-of-age novel.

- Another novel by Smith, *Maggie-Now* (1958), focuses on the lives of Irish immigrants in Brooklyn.

- Valerie Raleigh Yow's biography of the author, *Betty Smith: Life of the Author of "A Tree Grows in Brooklyn"* (2008), is an in-depth look at Smith's life and work.

- Alice McDermott's novel, *At Weddings and Wakes* (1992), is the story of three generations of an Irish American family living in Brooklyn.

- *The Fortunate Pilgrim* (1965), a semiautobiographical novel by Mario Puzo, is the story of an Italian immigrant family living in New York City.

- Michael Gold's work *Jews Without Money* (1930) is an autobiographical novel that reveals the harsh lives that Eastern European Jews endured in their struggle as new immigrants on Manhattan's Lower East Side.

- *Growing Up Ethnic in America: Contemporary Fiction about Learning to Be American* (1999), edited by Maria Mazziottf Gillan and Jennifer Gillan, is a collection of short stories that portrays the experiences of adapting to life in America for those who are not Caucasian. The editors include stories that depict the experiences of Hispanics, African Americans, Native Americans, and others.

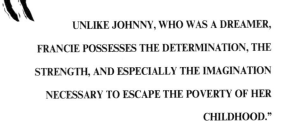

UNLIKE JOHNNY, WHO WAS A DREAMER, FRANCIE POSSESSES THE DETERMINATION, THE STRENGTH, AND ESPECIALLY THE IMAGINATION NECESSARY TO ESCAPE THE POVERTY OF HER CHILDHOOD."

earlier. Mary Rommely's comments to Katie when Francie is born illustrate her hope that her children and grandchildren will someday achieve the American dream. Mary tells Katie that she must read a page every day from the works of Shakespeare and a page from the Bible to her children. For Mary, these are the two great books that educated people read. Mary points out that in Shakespeare "all that a man has learned of beauty, all that he may know of wisdom and living are on those pages." Mary also tells Katie that she must immediately create a tin can bank and begin saving to buy land. Mary sees education and owning land as the surest ways of achieving the American dream. Although Katie challenges her mother, reminding her that her own children, including Katie, are poor and they will always be poor, Mary responds with a reminder that in the old country they had nothing. They were poor, and they were peasants and they starved, and while they are also poor in America, according to Mary, the reason they are now in America is that they are free, and their children are born in a free land.

In a sense, Francie is destined to succeed from her birth. She was born with a caul, a thin membrane that covers the face of some newborns. Folk tradition suggests that a baby born with a caul will have good luck, but Katie and Mary will not leave that good luck to chance. When Francie is born, Mary tells Katie that she needs to nurture Francie's imagination to help her create a secret world in which she can escape from the real world. Mary says that it is important for Francie to have a world that is not real, so that "when the world becomes too ugly for living in, the child can reach back and live in her imagination." As it turns out, Mary is right about imagination being a way for Francie to escape from poverty. It is imagination that will help Francie to escape the limitations of their Williamsburg neighborhood. One example of how imagination allows Francie to improve her life is in her determination to attend a school with more opportunities than the one in her neighborhood. Before she enters school for the first time, Francie imagines how wonderful school will be once she is old enough to attend. The reality is disappointing. Her neighborhood school is overcrowded, and the teachers are cruel to the children of immigrants. The school symbolizes a larger problem for the immigrant community. The flood of immigrants into some areas of New York City has put a strain on all public and social services. Children attend neighborhood schools, but when tenements and apartment buildings are crowded with families and many children, neighborhood schools become crowded, as well. The school that Francie initially attends has three times as many students as it was designed to hold. Two or three students share each desk. The classrooms are crowded and the teachers impatient and overworked. There are few bathrooms, and the poverty and cruelty in the children's lives create bullies, who limit the number of children who can use the bathrooms. It is a small thing, the inability to use a bathroom, but it creates accidents that lead to shame. Most children will stay and endure, but Francie finds another, much nicer school, one with grass, not concrete, and without fences encircling it. Francie imagines that she can attend the new school, and she imagines a way to make attending the new school possible. Her imagination allows her to see herself in a better world and as a result, she works to create that better world for herself.

It is common for the children of immigrants to fare better than their parents in many ways. Francie's ability to advocate for her own education and for a better school suggests that she will grow up with advantages that her parents did not have. The parents whose children attend Francie's new school have lived in the United States for many generations. They know their rights and their children's rights, and more importantly, teachers know that these parents will not tolerate abuse. Unlike Katie and Johnny Nolan, the parents at Francie's new school know enough to demand a better education for their children. The new school is not overcrowded. Francie has her own desk, and the new teachers, who are not forced to deal with too many students and poor facilities, are more generous with their time. In the old school, Francie was the only child in her class who could claim to be, in a sense, an American, since she was the only child whose parents were born in America. In the new school, all the children are Americans.

An important means for Francie's escape from her family's crushing poverty is education, but education does not come easily to immigrant children. Before children can begin school in Williamsburg, they must be vaccinated against smallpox. The vaccination rule creates a problem for immigrant families, who are told that education is free and a requirement for all

children. However, they are also told that their children must be vaccinated. If they are not, children cannot enroll in school, and if they do not enroll in school, the parents are breaking the law. Many parents are frightened by the idea of exposing their healthy children to an injection that might make them sick. Katie is so frightened by the vaccinations that she will not take the children to be vaccinated. She makes Francie take Neeley. To assuage Neeley's fear, Francie engages him in a game of mud pies, which means that when they arrive for their vaccinations, they are dirty. To the Harvard-educated doctor, forced to perform community medicine in a neighborhood of poor immigrant families, the Nolan children are an example of the filthiness of those who are poor. When he sees Francie, with her dirty arm, he exclaims, "Filth, filth, filth, from morning to night. I know they're poor but they could wash. Water is free and soap is cheap." The doctor uses the word "they" to mean the poor, the immigrants, those who live in the slum areas of Williamsburg. The doctor's cruelty when Francie goes for her vaccination is one more example of how easy it is for those who have forgotten their own immigrant roots to mistreat the poor. The doctor, who has achieved the American dream, no longer recalls that at some point, his family were immigrants. The story of Francie and Neeley's vaccinations and the fear that vaccination evokes in the immigrant community is a reminder that everything that immigrants encounter once they arrive in the United States is new to them and often quite frightening. Most immigrants came from rural areas and small villages, with poverty, little medicine, and high infant and child mortality rates, and where their children's good health was not taken for granted. Now they are being asked to surrender their healthy children for a vaccination that they think will reproduce the conditions that they have fled across the ocean to escape. To the new immigrant, vaccinations are just one more hurdle in reaching the American dream, but it is a hurdle that Francie can surmount, even though she is only seven years old.

Imagination allows Francie to envision a world beyond the Williamsburg tenements where she lives. She can imagine years filled with joy and the promise of a better life, rather than the exhaustion of spending each moment just trying to survive. The first step toward fulfilling the promise of the American dream is best illustrated near the end of the novel, when Francie and Neeley meet at the

Williamsburg Bridge connecting Brooklyn to Manhattan (© *Stephen Chernin | Getty Images*)

bank to have the first money they have earned converted into new dollar bills, which they can present to their mother. The act of taking money home to give to their mother symbolizes the expectation inherent in the American dream that children will have a better life than their parents. Johnny Nolan's failures nearly prevent his family from achieving the American dream. Katie will achieve only the dream for herself and for her youngest child, Laurie, by marrying McShane, who has already achieved the dream through his hard work as a policeman and as a politician and who, in paying for Francie and Neeley to attend college, opens the way for Katie's older children to achieve the American dream. In contrast, the American dream is never achieved by Francie's father, Johnny. Johnny has talent and might have succeeded, but very early in *A Tree Grows in Brooklyn*, readers learn that his love of drinking limits his future. Although Johnny is able to join the Waiters' Union and become an active member of the Democratic party—both signs that he has the ability to achieve the American dream—he never moves beyond his own personal fears. Achieving the American dream takes hard work, but Johnny is a dreamer, who imagines a better life but lacks the incentive and hard work to make the dream come true. The lesson he does teach Francie, though, is that there is a role for dreaming in her life; her imagination and the ability to imagine her own success help her fulfill her dreams. Francie

Nolan succeeds because while she may have her father's ability to dream of a better life, she also has the immigrant desire to work hard and create a better life. Francie embodies the American dream, which makes Smith's autobiographical novel, *A Tree Grows in Brooklyn*, the perfect venue to learn about the immigration experience and how hard some people struggled to make the American dream their own.

Source: Sheri Metzger Karmiol, Critical Essay on *A Tree Grows in Brooklyn*, in *Novels for Students*, Gale, Cengage Learning, 2010.

Geraldine DeLuca

In the following excerpt, DeLuca recommends A Tree Grows in Brooklyn *to adolescent readers for its authenticity and strong protagonist.*

Hemingway is often quoted as saying that all American literature comes from one book and that that book is *Huckleberry Finn*. Whether one agrees about "all American literature," it is clear that that is where Salinger's *The Catcher in the Rye* comes from. And one can say, in dubious celebration of Salinger, that *The Catcher in the Rye* is the one book that the adolescent novel comes from. It is a difficult, deceptive heritage: satirical and ostensibly designed to offer a clearer mode of life and thought than that which the heroes witness. But certainly in Salinger's case, and very possibly in Twain's before him, there

> SHE IS MOVED AND STIMULATED BY THE
> PEOPLE AROUND HER, BY THE LIFE THAT EXISTS FOR
> HER IN THE BOOKS SHE READS, AND BY THE WORKINGS
> OF HER OWN MIND. LIKE THE POOR COMMUNITY SHE
> LIVES IN, SHE HAS ENERGY AND PROMISE."

really are no alternatives. One's only salvation is to remain a child.

Even in his works about the Glass Family, where he has turned to the adult world, Salinger is still celebrating childhood. While the Glass family can get quickly under one's skin, the books ultimately do not satisfy because the characters never quite get past what Zooey himself termed their "tenth-rate nervous breakdowns," never accepting or confronting the ills of the adult world that so oppress them. The]*sic*[remain Salinger's children, sanctified and damaged by their sensibilities.

In all of Salinger's work, children alone offer solace to his tormented characters: twelve-year-old Esme is the only one of the narrator/Sergeant X's correspondents who can help him; Seymour Glass, the oldest of the Glass family children, now unhappily married, has a sad tryst in the ocean at Miami Beach with a little girl named Sybil before he blows his brains out. The family reminisces about Franny sitting in the kitchen as a child, having a small glass of milk with Jesus. And of course there is Holden's younger sister Phoebe, dressed in her pajamas with the elephants on the collar, urging Holden to face his parents—if not his problems. These are the ideal characters in Salinger's world, and adults are appealing insofar as they share the qualities and voice of childhood. Franny and Zooey, for all their sophistication, are still pained children. Zooey's small, beautiful back—observed mostly by his mother who sits talking to him as he takes a bath—suggests a child's; Franny recovers from her depression by listening, open-mouthed, on the phone to her brother Zooey, who disguises his voice as their brother Buddy's and tells her the old adage of their brother Seymour that she should live for the fat lady, because the fat lady is Christ. Seized and calmed by the truth of that simple notion, Franny climbs into her father's empty bed and

goes beatifically to sleep. How comfortably, innocently incestuous they all are. "It's a Wise Child," the radio program on which each of the Glass family in turn spouted their wisdom, might be the name of any of Salinger's works.

The casual reader might be beguiled into the belief that Salinger's nay-saying characters are simply confused and short-sighted and that the author is implying they can mature and change. Zooey's pep talks with his sister—self-mocking, ironic, good humored—sound optimistic. But Salinger's humor comes more from desperation than distance. The unhappiness Holden feels because of his intolerance for compromise and his discomfort with sexuality cannot easily be helped. There is no successful model for him. One either compromises or goes under. And none of the Glass family is doing much better. Their fat lady—in the prophetic Seymour's extended description—has cancer and sits on her porch listening to the radio. In the face of this dismal vision, the Glass family must simply bear up under their crown of thorns.

In terms of what he finds acceptable, Salinger is not, in fact, very far from Lewis Carroll. He has much more sympathy for the compromises of the common man, but no more hope. Yet, like Carroll, he is authentic. He may have descended from Twain, but he is not an imitator. Unfortunately, the same cannot be said of his descendants. The idiosyncrasies—not to say excesses—of his style, along with his simplifications and his celebration of innocence have been adopted by a host of followers. The fat lady has been succeeded by M.E. Kerr's Miss Blue, who hangs pictures of Jesus in the dormitory bathroom, and Paul Zindel's invalid Irene, who spits into a sputum cup all day, and writes doggerel verse which she sends to *The London Observer*. Almost all the adolescent novels use the familiar and by now too predictable first person narrator whose alienated-innocent voice confines, constricts, and dominates the work. They are all sanctified, all wise children. Salinger's gimmicks appear everywhere: in the lists, like the contents of Bessie Glass's medicine cabinet; the footnotes, that "aesthetic evil" for which Buddy Glass asks indulgence; the physical grotesques and caricatures, like Old Spencer, surreptitiously picking his nose, or Mr. Antolini, ambiguously stroking Holden's hair....

Somewhere during the last ten pages of the typical adolescent novel, its author may haul in a moral, but the morals, like the stories, are contrived and unconvincing. Often they are no more than a re-offering of what the adolescent originally rejected and ridiculed for most of the book. No matter how seriously the authors ask the readers to take themselves, their books are fundamentally disrespectful of their audience, diminishing and trivializing their existence, and offering them few authentic signs of hope in the adult world that awaits their coming.

It is easy, of course, to criticize, and obviously hard to write for that age group. The successful writers for younger children seem, as Sidney did, to need only "to look in their heart and write," while the writers for adolescents feels pressed to fulfill unusual demands, to shape their writing into patterns that adolescents have embraced in the past. And adolescents are a difficult audience. They are self-conscious, cautious, embarrassed both by their childishness and their maturity. Nonetheless, writers seem to have given themselves over too completely to the proven success formula. And the more the formula is used, the thinner and more exhausted it becomes, so that is products become too specifically about a place—a school or hospital—or a subject—drug abuse, divorce, sex—and about nothing else, nothing to suggest a microcosm, a universe of wider if similar concerns.

Where then do we find books that we can offer adolescents without misgivings—books that deal with their experiences, that they will find substantial as well as entertaining, that don't narrow and distort their world? Where do we find books that, in addition, are written with enough talent and grace to develop an adolescent's sense of aesthetics, to delight an adolescent with their own beauty? Where do we find books that offer adolescents a sense of options, a sense of balance and hope? While there are "adolescent novels" that satisfy these criteria, they are few in number. We need, then, perhaps as we have always done, to look elsewhere—to the children's books that are sophisticated enough to satisfy their tastes, and to the adult books that by virtue of subject matter and simplicity of narrative are accessible.

Somewhat arbitrarily, I've chosen three books that seem to me worth an adolescent's time and attention. They are simply three among many, but they help to establish criteria. The first, Mollie Hunter's *A Sound of Chariots*, is a bona fide children's book which shares the best qualities of autobiographical works for any audience. The other

two, Betty Smith's *A Tree Grows in Brooklyn* and Judith Guest's *Ordinary People*, are putatively works for adults. In fact, one might characterize them as adult novels that don't quite make it. But because they are clear and relatively unadorned, and because, without limiting their focus, they deal with adolescence, they are particularly suited to a young audience. . . .

The uniqueness and authenticity of *A Sound of Chariots* may stem from the fact that it is autobiographical. Absolutely uncontrived, it captures the mind of a young adolescent the way few adolescent novels do. And perhaps because it too is autobiographical, Betty Smith's *A Tree Grows in Brooklyn* has that same air of authenticity. It is a detailed, often unabashedly sentimental chronicle of the childhood and adolescence of Francie Nolan—whose life, like Bridie's, parallels its creator's. And there are other parallels between the books. Like Bridie, Francie grows up in poverty, loses her father, and feels alienated from her mother. She has similar desires to become a writer, although it is the stories—the allowed lying—that appeals to her rather than the words. (The distinction is apparent in the prose.) Like Bridie, Francie is forced to leave school to earn money, and finally, she too grows into womanhood with a sense of kinship with her mother and a faith in her own strength and talent.

The differences, however, are just as marked as the similarities. Whereas Hunter's book is a tight, one might almost say disciplined, story, *A Tree Grows in Brooklyn* weaves its casual way through the streets of Williamsburg for 420 pages with total abandon. Though the novel is divided into books, the division seems rather arbitrary and adds little aesthetically. But the book has other charms. Betty Smith seems less concerned with the shape of her story than with describing fully all the details of life in pre-World War I Williamsburg. Her story is full of vignettes about the Irish, the Jews, the provincial, angry women, the shrewd, exhausted storekeepers, the street-wise kids, the folklore. . . .

Francie is smart enough to see past the slogans, the propaganda, and the boat rides sponsored by the bosses from Tammany Hall. In that respect she is shrewder than her father. But there is a sense that, at least for a white, Irish child in Williamsburg things can change. Francie's grandmother marvels that Francie and her brother Neeley can read and write: that marks progress from her own generation.

She has faith in the penny bank she nails to the floor of the closet. And at the novel's end, Francie's mother puts away her scrubwoman's pail to marry the courtly police officer-cum-local politician Mister McShane. Their baby sister, Annie Laurie, will never have to collect junk the way she and Neeley did.

So it is an American fairy tale. But Smith tells it with her eyes open, and she rarely suspends her critical faculties. Francie knows, for instance, that her father is weak, that his talents—for charming people with his songs, his stories, and his frail good looks—are not marketable, that he is one of life's losers. In his happy moments he is like a lovable child full of illusions. He tries to convey to his skeptical daughter his reverence for America's union labels and its promises. And she, because she is a child, tries to believe him. The following dialogue between them, demonstrating all the limitations of Smith's style, is like an argument between two children.

> "Anybody," said Johnny, carried away by his personal dream of Democracy, "can ride in one of those hansom cabs, provided," he qualified, "they got the money. So you can see what a free country we got here."
>
> "What's free about it if you have to *pay?*" asked Francie.
>
> "It's free in this way: If you have the money you're allowed to ride in them no matter who you are. In the old countries, certain people aren't free to ride in them, even if they have the money."
>
> "Wouldn't it be more of a free country," persisted Francie, "if we could ride in them free?"
>
> "No."
>
> "Why?"
>
> "Because that would be Socialism," concluded Johnny triumphantly, "and we don't want that over here."
>
> "Why?"
>
> "Because we got Democracy and that's the best thing there is," clinched Johnny.

Francie's remarks may be just as simplistic as his, but the point is he lacks the understanding to sustain the discussion. Because he believes so absolutely in America the land of opportunity, he is confused and wounded by his own failures. An alcoholic almost by way of fulfilling his mother's prediction that none of her Nolan boys could survive a marriage, he finds America's elusive promise a bitter one. Lacking the purpose and energy to survive, in moments of

self-pity he unloads his misery on his daughter. "I am not a happy man," he tells her. "I got a wife and children and I don't happen to be a hard-working man. I never wanted a family." Francie absorbs this careless assault as she absorbs the love, wondering why she loves him: "Why did she like her father better than her mother? Why did she? Papa was no good. He said so himself. But she liked Papa better."

If the men in Francie's family lack energy, the women pick up the slack. Francie's mother, Katie Nolan, is bitter and hard edged, not even necessarily disillusioned but merely saddened by her beautiful husband's inability to help the family survive. Yet, like Bridie's mother, she has the will to keep going, and with the help of her own mother and her two sisters, she manages to earn enough money to survive until she remarries. More impressive and appealing, though, than Katie is her younger sister Sissy. She is a modern day Wife of Bath, an embodiment of the life force, marrying and remarrying—she regards divorce as superfluous since she never marries in church—loving each husband in turn with an honest exuberance but eventually leaving each because her babies are all stillborn. Finally, after ten pregnancies, and with the help of a hospital and a "Jewish doctor," the eleventh survives, and she begins to mellow. But throughout the work she lives by her instincts, a constant source of embarrassment to her more conventional sisters, a delight to Francie, and always life-affirming, sexual and nurturing in her choices. Juxtaposed against the tight-lipped women who line the tenement stoops, there is never any question about who has the greater sense of decency or who is happier.

Finally we come to Francie herself. Knowing full well that her mother loves her less than she loves her brother, watching her father die from alcoholism, being forced to leave school while her less imaginative brother is forced to continue because he is a boy, she still remains open and receptive to life, adapting, maintaining a sense of values, and rarely doubting her own strength. And the depiction does not seem unrealistic. People like Frantic do exist. She is one of those authentically strong individuals who have somehow gotten what they needed to survive. She is moved and stimulated by the people around her, by the life that exists for her in the books she reads, and by the workings of her own mind. Like the poor community she lives in, she has energy and promise. She is both a participant and an observer, neither narcissistic nor aloof. If she is occasionally ambivalent about the notion of progress, and cynical about the promises of America, she is nonetheless ready to see them through.

A Tree Grows in Brooklyn is a book about beginnings, about a community that grows, like that tree, despite its lack of soil and sunlight. It is a book about tenacity. . . .

Source: Geraldine DeLuca, "Unself-Conscious Voices: Larger Contexts for Adolescents," in the *Lion and the Unicorn*, Vol. 2, No. 2, 1978, pp. 89–108.

Katharine Jocher

In the following 1943 review, Jocher argues that A Tree Grows in Brooklyn *is a work of sociology that "should be read by every sociologist and social worker."*

Here there passes before us the panorama of a section of city life, together with the intimate details of family life, prepared for us not by a statistician with an array of facts and figures, not by a sociologist presenting a carefully prepared case history, not by a participant observer who has for a brief period lived among the group, nor by a psychologist, a historian, or an economist, but by one who naturally combines all of these—who, herself, is a member of the group about which she writes. Only one who had been born and bred in Brooklyn, who had been part of its warp and woof, could have had that ". . . *feeling* about it—Oh, I can't explain it. You've got to live in Brooklyn to know." To live "there" is always the best way to know, and to those of us who have lived in a city, Brooklyn or another, Betty Smith gives us incident after incident that can be matched at every turn. Analogous, and even identical, happenings are recalled and relived in the light of Miss Smith's penetrating interpretation. Brooklyn is the locale, but the tragedy and comedy, the pathos and humor, the sordidness and beauty—all can be and are duplicated again and again in any large city.

For the sociologist, of special significance in this series of pen sketches is the folk portraiture about which Miss Smith writes so earnestly and sympathetically, as well as poignantly. Page after page carries the wisdom, the beliefs, the courage, the aspirations of the folk. There is none of the futility of "Tobacco Road" folk, but there is always the looking ahead, the striving upward and onward, the desire that each generation shall rise upon the achievements—feeble though they may be—of the last. " . . . In the old country, a man is given to the past. Here he belongs to the future. In this land, he may be what he will, if he has the good heart and the way of working honestly at the right things." "The secret lies in the reading and the writing. You are able to read. Every day you must read one page from some good book to your child. Every day this must be until the child learns to read. Then *she* must read every day. I know this is the secret." Yet the lore of the folk must not be neglected but must be handed down, by word of mouth, from generation to generation. "And you must tell the child the legends I told you—as my mother told them to me and her mother to her. . . . " But "It is a good thing to learn the truth one's self. To first believe with all your heart, and then not to believe, is good too. . . . When as a woman life and people disappoint her, she will have had practice in disappointment and it will not come so hard. In teaching your child, do not forget that suffering is good too. It makes a person rich in character."

And finally, "Before you die, you must own a bit of land—maybe with a house on it that your child or your children may inherit." Here is the wisdom of the folk handed down by Francie's grandmother to her daughter, Katie, and thence on to Francie and to Neeley, her brother. With such a heritage of the good life, is it any wonder that Francie and Neeley spoke thus of their little sister, who would never know the pangs of hunger or any of the deprivation of poverty, who would naturally be "somebody" without the constant struggle to achieve or to maintain:

> "Laurie's going to have a mighty easy life all right."
>
> "She'll never have the hard times we had, will she?"
>
> "No. And she'll never have the fun we had, either."
>
> "Gosh! We *did* have fun, didn't we, Neeley?"
>
> "Yeah!"
>
> "Poor Laurie," said Francie pityingly.

A Tree Grows in Brooklyn is definitely not "a sour and sociological report," but it *is* sociology and should be read by every sociologist and every social worker, for its clear and understanding interpretation of why people are "that way." Miss Smith knows why and she tells it in simple, rhythmic prose that is frequently of the essence of poetry.

Source: Katharine Jocher, "Review of *A Tree Grows in Brooklyn* by Betty Smith," in *Social Forces*, Vol. 22, No. 2, December 1943, pp. 240–41.

SOURCES

Berger, Meyer, "Green Sunless Weed," in *New York Times*, August 22, 1943.

Burns, Ric, and James Sanders, *New York: An Illustrated Story*, Alfred A. Knopf, 1999, pp. 226, 237, 274, 470–480, 552.

Casey, Daniel J., and Robert E. Rhodes, eds., "Betty Smith," in *Modern Irish-American Fiction: A Reader*, Syracuse University Press, 1989, pp. 55–64.

Cornfield, Robert, "The Tree Still Grows in Brooklyn," in *New York Times*, January 3, 1999.

Daniels, Roger, "Pioneers of the Century of Immigration: Irish, Germans, and Scandinavians," in *Coming to America: A History of Immigration and Ethnicity in American Life*, 2nd ed., Perennial, 2002, pp. 121–84.

"Elizabeth-PA Marine Terminal," Web site of the Port Authority of New York and New Jersey, http://www.panynj.gov/DoingBusinessWith/seaport/html/pn_elizabeth.html (accessed May 15, 2009).

"Expanding Affordable Housing," Web site of the New York City Housing Authority, http://www.nyc.gov/html/nycha/html/expanding/expanding.shtml (accessed May 15, 2009).

Jocher, Katharine, Review of *A Tree Grows in Brooklyn*, in *Social Forces*, Vol. 22, No. 2, December 1943, pp. 240–41.

Johnson, Carol Siri, "The Life and Work of Betty Smith, Author of *A Tree Grows in Brooklyn*," City University of New York, 1994, http://web.njit.edu/~cjohnson/tree/index.html (accessed May 2, 2009).

Lye, John, "Fiction and the Immigration Experience," Brock University Department of English Language and Literature Web site, http://www.brocku.ca/english/courses/1F95/immigrant.php (accessed May 15, 2009).

Mooney, Jake, "Still a Warehouse Wonderland," in *New York Times*, February 3, 2008.

"Our Brooklyn: Williamsburg," Brooklyn Public Library, http://www.brooklynpubliclibrary.org/our-brooklyn/williams burg/ (accessed May 15, 2009).

Smith, Betty, *A Tree Grows in Brooklyn*, Harper Perennial Modern Classics, 1998.

Yow, Valerie Raleigh, *Betty Smith: Life of the Author of "A Tree Grows in Brooklyn,"* Wolf's Pond Press, 2008.

FURTHER READING

Brownstone, David M., Franck, Irene M., and Douglas Brownstone, *Island of Hope, Island of Tears*, Barnes & Noble Books, 1979.

> This book is a collection of stories drawn from only a very few of the 15 million immigrants who passed through Ellis Island between 1892 and 1954, when Ellis Island was closed as a port of entry.

Coan, Peter Morton, *Ellis Island Interviews*, Checkmark Books, 1997.

> This book is a collection of interviews with new immigrants, who describe the lives they have left and their hopes for the future.

Hamburger, Eric, *The Historical Atlas of New York City: A Visual Celebration of 400 Years of New York City's History*, 2nd ed., Holt, 2005.

> This book is an illustrated history of New York City, including the five boroughs.

Hopkinson, Deborah, *Shutting Out the Sky: Life in the Tenements of New York, 1880–1924*, Orchard, 2003.

> This book is designed for middle school readers. Five young immigrants tell the story of their lives as children in the crowded tenements of New York City.

Ledger, Victor, *Williamsburg NY*, Arcadia, 2005.

> Relying on photographs taken from the Brooklyn Historical Society, this book is an illustrated history of Williamsburg, Brooklyn, that shows the neighborhood's transition from a wealthy suburb in the nineteenth century to a crowded slum filled with new immigrants early in the twentieth century, and finally as the neighborhood rebuilds and reinvents itself later in the twentieth century.

Martinez, Ruben, *The New Americans*, New Press, 2004.

> This book is a companion to the Public Broadcasting Service series of the same title. The book traces the stories of seven new immigrant families that come to America in search of the American dream.

Reiss, Marcia, *Brooklyn Then and Now*, Thunder Bay Press, 2002.

> This book is a photographic history of Brooklyn, with oversized landscape-type photos of the city. This author shows the historical Brooklyn in old photographs and then shows the same scene as it appears currently.

When Rain Clouds Gather

BESSIE HEAD

1969

Bessie Head's *When Rain Clouds Gather*, published in 1969, is a story about people as well as about a land. The people in the book come from varied walks of life, with many of them being refugees from places that did not appreciate them. The main characters are looking for newer and better lives. The land is in the southern African country of Botswana, a harsh, mostly desolate place. As the characters work with the land they are living on, they study it in hopes of discovering what the land is capable of producing. In many ways, the characters are similarly studying themselves and their own abilities.

When Rain Clouds Gather was Head's first novel. Many of her characters are based on real people she met while she, like the people in this novel, was a refugee. While living in Botswana, Head lived in a village somewhat like the village she creates in her story. She became fascinated with the agricultural experiments that were going on in the village, so much so that she dedicates some of her story to describing the development of the land. The narrative that involves the agricultural processes, far from being a dry exploration of technical terms, reflects present-day concerns about the preservation and sustainability of the land.

At the heart of this novel, however, are the people and their need for freedom, love, respectability, and appreciation. Their lives are harsh in many ways, but they all have dreams of a better future. They also have the will and determination to work toward realizing their goals.

Bessie Head (Reproduced by the kind permission of the Estate of Bessie Head)

AUTHOR BIOGRAPHY

Bessie Head lived a tragic life, beginning with her birth. Head was born on July 6, 1937, in Pietermaritzburg, South Africa, in the province of KwaZulu-Natal, the child of a white woman and a black African man. She learned very little about her biological parents: she knew only that her father was black and that her mother (also named Bessie) was psychologically unstable, giving birth to her daughter while a patient in Fort Napier Mental Hospital. After birth, Head was briefly adopted by an unnamed white couple who returned her once they discovered she was biracial. Shortly afterward, Nellie and George Heathcote adopted Head, and they would become the only parents she would know. Head's biological mother died in the hospital when Head was six years old.

When she was fourteen, Head was sent away to school. While there, one of the school's administrators told Head that the Heathcotes were not her real parents. It was the first time Head had heard this, and the news traumatized

her; she sought comfort in reading. After graduating from high school, Head taught for two years but found she did not like teaching, and was more interested in writing. At the age of twenty-one, she found a job as a journalist for a small Cape Town newspaper, the *Golden City Post*. Though she had found her calling as a writer, Head suffered under apartheid, the system of extreme segregation and racism that plagued South Africa at that time. Undaunted, however, in 1959 Head sought a writing job at a larger paper in Johannesburg, the *Home Post*. During this time, she became more politically conscious and joined the Pan-Africanist Congress (PAC), which was working toward the elimination of apartheid. In 1960, Head was arrested because of her association with PAC. She attempted suicide and was hospitalized.

In 1961, Head married Harold, a fellow journalist. The couple had a son the next year. Though they did not divorce until decades later, Bessie and Harold separated in 1964. Head, hoping to find more personal freedom, took her son with her to Botswana and returned to teaching in the village of Serowe. Botswana, at the time, was only two years away from independence. Serowe was a meeting place for other political refugees from South Africa, and for a while Head felt at home.

In 1966, Head moved to Palapye, the center of the Bamangwato Development Association, where Head learned about agriculture (experiences she would later convey in the novel *When Rain Clouds Gather*). While working for the agriculture cooperative, Head wrote short stories. Her story "The Woman from America" was her first published piece (1966). A publisher in the United States read the story and suggested that Head try her hand at writing a novel. Three years later, *When Rain Clouds Gather* (1969) was published.

Head began to have hallucinations around this time. She believed they were visions from God. But she was diagnosed as suffering from a mental breakdown and spent time in and out of hospitals. In between, she wrote her second novel, *Maru* (1971). The following year, she wrote an autobiography called *A Question of Power*, published in 1973. The book brought her worldwide attention. She would continue to write and publish until her death on April 17, 1986, in Serowe, Botswana, of alcohol-induced hepatitis.

PLOT SUMMARY

Chapters I–III

Head's novel *When Rain Clouds Gather* begins in the small village of Barolong, at the border between South Africa and Botswana. The protagonist, Makhaya Maseko, is attempting to cross the border without being detected. Makhaya has been in trouble with the law in South Africa, having spent time in prison under suspicion for planning to sabotage the South African government. He belongs to a Zulu tribe, but he has grown frustrated by tribal thinking and exasperated by the harsh South African segregation policies known as apartheid. Makhaya hopes to find freedom in Botswana.

Once night falls, Makhaya makes a successful run into Botswana. He is not sure where he is going. He is only happy to be out of South Africa. He comes across an old woman, who offers Makhaya a hut for the night. Just before Makhaya falls asleep, a child appears in his hut and suggests that her grandmother wants her to sleep with Makhaya. Instead, Makhaya gives her money and sends her back to the old woman, who thinks Makhaya must be crazy. However, with this act, the author establishes Makhaya's moral character.

The next day Makhaya runs into a British police officer, who recognizes him. Makhaya's picture is on the front of a newspaper. The story in the newspaper refers to him as being dangerous. Makhaya denies this, and the officer, whose name is George Appleby-Smith, believes him and gives Makhaya permission to stay. George has a feeling that Makhaya will be good for the local village.

Next Makhaya meets Dinorego. The old man is impressed with Makhaya's obvious education and invites Makhaya to come to his home. He lives in the village called Golema Mmidi. Dinorego thinks Makhaya might be the perfect husband for his daughter, Maria.

Four hundred people live in Golema Mmidi, a unique place in Botswana. It is not like the tribal villages that usually contain many extended families. Golema Mmidi is an experimental village, where Gilbert Balfour, a British expatriate (someone who is living in a place other than his or her native country), is trying to change the way people in Botswana grow crops and raise cattle. Chief Sekoto, ruler of the area, offered Golema Mmidi to his younger brother, who once tried to assassinate him. Sekoto thought ruling Golema Mmidi would keep his younger brother, Matenge, busy so he would not bother him. But no one in Golema Mmidi likes the way Matenge rules, so there are always complaints that Sekoto has to deal with. Chief Sekoto sent Gilbert Balfour and all his new ideas for agriculture to Golema Mmidi, thinking that Gilbert and Matenge would drive each other nuts. Then Sekoto would be rid of both of them.

Gilbert takes an immediate liking to Makhaya and offers him a job if he will stay and educate the women of Golema Mmidi in new ways of farming. Gilbert does not speak the local language, so when he discovers that Makhaya does, he wants Makhaya to teach the women how to raise tobacco as a cash crop. Chief Matenge does not take to Makhaya or to Gilbert. As far as Matenge is concerned, Gilbert thinks too fondly of the people that Matenge would rather keep poor. Gilbert often tells the people that if they work together in a cooperative, they will make more money and no longer have to work as slaves for Matenge. Matenge's friend Joas Tsepe, a politically ambitious man, believes he knows how to get rid of both Gilbert and Makhaya. He tells Matenge that Gilbert is harboring a refugee (Makhaya), which is against the law.

Chapters IV–VI

Matenge goes to his brother and complains about Gilbert and Makhaya. Sekoto tells Matenge to take the matter to the inspector, George Appleby-Smith. George and Chief Sekoto are close friends. Before Matenge gets to the inspector, Sekoto goes to the police station to visit George. They talk about Matenge and wonder what to do with him. The inspector asks Sekoto if he would mind if he put Matenge in jail. The chief confesses that he would love to see his brother in jail for a long period of time. The inspector hopes to catch Matenge and his friend, Joas Tsepe, red-handed as they plot against the new government.

Joas continues to try to find a way for Matenge to be rid of Makhaya and Gilbert. Joas tells Matenge the two men are spies and are planning to recolonize all of Africa. Matenge waves Joas to the side when he sees Makhaya and Dinorego approaching Matenge's house. When Makhaya approaches him, Matenge tells Makhaya that he does not like refugees because they are known to sneak out of their huts at night and kill people. Matenge also says that Gilbert knows nothing about agriculture in Botswana. Matenge wants Gilbert to go back to England where he came from. If both of them, Gilbert and Makhaya, do not leave, Matenge says he will make it very difficult for them.

Makhaya becomes angry. Dinorego tells Makhaya not to worry about Matenge because he is not well and might die of high blood pressure soon enough. Makhaya responds, "The chief is not going to die of high blood pressure." Then he adds, "I am going to kill him." Dinorego is shocked by this response. He appeals to Makhaya's intelligence and suggests that Makhaya use his brain rather than a gun to defeat Matenge.

Dinorego introduces Makhaya to Mma-Millipede who asks Makhaya many personal questions, such as what kinds of food he is eating and how is his health. This makes Makhaya both uncomfortable and yet at ease. He is not used to talking to anyone about his private thoughts and daily habits. However, he enjoys the mothering that Mma-Millipede offers him.

In chapter VI, Paulina is introduced. She is a newcomer to the village, a woman with two children and no husband. Paulina is described as a woman who is determined to get on with her life despite her challenges. Paulina's hut is close to a path that Makhaya takes each night to watch the sun set. When Paulina's eight-year-old daughter, Lorato, invites Makhaya to tea with her mother, Makhaya refuses, saying he does not know the girl's mother. This makes Paulina think that Makhaya is interested in Maria, the unmarried and very independent daughter of Dinorego. Makhaya is attracted to Maria, but when he learns that Gilbert is interested in Maria, Makhaya backs away. Gilbert has indeed enjoyed his relationship with Maria, and one day he asks Dinorego's permission to marry Maria. Dinorego asks his daughter what she thinks about this. Maria agrees.

Chapters VII–IX
Mma-Millipede decides Paulina and Makhaya would make a nice match. When Gilbert informs Mma-Millipede that he wants Makhaya to educate the women of the village in new agricultural practices, Mma-Millipede sees a way to bring Makhaya and Paulina together. She indicates that Makhaya should teach the women through Paulina, telling her what needs to be done and having her lead the other women through the projects. In the days that follow, Makhaya teaches Paulina how to build huts in which to dry tobacco and in this way gets to know her. Once, at Paulina's hut, Makhaya notices a miniature village that

Paulina's daughter has made out of mud. The young girl is not around, but Makhaya thinks the play village needs some trees, so he makes some out of sticks. Through this act, Paulina begins to see Makhaya's tender side.

The more Makhaya works with Paulina, the more he comes to appreciate her. He encourages her to put away her limited concepts of the roles of women and men. For instance, when Makhaya says he wants some tea and gets up to start the fire, Paulina pushes him away, telling him that making a fire is a woman's job. Makhaya tells her she must start getting used to the idea that men live on earth, too. When he wants some tea, he tells her, he is capable of fixing it for himself.

Makhaya becomes more involved in Paulina's life. He asks about her son, Isaac, who is not living in the village. Rather, Isaac is out in the countryside watching over Paulina's herd of cattle. Makhaya thinks the boy, who is only ten, is too young to be doing this. When Paulina tells Makhaya that she cannot afford to pay an adult to watch the cows, Makhaya says that she should sell most of the animals. She will make much more money off the tobacco she will be growing.

Chapters X–XII
Chapter X begins with Chief Matenge and the anger he has bred over the progress of Golema Mmidi, the village he is supposed to rule. The narrator states that Golema Mmidi is not only thriving, but the people are also ignoring the chief. Because of this, Matenge feels threatened. The narrator adds, "There were too many independent-minded people there [in Golema Mmidi], and tragedies of life had liberated them from the environmental control of the tribe." The experiment at Golema Mmidi was the first of its kind: "Never before had people been allowed to settle permanently on the land" as Chief Sekoto was letting them do now. This was due to Chief Sekoto's interest in Gilbert's agricultural experiments. Previously, according to the narrator, anyone who tried to be a farmer had his or her huts burned to the ground. The independence of the farmers was always a threat to the authoritarian rule of the chiefs. This did not bother Chief Sekoto, but it was driving his brother mad.

The rainy season comes and goes without any precipitation. Soon the cattle begin to die because all the water holes have dried up. The men of the village, who have been away for several months because they take their cattle to other areas to graze, start arriving back in the village. Their tales of how many dead cows they have seen frighten everyone. Paulina, whose son tends her cattle, has not returned. So Paulina asks one of the men if he knows where her son is. She finds out that the last time someone saw Isaac, the boy had complained of having a cold. The narrator, however, tells readers that Isaac is actually sick with tuberculosis, which Paulina does not know. When Paulina tells Makhaya of her concern for Isaac, Makhaya tells her they will travel together to find out how Isaac is doing. For the first time, after hearing Makhaya's offer, Paulina tells him that she loves him. In response, Makhaya says that he has never known love, but he hopes, with her help, he will learn to love.

Gilbert decides he will drive Makhaya and Paulina to find Isaac. On the drive, all three of them are amazed at the number of dead animals they see. The full impact of the drought finally hits them. Vultures circle in the skies. When they reach the hut where Isaac lived, Makhaya, suspecting the worst, tells Paulina to wait in the car while he goes inside. When he enters the hut, he finds a pile of bones, all that is left of Isaac. Paulina wants to see the remains of her son after Makhaya tells her that her son is dead. Makhaya does not allow this. Paulina says she must because it is the custom of her people. At this, Makhaya tells her he is tired of old customs. Then he adds, "Can't you see I'm here to bear all your burdens?" On the drive home, Makhaya realizes how much he loves Paulina. The narrator exposes Makhaya's new awareness that "it was only people who could bring the real rewards of living, that it was only people who give love and happiness."

In the last chapter of the story, Paulina is surprised by a deep happiness she feels, in spite of the loss of her son. Mma-Millipede tells Paulina that it is all right to be happy. Not many women are given a man as good as Makhaya. The narrator explains that the typical African man does not love as Makhaya loves. Most African men either have many wives or one wife and many mistresses, she says. Women are possessions for these men. Paulina agrees that Makhaya is very different.

Paulina walks out into her yard one morning to find one of Matenge's servants waiting for her. He tells her that she has been summoned to meet with Chief Matenge. Paulina is concerned. A summons usually means that the person has done something that has angered the chief. All she can think of is that she has forgotten to report the death of her son to Matenge. As

Paulina begins her walk to the chief's residence, other villagers accompany her. The news has traveled fast. Soon the whole village is trailing behind her. The villagers are curious about what the chief wants, but they also want to see his face: "They wanted to see this man who had all the privileges, who had never known a day of starvation." They are not there to threaten Matenge or to forcibly take away his possessions. However, they do want him to understand that "it was only their lives they wanted to set right and he must not stand in their way." As the crowd gathers outside Matenge's house, the villagers are pleased with themselves. It is the first time they have all come together for the same cause.

When Matenge looks out at the crowd, he is frightened. He locks the doors and does not go outside. Meanwhile, noticing the deserted huts in the village, Gilbert and Makhaya drive quickly to Matenge's and ask the villagers what is going on. The people are all sitting quietly in the courtyard. Dinorego replies that they are waiting to see the chief. Makhaya, too impatient to wait, climbs the stairway to the chief's house and breaks down the door. Inside he finds Matenge hanging at the end of a rope. The chief has committed suicide.

Days later, after things have settled down, Paulina is cooking dinner for Makhaya. As he watches her, he finally remembers something very important: "I forgot to ask you if you'd like to marry me. Will you, Paulie?" And Paulina says that she will.

CHARACTERS

George Appleby-Smith

George is the British inspector who keeps the law in Golema Mmidi. He is a remnant of British colonial rule. He is kindhearted like Chief Sekoto. The two of them are close friends. George says he does not like people because they are always playing psychological games or not being honest about what they want. However, when he meets people who are sincere, he recognizes them for their straightforwardness and rewards them in any way he can. Thus, though he is reading a story about Makhaya in the newspapers as Makhaya makes his first appearance in the area, George does not believe the newspaper article that describes him as a criminal. He sees Makhaya's character traits and decides to trust him. George also likes the spirit of Gilbert and his progressive ideas to help the people.

Gilbert Balfour

Gilbert is a British citizen who is described as being very tall and having blues eyes. As a student, Gilbert visited Botswana and became very interested in the way the people lived. He returned to England to finish his studies. Upon graduating, he came back to Botswana and became friends with the British inspector, George Appleby-Smith. George was also friends with the powerful local leader, Chief Sekoto. The chief also liked Gilbert and granted him permission and some land on which to put his new agricultural ideas into practice.

Gilbert is consumed with his projects as he tries to bring the people of the village out of poverty. He sees how the cattle are destroying the land and tries to encourage the people to rely more on cash crops. Gilbert also pushes the idea of working through cooperatives, which takes some of the money away from Chief Matenge. Gilbert thus becomes at odds with Matenge, who tries to get rid of Gilbert.

Not only is Gilbert well educated, he is also intelligent. He is focused so much on his projects that he sometimes has trouble understanding people. But this has not kept the villagers from accepting and trusting him. The person who confuses Gilbert the most is Maria. He enjoys her independent nature and her natural intelligence, but he does not know how to get her to marry him.

Gilbert represents one good reason for the villagers to trust white men. This is especially true for Makhaya, who has lived under the apartheid system in South Africa, where he was born and raised. Gilbert's heart is pure, and he is very honest in his dealings with the people of Golema Mmidi.

Dinorego

Dinorego is one of the elders of Golema Mmidi. He is a soft-spoken man who makes blankets from animal skins for a living. Dinorego and Mma-Millipede are two of the most respected people in the village.

Dinorego refers to Makhaya as a son from the first time he meets him. He recognizes Makhaya's education as well as Makhaya's straightforwardness. Dinorego has been looking for a husband for his daughter, Maria. He believes Makhaya might be the right man. He takes Makhaya under his wing, counseling him when Makhaya's anger gets the best of him. Though Dinorego is an elder, he is progressive in his thoughts and therefore admires the ideas of Gilbert and Makhaya, who are looking for change.

Isaac

Isaac is the ten-year-old son of Paulina. He is never present in the story, but is talked about by some of the characters. He is away, living out in the bush, taking care of his mother's cattle. While away, Isaac becomes sick with tuberculosis and dies. His bones are discovered after Paulina and Makhaya travel into the bush to find out why Isaac has not come home when all the other men have deserted their posts. Isaac represents the tragedy of living in poverty. His unmarried mother did not have enough money to hire an adult to take care of her cattle.

Lorato

Lorato is the eight-year-old daughter of Paulina. Though Lorato has little to say in this story, her presence is felt when Makhaya helps Lorato build a miniature village out of mud. It is through Lorato that Makhaya first expresses his tenderness.

Maria

Maria is Dinorego's daughter. She is described as being very independent and unlike most of the other village women. Maria works with Gilbert and likes him, but she is concerned that she is not educated enough to become his wife. So for three years, she turns Gilbert's proposals down. Instead she asks that he teach her English. In turn, she tries to teach Gilbert her language. When she has mastered basic English, she tells Gilbert she will marry him.

Makhaya Maseko

Makhaya is the protagonist of this story. Although the narration often focuses on other characters, as well as on discussing various elements of the country of Botswana and its people and traditions, the novel begins and ends with Makhaya. Of all of the characters, Makhaya is the one who changes the most. He arrives in Botswana angry and emotionally closed but learns through the gentle guidance of the other main characters what it means to love and to care for other people.

Makhaya was born in South Africa into the tribal customs of the Zulu people, an ancient African group. He felt confined by the traditions of his people, but when he goes out into the world of white South Africans, he cannot stand the oppression that is placed on his lifestyle and beliefs. At one time, though the details not are thoroughly discussed, he rebels against the apartheid system of segregation and is put into prison. As the story opens, Makhaya is about to illegally sneak across the border between South Africa and Botswana. He is determined to find a better, less limited life.

Makhaya says that he wants to find peace of mind and a good wife who will bear his children. In the course of the story, Makhaya explains that he is attracted to independent thinkers. That is why he likes Gilbert and agrees to work with the British scientist. Makhaya understands that Gilbert is trying to improve the lives of the poor. Paulina teaches Makhaya how to love and care about a woman. Up until Makhaya meets Paulina, he thinks that prostitutes are the only African women who can think for themselves. Makhaya seriously dislikes the way tribal culture prohibits people from progressing. He believes that only free thinkers can progress.

Chief Matenge

Chief Matenge is a vicious, greedy man. He has no skills in dealing with people except as a dictator. He makes people give him part of everything they own and raise. Thus, he becomes rich, living in the only brick house in the village. He is proud of his fancy Chevrolet and expects no one to ever talk back to him.

Matenge is the younger brother of Chief Sekoto. He is also the opposite of everything that his older brother stands for. At one time, before the story begins, Matenge attempted to kill Sekoto. His brother not only forgave him, he also gave Matenge the land on which the village of Golema Mmidi lies. Matenge rules the people there poorly, and they have no respect for him. They ignore him, going to Sekoto when they have complaints.

Matenge would like to rid the village of Gilbert and Makhaya, but no matter what he tries, nothing works in his favor. In the end, Matenge panics when he sees all the villagers sitting outside his home. He is afraid of them because they have come together as one and he assumes they are against him. Instead of facing them, he hangs himself.

Mma-Millipede

Mma-Millipede is a close friend of Dinorego. She and Dinorego, in their youth, were engaged to be married. However, the chief of their village in northern Botswana decided he wanted Mma-Millipede for himself. So he threatened Mma-Millipede's family until Mma-Millipede agreed to marry him. Later, when the chief divorced Mma-Millipede, she accepted Dinorego's invitation to move south and live in Golema Mmidi.

At the time of the story, Mma-Millipede and Dinorego represent the wise elders of Golema Mmidi. The villagers often go to both of them for advice. In particular, Mma-Millipede counsels both Makhaya and Paulina, two of her favorite people. She also tries to bring them together, believing they would be good for one another. Though not a devoutly religious person, Mma-Millipede often reads the Bible, through which she attempts to interpret why people try to oppress others.

Chief Sekoto

Chief Sekoto is Matenge's older brother. The two of them could hardly be more different. Sekoto is often praised throughout the novel as having a positive outlook on life. He is kind hearted and does not rule with a tight hold on his people. He enjoys watching his subjects figure out solutions to their own problems. He especially likes Gilbert and has made the unchieflike promise that if Gilbert succeeds in his plans, Sekoto himself will go to work for him. Of course this is a joke, but it shows how much Sekoto hopes Gilbert will succeed.

Sekoto is said to like fast cars, pretty women, and food. His appearance in the novel is limited, though his presence is felt. The people know that they have a friend in Chief Sekoto, especially when his brother, Matenge, is acting badly.

Joas Tsepe

Joas is a coconspirator of Matenge's. His main goal is to get rid of the elected Botswana government. Even though the people approve of the government, Joas wants to incite a rebellion. He needs Matenge's help to do this. So he feeds Matenge stories of government corruption, spies, and people who want to kill him. Joas does not like Gilbert or Makhaya and what they are doing in the village. He wants Matenge to get rid of them. Little more is said about this character. He has no redeeming virtues.

THEMES

Tribalism versus Progress

Tribalism in Head's novel refers to the concept that everyone must follow the dictates of the tribal chiefs, who rule according to long traditional

TOPICS FOR FURTHER STUDY

- Read Chinua Achebe's 1965 novel *A Man of the People*. This story follows Odili, a Nigerian teacher, who is at first excited about Nigeria's independence from Britain but who becomes frustrated with the corruption of local politicians. Compare the protagonist, Odili, with Head's protagonist, Makhaya. Think about which character changes the most. What is each character's psychological attitude toward change? Which protagonist is most optimistic? Which of the two characters have the most effect on the other people in the novels? Write a 1,500-word essay about your study and turn it in to your teacher.

- Read Richard Tames's *The End of Apartheid: A New South Africa* (2001) or a similar book about apartheid. Who were the most important people involved in the struggle to end apartheid? What were the political parties representing black Africans? Were there significant events that empowered blacks to stand up and fight for their civil and human rights? What were they? After gathering the facts, search the Internet for pictures of the people involved and some of the news photographs of political clashes. Then present your findings to your class in a PowerPoint presentation so they can better understand what apartheid was, how it affected the people, and how it was ended.

- Research the effects of agriculture on Botswana's economy and its land. What has changed in the years since Head's novel was published? Have any of the ideas presented in the novel taken root in the country? Have the practices of cattle raising been converted to help protect the land? What are the major crops? What portion of the country's economy is based on agriculture?

Present your findings through a PowerPoint presentation to your class, comparing what was happening in the 1960s to what is happening now.

- Head provides vivid descriptions of various scenes in her novel. Create one to three sketches of what the village of Golema Mmidi might have looked like. Or choose the scene in front of Matenge's house when the villagers gathered to protest the chief's accusations against Paulina. Or make a sketch of the small railroad station where Makhaya is dropped off when he first arrives in Botswana. Create your sketches in a medium of your choice, then display and explain them to your class.

- Oral storytelling preceded written fiction in most cultures. Find electronic versions of African folktales on the Internet or look for books such as *African Folktales* by Roger Abrahams (1983), *Favorite African Folktales* by Nelson Mandela (2004), or the young-adult book *A Pride of African Tales* by Donna L. Washington (2004) at your library. Choose one or two tales, memorize them, and then present them as if you were a tribal storyteller, using your classmates as your audience. Remember that storytellers did more than just recite their stories. They used gestures and expressions as if they were acting out the tales they were reciting. Most of these folktales are also meant to convey lessons to the audience. So the role of storyteller is also that of a teacher. You might want to enhance your presentation by dressing in a robe, making you look more like an ancient tribal elder.

practices. These principles include the power of men over women; the division of labor, in which men tend to the cattle and women grow the crops; as well rules about the clothes people wear, the mannerisms people use, and the way they cook their food and what they eat.

Tribal women in Botswana (AP Images)

Makhaya, the protagonist, makes it very clear in the beginning of the story that he does not believe in the tribal ways. He does not even like his name because it is a tribal name. Makhaya represents a more progressive view. He is interested in what Gilbert is doing because Gilbert is always trying to push the people ahead and to make the village progress into the future. Gilbert represents the sciences and education, which have made him aware of better ways for the village people to live. For thousands of years the people have been destroying the land as well as themselves. The people raise cattle because that is what their forefathers did. They do not see that the cattle are turning their homeland into a desert. However, for many of the tribal people, progress is scary. It is unknown to them. Most of the people in Golema Mmidi do not have a formal education in the sciences, so they have to put all their faith in Gilbert, a white man. This is difficult to do for two reasons: first, white people have not always treated black Africans fairly, and second, traditions are hard to break. For example, an old man in the beginning of the novel tells Makhaya that it is his education that

makes him want progress over his traditional, tribal ways. The old man is afraid of change and represents the tribal elders, who have, in the past, made all the rules.

The conflict of tribalism versus progress is woven through much of this novel. The arguments for and against one side or the other are taken up either in the conversations of the characters or through long narration, which breaks into the plot line of the story. The whole village of Golema Mmidi is an experiment that sits in the middle of this conflict as the traditional village chiefs look on and observe the changes.

Poverty and Oppression

There are many images of poverty and oppression in *When Rain Clouds Gather*. One of the strongest occurs when the drought begins to kill off the animals. When the animals die, the people come home empty handed. They know that they too could die if the drought lasts much longer. When Paulina is summoned to face Chief Matenge, the people follow her to Matenge's house. They go for two reasons: first, they want to know why the chief has called Paulina. But second, and more importantly, they want to see what his face looks like when he sees that they are suffering and he still lives in the midst of his riches. His cattle are safe. His food lockers are as full as his belly. And yet his people are starving. The chief has kept a tight control of his people, demanding their labor and their goods to feed his greed. In the past, the people did as they were told because they were used to the oppression. It had become a way of life for them. Whether it was through the influence of Gilbert and Makhaya, the reader is not told, but something awakens these people to the unfairness of their situation. Poverty and oppression are not a natural way of life but become a habit for them, at least until that day when they went together, all of the same mind, to find out why the chief had so much and they had none. Head does not lecture on poverty and oppression, but she does use many examples to show the effect on people's lives. Examples include the apartheid system in South Africa and hints of the oppression the people experienced under colonial rule. What surprises some of the characters most is the oppression of black Africans by black Africans.

STYLE

Figurative Language

Throughout *When Rain Clouds Gather*, Head uses long passages of figurative language to enhance her story. Figurative language is the opposite of literal language, when an author expresses exactly what he or she means by using concrete words in the narrative. An example of Head's use of figurative language is found in the following passage in which she describes a sunrise in the flatlands of Botswana: "So sudden and abrupt was the sunrise that the birds had to pretend they had been awake all the time." This description is not to be taken literally. The birds were not really pretending anything. This is merely how Head chooses to describe the sudden appearance of the sun. The image of the startled birds enhances her meaning.

In another passage, Head wants to describe the mannerisms of some of the local tribal women. She refers to the way one woman out-talks another. In the middle of a conversation, one of the women manages a laugh, though the topic of conversation is very serious. This has an effect, which Head describes as an "unusual" sound, that creates the impression that "all the glass in the world were being hurled into a deep pit and shrieking in agony." Here, Head offers more than words to describe the unique laughter: she gives her readers a sound that they can almost hear. It is a startling sound, she states, one that gathers the attention of all who hear it, which, apparently, is exactly what the person who laughs wants to do.

When describing a young girl in the novel, rather than simply stating that the girl is thin and playful, Head writes that the girl "walked like a wind-blown leaf." In this simple phrase, the author suggests an image that many people have seen. There is a leaf that is picked up off the ground by a breeze. The leaf twirls in the wind, floating up, then down, and near, and then away. The leaf is light and free in its movements, with no care as to where it will land. From this picture that Head creates, readers can easily imagine a young girl skipping and hopping, free as a breeze, with few troubles to bog down her body or mind.

Setting as a Minor Character

The country of Botswana plays a minor character in this novel, through descriptions of how Gilbert is attempting to change the practices of the villagers in order to save the land and to improve their lives. There are also long discussions about the culture of the people of Botswana. Their tribal affiliations, the structure of their society, and the different roles that men and women play are all discussed.

The layout of the land, the crops that grow naturally in the ground, and the challenges of living in an arid place are also described in detail. The land is an integral part of the story because it represents the challenges that the main characters must face. The land is dying at the beginning of the story, but as Gilbert employs his knowledge and understanding about what the land is capable of producing, the land begins to change from wasteland to cropland. Without the land and the country in the background, this story would be far less complex.

HISTORICAL CONTEXT

Apartheid

Like her protagonist in *When Rain Clouds Gather*, Head also emigrated from South Africa to Botswana to escape the harsh conditions of apartheid. Although South Africa had been segregated for a long time, apartheid, the system of strict segregation laws that defined South Africa for more than forty years, only officially began in 1948. Black South Africans, who made up almost 75 percent

COMPARE & CONTRAST

- **1960s:** The British government accepts proposals for democratic self-government in Botswana. A constitution is written and the first general elections are held.

  Today: Botswana is one of the most politically stable governments of all African nations.

- **1960s:** Botswana is considered one of the poorest countries in the world.

Today: According to the CIA's *World Factbook*, Botswana has one of the world's highest economic growth rates at about 9 percent per year.

- **1960s:** Refugees from South Africa cross the Botswana border to escape the apartheid system in their country.

  Today: Refugees from Zimbabwe cross the Botswana border to escape the economic collapse of their country.

---

of the population, could receive only a limited amount of education, and they were told where to live and whom they could or could not marry. No marriages between whites and nonwhites were tolerated. All nonwhite people were required by law to carry passes on them at all times. These passes contained a photo identification, fingerprints, and information about where in the country they could or could not travel.

Discrimination against nonwhites grew stronger as time went on. In 1950, the white government passed new laws, restricting where black and all nonwhite people could live. The people's rights to vote were then limited to the areas in which they lived. They could no longer be involved in national politics and elections. In essence, all nonwhite people became foreigners in their own country.

The government clamped down even harder on the nonwhite population, declaring its right to detain anyone without a hearing. Thousands reportedly died while in prison. Many were victims of torture. Many others were ordered to leave the country, such as the famous singer Miriam Makeba. Some were executed. Others were imprisoned, such as Nelson Mandela, an activist for human rights, who was imprisoned for twenty-seven years.

Resistance to apartheid eventually led to the end of the system during the 1990s; the 1990 release of Nelson Mandela marked the beginning of the end. On April 27, 1994, the first democratic elections

were held in South Africa. Mandela was elected president, thus marking the end of apartheid.

Botswana

Botswana is a landlocked country in southern Africa. It is a bit smaller than Texas and is bounded by the countries of Namibia, South Africa, and Zimbabwe. Botswana is an arid country, with the Kalahari Desert making up most of its southern portion. Desertification, the process of land turning into desert, is a significant problem for Botswana. Less than 1 percent of the land is capable of sustaining crops. Making the situation worse, there was a series of droughts in the early years of the twenty-first century. Cattle, an important agricultural product, add to the problem because they have caused damage to the land through overgrazing, making the land even more susceptible to desertification.

Most of Botswana's population, almost two million people, live in the eastern part of the country. This is where the major cities such as Francistown, Selebi-Phikwe, Serowe, and Gaborone (the country's capital) are located. The earliest people to live in the area that is now Botswana were the San people, now referred to as the Bushmen, and the Khoi, or Khoikhoi (the name Hottentot, formerly used to describe this tribe, is now considered to be derogatory). Descendents of these ancient tribes still live in Botswana and not much has changed in their lifestyles for many thousands of years. Other tribal groups have since moved into

Rain clouds over an African savannah (*Image copyright Pichugin Dmitry, 2009. Used under license from Shutterstock.com*)

the country and the population today is a mix of these ancient tribes.

In the nineteenth century, European missionaries came to the continent of Africa, including Botswana. When the Botswana people had difficulties with the Dutch Boer settlers (most of whom came from South Africa), they appealed to Britain for help. In 1885, Botswana became a British protectorate. However, by the middle of the twentieth century, Botswana had grown tired of British rule and asked for independence, which the British granted in September 1966.

Though Botswana has been called a model African country because of its economic and political stability, there remain problems that need to be resolved. One is the rapid spread of HIV/AIDS, the worst on the continent, and another is the issue of recent human rights abuses in regards to the Bushmen, who have been forced off their traditional land.

Sub-Saharan African Literature, 1950–1980

Though the history of literature in Africa goes back to ancient times, most works were not written down. Oral storytelling, handed down from generation to generation, was the prevalent practice in the ancient cultures. It was not until colonization that writing and reading were introduced. Literacy of the people of African nations occurred mostly in the languages of the colonists, so most of the literature in the nineteenth century that came out of Africa was in English and French, not in the people's native tongues. Some of the first stories published were about slavery, colonization, the disruption of native culture, and emancipation. As the twentieth century progressed, more works emerged with themes of liberation and independence. Since the 1950s and 1960s, as more and more African nations attained their freedom, the literature written by authors in African countries has grown both in numbers and in popularity around the world.

Some of Head's contemporary authors include the Nigerian authors Chinua Achebe, best known for *Things Fall Apart*; Wole Soyinka, who won the Nobel Prize in Literature in 1986, the first African writer to do so; and Buchi Emecheta, known for writing fiction about women's issues.

CRITICAL OVERVIEW

Head's novel *When Rain Clouds Gather* marked the beginning of her illustrious career as an author. She was one of the first prominent female authors from Africa who was not afraid to write about the oppression black Africans were experiencing. Her work not only demonstrated her gift for writing but also exposed the tragedies experienced by the people of Africa.

When Rain Clouds Gather is not considered Head's best writing, but the novel set the tone for the books that would follow. In *When Rain Clouds Gather*, Head delves into the psychology of her characters as well as the politics that surround their lives. In many interviews, Head stated that she was not a political writer. Critics, however, disagree. As Pia Thielmann (writing for *Africa Today*) points out in her review of Maureen Fielding's essay found in *Critical Essays on Bessie Head*, "Head's writing gives testimony to the trauma of apartheid long before the creation of the Truth and Reconciliation Commission in 1996 to address the injustices of apartheid." This statement refers to Head's courage in creating characters such as Makhaya in *When Rain Clouds Gather* while apartheid in South Africa was at its height. In a *Publishers Weekly* review of Head's novel *The Cardinals*, a critic states that Head "may have been ahead of her time" in speaking out against oppression. In a second review of *Critical Essays on Bessie Head*, Femi Ojo-Ade (writing for *Research in African Literatures*) also refers to the essay of Maureen Fielding, pointing out how "Fielding uses the novel *When Rain Clouds Gather* to show how Bessie Head, instead of breaking down under the weight of trauma and oppression, wrote to liberate and to heal herself and her sick society." The politics of Head's life certainly seem to have influenced her writing.

Critics often debate whether Head wrote about personal relationships and the psychological struggles of her characters or wrote political statements about the countries in which she lived. One thing they agree on, though, is that her writing was skilled and powerful. Critic Charles Larson, writing for the *Washington Post Book World* says, "Bessie Head's achievement at the time of her death in 1986 was honorific: black Africa's preeminent female writer of fiction." Carole Boyce Davies, a critic for *Research in African Literatures* calls Head a "provocative writer." In the publication *Biography*, three reviewers (Margaret Lenta, Ruth Bhengu, and Fiona Moolla) refer to Head as "one of Africa's great letter writers as well as one of the continent's finest novelists."

CRITICISM

Joyce Hart

Hart is a published author and a creative writing teacher. In the following essay, she explores how various characters in When Rain Clouds Gather *represent Head's interpretation of the history and the future of African society.*

In *When Rain Clouds Gather*, Head tells the intertwining stories of several characters and circumstances. Readers follow the successes, failures, and challenges of a South African refugee, a British expatriate, local chiefs, a British inspector, and several Golema Mmidi villagers. Interspersed throughout this storytelling, however, the author (either through her narrator or her characters) often thinks about spiritual, philosophical, and psychological reasons for why life in Africa is the way it is. In the process, the narrator subtly lays out what might be called a history of life in southern Africa, relating what has gone on before to explain what still exists and what might occur tomorrow. Through various characters, she personifies the oppression, customs, trials, failures, successes, and hopes that she herself might have experienced. She also hints at what might lie ahead.

Taking on the discussion of oppression, Head offers the character of Matenge, chief of Golema Mmidi, and the system of apartheid in South Africa that overshadows the life of her protagonist, Makhaya. One might say that both Matenge and apartheid represent the worst of the past. In Matenge, readers witness the oppression of black people at the hands of a fellow black citizen. Matenge enslaves his people and keeps them in poverty to better rule them. He is a dictator with no compassion for his fellow man. Matenge is as greedy as he is strict. He lives in luxury off the labor of his people who often go without food. Matenge embodies what can happen when a ruler thinks only of his own comforts. In some ways, he also represents the oppression of the traditional tribal system.

Apartheid is related to Matenge's form of oppression with a few exceptions. With apartheid,

WHAT DO I READ NEXT?

- Head's second novel *Maru* (1971) describes the challenges an orphaned girl must face when she moves to a remote Botswana village to teach. She is looking for freedom but finds, instead, that people of her culture are treated as outcasts.

- Head's autobiography *A Question of Power* (1973) has been called one of the author's best works. It was this autobiography that made Head famous as a writer. Her life was tormented by mental breakdowns, problems adjusting to social norms, and in the end, alcoholism. In spite of these struggles, Head is now seen as one of the most important African female authors.

- Find out what it is like to be a South African teen who must move to California. In Ermila Moodley's young-adult novel, *Path to My African Eyes* (2007), you will share Thandi Sobukwe's struggles as she leaves friends behind and tries to create a new life. Self-doubt reigns as Thandi is thrust into the confusion of rejection and cultural transformation.

- Explore living in Botswana from a different point of view in Robyn Scott's account, *Twenty Chickens for a Saddle* (2008). Her family sought adventure when they moved to Botswana, so the author grew up in various locations in Botswana as well as in other African countries. Though parts of her childhood were ideal, as she grew older, the author witnessed the continuing effects of apartheid as well as the devastation of HIV/AIDS among the local residents.

- A white family in South Africa must flee as black insurgents plunge the country into chaos in Nadine Gordimer's novel *July's People* (1981). Gordimer is one of South Africa's most successful white female authors. Her characters in this novel, the Smales family, must learn to adjust to a black-dominated village society.

- *Things Fall Apart* (1958) by Chinua Achebe was one of the first internationally recognized works of fiction from Africa. Achebe, a native of Nigeria, is credited with helping to shape African literature. His book portrays the conflicts between African and European cultures and how these clashes affect people's lives.

- Buchi Emecheta's second book *Bride Price* (1976) tells the story of a young Nigerian girl, her challenges in negotiating some of the contradictions of her tribal laws, and the residual effects of colonial rule and customs.

- Wole Soyinka is best known for his plays. One of his most memorable is *A Dance of the Forests* (1963), a political play that warns Nigerian officials not to make the same corrupt mistakes that their predecessors did.

- Carol Matis's 2007 novel *The Whirlwind* describes the discrimination experiences of a World War II German Jewish refugee and his new Japanese American friend.

white people dominated blacks, the oppression was less personal than Matenge's, and the cruelties imposed were more aggressive. The results, however, were similar. Matenge's rule, for the most part, went unquestioned. The same was true for apartheid. Or to be more specific, those who did oppose apartheid were quickly silenced by death, torture, or life in prison. Under both systems, apartheid's and Matenge's, the people under the systems suffered, while the people favored by the system grew rich. Apartheid is a model for the most terrible aspects of colonialism (the exploitation of a weaker country by a stronger one) and extreme prejudice.

There is a pair of figures in this story who might represent a more benevolent past. However,

> MAKHAYA MIGHT BE HEAD'S IMAGE OF THE
> NEW BLACK AFRICAN. MAKHAYA ONLY WANTS
> PEACE OF MIND AND FREEDOM."

these two characters are presented more as transitional icons, tied to the past but looking toward the future. First, there is Chief Sekoto, the older brother of Matenge. He shares some of his brother's tastes for good food, lots of women, and big houses, but he rules his people with a gentler and more understanding attitude. He has compassion for their struggles and is curious about the changes that are happening in the village. He is also very forgiving, comprehending human nature in a much more liberal frame of mind than his more conservative brother. Head might be presenting Sekoto as the more modern chief, one who knows that his days are numbered because of the newly voted into power democratic government. Sekoto might be the product of the same oppressive history as his brother, but he sees more clearly what lies ahead for him and his country.

George Appleby-Smith is Chief Sekoto's Caucasian equivalent. George is a remnant of British rule. His country was once in charge of Botswana, making the rules as well as protecting the local people from invasions from land-grabbing warmongers from neighboring countries. George's authority is demonstrated when Matenge must appeal to George for support when Matenge tries to force Makhaya out of Golema Mmidi. George is the one who decides who stays and who leaves. But like Chief Sekoto, George also understands that he is an authority figure in transition. The rule of Britain is all but over. His role as law enforcement officer will soon end. Unlike Matenge, who desperately wants to hold onto his power, George has loosened his grip. Though he often states that he does not like people, George is a good judge of character. He senses that Makhaya will be beneficial for the village, just as he knows Matenge is up to no good. At one point, the narrator states that George looked upon people as crossword puzzles that he liked to figure out. George and Chief Sekoto also represent the transitional powers of black Africa working in concert with the

transitional roles of white outsiders. Though their backgrounds and interests differ, George and Chief Sekoto are best friends. They provide a glimmer of hope for progress in the relationships between blacks and whites.

At the heart of the story, however, is another black man and white man, Makhaya and Gilbert Balfour, who also work well together. Makhaya and Gilbert represent the present in Head's novel. It is a present that is leaning toward a future of its own making. Makhaya's life and psychology is marred by the consequences of both the apartheid system and traditional tribal conservatism. He is filled with anger when he arrives at Golema Mmidi for the harsh and unfair treatment he experienced in South Africa. He is determined also to release his mind from the confines of tribalism with which his Zulu tribal elders attempted to mold him. Makhaya might be Head's image of the new black African. Makhaya only wants peace of mind and freedom. Many times throughout Head's novel, Makhaya is praised for being different from the traditional African male. He is educated. He has progressive ideas. And he wants to learn how to love a woman, which makes him compassionate. It is when Makhaya meets Gilbert and settles in Golema Mmidi that he begins to fully explore his personal goals. He finds in Gilbert ideas that stimulate his imagination. Being an educated man, he appreciates the knowledge that Gilbert has attained and wants to work with him to improve the living conditions of the other villagers.

Gilbert, the white outsider, is not interested in making a name for himself or gaining wealth. All he wants is to teach the people of Golema Mmidi how to best use the resources they have been given. He wants to rid them of the burdens of tribalism in which they are bound to their chief and must sacrifice their own well-being for the benefit of one man. Gilbert is a scientific man who understands the underlying elements of agriculture. He knows how to make the arid land produce a livelihood for the people. Using old traditional ways of life is killing the land and starving the people. Though Gilbert's people skills are somewhat lacking because his mind is focused on the land, he is a compassionate man. He is never boastful and appreciates the gift that Makhaya offers, that of knowing the language of the people. Whereas Gilbert is the scientist, Makhaya is the communicator. Together, the novel suggests, the two men will

African village (*Image copyright Pichugin Dmitry, 2009. Used under license from Shutterstock.com*)

lead the villagers out of oppression and poverty. They are the transitional present moving toward the future.

Who in this novel best represents the future? There is no one better than children to do this. Head focuses on two children in her novel, the children of Paulina. Isaac is a ten-year-old living solidly in the adult world. On his small shoulders is placed a huge burden: he must keep his mother's cattle alive. In order to do this, Isaac sacrifices his youth and eventually his life. If Isaac represents the future of black African men, then Head is making a very strong statement. Isaac is sick and succumbs to his illness. Head might be saying that if the African male does not change his traditional ways, he too may die. In Botswana today, AIDS is wreaking havoc on the population. Head might not have foreseen this turn of events, but she did praise Makhaya for not treating women merely as sexual objects. For Isaac, though, it was the reliance on raising cattle for money that killed him. Or maybe it was Paulina's misguided belief that a ten-year-old could forsake his childhood and take on the duties of a man. Makhaya chides Paulina to let

go of the past customs that allowed this. The price for not doing so was the sacrifice of her son.

But there is another child in this story, Paulina's daughter, Lorato. She is only eight. However, she is the maker of a village. Though her village is made of mud and sticks, she is definitely portrayed as a creator. Is it through Lorato that Head puts forth her beliefs in the power of the African woman? Is the strength of the African woman the foundation of the future? With strong and loving parents, such as Paulina and Makhaya, to encourage her, the African woman could do well in molding the villages of the future. The concept is foreshadowed as the women build the huts for the drying of tobacco. While the men are tending the cattle many miles away, the women are being educated. They are being shown how to better their lives. The women represent progress and change. Head suggests that Lorato will emulate these women in the future to build better African villages.

Source: Joyce M. Hart, Critical Essay on *When Rain Clouds Gather*, in *Novels for Students*, Gale, Cengage Learning, 2010.

" IF IT IS BESET BY ROMANTIC ESCAPISM, IT IS SO BECAUSE ITS AUTHOR, PERSUADED BY HER OWN EMOTIONAL INSECURITY, STILL HOPES FOR THE POSSIBILITY OF HER HUMAN COMMUNITY.**"**

Coreen Brown

In the following essay, Brown explores the notion of human community in When Rain Clouds Gather.

In one of her letters, head states that out of all her writing, she likes best the description of an early morning sunrise in Botswana. She quotes:

> As far as the eye could see it was only a vast expanse of sand and scrub but somehow bewitchingly beautiful. Perhaps he confused it with his own loneliness. Perhaps it was those crazy little birds. Perhaps it was the way the earth had adorned herself for a transient moment in a brief splurge of gold. Or perhaps he simply wanted a country to love and chose the first thing at hand. But whatever it was, he simply and silently decided that all this dryness and bleakness amounted to home and that somehow he had come to the end of a journey. (Appendix 13)

This extract is from *When Rain Clouds Gather:* it describes Makhaya's response to his first dawn in Botswana. *When Rain Clouds Gather* was the first novel that Head wrote in exile in Botswana. There is sufficient evidence in Head's written accounts, both published and private, to show that Head grew to love the Botswanan landscape, and throughout her writing her evocation of the natural world is an affirmation of her belief in the restitutive quality of the natural as an antithesis to the social and the material. In *A Question of Power*, Elizabeth's first home in Botswana is a mud hut, and Elizabeth becomes intensely aware of the closeness of the living earth. Her work in the garden, like Maru's plans to grow his sunflowers, and like the General's dreams to be allowed to work his land (*TTP*, 102) are all means by which these characters seek redemption from the demands of an alienating world. Even in *The Cardinals*, a narrative dense with the imagery of the poverty of the slum dwellings of South Africa, Johnny and Mouse seek consolation in the margins of their urban environment, in the sky, the sea, and the mountains.

Thus, although there is no doubt that Head is describing the real, the visual, she is also providing what Jane Wilkinson defines (in her explanation of the South African landscape in Olive Schreiner's *The Story of an African Farm*) as a "moral landscape" (1991, 118). Makhaya, captivated by his first dawn in Botswana, is responding subjectively to the Botswanan landscape. This subjective response to the natural world has always been a characteristic feature of romanticism. It is explained by W. K. Wimsatt (using Samuel Taylor Coleridge's term) as the "*esemplastic* power which reshapes our primary awareness of the world into symbolic avenues to the theological" (1975, 25). So it is with the stress on the animism of this new environment that Makhaya can begin to "undo the complexity of hatred and humiliation that had dominated his life for so long" and reflect on the meaning of community in its displacement of his South African experience.

As a refugee from apartheid in South Africa, Makhaya is seeking "peace of mind" in rural Botswana, and it is here that he chances upon the experimental farming projects initiated by Gilbert, a British agronomist. The details of Gilbert's work are (as Head insists) all securely founded on practical, scientific knowledge, schemes that reflected not a "fancy or pretty-pretty, but a practical, busy world where people are planning for the future" (WDIW). It was this care taken to provide an accurate account of farming procedures that made *When Rain Clouds Gather* suggested reading for international volunteers intending to work in Botswana.

For his schemes to work, Gilbert needs the cooperation of the local inhabitants, their willingness to engage in communal enterprises:

> you had to start small, and because of this small start, co-operative marketing was the only workable answer, and its principle of sharing the gains and hardships would so much lessen the blows they had to encounter along the way.

Thus, communal farming is perceived by Gilbert to be the most efficient way of developing the natural resources of Golema Mmidi. He surveys the newly fenced pasture lands, the irrigation dykes, the fresh growth of grass on drought-stricken land, and declares to Makhaya. "'This is Utopia, Mack. I've the greatest dreams about it.'" Nonetheless, in spite of this caveat, Gilbert's "long discussions on the marvels and wonders of the earth" are primarily to convince his audience of

Botswana's potential as a "farmer's heaven," and the opportunity this presents to improve the living conditions of the community. Head, in a letter, recognizes that physical and material considerations are a priority: "I bow to Marxism and stand close to it in the sense that it is important to feed and clothe and house mankind" (Appendix 17).

But utopia for Makhaya means much more than this. Communal farming stresses "human" community; cattle farming near at hand strengthens family bonds and removes the necessity of enforced isolation for people who lived "like trees, in all the lonely wastes of Africa, cut off even from communication with their own selves." Indeed, Makhaya makes "a religion out of everything he found in Golema Mmidi":

> Golema Mmidi seemed a dream he had evoked out of his own consciousness to help him live, to help make life tolerable. But if it was a dream, it was a merciful one, where women walked around all day with their bare feet and there were no notices up saying black men could not listen to the twitter and chatter of birds.

In her first draft of the novel, Head used a first-person narrative voice, but with a male persona. When her publishers complained that the male narrator sounded too much "like a woman," Head resorted to a third-person voice in order, she explains, to "widen out the range and horizon" (Vigne 1991, 50). Nonetheless, as Huma Ibrahim argues, Head's letters attest to the fact that her exile is defined, just as it is for Makhaya, by the desire to find a home. Thus, she continues, "*When Rain Clouds Gather* is characteristic of an early stage in the development of an exile's system of desires and the consciousness out of which they emerge" (1996, 54). It is in this way that this early novel, "Makhaya's personal odyssey" to find "a few simple answers on how to live well and sanely" (*WRCG*, 71), is the author's portrayal of her own needs; Makhaya's "psychic power is analogous to the artistic imagination itself" (Brown 1979, 48). The narrative closes with Makhaya secure in his newfound home, having discovered, as Lloyd Brown suggests, "his own inner peace and sense of fulfilment" (46).

However, because in this novel, Head is describing her own firsthand experience of an experimental farm near Serowe—facts that Head claimed were drawn from reality, the "development of rural projects" (Appendix 29)—there is a danger that this novel might be read as an attempt to imitate reality. It is this assumption that leads Elaine Campbell to her conclusion when she argues that "these agricultural matters are not Eliot's objective correlative: external equivalents of inner emotional reality. Instead, they are subjective correlatives of the human lives with which they are intertwined" (1985, 82). This analysis might accurately describe Gilbert's relationship with his work, and indeed even explains why he seems more real than the other characters. However, the whole context of the narrative, including the other characters, serves for Makhaya, and his creator, as an objective correlative, an expression of acute and personal emotional need.

So Golema Mmidi is never a "real" community. It is "a place [God] had especially set aside to bring all his favourite people together" for "there was not anything he would not do for a village like Golema Mmidi." What is significant about this conception of community is that it has emerged from the same subjectivity that created the hero; Makhaya discovers his peace of mind simply because Head contrives to create a community in which he can do so. The other characters in the narrative, with the possible exception of Gilbert, only exist so that they can substantiate Makhaya's heroic stature and this often leads to what some readers may feel is an uncomfortable and somewhat mawkish adulation of the hero, Dinorego, one of the oldest residents of Golema Mmidi, immediately adopts him as his son; for Mma-Millipede, her friendship with Makhaya means that "a rich treasure had entered her life"; the women whom he teaches watch him with "thrilled eyes."

Lloyd Brown argues that Makhaya "grows into a dual perception, a complex synthesis of idealistic and realistic awareness that reflects the highly effective tension . . . between the visionary and the skeptic" (1979, 46). As literature of "process," the discursive style in which the novel is written does depend upon a frame of reference that defers mainly to the consciousness of the protagonist. But most readers would argue that even though Makhaya's consciousness portrays his disturbed reflections on past suffering, it does not necessarily follow from this that the developing consciousness is characterized by conflict or indeed tension, for the village that Makhaya "evokes out of his own consciousness" guarantees fulfillment for the hero. For Head, in this novel, usually tells and rarely shows. It is when she shows the consequences of the interaction of her characters, as she does in her short stories, that complexities and contradictions are allowed free play and tensions remain unresolved. This kind of autonomy for minor characters is never a possibility in those of her narratives that are dominated by the aspirations of a hero figure. So, after the routing of the chief villains, there is little to undermine the code by which Makhaya chooses to live, so completely are the subsidiary characters an extension of his needs. Within Golema Mmidi he discovers a surrogate mother and father, a woman eager to become his wife, and a white man with whom, through mutual understanding, Makhaya can forge a link between the black and white races, to combine "the good in Gilbert with the good in his own society."

Utopian writing has always been vulnerable to the charge that, as fantasy or chimera, it can have neither practical nor literary value. But, as Martin Buber explains, utopian writing is a response to "suffering under a social order that is senseless." If, Buber argues, this suffering should arouse the critical faculties of a writer, his/her recognition of "the perversity of what is perverted" endorses the creation of a Utopian picture of what should be and the "longing for that *rightness* ... is experienced as revelation or idea, and which of its very nature cannot be realized in the individual, but only in human community" (1949, 7–8). Makhaya's dreams in *When Rain Clouds Gather* are a reaction to the "torture and torment" (128) of human relationships within an oppressive society. As Buber suggests, the antidote to this is the realization of a "human community." Makhaya discovers that he "could run so far in search of peace, but it was contact with other living beings that a man needed most."

It is at this point that Head must romanticize, for these "living beings" must be of a certain type if they are to compensate Makhaya for the bitterness of past experience. This thematic, discursive style of writing that characterizes *When Rain Clouds Gather* is one in which the reader sympathizes with the needs of the protagonist; this means, in Frye's view, that pity is "involved or contained rather than purged." The implications of this are, as Frye argues, that "pity without an object" is "an imaginative animism which finds human qualities everywhere in nature, and includes the beautiful, traditionally the corresponding term to the sublime" (1990, 66). It is within this perspective that the characters in this narrative function; for Makhaya, and for the reader, they belong in a context that can provide significant meaning. Embodying this animism, which Rooney refers to as a "creative

mode of knowledge" (1991, 118), are Head's archetypes and motifs that define her good characters and the world they inhabit. They belong in a world that celebrates the consciousness of the child, the exile, the primitive, the asocial hero and heroine. It is a consciousness still attuned to a natural world, and it is with the development of these archetypes that Head can justify her implicit belief in the existence of human qualities and also assert that they are instinctive, natural, and essential. In *A Question of Power*, she shows the vulnerability of these instincts, how easily they can be flawed by socialization. But it is precisely this vulnerability for which the artistic imagination must compensate.

When Rain Clouds Gather marks the first stage in this process. If it is beset by romantic escapism, it is so because its author, persuaded by her own emotional insecurity, still hopes for the possibility of her human community. This really is the value of *When Rain Clouds Gather*. It is an introduction to the development of Head's artistic imagination. It may fail to convince the reader, or prove true for its creator, but this compels the author—literally and literarily in her later books—to delve more deeply into human consciousness. Makhaya is the hero who feels there is a world he can live in; Maru, the hero of Head's next novel, knows there is not. . . .

Source: Coreen Brown, "*When Rain Clouds Gather*," in *The Creative Vision of Bessie Head*, Fairleigh Dickinson University Press, 2003, pp. 53–70.

SOURCES

Central Intelligence Agency, "Botswana," in *Central Intelligence Agency: The World Factbook*, https://www.cia.gov/library/publications/the-world-factbook/geos/bc.html (accessed June 26, 2009).

Davies, Carole Boyce, Review of *A Woman Alone: Autobiographical Writings*, in *Research in African Literatures*, Vol. 23, No. 1, Spring 1992, pp. 210–12.

Davis, David Brion, *Inhuman Bondage: The Rise and Fall of Slavery in the New World*, Oxford University Press, 2006.

Garrett, James M., "Writing Community: Bessie Head and the Politics of Narrative," in *Research in African Literatures*, Vol. 30, No. 2, Summer 1999, pp. 122–35.

Head, Bessie, *When Rain Clouds Gather*, Heinemann Educational Publishers, 1969.

"Khoi," in *Encyclopedia of World Cultures*, edited by David Levinson, Vol. 9, *Africa and the Middle East*, edited by John Middleton and Amal Rassam, Hall, 1995.

Larson, Charles, "Bessie Head, Storyteller in Exile," in *Washington Post Book World*, February 17, 1991, p. 4.

Lenta, Margaret, Ruth Bhengu, and Fiona Moolla, Review of *Imaginative Trespasser: Letters between Bessie Head and Patrick and Wendy Cullinan, 1963–1977*, in *Biography*, Vol. 29, No. 1, Winter 2006, pp. 219–20.

Louw, P. Eric, *The Rise, Fall, and Legacy of Apartheid*, Praeger, 2004.

Ojo-Ade, Femi, Review of *Critical Essays on Bessie Head*, in *Research in African Literatures*, Vol. 36, No. 1, Spring 2005, pp. 127–28.

Review of *The Cardinals*, in *Publishers Weekly*, Vol. 243, No. 1, January 1, 1996, p. 68.

"Special Gallery: Historical Images of Apartheid in South Africa," in *United Nations Photo*, http://www.unmultimedia.org/photo/subjects/apartheid.html (accessed May 9, 2009).

Thielmann, Pia, Review of *Critical Essays on Bessie Head*, in *Africa Today*, Vol. 51, No. 3, Spring 2005, pp. 142–44.

U.S. Department of State, "Background Note: Botswana," in *Botswana (05/09)*, http://www.state.gov/r/pa/ei/bgn/1830.htm (accessed May 9, 2009).

FURTHER READING

Abrahams, Cecil, ed., *The Tragic Life: Bessie Head and Literature in Southern Africa*, Africa World Press, 1990.
 Abrahams provides a biography of Head, a study of her writing, and an overview of literature of southern Africa, which includes other Botswana works.

Currey, James, *Africa Writes Back: The African Writers Series and the Launch of African Literature*, Ohio University Press, 2008.
 Currey has put together a study of new and established African writers. In this book are portraits of the writers as well as an overview of their works.

Eilersen, Gillian Stead, *Bessie Head: Thunder behind Her Ears: Her Life and Writing*, Wits University Press, 2007.
 Described as an emotional biography of Head, Eilersen has been praised for unraveling some of the mystery that has surrounded Head's life story. In this book not only are Head's works explored but also her opinion, attitude, and ideas.

Leith, J. Clark, *Why Botswana Prospered*, McGill-Queen's University Press, 2005.
 Botswana has enjoyed a successful transition from colonized dependence to democratic independence. While other African countries around Botswana have been called political and economic disasters, why has Botswana enjoyed success? This is the question that the author explores, describing the evolution of Botswana's history.

Lewis, Desiree, *Living on a Horizon: Bessie Head and the Politics of Imagining*, Africa World Press, 2007.
 Lewis, a teacher at the University of the Western Cape in South Africa, explores the philosophy and writing style of Bessie Head in this study of the author's work. In particular, Lewis focuses on Head's use of myth and awareness of the history around her. Lewis also looks for feminist theories and cultural references in Head's body of work.

Sample, Maxine, ed., *Critical Essays on Bessie Head*, Greenwood Press, 2003.
 Sample has assembled a collection of essays on Head's life and work, including a discussion of *When Rain Clouds Gather*.

Seth, Willie, *Botswana and Its People*, New Africa Press, 2008.
 Seth provides a general introduction to the land and people of Botswana. Basic information about the geography, the nation's resources, and tourist attractions are also offered.

Zen and the Art of Motorcycle Maintenance

ROBERT PIRSIG

1974

Robert Pirsig's *Zen and the Art of Motorcycle Maintenance: An Inquiry into Values* is a novel, often described as semi-autobiographical, narrated in the first person (the narrator refers to himself as "I") by an unnamed man. The story he tells is described as a series of "Chautauquas." (A Chautauqua, in brief, is a series of stories or lectures intended to educate and entertain.) The narrator's story is a divided one, in part concerned with a cross-country motorcycle trip he is taking from Minnesota to California with his young son and a couple of friends. It is also the story of the narrator's former personality, whom the narrator identifies by the name of Phaedrus. In the course of describing his current journey, the narrator relates Phaedrus's journey toward insanity and eventual annihilation. Along the way, Phaedrus's ideas regarding the philosophical notion of "Quality" are explained, dissected, and elaborated upon by the narrator. The narrator claims that the purpose of the trip and his analysis of Phaedrus and Phaedrus's worldview is to finally bury Phaedrus properly. Through the course of the novel, however, it is revealed that the personality of Phaedrus, the personality the narrator presumes has been eliminated by the shock-therapy treatment he received in a mental facility, has not, in fact, been destroyed. Phaedrus still resides within the narrator's mind and, furthermore, is attempting to reestablish himself.

Found in both fiction and nonfiction sections of libraries and bookstores, *Zen and the Art of*

Meditation *(Image copyright Paul Prescott, 2009. Used under license from Shutterstock.com)*

Motorcycle Maintenance, originally published in 1974, is available in these more recent editions: the twenty-fifth anniversary edition, published in 1999 by First Quill and by Perennial Classics in 2000, and a 2008 edition published by Harper Perennial Modern Classics.

AUTHOR BIOGRAPHY

Pirsig, the son of a professor, was born on September 6, 1928, in Minneapolis, Minnesota. Many of the facts regarding Pirsig's life are comparable to the personal history of his narrator in *Zen and the Art of Motorcycle Maintenance*; this has led to the novel being described as a fictionalized autobiography. Like the narrator, Pirsig, as a child, was a gifted student with an IQ of 170 at the age of nine. He began a course of study at the University of Minnesota in 1943 and was expelled two years later due to academic failure.

In 1946, Pirsig enlisted in the army and served until 1948. His years of service included serving in Korea for some time.

After returning to the United States, Pirsig re-enrolled at the University of Minnesota, studied chemistry and philosophy, and earned a bachelor of arts degree in 1950. With the help of a tutor, Pirsig was granted a place at Benares Hindu University in India, where he studied Eastern philosophy. After his return, he married Nancy Ann James in 1954. The couple had two children, Christopher and Theodore. Pirsig earned his master of arts degree in journalism from the University of Minnesota in 1958.

Pirsig taught as an instructor of English composition at Montana State College (now University) from 1959 to 1961, where he renewed his interest in philosophy. His focus on a metaphysical notion of quality became single-minded. During this time, Pirsig battled severe anxiety and depression. He pursued graduate studies at the

University of Illinois, Chicago, and also taught there as an instructor in rhetoric from 1961 to 1962. During these years, Pirsig's internal struggles intensified. In interviews he has described his particular experience of sitting on the floor of his apartment for days, unmoving, alternately as enlightenment and as catatonic schizophrenia. (Schizophrenia is a severe mental disorder in which the patient has the following symptoms: loss of contact with environment, deteriorating ability to function, delusions, and hallucinations.) He was eventually committed by the court to a mental institution, where he was diagnosed with schizophrenia and received shock therapy (the administering of high-voltage alternating current through his brain). From 1961 to 1963, Pirsig spent time in and out of mental hospitals. He discontinued his treatment in 1964 and found employment as a technical writer.

The motorcycle trip described in *Zen and the Art of Motorcycle Maintenance* took place in 1968. Pirsig's manuscript was rejected over one hundred times, as Pirsig discusses in his afterward to the twenty-fifth anniversary of the novel, but it was finally published in 1974. Pirsig and his first wife divorced in 1978, and he was remarried later that year to Wendy L. Kimball, with whom he had a daughter, Nell. In the year following his second marriage, Pirsig's son Christopher was killed in a violent mugging. Pirsig wrote a sequel to *Zen and the Art of Motorcycle Maintenance* titled *Lila: An Inquiry Into Morals* (1991), in which his "metaphysics of quality" is further explored.

PLOT SUMMARY

Part One

CHAPTER ONE

Zen and the Art of Motorcycle Maintenance opens with the narrator riding his motorcycle through the Central Plains. His thoughts are interwoven with his conversation with his young son, Chris, who is on the motorcycle with him. The narrator explains his intention to use the westward journey from their home in Minnesota as an opportunity to discuss some of the things on his mind, and he envisions this experience as a series of "Chautauquas," or a series of lectures intended to entertain and educate. Traveling with the narrator and his son are family friends John and Sylvia Southerland. The narrator explores

MEDIA ADAPTATIONS

- *Zen and the Art of Motorcycle Maintenance: An Inquiry Into Values* was recorded as an unabridged audio CD, read by Michael Kramer and published by Macmillan Audio, 2006.

John's dislike of motorcycle maintenance as an example of a certain "disharmony" that plagues not just John but many people. He describes it as a split between those who value and embrace technology and those who approach life in a more romantic, intuitive manner. John and the narrator's attitudes toward motorcycle maintenance, the narrator explains, shed light on this split and are used to explore the larger implications of the split between rationality and romanticism. The narrator's philosophic approach to such issues in the first chapter sets the tone for the rest of the book.

CHAPTER TWO

The trip and the Chautauqua continue as the narrator observes the subtle change in the country they are riding through, a transition from the Central Plains to the Great Plains. The narrator offers further ruminations on the way motorcycle maintenance and one's attitudes toward it reflect larger issues within society as a whole.

CHAPTER THREE

The four cyclists (the narrator and his son Chris on one cycle, John and Sylvia on another) have ridden through the Red River Valley and are heading into an approaching storm. As the rain and thunder hit, the narrator has a flash of recognition. When various features of the landscape are illuminated he thinks, "He's *been* here!" This is one of the first clues the narrator offers regarding the alternate personality that has resided within him. The narrator becomes extremely cautious about proceeding in the bad weather, but his conversation with his son suggests that his cautiousness and trepidation are also a response to the resurgence of the other personality. Later, at the hotel where the four are staying, talk turns to ghosts. The narrator's mysterious comments about having known someone who chased a ghost, beat it, and then became a ghost himself foreshadow his later explanations of his relationship with his alternate personality.

CHAPTER FOUR

The narrator offers an extensive list and discussion of the items he has taken with him on this motorcycle trip. The four cyclists ride out of town early—at the urging of the narrator—on a cold morning. John, Sylvia, and Chris are angry with the narrator when they finally stop for breakfast. The mood shifts before they ride again.

CHAPTER FIVE

The riders approach the High Plains and stop in Hague, North Dakota, to plan their route across the Missouri River. The narrator recalls previous conversations with John about motorcycle maintenance and continues to contemplate John's negative reaction to the idea of a person learning the technical and intuitive details of maintaining one's own machine. In an attempt to account for John's attitudes, the narrator observes that there are two distinct realities that people perceive, "one of immediate artistic appearance and of underlying scientific explanation." The narrator observes how these two realities do not seem to fit together very well. After a brief stop, the cyclists continue on to the town of Lemmon. They are all fatigued, but Chris is excited about camping. They find a spot but have difficulties getting set up and preparing dinner. When Chris stalks off after complaining of stomach pains, John, Sylvia, and the narrator discuss his ailment. The narrator explains that Chris's stomach complaint is a recurring one for which they have found no medical explanation. Doctors have told the narrator and his wife that the issue is likely a symptom of mental illness. The narrator tries to explain why he stopped Chris's psychiatric treatments, but he falters, acknowledging only that it did not feel right. After Chris returns and the group falls asleep, the narrator dreams of a figure he describes as evil and insane. He identifies this figure as Phaedrus.

CHAPTER SIX

The narrator decides to discuss Phaedrus, claiming that to omit him from the story would be like running from him. He asserts that Phaedrus was never properly buried, and assumes that

is why he, the narrator, feels troubled by the renewed sense of Phaedrus's presence. The cyclists load their gear and head out into the hot day. Prefacing his comments with the statement that Phaedrus will not be praised but buried permanently, the narrator begins to flesh out Phaedrus's theories. Here he further explains ideas he alluded to earlier and discusses at length two modes of human understanding: classical and romantic. Much is made of the division between these two ways of perceiving the world. After commenting on the depths to which Phaedrus probed these ideas, the narrator informs us of Phaedrus's ultimate fate: a police arrest ordered by the court and removal from society. The narrator's thoughts are interrupted by periodic breaks in their journey for coffee and food. He continues to analyze Phaedrus's analytic approach to the classic/romantic split.

CHAPTER SEVEN

The narrator observes the oppressive heat in which they are riding. As the review of Phaedrus's analysis continues, the narrator stresses that Phaedrus was looking for a solution to the classic/romantic divide, a way to unite these two modes of understanding. He sought a theory that would explain and synthesize rather than dissemble and divide. The group passes into Montana, and the narrator explains that the ghost he spoke with Chris about was the "ghost of rationality" that Phaedrus pursued. As the oppressively hot day continues, the narrator rides more slowly to avoid overheating the motorcycle or blowing tires, but John and Sylvia are irritated with his slow pace. He thinks of the way Phaedrus's wife and family suffered due to his inattention. Interspersed with discussions of Phaedrus's thoughts—ideas the narrator claims to have discovered through Phaedrus's writings—are the narrator's recollections of having woken up in a hospital where it was eventually explained to him that he now had a new personality. The narrator further explains that Phaedrus, his former personality, was dead, after the court had ordered him institutionalized and he had undergone shock therapy (the administering of high-voltage alternating current through his brain). He speaks of the fear he feels now, of how he never knew Phaedrus, but everything he sees, he sees with his own eyes, as well as with Phaedrus's. After the slow, hot ride, a cooling rain refreshes the group.

Part Two

CHAPTER EIGHT

Sylvia, John, Chris, and the narrator are in Miles City, Montana. They have slept and bathed and the mood is good. The narrator applies his analysis of the classic/romantic divide to his current maintenance of his cycle. The group discusses their upcoming destination of Bozeman, Montana. As John discusses radical professors from the college in Bozeman, the narrator notes that he has been among them, observing silently that it was Phaedrus, not him, who was one of the professors under discussion. This observation highlights the peculiarities of the narrator's identity: he views himself as a different person entirely from the person he used to be (Phaedrus), but to all outward appearances he seems to be the same person.

CHAPTER NINE

Following the Yellowstone Valley, the group traverses Montana on their way to Bozeman. The narrator's Chautauqua for the day focuses on logic and its uses. He extensively discusses inductive and deductive reasoning.

CHAPTER TEN

The narrator notes that Phaedrus's break from mainstream rational thought can now be discussed. He outlines Phaedrus's thoughts regarding the formation of scientific hypotheses. Phaedrus's analysis led him always to more questions, to pondering the nature of truth. He reveals that Phaedrus, who entered college at the age of fifteen, was expelled by the age of seventeen for failing grades. He was unable to thrive in the academic community when he questioned the basic structures and models of what he was being taught. The narrator notes that Phaedrus at this point began to drift. The group arrives at Laurel, Montana, with the mountains in sight.

CHAPTER ELEVEN

Everyone seems excited and energized by the mountain air. They discuss their path to Bozeman, and they select a route that the narrator recalls Phaedrus having used a number of times. During the next phase of the trip, the narrator explores the truths Phaedrus sought after he left college. He notes that Phaedrus joined the Army and served in Korea and became interested in Eastern philosophy. After his return, Phaedrus renewed his studies at the university in Minnesota, from which he had previously been expelled,

focusing on philosophy. As the cyclists travel further into the mountains, the narrator discusses Phaedrus's philosophical journey, commenting on Phaedrus's study of philosophers such as Immanuel Kant and David Hume.

CHAPTER TWELVE

The group is conversing about the person they will be staying with, a former colleague of the narrator. Some anxiety is felt by all, as everyone realizes that the man, an art professor by the name of DeWeese, knew the narrator only as Phaedrus. Though the narrator remembers very little of DeWeese, a few conversations Phaedrus and DeWeese shared come back to him on their way to DeWeese's house. He also explains that between Phaedrus's undergraduate studies and his teaching stint in Bozeman, he spent some time living in India and studying Eastern philosophy at the Benares Hindu University. Following Phaedrus's return to the Midwest, he got a degree in journalism, married, and had two children, and worked as a technical writer. He had, the narrator observes, "given up."

CHAPTER THIRTEEN

The narrator notices how anxious he feels about being back in Bozeman, and recalls Phaedrus's extreme anxiety about teaching. Further recollections regarding Phaedrus's interest in protecting the college's accreditation requirements are related. For some colleagues it was a political issue, but for Phaedrus it was about the quality of the education the students were receiving.

CHAPTER FOURTEEN

The four travelers enter Bozeman, stop and eat, and then proceed to DeWeese's house where they are greeted by DeWeese and his wife. The narrator is aware that DeWeese still views him as Phaedrus. That evening, Chris tells his father that the previous evening, his father told him that it was lonely here. The narrator has no recollection of the conversation, and assumes Chris was dreaming. After dinner, other guests arrive, Jack and Wylla Barsness. Conversation turns to some of the same topics the narrator has been ruminating about, and he offers a brief lecture on the schism between art and technology.

CHAPTER FIFTEEN

Following some leisure time exploring a mining town, John and Sylvia decide to head back toward Minnesota. Chris and his father will hike into the mountains near Bozeman, then return for the motorcycle to continue their journey. The narrator and Chris walk to the school where Phaedrus used to teach. When the narrator decides to explore one of the buildings, the one containing his former classroom and office, Chris feels scared and runs outside. The narrator proceeds and is overcome with memories. He has the sensation that Phaedrus is present, not as a fragmented part of himself but seeing everything he himself sees. Having returned to the place where his obsession with the metaphysical notion of "Quality" began, the narrator is once again immersed in his former thought processes on the subject.

Part Three

CHAPTER SIXTEEN

Chris and his father begin their journey into the mountains. As they hike, the narrator explores Phaedrus's examination of the notion of Quality. He points out that he is not aware of everything that existed in Phaedrus's mind during this phase of his life, and is now attempting to piece together the remnants he has found. Interspersed with this extensive recollection of his classroom teachings are snippets of conversations with Chris, who appears to be struggling with the arduous hike.

CHAPTER SEVENTEEN

The narrator attempts to encourage Chris, who has grown increasingly frustrated. As their hike continues, the narrator returns to Phaedrus's classroom and his attempts to define and identify Quality. Chris's hiking efforts are defiant and angry.

CHAPTER EIGHTEEN

Phaedrus's quest toward understanding Quality progresses, the narrator informs us, when Phaedrus begins to view Quality as something undefinable. The benefits and pitfalls of this approach are reviewed, and along the way, the narrator continues to urge on his son, who stumbles up the mountain, falls often, and becomes ever more discouraged and angry. They camp for the night.

CHAPTER NINETEEN

Waking, the narrator recalls a dream, one that will recur throughout the rest of the novel in various versions, in which he is separated from Chris, Chris's brother, and mother by a glass door. Chris beckons his father to open the door, but he does not. When the narrator speaks with

Chris, Chris tells him that he, the narrator, kept Chris up all night talking about the mountain, and how he would meet Chris at the top. The narrator recalls nothing of this conversation. Once they are on the move again, the narrator returns to his Chautauqua, recalling Phaedrus's tackling of the question of whether or not Quality is subjective. The narrator reveals that Phaedrus began to view Quality as an event, the cause of subjects and objects. This represents a major breakthrough in Phaedrus's theories. Just then, Chris sees blue sky, and realizes they are near the top of the mountain.

CHAPTER TWENTY

Chris is in good spirits, as they have nearly reached the summit of the peak. They discuss Chris's claim that the narrator spoke to him about meeting him at the top of the mountain, and Chris suggests that the narrator sounded like he used to. The descent down the mountain begins, and the narrator declares that it is time to leave Phaedrus's path and explore some of his own ideas, paths that Phaedrus neglected. The narrator points out that for Phaedrus, the metaphysics of Quality were not channeled into everyday life. Rather, his approach focused on the moment of "nonintellectual awareness," the moment between the "instant of vision" and the "instant of awareness." Phaedrus was increasingly drawn to that in-between moment, when Quality is experienced but not intellectualized, a process which degrades the actual truth of the moment. This awareness, and his being able to link his view with that explored in the Eastern philosophy of the *Tao Te Ching* caused a "slippage" in Phaedrus's mind, a disconnection, the narrator explains.

CHAPTER TWENTY-ONE

Chris and his father struggle through thick brush on their way down the mountain. The narrator attempts to ground Phaedrus's theories and place the notion of Quality within the context of art, religion, and science. When Chris and his father reach the bottom of the mountain, they find other campers who offer them a ride into Bozeman, where they get a hotel room for the night.

CHAPTER TWENTY-TWO

After saying good-bye to the DeWeeses, Chris and his father head west. The narrator discusses the intersection of Phaedrus's philosophy with that of another philosopher, Jules

Henri Poincaré. Near Missoula, Montana, Chris and his father stop and eat and later find a place to camp.

CHAPTER TWENTY-THREE

This brief chapter is from Phaedrus's point of view. In the twenty-fifth anniversary edition of the book, all that is from Phaedrus's point of view is set in a font different from that of the rest of the book, to set it apart. Phaedrus recounts the dream the narrator had earlier in the book. In this version, Phaedrus understands that he is dead, and that Chris and Chris's mother and brother have come to pay their respects. Chris motions for Phaedrus to open the door, but when Phaedrus tries, a dark, shadowy figure moves between him and the door. He shouts to Chris, telling him he will see him at the bottom of the ocean because the mountain is gone.

CHAPTER TWENTY-FOUR

Waking up in Idaho, the narrator recalls the dream. He wakes Chris and the two head out, and he is eager to begin his Chautauqua. He explores the relationship between care and Quality, pointing out that someone who recognizes Quality, and is able to experience it when he works is someone who cares. The narrator then talks about obstacles to experiencing Quality, obstacles such as one's reaction to getting stuck in any particular activity, such as motorcycle repair.

CHAPTER TWENTY-FIVE

Riding through Idaho, the narrator now discusses the "ugliness of technology" that "traditional reason" has created. He advocates viewing technology as a union of the human and the natural into a new transcendent creation, and emphasizes that the transcendence one can experience is not particular to what can be achieved through motorcycle maintenance. He goes on to discuss inner peace of mind and the way it can be achieved in various levels of understanding. They arrive in western Idaho in a town called Cambridge and camp for the night.

CHAPTER TWENTY-SIX

Chris and his father arrive in Oregon. The narrator's Chautauqua focuses on a state of being that leaves one open to Quality, and that is having gumption. The obstacle to enthusiasm is identified as "the internal gumption trap of ego," which the narrator explores with respect to motorcycle maintenance. After a lengthy discussion, the narrator points out that in reality,

the metaphorical cycle he is speaking of is one's self. Chris and the narrator arrive at the West Coast and settle in for another night of camping after a long day of travel.

Part Four

CHAPTER TWENTY-SEVEN

This brief chapter opens with a dream, from Phaedrus's point of view. Phaedrus is attempting to attack the shadowy figure that comes between him and the door, him and Chris. Chris, frightened, wakes his father, who has been shouting. The narrator realizes that the person in the dream, the dreamer, is Phaedrus, and that he is the person in the shadows. He acknowledges to himself that Phaedrus is returning and that he must prepare Chris for this.

CHAPTER TWENTY-EIGHT

The narrator recalls being Phaedrus and driving with a young Chris in the car and not remembering where he was going or how to navigate in his surroundings at all. He fears endangering Chris again now. The narrator begins to recount Phaedrus's end, which began when he sought to explore Quality further in his graduate studies at the University of Chicago. While the narrator repeatedly turns to these thoughts, he and Chris arrive at Crater Lake National Park in Oregon. The narrator describes his classroom experiences in the philosophy courses in Chicago, challenging experiences with professors whose attitudes and beliefs incensed Phaedrus and drove him to further hone his understanding of Quality.

CHAPTER TWENTY-NINE

Chris, under his father's instruction, washes their clothes at the laundromat while the narrator repairs the motorcycle. His thoughts return to Quality, to his own individual view of it, and to Phaedrus's, which was larger and broader in scope. Detailed analyses of Phaedrus's clash with his professors regarding the thinking of ancient philosophers, including Aristotle, are provided by the narrator, who also pauses to note the progress of their journey into California. The narrator discusses Phaedrus's comparison of Plato's notion of the Good with his own view of Quality.

CHAPTER THIRTY

In the opening paragraph of this chapter the narrator promises to finish Phaedrus's story once and for all. He speaks of Phaedrus reading one of Plato's dialogues, the one featuring the character of Phaedrus. The solitude and aggression of the character appeal to Phaedrus. An account of the classroom discussion on the topic is presented. Phaedrus becomes increasingly withdrawn, no longer motivated to teach or to learn. He begins to feel that the more he desires to understand Quality, the more he attempts to define it, and Quality is defeated. He stops wandering and returns to his apartment, sitting cross-legged in his room for days. His consciousness dissolves; his sense of himself disintegrates. The narrator and Chris find a hotel for the night and Chris questions his father about where they are going and why he does nothing. Chris cries, rocking himself in the fetal position, claiming that he has lost an interest in wanting anything. The narrator is certain that Chris's main problem is that he misses Phaedrus.

CHAPTER THIRTY-ONE

Chris and his father leave the hotel and have breakfast. Chris expresses his desire to turn around and go home. The narrator insists that they will be heading south instead, and Chris begrudgingly climbs on the motorcycle behind his father. The narrator feels that Chris understands that his real father is no longer there. He states his feelings of having conformed. He attempts to persuade Chris to return home on a bus, and tells him he was insane for a long while, and is perhaps still insane. When Chris does not respond, the narrator also tells him of the possibility that he, Chris, may also suffer from some sort of mental illness. Chris, stunned as the import of what his father is saying sinks in, falls to the ground, rocking back and forth. A truck is approaching them, the narrator can hear it, and they are in its path. He cannot get Chris to move. When he next speaks, he recognizes the voice as not his own but Phaedrus's. It is the return of Phaedrus that prompts Chris to save his own life. Chris asks Phaedrus why he left, and if he was really insane. Phaedrus responds that they would not let him leave the hospital, and that no, he was not insane.

CHAPTER THIRTY-TWO

Chris and Phaedrus ride without helmets for the first time in the story. They can hear each other better now, and Phaedrus notes that they are connected in ways they do not even understand. Phaedrus concludes the story by stating his belief that things will be better now.

CHARACTERS

Jack Barsness

Jack Barsness and his wife Wylla visit the DeWeeses on the evening of the same day that the narrator, Chris, and the Sutherlands arrive. The narrator seems to recall that Barsness is a writer and English instructor at the University (where Phaedrus taught). An unnamed sculptor arrives at the DeWeeses after the Barsnesses appear.

Wylla Barsness

Wylla Barsness is the wife of English instructor Jack Barsness. The couple visits the DeWeeses the evening of the arrival of the narrator, Chris, and the Sutherlands.

Chris

Chris is the eleven-year-old son of the narrator. During the motorcycle trip, Chris is at times enthusiastic and happy, at other times angry; the narrator presumes these moods correspond with Chris's interpretations of and responses to his own feelings. Chris periodically complains of stomach pains, which the narrator informs the Sutherlands have no physical source but have been diagnosed as a possible symptom of mental illness. On a number of occasions throughout the journey, Chris tells his father of things his father said in his sleep and of conversations the narrator cannot recall the next day. The narrator suspects that Chris prefers his old personality of Phaedrus to his current self and begins to understand that Phaedrus is reemerging and trying to talk to Chris. At the novel's end, the narrator explains his former existence as one of insanity and tells Chris that the insanity is returning. He also tells Chris that he might have a similar mental illness. The narrator suggests that Chris return home alone. At this suggestion and upon hearing his father's description of his past life as "insane," Chris experiences a breakdown of sorts, collapsing in the road. As the narrator tries to coax him back to reality, Phaedrus emerges and speaks to Chris directly, telling him that they can at last be together. Chris's response is overwhelmingly joyful. When Chris tells Phaedrus that for all these years, he thought Phaedrus did not want to see him, Phaedrus responds that he had to do what he was told and that he was not allowed to return to his family. The narrator begins now to understand the problems Chris has had for so many years and comprehends the terror he has seen in Chris's eyes.

Phaedrus now insists that he was not insane. Chris replies, "I *knew* it." In the final chapter, Chris and his father ride with their helmets off, and Chris stands behind his father to see over his head and shoulders, explaining his new perspective, saying that everything is now different. Not only has his perspective on the motorcycle changed, but his perspective on his father has as well.

Chris's Father
See Narrator

Gennie DeWeese
Gennie DeWeese and her husband host the narrator, Chris, and the Sutherlands at their Bozeman, Montana, home. The narrator confides to the DeWeeses that he is considering writing a series of essays on the philosophy of the ancient Greek rhetoricians that Plato "vilified." He describes his notion of the "Church of Reason" (the analytic reasoning taught at the University, which is mistakenly believed to encompass the whole of human understanding) to the DeWeeses. Gennie encourages the narrator in his plan to write the essays and tells him he should not worry about "trying to get it perfect."

Robert DeWeese
DeWeese is an abstract impressionist painter and an instructor of fine art at the University in Bozeman, Montana, where Phaedrus taught. The narrator, Chris, and the Sutherlands spend several nights at his house. DeWeese knew the narrator only when the narrator was in his Phaedrus phase, and the narrator is anxious about meeting DeWeese again, because he realizes that DeWeese will see him as his former personality. The narrator recalls that Phaedrus regarded DeWeese as a man with a wealth of untapped knowledge and understanding. When the narrator, Chris, and the Sutherlands arrive at the DeWeese home, DeWeese introduces them to his other guests, an unnamed art instructor and his wife.

Narrator
The narrator of the novel is Chris's father. Years prior to the motorcycle trip, the narrator was a college instructor of rhetoric. He was a gifted child with a high IQ who entered college at the age of fifteen and was expelled two years later. He served in the army, in Korea, and returned to complete his education. After he began teaching in Bozeman, Montana, he pondered the philosophical questions he was so plagued by in his earlier years. Gradually he became obsessed with the metaphysical notion of Quality and its role as an organizing principle in the universe. Unable to find a way to incorporate his philosophy into his everyday life, he became increasingly withdrawn and isolated, a stranger to his family and friends. He was committed to a mental institution, diagnosed with schizophrenia, and treated with electro-shock therapy. When he returned to society, he had what his doctors described as a new and different personality. The narrator comes to view his old self as another identity entirely and names him Phaedrus, after a character in one of the Greek philosopher Plato's dialogues. The new personality—the narrator—is not identified by name. His son calls him Dad, and the other characters in the book never refer to him by name. References to emptiness and loneliness in the novel suggest that he feels cut off, isolated from his true self. He seems to want to put Phaedrus behind him for good, to "bury" him, yet he seems to be running toward Phaedrus at the same time, returning to his college office and classroom and following his route across the country and through the mountains. Throughout the novel, the narrator accesses more and more of the remnants of Phaedrus's thought and follows the philosophical paths created by Phaedrus to new directions that Phaedrus had not pursued. When the narrator understands at last, after a series of dreams, that Phaedrus is reemerging, he attempts to prepare Chris. He draws out the journey in order to spend more time with Chris and then tells his son some of the truth about his past, saying that he wants to send Chris home alone. Chris is unable to bear this news. The breakdown that follows draws Phaedrus out and reunites father and son. In the final chapter of the book, the narrator/Phaedrus concludes his narration with a declaration of victory. "We've won it," he says. "It's going to get better now."

Phaedrus
See Narrator

Sarah
Sarah is a woman the narrator recalls after he enters his old office at the college in Bozeman, Montana. Her office was adjacent to Phaedrus's, and it was her statement to him, "I hope you are teaching Quality to your students," that set Phaedrus on his obsessive quest for an understanding of Quality.

John Sutherland

John Sutherland and his wife, Sylvia, are friends of the narrator. They accompany the narrator and his son Chris on the motorcycle trip from Minnesota to Montana. While the couple provides amiable company for the narrator throughout much of the journey, the narrator also identifies areas in which his and John's approaches to motorcycles, and to life, are in opposition to one another. Due to this difference, John is used by the narrator as an example of the romantic, intuitive, anti-technological mindset as opposed to the classic, reasoning, technological one. Despite the deep differences in the philosophies of John and the narrator, the narrator observes that John is worth the effort of reasoning with and of trying to understand. The narrator also informs the reader that he and the Sutherlands have been on a number of motorcycle trips together in the past and that John is a musician.

Sylvia Sutherland

Sylvia Sutherland and her husband John are friends of the narrator who travel with him for some of the journey. She is depicted as contemplative, amiable, and pleasant, and in complete agreement with her husband in terms of their romantic approach to life, an approach that is disdainful of technology, according to the narrator. Sylvia expresses both concern about Chris and his stomach pains and occasional annoyance with Chris's behavior.

THEMES

Classicism versus Romanticism

In *Zen and the Art of Motorcycle Maintenance*, the narrator discusses two schools of thought—classicism and romanticism—and explores the reasons these branches of thinking have been set in opposition to one another throughout history. He advocates for a unification of these two ways of approaching the world, stating that "classic and romantic understanding should be united at a basic level." The narrator also explains that Phaedrus's quest was to solve this philosophical dilemma. The classical school of thought or mode of thinking, as the narrator describes it, is associated with analysis, reasoning, science, technology, and technological methods. Romanticism is associated with art, intuition, and the view that technology is ugly. The Sutherlands are identified by the narrator as representatives of romanticism.

Throughout the novel, the narrator offers examples of the ways these two modes of thought are viewed in terms of their opposition to one another. He speaks of the way abstract art is derided by the scientifically minded and how technical tasks such as motorcycle repair are feared by individuals with a more intuitive mind-set. He explains that romantics see things for what they are, appreciating the beauty of the object as it is, while classicists see things for what they do, appreciating the function of each component.

When the narrator is asked by Robert DeWeese to examine the instructions for putting together a rotisserie, the discussion arises again. DeWeese, an artist, is unable to make sense of the technical assembly instructions. The narrator claims that the reason for this is at least in part because the instructions were written without an appreciation for the rotisserie as a whole. The instruction writer focused on the pieces, while DeWeese focused on his desire for the completed whole. This points to the disconnection and resulting isolation the narrator spends much of the book discussing. Had the instruction writer appreciated the various ways the parts could be assembled to make a functioning unit, and had DeWeese had that same appreciation, rather than the impatience for only the end result, there would likely not have been a problem. As the narrator points out, "This divorce of art from technology is completely unnatural."

Metaphysical Quality

The narrator's gradual solution to the divorce of art and technology is the idea of Quality. Phaedrus arrives at a philosophical, metaphysical idea of Quality. (Metaphysics is a branch of philosophy dealing with the principles of reality and nature of being, as well as an exploration of concepts which the sciences accept as fact.) The notion of Quality, or Quality in the metaphysical way Phaedrus considers it, is his solution to the classic versus romantic split. He sees the notion of Quality as a "new spiritual *rationality*—in which the ugliness and the loneliness and the spiritual blankness" provided by traditional classic versus romantic thinking "would become illogical."

The narrator, however, takes a different approach, focusing instead on attitudes, making Quality "occur at the individual level, on a personal basis, in one's own life, in a less dramatic way." The ideas of care and of gumption are the more practical approaches to experiencing

TOPICS FOR FURTHER STUDY

- Some critics have compared *Zen and the Art of Motorcycle Maintenance* to the 1851 novel *Moby Dick* by Herman Melville. On the surface, these books seem very different, one centering on a cross-country motorcycle trip, the other set at sea and focusing on a whale hunt. Yet both the narrator of *Zen and the Art of Motorcycle Maintenance* and Ishmael of *Moby Dick* deal with issues of personal identity while exploring the nature of the universe and their places in it. Read *Moby Dick*. What themes does it share with *Zen and the Art of Motorcycle Maintenance*? How are the main characters and their concerns alike? How are they different? Compare the endings of the novels. How do the resolutions differ? What is the fate of the main characters? Write an essay on your findings.

- The motorcycle journey taken in *Zen and the Art of Motorcycle Maintenance* has become a popular route for motorcycle enthusiasts and fans of the novel. Using the book as your guide, plot the route taken first by Chris, his father, and the Sutherlands, and later by just Chris and his father. Create a Web page or PowerPoint presentation that maps their route and the stops the travelers made along the way.

- In *Zen and the Art of Motorcycle Maintenance*, the narrator has a history of mental illness, and he suggests that his son might also suffer from some degree of mental illness. Chris's stomach aches, we are told, are a symptom of such problems. Using both Internet and print sources, research schizophrenia, the mental illness with which the narrator was diagnosed. Study the ways in which such a diagnosis was treated during the 1950s and compare these methods, which the novel informs us included electro-shock therapy, with modern methods

of treatment. Create a PowerPoint or similar visual presentation in which you present the findings of your research. Be sure to include the proper documentation of your Internet and print sources.

- The young-adult novel *The Absolutely True Diary of a Part-Time Indian*, by Sherman Alexie, published in 2009 by Little, Brown Young Readers, is like *Zen and the Art of Motorcycle Maintenance* in that it is a semi-autobiographical work in which the narrator explores questions of his own identity and his identity within a larger community. Read Alexie's novel and compare its main character (Arnold Spirit) to both the narrator of *Zen and the Art of Motorcycle Maintenance* and to the narrator's son, Chris. In what ways are the characters' concerns about their personal identities similar? Note their similar senses of isolation and consider reasons for this common feeling. To what extent are Arnold Spirit's experiences of isolation generated by his racial identity? Prepare an oral or written report in which you compare the characters in these works.

- In *Zen and the Art of Motorcycle Maintenance*, the character of Chris is seen only from the eyes of his troubled father. We see the narrator's concern for Chris and understand at the novel's end how much the narrator believes Chris has helped him along his journey. Rewrite the ending of the book from Chris's point of view. Reflect on the whole journey up to this point from Chris's perspective. Examine the novel for clues regarding Chris's perceptions of his father. When does he fear him? When does he feel a sense of connection? How do experiences early on in the journey affect the events of the last three chapters?

Motorcyclist *(Image copyright Stephen Mcsweeny, 2009. Used under license from Shutterstock.com)*

Quality advocated by the narrator. Phaedrus and the narrator offer different details and structures to support their theories about Quality. For Phaedrus, the details include analyses of the philosophies of Immanuel Kant, David Hume, Aristotle, and Plato. He offers a reasoned approach to the existence of Quality despite its inability to be defined. As an instructor at the University, he proved that his students could identify Quality (in the writing of other students), even though they could not explain or define it. The narrator offers instead details regarding the specific features of various motorcycle repair jobs. He discusses a variety of parts, their functions, and the way to avoid a "gumption trap" like anxiety or ego, traps which inhibit Quality. He discusses "stuckness" and the meditative way this state can be approached in order to yield a more enlightened understanding of the motorcycle as a fusion of both art and technology.

The two take different approaches to the same goal. Phaedrus eventually comes to recognize Quality as the same concept as the Tao, the "Way," as explored in the *Tao Te Ching* by Lao Tzu. (Taoism is a Chinese philosophy that

focuses on achieving a spiritual harmony with nature.) The narrator comes to identify his meditative approach to his motorcycle and his life with the Zen Buddhist tradition. (Zen Buddhism is a Japanese philosophy advocating meditation as a path toward spiritual enlightenment.)

STYLE

First-Person Narrative

Zen and the Art of Motorcycle Maintenance is written as a first-person narrative describing the cross-country motorcycle trip of the narrator and his companions. The unnamed narrator refers to himself as "I." The sections of the book in which the account of the narrator's travels with his son are being directly related are written in present tense, as are the narrator's thoughts on motorcycle maintenance and his personal thoughts on the larger implications of motorcycle maintenance attitudes. The narrator's recollections of Phaedrus and the explanation of Phaedrus's thoughts are written in past tense, as this personality, his thoughts, and the events of his life occurred in the narrator's past.

In any first-person narrative, the reliability of the narrator is a subject for consideration: the reader has only the narrator's account of events as a guide. As this particular story unfolds, the reader realizes that the narrator has a history of mental illness, thereby calling into question the accuracy of all of his observations and thoughts. Yet the narrator of *Zen and the Art of Motorcycle Maintenance*, through both his awareness of his past mental illness and his calm, intellectual, and intelligent way of interacting and expressing himself, establishes a sense of trustworthiness. This view of the narrator as reliable is undercut by the existence of verbal exchanges with his son that he cannot recall, and readers are left to resolve this issue on their own, weighing his apparent intelligence and normalcy against his history of mental illness and the resurgence of his former personality. Readers must also ask whether or not his past or current insanity actually inhibits his ability to be trustworthy and reliable as a narrator.

Extended Metaphor

Throughout the novel, Pirsig uses motorcycle maintenance as a metaphor for the maintenance of the spiritual/philosophical well-being of an individual. A metaphor is a figure of speech in which two different objects or concepts are equated to one another. Pirsig, for example, early on in the narrator's journey, uses an oncoming storm as a metaphor for the emotional conflict the narrator is approaching.

A person would not normally refer to caring for himself as motorcycle maintenance. But Pirsig applies his ideas about a person's attitudes toward motorcycle maintenance to his attitudes about his spiritual and philosophical world view. Because he does this throughout the course of the novel, repeatedly drawing the reader's attention to these parallels, the metaphor is referred to as an extended metaphor. Pirsig directly addresses this relationship (between motorcycle maintenance attitudes and personal/spiritual/philosophical attitudes) when the narrator observes that

> the real cycle you're working on is a cycle called yourself. The machine that appears to be "out there" and the person that appears to be "in here" are not two separate things. They grow toward Quality or fall away from Quality together.

The narrator advocates looking at life in the same way that one looks at motorcycle maintenance—seeing the fusion of art and technology in all of humanity, approaching tasks with care, and focusing on the task itself without rushing or wishing to get to the final product or the next destination faster. At the novel's end, Chris asks about having a motorcycle when he is older. His father tells him he may have one, if he takes care of it. The narrator tells Chris that it is not difficult to properly care for a motorcycle "if you have the right attitudes. It's having the right attitudes that's hard." What these right attitudes are is what he has been explaining throughout the novel; his discussion of motorcycle maintenance dovetails with his thoughts on the integration and the transcendence of art and technology.

The extended metaphor of motorcycle maintenance provides overarching structure to the novel. In addition, Pirsig makes use of metaphorical language throughout the book. For example, the narrator's comparison of his former personality, Phaedrus, to a ghost, is another use of metaphor. This comparison encourages the readers to think that Phaedrus is dead and that his memory haunts the narrator in powerful ways. Similarly, the journey the narrator and his son take up the mountain serves as a metaphor for the narrator's journey toward a greater understanding of Phaedrus, toward his ultimate enlightenment. Significantly, the narrator refuses to reach the summit of the mountain, turning to make the descent before the full completion of the journey, much to his son's disappointment. He is not yet ready to completely face Phaedrus, and the failure to reach the summit is noted by Chris when he accuses his father of not being brave.

HISTORICAL CONTEXT

Conservative Reactions to Communist Fears in the 1950s

Zen and the Art of Motorcycle Maintenance was published in 1974, but it takes place in two different time periods. The Phaedrus phase of the narrator's life occurs in the 1950s. The real-life motorcycle trip Pirsig writes about in the novel took place in 1968, several years prior to the book's publication, but within the same general cultural atmosphere. The narrator relates a few things about both time periods. In Montana in the late 1950s, the place and time in which Phaedrus taught there, was what the narrator describes as "an outbreak of ultra-right-wing politics." Through his narrator, Pirsig

COMPARE
&
CONTRAST

- **1950s:** The United States is involved in a war against Communist aggression in Korea. Pirsig writes about serving in Korea (prior to the Korean War) in *Zen and the Art of Motorcycle Maintenance* and also about the conservative, anti-Communist attitudes pervasive in the United States at the time.

  1970s: The spread of Communism is now being fought, with the aid of the United States, in Vietnam. A cultural battle between conservatives who feel that Communism is a world-wide threat and anti-war liberals pervades the country. The opposing value systems at war are reflective of the classic/romantic divide Pirsig explores in his novel.

  Today: The United States is involved in a lengthy war in Iraq, a war which originally saw a considerable amount of popular support. This support has waned as the United States involvement has continued, and distrust toward people of Arab descent is not uncommon.

- **1950s:** There is a great deal of social stigma attached to mental illness, particularly forms more severe than anxiety or depression, such as the narrator's diagnosed schizophrenia in *Zen and the Art of Motorcycle Maintenance.* Society is, in general, intolerant of nonconformity.

  1970s: While there remains some stigma attached to mental illness, societal attitudes are less judgmental than in the 1950s. There is a trend toward deinstitutionalizing individuals who had previously been committed for various forms of mental illness, inspired in part by the desire of mental health professionals hoping to break the social stigma of

mental illness. Yet, many individuals suffer as a result of the loss of proper care and treatment.

  Today: The social stigma surrounding mental illness persists. Even individuals who receive proper care are sometimes denied employment. Social fears regarding the possible violent tendencies of individuals suffering from mental illness have increased since the 1950s. Despite the plethora of new medications designed to treat various mental illness, many individuals diagnosed with mental illness are not properly treated.

- **1950s:** In 1957, Jack Kerouac's *On the Road* is published by Viking Press. The work ushers in the modern road trip novel as an immensely popular genre. Kerouac's fictionalized autobiography receives immediate critical acclaim as well as popular success.

  1970s: The road trip genre thrives. In 1974, Pirsig's road trip novel, *Zen and the Art of Motorcycle Maintenance*, is beloved by many not only for its philosophical commentary but also for its beautifully written account of the motorcycle trip from Minnesota to California, a route fans of the book have followed religiously since the novel's publication. Like Kerouac's novel, Pirsig's book is a somewhat fictionalized account of his real-life experiences.

  Today: As a genre, the road trip novel remains appealing and successful. Modern examples of the genre include literary novels, such as *Ash Wednesday*, written by actor-director Ethan Hawke and published by Vintage in 2003, and young-adult fiction, such as the novel *Shift*, by Jennifer Bradbury, which features an account of a bicycle road trip taken by teens.

---

highlights some of the conservative policies of the University administration. He relates that the public statements of professors had to be approved by the administration, and the academic standards of

the college were, in Phaedrus's opinion, deteriorating in order to increase enrollment. The University's accreditation status would be affected unless the broad enrollment guidelines were enforced.

Phaedrus objected to this policy. The Montana State University Web site confirms that the expansion of the school was brought about by a lowering of academic standards, which the president of the university allowed but with which he apparently did not agree. According to Montana State University, the president (Roland Renne) was "forced to downplay his ideals in order to secure funds for the expansion" of the school.

While the narrator focuses on Phaedrus's particular concerns about the school's accreditation, the university's Web site also confirms the truth about a general atmosphere of fear and resulting conservatism and names the fear of Communism that began to seep across the country as a cause. Such heightened concern about Communism was generated in part by the Korean War and by McCarthyism and the Red Scare. The United States's involvement in the Korean War took place from 1950 to 1953 and was centered around the U.S. defense of South Korea against Communist North Korea. Fear of the spread of Communism became pervasive in the United States, as the Communist Union of Soviet Socialist Republics (U.S.S.R.) was becomingly increasingly powerful. Senator Joseph McCarthy was famous for claiming to have a list of accused Communists who worked for the U.S. State Department. His accusations were unproven, but he gained national support for his interest in finding and convicting suspected communists of treason.

Social Activism in the Late 1960s and Early 1970s

Whereas Pirsig, in his novel, offers specifics regarding the conservative atmosphere of the university setting in the 1950s, his portrayal of the cultural atmosphere of the late 1960s and early 1970s is more vague. And for neither time frame does he discuss national political events, such as the Korean War or the Vietnam War. He mentions that Phaedrus served in Korea, but the context provided, along with known biographical facts of Pirsig's life, shows that his service was prior to the war. With regard to the late 1960s and early 1970s, Pirsig's novel paints a picture of what is wrong with society in terms of general, negative reactions to technology. Pervading the novel is the idea that because so many people view the world in terms of the classic/romantic split, everyone suffers from the tension created. He speaks of the need to reform attitudes.

The Thinker, *by Auguste Rodin* (*Image copyright Vladimir Wrangel, 2009. Used under license from Shutterstock.com*)

This desire for societal reformation, the narrator insists, must be accomplished on a personal level before society can change, but the desire itself for inner peace and the longing to "reform the world, and make it a better place to live in," are reflective of the activism of the time period. The United States's involvement in the Vietnam War (1959–1975) was lengthy, and as U.S. military presence there grew, so did the opposition to it back in the United States. During the late 1950s, the most pervasive fear in the United States was the fear of communism. In the late 1960s and early 1970s, the deeper fear seems to have been with the way the United States was fighting the war against the spread of communism. War protesters learned from the activism of the everyday citizens involved in the civil rights movement, citizens who were successful in making changes to government policies. Both the civil rights and the anti-war movements focused on peaceful activities for advocating change: they staged marches, rallies, and parades; they spread their message through speeches and publications; and they petitioned the government for change.

The narrator directly contrasts the conservatism of the 1950s with the liberalism of the 1970s by stating, "This was the nineteen-fifties, not the nineteen-seventies. There were rumblings from the beatniks and early hippies at this time about 'the system' and the square intellectualism that supported it, but hardly anyone guessed how deeply the whole edifice would be brought into doubt."

CRITICAL OVERVIEW

Criticism of *Zen and the Art of Motorcycle Maintenance* tends to combine analysis of the work as a literary endeavor and as a philosophical treatise. Some earlier reviewers were quick to recognize the dual nature of the book. W. T. Lhamon, for example, in a 1974 review in the *New Republic*, observes the sluggish way the book, encumbered with its philosophical baggage, plods along, but comes together at the end. Lhamon praises the novel's way of tackling the big ideas of nature and technology, comparing Pirsig to Melville and, ironically, Thoreau, whom the narrator of *Zen and the Art of Motorcycle Maintenance* criticizes. The reviewer predicts, "There will be a lot of people reading this novel and it may well become an American classic." Likewise, Robert M. Adams, in a 1974 review appearing in the *New York Review of Books*, comments on the somewhat clunky way the story progresses. Yet Adams also praises Pirsig's rich prose, maintaining that even if the novel's "confused metaphysics" should fade, the novel's "wonder and fear" would persist. The book's dualities, it's attempt to balance the narrative regarding father and son with the philosophical doctrines of Phaedrus, were also noted by critic George Steiner. In his 1974 review for the *New Yorker*, he finds much to praise about Pirsig's novel, which he considers perhaps intentionally awkward.

In Una Allis's 1978 article for *Critical Quarterly*, the critic observes the warm critical and popular reception *Zen and the Art of Motorcycle Maintenance* received. Allis goes on to review the novel's philosophical content, and to assess it in terms of its realism. Taking another approach to understanding the novel, Richard H. Rodino, in a 1980 article for *Critique: Studies in Modern Fiction*, examines the irony inherent in the relationship between the novel's action and the commentary of the narrator. Rodino finds that in studying the instances of such irony, the reader must balance his understanding of what the novel seems to be teaching with the knowledge of the novel's warning regarding the "dangers of being taught." This practice, Rodino insists, reveals "new discoveries" that the reader makes alongside the narrator.

The narrator's insistence on the integration of art and technology, and his views on the split between the romantic and classic modes of thinking, have been explored by those in technical fields. In a 1975 article for *Science*, George Basalla assures readers that Pirsig's novel does not attack the fields of science and technology. Basalla explores the ways in which the narrator and Phaedrus seek unification, rather than preaching further division. James Willis writes in an article in a 2000 edition of *Journal of Medical Ethics*, "In the seventies it would have been thought madness to suggest that medical practice could be defined by rigid rules. Today it is our tragedy to live at a time when this bizarre idea is orthodoxy." Similarly, in a 1994 article in *Technical Communication*, Charles Beck examines Pirsig's use of "the rhetoric of technical communication" to study the finer points of the classic/romantic divide.

CRITICISM

Catherine Dominic

Dominic is a novelist and a freelance writer and editor. In this essay, she introduces a way of understanding the narrative, storytelling voice of Zen and the Art of Motorcycle Maintenance *as a synthesis of the character of the narrator and his past personality of Phaedrus.*

The "true" identity of the narrator of *Zen and the Art of Motorcycle Maintenance* is perhaps one of the most challenging aspects of the novel to understand. The novel depicts two personalities: the now-dead Phaedrus and the lonely, empty man who remained after undergoing shock therapy. The actual storyteller, it may be argued, is neither one of these personalities alone, but an integrated figure representing both the "old" Phaedrus and the unnamed man on the motorcycle trip. In order to distinguish these figures, the narrator's past personality shall be designated as Phaedrus; the narrator as the character who

WHAT DO I READ NEXT?

- Pirsig's sequel to *Zen and the Art of Motorcycle Maintenance* is *Lila: An Inquiry Into Morals* (published by Bantam in 1991). In this second novel, Pirsig continues the story of Phaedrus, who is now traveling the Hudson River by boat when he meets Lila, a woman with mental instabilities of her own. Phaedrus's relationship with Lila leads to insights that enable him to further shape his theory of Quality.

- *Zen and Now: On the Trail of Robert Pirsig and the Art of Motorcycle Maintenance*, by Mark Richardson, published by Knopf in 2008, is an exploration of Pirsig's life and his philosophy as expressed in *Zen and the Art of Motorcycle Maintenance*. It is also a travelogue of Richardson's motorcycle trek along Pirsig's former route from Minnesota to California, as Pirsig detailed the journey in his novel.

- *Zen Mind, Beginner's Mind*, by Shunryu Suzuki, published by Shambala in 2006, is a collection of excerpts from Suzuki's lectures on Zen Buddhism, presented with the beginner American Buddhist in mind. As an introduction to Buddhism for an American audience, the book helps explain the belief system Pirsig embraces in his novel.

- *Picture Perfect* is a young adult novel by Elaine Marie Alphin, published in 2003 by First Avenue Editions. A first-person narrative, the book is a psychological mystery in which the reader is exposed to three distinct personalities of the narrator. It offers an exploration of psychological issues similar to those examined in *Zen and the Art of Motorcycle Maintenance*, but is told from the perspective of a teenage boy.

- *Let Their Spirits Dance* by Stella Pope Duarte is, like *Zen and the Art of Motorcycle Maintenance*, a novel that utilizes the road trip format as a metaphor for the journey of confronting the past. It concerns a Hispanic American family and their grief over a family member who died serving in the Vietnam War. The book was published in 2003 by Harper Perennial.

- Actors Ewan McGregor and Charley Boorman, both motorcycle aficionados, realized it was possible to ride all the way around the world if they could be transported across the Bering Strait. Though their journey was possible, it was not without difficulties, and their resulting journey of over 20,000 miles in four months was recorded in *Long Way Round: Chasing Shadows across the World* (published by Atria in 2004). The memoir, like *Zen and the Art of Motorcycle Maintenance*, includes retellings of the adventures and introspections of the two actors as they found their lives changed by the experience.

embarks on the motorcycle journey with his son shall be designated as the man on the motorcycle (or motorcycle man); and the narrator, who is to be viewed as an integrated version of these two individuals, shall be referred to for purposes of this discussion as the narrator/storyteller. A close reading of the novel suggests that the motorcycle man's understanding of himself and of Phaedrus happened not just on the journey, but *after* the pivotal moment at the end of the book when man

on the motorcycle and Phaedrus are unified into a new personality. This new figure transcends both of the distinct isolated personalities the man used to be, and it is his voice that offers commentary on the two, earlier versions of himself.

Robert Pirsig's novel was inspired by events in his own life, and he uses a first-person narrator to tell the story. He states in his author's note that the story is "based on actual occurrences." He goes on to note that while "much has been

> THE NOVEL DEPICTS TWO PERSONALITIES: THE NOW-DEAD PHAEDRUS AND THE LONELY, EMPTY MAN WHO REMAINED AFTER UNDERGOING SHOCK THERAPY. THE ACTUAL STORYTELLER, IT MAY BE ARGUED, IS NEITHER ONE OF THESE PERSONALITIES ALONE, BUT AN INTEGRATED FIGURE REPRESENTING BOTH THE 'OLD' PHAEDRUS AND THE UNNAMED MAN ON THE MOTORCYCLE TRIP."

changed for rhetorical purposes," the essence of the story must be considered factual. What readers do not know is what exactly has been changed for "rhetorical purposes"—that is, what has been altered in order to improve the novel as a story. Readers are also left to wonder what should be considered factual essence. This statement, rather than specifying what is to be taken as truth, suggests that nothing is safe from doubt, and that even the identity of the narrator should not be presumed to be known. The narrator cannot be taken as Pirsig himself.

When considering Pirsig's first-person narrator, it should be noted that no one in the story refers to this character as "Robert" or "Mr. Pirsig." Chris calls him "Dad," and that is the only direct address the narrator receives. While the narrator is clearly meant to be associated with the author, in that the life experiences attributed to the narrator by Pirsig mirror those events in his own life, it may be argued that this man on the motorcycle is a fictionalized version of the author, a character crafted for the purposes of storytelling.

The way in which the story is told further suggests an overarching consciousness, a personality distinct from Phaedrus and from the man on the motorcycle. The motorcycle man's experiences—the actual events of the motorcycle trip—are related in present tense. The sections of the story pertaining to Phaedrus—the details regarding his existence, his philosophy, and his ultimate fate—are related in the past tense. The fact that two different stories are being told in two different ways further indicates the presence

of a figure—the narrator/storyteller—who is able to discuss both perspectives.

The narrator/storyteller is removed by both time and space from the character who is actually experiencing the events in the story. The man on the motorcycle discusses with the DeWeeses that he is considering writing a "series of lecture-essays—a sort of Chautauqua," and that he has been attempting to "work them out" in his mind on the trip. During the trip, he is not actually writing the Chautauqua. The story is what he produced after the trip was over. Yet something significant happens at the end of the trip, something suggesting that the final version of the story was produced by a different version of the narrator, by a different mind, than the one in the experiences of the story.

At the end of the trip, and the end of the novel, Phaedrus reemerges. In his "Introduction to the Twenty-fifth Anniversary Edition," of *Zen and the Art of Motorcycle Maintenance* Pirsig makes this clear. He states that in the end, "It is an honorable Phaedrus who triumphs over the narrator that has been maligning him all the time." He stresses additionally that the "dissembling narrator has vanished."

Rereading the novel's ending in this light, it is possible to see that while the fragmented, tormented man on the motorcycle has disappeared, the Phaedrus that emerges is not the same Phaedrus featured all along. The former identity of Phaedrus, like the former identity of the man on the motorcycle, has also disappeared. A new identity, one unifying these two fragmented parts, has emerged. Significantly, there is a recognition by this new version of Phaedrus that he is in fact the same "I" who has experienced the trip with Chris. Previously, the two identities were distinct. The "old" Phaedrus was completely Phaedrus, and the resulting person who remained after Phaedrus's destruction was aware of Phaedrus as a distinctly separate personality. At the novel's end, however, the two identities are no longer separated from one another's consciousness. They have finally integrated into one person. The "old" Phaedrus, upon his reemergence is recognized by the narrator as himself. Regarding Chris's "childish misunderstanding" about Phaedrus, the narrator says, "That's what Phaedrus always said—*I*— always said." There is recognition now that the two individuals presented as separate personalities throughout the story have united. They have, in fact, become a better version of both, in the sense that as a man and as a father, to be one person rather than two fragmented ones is an improved state of being. Phaedrus/the motorcycle man tells himself, "Be one person again!" Given that it is this unified individual who remains at the journey's end, it is clearly also this unified person who actually tells us the story.

This narrative voice empathizes both with Phaedrus and with the man struggling along on the motorcycle journey. Returning to the "Introduction," Pirsig explains that the "real Phaedrus" is not "a villainous ghost but rather a mild-mannered hyperintellectual." This real Phaedrus is the integrated Phaedrus. He is both the Phaedrus of the story with his obsessive philosophical drive toward Quality and the man on the motorcycle who strives toward a better understanding of himself and of his son. The integrated individual, the narrator/storyteller, shows the motorcycle man's fear of his former self through the man's dreams. But when the narrator/storyteller recounts Phaedrus's quest, it is with sympathy and respect, not with horror. He views Phaedrus as Chris does, as a noble hero, but one with fatal flaws.

As the storyteller presents it, when Phaedrus sat on the floor of his apartment for days, the event that precipitated his hospitalization, the experience was one in which Phaedrus's consciousness dissolved and he was able to truly perceive Quality, "and his soul [was] at rest." Phaedrus's truth-seeking was his undoing. Similarly, the man he became after leaving the mental institution sought, unconsciously at first, and later consciously, Phaedrus, or at least the remnants of his philosophy. His quest, too, was his undoing. Yet the resultant personality—a man who recognizes that he was both Phaedrus, and a "middle-class, middle-aged person getting along," that remained after Phaedrus was destroyed—is at last able to be the father that his son needs. He is able to examine Phaedrus's philosophical ideals and combine them with the man on the motorcycle's desire to ground Phaedrus's thought into a meaningful approach to everyday life. In the narrator/storyteller's presentation of Phaedrus's ideas and the man on the motorcycle's reaction to those ideas, we see the synthesis he has been advocating throughout the book. In exploring the way to "solve the conflict between human values and technological needs," which is what Phaedrus and the man on the motorcycle have been attempting to do, each in their own way, the narrator/storyteller insists that "barriers" must be overcome, specifically, the

barriers that prevent an understanding of technology as a "fusion of nature and the human spirit into a new kind of creation that transcends both." He further explains that this "transcendence should also occur at the individual level, on a personal basis, in one's own life."

This integration of two separate identities corresponds with what the narrator has been urging throughout the novel. In the man's motorcycle repair, just as in Phaedrus's philosophical endeavors, exists a quest for integration, for something that unified the romantic and the intuitive with the classic and analytical approaches. The narrator speaks also of the "separation of what man is from what man does" and of the disjunction between people who see things for what they are and people who see things for what they do. The unification of the disparate parts of the narrator emphasizes the possibility of greater unification. Early on in the novel, the narrator states that Buddha "resides quite as comfortably in the circuits of a digital computer or the gears of a cycle transmission as he does at the top of a mountain or in the petals of a flower." "That," he says, "is what I want to talk about in this Chautauqua." People's existence, he explains at the beginning of the book and throughout it, should be viewed as one of unity, not one of disintegration. This is reinforced through Phaedrus's notion of Quality and how he finds the same idea expressed in the ancient words of Lao Tzu in the *Tao Te Ching*. The narrator's approach to maintaining his motorcycle, an approach that involves analytic reasoning as well as such things as "care" and "gumption," also reinforces the notion of the necessity of integrating two schools of thought that only appear incompatible. The book's emphasis is perpetually placed on the idea of wholeness and unity, and on the peace that such integration has the potential to bring. When the old motorcycle man and the old Phaedrus have been unified, and Chris has been revived from his own disintegration, the troubled, anxious tone of the story is gone and is replaced by the joy experienced by both Chris and his father. The feeling, it is noted, is a new one. It is one "that was not here before, and is not just on the surface of things, but penetrates all the way through: We've won it. It's going to get better now." The new positivity may be viewed as a validation of the process of integration that is occurring for the new Phaedrus, the real Phaedrus.

Phaedrus believed "that he had solved a huge riddle of the universe," that he had transcended the dualistic, classic versus romantic way of looking at reality. The man on the motorcycle is trying to simply get by and improve his relationship with his son, and he considers himself "nothing special." The overarching tone of the book, however, is that of the narrator/storyteller, the integrated personality. He seeks to "reform the world, and make it a better place to live in." To do this, he advises a practical, individual approach: "The place to improve the world," he says, "is first in one's own heart and head and hands, and then work outward from there." His ideals are, like Phaedrus's, grand and noble, and his methods, like those of the father and motorcycle man, simple, straightforward, and personal.

Source: Catherine Dominic, Critical Essay on *Zen and the Art of Motorcycle Maintenance: An Inquiry into Values*, in *Novels for Students*, Gale, Cengage Learning, 2010.

Ronald J. Lee

In the following essay, Lee argues that the way Pirsig philosophizes in Zen and the Art of Motorcycle Maintenance *unites form and content.*

Robert Pirsig's story of the summer-time motorcycle journey of a father and a son has become one of the publishing successes of recent years. [*Zen and the Art of Motorcycle Maintenance*] is above all a very well told story: exciting, suspenseful, a little sentimental, tasting a bit of the old counter-culture fondness for debating the merits of man and his machines and for scrutinizing the different levels of consciousness by which we live. But many people put the novel aside in exasperation, refusing to trudge through the lengthy philosophical "digressions" or to accept the conventions of the romance quest narrative with which the novel operates. Those who do trudge through the philosophy often despair of finding a single, adequate definition of the idea of "quality" which is so central to the narrator's story. Herein lies the need for explication and clarification. Pirsig's thesis is that "quality" is too ambiguous to be defined in the philosophy, even though the philosophizing is important in an experiential way to the narrator, and that the definition or statement of what he means can finally emerge only in the *story* itself. The story is the *myth* which is, all at the same time, more profound, more ambiguous, and closer to life itself, than the *logos*, the mere words.

In a wry disclaimer at the beginning of the book, Pirsig says that what follows "should in no

> BUT THE NOVEL DOES NOT PRODUCE A CLEAR PHILOSOPHICAL STATEMENT; RATHER IT PRESENTS ITS *IDEA* IN A STORY OR *MYTH*. WE MIGHT SAY THAT, IN A SENSE, ART AND LIFE TRIUMPH OVER PHILOSOPHY."

way be associated with that great body of factual information relating to orthodox Zen Buddhist practice. It's not very factual on motorcycles, either." Indeed, the story is rather loose on both counts, but a central insight to the notion of quality does lie in his allusions to notions of Zen and specifically in a reference he makes to the *Tao*. The casual way in which "quality," Zen, and the Tao are linked indeed is typical of Pirsig's imprecise and suggestive way of proceeding, and the novel can be faulted for that. But in a rather bold and ingenuous way the novel stands formally as an assertion of its particularly contemporary, romantic content. Pirsig's heavily autobiographical story is presented as an argument for an alternative to the mere conceptualization of one's problems: the discovery of meaning through the somewhat mystical (and certainly romantic) notion of immersion in experience itself. Thus, although one cannot altogether excuse or condone the fuzziness of the philosophy, it is important to recognize the aesthetic "spine" to which the formal elements of the novel relate. For the narrator "quality" is something mystical, encountered and understood in experience itself, and likewise the meaning of the novel lies simply in the story. It is the story, the thing itself, in both its form and content which reveals the meaning. The several strands of the plot (the narrator's relationship to his travelling companions, his conflict with his son, his painful reminiscence about his own past, and his journey to his old haunts) are carefully woven together with the philosophical digressions by means of establishing allegorical parallels to the physical journey and psychological parallels to the inward search of the protagonist. And at the end of all this it is his particular experience of wholeness and integration that defines the meaning of quality.

In general terms one might say that what this novel is about is the divided self, and that, if one accepts its success, it takes its place in a line of twentieth century works which might include Eliot's "The Love Song of J. Alfred Prufrock," Samuel Beckett's *Murphy*, Ken Kesey's *One Flew Over the Cuckoo's Nest*, and Peter Shaffer's *Equus*. In works of this sort we have the presence of the romance narrative of the quest, an archetypal narrative pattern of action focusing on a central figure or hero whose journey consists of search, struggle, and discovery. In these contemporary works, however, the ancient pattern of romance is laced with irony, and the pleasure and the frustration of our encounter with the works derive from the inversions of the conventions of character and action and from the puzzling sensation that if the old world is turned upside-down it still might come out right-side-up. The specific device for inversion that Pirsig and his progenitors employ is madness, a contemporary ironic motif used as both a thematic element and a plot device by which the divided self is demarcated. In *Zen and the Art of Motorcycle Maintenance* the specific device for defining the divided self is the electroshock treatment to which the protagonist is subjected. This treatment effectively draws a curtain between the narrator's present self, which is quiet, withdrawn, and moody, and his former self, which was restless, rebellious, and active.

The story itself emerges from a complicated context, although it is unified throughout by the effort of the protagonist to find his former self, an effort which is ambivalent for him because of the fear and guilt associated with that self. The complicated narrative has three aspects to it. It begins in the context of a journey undertaken as an act of love for the motorcycle. From this derives the "Whole Earth Catalogue" kind of interest in do-it-yourself survival, as well as part of the framework for the discussion of romantic and classic consciousness. In this we also find a connection to the current popularity of "road stories," the most immediate roots of which go back to Jack Kerouac's *On the Road*. The journey is undertaken, secondly, as an effort on the part of the father to heal several layers of alienation: between himself and his son, between facets of his own psyche, and between himself and his environment. The third reason for the journey is incidental though yet significant: it is to be a sentimental journey to visit old haunts and former friends. From this purpose derives the means to bring together the

inward search of the protagonist for his other self, the travelling backwards in time through memory and past experience, and the outward geographical wanderings.

Most impressive, however, is the manner in which Pirsig *resolves* both the plot and the philosophical discussion. Near the end of the novel it appears that the narrative pattern of romance has gone ironic, for the journey seems to have failed and the quest seems to have led only to despair. But Pirsig reverses all this again with yet another irony. While the story appears to resolve itself with the father yielding to his shadow personality in the face of what he believes is defeat, in fact the yielding ironically is the means to the final integration that he has desperately been seeking.

As a result of the exploration in the narrative of both the consciousness and the unconscious, a potential integration is at hand. For the narrator, the struggle with ideas has been revived, and the shadow personality has been brought up from the unconscious near to the surface of consciousness. Of central importance is the presence of this shadow figure, Phaedrus. At one level he represents the former self of the narrator, the unbalanced person from whose condition he had been cured. The electroshock therapy was meant to sever the narrator forever from this previous self. At a deeper level Phaedrus represents the "shadow" as it is defined in a technical sense by Jungian or archetypal psychology.

The shadow in Jungian theory represents our other side, those qualities of our total self which have been repressed or which have remained undifferentiated, that is, which have not been brought into consciousness but remain in the realm of the unconscious. The shadow may be positive or negative: it may represent qualities we dislike and wish not to recognize in ourselves, or qualities which for one reason or another (guilt, for example, or insecurity) we will not recognize. The shadow is a figure existing in a close parallel relationship to our ego, and thus is a figure of the same sex as ourself. What is essential, from the point of view of Jungian psychology, is that ultimately the shadow be recognized, for to persist in repressing the shadow is to make oneself finally its victim. This victimization will occur through one or both of two means: the qualities of the shadow tend to be projected onto other people, and thus there is the inclination to blame or criticize others for characteristics of oneself; or refusing to recognize the presence of these qualities, we become subject to their influence in capricious and uncontrollable ways. In either case, the shadow becomes an enemy, rather than the source of a more complete personality.

Thus the idea of the divided self can be understood in terms of the separation between one's conscious ego and one's shadow, and the goal of psychic wholeness can be seen as the difficult and sometimes painful process of coming to terms with one's "other side." In Pirsig's narrative the most explicit suggestion of Phaedrus as the narrator's shadow comes through the recurring dream. At an early point in the novel, just after the narrator relates the Goethe poem about the father and his son, he speaks of his vision of Phaedrus:

> And in the fog there appears an intimation of a figure. It disappears when I look at it directly, but then reappears in the corner of my vision when I turn my glance. I am about to say something, to call to it, to recognize it, but then do not, knowing that to recognize it by any gesture or action is to give it a reality which it must not have. But it is a figure I recognize even though I do not let on. It is Phaedrus.

This figure reappears four times in the text, specifically in the context of the narrator's disturbing dream. Each time the dream is related a few details have been added or changed, as the narrator's comprehension of it develops. The essential details are these: the narrator is standing behind a glass door, on the other side of which stand his wife and children. His son, Chris, particularly stands out, for he is motioning to his father to come out to them. He almost seems to be smiling, but in fact he is very afraid. The father would like to move towards them, but he is held back by a figure standing near him in the shadows. In the last telling of the dream the father says that he lunges at the shadow figure and grasps him by the neck.

A key to the meaning of the father's experience lies in the irony of his own interpretation of the dream. At first it appears that the "loathsome" figure in the shadows in Phaedrus, the dark side whose return the father fears. But after the dream in which the dreamer attacks the figure in the shadows, the father believes that he is the one in the shadows, and the aggressive figure who is trying to get free to return to the child is Phaedrus. This frightens him even more, for it suggests how strong and how close Phaedrus is. Despite these

changing interpretations, what remains constant is the father's fear of the shadow figure and his desire to keep the shadow figure at bay.

The boy is the means to the final resolution. At the climactic moment near the end of the novel, when the father and son are at the edge of the sea and facing hopelessness, the boy reveals his awareness of the "dream," that in fact he was there at the glass door, and that it was the actual scene at the hospital after the father's breakdown. What had frightened him was his belief that the father did not come to him because he did not *want* to. He reveals further that he had loved Phaedrus, and that he actually longs for the return of that earlier self that had been his father. In this moment of startling revelation the father realizes that he can be one person again, that wholeness is possible, and that it lies in the acceptance rather than the rejection of his shadow. He is freed from his bondage to the assumption of a divided world. In the symbolism of the Goethe poem, but without its tragic ending, the wind from the life-giving ocean blows over the father and the son, and the fog begins to lift. The glass door, the dream symbol of alienation, disappears.

What Pirsig manages to bring together in this dramatic climax to the novel is a simultaneous revelation of the resolution to the conflict in the plot and an answer to the philosophical inquiry which has been progressing with the story. The device by which this is made possible is the dream; specifically, what is revealed to us is that the father's misunderstanding of the dream symbolizes his misunderstanding of life. At the end of the story, when the father succumbs to his despair, what he is really giving in to is that view of reality which assumes a divided world, a world of object over subject, of consciousness over the unconscious, or of ego over shadow. This was the philosophical position which Phaedrus had tried to resist and had failed, and which the narrator undertakes again to disprove in his discussion of "Quality." What the novel asserts is the inadequacy of the philosophical discussion as it might stand by itself. The wholeness or integration that the narrator seeks, and which seems to be embodied in the notion of "quality," cannot be grasped in a simple conceptual way, but rather must be lived and experienced.

Pirsig then is literally "doing" philosophy in this novel. The philosophizing that occurs is an integral part of the plot itself and also of the experiential struggle of the narrator to discover himself. But the novel does not produce a clear philosophical statement; rather it presents its *idea* in a story or *myth*. We might say that, in a sense, art and life triumph over philosophy. The narrator, both as his earlier and as his later self, struggles to conceptualize a holistic view of life, but he finds himself caught on the horns of a dilemma: the very process of conceptualization requires him to accept the thing he opposes, what he calls "this eternally dualistic subject-object way of approaching the motorcycle." The problem is with rationality itself, with the fact that "each year our old flat earth of conventional reason becomes less and less adequate to handle the experiences we have ... " He seems to have no other option: he must do philosophy in order to find an alternative to philosophy. The dilemma is resolved, however, through art, through the embodiment of the problem in the aesthetic form of the novel.

Source: Ronald J. Lee, "Pirsig's *Zen and the Art of Motorcycle Maintenance*: The Fusion of Form and Content," in *Western American Literature*, Vol. 14, No. 3, Fall 1979, pp. 221–26.

SOURCES

Adams, Robert M., "Good Trip," in *Guidebook to Zen and the Art of Motorcycle Maintenance*, by Robert L. DiSanto and Thomas J. Steele, William Morrow, 1990, pp. 240–337; originally published in *New York Review of Books*, June 13, 1974, pp. 22–23.

Adams, Tim, "The Interview: Robert Pirsig," in the *Observer*, November 19, 2006, Features Section, p. 4.

Allis, Una, "Zen and the Art of Motorcycle Maintenance," in *Critical Quarterly*, Vol. 20, No. 3, September 1978, pp. 33–41.

"Anti-Vietnam War Movement," in *MSN Encarta*, http://encarta.msn.com/encyclopedia_761589794/Anti-Vietnam_War_Movement.html (accessed May 1, 2009).

Basalla, George, "Man and Machine," in *Science*, Vol. 187, No. 4173, January 24, 1975, pp. 248–50.

Beck, Charles E., "The Most Famous Yet Unusual Technical Writer (Technical Writer Robert Pirsig)," in *Technical Communication*, Vol. 41, No. 2, May 1994, pp. 354–58.

Borinstein, Andrew B., "Public Attitudes toward Persons with Mental Illness," *Health Affairs*, Fall 1992, pp. 186–96.

Bump, Jerome, "Creativity, Rationality, and Metaphor in Robert Pirsig's *Zen and the Art of Motorcycle Maintenance*," in *South Atlantic Quarterly*, Vol. 82, No. 4, 1983, pp. 370–80.

Byrne, Peter, "Zen Rides Again: Robert Pirsig's *Zen and the Art of Motorcycle Maintenance*," in *Swans Commentary*, August 11, 2008, http://www.swans.com/library/art14/pbyrne78.html (accessed May 6, 2009).

"Chapter 1: Introduction and Themes," in *Mental Health: A Report of the Surgeon General*, United States Office of the Surgeon General Web site, http://www.surgeongeneral.gov/library/mentalhealth/chapter1/sec1.html (accessed May 6, 2009).

DiSanto, Ronald L. and Thomas J. Steele, "A Philosophical Backpack—Eastern Philosophy," and "A Philosophical Backpack—Western Philosophy," in *Guidebook to Zen and the Art of Motorcycle Maintenance*, William Morrow and Company, 1990, pp. 50–133, 134–204.

Lhamon, W. T., "A Fine Fiction," in the *New Republic*, Vol. 170, June 29, 1974, pp. 24–26.

"Montana State University History: 1950–1959," in *Montana State University* Web site, http://www.montana.edu/msuhistory/1950.html (accessed May 1, 2009).

Pirsig, Robert M., *Zen and the Art of Motorcycle Maintenance: An Inquiry into Values*, Perennial Classics, 2000.

Rodino, Richard H., "Irony and Earnestness in Robert Pirsig's *Zen and the Art of Motorcycle Maintenance*," in *Guidebook to Zen and the Art of Motorcycle Maintenance*, by Robert L. DiSanto and Thomas J. Steele, William Morrow, 1990, pp. 240–337; originally published in *Critique: Studies in Modern Fiction*, Vol. 22, 1980, pp. 21–31.

"Role of Deinstitutionalization" and "Inadequacies with the Current Mental Health System," in *Mental Health Association of Westchester* Web site, http://www.mhawestchester.org/advocates/agendao2702.asp (accessed May 6, 2009).

Steiner, George, "Uneasy Rider," in the *New Yorker*, April 15, 1974, pp. 147–50.

"Timeline: Iraq After Saddam," *BBC News*, http://news.bbc.co.uk/2/hi/middle_east/4192189.stm (accessed May 5, 2009).

"United States History: The Korean War," *MSN Encarta*, http://encarta.msn.com/encyclopedia_1741500823_29/united_states_history.html (accessed May, 1, 2009).

Willis, James, "A Personal Response to *Zen and the Art of Motorcycle Maintenance*," in *Journal of Medical Ethics*, Vol. 26, No. 6, December 2000, p. 110.

FURTHER READING

Garripoli, Garri, *The Tao of the Ride: Motorcycles and the Mechanics of the Soul*, HCI, 1999.

> Garripoli's work is a nonfiction exploration of the relationship between Eastern philosophy and motorcycle riding. While Garripoli uses the motorcycle journey as a metaphor for the journey of life, his descriptions of the motorcycle road trip focus on the details of the actual physical trip.

Hinshaw, Stephen P., *The Mark of Shame: Stigma of Mental Illness and an Agenda for Change*, Oxford University Press, 2006.

    Hinshaw offers an analysis of the stigma attached to mental illness and studies the way societal views and judgments have changed over the last fifty years.

Hoff, Benjamin, *The Tao of Pooh*, Dutton, 1982.

    Hoff provides an accessible introduction to the Eastern philosophy known as Taoism, which Pirsig references in his novel. Phaedrus observes the parallels between his own thinking and the *Tao Te Ching*, an ancient work composed by Lao Tzu. Hoff compares Taoism with the other Eastern philosophies of Buddhism and Confucianism, using the A. A. Milne children's book characters of Winnie the Pooh and Piglet.

Kerouac, Jack, *On the Road*, Viking, 1957.

    Kerouac's novel introduced a format and narrative style that many critics believe influenced Pirsig's novel.

Larsen, Karen, *Breaking the Limit: One Woman's Motorcycle Journey through North America*, Hyperion, 2004.

    Larsen offers an account of a cross-country motorcycle trip from a woman's perspective. Her work is a combination of essay and travelogue and is filled with Pirsig-like observations on the towns she stops in, the camping she does, and the road she travels.

Plato, *The Dialogues of Plato*, introduced by Erich Segal, Bantam Classic, 1986.

    This collection of several of Plato's philosophical dialogues includes *Gorgias*, featuring the character of Phaedrus, after whom the narrator names his alternate personality.

Glossary of Literary Terms

A

Abstract: As an adjective applied to writing or literary works, abstract refers to words or phrases that name things not knowable through the five senses.

Aestheticism: A literary and artistic movement of the nineteenth century. Followers of the movement believed that art should not be mixed with social, political, or moral teaching. The statement "art for art's sake" is a good summary of aestheticism. The movement had its roots in France, but it gained widespread importance in England in the last half of the nineteenth century, where it helped change the Victorian practice of including moral lessons in literature.

Allegory: A narrative technique in which characters representing things or abstract ideas are used to convey a message or teach a lesson. Allegory is typically used to teach moral, ethical, or religious lessons but is sometimes used for satiric or political purposes.

Allusion: A reference to a familiar literary or historical person or event, used to make an idea more easily understood.

Analogy: A comparison of two things made to explain something unfamiliar through its similarities to something familiar, or to prove one point based on the acceptedness of another. Similes and metaphors are types of analogies.

Antagonist: The major character in a narrative or drama who works against the hero or protagonist.

Anthropomorphism: The presentation of animals or objects in human shape or with human characteristics. The term is derived from the Greek word for "human form."

Anti-hero: A central character in a work of literature who lacks traditional heroic qualities such as courage, physical prowess, and fortitude. Anti-heroes typically distrust conventional values and are unable to commit themselves to any ideals. They generally feel helpless in a world over which they have no control. Anti-heroes usually accept, and often celebrate, their positions as social outcasts.

Apprenticeship Novel: See *Bildungsroman*

Archetype: The word archetype is commonly used to describe an original pattern or model from which all other things of the same kind are made. This term was introduced to literary criticism from the psychology of Carl Jung. It expresses Jung's theory that behind every person's "unconscious," or repressed memories of the past, lies the "collective unconscious" of the human race: memories of the countless typical experiences of our ancestors. These memories are said to prompt illogical associations that trigger powerful emotions in the reader. Often, the emotional process is primitive, even primordial. Archetypes are the literary images that grow out of the "collective unconscious." They appear in literature as incidents and plots that repeat basic patterns of life. They may also appear as stereotyped characters.

Avant-garde: French term meaning "vanguard." It is used in literary criticism to describe new writing that rejects traditional approaches to literature in favor of innovations in style or content.

B

Beat Movement: A period featuring a group of American poets and novelists of the 1950s and 1960s—including Jack Kerouac, Allen Ginsberg, Gregory Corso, William S. Burroughs, and Lawrence Ferlinghetti—who rejected established social and literary values. Using such techniques as stream of consciousness writing and jazz-influenced free verse and focusing on unusual or abnormal states of mind—generated by religious ecstasy or the use of drugs—the Beat writers aimed to create works that were unconventional in both form and subject matter.

Bildungsroman: A German word meaning "novel of development." The *bildungsroman* is a study of the maturation of a youthful character, typically brought about through a series of social or sexual encounters that lead to self-awareness. *Bildungsroman* is used interchangeably with *erziehungsroman,* a novel of initiation and education. When a *bildungsroman* is concerned with the development of an artist (as in James Joyce's *A Portrait of the Artist as a Young Man*), it is often termed a *kunstlerroman.*

Black Aesthetic Movement: A period of artistic and literary development among African Americans in the 1960s and early 1970s. This was the first major African-American artistic movement since the Harlem Renaissance and was closely paralleled by the civil rights and black power movements. The black aesthetic writers attempted to produce works of art that would be meaningful to the black masses. Key figures in black aesthetics included one of its founders, poet and playwright Amiri Baraka, formerly known as LeRoi Jones; poet

and essayist Haki R. Madhubuti, formerly Don L. Lee; poet and playwright Sonia Sanchez; and dramatist Ed Bullins.

Black Humor: Writing that places grotesque elements side by side with humorous ones in an attempt to shock the reader, forcing him or her to laugh at the horrifying reality of a disordered world.

Burlesque: Any literary work that uses exaggeration to make its subject appear ridiculous, either by treating a trivial subject with profound seriousness or by treating a dignified subject frivolously. The word "burlesque" may also be used as an adjective, as in "burlesque show," to mean "striptease act."

C

Character: Broadly speaking, a person in a literary work. The actions of characters are what constitute the plot of a story, novel, or poem. There are numerous types of characters, ranging from simple, stereotypical figures to intricate, multifaceted ones. In the techniques of anthropomorphism and personification, animals—and even places or things—can assume aspects of character. "Characterization" is the process by which an author creates vivid, believable characters in a work of art. This may be done in a variety of ways, including (1) direct description of the character by the narrator; (2) the direct presentation of the speech, thoughts, or actions of the character; and (3) the responses of other characters to the character. The term "character" also refers to a form originated by the ancient Greek writer Theophrastus that later became popular in the seventeenth and eighteenth centuries. It is a short essay or sketch of a person who prominently displays a specific attribute or quality, such as miserliness or ambition.

Climax: The turning point in a narrative, the moment when the conflict is at its most intense. Typically, the structure of stories, novels, and plays is one of rising action, in which tension builds to the climax, followed by falling action, in which tension lessens as the story moves to its conclusion.

Colloquialism: A word, phrase, or form of pronunciation that is acceptable in casual conversation but not in formal, written communication. It is considered more acceptable than slang.

Coming of Age Novel: See *Bildungsroman*

Concrete: Concrete is the opposite of abstract, and refers to a thing that actually exists or a description that allows the reader to experience an object or concept with the senses.

Connotation: The impression that a word gives beyond its defined meaning. Connotations may be universally understood or may be significant only to a certain group.

Convention: Any widely accepted literary device, style, or form.

D

Denotation: The definition of a word, apart from the impressions or feelings it creates (connotations) in the reader.

Denouement: A French word meaning "the unknotting." In literary criticism, it denotes the resolution of conflict in fiction or drama. The *denouement* follows the climax and provides an outcome to the primary plot situation as well as an explanation of secondary plot complications. The *denouement* often involves a character's recognition of his or her state of mind or moral condition.

Description: Descriptive writing is intended to allow a reader to picture the scene or setting in which the action of a story takes place. The form this description takes often evokes an intended emotional response— a dark, spooky graveyard will evoke fear, and a peaceful, sunny meadow will evoke calmness.

Dialogue: In its widest sense, dialogue is simply conversation between people in a literary work; in its most restricted sense, it refers specifically to the speech of characters in a drama. As a specific literary genre, a "dialogue" is a composition in which characters debate an issue or idea.

Diction: The selection and arrangement of words in a literary work. Either or both may vary depending on the desired effect. There are four general types of diction: "formal," used in scholarly or lofty writing; "informal," used in relaxed but educated conversation; "colloquial," used in everyday speech; and "slang," containing newly coined words and other terms not accepted in formal usage.

Didactic: A term used to describe works of literature that aim to teach some moral, religious, political, or practical lesson. Although didactic elements are often found in artistically pleasing works, the term "didactic" usually refers to literature in which the message is more important than the form. The term may also be used to criticize a work that the critic finds "overly didactic," that is, heavy-handed in its delivery of a lesson.

Doppelganger: A literary technique by which a character is duplicated (usually in the form of an alter ego, though sometimes as a ghostly counterpart) or divided into two distinct, usually opposite personalities. The use of this character device is widespread in nineteenth- and twentieth-century literature, and indicates a growing awareness among authors that the "self" is really a composite of many "selves."

Double Entendre: A corruption of a French phrase meaning "double meaning." The term is used to indicate a word or phrase that is deliberately ambiguous, especially when one of the meanings is risqué or improper.

Dramatic Irony: Occurs when the audience of a play or the reader of a work of literature knows something that a character in the work itself does not know. The irony is in the contrast between the intended meaning of the statements or actions of a character and the additional information understood by the audience.

Dystopia: An imaginary place in a work of fiction where the characters lead dehumanized, fearful lives.

E

Edwardian: Describes cultural conventions identified with the period of the reign of Edward VII of England (1901-1910). Writers of the Edwardian Age typically displayed a strong reaction against the propriety and conservatism of the Victorian Age. Their work often exhibits distrust of authority in religion, politics, and art and expresses strong doubts about the soundness of conventional values.

Empathy: A sense of shared experience, including emotional and physical feelings, with someone or something other than oneself. Empathy is often used to describe the response of a reader to a literary character.

Enlightenment, The: An eighteenth-century philosophical movement. It began in France but had a wide impact throughout Europe and America. Thinkers of the Enlightenment valued reason and believed that both the individual and society could achieve a state of perfection. Corresponding to this essentially humanist vision was a resistance to religious authority.

Epigram: A saying that makes the speaker's point quickly and concisely. Often used to preface a novel.

Epilogue: A concluding statement or section of a literary work. In dramas, particularly those of the seventeenth and eighteenth centuries, the epilogue is a closing speech, often in verse, delivered by an actor at the end of a play and spoken directly to the audience.

Epiphany: A sudden revelation of truth inspired by a seemingly trivial incident.

Episode: An incident that forms part of a story and is significantly related to it. Episodes may be either self-contained narratives or events that depend on a larger context for their sense and importance.

Epistolary Novel: A novel in the form of letters. The form was particularly popular in the eighteenth century.

Epithet: A word or phrase, often disparaging or abusive, that expresses a character trait of someone or something.

Existentialism: A predominantly twentieth-century philosophy concerned with the nature and perception of human existence. There are two major strains of existentialist thought: atheistic and Christian. Followers of atheistic existentialism believe that the individual is alone in a godless universe and that the basic human condition is one of suffering and loneliness. Nevertheless, because there are no fixed values, individuals can create their own characters—indeed, they can shape themselves—through the exercise of free will. The atheistic strain culminates in and is popularly associated with the works of Jean-Paul Sartre. The Christian existentialists, on the other hand, believe that only in God may people find freedom from life's anguish. The two strains hold certain beliefs in common: that existence cannot be fully understood or described through empirical effort; that anguish is a universal element of life; that individuals must bear responsibility for their actions;

and that there is no common standard of behavior or perception for religious and ethical matters.

Expatriates: See *Expatriatism*

Expatriatism: The practice of leaving one's country to live for an extended period in another country.

Exposition: Writing intended to explain the nature of an idea, thing, or theme. Expository writing is often combined with description, narration, or argument. In dramatic writing, the exposition is the introductory material which presents the characters, setting, and tone of the play.

Expressionism: An indistinct literary term, originally used to describe an early twentieth-century school of German painting. The term applies to almost any mode of unconventional, highly subjective writing that distorts reality in some way.

F

Fable: A prose or verse narrative intended to convey a moral. Animals or inanimate objects with human characteristics often serve as characters in fables.

Falling Action: See *Denouement*

Fantasy: A literary form related to mythology and folklore. Fantasy literature is typically set in non-existent realms and features supernatural beings.

Farce: A type of comedy characterized by broad humor, outlandish incidents, and often vulgar subject matter.

Femme fatale: A French phrase with the literal translation "fatal woman." A *femme fatale* is a sensuous, alluring woman who often leads men into danger or trouble.

Fiction: Any story that is the product of imagination rather than a documentation of fact. characters and events in such narratives may be based in real life but their ultimate form and configuration is a creation of the author.

Figurative Language: A technique in writing in which the author temporarily interrupts the order, construction, or meaning of the writing for a particular effect. This interruption takes the form of one or more figures of speech such as hyperbole, irony, or simile. Figurative language is the opposite of literal language, in which every word is truthful, accurate, and free of exaggeration or embellishment.

Figures of Speech: Writing that differs from customary conventions for construction, meaning, order, or significance for the purpose of a special meaning or effect. There are two major types of figures of speech: rhetorical figures, which do not make changes in the meaning of the words, and tropes, which do.

Fin de siecle: A French term meaning "end of the century." The term is used to denote the last decade of the nineteenth century, a transition period when writers and other artists abandoned old conventions and looked for new techniques and objectives.

First Person: See *Point of View*

Flashback: A device used in literature to present action that occurred before the beginning of the story. Flashbacks are often introduced as the dreams or recollections of one or more characters.

Foil: A character in a work of literature whose physical or psychological qualities contrast strongly with, and therefore highlight, the corresponding qualities of another character.

Folklore: Traditions and myths preserved in a culture or group of people. Typically, these are passed on by word of mouth in various forms—such as legends, songs, and proverbs—or preserved in customs and ceremonies. This term was first used by W. J. Thoms in 1846.

Folktale: A story originating in oral tradition. Folktales fall into a variety of categories, including legends, ghost stories, fairy tales, fables, and anecdotes based on historical figures and events.

Foreshadowing: A device used in literature to create expectation or to set up an explanation of later developments.

Form: The pattern or construction of a work which identifies its genre and distinguishes it from other genres.

G

Genre: A category of literary work. In critical theory, genre may refer to both the content of a given work—tragedy, comedy, pastoral—and to its form, such as poetry, novel, or drama.

Gilded Age: A period in American history during the 1870s characterized by political corruption and materialism. A number of important novels of social and political criticism were written during this time.

Gothicism: In literary criticism, works characterized by a taste for the medieval or morbidly attractive. A gothic novel prominently features elements of horror, the supernatural, gloom, and violence: clanking chains, terror, charnel houses, ghosts, medieval castles, and mysteriously slamming doors. The term "gothic novel" is also applied to novels that lack elements of the traditional Gothic setting but that create a similar atmosphere of terror or dread.

Grotesque: In literary criticism, the subject matter of a work or a style of expression characterized by exaggeration, deformity, freakishness, and disorder. The grotesque often includes an element of comic absurdity.

H

Harlem Renaissance: The Harlem Renaissance of the 1920s is generally considered the first significant movement of black writers and artists in the United States. During this period, new and established black writers published more fiction and poetry than ever before, the first influential black literary journals were established, and black authors and artists received their first widespread recognition and serious critical appraisal. Among the major writers associated with this period are Claude McKay, Jean Toomer, Countee Cullen, Langston Hughes, Arna Bontemps, Nella Larsen, and Zora Neale Hurston.

Hero/Heroine: The principal sympathetic character (male or female) in a literary work. Heroes and heroines typically exhibit admirable traits: idealism, courage, and integrity, for example.

Holocaust Literature: Literature influenced by or written about the Holocaust of World War II. Such literature includes true stories of survival in concentration camps, escape, and life after the war, as well as fictional works and poetry.

Humanism: A philosophy that places faith in the dignity of humankind and rejects the medieval perception of the individual as a weak, fallen creature. "Humanists" typically believe in the perfectibility of human nature and view reason and education as the means to that end.

Hyperbole: In literary criticism, deliberate exaggeration used to achieve an effect.

I

Idiom: A word construction or verbal expression closely associated with a given language.

Image: A concrete representation of an object or sensory experience. Typically, such a representation helps evoke the feelings associated with the object or experience itself. Images are either "literal" or "figurative." Literal images are especially concrete and involve little or no extension of the obvious meaning of the words used to express them. Figurative images do not follow the literal meaning of the words exactly. Images in literature are usually visual, but the term "image" can also refer to the representation of any sensory experience.

Imagery: The array of images in a literary work. Also, figurative language.

In medias res: A Latin term meaning "in the middle of things." It refers to the technique of beginning a story at its midpoint and then using various flashback devices to reveal previous action.

Interior Monologue: A narrative technique in which characters' thoughts are revealed in a way that appears to be uncontrolled by the author. The interior monologue typically aims to reveal the inner self of a character. It portrays emotional experiences as they occur at both a conscious and unconscious level. images are often used to represent sensations or emotions.

Irony: In literary criticism, the effect of language in which the intended meaning is the opposite of what is stated.

J

Jargon: Language that is used or understood only by a select group of people. Jargon may refer to terminology used in a certain profession, such as computer jargon, or it may refer to any nonsensical language that is not understood by most people.

L

Leitmotiv: See *Motif*

Literal Language: An author uses literal language when he or she writes without exaggerating or embellishing the subject matter and without any tools of figurative language.

Lost Generation: A term first used by Gertrude Stein to describe the post-World War I generation of American writers: men and women haunted by a sense of betrayal and emptiness brought about by the destructiveness of the war.

M

Mannerism: Exaggerated, artificial adherence to a literary manner or style. Also, a popular style of the visual arts of late sixteenth-century Europe that was marked by elongation of the human form and by intentional spatial distortion. Literary works that are self-consciously high-toned and artistic are often said to be "mannered."

Metaphor: A figure of speech that expresses an idea through the image of another object. Metaphors suggest the essence of the first object by identifying it with certain qualities of the second object.

Modernism: Modern literary practices. Also, the principles of a literary school that lasted from roughly the beginning of the twentieth century until the end of World War II. Modernism is defined by its rejection of the literary conventions of the nineteenth century and by its opposition to conventional morality, taste, traditions, and economic values.

Mood: The prevailing emotions of a work or of the author in his or her creation of the work. The mood of a work is not always what might be expected based on its subject matter.

Motif: A theme, character type, image, metaphor, or other verbal element that recurs throughout a single work of literature or occurs in a number of different works over a period of time.

Myth: An anonymous tale emerging from the traditional beliefs of a culture or social unit. Myths use supernatural explanations for natural phenomena. They may also explain cosmic issues like creation and death. Collections of myths, known as mythologies, are common to all cultures and nations, but the best-known myths belong to the Norse, Roman, and Greek mythologies.

N

Narration: The telling of a series of events, real or invented. A narration may be either a simple narrative, in which the events are recounted chronologically, or a narrative with a plot, in which the account is given in a style reflecting the author's artistic concept of the story. Narration is sometimes used as a synonym for "storyline."

Narrative: A verse or prose accounting of an event or sequence of events, real or invented. The term is also used as an adjective in the sense "method of narration." For example, in literary criticism, the expression "narrative technique" usually refers to the way the author structures and presents his or her story.

Narrator: The teller of a story. The narrator may be the author or a character in the story through whom the author speaks.

Naturalism: A literary movement of the late nineteenth and early twentieth centuries. The movement's major theorist, French novelist Emile Zola, envisioned a type of fiction that would examine human life with the objectivity of scientific inquiry. The Naturalists typically viewed human beings as either the products of "biological determinism," ruled by hereditary instincts and engaged in an endless struggle for survival, or as the products of "socioeconomic determinism," ruled by social and economic forces beyond their control. In their works, the Naturalists generally ignored the highest levels of society and focused on degradation: poverty, alcoholism, prostitution, insanity, and disease.

Noble Savage: The idea that primitive man is noble and good but becomes evil and corrupted as he becomes civilized. The concept of the noble savage originated in the Renaissance period but is more closely identified with such later writers as Jean-Jacques Rousseau and Aphra Behn.

Novel: A long fictional narrative written in prose, which developed from the novella and other early forms of narrative. A novel is usually organized under a plot or theme with a focus on character development and action.

Novel of Ideas: A novel in which the examination of intellectual issues and concepts takes precedence over characterization or a traditional storyline.

Novel of Manners: A novel that examines the customs and mores of a cultural group.

Novella: An Italian term meaning "story." This term has been especially used to describe fourteenth-century Italian tales, but it also refers to modern short novels.

O

Objective Correlative: An outward set of objects, a situation, or a chain of events corresponding to an inward experience and evoking this experience in the reader. The term frequently appears in modern criticism in discussions of authors' intended effects on the emotional responses of readers.

Objectivity: A quality in writing characterized by the absence of the author's opinion or feeling about the subject matter. Objectivity is an important factor in criticism.

Oedipus Complex: A son's amorous obsession with his mother. The phrase is derived from the story of the ancient Theban hero Oedipus, who unknowingly killed his father and married his mother.

Omniscience: See *Point of View*

Onomatopoeia: The use of words whose sounds express or suggest their meaning. In its simplest sense, onomatopoeia may be represented by words that mimic the sounds they denote such as "hiss" or "meow." At a more subtle level, the pattern and rhythm of sounds and rhymes of a line or poem may be onomatopoeic.

Oxymoron: A phrase combining two contradictory terms. Oxymorons may be intentional or unintentional.

P

Parable: A story intended to teach a moral lesson or answer an ethical question.

Paradox: A statement that appears illogical or contradictory at first, but may actually point to an underlying truth.

Parallelism: A method of comparison of two ideas in which each is developed in the same grammatical structure.

Parody: In literary criticism, this term refers to an imitation of a serious literary work or the signature style of a particular author in a ridiculous manner. A typical parody adopts the style of the original and applies it to an inappropriate subject for humorous effect. Parody is a form of satire and could be considered the literary equivalent of a caricature or cartoon.

Pastoral: A term derived from the Latin word "pastor," meaning shepherd. A pastoral is a literary composition on a rural theme. The conventions of the pastoral were originated by the third-century Greek poet Theocritus, who wrote about the experiences, love affairs, and pastimes of Sicilian shepherds. In a pastoral, characters and language of a courtly nature are often placed in a simple setting. The term pastoral is also used to classify dramas, elegies, and lyrics that exhibit the use of country settings and shepherd characters.

Pen Name: See *Pseudonym*

Persona: A Latin term meaning "mask." *Personae* are the characters in a fictional work of literature. The *persona* generally functions as a mask through which the author tells a story in a voice other than his or her own. A *persona* is usually either a character in a story who acts as a narrator or an "implied author," a voice created by the author to act as the narrator for himself or herself.

Personification: A figure of speech that gives human qualities to abstract ideas, animals, and inanimate objects.

Picaresque Novel: Episodic fiction depicting the adventures of a roguish central character ("picaro" is Spanish for "rogue"). The picaresque hero is commonly a low-born but clever individual who wanders into and out of various affairs of love, danger, and farcical intrigue. These involvements may take place at all social levels and typically present a humorous and wide-ranging satire of a given society.

Plagiarism: Claiming another person's written material as one's own. Plagiarism can take the form of direct, word-for-word copying or the theft of the substance or idea of the work.

Plot: In literary criticism, this term refers to the pattern of events in a narrative or drama. In its simplest sense, the plot guides the author in composing the work and helps the reader follow the work. Typically, plots exhibit causality and unity and have a beginning, a middle, and an end. Sometimes, however, a plot may consist of a series of disconnected events, in which case it is known as an "episodic plot."

Poetic Justice: An outcome in a literary work, not necessarily a poem, in which the good are rewarded and the evil are punished, especially in ways that particularly fit their virtues or crimes.

Poetic License: Distortions of fact and literary convention made by a writer—not always a poet—for the sake of the effect gained. Poetic license is closely related to the concept of "artistic freedom."

Poetics: This term has two closely related meanings. It denotes (1) an aesthetic theory in literary criticism about the essence of poetry or (2) rules prescribing the proper methods, content, style, or diction of poetry. The term poetics may also refer to theories about literature in general, not just poetry.

Point of View: The narrative perspective from which a literary work is presented to the reader. There are four traditional points of view. The "third person omniscient" gives the reader a "godlike" perspective, unrestricted by time or place, from which to see actions and look into the minds of characters. This allows the author to comment openly on characters and events in the work. The "third person" point of view presents the events of the story from outside of any single character's perception, much like the omniscient point of view, but the reader must understand the action as it takes place and without any special insight into characters' minds or motivations. The "first person" or "personal" point of view relates events as they are perceived by a single character. The main character "tells" the story and may offer opinions about the action and characters which differ from those of the author. Much less common than omniscient, third person, and first person is the "second person" point of view, wherein the author tells the story as if it is happening to the reader.

Polemic: A work in which the author takes a stand on a controversial subject, such as abortion or religion. Such works are often extremely argumentative or provocative.

Pornography: Writing intended to provoke feelings of lust in the reader. Such works are often condemned by critics and teachers, but those which can be shown to have literary value are viewed less harshly.

Post-Aesthetic Movement: An artistic response made by African Americans to the black aesthetic movement of the 1960s and early '70s. Writers since that time have adopted a somewhat different tone in their work, with less emphasis placed on the disparity between black and white in the United States. In the words of post-aesthetic authors such as Toni Morrison, John Edgar Wideman, and Kristin Hunter, African Americans are portrayed as looking inward for answers to their own questions, rather than always looking to the outside world.

Postmodernism: Writing from the 1960s forward characterized by experimentation and continuing to apply some of the fundamentals of modernism, which included existentialism and alienation. Postmodernists have gone a step further in the rejection of tradition begun with the modernists by also rejecting traditional forms, preferring the anti-novel over the novel and the anti-hero over the hero.

Primitivism: The belief that primitive peoples were nobler and less flawed than civilized peoples because they had not been subjected to the tainting influence of society.

Prologue: An introductory section of a literary work. It often contains information establishing the situation of the characters or presents information about the setting, time period, or action. In drama, the prologue is spoken by a chorus or by one of the principal characters.

Prose: A literary medium that attempts to mirror the language of everyday speech. It is distinguished from poetry by its use of unmetered, unrhymed language consisting of logically related sentences. Prose is usually grouped into paragraphs that form a cohesive whole such as an essay or a novel.

Prosopopoeia: See *Personification*

Protagonist: The central character of a story who serves as a focus for its themes and incidents and as the principal rationale for its development. The protagonist is sometimes referred to in discussions of modern literature as the hero or anti-hero.

Protest Fiction: Protest fiction has as its primary purpose the protesting of some social injustice, such as racism or discrimination.

Proverb: A brief, sage saying that expresses a truth about life in a striking manner.

Pseudonym: A name assumed by a writer, most often intended to prevent his or her identification as the author of a work. Two or more authors may work together under one pseudonym, or an author may use a different name for each genre he or she publishes in. Some publishing companies maintain "house pseudonyms," under which any number of authors may write installations in a series. Some authors also choose a pseudonym over their real names the way an actor may use a stage name.

Pun: A play on words that have similar sounds but different meanings.

R

Realism: A nineteenth-century European literary movement that sought to portray familiar characters, situations, and settings in a realistic manner. This was done primarily by using an objective narrative point of view and through the buildup of accurate detail. The standard for success of any realistic work depends on how faithfully it transfers common experience into fictional forms. The realistic method may be altered or extended, as in stream of consciousness writing, to record highly subjective experience.

Repartee: Conversation featuring snappy retorts and witticisms.

Resolution: The portion of a story following the climax, in which the conflict is resolved.

Rhetoric: In literary criticism, this term denotes the art of ethical persuasion. In its strictest sense, rhetoric adheres to various principles developed since classical times for arranging facts and ideas in a clear, persuasive, appealing manner. The term is also used to refer to effective prose in general and theories of or methods for composing effective prose.

Rhetorical Question: A question intended to provoke thought, but not an expressed answer, in the reader. It is most commonly used in oratory and other persuasive genres.

Rising Action: The part of a drama where the plot becomes increasingly complicated. Rising action leads up to the climax, or turning point, of a drama.

Roman à clef: A French phrase meaning "novel with a key." It refers to a narrative in which real persons are portrayed under fictitious names.

Romance: A broad term, usually denoting a narrative with exotic, exaggerated, often idealized characters, scenes, and themes.

Romanticism: This term has two widely accepted meanings. In historical criticism, it refers to a European intellectual and artistic movement of the late eighteenth and early nineteenth centuries that sought greater freedom of personal expression than that allowed by the strict rules of literary form and logic of the eighteenth-century neoclassicists. The Romantics preferred emotional and imaginative expression to rational analysis. They considered the individual to be at the center of all experience and so placed him or her at the center of their art. The Romantics believed that the creative imagination reveals nobler truths—unique feelings and attitudes—than those that could be discovered by logic or by scientific examination. Both the natural world and the state of childhood were important sources for revelations of "eternal truths." "Romanticism" is also used as a general term to refer to a type of sensibility found in all periods of literary history and usually considered to be in opposition to the principles of classicism. In this sense, Romanticism signifies any work or philosophy in which the exotic or dreamlike figure strongly, or that is devoted to individualistic expression, self-analysis, or a pursuit of a higher realm of knowledge than can be discovered by human reason.

Romantics: See *Romanticism*

S

Satire: A work that uses ridicule, humor, and wit to criticize and provoke change in human nature and institutions. There are two major types of satire: "formal" or "direct" satire speaks directly to the reader or to a character in the work; "indirect" satire relies upon the ridiculous behavior of its characters to make its point. Formal satire is

further divided into two manners: the "Horatian," which ridicules gently, and the "Juvenalian," which derides its subjects harshly and bitterly.

Science Fiction: A type of narrative about or based upon real or imagined scientific theories and technology. Science fiction is often peopled with alien creatures and set on other planets or in different dimensions.

Second Person: See *Point of View*

Setting: The time, place, and culture in which the action of a narrative takes place. The elements of setting may include geographic location, characters' physical and mental environments, prevailing cultural attitudes, or the historical time in which the action takes place.

Simile: A comparison, usually using "like" or "as," of two essentially dissimilar things, as in "coffee as cold as ice" or "He sounded like a broken record."

Slang: A type of informal verbal communication that is generally unacceptable for formal writing. Slang words and phrases are often colorful exaggerations used to emphasize the speaker's point; they may also be shortened versions of an often-used word or phrase.

Slave Narrative: Autobiographical accounts of American slave life as told by escaped slaves. These works first appeared during the abolition movement of the 1830s through the 1850s.

Socialist Realism: The Socialist Realism school of literary theory was proposed by Maxim Gorky and established as a dogma by the first Soviet Congress of Writers. It demanded adherence to a communist worldview in works of literature. Its doctrines required an objective viewpoint comprehensible to the working classes and themes of social struggle featuring strong proletarian heroes.

Stereotype: A stereotype was originally the name for a duplication made during the printing process; this led to its modern definition as a person or thing that is (or is assumed to be) the same as all others of its type.

Stream of Consciousness: A narrative technique for rendering the inward experience of a character. This technique is designed to give the impression of an ever-changing series of thoughts, emotions, images, and memories in the spontaneous and seemingly illogical order that they occur in life.

Structure: The form taken by a piece of literature. The structure may be made obvious for ease of understanding, as in nonfiction works, or may obscured for artistic purposes, as in some poetry or seemingly "unstructured" prose.

Sturm und Drang: A German term meaning "storm and stress." It refers to a German literary movement of the 1770s and 1780s that reacted against the order and rationalism of the enlightenment, focusing instead on the intense experience of extraordinary individuals.

Style: A writer's distinctive manner of arranging words to suit his or her ideas and purpose in writing. The unique imprint of the author's personality upon his or her writing, style is the product of an author's way of arranging ideas and his or her use of diction, different sentence structures, rhythm, figures of speech, rhetorical principles, and other elements of composition.

Subjectivity: Writing that expresses the author's personal feelings about his subject, and which may or may not include factual information about the subject.

Subplot: A secondary story in a narrative. A subplot may serve as a motivating or complicating force for the main plot of the work, or it may provide emphasis for, or relief from, the main plot.

Surrealism: A term introduced to criticism by Guillaume Apollinaire and later adopted by Andre Breton. It refers to a French literary and artistic movement founded in the 1920s. The Surrealists sought to express unconscious thoughts and feelings in their works. The best-known technique used for achieving this aim was automatic writing—transcriptions of spontaneous outpourings from the unconscious. The Surrealists proposed to unify the contrary levels of conscious and unconscious, dream and reality, objectivity and subjectivity into a new level of "super-realism."

Suspense: A literary device in which the author maintains the audience's attention through the buildup of events, the outcome of which will soon be revealed.

Symbol: Something that suggests or stands for something else without losing its original identity. In literature, symbols combine their literal meaning with the suggestion of an abstract concept. Literary symbols are of two types: those that carry complex associations of meaning no matter what their contexts, and those that derive their suggestive meaning from their functions in specific literary works.

Symbolism: This term has two widely accepted meanings. In historical criticism, it denotes an early modernist literary movement initiated in France during the nineteenth century that reacted against the prevailing standards of realism. Writers in this movement aimed to evoke, indirectly and symbolically, an order of being beyond the material world of the five senses. Poetic expression of personal emotion figured strongly in the movement, typically by means of a private set of symbols uniquely identifiable with the individual poet. The principal aim of the Symbolists was to express in words the highly complex feelings that grew out of everyday contact with the world. In a broader sense, the term "symbolism" refers to the use of one object to represent another.

T

Tall Tale: A humorous tale told in a straightforward, credible tone but relating absolutely impossible events or feats of the characters. Such tales were commonly told of frontier adventures during the settlement of the west in the United States.

Theme: The main point of a work of literature. The term is used interchangeably with thesis.

Thesis: A thesis is both an essay and the point argued in the essay. Thesis novels and thesis plays share the quality of containing a thesis which is supported through the action of the story.

Third Person: See *Point of View*

Tone: The author's attitude toward his or her audience may be deduced from the tone of the work. A formal tone may create distance or convey politeness, while an informal tone may encourage a friendly, intimate, or intrusive feeling in the reader. The author's attitude tward his or her subject matter may also be deduced from the tone of the words he or she uses in discussing it.

Transcendentalism: An American philosophical and religious movement, based in New England from around 1835 until the Civil War. Transcendentalism was a form of American romanticism that had its roots abroad in the works of Thomas Carlyle, Samuel Coleridge, and Johann Wolfgang von Goethe. The Transcendentalists stressed the importance of intuition and subjective experience in communication with God. They rejected religious dogma and texts in favor of mysticism and scientific naturalism. They pursued truths that lie beyond the "colorless" realms perceived by reason and the senses and were active social reformers in public education, women's rights, and the abolition of slavery.

U

Urban Realism: A branch of realist writing that attempts to accurately reflect the often harsh facts of modern urban existence.

Utopia: A fictional perfect place, such as "paradise" or "heaven."

V

Verisimilitude: Literally, the appearance of truth. In literary criticism, the term refers to aspects of a work of literature that seem true to the reader.

Victorian: Refers broadly to the reign of Queen Victoria of England (1837-1901) and to anything with qualities typical of that era. For example, the qualities of smug narrowmindedness, bourgeois materialism, faith in social progress, and priggish morality are often considered Victorian. This stereotype is contradicted by such dramatic intellectual developments as the theories of Charles Darwin, Karl Marx, and Sigmund Freud (which stirred strong debates in England) and the critical attitudes of serious Victorian writers like Charles Dickens and George Eliot. In literature, the Victorian Period was the great age of the English novel, and the latter part of the era saw the rise of movements such as decadence and symbolism.

W

Weltanschauung: A German term referring to a person's worldview or philosophy.

Weltschmerz: A German term meaning "world pain." It describes a sense of anguish about the nature of existence, usually associated with a melancholy, pessimistic attitude.

Z

Zeitgeist: A German term meaning "spirit of the time." It refers to the moral and intellectual trends of a given era.

Cumulative Author/Title Index

Cumulative Nationality/ Ethnicity Index

African American

Angelou, Maya
  I Know Why the Caged Bird Sings: V2
Baldwin, James
  Go Tell It on the Mountain: V4
Butler, Octavia
  Kindred: V8
  Parable of the Sower: V21
Cleage, Pearl
  What Looks Like Crazy on an Ordinary Day: V17
Danticat, Edwidge
  The Dew Breaker: V28
Ellison, Ralph
  Invisible Man: V2
  Juneteenth: V21
Gaines, Ernest J.
  The Autobiography of Miss Jane Pittman: V5
  A Gathering of Old Men: V16
  A Lesson before Dying: V7
Haley, Alex
  Roots: The Story of an American Family: V9
Hughes, Langston
  Tambourines to Glory: V21
Hurston, Zora Neale
  Their Eyes Were Watching God: V3
Johnson, James Weldon
  The Autobiography of an Ex-Coloured Man: V22
Kincaid, Jamaica
  Annie John: V3
Morrison, Toni
  Beloved: V6

The Bluest Eye: V1
  Song of Solomom: V8
  Sula: V14
Myers, Walter Dean
  Fallen Angels: V30
Naylor, Gloria
  Mama Day: V7
  The Women of Brewster Place: V4
Shange, Ntozake
  Betsey Brown: V11
Toomer, Jean
  Cane: V11
Walker, Alice
  The Color Purple: V5
Wright, Richard
  Black Boy: V1

Algerian

Camus, Albert
  The Plague: V16
  The Stranger: V6

American

Agee, James
  A Death in the Family: V22
Alcott, Louisa May
  Little Women: V12
Alexie, Sherman
  The Lone Ranger and Tonto Fistfight in Heaven: V17
  Reservation Blues: V31
Allende, Isabel
  Daughter of Fortune: V18
  Eva Luna: V29
  The House of the Spirits: V6

Allison, Dorothy
  Bastard Out of Carolina: V11
Alvarez, Julia
  How the García Girls Lost Their Accents: V5
Anaya, Rudolfo
  Bless Me, Ultima: V12
Anderson, Laurie Halse
  Speak: V31
Anderson, Sherwood
  Winesburg, Ohio: V4
Angelou, Maya
  I Know Why the Caged Bird Sings: V2
Asimov, Isaac
  I, Robot: V29
Auel, Jean
  The Clan of the Cave Bear: V11
Banks, Russell
  The Sweet Hereafter: V13
Baum, L. Frank
  The Wonderful Wizard of Oz: V13
Bellamy, Edward
  Looking Backward: 2000–1887: V15
Bellow, Saul
  Herzog: V14
  Humboldt's Gift: V26
  Seize the Day: V4
Blume, Judy
  Forever...: V24
Borland, Hal
  When the Legends Die: V18
Bradbury, Ray
  Dandelion Wine: V22
  Fahrenheit 451: V1

Cumulative Nationality/Ethnicity Index

Subject/Theme Index

Satire
  The Prince and the Pauper 185–186
  The Princess Bride: 170
  Reservation Blues: 212
Science
  The Bonesetter's Daughter: 14
  When Rain Clouds Gather: 310, 316
  Zen and the Art of Motorcycle Maintenance: 331
Science fiction
  Dune: 48, 49, 57, 59–60, 67, 74–78
Scottish history
  Ivanhoe: 80, 91–92
Seduction
  Reservation Blues: 224
Self control
  Dune: 58
Self destruction
  Reservation Blues: 212
Self doubt
  Speak: 258, 268
Self identity
  Cold Sassy Tree: 41–42
  The Prince and the Pauper: 172, 189–192, 192–196
Self image
  The Prince and the Pauper: 191
  Speak: 268
Self knowledge
  Zen and the Art of Motorcycle Maintenance: 338, 340, 342
Self realization
  Cold Sassy Tree: 41
Self worth
  The Prince and the Pauper: 191
  Speak: 265, 275
  A Tree Grows in Brooklyn: 281
Selfishness
  Reservation Blues: 207
  A Tree Grows in Brooklyn: 287
Selflessness
  Ivanhoe: 101
  Reservation Blues: 208
Sensory awareness. *See* Perception (Psychology)
Sensuality
  The Power and the Glory: 147
Sentimentality
  Ivanhoe: 94, 95
  The Scarlet Pimpernel: 233, 238
Servitude
  Dune: 73
  The Scarlet Pimpernel: 234, 235
Setting (Literature)
  The Bonesetter's Daughter: 11
  The Power and the Glory: 138, 148
  When Rain Clouds Gather: 311
Sex roles
  Dune: 72–74
  Ivanhoe: 90
  Speak: 274
  When Rain Clouds Gather: 309

Sexual behavior
  A Tree Grows in Brooklyn: 287
Sexuality
  Cold Sassy Tree: 32, 41
Shame
  The Prince and the Pauper: 178, 180
  Speak: 254, 255, 258, 259
  A Tree Grows in Brooklyn: 295
Sibling relations
  The Scarlet Pimpernel: 236, 248
  A Tree Grows in Brooklyn: 286, 300
Silence
  Dune: 70
  Speak: 254, 271, 275
Simplicity
  Cold Sassy Tree: 44–45
  Ivanhoe: 92
  Reservation Blues: 208
Sin
  The Power and the Glory: 136, 141, 146, 147, 151
  The Prince and the Pauper: 184
  Reservation Blues: 217
Skepticism
  The Power and the Glory: 136
Social change
  Cold Sassy Tree: 33–34, 35, 36, 39, 42
  Ivanhoe: 90, 93
  When Rain Clouds Gather: 307, 316, 317
  Zen and the Art of Motorcycle Maintenance: 337
Social class
  Dune: 64–65
  Ivanhoe: 95, 100
  The Prince and the Pauper: 172, 182, 184, 192–193
  The Scarlet Pimpernel: 239–240, 242, 245–246
Social commentary
  Cold Sassy Tree: 38
Social conventions
  Cold Sassy Tree: 29, 31, 32, 35, 40, 41
Social criticism
  The Prince and the Pauper 185–186
Social evolution
  Cold Sassy Tree: 40
Social identity
  The Power and the Glory: 137
Sociology
  A Tree Grows in Brooklyn: 293, 300–301
Sorrow
  Reservation Blues: 215, 217
Southern gothic
  Cold Sassy Tree: 37
Southern United States
  Cold Sassy Tree: 26, 33, 34, 36–37, 37–39, 45–46

Spirituality
  Cold Sassy Tree: 31, 40, 42
  The Power and the Glory: 140, 148, 152
  Reservation Blues: 209
  When Rain Clouds Gather: 314, 315
  Zen and the Art of Motorcycle Maintenance: 334
Stereotypes (Psychology)
  Dune: 63, 86
  Ivanhoe: 87–88, 89, 93
  The Namesake: 120
  Reservation Blues: 203, 212, 215, 216, 219
  Speak: 274
Stoicism
  The Namesake: 110
Storytelling
  The Bonesetter's Daughter: 16–23
  Reservation Blues: 207, 208, 212, 217
  A Tree Grows in Brooklyn: 286, 293
  Zen and the Art of Motorcycle Maintenance: 338–339
Strength
  The Bonesetter's Daughter: 10
  Ivanhoe: 83
  The Namesake: 110
  The Prince and the Pauper: 191
  The Princess Bride: 160, 162
  The Scarlet Pimpernel: 234, 244
  A Tree Grows in Brooklyn: 286, 289, 293, 298
Struggle
  The Power and the Glory: 152
  The Princess Bride: 163–164
  A Tree Grows in Brooklyn: 279, 293, 296
  When Rain Clouds Gather: 314
  Zen and the Art of Motorcycle Maintenance: 327, 342
Submission
  Ivanhoe: 87
Suburban life
  The Namesake: 106
Success
  Reservation Blues: 207, 217, 223, 224, 225, 226
  A Tree Grows in Brooklyn: 278, 289, 293, 294, 295–296
  When Rain Clouds Gather: 314
Suffering
  The Power and the Glory: 151
  The Princess Bride: 164
  A Tree Grows in Brooklyn: 293, 299
  When Rain Clouds Gather: 311, 315–316, 319, 320
Suicide
  The Bonesetter's Daughter: 4, 8, 13, 23

For Reference

Not to be taken from this room